Building a Strategic Air Force

Building a Strategic Air Force

Walton S. Moody

GOVERNMENT REPRINTS PRESS
Washington, D.C.

© Ross & Perry, Inc. 2001 All rights reserved.

No claim to U.S. government work contained throughout this book.

Protected under the Berne Convention. Published 2001

Printed in The United States of America
Ross & Perry, Inc. Publishers
717 Second St., N.E., Suite 200
Washington, D.C. 20002
Telephone (202) 675-8300
Facsimile (202) 675-8400
info@RossPerry.com

SAN 253-8555

Government Reprints Press Edition 2001

Government Reprints Press is an Imprint of Ross & Perry, Inc.

Library of Congress Control Number: 2001092605

http://www.GPOreprints.com

ISBN 1-931641-25-0

∞ The paper used in this publication meets the requirements for permanence established by the American National Standard for Information Sciences "Permanence of Paper for Printed Library Materials" (ANSI Z39.48-1984).

All rights reserved. No copyrighted part of this publication may be reproduced, stored in a retrieval system, or transmitted, in any form or by any means, electronic, photocopying, recording, or otherwise, without the prior written permission of the publisher.

To Those Who Stood Guard

Foreword

From 1946 to 1991 the Strategic Air Command (SAC) operated the intercontinental and nuclear strike forces of the United States Air Force. During much of this period SAC was the premier operational command of the service. The rising tensions of the Cold War with Soviet-directed world communism gave the command a crucial role as the main force deterring potential aggression against the United States and its allies. Even after the emergence of airborne strategic nuclear forces in the late 1950s, SAC's status as an Air Force major command and the Joint Chiefs of Staff specified command gave it the pivotal role in national strategy.

This volume deals with the early years of the Air Force's effort to build and maintain a strategic striking force, from 1945 through 1953. It discusses the period of reorganization in national defense in the years after the end of the Second World War, as the Army Air Forces dealt with questions of structure, doctrine, strategy, atomic weapons, and technology. Crucial decisions were made at the end of 1947 and the beginning of 1948, but fiscal austerity limited the new United States Air Force in implementing those decisions. Despite this, General Curtis E. LeMay, the SAC Commander, found means and developed methods to ensure a high state of combat readiness. The war in Korea triggered an expansion of the armed forces—including SAC—that culminated in the "New Look" of the Eisenhower administration. The New Look emphasized nuclear air power as the foundation of a national strategy of containment and deterrence.

Walton S. Moody's analytical work discusses the challenges facing Air Force leaders in this time of stringent budgets, interservice disputes, and technological change. In particular, it examines the role of that leadership in fostering the development of an effective war-ready yet peace-keeping organization. The issues it raises are still relevant today, in a time when the distinction between strategic and tactical air power is less clear-cut, and when the armed services of the United States are redefining roles for themselves in the Post-Cold War era.

Richard P. Hallion
Air Force Historian

Preface

On March 21, 1946, by order of Headquarters, Army Air Forces, Continental Air Forces received a new name, becoming the Strategic Air Command. This administrative procedure was intended to give some suggestion as to what the mission of that command was to be under the new structure of the air arm. One effect the order had was upon the American language. Very soon after that order was issued, "SAC"—pronounced as a word of one syllable—would be commonplace usage of everyone in or involved with the command. This volume recounts how the Army Air Forces and its successor organization, the U.S. Air Force, organized, trained and equipped strategic air forces for a worldwide mission during the years of the administration of President Harry S. Truman.

The period of history covered in this volume has been heavily studied. It is the opening era of the "Cold War" between the Union of Soviet Socialist Republics and the western countries led by the United States. There has been work on the diplomacy of the Cold War, the limited conflicts that arose from it, about the development of the United States and Europe, as well as the regions then largely under colonial rule. Students have examined issues of national strategy and defense organization. There have even been efforts to study developments within the Soviet bloc itself. In spite of profound disagreements and attempts to fix blame, a certain amount of common understanding of events has emerged. What perhaps has been lacking has been more detailed work to trace the development of military institutions, especially in the United States, to deal with what was in effect a new world situation. A major problem has been the secrecy understandably surrounding much of the information. Over the years, much material has been made available to researchers, and a certain amount has been written. This volume undertakes to give the experience of a particular service in these terms.

The strategic air force that emerged during the period under discussion was central to the nation's strategy. This was the case in part because many airmen themselves believed strategic air power to be the most important component of air power in general. It also was the obvious

Preface

means of delivering the most potent and revolutionary new weapon in the American arsenal, the atomic bomb. And because of the political difficulties (mainly fiscal) inherent in building and maintaining military forces in the United States, strategic air power was the one means by which the nation could be strong at a price it could afford. The development of this force was also seen as a deterrent which, if powerful enough, would overawe a potential aggressor (whether the Soviet Union or one of its proxies) and insure that war would not come.

The decision to develop a strong atomic intercontinental air striking force was made at the end of 1947. This was not a response to a specific recent crisis but to the situation that previous crises had highlighted, namely the rivalry between the United States and the Soviet Union, which carried a military danger so great as to justify a major effort to deter aggression and war. The timing resulted from the fact that the postwar reorganization of national defense had been difficult, and only after some time had the organization, resources, and techical knowledge existed to make the creation of a strategic air force possible. Although the Korean War, beginning in 1950, was essential to the fulfilling of the Air Force's own concepts, that any action at all was possible was due to the perceived urgency of the situation in a time of limited military budgets. A sense of this urgency grew over time, from the crises of 1948 to the Soviet atomic test late in 1949 and the onset of war in Korea.

What emerged was something not altogether new in American life. Before the twentieth century it was not American practice to maintain forces in peacetime ready for an important war. More recently, the Navy had emerged as the "M-Day force" (mobilization day) maintained in readiness for action, while only at the outset or serious threat of war did the nation start to build up land forces. But the Navy was to be ready to fight when war came, shielding the nation as it prepared. It was evident that a strong fleet could also deter an attacker, but its main rationale was that naval forces were likely to be the first to engage a foreign enemy and could not be created overnight in the face of an immediate challenge. Airmen also came to recognize that air forces could not be created overnight. But the new development had to do with the dynamics of deterrence. The decision to make strategic air power the means to act at the outset of war was based on the need to be so strong that war would in fact not come. The demands of an operational air force changed the nature of military organization in a number of ways, not the least in relation to the tensions inherent in a strategy of deterrence.[1]

---

[1] Allan R. Millett and Peter Maslowski, *For the Common Defense: A Military History of the United States of America* (NY: Free Press, 1984), pp 303–309.

Preface

It is worthwhile to point out that the Air Force embraced more than strategic bombers. The other elements of the service had their history, but there was a special urgency attached to the strategic force. On the other hand, this volume is not specifically a history of SAC itself, although the need for one still exists. Much that a work of that kind would need to cover will not be discussed here. Much of the detail of organizational and training matters, for example, would be revealing about the nature of what it was like to be in SAC. The account of the Hiroshima operation tells something of the complexity that early atomic operations would have entailed, but little of the way things changed later.

This volume presents a larger focus. It concerns the American air force's efforts to build a strategic force. The emphasis is on the leaders, the political context, programs, and forces. A significant element of the subject concerns air doctrine, but here this is seen primarily in terms of the experience the leadership of the air arm had had with air warfare. The struggle to create a coherent doctrine for the U. S. Air Force is well described elsewhere. As for the debate in the nation at large, this relates to the political context mentioned above.[2]

In the years after 1953, a school of expertise on national strategy developed outside the armed forces. That was the "golden age" of the civilian strategists. Their work had roots in the period discussed here, and some of the participants appear in these pages. They, too, have received coverage elsewhere. Often, however, the issues of direct concern to the Air Force are not given the same attention. It may be hoped that this work will cast light on this aspect of the question.

Military history often concerns itself with the interaction of great events and the operations of military forces. The strategic force here described was not only by 1953 the premier command of the Air Force. It was the centerpiece of national strategy. The intention here will be to connect the development of the strategy of atomic deterrence with the actual composition and nature of that force. The importance of the Air Force as an institution in American life, and the role of the strategic force in that institution, would seem to establish the importance of the subject.

A number of points need to be made by way of introducing the subject. One of these is the use of the word "strategic". That word is in the title of this volume, and it is in the title of the Air Force major command which stands at the center of the story. Yet objections to the word's use

---

[2] See especially Robert Frank Futrell, *Ideas, Concepts, Doctrine: Basic Thinking in the United States Air Force, 1907–1984* (Maxwell AFB, Ala: AU, 1971 [new imprint 1989]). An account of the civilian strategists can be found in Fred Kaplan, *The Wizards of Armageddon* (NY: Simon & Schuster, 1983).

Preface

in the sense intended continue to appear. In the fall of 1949 the *Air University Quarterly Review* printed an article by the British aviation writer J. M. Spaight. In this article the author suggested an alternative for the use of the word "strategic" as describing certain types of air forces and operations. The alternative was "counteroffensive," a term already used in a published report to the President of the United States. In a different vein, SAC's first commander, Gen. George C. Kenney, once observed: "I do not think that an airplane should be considered as a tactical airplane and a strategic airplane; I think it is an airplane."[3]

These objections have some grounds. The term "strategic" as applied to certain types of air forces can confuse thinking about strategy in broader senses, and about things pertaining to strategy. But the usage has become established. The best to hope for is care in distingushing special and general meanings of the word.

In the specialized sense the word strategic is used in distinction to "tactical." An early example of this distinction is found in the specifications adopted in February 1912 to replace those under which the Signal Corps of the U.S. Army had purchased its first Wright airplane. In these new specifications, two types of airplane were to be bought. The single-seat "Speed Scout" was for strategic reconnaissance, meaning the reconnoitering of enemy forces distant from one's own. The two-seat "Scout" on the other hand, was for tactical reconnaissance, observing hostile forces approaching or in contact with friendly units.[4] The distinction has to do with collecting information useful for furthering the commander's *strategy* or for aiding in decisions pertaining to *tactics*.

Strategic air power, for purposes of this volume, should be seen under three headings: strategic *weapon systems*, strategic *targets*, and strategic *forces*. Strategic weapon systems are those designed for long-range reconnaissance (like the Speed Scout) or bombardment. The connection logically would be that strategic objectives are more likely to require great range than tactical ones. Clearly, then, range is a major attribute of strategic weapon systems (the Soviet counterpart to SAC in those years was called "Long Range Aviation"). Strategic targets are those the destruction of which directly furthers the strategic design of the war. Strategic forces are those responding directly to the higher command direction of the war. That is, they are available to pursue a strategic objective rather than the tactical objectives of a local commander. Thus anomalies can

---

[3] Verbatim Report, 4th Meeting of the Air Board, Dec 3–4, 1946, p 179, RG 340, Proceedings of Air Board, Box 15, MMB, NA.

[4] Juliette A. Hennessy, *The United States Army Air Arm, April 1861 to April 1917* (Washington: USAF Hist Div, 1958 [new imprint, AFCHO, 1985]), p 58.

arise. The long-range bomber can be used against a tactical target and can be placed under a local theater commander. This can be done by the decision of the highest command authority. And "tactical" aircraft may be used against strategic targets. Both situations occurred in Southeast Asia during the 1960s.

Nonetheless, the central conception of strategic air power is fairly simple. It is to further the national strategy by striking at the interior of the enemy country. There the objective may be to demoralize the population, an objective for which the historical precedents are not promising (although Hiroshima and Nagasaki may be an exception). Or the attacker may seek to destroy the economic basis of the adversary's military power. Most official statements of doctrine—especially in the United States—tend to emphasize the latter.[5] In any case, a term often encountered, "strategic bombing," may be understood primarily as air attacks on strategic targets.

Another note on terminology may be in order on a more mundane level. This pertains to the organization of the American air force during the period covered by this volume. At the end of the Second World War, squadrons were the basic combat flying units. A B-29 squadron had ten aircraft, while other types had larger numbers. Three or four squadrons were assembled into a *group*, usually commanded by a colonel and having between 500 and 1,000 men. In large commands a *wing* consisted of several groups and might be commanded by a general officer. Normally a group operated from a single base.[6]

In 1947 the Army Air Forces began to reorganize in anticipation of independence. Their problem was that the combat base, with all of its service units, had become too unwieldy for a combat group headquarters to manage. All too frequently the solution had been to deny the group commander control of his own support units. Consequently a combat *wing* was created, with one combat *group* under it as well as the support elements. Ultimately the group disappeared altogether within the normal

---

[5] For definitions of "strategic air warfare," see JCS Pub 1 and AFR 1–1, *U.S. Air Force Basic Doctrine*. The Sep 1, 1970, edition of AFM 11–1, *United States Air Force Glossary of Standardized Terms*, Vol I, p 188, defined "strategic air warfare" as "Air combat and support operations, designed to effect, through the systematic application of force to a selected series of vital targets, the progressive destruction and disintegration of the enemy's war-making capacity to a point where he no longer retains the ability or will to wage war. Vital targets may include key manufacturing systems, sources of raw material, critical material, stockpiles, power systems, transportation systems, communication facilities, concentrations of uncommitted elements of enemy armed forces, key agricultural areas, and other such target systems."

[6] J. C. Hopkins and Sheldon A. Goldberg, *The Development of Strategic Air Command, 1946–1986* (Offutt AFB, Neb: SAC, 1986), pp 9, 31, 38.

Preface

wing structure. The level of command immediately above the wing became the *division*.[7]

In force planning, a subject of importance in this volume, staff officers described a tentative or approved program in terms of the number of combat groups it would provide, as with the "seventy-group program" discussed in the early chapters here. By 1950 reorganization had so far proceeded that the planners more and more spoke of wings in the same sense. That change in usage will be reflected in the text, but in terms of combat power, the *group* of 1946 is the same as the *wing* of 1952.

Some observations are in order as well on the character of the time covered in this volume. Since that time the relations of the United States with the Union of Soviet Socialist Republics have undergone remarkable evolution. In 1945, however, a number of American leaders had come to regard the Soviet Union and its leader, Josef Stalin, with the utmost suspicion. They perceived Stalin as possessed of an insatiable ambition and shared their compatriots' aversion to communism as a principle of government. The Soviet leader's reputation as a mass murderer and his actions at the time did nothing to allay these suspicions and aversions. In due course, the general public in the United States and most of Western Europe came to share this viewpoint. In people's minds, the Munich agreement of 1938 carried the lesson that making concessions to aggressive dictators did not prevent war. It was therefore necessary for the western nations to be strong in order to contain Stalinist aggression.

In this atmosphere, although intelligence analysts often doubted that Stalin actually wanted war, it still seemed possible. The deterrent force emerged from that fear. But deterrence might fail. Military men knew that there would be expectations that an atomic offensive against the Soviet Union could become necessary. As a result, American air leaders believed that the consequences of the air arm's not being ready to carry out such an offensive, through failure to plan or for any other reason, could be grave. These, then, were disturbing times. In this connection, there are many in the Soviet Union today who consider the practice of falsifying the historical record for current political purposes to have been one of the most corrupting factors in the life of that country. An improved international atmosphere should not conceal the realities of the past.

A further observation touches on a different set of suspicions, entirely domestic. The period of postwar reorganization in the American defense establishment after 1945 did not end with true consensus. Numerous viewpoints had been put forward during the debate, having in large part to do with the roles the various services and branches of the armed forces

---

[7] *Ibid.*

were to play. An act of Congress in 1947 could not be final proof that any particular position was correct. Consequently, debate continued, sometimes reaching a level of acrimony that appalled both participants and observers. At the same time, a rule of discourse seemed to require that every participant be speaking from a position of undiluted, self-effacing patriotism. According to these rules, it was totally unworthy of a serving officer to have any desire to advance his own career or the well-being of his particular service. The unbiased observer must make allowance for the existence of these rules and the unrealistic expectations they created. That an officer might feel that he and his service possessed special qualifications to serve his country can hardly be grounds to bring his patriotism into question. Likewise, that honest men might disagree in all sincerity would seem to be a fundamental tenet of debate in a democratic country. The words of an officer in the 1950s might be apt here: "How curious it is that the Congress *debates*, the Supreme Court *deliberates*, but for some reason or other the Joint Chiefs of Staff just *bicker*?"[8]

Furthermore, all was not acrimony. The different services were not hermetically sealed off from each other or arrayed as hostile camps. One of the figures who appears in this volume, Maj. Gen. Frederic H. Smith, was the son-in-law of the wartime Chief of Naval Operations, Admiral of the Fleet Ernest J. King. This relationship was perhaps unusual, but it should point up the links that bound those who had fought (and lost friends) in a common struggle, and shared a dedication to the safety and well-being of their country. Their forthrightness in expressing strongly held views should not then imply that they existed purely as adversaries.

---

[8] Quoted in Samuel P. Huntington, *The Common Defense: Strategic Programs in National Politics* (NY: Columbia Univ Press, 1961), p 170.

Acknowledgments

All official history is a cooperative effort, and this is as true in the U.S. Air Force as anywhere else. A book of this nature stands on the shoulders of giants as it were, and the debt owed to the unit and command historians of the years 1945 to 1953 contributed much more than might be supposed from a brief perusal of the notes. The book would have been quite simply impossible without their effort.

The prolonged work involved in preparing this volume necessarily required the direct assistance of a great many people. It was in fact initially undertaken in 1970 as a joint effort by the Office of Air Force History (now the Air Force History and Museums Program) and the Office of the Historian, Headquarters SAC. The originally assigned authors were Mr. Herman S. Wolk of the former office and Mr. Robert M. Kipp of the SAC Historian's Office. Subsequently Dr. John T. Greenwood, then of the Office of Air Force History, assumed responsibility for the project. The present author came into possession of an extremely useful draft of some early chapters. While he completely reworked the material, he remains supremely indebted to these historians, who accomplished an important part of the research on which the volume is based. Their work provided an invaluable foundation for the result, and while the author assumes responsibility for the final product, such merit as it may possess is attributable in large part to his predecessors.

The author was greatly assisted in research by a number of repositories. First among these was the National Archives. There the assistance of the staff in room 13W, currently the Military Reference Branch, overcoming all of the obstacles with which researchers at the National Archives are familiar, provided the untiring and considerate service absolutely essential to this undertaking. Those assisting included Messrs. Charles Shaughnessy, Gibson Smith, Wilbert Mahoney, and especially Edward J. Reese, who spent hours pursuing every kind of lead in the stacks. Mr. Leroy Jackson proved equally helpful in making documents available. Misses Terese E. Hammett and Angela M. Fernandez devoted hours to copying material.

Acknowledgments

Mr. Gary J. Kohn, formerly of the Manuscript Reading Room of the Library of Congress, and the rest of the staff there, were most helpful in providing access to their well-organized collections. At the Harry S. Truman Library, Independence, Missouri, Mr. C. Warren Ohrvall and the rest of the staff provided indispensable help. The Albert F. Simpson Historical Research Center (now the Air Force Historical Research Agency), Maxwell Air Force Base, Alabama, was of great assistance. The late Dr. Richard Morse, Ms. Lynn O. Gamma and their staffs supported this effort.

Mr. William C. Heimdahl, Chief of the Reference Branch of the Air Force History Support Office, gave of his incredible expertise on numerous occasions. To his support as manager, as expert archivist, and as friend, the author is especially indebted. Hardly less recognition is due to another friend, Mr. Sheldon A. Goldberg, who both as archivist at the SAC Historian's Office and in Washington, was endlessly supportive. Mr. Goldberg's help in the bewildering process of extracting this volume from the security review process virtually intact made all the difference. Dr. Henry Narducci of the SAC Historian's Office was also helpful. The late General Curtis E. LeMay, USAF (Ret), was most courteous in providing information. Brig. Gen. William G. Hipps, USAF (Ret) was helpful, and the late Brig. Gen. Noel F. Parrish, USAF (Ret), gave valuable information, insight, and support.

As one who had previously been an assigned author of the book, Herman S. Wolk, as Chief of the Histories Branch of the Office of Air Force History, was commendably forebearing in his support, the endless source of wise counsel, patience, and friendship. The outside members of the panel, the late Gen. Jack Catton, Professor David A. Rosenberg, Dr. Steven L. Rearden, Dr. Walter S. Poole of the Historical Division, Joint Chiefs of Staff, and Dr. Narducci also made other important contributions to improving this volume.

Professor John W. Huston, then on active duty in the rank of major general, USAFR, as Chief of the Office of Air Force History, originally assigned the authorship of this volume, and Drs. Richard H. Kohn and Richard P. Hallion, his successors, continued to provide his energetic support as well as a penetrating insight. The late Col. John F. Shiner, as Dr. Kohn's deputy, proved helpful in seeing the manuscript through final clearance for release. Mr. Jacob Neufeld was helpful, among other things, in arranging for keying the early chapters into the office's new software program. Among others, Ms. Ida J. Newman, Sgt. Glenn Reynolds, and SSgt. John Wyche typed the manuscript.

The cooperative nature of work of this sort could hardly be ignored either in the case of the numerous colleagues within the Air Force History and Museums Program who offered friendship and advice in an incredible variety of combinations. The author is especially indebted in this connec-

Acknowledgments

tion to Mr. Jacob Neufeld, Ms. Marcelle S. Knaack, Dr. Wayne W. Thompson, Dr. Rebecca Hancock Cameron, Dr. George M. Watson, Dr. Edgar F. Raines, Jr. (now of the U. S. Army Center of Military History), Dr. Daniel R. Mortensen, Mr. Warren A. Trest (now of the Air Force Historical Research Agency), Lt. Col. Vance O. Mitchell, Mr. Bernard C. Nalty, Major William C. Borgiasz, Drs. Benjamin F. Cooling, Mark Mandeles, and the late Robert P. Smith.

Contributors from other agencies—Dr. Marie E. Hallion of the U.S. Department of Energy, Mr. Brian Nicklas of the National Air and Space Museum, Mr. Joe Caver of the Air Force Historical Research Agency, and Mr. Mark Renovitch of the Franklin D. Roosevelt Library quickly and cheerfully provided photos from their various historical collections.

The author owes a particular debt of gratitude to the writer/editors of the Air Force History and Museums Program whose professionalism, keen insights, and rigorous standards made this a much livelier, more coherent book—Editorial Chief Anne Johnson-Sachs, Ms. Janett Gordon, and especially Ms. Mary Lee Jefferson, who in addition to editing the book, shepherded it through a complex production process, acquired photos, composed captions, and worked with the artists of Headquarters Air Force Graphics—Mr. Steve Gonyea, who designed and executed the book's cover, and Ms. Kathy Jones, who executed the charts and maps.

To all these colleagues, to such extracurricular combinations as the St. Mark's Players of Capitol Hill, and to his parents and family the author is obligated for those intangibles, not just of support and friendship, but of counsel and encouragement.

Contents

	Pages
Foreword	v
Preface	vii
Acknowledgments	xv

Part I

Postwar Reorganization, 1945 – 1947

I. Air Power and the Airmen: 1945 3
Air Power and Strategy
Building a Strategic Air Force, 1917–1945
The Postwar Challenge

II. The Case for a Postwar Air Force 29
A New Strategic World
Demobilization and Occupation
Planning for Strategic Air Power

III. The Beginnings of a Strategic Air Force 67
Air Power Deferred
The Strategic Force and Demobilization
The Strategic Force and the Fifty-five Group Program
Modernizing the Bomber Force

IV. The Uncertain Phase 113
Understanding the Bomb
Command of Strategic Forces
Planning for Atomic War

Part II

Austerity and Strategic Air Power, 1947 – 1950

- V. **Decision for a Strategic Air Force** 155
  Making the Case for Air Power: Finletter and Brewster
  A Program for Atomic Readiness: JCS 1745 / 5
  Aircraft for the Strategic Offensive

- VI. **The Year of Crisis**................................ 187
  Toward a Crisis Budget
  Roles, Missions, and Budgets
  The Berlin Crisis
  Containment, Deterrence, and NSC–20 / 4
  "The Hollow Threat" and LeMay

- VII. **The Priority Mission**............................. 235
  Aircraft for Deterrence
  Return to Austerity
  Modernization and Standardization

- VIII. **Challenges to Strategy**........................... 283
  The Challenge at Home
  Facing the Challenge
  The External Challenge: The Soviet Bomb
  The Strategic Force at the Ready: SAC in 1950

Part III

Expansion of the Strategic Force, 1950 – 1953

- IX. **Limited War, Atomic Plenty, and Rearmament** 339
  Deterrence at Risk
  Rearmament Begins
  The Role of Nuclear Weapons
  Expanding the Strategic Force
  An Investment in Air Power

- X. **"Never Before Surpassed"** 393
  Medium Bombers in Korea
  Expansion and Professionalism
  Planes and Weapons, 1950–1953
  Basing for a Global Strike Force
  From New Phase to New Look

Conclusion 463
Glossary 475
Bibliography 479
Index 497

Tables and Charts

Assignment and Stationing of B–29 Units, 1946 62
Flights of Experimental Bombers, 1946–1947 99
Proposed Aircraft Procurement Programs, 1947 111
Strategic Air Command, 1947 147
1949 Air Force Budget and Supplemental 198
Supplemental Aircraft Program, 1948 241
Bomber Programs 244
Strategic Air Command, 1948 296
Strategic Air Command, 1949 320
Air Force 143-Wing Program, 1951 391

Maps

SAC Units, Location and Type, 1950 356
SAC Deployment from the United States to Korea 382

Photographs

LITTLE BOY 8
FAT MAN 9
Enola Gay 11
Dawn of the Atomic Age 18
Strategists of the Air 25
Big Three at Yalta, 1945 28
U.S. Defense Leaders 36
Lt. Gens. Norstad and Vandenberg 45
Vannevar Bush and Leslie Groves 51
Gen. Ira C. Eaker 57
Maj. Gen. Curtis E. LeMay 64
Gen. George C. Kenney 75
Maj. Gens. McMullen and Streett 86
B–17 and B–24 96
B–29 107
AAF Task Group 1.5 119
B–36 131

Elmendorf Air Force Base	140
Changes at the Top	158
New Air Force Team	163
Air Policy Commission	167
Aerial Refueling	178
Advocates of Aerial Refueling	184
George F. Kennan	192
DARKHORSE War Planners	200
USS *United States*	206
Challenge in Berlin	213
Charles A. Lindbergh	228
New Era at SAC	232
New Needs, New Aircraft	242
Lucky Lady II	255
SAC and Training	262
Wherry Housing	268
SAC and Base Life	274
SAC and Maintenance	278
XB–35 Flying Wing	286
Secretary of Defense Louis A. Johnson	292
Newport Conference	301
Lt. Gen. Hubert H. Harmon	307
Soviet Threat	315
Gens. Fairchild and McNarney	324
U.S. political cartoon on the Soviet's Atomic Bomb	331
Secretary of the Air Force Thomas K. Finletter	343
Maj. Gen. Emmett O'Donnell	348
On Target	351
Lt. Gen. Nathan F. Twining	365
B–45	374
Gen. LeMay's New Wing Commanders	378
SAC and the Korean War	400
New and Improved Radar	404
A Crew of the 6th Bomb Wing	413
B–36s after the Carswell Storm	418
F–84E Thunderjets	423
The Jet Age	428
Maj. Gen. Archie J. Old, Jr.	433
Lt. Gen. George E. Stratemeyer	441
New Look Team	450
Gen. Vandenberg before Congress, 1953	459

Part I

Postwar Reorganization 1945–1947

Chapter I

Air Power and the Airmen: 1945

On Sunday, August 5, 1945, the combat forces of the United States for the first time had possession of an atomic bomb. At the "tech area" adjacent to North Field on the island of Tinian in the Marianas, airmen had been working for days on the final phase of assembling the weapon. This was the task of the 1st Ordnance Squadron, Special (Aviation), 509th Composite Group, 313th Bombardment Wing (Very Heavy), Twentieth Air Force, United States Army Strategic Air Forces.[1]

The technicians and ordnancemen at the assembly area constructed the bomb, dubbed LITTLE BOY, from components that had arrived during the previous two weeks. The uranium core was inserted, but the fusing mechanism was left unarmed. Then on the afternoon of August 5, airmen placed the weapon aboard a trolley, covered it with a tarpaulin, and towed

---

[1] The Twentieth Air Force was responsible for delivering the atomic weapon on target. The design, testing, and manufacture of the bomb was done under the auspices of the War Department's MANHATTAN PROJECT. Lee Bowen, *Project Silverplate, 1943–1946*, Vol I in Lee Bowen and Robert D. Little, eds, *The History of Air Force Participation in the Atomic Energy Program, 1943–1953* (Washington: USAF Hist Div, 1959), pp 106–107, 132–136. The Hiroshima mission has been described countless times. The most important works on the atomic project as a whole are Vincent C. Jones, *Manhattan: The Army and the Atomic Bomb* [The United States Army in World War II: Special Studies] (Washington: CMH, 1985); Richard G. Hewlett and Oscar E. Anderson, Jr., *The New World, 1939–1946*, Vol I of *A History of the Atomic Energy Commission* (University Park, Pa: Pa Univ Press, 1962; Leslie R. Groves, *Now It Can Be Told: The Story of the Manhattan Project* (NY: Harper & Row, 1962); William L. Laurence, *Dawn Over Zero: The Story of the Atomic Bomb* (NY: Knopf, 1946 [new imprint, Westport, Conn: Greenwood, 1977]); an account of the Hiroshima mission that is readable and generally accurate is Gordon Thomas and Max Morgan Witts, *Enola Gay* (NY: Stein & Day, 1977).

it by tractor under heavy guard to the loading area. There LITTLE BOY was moved down a ramp into a pit and a plane parked over it.[2]

The Commanding Officer of the 509th Composite Group, Col. Paul W. Tibbets, Jr., had already selected the aircraft to deliver the bomb. A Boeing B–29 Superfortress, serial number 44–86292, was one of the 509th's planes that had been modified under Army Air Forces (AAF) PROJECT SILVERPLATE to carry atomic weapons. Seventeen feet long and weighing nearly five tons, even without its electrical connections, LITTLE BOY would not fit in the bomb bay of a conventional B–29. Tibbets intended to fly the plane himself, and he named it *Enola Gay* after his mother. The bomb was hoisted into the B–29's bomb bay and secured, after which the doors were closed.[3]

Tibbets chose the crew for the crucial mission. Though it resembled a conventional Superfortress crew, there were some special features. The regular pilot of the plane was the copilot. Tibbets personally selected the navigator and bombardier and assigned the 509th's radar countermeasures officer, 1st Lt. Jacob Beser. Also on board were the enlisted members of the regular crew, including a flight engineer, radio operator, radar operator, mechanic, and tail gunner. Two key specialists were prepared for the mission: U.S. Navy Capt. William S. Parsons, a leading officer of the MANHATTAN PROJECT which designed the bomb, went as weaponeer, and 2d Lt. Morris R. Jeppson as his assistant. Parsons was responsible for arming the bomb during flight.[4]

At 0245 hours on Monday, a large crowd watched the *Enola Gay* take off. Other B–29s, carrying observers, followed it into the air. Tibbets headed his bomber in the direction of Japan. The primary target was Hiroshima, with Kokura as secondary and Nagasaki the tertiary. At 0815 hours Tibbets heard from the weather observer over Hiroshima and decided to attack the primary target. Captain Parsons had already armed the weapon. At 0911 hours the plane reached the initial point and the bombardier began his bomb run. At 0915 (0815 Hiroshima time) the bombardier released the weapon. Tibbets turned the bomber sharply and began his descent at high speed, thus placing himself at a slant range of fifteen miles from the detonation point. There was a flash, and shortly afterward two shock waves struck the plane. The *Enola Gay* then turned to circle the area and observe. Parsons considered the blast more impressive

---

[2] Jones, *Manhattan*, pp 535–536; Groves, *Now It Can be Told*, p 317; Thomas & Witts, *Enola Gay*, p 232.
[3] Bowen, *Silverplate*, pp 91–101, 157; Thomas & Witts, *Enola Gay*, pp 232–233.
[4] Bowen, *Silverplate*, pp 134–136, 157, 160.

visually than the test shot he had witnessed three weeks before.⁵ SSgt. George R. Caron, the tail gunner, recorded his impressions:

> A column of smoke rising fast. It has a fiery red core. A bubbling mass, purple-gray in color, with that red core. It's all turbulent. Fires are springing up everywhere.... There are too many to count. Here it comes, the mushroom shape that Captain Parsons spoke about.... It's maybe a mile or two wide.... It's nearly level with us and climbing. It's very black, but there is a purplish tint to the cloud. The base of the mushroom looks like a heavy undercast that is shot through with flames. The city must be below that. The flames and smoke are billowing out, whirling out into the foothills.⁶

Tibbets set an eastward course and began the journey home, radioing a report of his success. He touched down at North Field at 1500 hours. In the crowd waiting to greet him was Gen. Carl A. Spaatz, Commanding General, U.S. Army Strategic Air Forces (USASTAF). As Tibbets climbed out of the plane, General Spaatz approached and presented him with the Distinguished Service Cross.⁷

In Hiroshima the blast of the bomb generated vast heat, starting fires and inflicting enormous casualties. The shock wave destroyed nearly five square miles of the city. Even more devastating was the radiation in the huge cloud that engulfed Hiroshima. Eighty thousand died instantly or within a few days. At least as many more were injured. The prolonged effects of radiation exposure, however, meant that the actual toll would remain unknown for years.⁸

The shock of Hiroshima, while great, did not immediately lead to surrender. The Japanese government was paralyzed by the deteriorating military situation and the massive destruction inflicted on the homeland by all types of American bombing. On August 9 Japan learned that Soviet forces had attacked their positions in Manchuria. Within hours Nagasaki met the same fate as Hiroshima. Although the damage and loss of life were less, there was no doubt of the destructive power of the new weapon. Finally, late that night, in an exceedingly rare personal intervention, the

---

⁵ *Ibid.*, pp 136–137; Groves, *Now It Can Be Told*, p 322; Thomas & Witts, *Enola Gay*, pp 262–265.
⁶ Quoted in Thomas & Witts, *Enola Gay*, p 264. Beser carried a recording machine on the flight, and Caron was among those whose impressions were given. Thomas and Witts do not state whether the words are transcribed from the recording or Caron's recollection of what he said. If the latter is the case, it is nonetheless an eyewitness account.
⁷ Thomas & Witts, *Enola Gay*, p 269.
⁸ Jones, *Manhattan*, pp 545–547.

Emperor instructed the government to accept the Americans' terms for peace. Further discussion ensued, with another Imperial intervention, before hostilities concluded on August 15. The world's first nuclear war had ended in nine days. The world hoped that a second one would never start.[9]

The bomb used against Nagasaki was of a different design from LITTLE BOY. Of comparable weight, it had a greater diameter and so was called FAT MAN. The difference between the bombs represented two separate solutions to the engineering problems encountered by the three-year, $2 billion research and development effort known as the MANHATTAN PROJECT. In LITTLE BOY, a gun fired a quantity of uranium at another. When the two portions came together, "critical mass" occurred—the concentration of the amount of material necessary to make the explosion take place. FAT MAN achieved "critical mass" by implosion. The plutonium was placed in separate portions inside a layer of high explosive which, on detonation, forced the material together.[10] The fusing mechanism was designed to create an air burst by sending a radar signal to the ground to measure altitude. Lieutenant Beser's job had been to make sure that a Japanese radar did not set off the mechanism.[11]

Although the implosion bomb was more complex than the gun-type, and its ballistic properties were undesirable from a bombardier's viewpoint, it was more efficient in terms of yield of energy to the amount of fissionable material used. Since, as will be discussed later, the MANHATTAN PROJECT was concerned about the availability of fissionable uranium and plutonium, the FAT MAN was preferable. This was the design that had been tested in the very first atomic explosion at Alamogordo, New Mexico, on July 16, 1945.[12]

The Nagasaki mission on August 9 had not gone as smoothly as the previous one. Maj. Charles W. Sweeney, commander of the 393d Bombardment Squadron (Very Heavy), the 509th's combat element, flew the mission in *Bock's Car*, the plane normally flown by Capt. Frederick C. Bock. Lt. Cmdr. Frederick L. Ashworth, U.S. Navy, was the weaponeer. FAT MAN could not be armed in flight, but there were other tasks for Ashworth to do. Kokura had been designated the primary target, but poor weather dictated the shift to the secondary target. A less accurate drop and the

---

[9] Bowen, *Silverplate*, pp 147–149.
[10] Hewlett & Anderson, *New World*, p 235.
[11] Thomas & Witts, *Enola Gay*, pp 36–41.
[12] Bowen, *Silverplate*, pp 91–101, 111–113; Hewlett & Anderson, *New World*, pp 378–380.

hilly terrain of Nagasaki combined to reduce the damage to the city, despite the great power of the bomb.[13]

Meanwhile material for another weapon was being readied at the MANHATTAN PROJECT's weapons laboratory at Los Alamos, New Mexico. But the officer in charge of the project, Maj. Gen. Leslie R. Groves, anticipated that the enemy would surrender after Nagasaki. He accordingly delayed delivery, and the material was never sent. To Groves as to so many others at the time, the connection between the atomic bombings and the Japanese surrender seemed obvious.[14] Over the years, historians have debated this simple view of causation, and indeed controversy has surrounded the entire question of the wartime use of nuclear weapons. The divergence of opinion, however, does not alter the fact that key observers at the time believed that the atomic weapon ended the war.

One of the German atomic scientists commented that Hiroshima "...shows that the Americans are capable of real co-operation on a tremendous scale."[15] Particularly striking was the collaboration between the MANHATTAN PROJECT and the Army Air Forces. In the summer of 1943 Gen. Henry H. ("Hap") Arnold, Commanding General of the AAF, received a request from the project for assistance in testing the ballistics of the bomb. Arnold and Groves subsequently conferred about organizing a combat unit. The resulting PROJECT SILVERPLATE was conducted with maximum secrecy. Even in the 509th Group, few knew the true mission of the unit. Nevertheless, despite this and other obstacles, the group was ready on time to receive the first bomb.[16]

Those involved in the atomic project had little time to speculate on the implications of the weapon, but to the AAF commander and his staff, the atomic bomb confirmed the importance of technological advance in warfare. Bombs were the basic weapon of the air arm, and the employment of the atomic weapon called for the airmen to operate in familiar ways. Questions of the purpose, organization, control, and use of air power applied to this weapon as to any other. On the other hand, a bomb of such enormous power altered the entire mathematics of attacking a target.

Arnold's own experience with the evolution of the technology had prepared him well for the dramatic new advance. As one of the first three

---

[13] Bowen, *Silverplate*, pp 139–146.
[14] Groves, *Now It Can Be Told*, pp 352–355.
[15] Quoted in Groves, *Now It Can Be Told*, p 335.
[16] Bowen, *Silverplate*, pp 92–102; Jones, *Manhattan*, pp 519–520; Groves, *Now It Can Be Told*, p 253. Jones and Groves both describe Groves's meeting with Arnold, according to Jones "for the first time." Jones mentions that Arnold already knew about the project, and Bowen states that Groves "told" Arnold about the bomb in July 1943.

LITTLE BOY, the first atomic bomb dropped on Japan over Hiroshima, used a "cannon"-type triggering mechanism, measured 28 inches across and 128 inches long and weighed 9,000 pounds. It yielded the equivalent of approximately 12,500 tons of high explosive.

U.S. Army officers to become a certified airplane pilot (having learned to fly from the Wright Brothers in 1911), Arnold became an early advocate of air power.[17] He was thus one of the small group that set the Army on the path of a major innovation in the history of warfare. It was fitting that in 1943 he should become intimately involved with another revolutionary technology.

Air Power and Strategy

The surrender of the Japanese left the United States without an enemy and possessing an unprecedented level of global power. The wartime British prime minister, Winston S. Churchill, had referred to the United States as having "a Navy twice as big as any other Navy in the world.... The largest Air Force in the world, with bases in every part of the

---

[17] Juliette A. Hennessy, *The United States Army Air Arm, April 1861–April 1917* (Washington: USAF Hist Div, 1950 [new imprint, AFCHO, 1985]), pp 47, 50, 236.

FAT MAN, the second atomic bomb dropped on Japan over Nagasaki, was an implosion weapon, characterized by a near-spherical shape. Weighing 10,000 pounds, it measured 60 inches across and 128 inches long. It yielded the equivalent of 22,000 tons of high explosive.

world..." and "all the gold in the world...."[18] Churchill had also known as he spoke that the first power to build the atomic bomb would be the United States. The reference to gold highlighted the burgeoning American economy, which was supporting, seemingly without effort, more than twelve million men under arms and a national budget approaching $100 billion a year.[19] In contrast, Germany and Japan lay defeated and in ruins, destined for a period of military occupation. The strongest of the remaining powers, the Union of Soviet Socialist Republics, had a huge land army, but its industrial plant needed time to recover its prewar vigor, and even when it did its technological backwardness would remain a handicap. The British faced staggering economic problems if they were to maintain an

---

[18] Winston Churchill, Speech to the House of Commons, Jan 18, 1945, in *Parliamentary Debates, 1944–1945*, p 407: cols 425–426, cited in Albert Resis, "The Churchill-Stalin Secret 'Percentages' Agreement on the Balkans, Moscow, October 1944," *AHR* 83 (Apr 78), p 387.

[19] Allan R. Millett & Peter Maslowski, *For the Common Defense: A Military History of the United States of America* (NY: Free Press, 1984), pp 407–414; U.S. Department of Commerce, *Historical Statistics of the United States, Colonial Times to 1957: A Statistical Abstract Supplement* (Washington: GPO, 1957), p 718.

international position. Thus, America was the senior partner in the triumphant coalition, although strains had developed with the Soviets.

This situation made many Americans feel confident, although precisely because it was new, it was also disturbing. The nation needed fresh ideas as well as guidance based on past experience. For those, like Arnold, who had risen to positions of leadership, much had changed in just three decades. In 1911 the United States possessed relatively small armed forces and had only recently been recognized as one of several world powers. Victory in two world wars had fostered a realization of America's stature in international affairs, and the lessons learned during this period of rapid political, economic, and military change would aid the nation's leadership now.

Two of the events that molded the consciousness of American leaders appeared to have been crucial in bringing the country into World War II. The first, the Munich crisis, was an experience shared with other government officials in the West. The other, the attack on Pearl Harbor, affected U.S. military strategists especially. Together these incidents were considered warnings against the dangers inherent in appeasement and military unpreparedness.

At the Munich conference of September 1938, the leaders of France and Great Britain had yielded to pressure from the German dictator Adolf Hitler and allowed him the fruits of aggression against Czechoslovakia without having to fight. "Appeasement," at first considered a rational alternative to war, became an epithet for craven surrender. And the best argument for giving up the Sudetenland to Germany turned on the lack of sufficient military strength on the part of the European powers to stand up to the aggressor. The outbreak of war a year afterward seemed to demonstrate that weakness and appeasement merely postponed the inevitable. U.S. observers further pondered whether America's policy of isolation, its refusal to join the League of Nations, play a role in European affairs, or maintain strong military forces, had contributed to the crisis.[20]

---

[20] James L. Stokesbury, *A Short History of World War II* (NY: William Morrow, 1980), pp 57–63. Although this discussion of the evolution of the American outlook on strategic air forces relies on traditional sources, some of the new work on the subject must be noted. Ronald Schaffer, *Wings of Judgment: American Bombing in World War II* (NY: Oxford Univ Press, 1985) provides a valuable discussion of the extent to which American civilian and military leaders, including the airmen, wrestled with the moral issues of strategic bombing. Another work, Michael S. Sherry, *The Rise of American Air Power: The Creation of Armageddon* (New Haven, Conn: Yale Univ Press, 1987) is a comprehensive account of the role of strategic air power in American life through 1945. It contains a valuable discussion of the antecedents of the atomic strike force. The focus of the book, however, is primarily cultural, and it places the AAF and its predecessors in this much broader context.

The *Enola Gay*, *above*, and her crew, *below*, prior to take-off from Tinian for Hiroshima. *Standing, left to right:* Lt. Col. John Porter, ground maintenance officer, not on flight; Capt. Theodore Van Kirk, navigator; Maj. Thomas Ferebee, bombardier; Col. Paul Tibbets, pilot and commanding officer, 509th Bombardment Group; Capt. Robert Lewis, copilot; Lt. Jacob Beser, radar countermeasure officer. *Kneeling, left to right:* Sgt. Joseph Stiborik, radar operator; SSgt. George Caron, tail gunner; Pfc. Richard Nelson, radio operator; Sgt. Robert Shumard, assistant engineer; SSgt. Wyatt Duzenbury, flight engineer. *Not pictured:* ordnance officers Lt. Morris Jeppson and Capt. William Parsons, USN.

Strategic Air Force

The Japanese surprise attack at Pearl Harbor on December 7, 1941, had spread the war to America and traumatized the public. Though blame was cast in several directions, the disasters of the following months were clearly the price of failure to arm sooner. Mere potential strength no longer seemed enough. And for military personnel there was a pointed lesson for the future. Years later, Curtis Emerson LeMay, having risen to general rank and high command, would recall how the Army and Navy commanders in Hawaii, having failed to be ready for an attack, had been made scapegoats for the entire disaster.[21]

While possession of the atomic bomb had altered the context of American strategic thinking, it did not immediately affect the conclusions drawn from the experience of the Second World War. If the nation's avoidance of foreign entanglements had contributed to the outbreak of war, participation in the new United Nations would be essential to keeping the peace. Anticipating the defeat of the Axis powers, President Franklin D. Roosevelt had based his plans for the postwar era on the United Nations and on cooperation between the United States and the Soviet Union. For the President, as for many Americans, the cost of such involvement in world affairs seemed worthwhile if another catastrophe was thereby averted. Roosevelt envisioned including the British and even the Chinese (for whom he had great hopes) in a coalition with the Americans and Soviets. The "Four Policemen" would play a leading role in enforcing the peace,[22] and, as Roosevelt told Vyacheslav M. Molotov, the Soviet Minister for Foreign Affairs, "If any nation menaced peace...it could be blockaded and then if still recalcitrant, bombed."[23]

This concept presupposed the maintenance of military forces, especially at sea and in the air, and was thus consistent with the lessons that American military leaders had drawn from their experience of the war. Yet there had been a certain alteration in U.S. strategic thinking. In the past, advocates of peacetime military strength had spoken of "preparedness," which generally meant maintaining a regular army and reserves as a nucleus around which the manpower pool would be mobilized. The scheme also called for building stocks of munitions and critical raw materials, with a national industrial base available for conversion to war production. The Navy had won acceptance as the force to be ready immediately at the

---

[21] Thomas M. Coffey, *Iron Eagle: The Turbulent Life of General Curtis LeMay* (NY: Crown, 1986), pp 263–264.
[22] John L. Gaddis, *The United States and the Origins of the Cold War, 1941–1947* (NY: Columbia Univ Press, 1972), pp 25–30.
[23] Roosevelt-Molotov Conversation, May 29, 1942, in U.S. Department of State, *FRUS*, 1942, Vol III (Washington: GPO, 1961), pp 568–569.

outset of war, and it would serve as the shield for national mobilization.²⁴ Arnold and his colleagues had lived through the era of "preparedness," and they acknowledged the public's aversion to large standing armies and peacetime military spending. However, the United States had fallen short of the level of preparedness that many had urged during the 1920s and 1930s. This in itself seemed to have contributed to the outbreak of war and American involvement. Moreover, Pearl Harbor demonstrated the swiftness with which devastating results could be achieved in the age of air power. Even the proposed prewar levels of readiness might not have been enough to forestall a future conflict. And for airmen such as Arnold, naval forces were no longer the best choice to be the ready shield. Roosevelt's concept of a coalition of peacekeeping powers was compatible with such thinking. Planners in the AAF had already begun to discuss a future role for American air forces in a United Nations peacekeeping force.²⁵

The Joint Chiefs of Staff (JCS) were somewhat skeptical of the potential of the United Nations to enforce the peace, but they supported official policy. This doubt was shared by others, including diplomats and political leaders, who saw bipolar cooperation with the Soviets as the essential factor. The same skeptics were generally suspicious of the communist power and considered the possibility of war with the former ally as one worth examining. Fortunately, the Soviets' failure to develop a large long-range air force or ocean-going navy limited their power to attack America. Nonetheless, the huge Red Army, ground troops backed up by large tactical air forces, could threaten security throughout the Eurasian landmass. In view of the wide dispersal of Soviet industry, even proponents of air power questioned whether a strategic air offensive could be effective. These geopolitical and military factors combined to feed a growing distrust of Josef Stalin's motives on the part of American officials, both military and civilian.²⁶

Building a Strategic Air Force, 1917–1945

The immense Air Force that the United States possessed in August of 1945 included thirty-seven groups of B–29 Superfortresses, considered the

---

²⁴ Millett & Maslowski, *Common Defense*, pp 363–365.
²⁵ Memo, Walter E. Todd for Maj Gen L. Norstad, ACAS/Pl to DCAS, subj: US Air Force Contingent for Combined International Enforcement Action of the United Nations, Jul 26, 1945, RG 341, TS AAG File 21, Box 7, MMB, NA.
²⁶ Perry McCoy Smith, *The Air Force Plans for Peace, 1943–1945* (Baltimore, Md: Johns Hopkins Univ Press, 1970), p 53; Michael S. Sherry, *Preparing for the Next War: American Plans for Postwar Defense, 1941–1945* (New Haven, Conn: Yale Univ Press, 1977), pp 41–43, 159–167, 199–205.

world's preeminent strategic bomber.[27] America's leadership in strategic air power was a recent development. Just six years earlier, the nation's strategic fleet had consisted of scarcely a dozen Boeing B–17 Flying Fortresses. These had recently emerged from a service test, with many deficiencies normal in an original design.[28] Once earlier, in 1917 and 1918, the United States had tried to build a strategic bomber force, but the effort came to very little. The technological advances of the interwar years made success much more likely.

The effort to create a strategic air force during the First World War emerged slowly, as American airmen learned of the efforts of their allies in this direction. Even before the declaration of war against Germany on April 6, 1917, there had been some public awareness of the attacks by German zeppelins on Great Britain. The idea of striking the heart of an enemy nation by air had been a staple of science fiction writers over the years, and there was a historical precedent in actual warfare. In February 1871 the Germans attempted to end their conflict with France by bombarding Paris with artillery. In that case, the war-weariness of the French countryside had more influence on the cease-fire than the morale of the Parisians.[29] This problem of defining precisely how bombardment can effect a strategic decision would bedevil military airmen from the very beginnings of their profession.

From the start, the American air contribution to the Allied war effort in the First World War was plagued with unrealistic expectations. Before it became clear that the United States would have to send a field army to fight in France, a great wave of enthusiasm had produced an unprecedented appropriation of $640 million to build a vast aerial armada to strike at the Germans. However, at the time of the armistice on November 11, 1918, not one fully equipped American strategic bomber unit was in service.[30] The fundamental lesson of this effort could hardly be better expressed than by Col. Edgar S. Gorrell, who had played a major role in the effort to deploy an American strategic air force in France: "[I]t was only cold...experience which proved to the world the fact that money and men could not make an air program over night...."[31]

---

[27] *Army Air Forces Statistical Digest*, World War II, pp 7, 16, 135.
[28] Thomas H. Greer, *The Development of Air Doctrine in the Army Air Arm, 1917–1941* (USAF Hist Study 89, Maxwell AFB, Ala: 1955), pp 44–47.
[29] Michael Howard, *The Franco-Prussian War: The German Invasion of France, 1870–1871* (NY: MacMillan, 1961), pp 349–357, 361–167, 438–451.
[30] I. B. Holley, Jr., *Ideas and Weapons* (Hampden, Conn: Yale Univ Press, 1953 [new imprint, Washington: AFCHO, 1983]), pp 45, 157–158.
[31] Extract from History, Col E. S. Gorrell, 1919, in Maurer Maurer, ed, *The U.S. Air Service in World War I* (Maxwell AFB, Ala: AFSHRC, 1978), Vol II, p 157.

Air Power and Airmen

In the effort to develop the Air Service of the American Expeditionary Force (AEF), American aviators did acquire much information and experience. Both Gorrell and Brig. Gen. William ("Billy") Mitchell met with British, French, and Italian airmen and studied their bombing programs. Americans actually flew with the British Independent Air Force in its night operations and with the Italian forces on the southern front. Maj. Gen. Sir Hugh Trenchard, who eventually won a peerage and played a central role in the development of the Royal Air Force (RAF), was in fact a late convert to the potential of strategic bombing. The French had been less interested than the British in attacks on Germany, but they did develop a concept of interdiction focused on *points sensibles*, "sensitive points," the destruction of which would seriously weaken the enemy's logistics.[32]

Not until 1940 and the threat of involvement in another world war would a new effort to build an effective American strategic air force begin. In the meantime, the underpinnings of a strategic bombing doctrine began to emerge. Besides Mitchell's own writings, airmen welcomed the opinions of Trenchard and of the Italian Giulio Douhet, both of whom envisioned the potential of an air force that could strike at an enemy's heartland and thereby eliminate the ghastly stalemate of trench warfare characteristic of World War I. The RAF in particular would apply a variant of this concept in its colonial wars. The Americans developed a strategic concept of their own during the interwar years. Mitchell was influential, and one of his major contributions before his court-martial conviction for insubordination in 1925 was to help organize and train operational units as a pattern for the future. Gradually, during the 1930s, the United States doctrine on strategic air power crystallized at the Air Corps Tactical School at Maxwell Field, Alabama.[33]

---

[32] *Ibid.*, pp 152–153, 156, 187, 191–192; Holley, *Ideas and Weapons*, pp 52–59; Alfred F. Hurley, *Billy Mitchell: Crusader for Air Power* (NY: Franklin Watts, 1964), pp 22–32; Lee Kennett, *A History of Strategic Bombing* (NY: Scribner's, 1982), pp 18–29.

[33] Kennett, *Strategic Bombing*, pp 52–57; David MacIsaac, "Voices from the Central Blue: The Air Power Theorists," in Peter Paret, ed, *Makers of Modern Strategy, from Machiavelli to the Nuclear Age* (Princeton, NJ: Princeton Univ Press, 1986), pp 629–636; Greer, *Doctrine*, pp 30–60. In the 1918 reorganization of the War Department air program, the Aviation Section of the Signal Corps (descended from the Aeronautical Division created in 1907) was split into a Division of Military Aeronautics and a Bureau of Aircraft Production, which were subsequently consolidated into the Air Service. This new organization was given permanent status by the National Defense Act of 1920. The Act of 1926 renamed the service the Air Corps. The Army Air Forces was created in 1941. For comments on the role of Douhet's ideas in the development of Air Corps thinking, see also John F. Shiner, *Foulois and the U.S. Army Air Corps, 1931–1935* (Washington: AFCHO, 1983), pp 47–48.

Strategic Air Force

What characterized the American precision bombing concept was a specific explanation of how strategic bombing could actually produce a strategic result. Douhet, Trenchard, and the Europeans influenced by them tended to assume that generalized damage and shaken civilian morale would undermine a belligerent government. As Arnold later noted, the American public was reluctant to support pure morale bombing.[34] Airmen began to consider ways that specific damage to an enemy's economy could cripple and undermine its military effort. This goal required accurate and precise attacks on specific industrial facilities. As a theory, precision bombing depended on a number of assumptions. The offensive required detailed information about the enemy's war economy to allow for identification of targets. Accurate daylight bombing would be necessary to ensure the most efficient application of bomb tonnage, and therefore the bombers had to be able to strike at their targets after fighting their way in with acceptable levels of losses. Analysis at the time seemed to indicate that all these tasks could be done and that a self-defending formation of bomber aircraft could actually achieve penetration of enemy airspace.[35]

In keeping with its strategic doctrine, the Air Corps of the U.S. Army developed a new bomber, the Boeing B-17 Flying Fortress. This plane exploited the possibilities of increased range and payload, the key properties of a strategic bomber. The B-17 was also designed to carry heavy defensive armament, and considerable effort was spent developing a top-quality bombsight. By 1940 and 1941 newer designs—the Consolidated B-24, the Boeing B-29, and the Consolidated B-36—tried to push the evolving technology even farther.[36]

Another aspect of the concept of a strategic force related to command. At the end of 1917, Gorrell was Chief of the Strategical Aviation Branch at Headquarters, Air Service, AEF, and he was coordinating with Trenchard concerning the latter's planned "Independent Air Force." Gen. John J. Pershing, the AEF Commander-in-Chief, and Marshal Ferdinand Foch, Allied theater commander in 1918, both were concerned that this force would not be under their control. Gorrell's organization was accordingly renamed "General Headquarters (GHQ) Air Service Reserve." In

---

[34] Herman S. Wolk, *Planning and Organizing the Postwar Air Force, 1943–1947* (Washington: AFCHO, 1984), pp 19–20 & 20n.
[35] Greer, *Doctrine*, pp 30–60, 77–81.
[36] *Ibid.*, pp 44–47; Wesley Frank Craven and James Lea Cate, eds, *The Army Air Forces in World War II*, Vol I: *Plans and Early Operations, January 1939 to August 1942* (Chicago: Univ of Chicago Press, 1948 [new imprint, Washington: AFCHO, 1983]), pp 177–185, 249.

the postwar years, the command arrangements evolved further, and in 1934 a permanent peacetime General Headquarters Air Force was created as part of an upgrading of the Air Corps. Though not explicitly committed to bombing strategic targets, the force remained under the direct control of the Army's high command and could be concentrated against objectives in furtherance of strategy.[37]

In the light of these experiences began the expansion of American air power on the eve of World War II. General Arnold later recalled that the Munich crisis of 1938 focused attention on the importance of air power in international affairs. That autumn the Air Corps chief attended a meeting with President Roosevelt to discuss military increases.

> A new regiment of field artillery, or new barracks at an Army post in Wyoming, or new machine tools in an ordnance arsenal, he said sharply, would not scare Hitler one blankety-blank-blank bit! What he wanted was airplanes! Airplanes were the war implements that *would* have an influence on Hitler's activities.[38]

Arnold considered Roosevelt's decision to expand aircraft production the "Magna Carta" of the Air Corps. Still, for some time he had to face the dilemma of increased airplane production without adequate provision for bases, supplies, or trained manpower. The outbreak of war in Europe only exacerbated the problems.

Even as late as 1942, LeMay, then a colonel commanding a new group, the 305th, experienced firsthand the frustrations inherent in the lack of preparedness.

> [The Group] consisted almost 100 percent of inexperienced people. I had one major, who had been commissioned from the rank of master sergeant, an administrative clerk, and he was my group adjutant. I had two pilots, besides myself, who had flown B-17s before, and we three had to check off the other pilots, who came directly from single engine school. The armament officer was an ex-Marine corporal who had been...in Nicaragua [and] knew something about machine guns.... My prize was a first lieutenant who had been a line chief in B-17s as a tech[nical] sergeant.

---

[37] Kennett, *Strategic Bombing*, p 29; extract, Gorrell, in Maurer, *World War I*, Vol II, pp 152–153, 156, 187, 191–192; Greer, *Doctrine*, pp 45–47, 70–75.

[38] Henry H. Arnold, *Global Mission* (NY: Harper & Brothers, 1949), p 177 (emphasis in original).

The Dawn of the Atomic Age. December 7, 1941, had brought a surprise attack by Japanese air forces on the island of Oahu, Hawaii, *above*. Although the United States was caught off-guard and plunged into World War II not fully prepared, her leaders were able to step up mobilization and eventually lead the Allies to victory against the Axis. But, August 6, 1945, abruptly ushered in a new era of air weaponry and warfare with the atomic explosion over Hiroshima, *right*. That explosion and a second over Nagasaki three days later forced the surrender of Japan to the Allies, the end of World War II, and a reevaluation by U.S. military leaders of readiness and retaliation. The Agricultural Exposition Hall and its surroundings, *below*, in Hiroshima, photographed in October 1945, were directly below the blast and totally devastated.

> The navigators I got two weeks before we went overseas had had one ride in a B-17 before they navigated across the Atlantic.... The bombardiers had never dropped a live bomb.... The gunners...had never fired a gun from an airplane....
> I hope no American has to go through the exercise again.[39]

The main guidance for building a strategic air force to attack Germany, however, had appeared in the fall of 1941. Among its origins were two especially important factors: the need to provide more focus for President Roosevelt's vision of vastly expanded aircraft production and the British strategic bombing offensive already underway against Germany. Having been driven from the European continent in June 1940, Britain had no other means of striking at the enemy and retaliating for enemy air attacks on England. Casualties in daylight bombing proved prohibitive, so the Royal Air Force Bomber Command operated at night, foregoing any attempt at precision bombing in favor of night area attacks. During staff conferences between the British and Americans early in 1941, the prospect of a U.S. contribution to the bombing effort had inevitably arisen, especially since Arnold was attending these meetings as the counterpart to the RAF representative.[40]

In calling for an overall plan for mobilizing American industry in the event of war, Roosevelt initiated studies which included the War Department's Victory Program. Arnold had formed an Air War Plans Division (AWPD), which proceeded to prepare the AAF portion of that program, under the title AWPD-1, as its first plan. Led by Lt. Col. Harold L. George, with the assistance of Lt. Col. Kenneth N. Walker, Maj. Haywood S. Hansell, and Maj. Laurence S. Kuter, all of whom had had some association with the Air Corps Tactical School, this group outlined the production and manpower requirements for a victorious air war in Europe. Although the RAF's night bombing operations had already begun, AWPD-1 focused primarily on an American daylight precision campaign using massive numbers of B-17s and newer aircraft types. The planners identified major target systems in Germany, calculated the forces needed to destroy them, and added elements for other missions, such as defending base areas and supporting the amphibious invasion of the European continent that would exploit Allied success in the air.[41]

---

[39] Curtis E. LeMay, *et al*, "The Perceptions of Three Makers of Air Power History," in Alfred F. Hurley and Robert C. Ehrhart, eds, *Air Power and Warfare*. Proceedings of the 8th Military History Symposium, USAF Academy, Oct 18–20, 1978 (Washington: AFCHO, 1979), pp 197–198.
[40] Craven & Cate, *AAF*, Vol I: *Plans & Early Operations*, pp 99–100, 135–139.
[41] *Ibid.*, pp 92–100, 177–185, 249.

The Victory Program marked a major stage in the spectacular industrial mobilization of the United States in the Second World War. By 1943 this mobilization was beginning to hit its stride. Much of the leadership of the AAF (which was created to absorb the Air Corps in 1941), including Arnold himself, presided over this effort. Under Henry L. Stimson, the Secretary of War, a staff that included Robert A. Lovett, former New York investment banker with a ready wit and a firm grasp of industrial management, as Assistant Secretary of War for Air, provided much of the expertise needed. It should also be noted that Lovett, as a U.S. Navy pilot, had flown long-range bombing missions with the British in 1918. He supported AWPD-1 enthusiastically.[42] The air force that awed Churchill and so many others was one of the products of this mobilization effort, with all of its inefficiencies.

The first half of the twentieth century witnessed armed collisions, called world wars, that pitted major modern industrial powers against each other. The adversaries mobilized their full economic strength in the quest for victory. Many participants, believing their industrial and military machines to be fragile, were convinced that one well-placed blow could make the whole structure collapse. In fact these systems were robust, and only years of gruelling attrition could bring them down. But the quest for a new means of striking the decisive blow continued. During the 1920s advocates of air power and armored warfare sought new ways to overcome attrition warfare and the attendant stalemate. Ironically, during the Second World War these innovations evolved into more sophisticated, yet frustrating, means of attrition. The American precision bombing doctrine may have envisioned attrition taking place more rapidly than proved realistic, but the theory still involved wearing down the enemy war economy, although more efficiently. In that sense strategic bombing was better attuned to the realities of the coming war than some of the unofficial theorists might have expected.

The drafters of AWPD-1 envisioned a buildup of overwhelming force before launching the air offensive. In reality, pressure from the White House as well as from Arnold drove the airmen stationed in Europe to seek results as soon as possible. As the participants recalled, air leaders such as General Spaatz and Maj. Gen. Ira C. Eaker began operations determined to apply the concept of precision bombing. But many of the preconditions of success could not be met in the grueling air battles of 1943. Intelligence on the industrial targets of Germany, while surprisingly

---

[42] Jonathan F. Fanton, "Robert A. Lovett: The War Years," (Ph.D. Dissertation: Yale Univ, 1978), pp 8, 10-15, 144-147.

Strategic Air Force

good, often proved insufficient. Weather was frequently inhospitable to accurate bombing, although later in the war radar began to conquer clouds and darkness. But the battles themselves demonstrated the most serious problem with the doctrine. AWPD-1 did lay the groundwork for building up a bomber force that could bring destructive weights of bombs to bear. However, operations conducted with formations of 100 or 300 B-17s simply proved too small, and most critical, the forces could not fight their way to the target in daylight with acceptable losses. Arnold and Eaker pushed to achieve decisive results, but by the end of 1943 there was little evidence that Germany's war economy had been seriously affected, while American losses had been heavy.[43]

Finally in February 1944, after Spaatz gained command of the overall American strategic offensive against Germany, the campaign began to produce results. First came the defeat of the German Air Force, and eventually, late in the summer, the targeting of the German oil industry and transportation net began to undermine the enemy's war effort. After the war, General Spaatz described the strategic bombing campaign as the "fulfillment of a concept."[44] Indeed, the prewar doctrine of strategic bombing as a means to achieve important results against a hostile war economy was in a large sense fulfilled. On the other hand, Germany's defeat had also required the combined efforts of the Red Army and Allied landings in northwest Europe. Also, the methods needed to achieve results in the strategic bombing offensive did not always reflect the emphases of prewar thinking. Success demanded the scale of operations indicated in AWPD-1, and no lesser force would have proven adequate. In that sense AWPD-1 was transitional. The escort fighter envisioned by air planners did prove crucial. The almost fortuitous development of the North American P-51 Mustang, along with drop tanks for other fighters, afforded some protection to the bomber fleet. The true achievement of the American fighters, however, involved inflicting major losses on the German fighter defenses, which resulted in a long-term improvement in the bombers'

---

[43] Craven & Cate, *AAF*, Vol II: *Europe: TORCH to POINTBLANK, August 1942 to December 1943*, pp 707-758; Williamson Murray, *Luftwaffe* (Baltimore, Md: Nautical & Aviation Publishing, 1985), pp 161-169. Spaatz became a major general in January 1942 and a lieutenant general in March 1943. He was promoted to four-star rank in March 1945, along with George C. Kenney and Joseph T. McNarney. Kenney, as MacArthur's air commander in the Southwest Pacific, was made senior of the three, while McNarney, Marshall's deputy chief of staff for much of the war, was the third-ranking of the three air generals. Eaker attained the rank of lieutenant general by the end of the war.

[44] Carl A. Spaatz, "Strategic Air Power: Fulfillment of a Concept," *Foreign Affairs* 24 (Apr 46), pp 385-396.

ability to reach their targets. By the time the enemy's oil industry and transportation net began to undergo real devastation, Allied armies already were ashore in western Europe. Heavy and continued attacks were necessary to gain such results. The postwar United States Strategic Bombing Survey, with its mass of detailed evidence, sustained the argument that air power had been "decisive" in Europe, but not without acknowledging that not all of the air effort had been effective.[45]

The British night bombing campaign also contributed to victory, as area bombing gradually became more effective near the end of the war. Even at night air battles were often grueling, and the RAF Bomber Command sustained horrendous casualties. At Hamburg in August 1943, however, the night bombers produced a firestorm that momentarily shook German morale. Not until late in 1944, with the aid of radar, did the RAF begin to do enough damage to weaken significantly the enemy's ability and will to make war. In February 1945 the allies fire-bombed Dresden out of desperation with a beaten adversary that refused to surrender. Only with the death of Adolf Hitler did the war end.[46] The British had been forced to revise their doctrine, but their efforts also demonstrated the role that a powerful bombing offensive aimed at the industrial heart of a nation could play in winning a war.

A similar pattern of inadequate first efforts followed by devastating success characterized the American strategic bombing offensive against Japan. Curtis E. LeMay, who attained the rank of major general in Europe largely on the strength of his reputation as an achiever, was involved in the campaign against Japan from the start. The idea of basing B-29 Superfortresses in China had appealed to President Roosevelt both as a way to win the war and to bolster sagging Chinese morale. In reality, the early bombing program had to rely on underdeveloped Asian nations, and the

---

[45] Craven & Cate, *AAF*, Vol III: *Europe: ARGUMENT to V-E Day, January 1944 to May 1945*, pp 30-66, 715-782; David MacIsaac, *Strategic Bombing in World War II: The Story of the United States Strategic Bombing Survey* (NY: Garland, 1976), *passim*. See also Alfred C. Mierzejewski, *The Collapse of the German War Economy, 1944-1945: Allied Air Power and the German National Railway* (Chapel Hill, NC: Univ of NC Press, 1988), pp 177-187. Although the Soviets did not conduct major strategic bombing operations, they did establish a strategic air force, known as "Long Range Aviation." Further, the Soviet Union bombed Helsinki in February 1944 when the Finns were proving too slow in arriving at a peace settlement. See Earl F. Ziemke, *Stalingrad to Berlin: The German Defeat in the East* [Army Historical Series] (Washington: CMH, 1968), p 267.

[46] Noble Frankland, *The Bombing Offensive Against Germany: Outline and Perspectives* (London: Faber & Faber, 1965), pp 83-90; Kennett, *Strategic Bombing*, pp 156-162.

great distances over rugged terrain created a logistical nightmare. For example, two gallons of aviation fuel were consumed in transporting one gallon from India to China, when operations were going at their best. In the end the resources expended just to fly planes, fuel, and bombs into the bases in China for a single bombing mission made the bombing a grossly inefficient effort.[47]

Even when the naval and amphibious campaigns in the Pacific brought the Marianas into American hands, strategic bombing proved difficult. Brig. Gen. Haywood S. Hansell, one of the drafters of AWPD-1, commanded the XXI Bomber Command there. His efforts to achieve precision bombing were limited by a number of factors, including the high winds over Japan. At the B-29's normal combat altitude, close to 30,000 feet, the winds proved so strong that the Superfortresses could make little headway upwind and barely even reach the targets, while downwind the planes moved so fast that the bombsight could not be set up, and crosswinds produced huge errors. In January 1945 Arnold's frustrations led him to replace Hansell with LeMay.[48]

Sensing the strong pressure from Washington for results, LeMay changed tactics. On the night of March 9, he sent more than three hundred B-29s against Tokyo, stripped of their guns, loaded with incendiaries, and bombing by radar at low altitude. Japanese air defenses proved negligible, losses were few, and the Superfortresses burned out sixteen square miles of the city, with a loss of life well over eighty thousand. The American airmen now believed they had found the means to win the war.[49]

Indeed, by June 1945, when the B-29s had begun systematically to burn down Japanese cities, LeMay was convinced that this method alone would suffice to defeat the enemy by late in the year. The planned Allied amphibious attack on the home islands would not be necessary, and the MANHATTAN PROJECT's special weapon would not be needed either. Arnold supported this position, but Gen. George C. Marshall, the Army Chief of Staff, remained skeptical.[50] In the end, only after the use of atomic weapons and the Soviet entry into the war did Japan surrender. From that point on, whatever his views, LeMay's career would be intimately linked to the concept of nuclear bombs as strategic air weapons.

---

[47] Craven & Cate, *AAF*, Vol V: *The Pacific: MATTERHORN to Nagasaki, June 1944 to August 1945*, pp 58–130.
[48] *Ibid.*, pp 58–130, 507–546.
[49] *Ibid.*, pp 566–568, 608–617.
[50] Coffey, *Iron Eagle*, pp 174–176.

Air Power and Airmen

Strategists of the Air. Lt. Cols. Harold L. George and Kenneth N. Walker, *above, left and right,* with Majs. Laurence S. Kuter and Haywood S. Hansell, *below, left and right,* **formed an effective planning team, setting down in AWPD-1 U.S. resources required for the air war in Europe.**

Though the experiences of commanders such as LeMay, Spaatz, and Eaker modified some of the prewar theories, their earlier convictions were confirmed strongly in significant areas. The idea of the GHQ Air Force, of an independent air striking force under control of the highest directing authority of the nation's war effort, had always been in the forefront of the airmen's thinking. Spaatz had commanded United States Strategic Air Forces in Europe—a theater-wide command set up in January 1944, consisting of the Eighth Air Force in England and the Fifteenth in southern Italy. The unifying factor behind these two organizations was their mission, to operate over Europe against Germany. Nominally under the theater commander, Gen. Dwight D. Eisenhower, Spaatz was in fact guided by directives from the Anglo-American Combined Chiefs of Staff;

Strategic Air Force

although for much of the time his directive was to support Eisenhower's ground and tactical air operations.[51]

When Arnold began to organize the strategic bombing of Japan, he conceived of an air force with headquarters in Washington and himself as commander, under the direction of the American joint chiefs. Twentieth Air Force, as it became known, would include all B-29 forces attacking Japan. Lt. Gen. George C. Kenney, commanding the air force in the Southwest Pacific, had envisioned using the Superfortresses in his own theater, but Arnold opposed any dispersal of the B-29 effort. The units in India and China became the XX Bomber Command of the Twentieth Air Force, and those in the Marianas constituted the XXI Bomber Command, also of the Twentieth. LeMay at one time or another commanded both. Brig. Gen. Lauris Norstad, as Chief of Staff of Twentieth Air Force in Washington, was the link between Arnold and the bomber commanders overseas.[52]

In July 1945, as the Americans prepared for the final operations against Japan, with the war in Europe now ended, the strategic force in the Pacific was again reorganized. Spaatz became Commanding General, U.S. Army Strategic Air Forces, with headquarters at Guam. LeMay served as his Chief of Staff, with Lt. Gen. Nathan F. Twining, former Commander of Fifteenth Air Force in Europe, in command of Twentieth Air Force, now organized under Spaatz in the Marianas. (The Eighth was to operate B-29s from Okinawa.) On his way through Washington from Europe to take up his new command, Spaatz received the directive to begin atomic operations. This directive he brought with him.[53] Since he was equal to Admiral Chester W. Nimitz and Gen. Douglas MacArthur, who commanded respectively the Navy and Army ground and tactical air forces in the theater, it fell to Spaatz to brief them about the new weapon.

The Postwar Challenge

MacArthur's reaction to Spaatz's news of the plans to use an atomic bomb against Japan was: "That changes warfare."[54] Since 1939, as scientists and administrators became aware of the implications of nuclear fission, particularly its potential use in a bomb, and as the MANHATTAN PROJECT moved toward its final achievement, many had arrived at the

---

[51] Craven & Cate, *AAF*, Vol II: *TORCH to POINTBLANK*, pp 751-756; Vol III: *ARGUMENT to V-E Day*, pp 72-83.
[52] Craven & Cate, *AAF*, Vol V: *MATTERHORN to Nagasaki*, pp 507-546.
[53] *Ibid.*, pp 392-396, 676-689, 700-714.
[54] MacIsaac, *Strategic Bombing*, p 166.

same conclusion. However, most of the officials heavily engaged in planning for the postwar armed forces had not been privy to the secret. Thus the advent of the bomb radically altered the military situation just as postwar plans were about to be put into effect.

Possibly the most important aspect of postwar planning would not change. Most members of the armed forces had been making their own plans to leave the service and go home. This extended to the staff of the MANHATTAN PROJECT. For the leaders of the AAF, however, the overriding issue remained independence for air power. At the beginning of the war Marshall and Arnold had reached an understanding that agitation for a separate air force would cease for the duration. In return, Arnold would possess great latitude as head of the AAF. Marshall himself strongly supported equal status for air and ground arms, within a unified defense establishment. Thus, two major items for postwar planning were the creation of a separate air force and unification of the services.[55]

Marshall also favored universal military training (UMT) to facilitate mobilization of the Army in any future war, as did his designated successor after the war, General Eisenhower. Arnold was prepared to support universal military training so as to retain Marshall's and Eisenhower's support for an independent air force. But the AAF commander's foremost concern was that the air force be ready in the event of war. This was not merely a matter of numbers of men and planes. Arnold understood as well as anyone that aviation technology does not stand still. In November 1944 he asked the distinguished scientist Theodore von Kármán to direct a study of future directions for research and development. Completed in December 1945, *Toward New Horizons* contained a wealth of information on developments in a number of fields.[56]

In strategic air warfare, Arnold foresaw that the next bomber would be the Consolidated B–36. An experimental model was under construction in the company's plant at Fort Worth, Texas. Work had been slowed mainly to accommodate the large-scale production of less advanced types, particularly thousands of B–24s. Beyond the B–36, however, the von Kármán committee suggested that the very large long-range bomber was reaching a point of diminishing returns. Continued study would determine whether airplanes, guided missiles, or some other approach would best enable an air force to strike at an enemy's industrial base.[57]

---

[55] Smith, *Plans for Peace*, p 53; Sherry, *Preparing*, pp 41–43, 159–167, 199–205; Gaddis, *Origins of the Cold War*, pp 26–30.

[56] Wolk, *Planning and Organizing*, pp 39–40, 210–214.

[57] Report of Heavy Bombardment by Heavy Bombardment Committee Convened to Report to the USAF Aircraft and Weapons Board, Jan 48, RG 341, DCS/Dev, Dir Rqmts, Papers 1st AWB, Box 181, MMB, NA.

Strategic Air Force

President Franklin D. Roosevelt, flanked by Prime Minister Winston S. Churchill and Premier Josef V. Stalin at Yalta in 1945, had hoped that a United Nations steered by the United States, Great Britain, and the Soviet Union would become the primary shaper of the post-war world and guarantor of peace.

Arnold also realized that the AAF's goals would not be reached without controversy. While he and his colleagues were convinced that the war had validated their main philosophy, he recognized that events had not convinced everyone. As he wrote to Spaatz,

> We were never able to launch the full power of our bombing attack.... The power of these attacks would certainly have convinced any doubting Thomases as to the capabilities of a modern Air Force. I am afraid that from now on there will be certain people who will forget the part we have played.[58]

Arnold would do what he could to further the cause of air power in the coming disagreements. But his words were a valuable warning for Spaatz, destined to succeed Arnold on his retirement as air chief. Spaatz would inherit the task of orchestrating the many voices of the AAF in the immediate postwar years.

---

[58] Ltr, Gen H. H. Arnold, CG AAF, to Gen C. A. Spaatz, CG USSTAF, Aug 19, 1945, Spaatz Coll, File Aug 45, Box 21, MD, LC.

Chapter II

The Case for a Postwar Air Force

At the time of the Japanese surrender, the United States had forty conventional B–29 groups as well as the 509th Composite Group, with a total inventory of nearly three thousand Superfortresses. General Spaatz commanded directly over half of the operating very heavy bomber (VHB) force.[1] However, if traditional practices followed the armistice, this strategic air force would soon disappear. Most of the officers and enlisted members of the Army Air Forces expected to go home, and anyone with Arnold's and Spaatz's experience in aviation could foresee that eventually the bombers would deteriorate or become obsolete. The advent of the atomic weapon brought more complications to the postwar environment, as it raised fundamental questions about the future of air power. Thus the presence of a massive strategic bomber force in August 1945 did not guarantee its existence three years later. Maintaining such a force would require additional personnel, advanced equipment, and some fresh ideas.

In fact, during the two years after the ceasefire, the U.S. strategic air force was largely dismantled, and little progress was made in developing a new one. There were many reasons for this stagnation. From 1945 to 1947 the American armed forces endured a reorganization more turbulent than any that had followed previous wars. Fundamental questions about America's position in the world, the nature of her security problem, and the organization of her defense forces demanded answers in the midst of an unprecedented international situation. The nation's leaders would have to determine the kind of strategic air force, if any, the country would need in a reorganized defense establishment. For their part, the airmen had to develop and defend their concepts, especially with regard to atomic

---

[1] *Army Air Forces Statistical Digest*, 1946, pp 4, 10.

weapons. And within these parameters, they should be prepared to organize, train, and equip an effective air force and keep it in readiness.

At the end of two years of reorganization, the air leaders would finally be able to define the kind of strategic force required, but during that period America's power to threaten a potential enemy would be, to borrow the term of one historian, "hollow" indeed.[2] Funding uncertainties, conflicting priorities, and unresolved issues of command all combined to delay progress toward the creation of a strong, up-to-date bomber force. Still, by 1947 a number of basic decisions would make a clear direction possible.

It must be understood that the important task of defining long-term roles and strategies for the armed forces, including the AAF's efforts to promote air power in the postwar defense establishment, coexisted with the immediate priorities of demobilization and the occupation of former enemy countries. In fact, the sole on-going commitment for an active long-range bombing force involved supporting the occupation, and manning the units in the Pacific and Europe proved impossible. Reorganizing the defense establishment would have been a monumental challenge even without the manpower and logistical strains inherent in a massive demobilization and major commitments overseas.

The U.S. armed forces began the postwar period with an almost complete change of leadership at the top. Fortunately, all the new officeholders possessed considerable experience from wartime service in the government. President Harry S. Truman, in office for four months by August 1945, had been Chairman of the Senate Committee to Investigate the Defense Program during most of the war. (Secretary Stimson felt compelled to warn Senator Truman off an inquiry into a construction project of the MANHATTAN District.)[3] As a former National Guard and Reserve officer with combat service in the First World War, the President was also familiar with issues of manpower readiness.

To replace Stimson at the War Department, Truman selected Robert P. Patterson, the Undersecretary. W. Stuart Symington, a business executive who had entered the Roosevelt administration during the war, succeeded Robert A. Lovett as the Assistant Secretary of War for Air. For the Navy, on the other hand, no change was necessary; James V. Forrestal had been secretary since 1944 and was willing to stay on. Forrestal's role gained significance largely because of his attention to issues of international affairs, national security, and strategy. An avid reader, the secretary circulated many articles, news stories, and papers among his colleagues.

---

[2] Harry R. Borowski, *A Hollow Threat: Strategic Air Power and Containment Before Korea* (Westport, Conn: Greenwood Press, 1982), *passim*.
[3] Jones, *Manhattan*, p 337.

Forrestal, like Lovett, had flown long-range air operations with the British in 1918.⁴

The Joint Chiefs of Staff (JCS) likewise changed almost completely. Fleet Admiral William D. Leahy remained on as Chief of Staff to the President, but Eisenhower took over as Chief of Staff of the Army, and Fleet Admiral Chester W. Nimitz became Chief of Naval Operations. Arnold, having presided over the building of the world's mightiest air force, did not retire until February 1946, but by then Spaatz had been assuming more and more of the work, inheriting command of the AAF on the departure of his chief and friend.⁵ All of these officers remained throughout the entire reorganization period and brought a breadth of experience as well as continuity to the task ahead.

A New Strategic World

From the devastation of World War II had emerged a new strategic world—one that posed several problems for American security. To many citizens, the atomic bomb assured invincibility, but the future development of the weapon remained unresolved. Another issue addressed a potential conflict with the Soviet Union. A growing number of influential Americans believed that the United States could not return to its prewar isolationism and must assume a leading role in preserving world peace. Airmen were conscious of other critical factors: the importance of strategic air power and the possibility of long-range air attacks on America.⁶

During 1946 and 1947 answers began to arise to several strategic problems facing the country, though the nature of the risk of war with the Soviet Union remained uncertain. As the wartime coalition collapsed and the Soviet Union became more and more the single "potential enemy," the question of general war became vital. An officer on the Air Staff described the USSR as: "...the only power of the United Nations with whom it is conceivable (but assiduously to be avoided) that we might clash."⁷ The experience of Munich and the belief that a nation should be firm with

---

⁴ Steven L. Rearden, *The Formative Years, 1947–1950*, Vol 1 of *History of the Office of the Secretary of Defense* (Washington: OSD, 1984), pp 29–32.

⁵ Wolk, *Planning and Organizing*, p 78.

⁶ *Ibid.*, pp 209–214.

⁷ Memo, Walter E. Todd for Maj Gen L. Norstad, ACAS/Pl, to DCAS, subj: US Air Force Contingent for Combined International Enforcement Action of United Nations, Jul 26, 1945, RG 341, TS AAG File 21, Box 7, MMB, NA.

aggressors conflicted with the administration's desire to restore trust between the two allies. In any case, as war-threatening crises ensued, there were gloomy forecasts of inevitable hostilities.[8]

In 1945 few predicted the dissolution of most of the colonial empires and the armed struggles that would result. One AAF staff officer pointed to the Spanish Civil War as an analogue of potential conflicts, but most thinking centered on the threat of more general wars.[9] The Assistant Chief of Air Staff for Plans (ACAS–5) in July 1945 ruled out the use of a United Nations air force in petty local disturbances: "The problem has nothing to do with the insignificant number of aircraft necessary to coerce a recalcitrant minor power or chastise natives in a border dispute. [The United Nations force] will never be so used."[10] Such attitudes led to a concentration in all defense planning on a general war with the Soviet Union, with little attention to the possibility of small-scale hostilities.

The growing estrangement between the United States and the Soviet Union dashed the hopes of those Americans who believed that the United Nations could be effective in maintaining peace and that the atomic weapon could be turned over to the world organization. Prominent individ-

---

[8] The study of the origins of the Cold War went through a major revisionist phase in the 1960s and 1970s, followed by the work of a number of "post-revisionists." Work has stabilized since then. See Geir Lundestad, "Moralism, Presentism, Exceptionalism, Provincialism, and Other Extravagances in American Writings on the Early Cold War Years," *Diplomatic History* 13 (Fall 89), pp 527–545. Ironically, a valuable contribution to the subject appeared *before* much of the official documentation was available: see William H. McNeil, *America, Britain, & Russia: Their Co-operation and Conflict, 1941–1946* (London: Oxford Univ Press, 1953 [Reprint, NY: Johnson Reprint Corp., 1970]). A valuable interpretation along post-revisionist lines appeared in John L. Gaddis, *The United States and the Origins of the Cold War, 1941–1947* (NY: Columbia Univ Press, 1972). Gaddis's recent work—*The Long Peace: Inquiries into the History of the Cold War* (NY: Oxford Univ Press, 1987)—has generally sustained his earlier synthesis. Other works consulted included: Raymond Aron, *The Imperial Republic: The United States and the World, 1945–1973*, trans Frank Jellinek (Englewood Cliffs, NJ: Prentice-Hall, 1974); Daniel Yergin, *Shattered Peace: The Origins of the Cold War and the National Security State* (Boston: Houghton Mifflin, 1977); Lisle A. Rose, *Dubious Victory: The United States and the End of World War II* (Kent, Ohio: Kent State Univ Press, 1973); Louis J. Halle, *The Cold War As History* (NY: Harper & Row, 1967); and Eduard Mark, "October or Thermidor? Interpretations of Stalinism and the Perception of Soviet Foreign Policy in the United States, 1927–1947," *AHR* 94 (Oct 89). On Soviet demobilization, see Yergin, *Shattered Peace*, pp 269–271.

[9] Memo, Brig Gen A. R. Maxwell, Ch Rqmts Div, to Maj Gen E. E. Partridge, ACAS/Ops, subj: Retention of the Night Attack Program of the Army Air Forces, Mar 19, 1946, in RG 18, 1944–1946 Uncl Organization 9, Inactivation, Box 1510, MMB, NA.

[10] See Note 7.

Postwar Air Force

uals such as Navy Secretary Forrestal and George F. Kennan, a Foreign Service officer who returned from the embassy in Moscow early in 1946 to take increasingly important positions in the government, already distrusted the Soviets. For these officials, the tensions with the Soviets were no surprise at all. With the crises of 1946, even the optimists began to recognize that Stalin was refusing to cooperate in building a peaceful world. The Soviet Union's delay in withdrawing its wartime garrisons from Iran precipitated a crisis in March, and in August Yugoslavia (then considered by many little more than a Soviet puppet) shot down two American transports. Likewise, Stalin's failure to support the United States' plan for international control of atomic energy contributed to the gradual disillusionment. By then the American public was extremely suspicious of Soviet behavior. Over the next few years Americans once sympathetic with the Moscow regime fell successively silent.[11]

The strategic situation, increasingly bipolar, demanded a reassessment of the role of the nation's armed forces. Some traditional ideas still seemed valid. The Navy envisioned maintaining a large operating force, built around aviation and large aircraft carriers of a new design. Representing the Army's point of view, Marshall favored universal military training (UMT) as a way of providing the skeletonized ground forces with a pool of trained manpower in the event of mobilization. But, as Truman's trusted adviser, Marshall also preferred air forces to naval forces as the "M-Day" (mobilization day) organization, the ready operating force in peacetime. Each military arm thus developed a postwar scheme emphasizing its own priorities and capabilities. The Army advocated universal military training, the Navy the supercarrier, and the AAF a strong ready air force.[12]

Concurrent with these plans was a debate over a major reorganization of the armed forces. Advocates of change believed that the separate War and Navy Departments, coordinated by the Joint Chiefs of Staff, despite their apparent success in the Second World War, would no longer suffice. Even in the Navy, where the existing system found ready defenders, Secretary Forrestal was convinced that interservice coordination needed to be improved. On the other hand, advocates of air power believed the war demonstrated the need for an autonomous air force. Late in 1945 Congress

---

[11] Gaddis, *U.S. and Origins*, pp 274, 306; Mark, "October or Thermidor?" p 951; James F. Schnabel, *The History of the Joint Chiefs of Staff: The Joint Chiefs of Staff and National Policy*, Vol I: *1945–1947* (Washington: JCS, 1979), pp 71–75, 81–99.

[12] Sherry, *Preparing*, pp 73–90; memo, JCS to SWNCC (282), subj: Basis for the Formulation of a U.S. Military Policy, Mar 27, 1946, in *FRUS*, 1946, Vol I, pp 1160–1165.

resumed hearings on defense organization that had begun the previous year. The War Department, in the Collins Plan, adopted the position agreed upon between Generals Marshall and Arnold during the war—a single department of defense with coequal army, navy, and air force. Needless to say, there were differences of perspective. The AAF saw autonomy as its primary goal, supporting unification of the services to ensure Army support. The Navy expressed its reservations in the Eberstadt Report, calling for a less centralized structure. Naval leaders feared the consequences to the nation's sea power if their service lost its independence.[13]

In the 1945 hearings, the AAF witnesses included such well-known airmen as Arnold, Spaatz, Doolittle, and Kenney. They all spoke from their experience about the importance of air power. General Arnold, testifying in October, keynoted the campaign with the basic arguments for independent air power. Winning the battle for air superiority, essential to all other operations, required a single commander. For this job a particular expertise was needed, and only an air commander could exploit the versatility and flexibility of the air arm. At the national level, air warfare, particularly air defense, required unified direction also. Arnold claimed that any part of the United States could be attacked from the air:

> Such developments as the atomic bomb, the V-2 and the whole range of radio directed and homing missiles accentuate the security problem of the air. At this time these weapons will be delivered through the air. The basic defense against such a plan of attack must lie in the ability to mount rapid, powerful offensive action against the source. Responsibility for this defense will rest on the Air Force.[14]

Finally, air power needed an institutional voice to ensure that a qualified person made key decisions. These conditions would ensure "that status necessary to our air power to maintain national security and world peace."[15]

---

[13] Paul Y. Hammond, *Organizing for Defense: The American Military Establishment in the Twentieth Century* (Princeton, NJ: Princeton Univ Press, 1961), pp 196, 213–220; Wolk, *Planning and Organizing*, pp 86–98.

[14] Statement by General of the Army H. H. Arnold Before the Committee on Military Affairs of the United States Senate Concerning the Unification of the War and Navy Departments, Oct 19, 1945, RG 165, Decimal 320 (Sep–Dec 1946), MMB, NA.

[15] *Ibid.*

Unlike his chief, General Spaatz did not specifically mention retaliatory air strikes. In fact he appeared to de-emphasize strategic bombing.

> There has been a tendency to over-emphasize long range bombardment, and to ignore the versatile application of Air Power. Our Air Forces were used [in the war] for any mission considered important, at any given moment. Especially misleading is the distinction made between Strategic and Tactical Air Forces. That distinction is not valid in describing the use of Air Power as a whole, day after day.[16]

Spaatz did argue that the unity of air command allowed the massing of all air forces for decisive action, avoiding the evil of breaking these forces into penny-packets for local use. He also pointed out that the entire country constituted the air frontier of America. Furthermore, the Arctic frontier was now accessible by air and could only be defended in that medium. And to develop the resources of air power required a single, autonomous directing agency. In a final appeal to senators aware of the popular enthusiasm for air power, Spaatz said, "The Air Force should have authority commensurate with its responsibility in the eyes of the American people."[17]

Thus, not all advocates of an autonomous air force emphasized the "independent mission" of strategic bombing. Those who disagreed on the bombing issue, however, did stress the need for unity of command in the air and argued that air power was too important to be subordinated to the land service. No longer could the nation afford to have decisions essential to air power vetoed by a ground-oriented General Staff.

Though critical, independence for the Army Air Forces represented only the first step toward building a strong, ready air arm. The AAF spokesmen shared a widespread view that the mere skeleton forces and mobilization base of the interwar years had failed to deter the Axis powers. As Secretary of State James F. Byrnes wrote: "Our military potential, demonstrated in 1917–1918, was not enough to keep us out of World War II."[18] The joint chiefs certainly agreed that cooperation with the British and the Soviets was the best means of securing the peace, but they realized that diplomacy could falter. In this case, potential military strength mat-

---

[16] Statement by Gen Carl Spaatz Before the Military Affairs Committee, Senate, on Nov 15, 1945, RG 165, Decimal 320 (Sep–Dec 1946), MMB, NA.
[17] *Ibid.*
[18] Ltr, James F. Byrnes, Sec State, to R. P. Patterson, Sec War, Nov 29, 1945, with encl: Answers to Questions Contained in the Memorandum Dated Nov 1, 1945 From the Secretary of War to the Secretary of State, in *FRUS*, 1946, Vol I, p 1132.

U.S. Defense Leaders in a New Strategic World. *Clockwise from above, left:* **Following the end of World War II Robert P. Patterson succeeded Henry L. Stimson as Secretary of War, W. Stuart Symington succeeded Robert A. Lovett as Assistant Secretary of War for Air, Dwight D. Eisenhower followed George C. Marshall as Army Chief of Staff, and Carl A. Spaatz took over as Chief of the AAF on the retirement of Henry H. Arnold. James V. Forrestal continued as Secretary of the Navy.**

tered little; actual force in being was the only insurance. United States military leaders recognized the dilemma: deterring war meant maintaining forces that, if strong enough, would never be used.[19]

In a similar vein General Spaatz testified:

> (T)he blessing of a time lag which we enjoyed in two World Wars is gone, perhaps forever. As top dog America becomes Target Number 1. There will be no time lag. The Airplane will possibly exceed the speed of sound. The possibilities for surprise are thus multiplied beyond measurement.[20]

Never again could the nation wait for the outbreak of war before undertaking the time-consuming business of building an air force. General Norstad, the Assistant Chief of Air Staff for Plans, wrote in September:

> The day of forming, equipping and training an Army and in particular an Air Force almost overnight is passed. Due to training specialization required and increased production problems of technical equipment, we must have sufficient strength in trained personnel and modern equipment to engage an enemy without being allowed time to build up an Air Force. In the last two wars we have fortunately been afforded up to two years to gear for war. With the character of modern warfare changed so radically in this last war, particularly by new weapons, in the next war we will be in the midst of an all-out war from the start. Our only salvation will be in immediately available modern weapons with sufficient personnel adequately trained in their use.[21]

There were other defense needs to which all of the services, particularly the AAF, could agree. America had to have the most advanced weapons possible. A vigorous program of research and development would exploit the nation's technological and industrial strength. Also, in view of the loss of the precious cushion of time, advance warning of aggression became more important than ever. An effective intelligence service was deemed essential to avoid an "atomic Pearl Harbor," and this consideration marked a clear break with past American practice. Indeed, in an age of atomic and chemical weapons, even an expected attack would be devastating. Therefore, the Joint Chiefs of Staff made a somewhat veiled

---

[19] Memo, JCS to SWNCC (282), subj: Basis for the Formulations of a U.S. Military Policy, Mar 27, 1946, in *FRUS*, 1946, Vol I, pp 1160–1165 & 1160N.
[20] See Note 16.
[21] Memo, Maj Gen L. Norstad, ACAS/Plans, to Lt Gen H. L. George, CG ATC, subj: Arguments for Justification of 70-Group Post-War Air Force, Sep 10, 1945, RG 341, TS OPD 320.2 (Apr 4, 1944), TS Supp Box 129A, MMB, NA.

reference to the need to be able to strike at potential aggression. The new emphasis on military preparedness translated into a requirement for a long-term presence overseas, and in November the joint chiefs advised the State Department of their needs for bases worldwide. Prime locations included U.S. possessions (including the Philippines, where negotiations were in progress to gain basing rights after the islands became independent) as well as occupied territories and the bases in the Americas leased from the British in 1940. The nation could gain control over the former Japanese Mandates in the Pacific, but it would also have to approach several foreign countries, especially colonial powers, to ensure access to other vital base areas.[22]

Much of the debate over defense organization was plagued with uncertainties about the atomic bomb. Questions of novelty, secrecy, and scarcity made informed discussion difficult. A new weapon only used twice, the bomb could be "just another weapon" or "the absolute weapon," as a young scholar at Yale University named Bernard Brodie called it in the title of a book published in 1946.[23] Information was scarce; much of it was still a secret being kept by a few. As Lt. Gen. Hoyt S. Vandenberg, the AAF's Assistant Chief of Air Staff for Operations, Commitments, and Requirements, commented: "There are few people in the world today who realize, even remotely, the full implications of the use of atomic power in warfare."[24] Likewise, it was uncertain how widely the secret had to be shared, and that affected the number of weapons that would be needed or available. Finally, strategists considered what to do about the American monopoly over atomic technology. Who should or would have the weapon? Without American assistance, when would the Soviet Union get the bomb? Or should the United States transfer the entire technology, secret and all, to the United Nations?

Not until 1947 did the general outlines of an American atomic program become clear: to preserve the monopoly as long as possible, to have a military program, but with development and production of weapons managed by a civilian agency, and to give access to classified information

---

[22] Sherry, *Preparing*, pp 73–90; memo, JCS to SWNCC (282), subj: Basis for the Formulation of a U.S. Military Policy, Mar 27, 1946, in *FRUS*, 1946, Vol I, pp 1160–1165; memo, JCS to Sec State (SWNCC 38/25), subj: Over-all Examination of U.S. Requirements for Military Bases and Rights, Nov 7, 1945, in *FRUS*, 1946, Vol I, pp 1112–1117.

[23] Bernard Brodie, *The Absolute Weapon: Atomic Power and World Order* (NY: Harcourt Brace, 1946), *passim*.

[24] R & R Sheet, Lt Gen H. S. Vandenberg, ACAS/Ops, to Rqmts Div, Effects of Atomic Bomb on the Future AAF Programs, Aug 22, 1945, RG 341, OPD, Asst for AE, 1945, 322 (Atomic Bomb Striking Force), Box 1, MMB, NA.

Strategic Air Force

on a "need to know" basis. Even then, much remained unsettled, and the AAF continued to manuever through a complex set of issues.

At the outset, secrecy reigned. Truman's Executive Order of August 15, 1945, severely restricted the circulation of information. On the other hand, the basic scientific principles of nuclear fission appeared in a report by Professor Henry D. Smyth of Princeton University. Published soon after Hiroshima, the Smyth Report showed that atomic energy could be used not only for explosives but also as a source for other forms of energy, useful for aircraft propulsion and commercial purposes of a great variety.[25] This potential seemed to offer great hope for humanity in spite of the bomb's dreadfully destructive power.

Although little information came from the MANHATTAN Engineer District, military leaders surmised some of the pertinent facts that had impact on the future of warfare. From the Smyth Report and from a look at the ground at Hiroshima and Nagasaki, they could expand their limited knowledge. It appeared that the atomic bomb had a yield of 20 kilotons (equal to 20,000 tons of TNT), and a more powerful bomb could be built. It did its damage through blast, heat, and radiation. A ground burst would so disseminate radiation that the area of the explosion would be impassable to humans for hours or days. Likewise, the distribution of radioactive material could deny an area to an enemy, although this tactic seemed somewhat impractical in most cases. The bomb could only be delivered by a large airplane—smuggling components for clandestine assembly at the target would be exceedingly difficult—or by missiles as yet not developed. Uranium had now become a strategic raw material. If a secret existed, it seemed to lie in the engineering of bomb construction. Building the bomb would be a formidable task for any country, even the world's number one industrial giant.

As for use in war, there was no sure defense. As Bernard Brodie of the Yale Institute of International Studies pointed out, effective defense required not only the ability to damage the attacker but also the capacity to take punishment. Almost nothing could survive even a near miss from

---

[25] Memo, Maj Gen E. M. Powers, ACAS/Mat, to CAS, subj: Dissemination of Atomic Energy Data, Sep 14, 1945, RG 341, OPD, Asst for AE, 1945, 312.1 (Atomic Energy) Box 1, MMB, NA; memo, JCS (SM-4810) to SWNCC, subj: Guidance as to the Military Implications of a United Nations Commission of Atomic Energy, Jan 23, 1946, with atch JSSC/JPS report, in *FRUS*, 1946, Vol I, pp 738–749; Bernard Brodie, *The Atomic Bomb and American Security*, Yale Institute of International Studies Memo No. 18 (New Haven, 1945).

an atomic bomb. Thus emerged the theoretical possibility for two countries to destroy each other.[26] Under such circumstances, deterrence assumed a central role in international relations.

Others seeking to understand the implications of the bomb included the scientists who had developed the technology and, therefore, had considerable prestige as experts. In September 1945 the University of Chicago, where the MANHATTAN PROJECT had conducted the first nuclear chain reaction, sponsored a conference on atomic energy for scientists and other interested scholars, Brodie being one of those attending. The conferees discussed the issues of secrecy and the revolutionary implications of atomic warfare. Most predicted that the Soviets could develop the bomb in a few years. Professor Jacob Viner of Chicago, an economist with an interest in international relations, emphasized the deterrent effect of building an atomic arsenal and the possibility of achieving world stability through mutual deterrence.[27]

In August General Marshall proposed a study by the Joint Staff Planners. This group turned to two men who had been involved with the MANHATTAN PROJECT since its inception: Vannevar Bush, former head of the Office of Scientific Research and Development and responsible for much of the early research, and General Groves, the Officer in Charge of the project. Though Bush dismissed the possibility of long-range guided missiles with atomic warheads, he noted the revolutionary implications of the bomb. He agreed that there was no defense against atomic attack. Once two nations had large atomic forces, neither would attack the other for fear of retaliation. This situation, Bush said, would not arise at once because it would take the Soviet Union several years to develop its own bomb. This was due to the inhibiting effect of totalitarian politics on research. Groves offered a quite similar view. He was more sanguine than Bush about the potential of missiles. As a soldier, he stressed the need for the United States to exploit its lead by establishing bases and building an

---

[26] See note above. The actual yield of the Hiroshima bomb was 12.5 kilotons and that at Nagasaki 22. The official press release announcing Hiroshima said the bomb had the force of 20,000 tons of TNT. See Richard G. Hewlett & Francis Duncan, *Atomic Shield, 1947–1952*, Vol II of *A History of the United States Atomic Energy Commission* (University Park, Pa: Pa State Univ Press, 1962 [new imprint, Washington: U.S. Atomic Energy Commission, 1972]), p 672.

[27] Fred Kaplan, *Wizards of Armageddon*, pp 24–30; David E. Lilienthal, *The Journals of David E. Lilienthal*, Vol II: *The Atomic Energy Years, 1945–1950* (NY: Harper & Row, 1964), pp 637–641.

atomic stockpile. As a key figure in the atomic enterprise, he also foreshadowed a major problem in the atomic program when he refused to divulge the number of bombs on hand.[28]

In October the Joint Strategic Survey Committee concluded its own study with a report to the JCS. The committee reflected much of Bush's thinking, maintaining that America had at least a five-year lead in atomic energy over any other country. However, once other nations had the bomb, the United States would be in serious danger. The Soviet Union, by virtue of its size, the dispersal of its industry, and the remoteness of its borders, was less vulnerable to atomic attack than the United States. While the committee agreed that the bomb was primarily an air weapon, it emphasized that the nation needed land and naval forces to seize and hold bases. These bases were essential even though vulnerable to atomic attack. Atomic power was the sum of a stockpile, an organization to maintain the stockpile, and a strategic air force. Other essential ingredients included control of uranium sources, research and development, intelligence, and protection of atomic secrets. Vulnerability placed a premium on surprise, and the report therefore suggested that "Effective action at its source would normally require us to 'strike first.'" In any event the bomb would be most decisive through its power to intimidate, rather than through actual damage. Owing to what was then considered a relatively small worldwide supply of raw material, the supply of bombs would probably always be limited.[29]

If the Joint Staff granted the AAF its obvious role in atomic matters, Groves was not as ready to do so. At the end of 1945, he prepared a paper on "Our Army of the Future." The head of the MANHATTAN PROJECT examined the implications of a successful international agreement banning atomic weapons and conversely, of the failure to reach such an agreement. Since a war would surely cause the breakdown of an agreement, it was necessary to abolish war to avoid an atomic arms race. If the nation retained its atomic weapons, Groves saw the Tinian operation as the model for their use. The bomb would remain in short supply, and only a few select air crews, assigned to ready, mobile units in the continental United States, would be needed to deliver the bombs that the MANHATTAN District provided. Groves viewed the bomb as "...a weapon of tremendous, devastating power...." It was an offensive weapon, able to cause "rapid attrition," eliminating entire countries with "suddenness, complete-

---

[28] Schnabel, *JCS, 1945–1947*, pp 137–140, 276–277.
[29] Rprt, JSSC to JCS (1477/1), Over-All Effect of Atomic Bomb on Warfare and Military Organization, Oct 30, 1945, RG 341, TS OPD (Aug 17, 1945), 384.3 (Atomic), Sect 1, MMB, NA.

ness, and totality." "Its very existence should make war unthinkable." The nation had a lead of five to ten years and would have to keep it: "We must have the best, the biggest, and the most...." Any agency charged with managing the nation's atomic program would, in Groves's view have to regard national security as its first duty.[30]

Groves supported the conventional view that the bomb would not be used alone. Other forces would be necessary to gain and hold bases, occupy territory, and control the sea. Armies could remain small, although the population would have to be mobilized for civil defense and reconstruction. The general reiterated the arguments for an intelligence system and research into new weapons. He, too, hinted at the need for preemption. While contending that America would need a large navy, he said little about air forces.[31]

At Eisenhower's instigation, the joint chiefs continued debating the relationship between the atomic bomb and national strategy into 1946. The Army Chief of Staff had sought a thorough study of the issue, coordinated with the Navy, in order to present a unified position before Congress. What emerged, however, amounted to little more than a compromise statement with minor impact. Eisenhower thought that the first effort failed to account for the nation's policy of seeking international control of atomic energy, and the second version of the report, in the eyes of Assistant Secretary of War Howard C. Peterson, seemed to dismiss atomic weapons solely to protect traditional strategies and budgets. Eisenhower offered Groves's study, although he did not fully agree with it. General Arnold could not win an endorsement of the principles of strategic bombing or of the need for an air striking force. The JCS report, as finally approved, merely advocated ready offensive forces and underlined the principle of "balanced forces." The highest priority went to intelligence and forward bases. Secrecy was necessary to protect the (this time) ten-year American lead, although the JCS did support efforts for international control. The new weapon was so destructive that war had to be

---

[30] Memo, Maj Gen L. R. Groves, OIC, Manhattan Project, subj: Our Army of the Future—As Influenced by Atomic Weapons, Jan 2, 1946, in *FRUS*, 1946, Vol I, pp 1197–1203; memo, CSA to JCS (1477/6), subj: Statement of Effect of Atomic Weapons on National Security and Military Organization, Jan 21, 1946, with atch paper, RG 341, TS OPD (Aug 17, 1945), 384.3 (Atomic), MMB, NA. The attached paper in JCS 1477/6 is virtually identical to the Groves paper in *FRUS*.

[31] Memo, Maj Gen L. R. Groves, OIC, Manhattan Project, subj: Our Army of the Future—As Influenced by Atomic Weapons, Jan 2, 1946, in *FRUS*, 1946, Vol I, pp 1197–1203.

Strategic Air Force

prevented, if not by international accord, then by deterrence. But the means of deterrence were deliberately kept vague.[32]

Many in the War Department probably shared Eisenhower's desire for a more serious study. For its part, the Air Staff disagreed with the lack of emphasis on air power. Brig. Gen. Alfred R. Maxwell, Chief of the Requirements Division of the Air Staff, pointed out that a detailed study was needed to dispel public misunderstanding. He argued that exaggerating the bomb's destructiveness could be damaging to the nation's security. "The atomic bomb is in fact an experimental weapon...," he wrote in December 1945; "...it is at present only another weapon." He admitted the bomb's devastating potential, but he speculated that at probable rates of public funding, atomic warfare with guided missiles lay fifty years in the future. Much of the current thinking lacked a basis in history and failed to "face the hard physical facts of the brains, money, energy and *time* required to revolutionize warfare with fantastic new and complicated equipment." Until such a revolution took place, the nation would need conventional air power.[33]

Maxwell believed that the statements of prominent scientists, combined with the effects of excessive secrecy, had fostered a public misunderstanding. Also, the "overeagerness on the part of the Air Forces' publicity program" deserved a major share of the blame. Exaggerated claims for atomic air power encouraged hysterical defeatism or overconfident bellicosity, in either case detrimental to the Air Forces' real political interests. No country was going to attack the United States until it had sufficient air power and atomic weapons. A war might well last longer than people expected; even with the bomb, victory would be difficult to attain. Maxwell saw the radius of escort fighters (1,000–1,500 miles) as the limiting factor

---

[32] Memo, H. C. Peterson, Asst Sec War, to CSA, subj: JCS 1477/5, Jan 15, 1946; memo, CSA to JCS, subj: National Security and Military Organization, Jan 21, 1946; memo, CG AAF to JCS (1477/8), subj: Statement of Effect of Atomic Weapons on National Security and Military Organization, Feb 6, 1946; memo, CNO to JCS (1477/9), subj: Statement of Effect of Atomic Weapons on National Security and Military Organization, Mar 13, 1946; rprt, JCS 1477/20, Statement of Effect of Atomic Weapons on National Security and Military Organization, Mar 31, 1946, all above documents in RG 341, TS OPD (Aug 17, 1945), 384.3 Atomic, Box 448, Sects 1, 3, 4, MMB, NA.
[33] Memo, Brig Gen A. R. Maxwell, Ch Rqmts Div, to Lt Gen H. S. Vandenberg, ACAS/Ops, subj: Publicity on the Atomic Bomb, Dec 13, 1945, RG 341, TS OPD (Aug 17, 1945), 384.3 (Atomic), Sect 1, Box 448, MMB, NA. Emphasis in original.

Lt. Gens. Lauris Norstad, *left,* Assistant Chief of Air Staff for Plans, and Hoyt S. Vandenberg, *right,* Assistant Chief of Air Staff for Operations, served as advisers to General Spaatz and his special board investigating the atomic bomb and its significance to structuring, equipping, and training in the post-war air forces.

in AAF striking power. He challenged the obsession with secrecy and contended that America's technological lead could not last:

> We do not have a monopoly on resources; there is no such thing as a monopoly on brains; our national realism, morale and organization is seriously open to question.... The Germans were in fact defeated more by the stupidity and dissensions of their leaders than by military or technical inferiority. For us to assume that we can maintain our lead in anything but the ingenuity and resourcefulness of the free man in a democratic state is the worst kind of walking on clouds.[34]

The testimony and reports of various experts on the atomic weapon reflected widespread uncertainty on how long the U.S. monopoly could last. Few believed that the technology was totally beyond the capacity of the Russians, although Truman at times entertained a low private opinion of their chances. Groves had maintained that the worldwide lack of raw material (uranium) would handicap the Soviets and ensure an American lead of twenty years. Deposits in Czechoslovakia, however, might come under Soviet control, and even before the communist coup in Prague in

---

[34] *Ibid.*

Strategic Air Force

1948 Groves was modifying his stance. A gradual emerging consensus predicted the first Soviet bomb in 1952 or 1953. The Central Intelligence Group, established to fill the gap left by the disappearance of the wartime Office of Strategic Services, postulated a date as early as 1950, and some even suggested 1949. The AAF included pessimists, and the Bikini tests of methods to detect atomic explosions interested such persons greatly. In any case, observers later noted the tendency to keep postponing the date when the U.S. monopoly would end.[35]

The Central Intelligence Group also foresaw series production of the Tu–4 (the Tupolev version of the B–29) in 1948, operational units in 1951, and a significant atomic delivery capability soon after. In the immediate future, this posed relatively little threat. The Boeing plant in the Seattle area and the atomic facility at Hanford, Washington, were the most vulnerable to a one-way mission by a Tu–4. For the long term, however, strategists who debated the implications of two opponents armed with atomic bombs had a dreadful real-world situation to consider.[36]

The position of the JCS and the War Department on control of atomic energy had largely been dictated by Truman's foreign policy. On November 15, 1945, the President obtained the agreement of the British and Canadian governments to the quest for international control under the auspices of the United Nations, and two months later, in January 1946, the UN created an Atomic Energy Commission. Under Secretary of State Dean G. Acheson had assembled a committee to draft a U.S. proposal to the United Nations body, with David E. Lilienthal, Chairman of the Tennessee Valley Authority, heading the Board of Consultants. The Acheson-Lilienthal Report appeared in March. In the meantime, the President named Bernard M. Baruch, a seventy-six-year-old businessman and consultant on public affairs, to represent the United States on the United Nations Atomic Energy Commission, with the mission of presenting the American plan.[37]

The Acheson-Lilienthal report favored an agency of the United Nations to control all atomic activities, with a strong inspection program to enforce compliance with its decrees. When consulted by Baruch, the

---

[35] Vance O. Mitchell, "The World War II Legacy and the Early Postwar Period, 1945–1948," Chapter I of draft study, *The United States Air Force and Intelligence, 1946–1953*, 1989, *passim*, CAFH.

[36] *Ibid.*

[37] Hewlett & Anderson, *New World*, pp 420, 444, and *passim*. The body created by the United Nations should not be confused with the U.S. Atomic Energy Commission created at the end of 1946 by the McMahon Act (see page 48). The UN-related International Atomic Energy Agency was not created until 1956, although the impetus for it lay in part in the earlier international group.

military leaders took strong positions on enforcement.[38] Admiral Nimitz wrote that the United States should exploit its monopoly to win effective international control.[39] Leahy noted that the "fear of punishment" would deter countries from violating any ban on atomic armaments.[40] Eisenhower's remarks were especially pointed. Atomic weapons were needed to prevent the use of atomic weapons. "There must exist for deterrent purposes, provisions for retaliation.... The existence of the atomic bomb in our hands is a deterrent, in fact, to aggression in the world."[41] Spaatz noted that the United Nations might have to take concerted retaliatory action.[42] But until effective international control was achieved, the military leaders agreed that the United States would have to defend itself and keep the peace, unilaterally if necessary.

They were not alone in this opinion. Aside from public support for such a position, the American members of the Military Staff Committee at the UN found sympathizers in Baruch's delegation. Baruch himself confessed to being "struck" by General Arnold's idea of a chain of bases at key points around the world. Fred Searls, Jr., a member of the delegation, proposed siting four to six atomic bombs at each of these bases, with sealed orders for the commander.[43]

When Baruch submitted the American plan to the United Nations on June 14, 1946, it not only called for international inspection, but also denied a veto by any member nation on sanctions by the atomic energy agency. This gave the Soviets an additional ground for opposition, over and above their objection to the inspection provisions. Few in the American administration doubted, as the deliberations of the United Nations became increasingly deadlocked, that the Soviets were attempting to develop an atomic arsenal of their own and had no intention of allowing inspection. Kennan observed that the Soviets were unwilling to agree to guarantees until the United States destroyed its stockpile, and conversely America

---

[38] *Ibid.*

[39] Ltr, Adm C. L. Nimitz, CNO, to B. Baruch, US Rep AEC, Jun 11, 1946, in *FRUS*, 1946, Vol I, pp 853–854.

[40] Ltr, Adm W. D. Leahy, CS CINC, to B. Baruch, US Rep AEC, Jun 11, 1946, in *FRUS*, 1946, Vol I, pp 851–853.

[41] Ltr, Gen D. D. Eisenhower, CSA, to B. Baruch, US Rep AEC, Jun 14, 1946, in *FRUS*, 1946, Vol I, pp 854–856.

[42] Draft ltr, Gen C. A. Spaatz, CG AAF, to B. Baruch, US Rep AEC, n.d. [Jun 46], RG 341, DCS/Ops, OPD S, Asst for AE, 1946, 452.1, MMB, NA; Hewlett & Anderson, *New World*, p 575.

[43] Memo, US Rep MSC to JCS, subj: Visit to Office of Mr. Bernard Baruch, Jun 7, 1946, in *FRUS*, 1946, Vol I, pp 843–846.

would not give up its weapons program without guarantees. By the summer of 1947 it was clear that international control was going nowhere.[44]

The prospect of international control raised the hope that the nonmilitary uses of atomic energy would outweigh military ones. This was one of the factors leading to pressure for a civilian agency to manage the domestic atomic program. The War Department moved quickly at the end of 1945 to sponsor legislation to provide the postwar successor to the MANHATTAN PROJECT. Although the bill envisioned an independent agency, opposition began to form, particularly among the atomic scientists. The issue divided along the lines of military versus civilian control. Not until August 1, 1946, did President Truman sign the Atomic Energy Act. The final bill, originally proposed by Senator Brien McMahon of Connecticut, established a five-member, all-civilian Atomic Energy Commission (AEC), to assume most of the functions of the MANHATTAN PROJECT at the end of the year. The commission would manufacture weapons, if necessary, and retain custody of them until the President ordered them transferred to the armed services. A Military Liaison Committee would represent the services. The commission would also sponsor research into non-military aspects of atomic energy and ensure proper safeguards for its use in industry. Provisions with regard to security were stringent, heavily reflecting General Groves's views on the matter.[45]

While the future of the atomic weapons program came under scrutiny, the MANHATTAN PROJECT continued to function, albeit haltingly. Demobilization posed a serious problem for the project. Those scientists who remained, distracted by the questions as to the future organization, worked as best they could to produce some weapons. By June 30, 1946, the stockpile included the components of nine bombs.[46] Meanwhile, the project's efforts were largely directed toward a test program. The Navy had advocated research on the effect of the bomb on naval vessels. This would prove to be the path to a better understanding of the possible implications of the weapon.[47]

---

[44] Hewlett & Duncan, *Atomic Shield, 1947–1952*, pp 261–267.
[45] Hewlett & Anderson, *New World*, pp 482–530.
[46] Ltr, J. M. Holl, Hist Dept Energy, to J. R. [sic] Bohn, Hist SAC, Mar 22, 1982, with encl, in SAC/HO; Hewlett & Anderson, *New World*, pp 624–626.
[47] Memo, Lt Gen H. S. Vandenberg, ACAS/Ops, to ACAS/Pl, subj: Atomic Bomb Striking Force, Nov 15, 1945, RG 341, OPD, Asst for AE, 1945, 322 (A-Bomb Striking Force), Box 1; memo, Maj Gen L. R. Groves, OIC Manhattan Proj, to Brig Gen W. A. Borden, Dir New Dev Div, WD Spec Staff, subj: War Department Research and Development Program for the Employment of Atomic Energy, Nov 8, 1945, RG 341, TS OPD, Asst for AE, 1945, 312.1, Box 1, both in MMB, NA; Hewlett & Anderson, *New World*, pp 624–626.

Postwar Air Force

Demobilization and Occupation

With the war ended, the primary immediate role of the armed forces was the occupation of Germany and Japan. Senior officials and diplomats also recognized that the nation would have more standing in postwar negotiations if its forces remained strong. But rapid demobilization threatened to deprive the forces of any capability for either purpose. The very heavy bomber force, for which a role in the occupation had been developed during the war, proved especially vulnerable. The growing estrangement with the Soviet Union also subtly altered the leaders' perceptions of the purpose of the occupation forces. Ironically, in the role for which the very heavy bombers were intended, they were never really needed, while they quickly lost the capacity to deter the new potential enemy.

The long-range bomber had potential value in the occupation force because it could be stationed outside of the occupied country, safe from harassment or outright attack from a resurgent enemy and could intervene if needed. Flyovers of the occupied country could then have a deterrent effect. In the Pacific, the bases in the Marianas served the purpose. In Europe, however, the AAF devised the Peripheral Basing Plan to obtain or keep bases in allied countries during the period of occupation.

The planners arrived at a strength of five groups of heavy bombers for the occupation force in Europe. As the B–29, the AAF's most advanced long-range bomber, was scheduled to replace the B–17 and B–24, Superfortress units would need to deploy to the area. From this arose PROJECT WONDERFUL to ready and dispatch B–29 units to Europe. Meanwhile the joint chiefs would seek assistance from the State Department to get bases in Italy, France, Denmark, and Norway.[48]

Continental Air Forces (CAF), with headquarters at Bolling Field in the District of Columbia, received the task of preparing the occupation forces. Organized in 1944 to manage the AAF redeployment from Europe to the Pacific, the CAF also had the mission of furnishing the air component of the Army's Strategic Striking Force, understood in the older sense of a central reserve of ground and supporting air forces ready to move to a

---

[48] Rprt, ACAS–5 (Ops) to Gen C. A. Spaatz, CG AAF, Briefing Material for European Trip, Jun 21, 1946, Spaatz Coll, Box 265, MD, LC; doc, Consolidated List of Units Committed for Overseas Movement, Sep 8, 1945, RG 18, AAG, 1945, 322 Units Misc, Box 1/14, MMB, NA.

threatened area. With its staff in Washington, Arnold had assumed direct command of CAF.[49]

Shortly after Hiroshima, the command called a major alert for five groups in training at fields in Iowa, Nebraska, and Kansas. Despite the elaborate planning for that event, Gen. Leon W. Johnson, recipient of the Medal of Honor for his valorous leadership during the attack on the oil fields at Ploesti, Romania, on August 1, 1943, later recollected the uneasiness that was beginning to develop in the Pentagon. Then a brigadier general working for the Assistant Chief of Staff for Personnel, he pondered the question: "What if the American people demand that they [the men in the services] get out?" His answer was, "Well our plan will be shot; it won't work." Johnson's account of demobilization was fairly succinct: "So we fell apart .... It was just a riot, really ...."[50]

In October and November 1945 demobilization reached its peak. The Army's strength fell by over a million in each month, November's figure being 1,153,075. Since the Army was still inducting draftees and (after legislation was passed in October) enlisting volunteers, the actual number of separations was still greater. For the AAF October marked the greatest decline in strength. A decrease of 493,093 reduced the air forces to a little over 1.5 million. Air force strength overseas fell from 1 million at the time of Hiroshima to 385,000 at the end of December.[51]

More telling than the numbers, however, was the decline in quality. The War Department had devised a system of "points" that gave precedence for separation to men with long service overseas and family responsibilities. Thus the most experienced and mature men were the first to go. Replacing seasoned workers with new recruits compounded the manpower problem, and the AAF, so dependent on skilled maintenance men, was especially hard hit. A year after the ceasefire, the number of qualified aircraft maintenance personnel had plummeted from 350,000 to 30,000. By then, as a result, only 18 percent of the aircraft were operationally ready. This trend had already started at the end of 1945, and by November 1946 air units overseas were generally less than fifty percent effective. Furthermore, the redeployment of air units from Europe to the Pacific had resulted in large combat forces being held in the continental United States

---

[49] Wolk, *Planning and Organizing*, pp 114–120; hist, Hq Continental Air Forces, Organization and Missions, Hq Continental Air Forces, Dec 15, 1944–Mar 21, 1946, pp 59–71, 78–79, AFHRA 415.01.
[50] USAF OHI, # 609, Arthur K. Marmor, AFCHO, with Gen Leon W. Johnson, Ret, Apr 14, 1965, p 23, AFHRA.
[51] *The Army Almanac* (1950), p 627; *Army Air Forces Statistical Digest*, 1946, p 14.

Postwar Air Force

Manhattan Project principals Vannevar Bush, *left,* **and Maj. Gen. Leslie Groves,** *right,* **were consulted on the future of the atomic bomb by the Joint Staff during early post-war strategic planning initiatives.**

awaiting overseas shipment at the moment the war ended. These units quickly lost their best men to the separation centers, devastating the potential strategic reserve.[52]

Overseas, metaphorically speaking, the victorious armies stacked arms and headed for the ships. They left behind billions of dollars worth of equipment and supplies, exposed to pilferage, rust, and rot on virtually abandoned airfields and supply dumps. After two years of demobilization the disposal of surplus property would still be the main unfinished job of the overseas commands. And the men who remained in service, frustrated by their working conditions and anxious to leave, became increasingly ill-tempered. In January 1946 the War Department tried to stanch the hemorrhaging of the occupation forces, but the new rules raised a public outcry, with demonstrations and disorders among the troops from Manila to Frankfurt.[53]

Frustration and anxiety soon spread to the higher levels of command. In October and November 1945 the Joint Strategic Survey Committee warned of the harmful effects of demobilization on national security.

---

[52] John C. Sparrow, *History of Personnel Demobilization in the United States Army* (Washington: Ofc of Ch of Mil Hist, 1951) pp 360–363; Alfred Goldberg, ed, *A History of the United States Air Force, 1907–1957* (Princeton, NJ: Van Nostrand, 1957), p 105; Harold B. Hinton, *Air Victory: The Men and the Machines* (NY: Harper, 1948), p 346.

[53] Sparrow, *Personnel Demobilization*, pp 360–363, 521.

Strategic Air Force

Secretary Byrnes approached his negotiations with the Soviets uneasily aware of how little armed strength he had to support his position.[54] In his November testimony to Congress, General Spaatz saw

> our Air Force disintegrating before our eyes. We see almost hysterical demobilization. We see the rising curve of flying accidents, due to the loss of experienced ground personnel.

He called for an immediate effort to reconstitute the nation's air power.[55]

The units designated to deploy to Europe under PROJECT WONDERFUL exemplified the problems of demobilization for the armed forces. As many men already had the points for separation from service, replacements were urgently needed. The resulting reshuffle of personnel compounded the increasing chaos. From commanders to mechanics, demoralization was general. One irate group commander telephoned Headquarters Second Air Force to find out what the policy was on removing men eligible for separation from WONDERFUL units. A personnel officer told him he thought that the commanding general had said, "...take out everybody that's unhappy." To this the group commander replied sourly, "Well, I can take out the whole god damn group then."[56] The constant changes in criteria for separation from the Army or for transfer overseas continually undid every arrangement to man the groups. The confusion forced postponement of the move, first from September 1 to October 1, then to December 1. In November Headquarters AAF suspended PROJECT WONDERFUL pending further study.[57] The officer monitoring the project on the Air Staff pointed out that the new War Department policy of releasing men with two years' service would make it impossible to find trained people.[58] Finally, in January 1946 Headquarters AAF announced the suspension of PROJECT WONDERFUL until summer.[59] The frantic demobilization had thus limited American military power in a quite specific way.

---

[54] Schnabel, *JCS, 1945–1947*, pp 212–218.
[55] See Note 16.
[56] Telecon, Col C. P. Ashworth, CO 489 Bomb Gp, with Maj R. P. Harman, Pers Plng Off, 2 AF, Aug 18, 1945, quoted in hist, 2 AF, Sep 1945–Mar 1946, pp 48–49.
[57] Sanders, *Redeployment and Demobilization*, pp 43–45; ltr, Brig Gen W. F. McKee, Dep ACAS/Ops, to CG ATSC, subj: VIII Bomber Command and Associated Units, Nov 24, 1945, RG 18, AAG, 1945, 322 Commands, 2/104, MMB, NA.
[58] Memo, Col L. P. Dahl, Ch Ofc Prog Monitoring, to ACAS/Pl, subj: Material for Briefing General Eisenhower, Dec 4, 1945, RG 341, OPD (Aug 17, 1945), 009, Anx 1/22, MMB, NA.
[59] Ltr, Brig Gen W. A. Matheny, Ch Commitment Div, ACAS/Ops, to CG CAF, subj: Deferment of VIII Bomber Command and Five VHB Groups, Jan 3, 1946, RG 18, AAG, 1946–1947, 322 Commands, Box 604, MMB, NA.

Postwar Air Force

Postponement might allow the AAF more time to prepare units eventually for deployment, but it would not resolve a policy contradiction inherent in PROJECT WONDERFUL. In November 1945 the State Department estimated that 200,000 troops in Germany—the number estimated to be in the country at the end of the coming June—would not be enough to deter, let alone oppose, a "militant enemy."[60] It would nonetheless be larger than necessary for simple occupation duties. Eisenhower, still theater commander in Europe, argued that he needed no more than two groups of very heavy bombers for "his assigned mission of *maintaining security within Germany*."[61] The AAF disagreed: "... retention of the five (5) VHB groups in the European theater is necessary to combat any possible threat from the East."[62] But U.S. policy toward the Soviet Union was not yet firmly enough established to justify maintaining such a force.

A further problem lay in the Peripheral Basing Plan itself. The State Department reported difficulties in obtaining access to the areas in question. Work might begin at Amendola, one of the Fifteenth Air Force's fields near Foggia, Italy,[63] but eventually the Allies would leave Italy and the problem of rights would arise again. Denmark and Norway feared Soviet pressure for similar rights if they let the Americans set up bases. France was equally reluctant.[64] As the stated rationale for the bases was the occupation, which appeared to most planners as a temporary phase, the Americans would eventually leave. So the whole program lingered on in uncertainty. The first postwar attempt by the United States to organize and maintain a strategic air force for deterrent purposes was falling

---

[60] Ltr, James F. Byrnes, Sec State, to R. P. Patterson, Sec War, Nov 29, 1945, with encl: Answers to Questions Contained in the Memorandum Dated Nov 1, 1945, From the Secretary of War to the Secretary of State, in *FRUS*, 1946, Vol I, pp 1128–1133.

[61] Emphasis in original.

[62] Memo, Lt Gen H. S. Vandenberg, ACAS/Ops, to Dep Comdr AAF, subj: Occupational Air Force Troop Basis, n.d. [Sep 45], RG 341, TS AAG File 21/7, MMB, NA.

[63] R & R Sheet, Cmt 1, Lt Gen I. C. Eaker, Dep CG AAF, to Maj Gen L. Norstad, ACAS–5 (Pl), Additional Requirements for USAFE, Apr 21, 1946, and Cmt 2, Norstad to Eaker, Apr 26, 1946, RG 341, TS AAG File 22, Box 7; memo, Norstad to Gen C. A. Spaatz, CG AAF, subj: Deployment of VHB Units in the Occupation of Germany, May 16, 1946, RG 341, TS AAG File 22, Box 7; memo, Brig Gen F. H. Griswold, Dep ACAS–3 (Ops), to Spaatz, subj: VHB Groups for ETO, May 23, 1946, RG 341, TS AAG File 25 (E–267), Box 8, all in MMB, NA.

[64] Rprt, ACAS–5 (Ops) to Gen C. A. Spaatz, CG AAF, Briefing Material for European Trip, Jun 21, 1946, Spaatz Coll, Box 265, MD, LC; Elliot V. Converse, "United States Plans for a Postwar Overseas Base System, 1942–1948," (Ph.D. Dissertation, Princeton Univ, 1984), pp 173–174.

victim to the realities of American peacetime politics and international diplomacy.

The tribulations of Continental Air Forces in PROJECT WONDERFUL paled in the light of the massive restructuring underway at the Pentagon. The Japanese surrender had taken place two months into fiscal year 1946 (ending in those days on June 30, 1946). Heavy reductions in military spending were expected, and in September 1945 President Truman submitted proposals to Congress. The Army's goal involved cutting strength from over eight million to two million. In planning this force, the War Department allocated a strength of 574,000 to the AAF. This number was subsequently reduced to 400,000. General Arnold considered that a force this size would provide a total of seventy combat groups. From then until 1951, seventy groups became the airmen's definition of adequate air power for the nation. While arrived at after the fact, the number had the virtue of being an agreed level easily described. As demobilization progressed, this force was never attained until 1951, by which time larger figures were under consideration. Arnold allocated these forces for the occupation, but he hoped to make the goal one for the peacetime force as well.[65]

The continuing demobilization forced the services to revise their planned force levels repeatedly. By February 1946 the joint chiefs approved goals of 400,000 personnel and seventy groups for the AAF throughout fiscal 1947, with a reduction of the rest of the Army over the same period from 1,150,000 to 670,000. A month later AAF manpower dropped to 500,000 with seventy-one groups. As the universal military training bill languished on Capitol Hill, the President asked for extension of selective service to enable the services to maintain their forces. For the time being, the seventy-group program seemed secure.[66]

Planning for Strategic Air Power

While contending with the current problems of demobilization and occupation, the leaders of the AAF also needed to start looking ahead. At the core of the proposed seventy-group air force were the twenty-five VHB groups. For these the B–29 would be the basic aircraft for the immediate future. Planned improvements would produce the B–29D, redesignated

---

[65] Schnabel, *JCS, 1945–1947*, pp 233–237; Wolk, *Planning and Organizing*, pp 61–68.
[66] Sparrow, *Personnel Demobilization*, pp 316–322, 360–363, 519–523; Sherry, *Preparing*, p 225; *Army Air Forces Statistical Digest*, 1946, pp 4–5, 14, 123.

the B–50 in December 1945. Also unresolved at war's end was the role of atomic weapons in the VHB force and what command structure would best control that force. These questions extended to matters of relationships with the rest of the War Department, especially the MANHATTAN PROJECT, and the overall defense establishment. During the last months of 1945 and early 1946, these issues became a major part of the work of the Air Staff, particularly for Hoyt Vandenberg as Assistant Chief of Air Staff for Operations, Commitments, and Requirements, and Lauris Norstad, now a major general and Assistant Chief of Air Staff for Plans.

Uncertain as everyone was of the true significance of atomic weapons, some answers had to be found soon. Airmen tended to see the bomb as transforming the potential of the strategic air offensive as a weapon of war. General Eaker, Deputy Commanding General of the AAF, later explained that the bomb offered the "opportunity to put warfare on an economical, sensible, reasonable basis."[67] Atomic weapons, most airmen thought, gave strategic air power the means to achieve its objectives and be truly decisive. The new technology did not alter the basic principles of air power. Different tactics and techniques might be required, but the factors of range and offensive action remained all-important. Realizing that the side attacking first in an atomic air war would have an advantage, airmen also knew that this would be an extremely sensitive subject. Above all, they argued, the atomic bomb was a strategic air weapon, primarily to be delivered by large bombers at the most important targets.

LeMay supported the AAF's claim to the new technology when he sent a message to Eaker from the Pacific. The USASTAF Chief of Staff began by noting:

(A) The efficacy of the atomic bomb has been established.
(B) It is essential to national security that U.S. leadership in this field be maintained.
(C) The atomic bomb is essentially an air weapon, and therefore, it is incumbent upon the Army Air Forces to provide full cooperation to insure U.S. leadership.

LeMay recommended that the 509th Composite Group not be dismantled in the demobilization. In the longer term the AAF had to have a force, "probably a wing," that could deploy anywhere in the world on short notice for atomic operations. Experienced people should be kept in the atomic program, and the training curriculum should include some science. Future aircraft development would have to take the bomb into account:

---

[67] USAF OHI, # 627, Charles H. Hildreth & Alfred Goldberg, AFCHO, with Lt Gen Ira C. Eaker, Ret, May 1962, p 6, AFHRA.

"The design of the bomb and the design of the airplane to carry the bomb, probably will be closely related as long as the bomb remains heavy and awkward." He recommended that either Palm Springs or Victorville, California, be the center of a base area for the force, using the California desert for testing and training. This area was remote but not isolated, and accessible to scientific centers.[68]

On September 14 General Arnold asked General Spaatz, recently returned from the Pacific, to chair a board to study the question of atomic weapons in the AAF. Vandenberg and Norstad were to serve with him. Meeting in the utmost secrecy, the Spaatz Board submitted its report on October 23. In the meantime Arnold took action to safeguard the AAF's atomic capability. The 509th Composite Group left Tinian for the United States, destined for Roswell Field, New Mexico, which had a less severe housing shortage than the California bases suggested by LeMay. Kirtland Field, ideally located for cooperation with Los Alamos, was rejected because its airfield was a municipal airport, and security would be compromised.[69] Possibly aware of the Spaatz Board's thinking, General Arnold was determined that the AAF's voice be heard on atomic matters. On October 22 he sent a memorandum to Robert P. Patterson, Secretary of War, asking for AAF representation in all War Department planning with regard to atomic energy and that military representatives, including an air officer, be included in any commission for the control of atomic energy.[70]

The basic recommendations of the Spaatz Board were quite similar to Arnold's memorandum, though less specific. The board concluded that the atomic bomb did not at the time impose radical changes on the AAF. Although improvements over the coming ten years could be foreseen, and a stockpile would be developed, the bomb would remain bulky, heavy, expensive, and in short supply. Therefore the AAF's very heavy bombers would still be the only effective means of delivery. Numbers would be too small to justify use of the bomb against tactical targets. A nation seeking to

---

[68] Msg, CG USASTAF to CG AAF (Personal LeMay to Eaker) 3505, 300901Z Aug 45, subj: Postwar Atomic Bomb Program, RG 341, OPD TS, Asst for AE, 1945, 373 Crossroads, Box 2, MMB, NA.

[69] Memo, Maj Gen E. M. Powers, ACAS/Mat, to ACAS/Pl, subj: Kirtland Field, Sep 4, 1945, RG 341, TS OPD, Asst for AE, 1946, 373 Crossroads, Box 2, MMB, NA; Maurer Maurer, *Air Force Combat Units of World War II* (Washington: GPO, 1961 [new imprint, Washington: AFCHO, 1983]), pp 371–372.

[70] Memo, Gen H. H. Arnold, CG AAF, to Sec War, subj: Policy on Atomic Energy, Oct 22, 1945, RG 341, OPD, Asst for AE, 1945, 312.1 AE, Box 1, MMB, NA.

Lt. Gen. Ira C. Eaker, Deputy Commander, AAF, saw in the atomic bomb the AAF's "opportunity to put warfare on an economical, sensible...basis."

defend itself against atomic attack would try to disperse its industry and thereby reduce the number of profitable targets. Also, the attacking force might have to use conventional bombing as well in achieving penetration. Therefore, the board concluded: "The atomic bomb has not altered our basic concept of the strategic air offensive but has given us an additional weapon." The bomb also made the AAF the primary customer of the MANHATTAN DISTRICT.[71]

The Spaatz report raised no challenge to the seventy-group air force. As for policy, the likelihood of another country developing the bomb compelled the nation to prepare for an atomic war. No country that lacked the bomb was likely to attack America. The board agreed that the only defense against the bomb was to destroy the bomb carrier in the air or on the ground. Therefore, "We must be prepared for: (1) Preventive or retaliatory action. (2) Defense against attacks of all kinds." The United States needed forward bases for three reasons. First, a forward defense would be more effective than a point defense. Second, it was necessary to deny other countries key bases for an attack on the United States. Thirdly, America would use these bases for its own strategic air offensive. The

---

[71] R & R Sheet, Gen H. H. Arnold, CG AAF, to Dep Comdr AAF, Board Report re Policy on Atomic Energy, Oct 23, 1945, with atch report, RG 341, TS OPD (Aug 17, 1945), 384.3 (Atomic), Sect 1, Box 448, MMB, NA.

Strategic Air Force

board supported the JCS view that intelligence and research and development were essential.⁷²

The actual recommendations were brief. The Spaatz Board called for a senior officer charged with representing the AAF in all atomic and research matters:

> His duties should embrace not only the exploitation of atomic energy, but also should include the direction of research and development of all air weapons of the future. He should be a participating member of the Manhattan District project and represent the Air Force in the highest councils of research and development.⁷³

The board then proposed appointing to this position "an officer of the caliber of Maj. Gen. Curtis E. LeMay."⁷⁴

The "officer of the caliber of Curtis LeMay" was then in Dayton, Ohio, taking charge of the Air Technical Service Command. LeMay had returned from the Pacific theater the previous month, landing at Chicago on September 19 after a 5,995-mile nonstop flight aboard a stripped-down B–29 from the Japanese island of Hokkaido. During the years before the war, Army aviators had often sought publicity through record-breaking flights; now the AAF was back in that business.⁷⁵

Called to Washington, LeMay became a member of the Army-Navy Advisory Committee to General Groves. He represented the AAF, with Col. Roscoe C. Wilson as his alternate. On December 5 LeMay received his official appointment as Deputy Chief of Air Staff for Research and Development. He was already establishing a small coordinating office to focus mainly on building an atomic energy program for the AAF.⁷⁶

---

⁷² *Ibid.*
⁷³ *Ibid.*
⁷⁴ *Ibid.*
⁷⁵ *New York Times,* Sep 21, 1945, pp 1, 4.
⁷⁶ R & R Sheet, Cmt 2, Gen C. A. Spaatz to Dep Comdr AAF, Dissemination of Atomic Energy Data, Nov 13, 1945, RG 341, TS OPD, Asst for AE, 1945, 312.1, Box 1, MMB, NA; Robert D. Little, *Foundations of an Atomic Air Force and Operation Sandstone, 1946–1948,* Vol II of *The History of Air Force Participation in the Atomic Energy Program, 1943–1953* (Washington: USAF Hist Div, 1954), pp 55–56 (note 1), 541ff (note 2); Curtis E. LeMay and MacKinlay Kantor, *Mission with LeMay: My Story* (Garden City, NY: Doubleday, 1965), p 395. This work, although presented as LeMay's own memoirs, needs to be used with considerable care.

Two days before LeMay's appointment, Eaker had acted to ensure that his new deputy would be included in the planning for an atomic strike force. By November these plans had begun to solidify. Vandenberg's staff had developed a plan for four of the twenty-five proposed VHB groups to be composite units along the lines of the 509th.[77] Subsequently reduced to three groups, this force would rely on the 509th as a nucleus around which an atomic strike capability would develop, while keeping some kind of ready element at all times. As Norstad pointed out, security reasons dictated avoiding the word "atomic" in the title of any organization.[78] Eaker cited a further reason, especially if there were only going to be three or four groups in the striking force:

> Are we not making an error in designating one wing as an atomic bombing force? Would it not be better to have all our long range bomber units employed for this purpose? It strikes me we are very likely to find the attitude of the War Department and of the Congress to be that the atomic bombing force is the only strategic Air Force we will require. If one wing will do the job, then one wing will be the size of the strategic force.[79]

The Deputy Commander of AAF agreed that a ready force was needed, but it should also help in "coaching the other long range groups as they become available."[80]

On December 12 Vandenberg, Norstad, LeMay, and Maxwell met with Maj. Gen. St. Clair Streett, the Deputy Commander of the Continental Air Forces, to design the new organization.[81] Two days later Norstad informed Streett of the rationale for the agreed plan, which accommo-

---

[77] Memo, Lt Gen H. S. Vandenberg, ACAS/Ops, to ACAS/Pl, subj: Atomic Bomb Striking Force, Nov 15, 1945, RG 341, OPD, Asst for AE, 1945, 322 A-Bomb Striking Force, Box 1, MMB, NA.

[78] Memo, Maj Gen L. Norstad, ACAS/Pl, to CAS, subj: Atomic Bomb Striking Force, Nov 24, 1945, RG 341, OPD, Asst for AE, 1945, 322 A-Bomb Striking Force, Box 1; R & R Sheet, Cmt 2, Brig Gen J. A. Samford, Dep ACAS/Intel, Atomic Bomb Striking Force, Dec 6, 1945, RG 18, AAG, 1945, 370.22 Campaigns and Expeditions, 178, both in MMB, NA.

[79] R & R Sheet, Cmt 1, Lt Gen I. C. Eaker, Dep Comdr AAF, to ACASs, Atomic Bomb Striking Force, Dec 3, 1945, RG 341, OPD, Asst for AE, 1945, 322, Box 1, MMB, NA.

[80] *Ibid.*

[81] R & R Sheet, ACAS/Ops to Dep Comdr AAF, Atomic Bomb Striking Force, n.d. [Dec 45], RG 341, OPD, Asst for AE, 1945, 322, Box 1, MMB, NA.

dated Eaker's criticism. There would be a specialized striking force at the beginning, but:

> It will be necessary in our dealings with other agencies of the government such as the War Department and the Congress, to emphasize the fact that the atomic bomb actually does not enable the elimination of any portion of our air force.[82]

Conventional bombers would be needed to attack enemy air defenses, to convoy the atomic carriers, and for diversionary attacks; in other words, to ensure penetration. Thus the actual atomic force had to be ready to go into action immediately in conjunction with conventional units, while at the same time it provided the nucleus for future development.[83]

During December the Air Staff worked out the details of a plan for the force, which received final Air Staff approval on January 7, 1946. The atomic force would carry the designation of the 58th Bombardment Wing. This wing's headquarters had recently arrived from the Pacific at March Field, California, under the command of Brig. Gen. Roger M. Ramey. The 58th would include the 509th Composite Group and two additional groups converted from conventional very heavy units. All groups would eventually be stationed near Los Alamos. The wing headquarters would train the units, coordinate technical support (including the movement of scientists and technicians to operating bases in wartime), conduct liaison with the MANHATTAN District, and support the district's flight tests. The planners expected that officials close to the President would take the keenest possible interest in atomic operations, so that control of them had to be responsive. In the event of war, a group or groups would deploy to an active theater and come under the control of the theater commander. All bombers would be available for conventional bombing until needed for an atomic mission. Transport units (possibly using C–97 cargo planes especially modified) would deliver the bomb to the B–29 base. The Tinian operation served as the model. However, now one could expect hostile defense to be a great deal more concerned than in the past at individual penetrations by B–29s. Tactics had to take this into account. The atomic carrier might have to accompany a mass raid or attack at night, either infiltrating or with the bombers flying in a stream. Newer aircraft, such as

---

[82] R & R Sheet, Cmt 2, Maj Gen L. Norstad, ACAS/Pl, to Dep Comdr AAF, Atomic Bomb Striking Force, Dec 14, 1945, RG 18, AAG, 1945, 370.22 Campaigns and Expeditions, 178, MMB, NA.
[83] Ibid.

the B-36, might be able to operate from the continental United States, but for the time being, forward bases were essential to atomic operations.[84]

If, during the occupation period, Continental Air Forces was to have five groups, the three planned atomic groups would represent the bulk of its strength. However, with the suspension of PROJECT WONDERFUL in January 1946, the deployment of units stopped, and the command inherited the majority of the AAF's B-29 units. The last VHB group to return from the Pacific reached California in December 1945. By February 1946 the CAF consisted of thirteen marginally effective VHB groups (See chart) and several headquarters, some only on paper. Besides the 509th, the command controlled two additional atomic groups: the 40th and the 449th.[85]

Another important consideration involved the CAF's position in the overall AAF command structure. In December 1945, as plans for the postwar organization began to emerge, an ad hoc committee on reorganization proposed the establishment of a combat command and a training command. The reorganization committee opposed spreading the long-range bomber force around the world and favored concentrating as much as possible of it under Air Force Combat Command for greater flexibility.[86]

At the same time, Eaker supported a plan to consolidate tactical air units in the continental United States under a single command. This organization would work with the Army Ground Forces in joint training. The idea of such a tactical force remained a constant theme throughout the months following the end of the war. Since many air officers feared that the Ground Forces would try to create their own air force, the AAF had to demonstrate its determination to furnish the needed air support.

---

[84] See Note 81; R & R Sheet, Cmt 2, Col J. G. Moore, Dep ACAS/Mat, to Dep Comdr AAF, Atomic Bomb Striking Force, Dec 11, 1945, RG 341, OPD, Asst for AE, 1945, 322, Box 1; memo, Lt Gen H. S. Vandenberg, ACAS/Ops, to Lt Gen I. C. Eaker, Dep Comdr AAF, subj: The Establishment of a Strategic Striking Force, n.d. [Dec 45], RG 341, OPD, Asst for AE, 1945, 322 A-Bomb Striking Force, Box 1; memo, Lt Col J. A. Derry, Manhattan Dist, to Maj Gen L. Norstad, ACAS/Pl, subj: Request for Two C-97 Airplanes, Nov 14, 1945, RG 341, OPD, Asst for AE, 1945, 452.1 Acft, all in MMB, NA.

[85] Maurer, *AF Combat Units*, pp 96-97, 101-103, 160-162, 318-319, 322, 324, 337, 342-344, 356, 364-366, 371-372, 386-387, 399-400, 407; ltr, Maj Gen St. Clair Streett, Dep Comdr CAF, to CG AAF, subj: Location of VHB Units, n.d., with 1st Ind, CG AAF to CG CAF, Dec 18, 1945, RG 341, TS OPD (Aug 17, 1945), 384.3 Atomic, Sect 1, Box 448, MMB, NA; ltr, Brig Gen W. A. Matheny, Ch Commitments Div, ACAS/Ops, to CG AAF, subj: VHB Units for SSF and General Reserve, Dec 27, 1945, with chart, RG 18, 322 O & T Units, Vol 9, 1945/114, MMB, NA.

[86] Wolk, *Planning and Organizing*, pp 124-133.

Assignment and Stationing of B-29 Units, March 1946

Planned Very Heavy Bomb Groups, 70-group Air Force, Occupation Period

Pacific	12
Alaska	1
Caribbean	2
Europe	5
CONUS	5
Total	25

Actual Assignments, CAF
Second Air Force
VIII Bomber Command[a]

44	VHB	Gp Smoky Hill, Kansas
485	VHB	Gp Smoky Hill, Kansas
93	VHB	Gp Clovis, New Mexico
467	VHB	Gp Clovis, New Mexico
448	VHB	Gp Ft Worth, Texas
449	VHB	Gp Grand Island, Nebraska

Third Air Force
73d Bombardment Wing – MacDill, Florida

497	VHB	Gp[b] MacDill, Florida
498	VHB	Gp[b] MacDill, Florida

Fourth Air Force
58th Bombardment Wing – March, California

40	VHB	Gp March, California
444	VHB	Gp Castle, California
509	VHB	Comp Gp Roswell, New Mexico
462	VHB	Gp[b c] MacDill, Florida
468	VHB	Gp[b c] Ft Worth, Texas

[a] VIII Bomber Command Headquarters not operational
[b] Inactivated March 31, 1946
[c] Temporarily assigned to 58th Wing

NOTE: In the March reorganization, First, Second, and Fourth Air Forces were among those assigned to the Air Defense Command. Third Air Force went to the Tactical Air Command.

Spaatz, a firm believer in the unity of air power, saw the creation of a new air force under the ground generals as unacceptable. As Eisenhower's airman in Europe, he had learned how to balance strategic and tactical requirements while winning his leader's confidence. General Eisenhower had become an enthusiastic partisan of air power. Thus by January 29, 1946, the AAF's Commander-designate and the Army's new Chief of Staff had reached a basic agreement about the proper organization in the air. The combat air forces in the continental United States would consist of three functional commands: strategic, tactical, and defense. The new Air Defense Command (ADC) would assume responsibility for reserve forces and regional activities. All three commands would focus on combat readiness, with a separate command for individual training. Spaatz ordered the new organization into effect as of March 21.[87]

Under the planned realignment, the new Strategic Air Command (SAC) would take over the CAF headquarters and staff at Bolling, while ADC and the Tactical Air Command (TAC) would establish new headquarters. Two numbered air forces, the Eighth and Fifteenth, would be allocated to SAC. The headquarters of these two air forces would be at Fort Worth, Texas, and Colorado Springs, Colorado. The headquarters building under construction at Andrews Field, Maryland, would house Headquarters SAC.[88]

The decision to situate SAC's headquarters in the Washington area reflected the bombers' status as the premier element of an air force. Likewise, in naming a commander, Spaatz turned to the man who was senior to him by four days and the senior general in the AAF, George C. Kenney. Since Kenney was serving on the Military Staff Committee of the United Nations, and since many Americans envisioned the U.S. bomber force as the principal American contribution to a UN police force, Kenney was well placed for a pivotal role.[89]

---

[87] *Ibid.* During the Second World War the U.S. Army had been organized at home into three major commands, Army Ground Forces, Army Air Forces, and Army Service Forces. This structure was somewhat changed after 1945, but Army Ground Forces persisted in some form even after the Air Force became a separate service.

[88] *Ibid.*, pp 133–137; ltr, Maj Gen E. F. Witsell, TAG, to CG AAF, subj: Establishment of Air Defense, Strategic Air and Tactical Air Commands, Redesignation of the Headquarters, Continental Air Forces and Certain Other Army Air Forces Units, AG 322 (Mar 21, 1946) OB-I-AFCOR–(971(d))–M; Activation, Inactivation and Assignment of Certain Army Air Forces Units, in hist, Hq Continental Air Forces, Organization and Missions, Hq Continental Air Forces, Dec 15, 1944–Mar 21, 1956, Doc 60, AFHRA 415.01.

[89] Borowski, *Hollow Threat*, pp 33–35.

Strategic Air Force

Maj. Gen. Curtis E. LeMay, appointed Deputy Chief of Air Staff for Research and Development in December 1946, would focus on building the AAF's atomic force.

In spite of the fact that Kenney had not been directly involved in the great strategic air campaigns of the war, his association with Gen. Douglas MacArthur had given him much publicity and prestige. He had commanded the air forces in the Southwest Pacific throughout the war, demonstrating brilliance as an improviser and tactician. Kenney's first and greatest achievement had been to win MacArthur's confidence, and he had served him well, eventually becoming the Army tactical air commander in the Pacific theater. His engineering background (having attended the Massachusetts Institute of Technology) had won him a strong reputation and would serve him well in any job.[90]

Kenney's only reservation with his new position was that he did not also control the tactical forces. Unaware of Spaatz's desire to create a separate Army support force in Tactical Air Command, Kenney wrongly assumed he would receive the Air Force Combat Command. As he openly considered the distinction between tactical and strategic air power to be largely arbitrary,[91] Kenney objected to his being confined merely to the former.[92]

---

[90] Herman S. Wolk, "George C. Kenney: The Great Innovator," in John L. Frisbee, ed, *Makers of the United States Air Force* (Washington: AFCHO, 1987), pp 127–150.
[91] See Preface, p. x.
[92] USAF OHI, #239.0512-729, Tom Sturm & Hugh N. Ahmann, AFCHO, with Gen Earle E. Partridge, Ret, Apr 23-25, 1974, p 486, AFHRA. A sidelight on Kenney's almost mystical sense of the men who served under him in the war is the fact that, in addition to his war memoirs, Kenney wrote books on two of the fighter aces of his command, Capt. Richard I. Bong and Col. Paul I. Gunn.

In spite of his new appointment, Kenney remained at the United Nations for the time being. The Deputy Commander of the CAF, Maj. Gen. St. Clair Streett, assumed the same duties with SAC and continued to run the command. He had served under Kenney before, when he commanded Thirteenth Air Force in the Far East. An aviator in the First World War, Streett had led the Army flight from New York to Nome, Alaska, in 1920.[93]

The new Strategic Air Command inherited the lion's share of the CAF's resources. On March 31, ten days after the command had been established, it had a strength of 84,231, while TAC acquired 26,000 personnel and ADC 7,000. The strategic force consisted of 1,300 airplanes, although only 221 of these were B-29s. The headquarters, occupying three temporary buildings at Bolling Field, accommodated a staff of 1,000.[94]

In reality, the fledgling command was a hodgepodge of organizations, as lacking in capability as in orderly structure. Devastated by demobilization, the bomber groups could barely maintain half of their Superfortresses. The 509th Composite Group at Roswell had scarcely 20 SILVERPLATE aircraft. The historian of the 449th Bombardment Group reported a situation which even then must have been extraordinary:[95] "Due to the fact that there are but 17 enlisted men assigned to Aircraft Maintenance Division instead of the 473 authorized, efficient maintenance has been impeded, to say the least."[96]

As the CAF had previously recognized, SAC's main task was to bring order out of chaos. Now, however, the final goal was clearer. On March 12 General Spaatz issued a letter defining SAC's mission:

> The Strategic Air Command will be prepared to conduct long range offensive operations in any part of the world either independently or in cooperation with land and naval forces; to conduct maximum range reconnaissance over land or sea either independently or in cooperation with naval forces; to provide combat units capable of

---

[93] Hq AAF GO 41, Apr 1, 1946; Robert P. Fogerty, Biographical Data on Air Force General Officers, 1917–1952, USAF Study No. 91, 1953.
[94] *Army Air Forces Statistical Digest*, 1946, pp 27, 28, 30, 31; SAC Statistical Summary, Aircraft and Maintenance Section, June 1, 1946; hist, 15 AF, Apr–Dec 1946, Pt I, pp 22, 25–26, 45–56; hist, SAC, 1946, pp 13–14.
[95] Hist, 2 AF, Sep 1945–Mar 30, 1946, p 111.
[96] Memo, Brig Gen F. H. Griswold, Dep ACAS/Ops, to Gen C. A. Spaatz, CG AAF, subj: Combat Effectiveness of PACUSA Tactical Units, Apr 17, 1946, RG 18, AAG, 1946–1947, 322 O & T Units, 1/605, MMB, NA.

Strategic Air Force

intense and sustained combat operations employing the latest and most advanced weapons; to train units and personnel for the maintenance of the Strategic Forces in all parts of the world; to perform such special missions as the Commanding General, Army Air Forces may direct.[97]

This directive formally resolved, at least for the moment, questions concerning the nature and purpose of the heavy bomber force in the continental United States. Beyond the two immediate tasks, the transfer of groups to Europe and the support of the upcoming atomic tests, the Strategic Air Command had now been given a long-term, global mission.

---

[97] Ltr, Gen C. A. Spaatz, CG AAF, to CG SAC, subj: Interim Mission, Mar 12, 1946, in hist, Hq Continental Air Forces, Organization and Missions, Hq Continental Air Forces, Dec 15, 1944–Mar 21, 1946, Doc 59, AFHRA 415.01.

Chapter III

Beginnings of a Strategic Air Force

A major obstacle in building a strategic air force involved the uncertainty surrounding the questions of scale and equipment. Plans for the seventy-group program initially called for SAC to have a small number of units (five groups of very heavy bombers out of twenty-five). Most B-29 groups would be stationed overseas in support of the occupation forces. With the end of the occupation, these bomber units could finally be concentrated in the continental United States. For the time being, SAC would serve as a reserve of strategic bombers. The decision to equip three groups with SILVERPLATE aircraft confirmed this important mission, as it gave that reserve the means to use the most powerful weapon in the American arsenal.

The actual strategic force in the continental United States at the beginning of 1946 had essentially three tasks. One involved fulfilling a commitment on the part of the 509th Group to support the bomb tests at Bikini. Another was support of PROJECT WONDERFUL, the plan to deploy five B-29 groups to Europe. The third called for sending a group to Alaska to begin training for Arctic operations. The tests at Bikini were, of course, an essential early step in developing an atomic air strike force. The deployment to Alaska encountered problems that were overcome. But PROJECT WONDERFUL proved a complete dead end; it collapsed from the bottom and the top. Not only was the AAF unable to man and train the groups, but the political assumptions on which the plan had been based rapidly disappeared. The B-29 had no true role in the occupation forces, and the commitment was finally canceled. The very heavy bomber forces in the Pacific were also cut back drastically for similar reasons.

With demobilization taking its toll, 1946 ended with a Strategic Air Command of six B-29 groups, half making up the planned atomic force

Strategic Air Force

and half envisioned as a reserve of conventional bombers to be trained to deploy anywhere in the world. After a seemingly interminable sequence of reorganizations, this force was organized into two air forces, whose respective missions reflected the two different tasks. Far East Air Forces continued to operate B–29s as well, but SAC planners were definitely looking toward basing all strategic bombers in the continental United States, deploying them overseas on rotation as needed or in the event of war. The end of 1946 also saw Kenney taking command of SAC in person and beginning to build up the force to the level called for in the fifty-five group program, the supposed intermediate step toward seventy groups. Throughout the period of postwar defense reorganization, Spaatz and the air leaders continued to argue that the nation's security required an independent, strong air force. Events tended to support their position. The tensions with the Soviet Union, now considered a plausible enemy, made a case for a force that could deter aggression and resist it should deterrence fail. Advances in bomber technology had evoked the spectre of intercontinental atomic warfare, making a strategic air force a necessity. But obstacles were bound to arise to such an unprecedented course of action as building a powerful air force in peacetime. Though some Americans feared provoking the Soviets, far more significant were the strains on the national budget. Under the inflationary pressures of the postwar economy, the cost of the undertaking would spark intense debate. And in the long-anticipated conversion to a civilian economy, a new military program was destined for scrutiny.

The goal of building a seventy-group AAF remained elusive. The Strategic Air Command struggled with obsolescent equipment and experienced the same shortages of trained manpower as the rest of the armed services. The AAF as a whole faced the dilemma of whether to man too many units inadequately or maintain too few units to support an expansion to seventy groups. Kenney and his staff had to meet the formidable challenge of organizing a large combat-ready force with extremely limited resources.

As for obsolescent equipment, the AAF leaders were concerned about maintaining a lead over other nations in the quality and modernity of their weapons. Americans could not expect to match the Soviets in the sheer size of their forces. Only the best, most modern weapons could assure the nation's ability to deter or defeat the potential enemy. For the strategic force, the next step was obviously the B–36 project, already in progress at the end of the war. In the years to come, further advances in jet engines, electronics, and the atomic weapon itself, could help the United States maintain its technological edge.

Beginnings

Air Power Deferred

As the Truman administration assessed its deteriorating relations with the Soviet Union early in 1946, it began to look beyond demobilization to the need for military strength to back up its diplomatic position. One official in the State Department wrote that the time had come to "reconstitute our military establishment."[1] Doing this, however, raised questions as to how much and what kind of forces were needed and whether Congress could be persuaded to fund them. The debate would continue over the next two years, with the future of the AAF very much a part of the discussion.

Meanwhile, reconstituting the strength of the air arm had to start at a basic level. Maj. Gen. Earle E. Partridge, the Assistant Chief of Air Staff for Operations, noted that he did not even have full reports on the readiness of units. In April 1946 Partridge told the Air Board: "It is a terrible admission for A-3 to make, but that is a fact." The operations chief admitted that accurate data would reveal how unready the AAF actually was.[2] In the face of such a challenge, Spaatz ordered the Air Staff to start building up the AAF one group at a time.[3]

It was the responsibility of Congress to provide the raw materials for this build-up. Having approved a strength of 1,070,000 for the Army at the end of fiscal 1947 (400,000 for the AAF), Congress extended Selective Service to September 1, 1946, and then in June it voted a further extension, until March 31, 1947. Still, the Army hoped to free itself from the draft through an adequate number of voluntary enlistments and had undertaken a recruiting program.[4] At the end of June 1946 the AAF had reason for optimism; since the end of the war 360,000 men had enlisted or reenlisted in its ranks.[5]

On financial matters, the AAF worked closely with the War Department. Its own appropriation was for the "Air Corps" program; that is, mainly for aircraft and aircraft engines, aviation fuel, air research and

---

[1] Memo, H. Freeman Matthews, Actg State Mem SWNCC, to SWNCC, subj: Political Estimate of Soviet Policy for Use in Connection with Military Studies, Apr 1, 1946, in *FRUS*, 1946, Vol I, pp 1167–1171.
[2] Verbatim rprt, 1st Meeting of the Air Board, Apr 16–18, 1946, p 36, RG 340, Air Bd, Mins of Mtgs, Box 13, MMB, NA.
[3] R & R Sheet, Maj Gen C. C. Chauncey, DCAS, to ACAS-3 (Ops), Building-Up of the Air Force, Apr 30, 1946, RG 18, AAG, 1946–1947, 321, AAF 1, Box 603.
[4] Schnabel, *JCS, 1945–1947*, p 237; Sparrow, *Personnel Demobilization*, p 523.
[5] *Army Air Forces Statistical Digest*, 1946, p 21.

development, and civilian employees at AAF installations. Other items, such as pay for military personnel, construction, and weapons, were considered "indirect," meaning that they were budgeted by appropriate Army agencies, which took AAF requirements into account.[6]

When the War Department and Congress were cutting the fiscal 1946 program,[7] AAF representatives emphasized the importance of continuing research and development and acquiring some new aircraft. The Air Coordinating Committee, an interdepartmental body for establishing federal policy in air matters, had concluded in the fall of 1945 that the government needed to buy 3,000 airplanes a year to keep the manufacturing industry in good health. The AAF could use a large share of these purchases. It calculated that the seventy groups would need 6,000 airplanes, plus more for the reserve forces and a reserve in storage. To keep this force up to date, planners proposed systematically replacing the aircraft with new models. Ideally, for example, a fighter should be replaced at the end of three years, a very heavy bomber after six. On this basis the AAF could estimate the number to be bought annually, envisioning a total Air Corps budget of $1.75 billion per year.[8]

This plan proved entirely too optimistic. By the time the War Department submitted a proposed budget for fiscal 1947 the Air Corps item was trimmed to $1.6 billion. The Bureau of the Budget then cut the amount to $1.2 billion, reducing the number of new aircraft from 1,192 to 1,020. The new budget would also force the AAF to decrease its civilian work force from 200,000 to 170,000. In May 1946 the War Department defended the budget before Congress. Counting the indirect appropriations, Truman was requesting $3 billion for the air arm and $3.5 billion for the ground army. Compared to other Army elements, the AAF was in fact doing well, but measuring by the seventy-group standard the budget still fell short.[9]

---

[6] Verbatim rprt, 2d Meeting of the Air Board, June 4–6, 1946, pp 42–46, RG 340, Air Bd, Mins of Mtgs, Box 13, MMB, NA.

[7] During this period the federal government's fiscal year ran from July 1 to June 30. Fiscal 1946 ended in June of that year and accordingly had included the last two months of the war with Japan.

[8] Hearings before the Subcommittee on Appropriations, House of Representatives, *2d Supplemental Surplus Appropriation Rescission FY 46*, 79th Cong, 2d sess, Feb 8, 1946, p 443; hearings before the Subcommittee on Appropriations, House of Representatives, *Military Establishment Appropriation FY 47*, 79th Cong, 2d sess, May 20, 1946, pp 400–486.

[9] Hearings before the Subcommittee on Appropriations, House of Representatives, *Military Establishment Appropriation FY 1947*, 79th Cong, 2d sess, May 20, 1946, pp 3–26, 26–68, 400–486; verbatim rprt, 2d Meeting of the Air Board, Jun 4–6, 1946, pp 45–46, RG 340, Air Bd, Mins of Mtgs, Box 13, MMB, NA.

Among the indirect items, those pertaining to improved living conditions for the troops particularly interested the AAF, which was intent on retaining trained men. At that moment, housing had a higher priority than pay. The training camps that had sprung up all over the country during the war had been built economically, to say the least. Barracks would start falling apart in a few years, and accommodations for families were extremely limited. As a result, in the AAF and the rest of the Army, officers and noncommissioned officers (NCOs) had to cope with appalling conditions. Where they could find adequate housing off post, landlords called the tune. The group commander at Castle Field, for example, was living in a hotel in Merced and paying $275 a month (1946 prices). Although the ninety airfields proposed for the continental United States would require construction of runways and hangars, the AAF for the time being supported the Corps of Engineers in its priority request for funds for family housing.[10]

Meanwhile General Spaatz approved a revised structure for the seventy-group AAF at a strength of 400,000. By April 1946 the plan called for a reduction in the number of separate squadrons and realigned the different types of groups. Twenty-six groups would be equipped with very heavy bomber types—the B-29 and its reconnaissance version, the F-13. This total would include two weather reconnaissance groups, one very long range (VLR) mapping group, two VLR reconnaissance groups, and twenty-one standard very heavy bomber groups, including the 509th. Fighter groups of all types were to number twenty-five.[11]

The on-going congressional hearings posed few problems, and the AAF budgeteers were hopeful, but Col. Edward H. White, Chief of the AAF Budget and Fiscal Office, cautioned the Air Board in April 1946:

> I strongly advise that we start spending our money...instead of waiting until the last few months of the [fiscal] year...because... action may be taken after it has been appropriated by Congress.[12]

---

[10] Hearings before the Subcommittee on Appropriations, House of Representatives, *Military Establishment Appropriation FY 1947*, 79th Cong, 2d sess, May 20, 1946, pp 3–26, 26–68, 400–486; hist, SAC, 1946, pp 32–38. In 1986 prices, $275 would be $1,570.

[11] Verbatim rprt, 2d Meeting of the Air Board, June 4–6, 1946, p 67, RG 340, Air Bd, Mins of Mtgs, Box 13, MMB, NA.

[12] MR, Maj Gen E. E. Partridge, ACAS-3 (Ops), subj: Meeting with General Spaatz and General Eaker (Apr 17), Apr 17, 1946, RG 18, 1944–1946 Unclas Operations 5, Post War Planning Jan–Apr 46, Box 1513; R & R Sheet, Lt Gen I. C. Eaker, Dep Cmdr AAF, to Air Staff, Composition of the Interim and Peacetime Air Force, Apr 22, 1946, RG 18, 1946–1947 AAG, 321 Interim Postwar and Peacetime Air Forces, Vol 1, both in MMB, NA.

Strategic Air Force

Colonel White's instincts proved correct. Congress set the Air Corps total at $1.2 billion, but in August, with an election approaching and wartime price controls turned off, inflation was becoming a major political issue. The flow of cash out of the Treasury not only fueled inflation but worried the voters. With the cost of government on the rise, Congress had voted a fourteen percent increase in civil service salaries without providing the means to pay for it.[13] For the President there was only one course. Navy Secretary Forrestal, the one-time investment banker, called Truman "a hard-money man if I ever saw one."[14] On August 2 the President ordered stringent limits on current spending for items such as travel and the reallocation of available funds to meet the pay increase. General Eisenhower immediately directed a review of the War Department budget for the year. Forced to cut its direct expenditures by $60 million, the AAF took $30 million from aircraft procurement, $30 million from other items, and left research and development intact. Some equipment expenses could be deferred because the buildup to seventy groups seemed to be going more slowly than anticipated.[15]

The financial squeeze continued into the next year. The fall elections returned a Republican Congress, the first since 1931, and talk of tax cuts was in the air. Though many Republicans had denounced communism in their campaigns, they would not necessarily support a strong defense.[16] The hope that the cuts made in fiscal 1947 could be recouped in the next budget quickly vanished; the War Department would have to make more reductions to keep the budget in line. Under pressure from the Bureau of the Budget, which was inclined to challenge the imbalance between research and current programs, the AAF trimmed its research and development funds, up to now sacrosanct. Total funds programmed at $210

---

[13] Ltr, Gen C. A. Spaatz, CG AAF, to AAF, subj: Current AAF Plans and Programs, Nov 18, 1946, with encls, RG 18, 1946–1947 AAG, 321 AAF, File 1, Box 603; verbatim rprt, 4th Meeting of the Air Board, Dec 3–4, 1946, pp 47–73, RG 340, Bds & Cmtes, Rcrds of Air Bd, Box 15, both in MMB, NA. The Consumer Price Index (1967 = 100) rose from 53.9 in 1945 to 58.5 a year later.

[14] James V. Forrestal, *The Forrestal Diaries* (NY: Viking, 1951), p 536.

[15] Ltr, Gen D. D. Eisenhower, CSA, to Dirs War Dept Gen Staff, Chs War Dept Spec Staff, *et al*, subj: Enforcement of Economies, Aug 22, 1946, in Tab 8 to ltr, Gen C. A. Spaatz, CG AAF, to AAF, subj: Current AAF Plans and Programs, Nov 18, 1946, RG 18, 1946–1947 AAG, 321 AAF, File 1, Box 603; verbatim rprt, 4th Meeting of the Air Board, Dec 3–4, 1946, pp 47–73, RG 340, Bds & Cmtes, Rcrds of Air Bd, Box 15, both in MMB, NA.

[16] Gaddis, *Origins of the Cold War*, pp 260–262, 306.

million fell to $135 million. The Air Staff subsequently reported that this had delayed the development of new weapons by eighteen months.[17]

Financial constraints also affected the Army's demobilization and threatened the seventy-group program. By the end of 1946 total AAF personnel had dropped to 340,000 in an Army of 1,320,000. A reduction to the planned 1,070,000 men would not be enough to keep the pay account within budget; if the Army was to have enough money to pay its men, strength reductions were inevitable. It became clear that the draft would not be needed beyond March 31, 1947, since there was no money to pay the extra personnel. At Eisenhower's bidding, the troop basis was cut across the board, except ground forces overseas. The AAF was left with a basis of 364,000, far too few to man seventy groups even at reduced strength.[18]

The fiscal 1948 budget then under consideration offered no relief. The AAF asked the War Department for $2.6 billion in direct appropriations. In order to keep the Army budget in line, the request was reduced to $1.6 billion. Even this figure proved unacceptable to the Bureau of the Budget, and the Air Corps program declined to $1.130 billion, with only $850 million available in cash (meaning that the rest could only be committed under contract and paid out in later years). The Army's budget went to Congress at $5.9 billion.[19] At this level, the Air Staff did not believe more than fifty-eight groups could be operated. Spaatz was willing to maintain twelve groups at skeleton strength to allow an easier buildup if more money ever surfaced.[20] But when, if ever, that would occur no one could foresee.

Thus at the beginning of 1947 there seemed little possibility of meeting the AAF's definition of adequate strength. New developments did

---

[17] Jacob Neufeld, *The Development of Ballistic Missiles in the United States Air Force, 1945–1960* (Washington: AFCHO, 1990), pp 26–27; hearings before the Subcommittee on Appropriations, House of Representatives, *Military Establishment Appropriation 1948*, 80th Cong, 1st sess, Mar 6, 1947, pp 599–619, 626–633; hearings before a Subcommittee of the Committee on Appropriations, Senate, *Military Establishment Appropriations Bill 1948*, 80th Cong, 1st sess, Jun 24, 1947, pp 1–11, Jun 27, 1947, pp 263–267.

[18] Sparrow, *Personnel Demobilization*, pp 351–358.

[19] Hearings before the Subcommittee on Appropriations, House of Representatives, *Military Establishment Appropriation 1948*, 80th Cong, 1st sess, Mar 6, 1947, pp 599–619, 626–633; hearings before a Subcommittee, Committee on Appropriations, Senate, *Military Establishment Appropriations Bill 1948*, 80th Cong, 1st sess, Jun 24, 1947, pp 1–11, Jun 27, 1947, pp 263–267.

[20] Verbatim rprt, 4th Meeting of the Air Board, Dec 3–4, 1946, pp 47–73, RG 340, Bds & Cmtes, Rcrds of Air Bd, Box 15, MMB, NA.

nothing to change this assessment. Truman's commitment to fiscal solvency even led him in 1948 to veto a tax cut; a President willing to run such a political risk could be taken at his word on the issue of a balanced budget. There was little chance that a Republican Congress would vote more money than the President requested. And the nature of the administration's response to the Soviet threat, primarily relying on diplomacy, seemed to preclude large expenditures on air power.

In fact, in 1947 the two major new initiatives in foreign affairs threatened additional pressure on a tight budget. The Truman Doctrine and the Marshall Plan arose as separate responses to the desperate economic conditions in Europe over the winter of 1946-1947. The British were on the verge of economic collapse, and, unable to afford continued aid to a Greek government embattled against communist insurgents, the government in London turned to America. Also concerned by Soviet pressure on Turkey, Truman called on Congress on March 12 to authorize military aid to the Greeks and Turks. The evolving "Truman Doctrine" proposed economic aid to free nations resisting aggression. Meanwhile, the virtual halting of a slow and painful recovery throughout the free countries of Europe led to fears of communist takeovers. Accordingly, in June Secretary of State George C. Marshall addressed the more general problem with a plan to provide large-scale economic aid.[21] If such a policy were adopted, the demands on the budget would create more pressure on military spending. This is not to imply that Truman Doctrine military assistance or Marshall Plan aid were approved *instead* of military spending. But clearly, in Truman's efforts to limit spending, he had given priority to these two initiatives and not to the U.S. armed forces.

The rationale for the existing policy was outlined in an article that appeared in the July issue of *Foreign Affairs*. Entitled "The Sources of Soviet Conduct" and ostensibly written by "X," the essay held out the hope that "containment" of Soviet pressure would insure peace. As it soon became known that "X" was none other than George F. Kennan, now head of Secretary Marshall's Policy Planning Staff, the public could see the connection between the idea of containment and existing policies. The man who advocated the theory had presumably some influence on the practice. But when it came to the military aspects of containment, the only specific proposal in the "X" article involved having forces ready to move into a threatened area. Complicating matters further, one of the administration's most outspoken advocates of overall military strength was James

---

[21] Lilienthal, *Journals*, p 131; Gaddis, *Origins of the Cold War*, pp 336-353.

Beginnings

Gen. George C. Kenney, first leader of Strategic Air Command.

Forrestal. He might not be opposed in principle to a strong air force, but no sane person could expect the Navy Secretary to support one at the cost of his own shipbuilding program.[22]

And Congress was proving as inhospitable to military spending as might have been expected. A budget committee on Capitol Hill, meeting in February, had proposed a reduction of $1 billion in the War Department appropriation. The House Appropriations Committee and its chairman, John Taber of New York, did not cut quite so deeply, but the Air Corps item was still decreased by $116 million to little over $1 billion—a disproportionately large reduction. However, airmen could take heart from the readiness of some members to resort to the hoary technique of inviting witnesses to ask for more money than was in the budget. On June 4 the House of Representatives debated the military appropriation, and some influential members of the Armed Services Committee spoke in support of air power. In view of the "Russian situation," congressmen either viewed armed might as a deterrent or a provocation. Military spending would either bankrupt the economy or it would rescue failing industries. Proponents of deterrence and help for airplane manufacturers won a qualified victory when the House restored most of the President's request for

---

[22] Gaddis, *Origins of the Cold War*, pp 336–353; "X" [George F. Kennan], "The Sources of Soviet Conduct," *Foreign Affairs* XXV (Jul 47), pp 566–582.

aircraft procurement. In the end, the Army budget was trimmed by only $435 million. The total Air Corps amount stood at $1.053 billion.[23]

Before the Senate Subcommittee, General Vandenberg, now acting as the AAF Deputy Commander in place of Eaker, who was soon to retire, asked for restoration of the full Air Corps amount. He needed the money to buy spare parts and fuel for training and to pay civilians to bring planes out of storage. Secretary of War Patterson came to Vandenberg's support with the argument that the precarious international situation did not justify the House reductions. General Eisenhower warned that the AAF would not be able to build up to seventy groups even with the money requested, and he also noted the depressed state of the aircraft industry.[24] Further help came from James E. Webb, Director of the Bureau of the Budget, who supported a request for another $100 million in authority to sign contracts for aircraft. The Senate went even further. The final appropriation allowed the AAF to commit $550 million for aircraft and parts. Part of this would come out of the cash appropriation of $830 million. Yet despite the restored funding, this was an austere budget, and the AAF was allowed to operate only fifty-five groups during the coming fiscal year.[25]

At the time Truman was announcing his "doctrine," the strategic forces of the United States consisted of SAC's six B–29 groups, including one atomic group, and some ill-equipped units in the Pacific region. Yet the strength of the armed forces was still declining. In the AAF it fell to 303,000 in May 1947, with thirty-eight groups manned and equipped in some fashion.[26] This declining strength had been anticipated, and in April the Deputy Chief of Air Staff, Maj. Gen. C. C. Chauncey, had warned that

---

[23] Forrestal, *Diaries*, pp 197–201; hearings before the Subcommittee on Appropriations, House of Representatives, *Military Establishment Appropriation 1948*, 80th Cong, 1st sess, Mar 6, 1947, pp 599–619; verbatim rprt, 5th Meeting of the Air Board, Jun 5–6, 1947, RG 340, Bds & Cmtes, Mins of the Air Bd, Box 13, MMB, NA.

[24] Hearings before the Subcommittee on Appropriations, Senate, *Military Establishment Appropriations Bill 1948*, 80th Cong, 1st sess, Jun 24, 1947, pp 1–11; Jun 27, 1947, pp 260–263, 273–274, Jun 28, 1947, pp 289–301.

[25] *Ibid.*; verbatim mins, 1st Meeting—USAF Aircraft and Weapons Board, First Day: Aug 19, 1947, pp 123–124, RG 341, DCS/Dev, Rqmts Div, First AWB, 1947–1948, Box 181, MMB, NA; *Air Force Statistical Digest*, 1947, p 249; memo, Maj Gen E. W. Rawlings, Air Comptr, to Civ Air Div, ACAS–5 (Pl), subj: Briefing to Mr. Symington for Testimony before President's Air Policy Commission, Sep 6, 1947, RG 341, DCS/Comptr, Admin Div, 1942–1953, 452.1 Acft Cmtes, File 63, Box 209, MMB, NA.

[26] Forrestal, *Diaries*, pp 197–201; *Air Force Statistical Digest*, 1947, p 16; hearings before the Subcommittee on Appropriations, Senate, *Military Establishment Appropriation Bill 1948*, 80th Cong, 1st sess, Jun 27, 1947, pp 260–263.

the commands would be short-handed for some time. War Department ceilings would force them to let many qualified officers go. However, Chauncey maintained that "In many respects this understrength condition is desirable in that it furnishes a solid foundation of long-term retainable personnel on which to build the desired structure." The AAF would force all functions except weather services and airways communication to share in reductions.[27] The civilian workforce, numbering 125,000 at the end of 1946, dropped to 110,000 by June 1947.[28] This was truly a time of austerity.

The decision to man and equip fifty-five groups during fiscal 1948, while a setback for the AAF, was optimistically called the "fifty-five-group phase" of the seventy-group program. The airmen were confident they could recruit all the three-year volunteers they needed, but the War Department limited total strength to 364,000 for the first six months of the fiscal year and 386,000 for the second half. It should be noted that, in spite of the ceilings, the AAF was the only service scheduled for a manpower increase. Even with the budget reductions, enough airplanes could be purchased or brought out of storage for fifty-five groups. The AAF therefore decided to go ahead and activate units for the seventy-group force, though fifteen groups would exist only on paper.[29]

It fell to the Air Staff to allocate the reductions within the seventy-group program. Among the most vulnerable units were the sixteen very heavy bomber groups scheduled for SAC and the five in the Pacific. A committee of the Air Staff[30] had noted that the current war plans called for seventeen VHB groups to be overseas nine months after the beginning of mobilization. Since it took nine months to build up a group to operational readiness, the committee argued, the AAF did not need any more than seventeen. On the other hand, the first phase of a war would require large forces of fighters to defend key areas. Thus the committee suggested revising the seventy-group program to reduce the VHB force, but did not make a firm recommendation, and the program temporarily remained the

---

[27] Ltr, Maj Gen C. C. Chauncey, DCAS, to CG SAC, subj: Reduced Manning Level, Apr 18, 1947, RG 18, 1946–1947 AAG, 320 Orgn of Army, Box 598, MMB, NA.

[28] *Air Force Statistical Digest*, 1947, p 73; chart, United States Air Force Program, Aug 27, 1947, RG 18, 1946–1947 AAG, 320.2 AAF Program, Vol 2, Box 559, MMB, NA.

[29] Rprt, Reprogramming Cmte AAF, Report on the Long Range AAF Program, Feb 15, 1947, RG 341, DCS/Ops, OPD, 320.2 (Apr 4, 1944), TS Supp, Box 129A, MMB, NA; hearings before the Subcommittee on Appropriations, House of Representatives, *Military Establishment Appropriation 1948*, 80th Cong, 1st sess, Mar 6, 1947, pp 599–736.

[30] See pp. 33–34.

same.[31] In the end, the deciding factor was the War Department's policy of maintaining the occupation forces. Both Patterson and Eisenhower had argued that the occupation of Germany and Japan was the Army's first priority. Overseas, the only cuts were in VHB units in the Pacific, reduced to a mere two groups. The other cuts were made stateside, concentrated in Strategic Air Command and Tactical Air Command. The resulting SAC program consisted of a total of seventeen groups—eleven of VHBs, one for reconnaissance, and five of fighters.[32]

The Strategic Force and Demobilization

In the seventy-group plan adopted in late 1945, there was to be a reserve of five VHB groups in the continental United States, while the rest of the bomber force was stationed overseas. The evolution from this plan to the idea of a U.S.-based strike force with a worldwide role occurred during 1946, largely as a result, not of planning, but of the pressures of demobilization. The AAF's failure to hold or gain trained manpower led to a sequence of declining expectations, until by the end of the year the VHB force in the continental United States numbered essentially six groups with relatively little bomber strength overseas.

Within SAC there was often the impression of a lack of urgency. Kenney himself decided to continue his work at the United Nations. His deputy, Maj. Gen. St. Clair Streett, wrote in July: "No major strategic threat or requirement now exists, in the opinion of our country's best strategists nor will such a requirement exist for the next three to five years."[33]

At the time that Continental Air Forces became SAC, the command had three main commitments. One was to organize the "atomic" force of three groups, including the 509th. Another was to support the upcoming atomic bomb tests at Bikini. And finally, it was necessary to man and equip

---

[31] Rprt, Reprogramming Cmte AAF, Report on the Long Range AAF Program, Feb 15, 1947, RG 341, DCS/Ops, OPD, 320.2 (Apr 4, 1944), TS Supp, Box 129A, MMB, NA.

[32] Hearings before the Subcommittee on Appropriations, Senate, *Military Establishment Appropriation Bill 1948*, 80th Cong, 1st sess, Jun 24, 1947, pp 1–11, Jun 28, 1947, pp 289–295; chart, United States Air Force Program, Aug 27, 1947, RG 18, 1946–1947 AAG, 320.2 AAF Prog, Vol 2, Box 559, MMB, NA.

[33] Ltr, Maj Gen St. C. Streett, Dep CG SAC, to CG AAF, subj: Operational Training and Strategic Employment of Strategic Air Command, Jul 25, 1946, SAC/HO.

groups for service overseas. And yet, on March 31, 1946, ten days after the creation of SAC, the command inactivated a large number of paper units, leaving it with ten groups of B–29s. These units were themselves in little condition for overseas duty.[34]

The biggest overseas commitment remained PROJECT WONDERFUL, the dispatch of five B–29 groups to Europe. By April 1946 it was clear that no American combat troops would be stationed in France. Indeed, the prospects for VHB units being anywhere but Germany were fast fading. And, just as Eisenhower had opposed stationing B–29s in Europe when he commanded the occupation forces, his successor, Gen. Joseph T. McNarney, also objected. The theater commander saw no role for B–29s in the occupation force. Without adequate air defenses or base security, the bombers were hardly likely to be much help if the Soviets attacked.[35]

In April McNarney suggested a plan for periodic training visits by B–29 units. Maj. Gen. Lauris Norstad, the Assistant Chief of Air Staff for Plans (A–5), proposed a compromise. Only two groups would deploy, and they would be based in Germany. The Peripheral Basing Concept was scrapped.[36] McNarney held firm in his objections, and the joint chiefs authorized Spaatz to discuss the matter during his visit to Europe at the end of June. The AAF commander also planned to meet with the British, and when he finally saw McNarney he had an understanding that a prospect for bases in England existed. Pending such an arrangement he agreed to cancel PROJECT WONDERFUL altogether. Spaatz's staff, however, worried that the inactivation of the remaining B–17 units would leave no U.S. bombers at all in Europe, and the arrival of B–29s on rotation later on would appear too much of a novelty. But none of the WONDERFUL units

---

[34] Ltr, Brig Gen W. A. Matheny, Ch Ops Div, ACAS–3 (Ops), to CG SAC, subj: Reduction of Manning Requirement for Tactical Units, Mar 29, 1946, in hist, SAC, 1946, Ex 20.

[35] Memo, Maj Gen L. Norstad, ACAS–5 (Pl), to Gen C. A. Spaatz, CG AAF, subj: Deployment of VHB Units in the Occupation of Germany, May 16, 1946; memo, Brig Gen C. B. Ferenbaugh, Dep Ch Theater Gp, OPD, War Dept, to CG AAF, subj: Security of VHB Bases, European Theater, Apr 24, 1946, atch to memo, Maj Gen C. C. Chauncey, DCAS, to Asst CS, OPD, War Dept, same subj, Apr 29, 1946, both in RG 341, TS AAG File 22, Box 7, MMB, NA.

[36] R & R Sheet, Cmt 1, Lt Gen I. C. Eaker, Dep CG AAF, to Maj Gen L. Norstad, ACAS–5 (Pl), Additional Requirements for USAFE, Apr 21, 1946, and Cmt 2, Norstad to Eaker, Apr 26, 1946, RG 341, TS AAG File 22, Box 7; memo, Norstad to Gen C. A. Spaatz, CG AAF, n.d., RG 341, TS AAG File 22, Box 7; memo, Brig Gen F. H. Griswold, Dep ACAS–3 (Ops), to Spaatz, subj: VHB Groups for ETO, May 23, 1946, RG 341, TS AAG File 25 (E–267), Box 8, all in MMB, NA.

was ready, and only a token deployment could take place before the end of 1946.[37]

The plans for the occupation period also envisioned stationing a B–29 unit in Alaska. This was for the purpose of developing the Arctic region for long-range bomber operations in keeping with the idea of the Polar air frontier. The deployment encountered delays, but the 28th Bombardment Group left Grand Island, Nebraska, for Elmendorf Field near Anchorage in October 1946. When the 28th's predecessor unit had first been manned, most of those assigned were expecting to go to Europe. In July Maj. Gen. Charles F. Born, commanding Fifteenth Air Force, went to Grand Island to investigate the problem. He told the men that they were the only unit in the AAF that knew where they were going. Agreeing to transfer those who desired it, he was able to persuade half the men to remain in the unit. This then led to remanning and retraining before the group was ready to go.[38]

The problem at Grand Island illustrated the problems SAC was encountering in outfitting units for overseas deployments. The inevitable confusion, as WONDERFUL was postponed, cut to two groups, and finally canceled, led to discontent among the personnel. In March Born had told his staff that the wartime practice of constant moves and reassignments would not work in peacetime. "Morale is shot...our experience with the Wonderful project has been a lesson...."[39]

In any case, getting the necessary units ready for deployment would have strained SAC's resources to the limit. By the end of June the command had fewer than 37,000 officers and enlisted men, less than half

---

[37] Memo, Brig Gen F. H. Griswold, Dep ACAS–3 (Ops), to Gen C. A. Spaatz, CG AAF, subj: VHB Groups for ETO, May 31, 1946, RG 341, TS AAG File 25 (E–273), Box 8; memo, Lt Gen I. C. Eaker, Dep CG AAF, to ACAS–3 (Ops), subj: Cable to CG USFET, re Peripheral Base Plan and Deployment of VHB Units to ETO, Jun 18, 1946, with encl draft msg, RG 341, TS AAG File 25 (E–312), Box 8; memo, Lt Gen I. C. Eaker, Dep CG AAF, to ACAS–5 (Pl), subj: Inclosed Cable # S4694, May 31, 1946, RG 341, TS AAG File 25 (E–276), Box 8; ltr, Maj Gen I. H. Edwards, CG USAFE, to Eaker, Jul 22, 1946, RG 341, TS AAG File 23, Box 7; memo, Maj Gen C. Bissell, Mil Att London, to Spaatz, subj: Reminder on Decisions Taken during London Visit (Jul 4–6), Jul 6, 1946, atch to R & R Sheet, Eaker to Air Staff, Decisions Reached in London between Gen Spaatz & Air Ministry (Jun 46), Jul 21, 1946, RG 341, TS AAG File 23, Box 7; memo, Maj Gen O. P. Weyland, ACAS–5 (Pl), to Spaatz, subj: Rotation of VHB Groups in ETO, Aug 6, 1946, with encls, RG 341, TS AAG File 23, Box 7; memo, Eaker to ACAS–3 (Ops), subj: VHB Groups, Jul 9, 1946, RG 341, TS AAG File 25 (E–368), Box 8, all in MMB, NA.

[38] Hist, 449 BG, Jul 46, pp 1–2; hist, SAC, 1946, Vol I, p 93.

[39] Record of Staff Conference, Hq 2 AF, cited in hist, 2 AF, Sep 45–Mar 1946, p 66.

of its strength the previous March. Nor was the reduced force especially well-trained. The entire AAF had fewer than 19,000 airplane mechanics in the continental United States. Nearly half the enlisted men were not qualified in any specialty.[40] Many new recruits had marginal scores on the Army General Classification Test (AGCT)—meaning that they were thought to be unteachable in any but the most menial skills. One bombardment group had thirty planes and four qualified crew chiefs. As of September, only nine men in the Fifteenth Air Force were qualified to care for the standard radar equipment on the B-29. About half the B-29s were therefore out of commission at any one time. There were plenty of experienced officers to man the bombers, but providing them the planes to fly was the problem. The group bound for Alaska put officers on duty as crew chiefs, though this was only a temporary expedient.[41]

If SAC lacked trained manpower, other problems of facilities and organization seemed to pose further obstacles to any kind of combat readiness. The 509th Group was tied up for the better part of summer supporting the atomic tests in the Pacific. As for facilities, conditions remained abysmal. None of the Army's six best air bases belonged to SAC. Considering the basic criteria of housing and proximity to town, plus suitability for B-29 operations (runway length and durability, together with adequate parking, hangar, and shop space), SAC had only eleven of the twenty-five bases it considered desirable.[42] Housing was particularly a problem if the command expected to retain trained men.

Several organizational complications resulted from the shifting commitments of SAC and from the length of time required to organize two fully operational air force headquarters. The 58th Bombardment Wing at Fort Worth was the atomic force, containing the 509th as well as the two other groups so far earmarked for the atomic role. The VIII Bomber Command was created for PROJECT WONDERFUL and closed down when that operation was canceled. Finally in November SAC had its two air

---

[40] *Army Air Forces Statistical Digest*, 1946, pp 25, 27; ltr, Brig Gen W. E. Hall, Dep ACAS-1 (Pers), to CG SAC, subj: Manning of VHB Units, Apr 24, 1946, RG 18, 1946–1947 AAG, 320 Orgn of Army, Box 598, MMB, NA.
[41] Transcript of telecon, Col C. Sommers, CS 15 AF, with Col F. J. Sutterlin, A-1 (Pers) SAC, Dec 6, 1946, in hist, 15 AF, Apr–Dec 1946, Supporting Docs, Pt II, Personnel Problems & Policies; SAC Statistical Summary, Jun 46, pp 15, 18–24; hist, 15 AF, Apr–Dec 1946, Pt III, pp 16–18; ltr, 2d Lt H. A. Wagner, Actg Asst AG, SAC to CG AAF, subj: Critical Shortages of Radar Maintenance Personnel, Sep 9, 1946, in hist, SAC, 1946, Ex 55.
[42] Memo, Col W. G. Hipps, Actg A-5 (Pl) SAC, to Maj Gen St. C. Streett, Dep CG SAC, subj: Status of the Strategic Air Command, May 10, 1946, in hist, SAC, 1946, Ex 19.

Strategic Air Force

forces functioning. The Eighth, with Headquarters at Fort Worth, included the three groups of the inactivated 58th Wing, while the Fifteenth continued at Colorado Springs with two B–29 groups and two fighter groups, as well as the 311th Reconnaissance Wing, which had negligible operating forces.[43]

A further obstacle to readiness arose because of the perennial urge in the government to move agencies, especially line organizations, out of Washington. Spaatz was especially concerned at the large numbers of flying officers concentrated in the capital because of the presence of operational headquarters. As for the logic of the premier command of the AAF, with its worldwide interests, having its headquarters either at the geographical center of the country or the political capital, opinions might differ. Spaatz seemed to favor the geographical center, Kenney the political. On July 15, 1946, Headquarters AAF ordered SAC Headquarters to Colorado Springs. Within the month Kenney managed to have the order canceled, but by then many staff officers had sold houses, found quarters in Colorado Springs, and shipped their household goods. Civilian employees had found new jobs. In short, the changes wrought maximum disruption of headquarters operations and private lives and necessitated a new hiring program.[44]

Under the circumstances, it is not surprising that the few units that could be manned were far from combat ready. In September 1946 the Air Inspector, Maj. Gen. Junius W. Jones, toured Fifteenth Air Force units and concluded that there had been no meaningful training for air crews since July. Ground crew training was so inadequate that he saw little hope of soon getting enough bombers into commission to meet the need. Streett only partly concurred in the inspector's observations on poor management, but neither officer denied that a problem existed.[45]

Evidence mounted that all was not well in the command. The traditional fever-charts of morale were disturbing. In Fifteenth Air Force the court-martial rate increased steadily during 1946. Also that year the number of cases of venereal disease per thousand hospital admissions in

---

[43] Hist, SAC, 1946, Vol I, pp 19–24, 88–91, 123–130; Maurer, *AF Combat Units*, p 119; ltr, CG SAC to CG AAF, subj: Operational and Administrative Control of the 311th Reconnaissance Wing and its Associated Units, Aug 15, 1946, in hist, SAC, 1946, Ex 17; hist, 311 RW, May 46, pp 9–15.

[44] Hist, SAC, 1946, Vol I, pp 13–16; Minutes of Air Staff Meeting (Oct 23, 1946), Oct 25, 1946, Spaatz Coll, Mins of Air Staff Mtgs, Box 261, MD, LC.

[45] Ltr, Maj Gen St. C. Streett, Dep CG SAC, to Maj Gen C. F. Born, CG 15 AF, Sep 30, 1946, in hist, SAC, 1946, Ex 62; hist, SAC, 1946, Vol I, pp 186–190; ltr, Gen C. A. Spaatz, CG AAF, to CG SAC, subj: Standards of Discipline, Nov 8, 1946, SAC/HO.

Beginnings

SAC rose from sixty to nearly one hundred. The relaxation of wartime controls on prostitution, along with reduced workloads, could be blamed for this increase. But Streett also considered the extreme youth of many of the recruits and the number of low AGCT scores as contributing to this and other problems.[46]

Despite these barriers, the early months of 1946 did show some progress. The mission statement for SAC clearly implied a worldwide role. Col. William G. Hipps, the command Plans Officer (A-5), foresaw the evolution of SAC from

> ...the interim state of unmanned, untrained, widely dispersed and loosely controlled units into a compact, centrally controlled, strategic striking force, based entirely within the Continental United States but capable of deploying any or all of its units to designated points of the globe from which a concentrated mass of air power could be launched at an enemy.[47]

Hipps proposed that SAC should encompass the AAF's planned twenty-four very heavy bomber and long-range reconnaissance groups, together with twelve fighter groups. Each unit would have a permanent home base in the states and would be detailed on rotation to fields in the North Atlantic region, Alaska, and the Far East. The SAC staff began to identify the home stations for these units. Organizationally the service units on these bases should have enough resources to operate the field and allow the combat group to be able to leave on a moment's notice. The basic plan for this U.S.-based force appeared in May 1946.[48]

While this plan diverged in some respects from the underlying concept of the seventy-group program, it responded to some of the problems the AAF was actually facing. The deteriorating prospects for PROJECT WONDERFUL altered the outlook for the existing deployment plan. The number of B-29 groups in the Pacific and Far East had already had to be cut to six and would probably be reduced to three.[49] Planned deployments also fostered morale problems. Assistant Chief of Air Staff for Personnel,

---

[46] Hist, SAC, 1946, Vol I, pp 181, 190; SAC Statistical Summary, Jan 1947, p 160 *passim*; hist, 15 AF, Apr-Dec 1946, Pt II, pp 15-16.

[47] Program for the Development of the Organization and Development Strategic Air Command, May 28, 1946, quoted in hist, SAC, 1946, Vol I, p 34.

[48] *Ibid.*; plan, Operational Training and Strategic Employment of Units of Strategic Air Command, Jul 18, 1946, encl to ltr, Maj Gen St. C. Streett, Dep CG SAC, to CG AAF, same subj, Jul 25, 1946, SAC/HO.

[49] Memo, Maj Gen O. P. Weyland, ACAS-5 (Pl), to CAS, subj: Proposed Revision of Peacetime Air Deployment for the Pacific, Jul 13, 1946, RG 341, TS AAG File 25, Box 8, MMB, NA.

Strategic Air Force

Maj. Gen. Frederick L. Anderson observed: "The average individual regards overseas duty as undesirable."[50] The Air Staff wanted to place a ceiling of thirty percent on the total AAF strength overseas.[51] A rotation plan such as Hipps proposed would go still further toward easing the problem of maintaining forces overseas.

In addition, not all the manpower figures were bleak. Enlisted strength in SAC stabilized and even increased from a low of 27,000 in May to over 34,000 in November. On-the-job training began to compensate for the chaotic state of the schools in the Training Command. Officer strength in fact had been too high, but the AAF had begun reductions, releasing officers with low performance ratings. A new AAF Training Standard established guidelines for improving the skills of the force.[52] These were all signs of progress in building up an effective postwar air force.

In the meantime, Kenney became aware of the problems Streett was experiencing at Bolling. Clearly, Kenney needed to join his command. The abortive move of the headquarters may have been the last straw. In any case, the prospects for a United Nations force were growing dim indeed. Lt. Gen. Ennis C. Whitehead, commanding the Far Eastern Air Forces in the Pacific, wrote Kenney to say that the world organization was a "dead pigeon." He warned Kenney that he had in his position as Commander of SAC the most critical mission in the AAF. If SAC and the AAF were not combat ready soon, the Navy would launch a publicity campaign hinting at the lack of return on the taxpayer's dollar. By October 15, 1946, Kenney had given up his responsibilities in New York and was assuming personal direction of SAC.[53]

Reaching his headquarters, Kenney found it in the throes of a move and yet another command reorganization. The new building at Andrews Field was ready, and the staff was starting to move in. At the same time the organization of SAC into two air forces was being completed. With

---

[50] Memo, Maj Gen F. L. Anderson, ACAS–1 (Pers), to CAS, subj: Distribution of AAF Personnel, Jan 3, 1946, atch to R & R Sheet, Cmt 2, Anderson to ACAS–3 (Ops), The Post War Air Force (Organization and Disposition), Apr 30, 1946, RG 18, 1946–1947 AAG, 321 AAF 1, Box 603, MMB, NA.

[51] *Ibid.*; R & R Sheet, Maj Gen E. E. Partridge, ACAS–3 (Ops), to Dep CG AAF, Permanent Peacetime Personnel Deployment Overseas, Mar 21, 1946, RG 18, 1946–1947 AAG, 370 Deployment Etc Misc, Vol 1, Box 632, MMB, NA.

[52] *Army Air Forces Statistical Digest*, 1946, p 29; hist, SAC, 1946, Vol I, pp 88–92, 97, 111–112, 159–160, 171–177; hist, 15 AF, Apr–Dec 1946, Pt V, pp 10–11; Kenneth L. Patchin, *SAC Bombardment Training Program, 1946–1959* (SAC Hist Study 80, Offutt AFB, Neb, 1960), p 16.

[53] Borowski, *Hollow Threat*, pp 40–41; Hopkins & Goldberg, *Development of SAC*, p 1.

this, Kenney had 150 B-29s in six groups, one temporarily assigned to Alaskan Air Command. The staff was also retaining three B-29 groups on paper to keep a claim to some airfields for future expansion. The Eighth Air Force was specifically charged with the atomic mission, while the Fifteenth was to support overseas deployments.[54]

The Strategic Force and the Fifty-five Group Program

Besides taking charge of SAC's reorganization, George Kenney was also assuming responsibility for the command's share of the "fifty-five-group phase" of the AAF program. He was to increase the VHB force from six equipped groups to eleven, the fighters from one group to five, along with forming a new reconnaissance group. The original target date of August 1947 proved unrealistic. For example, the plan called for 300 B-29s in service, and Kenney only had 148 as of the end of 1946. The remaining aircraft would have to be taken out of storage, and this did not begin until September 1947. Command strength only began to increase during the spring, rising to 32,000 in June 1947.[55] The job of building an effective postwar air force would take time.

Kenney soon assumed another role. As one of the top air generals in the war and a good speaker, he was much in demand for public appearances. Secretary of the Navy Forrestal called him "...very active as a proponent of an independent Air Force."[56] Busy with speeches and frequent visits to his units, Kenney needed someone as his deputy who enjoyed his full confidence. He found such a man in his friend Maj. Gen. Clements McMullen, a gifted, tough, and resourceful officer, known in the service by his nickname, "Concrete." In an atmosphere in which austere budgets imposed the strictest economies, McMullen's experience in maintenance and supply would serve him in good stead. During the war Kenney finally managed to turn over his depot organization to McMullen. Then, as he put it, he could relax, for McMullen "was just about the best in that

---

[54] Hopkins & Goldberg, *Development of SAC*, pp 1–3; hist, 15 AF, Apr–Dec 1946, Pt II, pp 8, 27–28; hist, SAC, 1946, Vol I, pp 21–23.
[55] Ltr, CG AAF to CG SAC, subj: Current AAF Plans and Programs, Oct 24, 1946, in hist, SAC, 1946, Ex 38; memo, Maj Gen E. E. Partridge, Act DCS/Ops USAF, to Gen C. A. Spaatz, CSAF, subj: General Kenney's Letter Re 55-Group Objective, Oct 10, 1947, RG 18, 1946–1947 AAG, 380 55–Gp Prog, Vol 1, Box 638, MMB, NA; Hopkins & Goldberg, *Development of SAC*, p 1.
[56] Forrestal, *Diaries*, p 227.

Strategic Air Force

Maj. Gen. Clements McMullen, *left,* who replaced Maj. Gen. St. Clair Streett, *right,* as Deputy Commander, Strategic Air Command, in January 1947, instituted severe fiscal restraints throughout the organization in response to the postwar drawdown of U.S. military forces.

game."[57] The new Deputy Commander of SAC replaced Streett on January 10, 1947.[58]

McMullen lived up to his reputation for firmness. He expected the AAF to revert to prewar conditions, with a small group of versatile professionals forced to economize in everything and do everything. He disliked large staffs, recalling that in 1935 the commander of GHQ Air Force had managed to run nine groups on six major bases with just 30 staff officers and 150 enlisted men. He told Maj. Gen. Roger M. Ramey, the Eighth Air Force Commander, that since people were just as smart as they had been then, Headquarters Eighth Air Force could be about the same size as the prewar GHQ Air Force. McMullen cut back the SAC staff by way of example, and his assuming the Chief of Staff's duties in March served to symbolize his approach.[59]

For the combat units McMullen also had a plan for operating at reduced strengths. He proposed a scheme for cross-training officers, in part as an attempt to follow AAF policy, but also as a way to recreate the GHQ Air Force of the thirties. At that time, most Air Corps officers had been pilots. The other positions on bomber crews, such as navigator and bombardier, and the jobs on the ground had been filled by pilots. (LeMay,

---

[57] George C. Kenney, *General Kenney Reports* (NY: Duell, Sloan, & Pearce, 1949 [reprint, Washington: AFCHO, 1987]), p 442.

[58] Hist, SAC, 1947, pp 1–5.

[59] *Ibid.*; ltr, Maj Gen C. McMullen, Dep CG SAC, to Brig Gen R. M. Ramey, CG 8 AF, Mar 11, 1947, SAC/HO.

as a young pilot in GHQ Air Force, had learned navigation and become one of the foremost navigators in the service). Everyone learned a variety of jobs, and this system produced a cadre of broadly trained professionals able to assume high positions in different fields when war came. In combat there had been no time to train people so extensively, and as a result specialization had set in and large numbers of additional non-rated (non-flying) officers were needed.[60] McMullen now saw his task as reviving peacetime practices.

In January 1947 Spaatz stated that 70 percent of the officers of the AAF were to be rated, although the actual need for them in air crews was lower. The extra number would provide a cushion and learn other jobs. The stringent limitations on officers that the Air Staff anticipated for the year made cross-training even more necessary.[61] As Maj. Gen. C. C. Chauncey, the Deputy Chief of Air Staff, explained, cuts would force "...cross training and utilization of officers on more than one duty assignment, consolidation of duty functions, and an overall review of officer requirements."[62] To that extent, McMullen's actions clearly mirrored overall policy.

But then, Kenney and McMullen decided to go the headquarters one better. Kenney wrote: "It is not reasonable to expect that officers will remain as pilots, co-pilots, bombardiers, navigators, flight engineers, radar observers, or any other of the many specialties within the Air Forces during their anticipated career of 30 years."[63] Cross-training would thus help develop the officer corps while at the same time very heavy bomber squadrons in the Eighth Air Force, then authorized 81 officers, could function with 34. SAC could man its seventeen groups with 3,772 officers and 37,500 enlisted men, saving 2,300 officers. Eighty percent of the officers in SAC would have to be rated; thus many of the current non-rated personnel would have to be separated. From this scheme came the so-called "McMullen ceilings," limits on strength below the officially authorized level. Along with these ceilings, SAC introduced a plan for

---

[60] See note above; Johnson OHI (with Marmor), pp 139–141; USAF OHI, #K239.0512–734, Robert M. Kipp, SAC/HO, with Lt Gen Clarence S. Irvine, Ret, Dec 17, 1970, pp 15–16, both in AFHRC; LeMay & Kantor, *Mission with LeMay*, p 431.
[61] Ltr, Gen C. A. Spaatz, CG AAF, to Gen G. C. Kenney, CG SAC, Jan 1, 1947, SAC/HO.
[62] Ltr, Maj Gen C. C. Chauncey, DCAS, to CG SAC, subj: Reduced Manning Level, Apr 18, 1947, RG 18, 1946–1947 AAG, 320 Orgn of Army, Box 598, MMB, NA. In the original, brackets have been penciled in around the passage quoted.
[63] *Ibid.*, with 1st Ind, Gen G. C. Kenney, CG SAC, to CG AAF, n.d., with atch charts.

cross-training officers in August 1947. Pilots were to learn all the other jobs in a B-29 unit so that eventually anyone could fill any position.[64]

Many SAC officers were skeptical of the proposed scheme. SAC's chief operations analyst predicted that most units would give cross-training low priority because of a shortage of instructors and the need to get required flying done.[65] At Davis-Monthan a survey of three crews of the 43d Bombardment Group showed that they were spending so much time away from base flying that they could not receive the basic instruction.[66] Especially disturbing was the contradiction with Spaatz's policy of attracting good non-rated officers into the new Air Force. As one officer observed, "McMullen had an obsession that only pilots were any good."[67] Brig. Gen. Leon W. Johnson, Commander of Fifteenth Air Force, bristled at being forced to get rid of excellent non-rated officers. Nevertheless, the plan was adopted, and each group was directed to have ten pilots fully cross-trained by July 1, 1948.[68]

In time-honored fashion, the training of a B-29 group progressed from crew-level practice, learning to work together flying a complex piece of equipment, through squadron exercises, to group-sized missions. The culmination would be an evaluation by the Air Inspector along the lines of the old POM (preparation for overseas movement) inspection. The SAC operations staff emphasized learning to take off in any kind of weather, instrument flying, gunnery, assembly for mass flights, navigation, and cruise control. McMullen brought in Col. Clarence S. Irvine, who had pioneered B-29 cruise control techniques in the Marianas, as his deputy, specifically charged with instructing the crews in long-range flying.[69]

Training since August 1945 had been hampered by the loss of skilled mechanics and the resulting inability to get enough planes in commission to do the needed flying. The postwar attitude also played a part, as there

---

[64] *Ibid.*; notes of intvw, G. Dubina, with Col R. T. King, Dir Pers SAC, Jan 20, 1949, in hist, SAC, 1947, Ex 38.

[65] Rprt, C. L. Zimmerman, Ch Ops An, SAC, Proposed Cross Training Program, Aug 22, 1947, SAC/HO.

[66] Hist, SAC, 1948, pp 261–262; ltr, 1Lt H. L. Luxon, Asst Adm, Davis-Monthan AAF, to CG 8 AF, subj: Diary of Combat Crew Activities, Aug 4, 1947, SAC/HO.

[67] Irvine OHI, p 15.

[68] Johnson OHI (with Marmor), pp 139–142; hist, SAC, 1948, pp 263–264.

[69] Ltr, Brig Gen L. W. Johnson, CG 15 AF, to CG 52 CBW(P), Oct 6, 1947; ltr, Col W. A. Adams, Dir Intel SAC, to Maj Gen C. P. Cabell, Dir Intel USAF, Apr 20, 1950; rprt, 7 BG, History of Wendover Maneuvers, Jun 17–Jul 6, 1947, all in SAC/HO; hist, SAC, 1947, pp 193–197, 1948, pp 279–280; Irvine OHI.

was a lack of enthusiasm and a reluctance to take risks that discouraged complete training. In addition, during 1947 SAC units participated in a series of public demonstrations of strategic air power, such as a flight over Kansas City by 70 B-29s in a mock attack, or one of 101 bombers over New York in May. These stunts served, perhaps, as valuable propaganda, but their value for training was limited.[70]

The effort to emphasize bombing by radar instead of optical bombsights compounded the difficulties of the training program. In 1946 Vandenberg had advised that in the atomic air force "reliance on visual bombing should be discarded altogether...accurate radar bombing *can* and *must* be attained and relied upon as a primary method of dropping."[71] This belief persisted depite the frustrations of using equipment and techniques developed during the war. The faults and frequent breakdowns of the AN/APQ-13 radar equipment and the short supply of trained repairmen delayed training in these techniques. While the Air Staff worked on methods to train operators and improve the hardware, SAC had to make do with what was available.[72]

One aid to effective training for radar bombing involved the use of ground equipment to score the accuracy of a simulated bomb release. Radar bomb scoring (RBS) had been developed late in the war by the AAF Tactical Center. In 1946, in keeping with Vandenberg's recommendations, SAC inherited all of the operational RBS equipment and set up five detachments. Still, it was some time before crews began to use the method. Early in 1947 the circular errors of the few crews that used the sites at Fort Worth and Kansas City varied from 2,600 to 4,440 feet, understandable results given the circumstances, but unacceptable against precision targets. In October 1947 Headquarters SAC ordered that all training

---

[70] Irvine OHI, pp 11–15; hist, 15 AF, Apr–Dec 1946, Pt III, pp 13–14; hist, 8 AF, Jan–Apr 1947, pp 39–41; hist, SAC, 1947, pp 186–187; ltr, CG SAC to CG 15 AF, *et al*, subj: Eastern Seaboard Mission (May 16, 1947), Jun 4, 1947, SAC/HO; ltr, Maj Gen L. W. Johnson, CG 15 AF, to CG SAC, subj: Participation in Aerial Demonstrations, Jun 10, 1948, SAC/HO.

[71] Memo, Lt Gen H. S. Vandenberg, ACAS/Ops, to Lt Gen I. C. Eaker, Dep Cmdr AAF, subj: The Establishment of a Strategic Striking Force, n.d. [Dec 45], RG 341, OPD, Asst for AE, 1945 S, 322 A–Bomb Striking Force, Box 1, MMB, NA.

[72] J. R. Loegering, Radar Bomb Scoring Activities...Origins and Growth Through 1951 (SAC Hist Study 59, Offutt AFB, Neb, 1952), pp 4–7; 1st Ind, Brig Gen T. S. Power, Dep ACAS–3 (Ops), to CG AAF, Mar 17, 1947, to ltr, Brig Gen F. H. Smith, CS SAC, to CG AAF, subj: Bikini Bombing Accuracy, Jan 20, 1947, RG 18, 1946–1947 AAG, 353.41 Bombing, Box 629, MMB, NA.

missions include an RBS run, but only the Eighth Air Force really met this requirement.[73]

As the operational effectiveness of the bomber units increased, SAC began to set more demanding goals for its rotational training missions overseas. Since the collapse of plans for deploying units to Europe, SAC had begun to envisage a more restrained program. The possibility of a visit of a few B–29s to Europe began to take form.

Planning for this mission took on a new dimension in August 1946, when Yugoslav gunners shot down two AAF C–47s. As a warning to the Soviets, Secretary of the Navy Forrestal announced that U.S. naval vessels in the Mediterranean were not there simply for training. He saw this as a show of force, but Assistant Secretary of War for Air W. Stuart Symington was appalled. In particular, a warship in the confined waters of the Adriatic would be vulnerable to massive attack by land-based air. In Symington's words: "We all know this is like putting a mouse in a trap, as no doubt do the [Yugoslavs]." He proposed a demonstration of air power, such as a round-the-world flight by a B–29. The State Department, which would have to obtain clearances from the countries to be visited, took no action at the time.[74]

By the time Symington's proposal had been blended with SAC's own plans, the State Department had obtained some clearances for a visit to Europe. The airmen were instructed that on arrival, the B–29s should not travel in flights of more than two planes. On November 15 six aircraft of the 43d Bombardment Group, at Davis-Monthan Field, Arizona, began a flight via Florida and the Azores to Rhein-Main Air Base near Frankfurt, Germany. From there the bombers visited a number of fields in Europe. The stated purpose was training in European flying conditions, and assessing the ability of the installations in Germany to support very heavy bombers.[75]

---

[73] J. R. Loegering, Radar Bomb Scoring Activities...Origins and Growth Through 1951 (SAC Hist Study 59, Offutt AFB, Neb, 1952), pp 1–7; memo, C. Zimmerman, Ch Ops An, SAC, subj: Operation Analysis Projects (Mar–Apr 1947), Apr 19, 1947, SAC/HO; ltr, Brig Gen D. W. Hutchison, ACS/Ops SAC, to CG 8 AF, 15 AF, *et al*, subj: Radar Bombing, Oct 21, 1947, SAC/HO; hist, 15 AF, 1947, Pt IV, pp 67–68; ltr, Brig Gen L. W. Johnson, CG 15 AF, to Brig Gen T. S. Power, Asst DCS/Ops USAF, Oct 29, 1947, SAC/HO.

[74] Memo, W. S. Symington, ASW/A, to Gen C. A. Spaatz, CG AAF, Aug 7, 1946; memo, W. S. Symington, ASW/A, to Gen C. A. Spaatz, CG AAF, n.d., both in Spaatz Coll, Assistant Secretary of War For Air, Box 256, MD, LC; Futrell, *Ideas*, pp 109–110.

[75] Futrell, *Ideas*, pp 109–110; ltr, Col J. C. Selser, CO 43BG, to CG 8 AF, subj: Report of B–29 Project 931995; Flight of Six B–29 Aircraft and Two C–54 Aircraft to Frankfort, Germany..., Dec 13, 1946, SAC/HO.

The results of the first visit were encouraging, and as soon as the bombers had returned home SAC planners outlined a more ambitious schedule. Early in 1947 the Air Staff approved plans for regular rotation of squadrons and then groups, and in June the 340th Bombardment Squadron deployed from Smoky Hill, Kansas, to Giebelstadt, Germany, where it spent a month. The squadron returned home only to turn around and head once again for Germany with the rest of the 97th Group. While in Germany, the 340th had made a ceremonial visit to England and the RAF Bomber Command. The group's two-week deployment in July included flights to several cities, although Copenhagen and Paris were scratched from the list for diplomatic reasons. (The meeting on the Marshall Plan was opening in Paris.) Because of Soviet objections, the B-29s that visited Berlin did not fly in formation. The 97th returned home on July 19. Through the middle of September three other groups made short trips to Europe, making flights as far afield as Italy and the south shore of the Mediterranean. Eventually, Headquarters SAC objected that these operations were interfering with training, and they were stopped. In their place, squadron-sized, thirty-day missions were run in November and December, with units from the 28th and 307th taking part. For the latter, the overseas base was shifted to Fürstenfeldbruck, which had better facilities than Giebelstadt. The squadron of the 307th visited Dhahran, Saudi Arabia. All of these deployments brought the units under the control of Headquarters United States Air Forces in Europe (USAFE).[76]

These European flights involved a minimum of publicity. The AAF stated that they were routine training and in support of the occupation forces. No statements were made except in reply to inquiries. This was designed to avoid trouble with the countries that held the transit stations, such as the Azores, since the agreements for access to these fields had been granted solely for the purpose of the occupation. Partridge cited another reason to avoid diplomatic trouble: "It is highly desirable that [these flights] gradually establish a precedent for our use of long distance air routes by bombardment units either for training or in the national interest."[77]

There was less likelihood of international trouble over the deployments to Japan, where the Americans were virtually the sole occupying power. Lt. Gen. Ennis C. Whitehead, Commanding General of Far East

---

[76] Hist, SAC, 1947, pp 139–166, 170–180.

[77] Ltr, Maj Gen E. E. Partridge, ACAS-3 (Ops), to CG SAC, subj: Employment Directive on Short Training Flights to Germany, Jul 2, 1947; ltr, Partridge to CG SAC, subj: Short Training Flights to Germany, Jun 19, 1947, both in SAC/HO; hist, 15 AF, 1947, p 26; hist, SAC, 1947, pp 158–159, 163–164.

Strategic Air Force

Air Forces (FEAF), asked for a squadron on rotation to augment his permanent VHB force. Approved in May, flights began soon after. Six squadrons spent a month each at Yokota, Japan, until a shortage of fuel on Hawaii led to cancellation of the deployments in November. On these moves, the B-29 crews received training in transoceanic flying and navigation and practiced dropping some live bombs on small desert islands. The flights also helped the squadron staffs learn to operate on their own.[78]

Another benefit of these trips to Japan involved testing the Eighth Air Force's mobility plan. A base overseas was likely to have a good deal of equipment on hand, for handling bombs, for instance, together with ammunition, food, fuel, and an adequate runway. But a unit under deployment would have to transport spare engines and parts that it might need before normal supply channels started functioning. Mechanics would have to come along to install the parts. Based on planned operations from the Marianas, the staff at Fort Worth compiled a list of items needed and designed a storage bin that could be carried in the bomb bay of a B-29. With a few C-54 transports supplementing the bombers, a unit could transport these bins, spare engines, and mechanics to a field overseas and set up an operation in short order. A squadron of the 7th Bombardment Group tested the kit on a trip to Japan; the Air Staff approved the Eighth's Mobility and Supply Plan; and Air Materiel Command (AMC) started to procure the "flyaway kits," as they came to be called.[79]

The fact that SAC units were in condition to deploy overseas indicated that much progress had taken place. Along with the buildup came some changes in unit structure that promised a more effective organization. Since the war, there had been strong dissatisfaction in the AAF with the existing relations between combat and support units. The main problem was that the commander of a combat group did not control all of the support units necessary for his mission. A number of AAF commands were considering various ways to reorganize, and SAC took a lead in the effort. Several plans had been produced and some even tested. At the same time, Col. Kenneth B. Hobson, Chief of the AAF Organizational Division on the Air Staff had developed a plan of his own, based on extensive study.[80]

---

[78] Ltr, Maj Gen C. McMullen, Dep CG SAC, to CG AAF, subj: Operational Training of Strategic Air Command Very Heavy Bombardment Units in the Pacific Theater, Feb 27, 1947, with 1st Ind, Maj Gen C. C. Chauncey, DCAS, to CG SAC, Apr 21, 1947; ltr, Lt Col J. J. Catton, CO 65 BSq, to CG Davis-Monthan AAF, subj: Report of Maneuvers of 65th Bomb Squadron at Yokota AB, Japan, Jul 10, 1947, both in SAC/HO; hist, SAC, 1947, pp 164–170.

[79] Hist, SAC, 1947, p 165; hist, SAC, 1951, Vol IA, pp 122–129.

[80] Borowski, *Hollow Threat*, pp 61–68.

Hobson's plan envisioned doing away with the wing as a level of command over several combat groups and instituting a new type of wing as a combat organization, containing the necessary support elements and intended to operate from a single base. The combat group would be merely one element of the wing, and the responsibility for the entire combat mission would be fixed squarely on the wing commander. Besides the combat group, a wing would have three support groups: maintenance and supply, airdrome, and medical.[81]

The Hobson plan became standard for the AAF in July 1947, but SAC had much work to do to make it function effectively. By the end of the year, however, most of the bases had a form of the wing-base system in effect. There were twelve operating bases in SAC (not including Bolling but including Andrews). Five of these had two combat groups, and a provisional consolidated wing headquarters was established at each location.[82] Some of SAC's trouble in the transition to the new structure arose because McMullen sought to retain the personnel ceilings, and units could not always fill all the positions the new structure seemed to require. Still, the organization promised to be a considerable improvement.[83]

By the end of 1947 Kenney had manned and largely equipped ten groups. Using a squadron from one of the existing groups as a cadre, a new group would acquire personnel from the schools, and as soon as planes arrived from storage, they could start training. Unfortunately, the withdrawals from storage had been done with such haste that the Air Materiel Command had been unable to make many of the modifications that would update the specific models. In particular, one of the most important modifications to the B-29 involved replacing carburetors with fuel injection systems, but many of the planes still arrived with carburetors. Although SAC by December 31, 1947, had a strength of 44,000, equipped with 319 B-29s in eleven groups and 350 fighters, only two groups were fully operational, and only one of these had atomic capable B-29s.[84] If the

---

[81] *Ibid.*
[82] *Ibid.*; Hopkins & Goldberg, *Development of SAC*, p 9.
[83] Borowski, *Hollow Threat*, pp 65–68.
[84] Ltr, Gen G. C. Kenney, CG SAC, to Gen C. A. Spaatz, CSAF, Sep 29, 1947, atch to memo, Maj Gen E. E. Partridge, Actg DCS/Ops, USAF, to Spaatz, subj: General Kenney's Letter Re 55-Group Objective, Oct 10, 1947; memo, Lt Gen H. A. Craig, DCS/Mat USAF, to CSAF, subj: Condition of B-29 Aircraft for the 55 Group Program, Oct 18, 1947, both in RG 18, 1946–1947 AAG, 380 55-Gp Prog, Vol 1, Box 638, MMB, NA; SAC Statistical Summary, Jan 48, pp 6, 28; hist, SAC, 1947, pp 198–199; 1st Ind, Lt M. Thompson, Actg Asst AG, to CG AAF, Sep 16, 1947, to ltr, Brig Gen A. H. Gilkeson, Dep AIG, to CG SAC, Sep 9, 1947, SAC/HO.

international situation were to deteriorate in the near future, there would be little that SAC could do.

Modernizing the Bomber Force

In the immediate postwar years the Boeing B–29 Superfortress was the pre-eminent symbol of American air power. It had the reputation both as a proven combat airplane and an aviation pioneer. It was the mainstay of SAC. But aviation technology was moving on, from the era of the propeller to the era of the jet, and the pioneer of one day would be the dinosaur of the next. The search for a suitable design for new bomber types was one of the principal tasks facing the AAF at the end of the Second World War. The results of that search had to take into account issues of national strategy as well as considerations of air doctrine and operations.

Boeing's Superfortress had itself begun as a further development of its B–17, but it emerged as a radically different airplane. At 70,000 pounds, an empty B–29 weighed more than a B–17G fully loaded. Its range was twice that of a Flying Fortress, giving it a combat radius that could be extended to 2,000 miles or more. Its four Wright R–3350 engines were rated at 2,200 horsepower each, contrasted with 1,200 each for the B–17's engines. It could climb higher and go faster than the older bomber, with altitudes above 30,000 feet and a speed of 350 miles per hour.[85] But for the crew the difference meant more than numbers. The degree of teamwork required went well beyond any previous experience in the AAF. One man who had flown a great deal before learning to pilot a B–29 said:

> Maybe Jimmy Doolittle could have flown it alone, but not...lesser mortals. The pilot, the copilot, and the flight engineers all had specific, coordinated functions in flying the airplane. The airplane commander called for power settings, much as the captain of a ship

---

[85] Carl Berger, *B–29: The Superfortress* (NY: Ballantine's, 1970), pp 102–103; Gordon Swanborough and Peter M. Bowers, *United States Military Aircraft since 1909* (Washington: Smithsonian Institute Press, 1989), pp 113–119; Mary R. Self, *History of the Development and Production of U.S. Heavy Bombardment Aircraft, 1917–1949* (Wright-Patterson AFB, Ohio: AMC, 1950), pp 72–73.

calls for engine performance and wheel corrections. The gunners had flight functions as lookouts, since the pilots could not see toward the rear quarters.... The last vestiges of the "daring young man in the flying machine" finally disappeared. Gone were the black silk stocking fastened to the leather helmet and the white strip of parachute silk worn as a scarf.... In their place was a very determined and rather serious young man in a prosaic cloth flying suit; his swagger stick had given way to a slide rule....[86]

Since the B-29 operated at high altitude, the crew of eleven inhabited three pressurized compartments linked by crawl-spaces. The standard crew had five officers: a pilot, a copilot, a flight engineer, a bombardier, and a navigator. These plus the radio operator normally worked in the forward compartment, while the one aft housed gunner-mechanics, whose guns operated by remote control, and a radar operator. The tail gunner was alone in the smallest compartment. Since missions could last ten hours and more, the need for teamwork was heightened by the requirement that the crew members spell each other on important jobs.[87]

The Superfortress, like the B-17, was one of those planes that continually exceeded expectations. Because of the altitudes it reached, B-29 crews over Japan were among the first to ride the jet stream.[88] In December 1945 a B-29 averaged 451 miles per hour riding a jet stream eastward across the United States. But the B-29's *raison d'etre* was its range. It was this feature which dictated the nature of the record flights undertaken by the AAF when the war was over and secrecy was eased. LeMay's historic return to America from the Far East in September 1945 was made in one of three B-29s which took off, headed for Washington, from Mizutani Air Base on the Japanese island of Hokkaido. The Superfortresses had to land for fuel at Chicago, but the distance covered totaled 5,995 miles. In November Brig. Gen. Frank A. Armstrong flew the same course and reached Washington. The same month, Col. Clarence S. Irvine flew the B-29 *Dreamboat* from Guam to Washington, a distance of 8,198 miles, breaking the world record of 1938. Almost a year later Irvine broke his own record, flying 10,925 miles from Hawaii to Cairo, over the polar region, in the *Pacusan Dreamboat*. These flights, though they were stunts

---

[86] Haywood S. Hansell, Jr., "B-29 Superfortress," in Robin Higham & Abigail Siddall, eds, *Flying Combat Aircraft of the USAAF-USAF* (Ames, Iowa: Iowa State Univ Press, 1975), pp 21-22.

[87] Berger, *B-29*, p 50; AAF Tactical Center, Tactical Doctrine, Very Heavy Aircraft, Nov 20, 1944, AFHRC.

[88] C. H. Hildreth & Bernard C. Nalty, *1001 Questions Answered About Aviation History* (NY: Dodd Mead & Co, 1969), p 331.

The Boeing B-17 Flying Fortress, *above*, and Consolidated B-24 Liberator, *below*, the AAF's premier bombers of World War II.

Beginnings

using specially-equipped planes, still convinced Irvine that combat-loaded B-29s had yet to reach their full potential.[89]

When the war ended, the B-29 became the AAF's sole strategic bomber. The B-17s and B-24s gradually went out of service, with only a few units retained temporarily for mapping and charting projects.[90] Nearly 4,000 B-29s had come off the assembly lines during the war, and at the end of 1945 there were 3,000 left in the AAF's inventory. A year later most of these were in storage with the Air Materiel Command as a reserve for mobilization. A few F-13s, a version used for reconnaissance, also remained in use.[91]

But, despite the B-29's success, the AAF was looking to new designs, as General Arnold had so often urged. American airmen anticipated that future bombers would outdo earlier ones in speed, range, and bomb loads, although the new aircraft were reaching the highest altitudes that were safe for the crew. The B-50 had originally been called the B-29D and resembled the original Superfortress. The B-36 had resulted from planning begun in 1941. Indeed AWPD-1 had envisioned use of the B-36 against Germany. Its rationale was to be able to reach Berlin from the North American continent, should England fall to the Nazis.

The B-36 would be considerably larger than the B-29. To call both "very heavy bombers" seemed increasingly questionable. The AAF preferred the distinction between "heavy" and "medium," with the B-29 in the latter category. The most formidable engineering challenges for the heavy bombers of the future involved speed and size. Unless the aircraft

---

[89] Coffey, *Iron Eagle*, p 181; *New York Times*, Sep 20, 1945, pp 1, 4; Irvine OHI, pp 10-15; ACSC Paper, Lt Col V. M. Cloyd, "The Utilization of the Present B-29 Type Aircraft in Individual Operations Against Strategic Targets Within Soviet Russia," Dec 1948, AFHRC; Maj J. M. Boyle, "This Dreamboat Can Fly!" *Aerospace Historian* XIV (Summer 67), pp 85-92. According to *The United States Air Force Dictionary* (Woodford A. Heflin, ed, Princeton, NJ: Van Nostrand, n.d.), cruise control "consists essentially of power settings for cruising speed, as well as propeller settings when propellers are used, so as to attain the maximum efficiency in terms of desired speed or range." "Pacusan" refers to PACUSA—Pacific Air Command, U.S. Army.

[90] *Army Air Forces Statistical Digest*, 1946, pp 163; ltr, H. L. Stimson, Sec War, to President, Sep 11, 1945, RG 341, TS AAG File 21, Box 7; chart, Activation, Deployment, and A/C Authorizations of AAF Units, Tab 2 to ltr, Gen C. A. Spaatz, CG AAF, to Cmdrs, subj: Current AAF Plans and Programs, Nov 18, 1945, RG 18, 1946-1947 AAG, 381 AAF 1, Box 603, both in MMB, NA.

[91] *Army Air Forces Statistical Digest*, 1946, pp 100, 123, 163; memo, Maj Gen G. Gardner, Dep ACAS-4 (Mat), to Asst Sec War (Air), subj: Cost of B-29 Program, Nov 22, 1946, RG 341, DCS/Mat, Exec Ofc 1948-1949, 452.1 B-29 (1949), Box 9, MMB, NA.

could be made fast enough to outrun fighters, it would have to carry armor, guns, and self-sealing fuel tanks, which all added to the weight. To achieve intercontinental range, it had to be big enough to carry vast amounts of fuel.[92] Although the super-bomber was considered fuel-efficient, the von Kármán Committee warned that the technology was approaching the point of diminishing returns, with vast increases in weight for small gains in performance.[93] The truth of this observation would soon become apparent to the AAF.

Early in 1946, Brig. Gen. Alfred R. Maxwell, the Chief of Requirements Division, under the Assistant Chief of Staff for Operations, outlined the future roles of both the heavy and medium types. Clearly, the large size of a heavy bomber would make it expensive and time-consuming to produce, so that it could not be acquired in large numbers. Thus the medium bomber, comparable to the B–29, would serve as a "workhorse." Maxwell also suggested another potential use for the heavy bomber—as a host for a parasite fighter. This concept involved transporting a small fighter in the bomb bay of a large bomber. The fighter could then be launched in the target area, overcoming the problem of range for escort fighters.[94]

The development of jet engines further compounded the problem of bomber performance. While jet propulsion increased the speed of airplanes, it consumed more fuel than conventional engines. This made longer range still harder to attain. Perhaps in future years technology could overcome this difficulty, but in the meantime the Air Staff envisioned turboprop engines as the solution for heavy bombers. For the medium bombers, the turbojet would be appropriate.[95]

The Army emerged from the war with contracts for several experimental jet bombers. These included a purely experimental contract with the Douglas Aircraft Company and development models expected from North American Aviation, Incorporated; the Consolidated Vultee Aircraft (Convair) Corporation; the Boeing Aircraft Company; and the Glenn Martin Company. Northrop Aircraft, Incorporated, had received AAF

---

[92] Rprt, ATSC, Trends and Problems in Bomber Design, Jan 18, 1945, atch to ltr, Col M. S. Roth, Ch Acft Proj, Eng Div AAF Mat Ctr, to Ch Svc Eng Sect, Eng Div AAF Mat Ctr, subj: Report for von Kármán Committee, Jan 19, 1945, RG 18, OCAS, Scientific Advisory Gp, 1941–Aug 1947, Misc Rprts #370, Box 9, MMB, NA.
[93] Report on Heavy Bombardment Committee Convened to Report to the USAF Aircraft and Weapons Board, Jan 48, RG 341, DCS/Dev, Dir Rqmts, Papers 1st AWB, Box 181, MMB, NA.
[94] Futrell, *Ideas*, p 110.
[95] See Note 92.

approval to put jets on two of its B-35 Flying Wings.[96] The Air Staff had also envisioned a heavy bomber more advanced than the B-36, issuing military characteristics in November 1945. This airplane would have to be able to carry 10,000 pounds of bombs a distance of 5,000 miles and return, cruising at 35,000 feet at a speed of 300 miles an hour. Boeing, Martin, and Convair turned in designs. Brig. Gen. Laurence C. Craigie, Chief of the Engineering Division of Air Materiel Command, recommended the Boeing design in May 1946 because, though its proposed radius was little more than 3,000 miles, it was, nonetheless, better than the others. The XB-52, as the experimental model was designated, would weigh 360,000 pounds, three times the weight of the B-29 and half again as heavy as the B-36. With six turboprop engines it would be faster than the B-36. On June 28, 1946, Boeing and the AAF agreed to a letter contract for a design study and mockup, for which the AAF allocated money from the fiscal 1946 appropriation.[97]

Flights of Experimental Bombers, 1946–1947

XB-43	Douglas	17 May 46	(Jet)
XB-35	Northrop	25 Jun 46	(Flying Wing)
XB-36	Convair	8 Aug 46	(Production contract)
XB-45	North American	17 Mar 47	(Jet)
XB-46	Convair	1 Apr 47	(Jet)
XB-48	Martin	22 Jun 47	(Jet)
B-50	Boeing	25 Jun 47	(Production contract)
YB-49	Northrop	21 Oct 47	(Jet Flying Wing)
XB-47	Boeing	17 Dec 47	(Jet)

But the most eagerly awaited event in the field of bomber development was the roll-out of the XB-36, then under construction at the Convair-operated plant in Fort Worth. Contractor personnel nicknamed the XB-36 the "Jesus Christ airplane," not because of any messianic

---

[96] Study, ARDC, *Air Force Developmental Aircraft*, 1957, CAFH.
[97] 5. Marcelle Size Knaack, *Post-World War II Bombers, 1945–1973* [Vol II of *Encyclopedia of U.S. Air Force Aircraft and Missile Systems*] (Washington: AFCHO, 1988), pp 205–208; Margaret C. Bagwell, *The XB-52 Airplane* (Wright-Patterson AFB, Ohio: AMC, 1949), pp 1–7, with ltr, Brig Gen L. C. Craigie, Ch Eng Div, AAF Mat Ctr, to CG AAF, subj: Design Composition, Heavy Bombardment Aircraft, May 23, 1946, with atch doc.

expectations, but in honor of the common expression of visitors when they first saw the huge bomber. Other aircraft, such as Howard Hughes's HK-1 Hercules Flying Boat (the famous, if misnamed, "Spruce Goose") were also called the "Jesus Christ airplane." In May 1946, Secretary of War Robert P. Patterson told a House subcommittee that the plane was "due to fly next month,"[98] and this prediction, repeated over and over again, indicated the continual delays caused by production difficulties. In fact, Convair was having trouble meeting the specifications. Inexperienced work crews had frequently substituted inferior materials in the construction, and it took time to correct this. In August 1945 Craigie had written a blistering letter to the president of Convair, but the AAF hesitated to penalize the company for poor performance.[99] After the war, the Fort Worth plant was hit by strikes, and labor trouble at the Aluminum Company of America held up shipments of materials.[100] The May 1946 completion date came and went. Secretary Patterson proved overly optimistic. Meanwhile, other experimental bombers made their first flights. Finally, on August 8, 1946, the giant bomber took off from Fort Worth for a 37-minute flight.[101]

The early flight testing of the XB-36 offered the usual mixed message of most initial flight test programs. As was common with successful test programs, reports on early flights of the YB-36 uncovered numerous deficiencies. The aircraft failed to perform up to design expectations, and various malfunctions surfaced. However, there was every reason to believe the experimental version, or at least the production models, could do better.[102] George Kenney remained unimpressed. In December he wrote to Spaatz recommending a reassessment of the production program and arguing that the B-36 was not an intercontinental bomber. It would be vulnerable in enemy territory because its fuel tanks were not fully self-sealing. Correcting this would add weight and reduce fuel capacity, further limiting speed and range. Drawing on his combat experience, General

---

[98] Hearings before the Subcommittee on Appropriations, House of Representatives, *Military Establishment Appropriation, 1947*, 79th Cong, 2d sess, May 8, 1946, p 23.
[99] *Case History of XB-36, YB-36, and B-36 Airplanes* (Wright-Patterson AFB, Ohio: AMC, 1948) pp 6-13, with atch ltr, Brig Gen L. C. Craigie, Ch Eng Div, AAF Mat Ctr, to Harry Woodhead, Pres Convair, Aug 29, 1945; *Case History of XB-36 Airplane Project* (Wright-Patterson AFB, Ohio: AMC, 1946), passim, both in AFHRA.
[100] R & R Sheet, Col G. Schaetzel, Ch Acft Proj Sec, to Maj Gen E. W. Rawlings, Ch Proc Div ATSC, Aluminum Shortages—B-36 Aircraft, Mar 26, 1946, in *Case History of XB-36 Airplane Project*, AFHRA.
[101] Knaack, *Bombers*, p 13; study, ARDC, *Air Force Developmental Aircraft*, 1957, CAFH.
[102] Knaack, *Bombers*, p 13.

Beginnings

Kenney asserted that to outrun enemy fighters the B-36 would have to burn a lot of fuel going full throttle. Its range would thus actually be 6,500 miles, or a combat radius of less than 3,000 miles. From Alaska or the continental United States it could not reach vital targets in the Soviet Union. In other words, the B-36 offered the AAF little that the B-29 and B-50 did not, and it was not as good as they were in other ways. It would be better, Kenney suggested, to save the money and develop a better bomber.[103]

Despite these reservations, the Air Staff and AMC did not waver in their commitment to producing the B-36. The Assistant Chief of Air Staff for Materiel asked Lt. Gen. Nathan F. Twining, Commander of AMC, for comments on Kenney's letter. In his reply, Twining asserted that the B-36 marked an important step toward acquiring intercontinental range and would provide practical experience in operating a very large bomber. He believed that many of the B-36's deficiencies could be corrected. Most models would feature a new type of water-injection engine, for example. In the long run, the only solution to the problem of low speed in all large bombers lay in reducing the fuel consumption of jet engines. From a strategic standpoint, the B-52 would offer better performance, but it would not be in service before 1954. Twining argued that, in any case, the B-36 would be able to reach a radius of 4,000 miles. He defended the decision not to leak-proof all of the fuel tanks but said little about the question of survival over target. Striking hard at the tone he detected in Kenney's letter, Twining noted that the nation had almost decided at one time or another against producing the B-17, the B-26, the P-47, the P-51, and the B-29, all successful airplanes in the war, "because of the same type of reasoning and arguments now being used against the B-36." All had proved better than early testing had indicated.[104]

General Spaatz advised Kenney that production of the B-36 would proceed. He attributed the limitations on range and speed to the state of engine development and predicted that eventually gas turbines would solve this problem. For the time being, the B-36 was the best available heavy bomber:

> As you probably know better than most, we would never have bought a single combat type, including the B-17, if we had waited

---

[103] Ltr, Gen G. C. Kenney, CG SAC, to Gen C. A. Spaatz, CG AAF, Dec 12, 1946, RG 341, DCS/Comptr, Admin Div 1942-1953, 452.1s Acft, B-36 Spec File, Box 212, MMB, NA.
[104] Ltr, Lt Gen N. F. Twining, CG AMC, to ACAS-4 (Mat), subj: Suitability of B-36 Airplane, Dec 27, 1946, RG 341, DCS/Comptr, Admin Div 1942-1953, 452.1s Acft, B-36 Spec File, Box 212, MMB, NA.

Strategic Air Force

for a better type we knew was just around the corner. If we stumble into the pitfall at one stage of three to five years, your strategic Air Forces will be without equipment.... Obviously, it was not possible for your ideas and mine to have been incorporated... into the B-36 for we were away at war when it was developed. It seems to me, however, that Arnold and his staff and the Materiel Command under his supervision did very well in the experimental field considering all the things he had to do in keeping you and me supplied with weapons to win the Air war in Europe and the Pacific.[105]

The AAF commander assured Kenney that the B-36 would improve. He had reason to expect this, for Convair planned to install a new four-wheel landing gear on the production models, enabling it to land on virtually any field that could accommodate a B-29. Most B-36s would feature an updated version of the Wright R-4360 engine that could generate 500 horsepower more than the previous model. A still more promising engine, equipped with a variable discharge turbine (VDT), would further improve performance. Convair wanted to install the VDT engines on one B-36, reducing total production by three airplanes in order to stay within the budget. These developments might correct some deficiencies and help answer some objections to the giant bomber.[106]

At the same time that Kenney was raising doubts about the B-36, its proposed successor became an issue as well. Partridge's staff expressed reservations about building an airplane as big as the B-52 was likely to be. To meet range and bomb load specifications, it would have to have a gross weight of 400,000 or 500,000 pounds. In October 1946 Boeing delivered a design that would yield a weight of 230,000 pounds, but LeMay, then Deputy Chief of Air Staff for Research and Development, noted that its range would be too short. The AAF needed a bomber of intercontinental range, whatever its size.[107] The contractor was asked to study the feasibility of a bomber capable of flying 400 miles per hour and 12,000 miles, if the gross weight did not exceed 480,000 pounds. Also in October, Boeing submitted designs for an intercontinental bomber that could carry the atomic bomb.[108]

---

[105] Ltr, Gen C. A. Spaatz, CG AAF, to Gen G. C. Kenney, CG SAC, Jan 16, 1947, RG 341, DCS/Comptr, Admin Div 1942-1953, 452.1s Acft, B-36 Spec File, Box 212, MMB, NA.

[106] See Note 104; Knaack, *Bombers*, pp 14-15.

[107] Knaack, *Bombers*, pp 208-209; Bagwell, *XB-52 Airplane*, pp 1-7, with ltr, Maj Gen L. C. Craigie, Ch Eng Div, AAF Mat Ctr, to CG AAF, subj: Conference at Wright Field with A-3 Personnel on XB-51, XB-52, XB-53 and Military Characteristics in General, Nov 26, 1946.

[108] Knaack, *Bombers*, pp 208-209.

Beginnings

Reinforcing the concerns of the operations staff was an analysis by the Douglas Aircraft Company's Project RAND. The RAND engineers examined Boeing's proposals and determined that such an aircraft would have to weigh 600,000 pounds at the very least. Analysts suggested that a smaller, cleanly designed airplane with bomb and fuel in jettisonable pods would have a better chance of attaining the necessary range. Maxwell regarded the conflict between the Boeing and Douglas engineers as disturbing: "It looks as if we are on very thin ice, considering the ultimate cost of the project...."[109] Brig. Gen. Alden R. Crawford, Chief of the Research and Engineering Division, Assistant Chief of Air Staff for Materiel, defended the Boeing project. He had spoken to the company's engineers, and "While their conclusions are somewhat alarming...," they were working on the problem. Representatives of Boeing, Douglas, and Northrop planned to meet and consider the engineering aspects of bomber development. Among the alternatives they would discuss was some encouraging data on the Flying Wing. Less attractive was the delta-wing design, which Crawford considered unproven and too risky, although Maxwell had mentioned it.[110]

Although no one really wanted to dismiss unproven ideas without study, the stringency of the research budget for fiscal 1948 forced the AAF to reject some of the recent proposals. Twining's staff struggled to establish priorities among several different alternatives: a future intercontinental bomber, a medium bomber obtainable in the short term, modification of current bombers, and the VDT engine or the T-35 turboprop then under development. In Washington a number of key members of the Air Staff met in LeMay's office on May 6, 1947, to devise guidelines for the Materiel Command. Reversing earlier decisions, the group agreed to give the XB-52 first priority for development. Fiscal 1948 money would also be allocated to a new medium bomber. The staff agreed to install VDT engines on a single B-36 and a B-50, the latter also slated for new wings. By using production model airplanes, the AAF could avoid charging the installation of VDT engines to the research budget.[111]

---

[109] R & R Sheet, Brig Gen A. R. Maxwell, Ch Rqmts Div ACAS-3 (Ops), to R & E Div ACAS-4 (Mat), XB-52 Performance, Apr 21, 1947, in Bagwell, *XB-52 Airplane*. RAND (Research and Development) had been established at Douglas under an AAF contract in May 1946, following an initiative by Arnold. The RAND Corporation separated from Douglas in 1948.
[110] R & R Sheet, Cmt 2, Brig Gen A. R. Crawford, Ch R & E Div ACAS-4 (Mat), to Rqmts Div ACAS-3 (Ops), XB-52 Performance, Apr 23, 1947, in Bagwell, *XB-52 Airplane*.
[111] Ltr, Maj Gen E. M. Powers, ACAS-4 (Mat), to CG AMC, subj: Medium Bombardment Aircraft, May 8, 1947, in Bagwell, *XB-52 Airplane*.

103

Reporting these decisions to Twining, LeMay reiterated the Air Staff view on bomber development and explained the necessity for supporting several new aircraft programs simultaneously. In an era of tight budgets, the AAF might have to justify to Congress its recommendation to continue buying B-50s and B-36s. Air Staff members believed that a future heavy bomber could not be purchased in quantities much above 100.

> I feel that the B-52, or any other airplane capable of doing the job for which the B-52 is intended, will of necessity be of such size and of such cost that neither the aircraft industry nor our future budget will permit its production and procurement on other than a very limited scale.[112]

On the other hand, the medium bomber would be cheaper and available in greater numbers. This "workhorse" aircraft, like the B-29, could be operated from overseas bases. LeMay hoped that a gross weight of 170,000 pounds would be possible.[113]

Though the Research and Development chief favored the XB-52 project, he urged that the AAF wait about six months before committing itself. This would allow more progress on development of the T-35-3 engine, on which the plane depended. Another factor involved encouraging technological competition in the industry:

> In this connection I have learned that Douglas, Northrop, and Consolidated have suddenly awakened to the fact that though they were uninterested in bidding on an airplane of the B-52 type when this project was started, they realize now that a large part of our production funds will go into such an airplane, and they are now out in the cold. It appears, therefore, that we must take a good look at any proposals that may now exist in the minds of the late starters in order to make sure that if the B-52 is the horse we intend to back, such action is firmed after all other possibilities have been considered and eliminated.[114]

In June 1947 the AAF issued new military characteristics for a heavy bomber to carry the atomic bomb. In this case especially, weight would be critical; the atomic carrier might even have to dispense with guns and armor in order to attain the speed and altitude necessary to assure its

---

[112] Ltr, Maj Gen C. E. LeMay, DCAS/R & D, to Lt Gen N. F. Twining, CG AMC, May 15, 1947, in Bagwell, *XB-52 Airplane*.
[113] *Ibid*.
[114] *Ibid*.

survival.[115] At the same time, LeMay's office hoped to look at alternatives to the heavy bomber. In July he discreetly warned Twining not to allow construction of the XB-52 to start without word from the AAF commander, who would consult with the Joint Chiefs of Staff before taking action. Meanwhile, Materiel Command planned to study various approaches, such as the one-way mission, landing overseas after a mission from the States, ditching, pilotless aircraft, and anything else the RAND people might suggest. As LeMay put it:

> The intent ... is not to stop progress on the present XB-52, nor to add to its difficulties, but to ascertain that Air Materiel Command understands the possibility of change occurring in this program. The strategic mission remains firm but the method of accomplishment is not fixed.[116]

Meanwhile, less theoretical designs were becoming reality. Though the Boeing B-50, which first flew on June 25, 1947, resembled the B-29 and also bore the name Superfortress, it did represent a new design, about 75 percent changed from its predecessor. It featured a new vertical fin and rudder assembly and more powerful engines. In addition to the sixty planes ordered with fiscal 1946 money, the AAF had committed 1947 funds for another seventy-three. The Air Staff scheduled the 43d Bomb Group at Davis-Monthan to receive the first B-50s.[117]

Building a modern strategic force, however, required more than bombers. For fighters the next move was to jet engines for increased speed and range. For the reconnaissance force, the traditional mounting cameras on existing models of bombers and fighters no longer seemed suitable. In the light of the abysmal state of intelligence about the Soviet Union, a high-speed, long-range photographic plane was urgently needed. Existing strategic reconnaissance units were in a totally unacceptable condition,

---

[115] Knaack, *Bombers*, p 209; MR, Maj W. C. Brady, subj: XB-52 Conference, Jan 7, 1947; memo, Maj Upson to Maj Gen C. E. LeMay, DCAS/R & D, subj: Defense Armament in Bombardment Aircraft, Mar 5, 1947, both in Bagwell, *XB-52 Airplane*.

[116] Ltr, Maj Gen C. E. LeMay, DCAS/R & D, to Lt Gen N. F. Twining, CG AMC, subj: XB-52 Program, Jul 14, 1947, in Bagwell, *XB-52 Airplane*.

[117] Swanborough, *U.S. Military Aircraft*, p 120; Self, *Heavy Bombardment Aircraft*, pp 72–73; study, ARDC, *Air Force Developmental Aircraft*, 1957, CAFH; chart, Activation, Deployment, and A/C Authorizations of AAF Units, Tab 2 to ltr, Gen C. A. Spaatz, CG AAF, to AAF, subj: Current AAF Plans and Programs, Nov 18, 1946, RG 18, 1946–1947 AAG, 321 AAF, File 1, Box 603, MMB, NA.

and the search continued for a plane designed specifically for reconnaissance. The four-engine Republic XF-12 was identified as the possible solution.[118]

The need for advanced equipment took on a certain urgency as the AAF's leaders contemplated the rivalry with the Soviets. Technical problems blended with questions of strategy. A bomber "gap" appeared likely around 1952, when the B-29 would be obsolete and the B-36 and B-50 would approach obsolescence. Yet at that time, only the B-52 would be coming off the assembly line, and it would be months before the few of those obtainable were combat ready. No other bombers could be made operational for the strategic mission before 1954. Unfortunately, the very size of the B-52 raised questions the AAF was reluctant to face. Vandenberg believed that better engines would solve the problem, but it would be five years before an engine could be built that combined the power and speed of the jet with the fuel economy of the piston so as to carry a heavy bomber on its long-range mission. Turboprops appeared to be the short-term answer, but no one was sure. Technical uncertainties thus combined with the problem of lead time to complicate all decisions.[119]

Tactics also had an impact on development plans. In view of the lack of intelligence about the Soviet Union, nobody could be sure what the bombers would actually face in a war. Would it be possible for them to fly fast enough and high enough to evade the interceptors? Or would they still need to bristle with guns? If the latter were true, development became more complex. Bulky turrets had to be eliminated for aerodynamic reasons, while fire control systems had to cope with high speeds. Besides, armament increased the weight of the airplane. And if the potential enemy had a fighter with flexible guns, it would be impossible to rely on speed for protection.[120]

The broad ideas about bomber design led to a concept all the same. It seemed possible that the United States would have no bases overseas soon after a war started. An atomic offensive over the North Pole would then be the only means available to retaliate with any hope of victory in the near future. This intercontinental mission was the greatest technical challenge

---

[118] Hist, SAC, 1946, pp 150-152; ATSC Hist Div, Case History of XF-12 Airplane, Jan 46, AFHRA. See also Richard P. Hallion, "Twilight of the Piston-Powered Airplane: The Republic XF-12/RC-2 Rainbow" *Aviation Quarterly* III, No. 1 (Spring 77), pp. 62-86.

[119] Verbatim mins, 1st Meeting—USAF Aircraft and Weapons Board, 1st Day: Aug 19, 1947, pp 1-14, Last Day: Aug 21, 1947, p 774, RG 341, DCS/Dev, Rqmts Div, 1st AWB, 1947-1948, Box 181, MMB, NA.

[120] *Ibid.*, First Day: Aug 19, 1947, pp 4-14, Last Day: Aug 21, 1947, pp 531-545.

The long-range Boeing B–29 Superfortress entered World War II in 1944 and was at first disappointing at high altitudes because of its four fire-prone 18-cylinder Wright R–3350–23 engines. It proved menacing at low altitudes over Japan, however, destroying nearly one-quarter of the city of Tokyo in March 1945 during a single incendiary raid. Two modified B–29s, *Enola Gay* and *Bock's Car*, dropped atomic bombs on Japan in August 1945. In the uneasy transition from hot to cold war, when budget slashing, rapid demobilizing, occupying Germany and Japan, facing Soviet ambition and adventurism, fighting for service autonomy, and building the atomic force beleaguered the nation's air leaders, the Superfortress remained the backbone of medium bomber capability and was phased out only at the end of the Korean conflict.

Strategic Air Force

facing the new Air Force. Should it fail, the nation would have to reconquer bases and begin a laborious strategic offensive with large numbers of airplanes and conventional bombs. The Air Staff conceived of the medium bomber in this role.[121]

At the time, the official answer to the question of intercontinental bombing was the B-36. The B-52 would be its successor, and the staff of Project RAND was studying such radical long-term solutions as guided missiles.[122] LeMay described the B-36 as "essential," but in a tight budget even an essential airplane had tough going. If the B-36 could not perform as advertised, its value was marginal. Also, the Air Staff had to decide how many to buy and whether to install the VDT engine. Atomic bombs would eventually be available in hundreds, and the scarcity of the weapon would no longer justify buying just a few planes.[123] Despite these unresolved questions, the AAF continued to support the basic design.

Should the B-36 fail to perform as an intercontinental bomber, the AAF would need a ready alternative. Kenney suggested trying to fit the B-29 with tractor-type, endless tread landing gear, which would enable it to land on undeveloped fields, possibly staging through Arctic stations. The Air Materiel Command pursued this project for some time, with little sign of progress.[124]

Related to this idea was Spaatz's promotion of the Arctic theater. During the winter of 1946-1947, the 28th Bombardment Group deployed to Alaska to gain practical experience in Arctic operations. The results showed that much work was needed for the AAF to be able to operate effectively from bases in the far north. The 28th itself had been poorly prepared for the special working conditions in a climate of extreme cold. Alaska's isolation and Alaskan Air Command's lack of supplies and facilities impeded effective flying. With a lack of flying time, the morale of the air crews suffered. Furthermore, the peculiar navigational problems of the polar region substantially increased the danger of a plane getting lost and running out of fuel in the midst of trackless, frigid, wasteland. One B-29 of the 28th did indeed disappear, never to be seen again. A second

---

[121] *Ibid.*

[122] Charts, USAF Airplane Procurement Programs, atch to memo, Col L. O. Peterson, Act Sec AWB, to CG AAF, subj: Fiscal Year 1948 Aircraft Procurement Program, Aug 25, 1947, RG 341, DCS/Dev, Dir Rqmts, 1st AWB, 1947-1948, Papers, Box 181, MMB, NA.

[123] Verbatim mins, 1st Meeting—USAF Aircraft and Weapons Board, Last Day: Aug 21, 1947, pp 618-628, RG 341, DCS/Dev, Rqmts Div, 1st AWB, 1947-1948, Box 181, MMB, NA.

[124] Memo, W. S. Symington, Sec AF, to Gen C. A. Spaatz, Jan 27, 1948, Spaatz Coll, Secretary of Air Force (2), Box 264, MD, LC.

had a malfunction and the crew had to bail out. One crewman died before rescuers could find the survivors.[125]

Another alternative to the intercontinental bomber was the "one-way mission." A B-29 or B-50 could reach as many as eighty percent of the targets in the Soviet Union if it did not have to return home. In some cases the bomber could reach a friendly or neutral country, but the usual scenario called for the crew to crash land in a remote area and attempt to survive until somehow rescued.[126] An article by Col. Dale O. Smith in the fall 1947 issue of *Air University Quarterly Review* publicized the idea. Smith contended that if the atomic offensive succeeded, the war would soon end and chances of rescue would be good.[127] Partridge, however, harbored few illusions:

> We can afford, in the economy of the country, to build, in my opinion..., light bombers for every bomb there is. Easy. It will be the cheapest thing we ever did. Expend the crew, expend the bomb, expend the airplane all at once. Kiss them goodbye and let them go. That is a pretty cold-blooded point view, but I believe that it is economically best for the country.[128]

The implications were not lost on crews that would be affected. In one squadron operations office of the 509th Bombardment Group a poster appeared at about this time. Two crew members with long white beards were sitting in the Ural Mountains awaiting rescue, over the caption, "Survival Can be Fun."[129] Brig. Gen. Thomas S. Power, the Deputy Assistant Chief of Staff for Operations, doubted the soundness of the one-way concept. He said that the crews "are not stupid...they might change the plans many times along the way."[130] Thus the various alternatives to the B-36 either required more work or were decidedly unappealing.

---

[125] Borowski, *Hollow Threat*, pp 77–87.
[126] Verbatim mins, 1st Meeting—USAF Aircraft and Weapons Board, Last Day: Aug 21, 1947, pp 618–628, RG 341, DCS/Dev, Rqmts Div, 1st AWB, 1947–1948, Papers, Box 181, MMB, NA.
[127] Col. Dale O. Smith, "One-Way Combat," *AU Quarterly Review* I (Fall 47), pp 3–8.
[128] Verbatim mins, 1st Meeting—USAF Aircraft and Weapons Board, Last Day: Aug 21, 1947, pp 623–627, RG 341, DCS/Dev, Rqmts Div, 1st AWB, 1947–1948, Box 181, MMB, NA.
[129] Intvw, Robert M. Kipp, Hist, Hq SAC, with Maj Gen W. C. Kingsbury, Dec 16, 1970, p 18, SAC/HO. CHECK AGST PAGE 107
[130] Verbatim mins, 1st Meeting—USAF Aircraft and Weapons Board, Last Day: Aug 21, 1947, pp 623–627, RG 341, DCS/Dev, Rqmts Div, 1st AWB, 1947–1948, Box 181, MMB, NA.

Strategic Air Force

Less urgent but no less complex was the matter of designing an effective medium bomber. Military characteristics issued in June 1947 called for a radius of 2,500 miles, but such an aircraft was expected to weigh 250,000 pounds, still too much. Jets like the B–47 had yet to prove that they could meet the requirement. To get a bomber built soon, the Air Staff had to sacrifice at least one factor: range, speed, or armament. The SAC staff considered high speed over the target essential. As McMullen told the Aircraft and Weapons Board: "That's what brings the boys home." Vandenberg tended to agree. The B–50 was expected to have a radius of 2,500 miles and a speed of 360 miles per hour, and a newer medium bomber could attain 420 miles an hour by cutting its radius to 2,000 miles. To the new deputy commander of AAF this seemed a good compromise. Such an aircraft could reach most targets on a one-way mission, and from England, Egypt, or Lahore (British India, later Pakistan) it could get to 80 percent of them and return. Still higher speeds were thought possible with no loss of range. LeMay, however, expressed his doubts, fearing that loading on armament would make the problem insoluble. To the Research and Development chief, the 2,000-mile radius represented the lowest desirable range. Some sacrifice of speed might prove necessary as guns were added. Though for the time being the AAF was willing to leave the question open in the hopes of a more promising design, the hard decisions might still have to be made.[131]

With the passage of the National Security Act of 1947, the soon-to-be independent air force had little time to enjoy the reward for its years of effort. Politically sensitive investigations were now added to the challenges of aircraft development. Formulating the official Air Force position on these problems required serious thought. For this purpose, General Spaatz called together key officers of the Air Staff and major commanders to form the Aircraft and Weapons Board. First meeting on August 19, 1947, the board was to advise him on matters of procurement.[132]

Initially, the Aircraft and Weapons Board focused its inquiry on a briefing on strategic bombardment presented by Partridge's requirements staff. The briefing team presented data on engine design, intercontinental bombing, and the questions of speed, range, and armament of medium bombers. In its report, the board recommended buying about 650 aircraft with fiscal 1948 money. Among these would be 83 B–50s, one of which would have the VDT engine, 25 Republic F–12 reconnaissance planes, and 344 jet fighters. Any remaining funds could be used to purchase another 10

---

[131] *Ibid.*, First Day: Aug 19, 1947, pp 4–14, Last Day: Aug 21, 1947, pp 531–547, 564.
[132] Wolk, *Planning and Organizing*, p 182.

Proposed Aircraft Procurement Programs
August 1947

	Fiscal Year							
Type	46	47	48	49	50	51	52	Total
B-36	100							100
B-50	60	73	83*	153	204	204	60	837
B-X (Heavy)							105	105
P-80	915	80						995
P-84	214	191	154	359				945
P-86		33	190	551	236			1,010
P-88					464	409	409	1,282
P-90					205	540	540	1,285
F-12			25	15	11	11	11	73

* Plus up to 10 if extra money remained.

B-50s. No major decisions were made concerning the future of the B-36, except that the existing order would continue and one aircraft would be fitted with the VDT engine. This decision would avoid slowing down production, which had to be completed before June 1948, the end of the fiscal year. For the long term, the problems of the medium bomber and the B-52 remained essentially unresolved. The Air Staff reported that it hoped to receive over $1 billion in fiscal 1949 and over $1.6 billion in 1950. Meanwhile the service planned to follow its existing priorities: to buy more than 800 B-50s (enough to replace all B-29s in the active force), develop a heavy bomber by 1952, continue research on the "workhorse" bomber, and encourage RAND to look for alternatives.[133]

As for other types of planes, the board determined that the F-12 would meet vital intelligence needs. In time the P-84 and P-86 would replace the Mustang and the P-80. Research would continue with the

---

[133] Verbatim mins, 1st Meeting—USAF Aircraft and Weapons Board, First Day: Aug 19, 1947, pp 4-14, Last Day: Aug 21, 1947, pp 578-594, 610-611, 628; memo, Col L. O. Peterson, Actg Sec AWB, to CG AAF, subj: Fiscal Year 1948 Aircraft Procurement Program, Aug 25, 1947, with atch charts, USAF Airplane Procurement Programs, both in RG 341, DCS/Dev, Rqmts Div, 1st AWB. 1947-1948, Box 181, MMB, NA.

Strategic Air Force

P-88 and P-90, but there were no funds for the P-85 "parasite" fighter, to be launched from the B-36 in flight.[134]

One significant result of the August 1947 meeting of the Aircraft and Weapons Board was a decision to set up a special study committee on bombardment. Reflecting the on-going concerns of the air arm, the committee would focus on the intercontinental mission and also consider the design of medium bombers.[135] It would report its findings at the next board meeting scheduled for the beginning of 1948. Thus as the birth of the new Air Force approached, its leaders were still struggling to solve their basic strategic problem.

---

[134] Verbatim mins, 1st Meeting—USAF Aircraft and Weapons Board, 3d Day: Aug 21, 1947, pp 415–440, Last Day: Aug 21, 1947, p 774, RG 341, DCS/Dev, Rqmts Div, 1st AWB, 1947–1948, Box 181, MMB, NA.

[135] Report on Heavy Bombardment by Heavy Bombardment Committee Convened to Report to the USAF Aircraft and Weapons Board, Jan 48, RG 341, DCS/Dev, Dir Rqmts, Papers 1st AWB, Box 181, MMB, NA

Chapter IV

The Uncertain Phase

The reorganization of the atomic program that accompanied the creation of the Atomic Energy Commission at the beginning of 1947 made it increasingly difficult to postpone decisions about the role of the bomb in national strategy. The previous year had witnessed the Bikini tests and the initiation of studies of the results. The commission devoted much of 1947 to assuming control of the production program and outlining its first goals. The facility at Los Alamos had been as affected by demobilization as the armed forces themselves, and the manufacture of bombs required a revitalization of the staff there. At the same time, the Bikini tests, with the controversy over an inaccurate air drop, had confirmed the need to improve the design of the bomb, so the commission also began to plan a new series of tests. This would further complicate the production program. Under the MacMahon Act, the scale of production was set by the President, but Congress controlled the budget. There the Joint Committee on Atomic Energy had acquired a position of great strength, and among its ranks were a number of members committed to seeing a growth in the nation's atomic arsenal. The fading hope for international control reinforced their concerns.

The importance of atomic weapons was also affected by the danger of war with the Soviet Union. While informed observers in 1947 still considered a war unlikely, the Truman Doctrine and the Marshall Plan seemed to assume some risk. In any event, should war come, the situation in Europe would be so grave that the failure to prepare for it seemed an invitation to disaster. The idea of the atomic bomb as the means to offset the Soviet superiority in ground forces won widespread acceptance. But the bomb was itself of little significance in an actual war without the means of delivery. In 1947 this was still the concern of the AAF, which was taking its responsibility in the matter seriously.

Strategic Air Force

The armed forces made progress in 1947 in being able to meet their commitments with regard to atomic weapons. The magic circle of those cleared for crucial information was growing, and officers were being trained to handle the tasks associated with arming and dropping the weapon. The AAF and SAC's Eighth Air Force managed to establish liaison with the new structure created under the MacMahon Act. Also, the prospect of increased production suggested that there might be a companion requirement for an increased delivery force. Thus the three-group atomic force, though not yet attained, might be superseded by an expanded modification program.

Because of the importance of the strategic air force, especially should an expanded atomic production be approved, the AAF was able to make the case for one of its most cherished concepts, the direct control of the strike force. During World War II, Twentieth Air Force and Spaatz's U.S. Strategic Air Forces in Europe had set precedents for a single strategic air element directly responding to the joint chiefs. During 1946, as the armed services worked out the concepts for the postwar command structure, the AAF urged a unique standing for SAC. By the end of the year, as the Air Force itself moved towards independence, the new Unified Command Plan had granted the strategic force its special position, free of control by theater commanders.

War planning, one of the key functions of the armed forces in peacetime, evolved slowly after 1945. The Soviet Union was the obvious potential enemy, but given so much uncertainty in the international situation and the turmoil of reorganization, it took time to start work. By late 1947 some progress had been made, but as yet no approved joint plan existed. Still, several studies had suggested the broad outlines of a plan. Though many issues remained undecided, it was becoming clear that the bomb offered the only means to offset Soviet superiority on the ground in Europe. Obviously, for the immediate future, the bomb's primary use would be as a strategic air weapon. Thus the atomic air offensive was gaining a central place in American strategic thinking.

As SAC became the focal point for American atomic capability, its requirements for men, planes, and bases received more attention. Without an intercontinental bomber force, overseas bases would play a pivotal role for the near future, and negotiations would be required to obtain some. England seemed to be the one place where bases were readily available and less vulnerable to ground attack. Egypt, still in British hands, offered another possibility, and the Air Staff was beginning to look elsewhere. The question of bases and range would continue to bedevil planners of the strategic air offensive for years to come.

The importance of the atomic bomb received further emphasis in the summer of 1947 when the Compton Board report on the Bikini tests finally appeared. Commissioned by the joint chiefs, the board determined that the bomb was indeed a strategic air weapon of great power. Its findings stated that the United States had the option of developing a deterrent force equipped to strike rapidly against strategic targets in the Soviet Union. Thus, by the time the White House and Congress began to investigate the potential of atomic air power at the end of 1947, the armed services were prepared to discuss the capabilities of a strategic atomic force and how it could be built.

Understanding The Bomb

Whatever their expectations for international control of atomic weapons, air leaders continued to press for a striking force under their full control. When he became Deputy Chief of Air Staff for Research and Development, LeMay established the goal of "complete Air Force responsibility for transport, assembly, testing, loading and dropping of the bomb."[1] In 1946 the AAF had little of this responsibility, mainly providing the plane and the crew to carry the bomb. The situation, as General Ramey, Commander of the 58th Bombardment Wing, described it, left the AAF "dependent upon engineers and scientists to use its major weapon."[2]

The first step towards control involved learning as much as possible about atomic weapons. The MANHATTAN PROJECT guarded the technological secrets and was reluctant to share them with outsiders. Also, even after Hiroshima and Nagasaki, further testing was necessary to gauge the bomb's power and the optimum methods of delivery. In this effort, the agency charged with dropping the bomb would have an important role to play. It took well over a year after Hiroshima to accumulate a new body of data that could be used to make policy decisions. Testing by itself was not enough; equally important was a thorough evaluation of the results. In retrospect the delay in developing atomic air power immediately following

---

[1] Ltr, Maj Gen C. E. LeMay, DCAS/R & D, to Brig Gen R. M. Ramey, Cmdr TG 1.5 (Prov), Apr 4, 1946, RG 341, OPD S, Asst for AE, 1946, 471.6 A-Bomb, Box 4, MMB, NA.
[2] Ltr, Brig Gen R. M. Ramey, Cmdr TG 1.5 (Prov), to Maj Gen C. E. LeMay, DCAS/R & D, Mar 29, 1946, RG 341, OPD S, Asst for AE, 1946, 471.6 A-Bomb, Box 4, MMB, NA.

the war did not indicate inertia or a lack of commitment; the agencies involved were simply marking time until the facts were in.

After the war the MANHATTAN PROJECT continued to be responsible for assembling the bomb and turning it over to an AAF loading crew at the combat base. It also provided the weaponeers to arm the bomb in flight. As the legislation emerged to create a civilian nuclear agency, it became clear that the MANHATTAN PROJECT or its successor would retain these functions. Groves prided himself on the rigor of the project's security program. His staff controlled and compartmentalized the data and approved security clearances.[3] With this level of institutional control, it would be difficult for the AAF to gain the kind of autonomy it sought.

In fact, the Air Staff found obtaining clearances to be a complicated process. A detailed justification had to accompany each request for a specific item of information, but the AAF often lacked the knowledge upon which to base the justification. And background investigations for clearances also proved time-consuming. As late as September 1946 a joint AAF-MANHATTAN PROJECT meeting could not complete its agenda because a few key participants had not yet been cleared.[4] A first step towards more cooperation occurred in early 1946 when Groves agreed to train six AAF colonels and five junior officers as weaponeers. These officers soon informed Ramey that, although they lacked confidence in the direction of their training, they were acquiring useful information. Ramey met with the future weaponeers and reported to LeMay: "[A]s you and I expected, those duties are not nearly so complicated as we have been told. As a matter of fact, I have made some little study of them myself and believe, in a pinch, I could tell whether the bomb was ready to go."[5]

Once Ramey had his units in place, planners began to consider how to organize the atomic strike force. On April 15, 1946, SAC representatives and Air Staff officers at the Pentagon started developing the general plan which would serve as the basis for tables of organization and equipment,

---

[3] See Note 1; Groves, *Now It Can Be Told*, pp 140–145.

[4] Memo, Maj Gen L. R. Groves, OIC Manhattan Proj, to CG AAF, subj: Coordination of Security Matters Arising from AAF Participation in Atomic Energy Program, May 25, 1946, RG 341, OPD S, Asst for AE, 1946, 380.01 Security Pol, Box 4; rprt, Col J. G. Armstrong, Chmn Ad Hoc Plng Cmte, Army Air Forces-Manhattan Project Coordination of Effort, Nov 5, 1946, RG 341, DCS/Ops S, Asst for AE, 1947, 334 Cmte of AE, Box 7; MR, Col E. J. Rogers, Jr, Ch Pol Div ACAS-5 (Pl), subj: Coordination of Information on Atomic Bomb, Sep 3, 1946, RG 341, DCS/Ops, OPD, 384.3 Atomic (Aug 17, 1945), Sect 6, Box 449, all in MMB, NA.

[5] See Note 2.

manning programs, and deployment plans. The conference defined the purpose of the atomic force:

> Consistent with our national policy it is unlikely that we will attack any nation until we have first been attacked. In such an event, we must have available a unit trained and capable of immediate retaliation against the aggressor nation with our most destructive weapon to effect as much or more destruction than we experienced.[6]

According to the basic plan, the 58th Wing would have 108 atomic-capable bombers in nine squadrons. Additional transport aircraft were needed to carry the bombs and technical equipment to the forward base from which the atomic attack would be launched. Once deployed, an ordnance company would be responsible for assembling the bombs. Personnel requirements involved training over one hundred bomber crews, including weaponeers, for both atomic and conventional bombing. The conferees further recommended giving the wing a manning priority second only to the occupation forces overseas. Because the bomber groups would be expected to deploy rapidly, the appropriate overseas bases needed to be stocked ahead of time.[7] On June 13 LeMay issued a mission statement for the 58th Wing—"and other wings to follow...." The 58th was

> to be capable of immediate and sustained VLR [very long range] offensive operations in any part of the world, either independently or in cooperation with land and naval forces, utilizing the latest and most advanced weapons.[8]

Meanwhile, the Air Staff was working on a plan for security. The AAF had received recommendations from Groves, and adopted most of them on June 27, 1946, in the hope that cooperation might improve the flow of information.[9] But any further action would have to wait, because by this time Ramey and much of his command were in the Pacific participating in the atomic tests at Bikini Atoll in the Marshall Islands.

---

[6] Memo, Maj Gen E. E. Partridge, ACAS–3 (Ops), to CAS, subj: Conference of Reorganization of the 58th Wing, Apr 26, 1946, with encl, Organization and Deployment of the 58th Bombardment Wing, RG 341, DCS/Ops, OPD S, Asst for AE, 1946, 008 Policy, Box 2, MMB, NA.

[7] *Ibid.*

[8] Ltr, Maj Gen C. E. LeMay, DCAS/R & D, to CG SAC, subj: Mission of the 58th Bombardment Wing, Jun 13, 1946, in hist, SAC, 1946, Ex 13.

[9] AAF Ltr 46–22, subj: Security Plan for AAF Participation in Atomic Energy Program, Jun 27, 1946, RG 341, DCS/Ops, OPD TS, Asst for AE, 1947, 380.01 Security Pol, Box 4, MMB, NA.

Strategic Air Force

The basic concept for the Bikini tests, codenamed OPERATION CROSSROADS, dated back to September 1945. The Navy took a keen interest from the start, for a major objective was to determine the bomb's effect on ships. The targets were to included the remnants of the Japanese navy. Plans called for three shots: an air burst and two underwater detonations, one at great depth. The AAF would drop the weapon for the air burst and also provide a wide variety of other support.[10]

President Truman approved the plan for the test on January 10, 1946, and the next day Vice Adm. William H. P. Blandy became commander of the testing organization, Joint Task Force 1. Maj. Gen. William E. Kepner, the former Eighth Air Force fighter commander, was Blandy's Deputy for Army and Navy Aviation. Ramey commanded the AAF element assigned to the force, known as Task Group 1.5. To Ramey fell the responsibility for major aspects of CROSSROADS: air transport for the test, drone aircraft to test weapons effects, aerial photography, and collection of air samples. Task Force 1.5 would also drop the bomb in the first test, shot ABLE.[11]

The AAF leadership hoped to gain practical experience and some favorable publicity in CROSSROADS. Though the experience proved beneficial, the task force encountered many operational problems which led to some unfortunate publicity. The key issue was accuracy. The very name of the test bomb—FAT MAN—suggested the awkward egg shape that gave it questionable aerodynamic properties. An accurate drop would require careful planning, close calculations, and rigorous training. Despite the determined efforts of the 509th Composite Group, the end result proved frustrating.

The 509th, based at Roswell, New Mexico, began training flights in February 1946, dropping facsimiles of the weapon on a range near Albuquerque. It became evident that new bombing tables were needed. The tables in use—giving the proper bombsight settings for different altitudes and aircraft speeds—had been designed during wartime for the climate of Japan. The officer who had prepared them, Capt. David Semple, had since left the MANHATTAN PROJECT to become a bombardier in the 509th. He developed new tables, but not without a direct request from LeMay to Groves for the data on the Marshall Islands. In the meantime, on March 7, Semple was killed in a B–29 crash. He had not been flying with his regular crew at the time, so the pilot, Maj. Woodrow P. Swancutt, replaced him

---

[10] Msg, CG USASTAF to CG AAF, 4840, 140730 Sep 1945, subj: Use [*sic*] Atomic Bombs in Destruction Remnants Japanese Fleet, RG 341, DCS/Ops, OPD TS, Asst for AE, 1945, 373 Crossroads, Box 2, MMB, NA; Bowen, *Silverplate*, pp 161–167.

[11] Bowen, *Silverplate*, pp 164, 236–238.

Uncertain Phase

Clockwise from above: **Vice Adm. William H. P. Blandy, leader of Joint Task Force 1; Maj. Gen. William E. Kepner, task force Deputy for Army and Navy Aviation; and Maj. Gen. Roger M. Ramey, leader of AAF Task Group 1.5.**

with Maj. Harold E. Wood. The crew dubbed their plane *Dave's Dream* in honor of their former bombardier.[12]

By the time the crews reached the CROSSROADS base at Kwajalein Island, the new bombing tables were finally available. Well-trained and prepared, the airmen anticipated a good drop on the test day. After a number of practice missions, airmen began to expect that on ABLE Day the bomb would land within 500 feet of the aiming point, the battleship USS *Nevada*. On June 15 Swancutt learned that his crew would make the drop. In a dry run on July 24 the bomb landed within 400 feet of the *Nevada*.[13] This was encouraging, but another requirement involved calculating the effect of wind on the fall of the bomb, so as to allow for corrections before

---

[12] *Ibid.*, pp 258–277.
[13] *Ibid.*, pp 258–282.

the actual drop. Unfortunately, the forecast for ABLE Day did not have accurate readings for the winds, and Major Wood would have to rely on his own judgment. Thus in some uncertainty *Dave's Dream* took off on the morning of July 1.[14]

The B-29 reached its position over the target area at 30,000 feet on schedule, and just before 0900 local time Wood released the weapon. The burst of the bomb shrouded the target array in smoke. But when it began to clear, the *Nevada* was still afloat. The shot appeared to have failed.[15] The co-pilot of a Navy plane observing the test expressed the view of many: "Well, it looks to me like the atom bomb is just like the Army Air Force [*sic*]—highly over-rated."[16] In fact, however, though only three ships sank, closer examination revealed heavy damage. Had the ships within a mile or so of the blast been manned, the heat and radiation would have killed or incapacitated the crews.[17]

Still, speculation began at once that the bomb had missed the aiming point. On July 2 one observer described "a bad error left and short" of the target (relative to the path of the bomber).[18] Two days later Kepner ordered an investigation, which revealed that the bomb had detonated 2,000 feet from the target, though the altitude of the burst, 550 feet, had been correct. Why was the bomb that far from the aiming point? A subsequent series of investigations never fully answered the question. While Wood may have been nervous, the AAF firmly rejected any suggestion of error on the part of the crew. Brig. Gen. Thomas S. Power, Kepner's Assistant Deputy Commander, noted that the bombsight could have malfunctioned or the bomb had fallen erratically.[19] LeMay soon directed a study of the photographs and tests with the same airplane at Albuquerque. Ruling out a faulty bombsight, the report concluded that "some unusual force affected the bomb causing it to veer off in an

---

[14] *Ibid.*, pp 282-282.
[15] *Ibid.*, pp 285-286, 289-290.
[16] Quoted in David Bradley, *No Place to Hide* (Boston: Little, Brown, 1948), p 58.
[17] Bowen, *Silverplate*, pp 299-313.
[18] *Ibid.*, p 300.
[19] *Ibid.*; ltr, Col H. G. Montgomery, Col J. J. Preston, R. Dorfman to Maj Gen C. E. LeMay, DCAS/R & D, subj: Bombing Analysis, Aug 1, 1946; ltr, Brig Gen T. S. Power, Asst Dep Cmdr Avn, JTF-1, to Maj Gen W. E. Kepner, Dep Cmdr Avn, JTF-1, subj: Analysis of Able Day Bombing, Jul 11, 1946, both in RG 341, DCS/Ops, OPD TS, Asst for AE, 1946, 384.3 Bombing Analysis, Box 2, MMB, NA.

unpredictable manner, giving a point of impact somewhere left and short of the theoretical one."[20]

The report was explicit about the implications of such a finding, recommending that the design of the bomb be changed to improve its ballistics. The historian of the Joint Task Force challenged the objectivity of the AAF study, but Kepner refuted the argument. The Army ran some tests of its own at Muroc Field, California, with inconclusive results. Neither the MANHATTAN District nor the Atomic Energy Commission acknowledged a faulty design, but the commission later cited improved ballistics as one of its goals in weapon design. Thus the AAF received some unspoken support for its strongly held view that the design needed improvement.[21]

The Bikini tests concluded on July 25 with shot BAKER, in which the bomb was suspended one hundred feet under water. Air units otherwise provided the same support as in the previous shot. The blast and heat were in fact less than in the previous test, and the radiation less strong, but the radioactive water thrown up contaminated everything it touched. With such a small stockpile of weapons, nine before ABLE shot, the amount of data a third shot would yield did not seem to justify expending precious resources, and test CHARLIE was canceled.[22]

In a test of the scale of CROSSROADS, with forty thousand personnel, the numerous reports—on every topic from bomber operations to the detection of atomic explosions and the scientific results—were the true justification for the undertaking. The joint chiefs appointed a panel of distinguished citizens to evaluate the tests and submit a thorough report. The chairman was Karl T. Compton, President of the Massachusetts Institute of Technology (MIT) and a leading organizer of scientific work during the war. Among the members was Lt. Gen. Lewis H. Brereton of

---

[20] Ltr, Maj Gen W. E. Kepner, Dep Cmdr Avn, JTF-1, to CG AAF, subj: Analysis of Able Day Bombing, Jul 11, 1946, RG 341, DCS/Ops, OPD TS, Asst for AE, 1946, 384.3 Bombing Analysis, Box 2, MMD, NA; Bowen, *Silverplate*, pp 307-311.

[21] Bowen, *Silverplate*, pp 311-313; R. D. Little, *Foundations of an Atomic Air Force and Operation Sandstone, 1946-1948*, Vol II in Bowen, Little, et al, *A History of the Air Force Atomic Energy Program, 1943-1953*, Pt II, pp 472-478.

[22] Bowen, *Silverplate*, pp 321-333; msg, JCS Eval Bd Atomic Test to JCS, 300558Z Jul 46, subj: Preliminary Report following Second Atomic Bomb Test, RG 341, TS AAG File 25, Box 8, MMB, NA; Hewlett & Anderson, *New World*, p 580; ltr, J. M. Holl, Hist Dept Energy, to J. R. [sic] Bohn, Hist SAC, no subj [classification of data], Mar 22, 1982, with encl, SAC/HO.

the AAF.[23] The Evaluation Board, as the Compton group was called, submitted its final report after nearly a year of effort.

In the meantime, however, the 509th found that its operations against Japan and involvement in the Bikini test had familiarized it with the basic requirements of its mission. By September the group's commander, Col. William H. Blanchard, could recommend that the unit was ready to begin serious training.[24] Blanchard and his staff recognized that more research was needed on radiological safety, and that there had been no multiple-strike atomic operations. Still, the broad outlines now existed for designing an atomic bombing mission. In fact much of the work and many of the techniques differed little from a conventional unit. There were specialized considerations, to be sure. The pilot had to understand how the heavy bomb affected the plane's center of gravity, and the bombardier had to deal with the challenge of dropping the FAT MAN accurately. The breakaway maneuver demanded more from the entire crew. In addition, there were two special crew positions in the atomic force, the bomb commander and the weaponeer. The former was usually a colonel, responsible for coordinating bomb assembly and delivering the bomb at the loading site. The bomb commander also supervised the weaponeer and certified the bomb as ready. The weaponeer in turn armed the bomb.[25]

The training of atomic officers received special attention at a meeting in September 1946 between representatives of the MANHATTAN District and AAF planners. The general concept called for bomb commanders to be colonels assigned to atomic units or key staff positions following a short course. Weaponeers would be younger officers and receive more technical training.[26] Although Groves had trained AAF officers before, he adopted a new emphasis, establishing the 2761st Engineer Battalion (Special) at Sandia, New Mexico, and assembling twenty-seven promising young engineer officers to train as weaponeers. He evidently intended to create a pool of these officers to assign for specific missions. The battalion itself would also be responsible for assembling the bombs. Determined to

---

[23] Bowen, *Silverplate*, pp 281–282; rprt, JCS 1691/10, Proposed Release of an Extracted Version of the Final Report of the JCS Evaluation Board on Operation Crossroads and the Related Proposed Press Release, Dec 29, 1947, RG 341, DCS/Ops, OPD TS, 384.3 (Aug 17, 1945), Sect 9, Box 450.

[24] Rprt, 509 BG, Atom Bombing with B–29s, n.d. [Aug 46], in hist, SAC, 1946, Ex 47; ltr, Col W. H. Blanchard, CO 509 BG, to Maj Gen C. E. LeMay, DCAS/R & D, Sep 24, 1946, RG 341, DCS/Ops, OPD S, Asst for AE, 1946, 353 Bomb Cmdrs & Weaponeers Tng, Box 3, MMB, NA.

[25] Rprt, 509 BG, Atom Bombing with B–29s, n.d. [Aug 46], in hist, SAC, 1946, Ex 47.

[26] MR, Col E. J. Rogers, Jr, Ch Pol Div ACAS–5 (Pl), subj: Coordination of Information on Atomic Bomb, Sep 3, 1946, RG 341, DCS/Ops, OPD, 384.3 Atomic (Aug 17, 1945), Sect 6, Box 449, MMB, NA.

increase its atomic role, the AAF insisted that weaponeers be air officers and full members of the air crew. Norstad, now Director of the War Department's Plans and Operations Division, believed that the engineer officers as a group were better qualified technically than the possible AAF candidates, but he conceded that the argument for a close link between the weaponeer and the air crew was a point in the AAF's favor. These essential issues would require compromise.[27] As Brig. Gen. George A. Lincoln, Norstad's Chief of Plans and Policy, wrote: "I do not consider it makes any particle of difference whether the weaponier [sic] wears wings or engineer castles or running shorts...."[28] General Spaatz saw no point in objecting to Groves' training his Army engineers, but the MANHATTAN District should *also* train air officers, and the AAF would try and recruit the engineer officers as well.[29]

In November the Air Staff finally reached an agreement with the MANHATTAN District. The training schedule would provide bomb crews as the B-29s being modified for SILVERPLATE became available. The district would train thirty AAF officers in a three-week course for bomb commanders. The twenty-four-week weaponeers' course was to produce forty-five AAF officers, and the engineer officers in the course were required to become familiar with B-29 operations. The AAF would offer jobs to them, but Groves insisted on making it clear that no engineer with the MANHATTAN District was obligated to transfer to the Army Air Forces. Finally, and most significantly, the two agencies agreed that weaponeers should normally be AAF officers. The schedule of courses devised under the agreement ran through 1947.[30]

---

[27] Memo, Brig Gen G. A. Lincoln, Ch Pl & Pol Gp, P & O, War Dept, to Col C. E. Combs, P & O, War Dept, Oct 15, 1946; memo, Lincoln to Maj Gen L. Norstad, Dir P & O, War Dept, Oct 16, 1946, both in NA 341, DCS/Ops, OPD, 353 (Oct 15, 1946), Box 250, MMB, NA; Little, *Foundations*, Pt I, pp 87–88.

[28] Memo, Brig Gen G. A. Lincoln, Ch Pl & Pol Gp, P & O, War Dept, to Maj Gen L. Norstad, Dir P & O, War Dept, Oct 16, 1946, in RG 341, DCS/Ops, OPD, 353 (Oct 15, 1946), Box 250, MMB, NA.

[29] Memo, Col E. L. Sykes to Brig Gen W. L. Ritchie, Ch WPD ACAS-5 (Pl), Oct 25, 1946, RG 341, DCS/Ops, OPD, 353 (Oct 15, 1946), Box 250, MMB, NA.

[30] DF, Maj Gen C. E. LeMay, DCAS/R & D, to Maj Gen L. Norstad, Dir P & O, War Dept, Training of Bomb Commanders and Weaponeers, Nov 18, 1946, with encl MR, Col J. G. Armstrong, Nov 14, 1946, and Cmt 3, Maj Gen L. R. Groves, OIC Manhattan Proj, to Col J. McCormack, P & O, War Dept, Dec 10, 1946; MR, Armstrong, subj: Training of Weaponeers, Nov 20, 1946; ltr, Col D. Canterbury, DCAS/R & D, to CG Manhattan Proj, subj: Training of Bomb Commanders and Weaponeers, Nov 25, 1946, all in RG 341, DCS/Ops, OPD TS, Asst for AE, 1946, 353 Weaponeer Tng, Box 2, MMB, NA; memo, Col W. M. Garland, Dep ACAS-3 (Pl/Tng), to Brig Gen A. W. Kissner, Dep ACAS-5 (Pl), subj: Requirements for AAF A-Bomb Commander and Weaponeer Training, Oct 25, 1946, RG 341, DCS/Ops, OPD, 353 (Oct 15, 1946), Box 250, MMB, NA.

Overshadowing these discussions was the impending dissolution of the MANHATTAN PROJECT. The Atomic Energy Commission would assume most of the project's functions, and the armed services were wrestling with the problem of how to absorb the rest. In the fall of 1946 Brereton became Chairman of the AEC Military Liaison Committee. The commission insisted on acquiring the Z Division of the MANHATTAN District, which built the bombs at Los Alamos. Everything the services retained became the Armed Forces Special Weapons Project (AFSWP), directed by the Chief of Staff of the Army and the Chief of Naval Operations. Rather than combine support and operational forces under the Special Weapons Project, as Groves recommended, Norstad and the Plans and Operations Division advocated confining the project to a support role, with AAF retaining the operational units. The Special Weapons Project would be responsible mainly for special training, coordination with the AEC on weapons development, and radiological safety. At the end of 1946 the issues of custody, assembly, and delivery of bombs remained unresolved. Groves was named Chief of the Special Weapons Project as well as a member of the Military Liaison Committee.[31]

Even before the establishment of the Special Weapons Project, the Air Staff had favored maintaining its own liaison arrangements. In September there was a proposal to establish a tactical and technical liaison committee to represent the AAF in its dealings with the atomic agencies. Two months later a committee chaired by Col. John G. Armstrong of Partridge's Operations staff submitted a report that supported the proposal and suggested an internal realignment of responsibility for atomic matters. LeMay's charter now seemed narrow, since the atomic bomb was no longer simply an experimental weapon. The Armstrong committee further proposed the appointment of an assistant to the Commanding General of the AAF with overall coordinating powers.[32] Reviewing the recommendations, Spaatz supported the idea of a tactical and technical liaison committee, and LeMay approached Groves about setting it up. As for the question of internal organization, Spaatz decided that LeMay would remain the AAF's principal coordinator of atomic matters as well as the Chief of Research and Development.[33]

---

[31] Little, *Foundations*, Pt I, pp 20–28, 48–56, 77–87.
[32] See Note 26 above; rprt, Col J. G. Armstrong, Chmn Ad Hoc Plng Cmte, Army Air Forces-Manhattan Project Coordination of Effort, Nov 5, 1946, RG 341, DCS/Ops S, Asst for AE, 1947, 334 Cmte on AE, Box 7, MMB, NA.
[33] Ltr, Maj Gen C. E. LeMay, DCAS/R & D, to CG Manhattan Proj, subj: Army Air Forces Liaison with Manhattan Project, Oct 28, 1946, RG 341, DCS/Ops, OPD S, Asst for AE, 1946, 312.1 Manhattan District, Box 2; R & R Sheet, Cmt 1, Brig Gen R. C. Hood, DCAS, to DCAS/R & D, AAF Participation in the Atomic Bomb Program, Dec 24, 1946, RG 341, DCS/Ops, OPD TS, Asst for AE, 1947, 334 Bds, Commissions & Cmtes, Box 3, both in MMB, NA.

Uncertain Phase

The Armstrong Committee also hoped to develop a new approach to the problem of secrecy. It suggested dividing atomic information into several categories and clearing individuals for each specific category. These would range from high level planning factors to operational data and technical material. At the same time, the Air Staff was exploiting the new organizational structure to gain more access to classified information. This was especially important because secrecy could be detrimental to efficient operations. For example, some of the equipment used in loading the bomb was so highly classified that it was available to only a few men in the Eighth Air Force, who had been cleared with great difficulty by a backlogged Federal Bureau of Investigation.[34]

Under the reorganization of SAC late in 1946, the Eighth Air Force succeeded the 58th Bombardment Wing as the three-group "atomic" force, with headquarters at Fort Worth. The new organization was understandably frustrated by the shortage of atomic-capable aircraft. Of the forty-six aircraft modified in PROJECT SILVERPLATE, only twenty-three remained in service by late 1946. Four had been lost to crashes or fires, and the rest had been stripped of their special equipment and either stored or assigned to museums. Fewer than twenty belonged to the 509th Group, while several were used at Kirtland for flight testing.[35] In July 1946 the AAF had begun modification of another twenty-five aircraft, the work to be done at the Sacramento Air Materiel Area. In the course of this ultra-secret project, so full of improvisation, there had been no standard design. All the various changes made each SILVERPLATE airplane unique. Maj. Robert L. Roark of the Materiel Center at Wright Field, Ohio, had years of experience with the project, and late in 1946 he prepared a manual for a standard modification. In December the first B–29 under the new standard came off the line. Though the number to be modified had been reduced to nineteen, enough planes would now be available to equip a full combat group of thirty B–29s and provide a few for the other groups of the Eighth.[36]

---

[34] Rprt, Col J. G. Armstrong, Chmn Ad Hoc Plng Cmte, Army Air Forces-Manhattan Project Coordination of Effort, Nov 5, 1946, NA 341, DCS/Ops S, Asst for AE, 1947, 334 Cmte on AE, Box 7; memo, Maj Gen C. E. LeMay, DCAS/R & D, to Lt Gen L. H. Brereton, Chmn MLC, subj: Declassification of Certain Material Which Affects the Training of Army Air Forces Tactical Units, Jan 9, 1947, with encls, RG 341, DCS/Ops, OPD TS, Asst for AE, 1947, 380.01, both in MMB, NA.

[35] R & R Sheet, Cmt 2, Col K. H. Gibson, ACAS–3 (Ops), to Spec Asst to ACAS–3 (Ops), Silverplate Airplanes, Jan 24, 1947, RG 341, DCS/Ops, OPD S, Asst for AE, 1947, 452.01 Mod of Saddle Tree and Silverplate, Box 9, MMB, NA.

[36] Bowen, *Silverplate*, pp 362–364.

Strategic Air Force

The leisurely pace of PROJECT SILVERPLATE could be attributed to a number of factors, including the scarcity of bombs, the persistent difficulties in handling the weapon, and the secrecy surrounding manufacture and operations. Not all these problems were the direct responsibility of the AAF. At the end of 1946 the MANHATTAN District, nearing its own demobilization, apparently still possessed only nine bombs, not all fully assembled.[37] The time-consuming tasks of assembling and loading the weapon had changed little since the days at Tinian. Once ready, the bomb had to be moved on a cart and unloaded into a pit, over which the airplane was parked. The weapon would then be hoisted into the bomb bay, secured, and connected with the electrical circuits used to test it and control its release. Security required that most personnel be kept away during the process and that any modifications be conducted with the highest secrecy. Largely because of security considerations, four thousand man-hours were expended on the B–29 modifications, and estimates for the B–36 conversion totaled eight thousand.[38]

The AAF had built its case on the assumption that for the foreseeable future the atomic weapon would remain scarce. The bomb would be a strategic weapon that the military could not afford to expend on troops or warships. For this reason, it belonged in the hands of the strategic air forces. On the other hand, some planners speculated that bombs might soon become available in greater numbers. The Joint Research and Development Board, for example, discussed the implications of manufacturing three thousand atomic bombs, and Brig. Gen. George A. Lincoln, Chief of the Plans and Policy Group of the War Department Plans and Operations Division, urged that atomic weapons be considered for a tactical role.[39] But it would be years before such a program could start. The breakup of the wartime scientific and technical staff at Los Alamos had nearly stopped bomb production. The fledgling Atomic Energy Commision would have to start over. By June 1947 the commission's stock of bombs totalled only thirteen. After some debate early in 1947, the commission assumed legal custody of the bombs, although the Armed Forces Special Weapons Project, soon to be under Groves's command, guarded

---

[37] Ltr, J. M. Holl, Hist Dept Energy, to J. R [sic] Bohn, Hist SAC, Mar 22, 1982, with encl, SAC/HO.

[38] Little, *Foundations*, Pt 2, pp 415–428; draft ltr, Dir R & E ACAS–4 (Mat), to Chmn MLC, subj: Modification of Aircraft to Fake the A-Bomb, Aug 11, 1947, RG 341, DCS/Ops, OPD S, Asst for AE, 1947, 452 Acft, Fighter, Bombardment, Etc, Box 9, MMB, NA.

[39] Memo, Brig Gen G. A. Lincoln, Ch Pl & Pol Gp, P & O Div WDGS, to Brig Gen A. W. Kissner, Dep ACAS–5 (Pl), Jan 19, 1947, RG 341, DCS/Ops, OPD TS, Asst for AE, 1947, 373 Crossroads, Box 4, MMB, NA.

and maintained them. Only by order of the President could a military organization take custody of the weapons. The President also determined the number of bombs and the amount of fissionable material to be produced. In February 1947 the Joint Strategic Survey Committee studied the armed forces' needs and concluded that it would be years before they could be met at the rates of production currently feasible. Supporting this position, the joint chiefs advocated making national defense virtually the sole objective of the AEC. In April the War and Navy Departments and the AEC agreed on a production program for fiscal 1948. They submitted the program to President Truman, gave him the disturbing facts about the small stockpile, and obtained his approval on April 16. The AEC also began studying possible design improvements and scheduled a test for the summer of 1948.[40]

As the AEC's main customer, the AAF wanted to deal with the commission as closely as possible, especially to overcome obstacles to the delivery, assembly, and transfer of bombs. But the Special Weapons Project at Sandia, New Mexico, would intervene frequently in these dealings under Groves and his deputy, the weaponeer of the *Enola Gay*, now Rear Admiral, William S. Parsons.[41] In February, a study by an ad hoc committee of the Air Staff asserted that "The AAF has the paramount military interest in the Atomic Energy Program," yet concluded that the air arm had no clear role. The committee proposed that the AAF's representation on the Military Liaison Committee and the Special Weapons Project be increased and further, that Maj. Gen. William E. Kepner, who had run the air operation at Bikini, replace Groves. LeMay passed these recommendations on to General Spaatz, along with a draft order making atomic energy the AAF's number one priority. For the time being, however, the commanding general took no action.[42]

---

[40] Hewlett & Duncan, *Atomic Shield, 1947-1952*, Vol II of *A History of the United States Atomic Energy Commission* (University Pk, Pa: 1969 [new imprint, Washington: U.S. Atomic Energy Commission, 1972]), pp 65-66, 136-137; Schnabel, *JCS, 1945-1947*, pp 290-295; Little, *Foundations*, Pt 2, pp 472-480; ltr, J. M. Holl, Hist Dept Energy, to J. R. [*sic*] Bohn, Hist SAC, no subj [classification of data], Mar 22, 1982, in SAC/HO.

[41] Little, *Foundations*, Pt 1, pp 81-84.

[42] R & R Sheet, Cmt 1, Lt Gen I. C. Eaker, Dep Cmdr AAF, to Maj Gen C. E. LeMay, DCAS/R & D, AAF Participation in the Atomic Energy Program, Feb 25, 1947, with notes & atch memo, LeMay to Gen C. A. Spaatz, CG AAF, same subj, Feb 21, 1947, with atch Report of Ad Hoc Committee, Feb 21, 1947, RG 341, DCS/Ops, OPD TS, Asst for AE, 1947, 360.2 AAF Participation in AE Prog, Box 4, MMB, NA.

Strategic Air Force

The AAF's existing channel with Los Alamos was through the Tactical and Technical Liaison Committee (T & TLC) at Kirtland Field, New Mexico, and the Air Materiel Command. The Chairman of the T & TLC, Col. Howard G. Bunker, reported that tension between the AEC element at Sandia and the Special Weapons Project offered him an opportunity to build closer ties with the civilian agency. Bunker's committee would need a firm charter to protect it from interference from the Special Weapons Project. This news could not have been a surprise in Washington, where ill-will was growing between Groves and David E. Lilienthal, the AEC Chairman. Indeed, at Sandia the AAF representatives "tended to think of themselves as an innocent third party caught in the crossfire between the civilian scientists [the AEC] and the Army [the Special Weapons Project]."[43] Groves was quoted as predicting that the AEC would be unable to handle its job, and the Army would have to take it over again. In any case, LeMay and Groves's staff worked out a charter for the T & TLC in July. Unfortunately for the AAF, the Special Weapons Project would retain its role in supervising the committee.[44]

Although Spaatz hesitated to declare the atomic program the AAF's first priority, he did agree to expand the program at the Air Staff level, appointing Kepner Chief of the Atomic Energy Division under LeMay on July 30, 1947. This was an interim arrangement pending the reorganization of the Air Force headquarters.[45] Ultimately, the creation of the independent Air Force offered more opportunity for equality in joint organizations such as the Military Liaison Committee as well as the best hope for a larger share of the atomic mission.

In the meantime, the military and the Atomic Energy Commission began to cooperate to solve some operational problems. The Atomic Energy Act gave the AEC the authority to define restricted data, that is to say, classified information about atomic weapons. If any equipment on SILVERPLATE aircraft remained restricted data, all mechanics who went near them had to be individually cleared, and this involved a time-consuming check by the FBI. When 8,500 men of the Eighth Air Force needed such clearances, the magnitude of the problem became evident. With support from the Military Liaison Committee, the AAF was able to

---

[43] Hewlett & Duncan, *Atomic Shield, 1947–1952*, p 139.
[44] Ltr, Col H. G. Bunker, Chmn T & TLC, to Col J. G. Armstrong, DCAS/R & D, subj: AAF Participation in AFSWP and AEC Activities, Jun 25, 1947, RG 341, DCS/Ops, OPD S, Asst for AE, 1947, 353 Bomb Cmdrs & Weaponeers, Box 8, MMB, NA; Lilienthal, *Journals*, pp 12, 136, 203, 236, 247–252.
[45] Memo, Maj Gen C. E. LeMay, DCAS/R & D, to Gen C. A. Spaatz, CG AAF, subj: Air Force Participation in the Atomic Energy Program, Aug 6, 1947, RG 341, DCS/Ops, OPD S, Asst For AE, 1947, 360.2 AAF Participation in AE Prog, Box 8, MMB, NA.

negotiate a compromise during the summer and fall of 1947. Restrictions were removed from all but a few easily-removable items. Major Roark also helped by devising a simple method to remove critical items from the aircraft during routine maintenance.[46]

Although Lilienthal was impressed with the AAF's willingness to widen access to atomic information, in contrast to Groves, the Atomic Energy Commission remained firm. It could not allow the War Department do its own background investigations for security clearances. An interagency panel under the auspices of the Military Liaison Committee supported the commission's position, but the AAF still hoped to overcome this obstacle and eliminate the backlog.[47]

Another unresolved issue directly affected SAC's operational readiness: the training of atomic personnel. The AAF continued to depend on the Special Weapons Project to supply trained bomb commanders and weaponeers as well as assembly teams. Late in 1947 only two assembly teams existed. The T & TLC estimated that, once a bomb was ferried to a combat base, it would take sixty hours to have it loaded in a B–29 and ready to go, and that more than a day would be required to assemble and load each additional bomb. Planners speculated that bombs could either be assembled fully at a rear base and ferried forward or partially assembled and then completed at the forward base. Further complicating the process, neither the Special Weapons Project nor the AEC had conducted training in the procedures for turning bombs over to the 509th.[48]

According to Air Staff calculations, the AAF needed about 200 weaponeers and 180 bomb commanders to man the strategic air force. The Special Weapons Project's program to train these specialists continued during 1947, but in August Groves canceled the bomb commanders' course on the grounds that the original quota had been met. When LeMay objected and submitted an AAF requirement to train another 114, the Chief of the Special Weapons Project announced that such a large number would endanger security. Groves and LeMay subsequently reached a compromise: the project would conduct a short orientation course for staff officers and resume training of bomb commanders for the atomic

---

[46] Memo, Lt Gen L. H. Brereton, Chmn MLC, to Secs War, Navy, subj: Recommendation for Declassification of Special Modifications for Atomic Bomb Carrying Aircraft, Jan 14, 1947; ltr, Lt Gen L. H. Brereton, Chmn MLC, to Secs War, Navy, subj: Declassification of Special Modifications for Atomic Bomb Carrying Aircraft, May 15, 1947, both in RG 341, DCS/Ops, OPD S, Asst for AE, 1947, 452.01 Mod of Saddle Tree and Silver Plate, Box 9, MMB, NA; Little, *Foundations*, Pt 2, p 392.

[47] Lilienthal, *Journals*, p 185; Little, *Foundations*, Pt 2, pp 415–428.

[48] Little, *Foundations*, Pt 2, pp 521–527.

squadrons. On the other hand, the course for weaponeers fell behind schedule because of the difficulty of finding qualified people.[49]

Lack of information also impeded the development of new bombers to carry the atomic bomb. The B–45 four-engine jet, under order for use as a light bomber, had been modified to carry the weapon, but the design had been incorrect, based on faulty data, and further modification was needed. In May of 1946 the Air Materiel Command had studied the whole problem of which aircraft could accommodate the atomic weapon. Some bombers, such as the B–50 and the Flying Wing, might lose range and speed when loaded with the weapon. On the other hand, the giant B–36 could easily carry several bombs, and the XB–47 looked promising if the bomb bay door were modified. In November 1946 the Assistant Chief of Air Staff for Materiel directed that the B–52 and all subsequent bombers be designed from the beginning to accommodate the bomb. Earlier types would be modified after production if the work was not too costly and performance did not seriously suffer. By the end of 1947 the AAF had a schedule for modifying existing B–36s and B–50s. This plan would give the AAF six atomic groups by 1949: three of B–36s, two of B–50s, and one of B–29s. At that point, no more B–29s would be modified. Work would be speeded up if depots besides Sacramento could be cleared to do it.[50]

Meanwhile, in May 1947 the modification program changed its name. SILVERPLATE had never been an official codeword but rather an informal nickname that was used widely and with some confusion. At times SILVERPLATE had referred to the 509th Group, the modification of the aircraft, the AAF atomic energy program, or even the entire national atomic effort. Suspecting that the term had become too well known, the Air Staff gave the name SADDLETREE to the modification project.[51]

---

[49] *Ibid.*, Pt 1, pp 357–369; memo, Col W. M. Garland, Dep ACAS–3 (Ops/Tng), to Brig Gen A. W. Kissner, Dep ACAS–5 (Pl), subj: Requirements for AAF A-Bomb Commander and Weaponeer Training, Oct 25, 1946, RG 341, DCS/Ops, OPD, 353 (Oct 15, 1946), Box 250; MR, Col J. G. Armstrong, Asst Ch AE Div, Training of Air Force Personnel by AFSWP, Aug 21, 1947, NA 341, DCS/Ops, OPD TS, Asst for AE, 1947, 353 Weaponeer Tng, Box 3, both in MMB, NA.

[50] Memo, Col W. M. Garland, Dep ACAS–3 (Ops/Tng), to Brig Gen A. W. Kissner, Dep ACAS–5 (Pl), subj: Requirements for AAF A-Bomb Commander and Weaponeer Training, Oct 25, 1946, RG 341, DCS/Ops, OPD, 353 (Oct 15, 1946), Box 250; rprt, Planning Factors for Atomic Bomb Requirements, n.d. [late 47], RG 341, DCS/Ops, OPD TS, Asst for AE, 1947, 471.6 Outline of Plng Factors for A-Bomb, Box 4, both in MMB, NA; Amy C. Fenwick, *History of Saddletree Project* (Wright-Patterson AFB, Ohio: AMC, 1953).

[51] Bowen, *Silverplate*, pp 366–367; Fenwick, *Saddletree Project*, with atch ltr S, Maj R. L. Roard, Eng Div AMC, to Col L. V. Harman, T & TLC, subj: Modification of B–50 Aircraft, May 6, 1947.

The AAF saw the gigantic six-engine Consolidated B–36 Peacemaker, *above*, as the principal deliverer of its long-range striking force in the decade following World War II. It dwarfed its contemporaries, like the B–29 shown next to it, *below*.

Strategic Air Force

As the AAF approached its incarnation as the independent U.S. Air Force, its atomic force amounted to little more than a single group, though modifications to the B-50 and B-36 would provide planes for the other two groups. To expedite development of the necessary equipment, the AAF continued to seek greater control over its relationship with the Atomic Energy Commission. In addition, its future status as a separate department might give the Air Force an advantage in its duel with the Special Weapons Project over the atomic weapon. However, despite the disagreements and organizational rivalries, circumstances would soon push all the principal groups, the Air Force, the Military Liaison Committee, the Special Weapons Project, and the Atomic Energy Commission, toward the most ambitious effort undertaken since the building of the bomb itself.

Command of Strategic Forces

The atomic force in SAC, though small in size, was clearly becoming one of the nation's major means for security. Meanwhile, the rest of the command was engaged in laying the groundwork for the day when all bomb units were atomic-capable. Until then, the B-29 force provided a capability to drop a substantial load of conventional bombs on a trouble spot anywhere in a large part of the world. But to employ SAC in a truly worldwide role would require establishing bases overseas. Questions naturally arose concerning the control of these bases as well as the nature of the forces operating from them.

Airmen tended to have a definite response to the issue of command structure. From the "GHQ Air Service Reserve" of 1918, through the GHQ Air Force, to the Twentieth Air Force and Spaatz's U.S. Strategic Air Forces in August 1945—various air organizations offered models of the approach that seemed most conducive to the effective command of strategic air force: a centrally controlled air striking force answering directly to the highest level of command.[52] On the other hand, one of the "lessons" of the Second World War was the need for unity of command in each theater. The division of command in the Pacific between General Douglas MacArthur and Admiral Chester W. Nimitz was often considered an unfortunate deviation from this principle. Likewise, although the Navy had accepted the creation of Twentieth Air Force during wartime, airmen doubted whether such agreement would be forthcoming in the future.

---

[52] See Chapter I.

Uncertain Phase

The Pacific remained a bone of contention between the Army and Navy even after the war, and during 1946 the chiefs staged a continuing debate over a plan for theater commands.[53] One of the crucial issues appeared to be the status of MacArthur in Japan.[54] Ironically during the Army-Navy disagreements, the leaders of the future independent Air Force began to formulate a concept of command structure that would further complicate the discussion.

Besides the Pacific theater, the Arctic frontier also posed a peculiar problem for command arrangements. Because of the increasing range of airplanes, AAF spokesmen foresaw the day when the polar icecap would no longer be an obstacle to attack, and air power would predominate in that region. Norstad suggested that the whole Arctic side of North America, from the Aleutians to Greenland, should be considered a single theater of war.[55] However, a more traditional view held that Alaska and the islands of the North Atlantic represented two different avenues along which the continent could be attacked or defended. As such, the JCS continued to think of Alaska and the North Atlantic as two separate theaters. No matter what the division, the AAF began to plan training for operations in the cold, ice, and long days and nights of the polar regions. In order to carry out its Arctic missions, the AAF would have to be involved in exploration and cold weather research. All, or at least two-thirds, of SAC's units would have to train in northern latitudes. Plans called for rotating units for summer training in Greenland as well as for year-round operations in Newfoundland and Alaska. As previously noted, the 28th Bomb Group went to Elmendorf in October, but a shift of funds prevented sending a unit to Newfoundland in 1946.[56]

There could be no doubt what command arrangements the Air Staff preferred for the Arctic forces. In September 1946 Brig. Gen. Thomas S.

---

[53] Schnabel, *JCS, 1945–1947*, pp 171–174.
[54] *Ibid.*, pp 173–181.
[55] Extract from Mins, JPS 240th Mtg, Tentative Over-all Strategic Concept and Estimate of Initial Operations, Short Title "Pincher," Jun 18, 1946, RG 341, DCS/Ops, OPD, 381 Russia "Pincher" (Mar 2, 1946), Box 949, MMB, NA.
[56] R & R Sheet, Cmt 1, Lt Gen I. C. Eaker, Dep Cmdr AAF, to ACAS–3 (Ops), Summer Maneuvers and Other Activities in Greenland, Apr 2, 1946, RG 341, TS AAG File 22, Box 7; R & R Sheet, Col A. P. Tacon, Jr, Theater Br ACAS–3 (Ops), to Allocation Br ACAS–3 (Ops), Cancellation of Plans for Deployment of the 307th VHB Gp to Newfoundland, Nov 15, 1946, RG 18, 1946–1947 AAG, 370 Deployment, Etc, Misc, Vol 2, Box 632; memo, Brig Gen T. S. Power, Dep ACAS–3 (Ops), to Gen C. A. Spaatz, CG AAF, subj: AAF Situation in Alaska, Sep 27, 1946, RG 341, TS AAG File 23, Box 7, all in MMB, NA.

Strategic Air Force

Power, Deputy Assistant Chief of Air Staff for Operations under Partridge, voiced the the AAF's position. VHB units in Alaska should report directly to the Commanding General of SAC, receiving administrative support from the theater headquarters.[57] In November General Spaatz proposed this structure for both Alaska and the proposed Northeast Command (Newfoundland, Labrador, and Greenland) before the Joint Chiefs of Staff. Responding to objections from Nimitz, the AAF chief argued that with long range bombers a theater became merely a staging base for strategic forces headquartered in the United States. The Navy chief then pointed out that this gave the joint chiefs an interest in the operations of forces in the continental United States, an argument that Spaatz accepted. The air chief further proposed that he be appointed the executive agent for the JCS to operate SAC. To settle the matter Norstad, representing the War Department, met with Vice Admiral Forrest P. Sherman, Deputy Chief of Naval Operations, and an aviator, to work out the details of a Unified Command Plan. With Eisenhower sponsoring various compromises, the chiefs adopted this plan on December 12, 1946.[58]

As approved by President Truman on December 14, the Unified Command Plan established several theater commands. In each one, the theater commander was responsible to the JCS for the operations of all Army and Navy forces assigned to him, while the individual services provided administrative support for their own forces. Besides the units within the joint theater commands, the Strategic Air Command would be "comprised of strategic air forces not otherwise assigned" and normally stationed in the continental United States. The SAC Commander, like the theater commanders, was directly responsible to the JCS.[59] This plan did not resolve all problems in actual command relations, even in Alaska, but it did serve as grounds for eventually giving SAC control of forces overseas. The strategic force was acknowledged as a major arm of national strategy. In the years that followed, the term "specified command" came into use, partly to describe SAC's unique position. However, the command's early link to the JCS, forged in December 1946, marked the first steps towards its emergence as a separate, powerful national strategic organization.

---

[57] Memo, Brig Gen T. S. Power, Dep ACAS-3 (Ops), to CG AAF, subj: AAF Situation in Alaska, Sep 27, 1946, RG 341, TS AAG File 23, Box 7, MMB, NA.
[58] Schnabel, *JCS, 1945–1947*, pp 181–185; Wolk, *Planning and Organizing*, pp 158–160.
[59] JCSM-1259-27, to President, Dec 12, 1946, cited in Schnabel, *JCS, 1945–1947*, pp 184–185.

Uncertain Phase

Planning for Atomic War

Although the Joint Chiefs of Staff had no statutory basis until the passage of the National Security Act of 1947, they had evolved as the principal forum for the War and Navy Departments to arrive at common policy and strategy. With their origins in the prewar Joint Board, the chiefs had been the logical agency to develop a joint war and mobilization plan after World War I. The COLOR plans that culminated in the RAINBOW series of 1939–1940 had envisioned a range of threats, although the RAINBOW plans appeared when the situation was clearer and the threat was from the Axis powers.[60] The postwar situation appeared simpler because there was only one plausible enemy. But, despite the growing estrangement between the United States and the Soviet Union in 1946–1947, war seemed unlikely in the near future. The Joint Staff conducted some studies of the strategic problems involved in such a conflict, the individual services drafted plans for their own use, and toward the end of 1947 the joint chiefs actually began to discuss proposals for a complete joint plan. Thus planning made limited progress during the period of postwar reorganization.

The COLOR plans of the interwar years had been largely requirements plans. In other words, planners devised a strategy and then determined the size of the forces needed to carry it out.[61] The postwar situation, characterized by fear of another "Pearl Harbor"—the possibility of a surprise air attack opening the war—lent importance to a second type, known as capabilities planning, which outlined actions that existing forces should take in an emergency.[62] Capabilities plans thus presupposed forces in being. This awareness stimulated concern in the services about America's military strength and in turn fostered an interest in new requirements planning for maintaining forces and budgeting for defense needs.

Certainly the military power of the USSR was formidable. Two years after the war, air intelligence officers admitted that the Soviets' long-range air force had little potential as a strategic bombing force, especially

---

[60] Mark S. Watson, *The Chief of Staff: Prewar Plans and Preparations* [*The United States Army in World War II: The War Department*] (Washington: GPO, 1950), pp 87–88, 103–104.
[61] *Ibid.*
[62] Memo, CSA to JCS (1630), subj: Strategic Guidance to Facilitate Planning within the Joint Agencies, Feb 19, 1946, with encl, RG 341, DCS/Ops, OPD, 381 Strat Guid (Feb 19, 1946), Box 382, MMB, NA.

135

because it lacked long-range escort fighters. On the other hand, the massive Soviet Army, supported by enormous tactical air forces, inspired something like awe in the Americans. The Intelligence Staff (Director of Intelligence) of the War Department believed that the Soviet Union could mobilize ten million men in thirty days, and a very large part this force would be effective at the onset of a war. Estimates of the current active force totaled four and half million men in over two hundred divisions. The air forces had 15,500 planes in operating units. The 1,100 bombers of the long-range force, for the most part twin-engined, had a combat radius of about 750 miles, although four-engine bombers such as the Tu (Tupolev)-4 (thought to be copied from a B-29 that had landed and been detained in the Soviet Union), with a radius of over 1,000 miles, were believed to be in the inventory. The Air Intelligence Division thought that the Soviets needed to overhaul their air force completely and expected that they would do so.[63]

American analysts attributed to the Soviet forces a frightening potential to overrun Europe, at least to the Alps and the Pyrenees. They might not be able to obtain bases from which the Mediterranean could be closed, but certainly northern Europe and especially England would be vulnerable to air attack by the Soviets' long-range force virtually at the outset of a war. U.S. occupation forces in Europe would have to withdraw somehow (hence McNarney's reluctance to build a large command). The European states lacked the means to resist the Red onslaught. Another Soviet objective would be the Middle East, where they could deny the West air bases and oil.[64]

Attacking the USSR by air would be difficult and was expected to grow tougher as the Soviets improved their air arm. At the time, military intelligence believed that Russians had few night fighters, but for day defense Soviet jet fighters superior to the Germans' wartime Messerschmitt 262 might be in production. German radar scientists, caught behind Russian lines, were thought to be working on an air defense

---

[63] Air Intel Rprt 100-10/5/1-79, 34, ACAS-2 (Intel), Estimate of the Capabilities of Potential Enemies to Conduct Air Attack against the United States in the Period to 1955, Nov 5, 1946, RG 341, TS AAG File 26, Box 9; Air Intel Rprt 100-153-34, ACAS-2/ONI, Intelligence Estimate of Soviet Air Force Mobilization Potential (1951), Mar 27, 1947, RG 341, TS AAG File 27, Box 9, both in MMB, NA. The Air Intelligence Division, the author of these reports, was an agency of the ACAS-2 (Intel), but it contained an Air Intelligence Group, manned equally by Army and Navy air officers.

[64] Briefing, Maj Gen L. Norstad, Dir P & O, War Dept, to President, Postwar Military Establishment, Oct 29, 1946, RG 341, TS AAG File 28, Box 9; Air Intel Rprt 100-62-34, ACAS-2/ONI, Estimate of Russian Capabilities in the Mediterranean, May 9, 1946, RG 341, TS AAG File 26, Box 9, both in MMB, NA. See also Steven Ross, *American War Plans*.

Uncertain Phase

system. Furthermore, within a few years the Soviets could start to build a large part of their industrial plant underground.[65]

In a future war, U.S. military planners envisioned relying on the traditional strategy of mobilization. When they were ready, America and its allies would launch a counteroffensive. Planning for such a contingency was complicated because its long-term objectives depended on political direction that had not yet been received.[66] The immediate focus therefore was on the early stages of a war, when key positions had to be defended and the sea lanes kept open. Naval planners argued that the fleet would continue its customary role as the first line of defense, but the War Department foresaw that an offensive could be conducted from the outset with strategic bombers.[67] At the other end of the spectrum, AAF officers believed that they possessed "the *only* major strategic U.S. force capable of conducting sustained, effective operations against the enemy..." during the opening months.[68] Thus the strategic air offensive became the centerpiece of AAF thinking about the next war.

In fact the air offensive was one of the most striking new notes in a planning process largely based on concepts from the 1930s. Logistical plans contained many references to "educational orders" and stockpiles of raw materials, the staples of prewar mobilization planning.[69] Even more impor-

---

[65] Air Intel Rprt 100-136-34, ACAS-2 (Intel), Significant Developments of Scientific Warfare in Russia, Nov 29, 1946, RG 341, TS AAG File 26, Box 9; memo, Brig Gen T. S. Power, Dep ACAS-3 (Ops), to Brig Gen W. L. Ritchie, Ch WPD ACAS-5 (Pl), subj: Present VHB Capabilities Against USSR Oil Targets, Oct 4, 1946, RG 341, DCS/Ops, OPD, P & O 381 (Sep 10, 1946), Box 380, both in MMB, NA.

[66] Memo, Lt Col R. C. Richardson III, Strat Br ACAS-5 (Pl), subj: Strategic Guidance for Mobilization Planning, n.d. [Dec 46], RG 341, DCS/Ops, OPD, 381 Strat Guid (Feb 13, 1946), Box 382, MMB, NA.

[67] Memo, RAdm C. D. Glover, Op-30, to Brig Gen G. A. Lincoln, Ch Pl & Pol Gp, P & O, War Dept, Brig Gen A. W. Kissner, Dep ACAS-5 (Pl), subj: Notes for Strategic Guidance in Planning, Dec 4, 1946, RG 341, DCS/Ops, OPD, 381 Strat Guid (Feb 19, 1946), Box 382; Extract from Mins, JPS, Concept of Operations for "Pincher," Mar 6, 1946, RG 341, DCS/Ops, OPD, 381 Russia "Pincher" (Mar 2, 1946), Box 949, both in MMB, NA.

[68] Memo, Col E. Vandevanter, Jr., AAF, to Col R. F. Tate, OPD, War Dept, subj: Proposed Composition and Deployment of United States Air Force during the Period 1946-1950 and after 1950, Jan 21, 1946, RG 341, DCS/Ops, OPD, P & O 320.2 (Apr 4, 1944), TS Supp, Box 129A, MMB, NA.

[69] Rprt, JLC 395/1 to JSSC, Strategic Guidance to Facilitate Planning within the Joint Agencies, Mar 22, 1946, with encl, RG 341, DCS/Ops, OPD, 381 Strat Guid (Feb 19, 1946), Box 382, MMB, NA. Educational orders were token orders of new equipment designed to allow manufacturers to learn what tooling they would need to produce at wartime levels.

Strategic Air Force

tant, the vision of total war that had developed out of the whole experience of the twentieth century remained largely intact. Atomic weapons simply made the great war of the future more destructive and total. In postwar planning, there was only a glimmer of the idea of intervention in limited, local wars. Secretary Forrestal's voice was among those advocating more attention to this possibility, but most strategists saw the Soviet threat in terms of its capability for total war.

Strategic air power, while it obviously had a place in a concept of total war, was a newer phenomenon than total war itself. Although Army planners recognized the importance of strategic air power, in September 1946 one staff officer told Brig. Gen. Frank F. Everest, the Deputy Assistant Chief of Air Staff for Plans, that only persistent pressure from the AAF kept the War Department aware of it. He noted, "Now it seems that the same old thinking of World War II is coming up again with the result that Air Power is treated as an adjunct to Ground and Sea Power."[70]

Also driving the planners of all services toward an appreciation of the need for a strategic air offensive was their perception of overwhelming Soviet strength on the ground. As Brig. Gen. Reuben E. Jenkins of the War Department Plans and Operations Directorate noted: "combined United States and British manpower cannot possibly defeat Russia on the field without a preliminary air effort of maximum violence."[71] In a series of planning studies prepared by the Joint Staff during 1946, known as PINCHER, the one major offensive operation envisioned for the early months of a war with the USSR was the strategic air offensive. For the rest, U.S. land and sea forces would have to concentrate on withdrawing from Germany, securing key bases for the counteroffensive, and keeping the sea lanes open. At the start, the strategic air offensive would attempt to destroy the enemy's warmaking potential in preparation for the next stage. During the mobilization phase, the nation would reinforce the strategic bombing force and develop forces for the counteroffensive.[72]

Naval planners did not deny the importance of the strategic air offensive. In planning for total war, their objective seemed to be to ensure parity for naval and strategic air forces. Naval strategists regularly emphasized the need for control of the Mediterranean so as to ensure access to

---

[70] Memo for Brig Gen F. F. Everest, Dep ACAS–5 (Pl), Sep 6, 1946, RG 341, DCS/Ops, OPD, 381 Russia "Pincher" (Mar 2, 1946), Sect 3, Box 949, MMB, NA.

[71] Extract from Mins, JPS, Concept of Operations for "Pincher," Mar 6, 1946, RG 341, DCS/Ops, OPD, 381 Russia "Pincher" (Mar 2, 1946), Box 949, MMB, NA.

[72] Rprt, JWPC 432/6, Tentative Over-all Strategic Concept and Estimate of Initial Operations, Short Title "Pincher," Jun 10, 1946, RG 341, DCS/Ops, OPD, 381 Russia "Pincher" (Mar 2, 1946), Box 949, MMB, NA.

the oil and air bases of the Middle East. However, should the Soviets reach the English Channel, air bases in the British Isles would be vulnerable, bringing their value into question. Thus the Navy outlined a major defensive role for the fleet.[73]

Whether the strategic bombing offensive would use atomic bombs was so far a largely academic question. Few planners had much information, and the stockpile was, for the time being, small. Nevertheless, by September 1946 some discussion of possible targets was under way.[74] Despite the uncertainties, few wanted to eschew the "decisive advantage" atomic weapons afforded.[75] Admirals Nimitz and Leahy objected to mentioning the bomb in the PINCHER documents. The stated reason was that the bomb might be outlawed, but Leahy intimated that his real concern was for the danger that a "leak" about atomic war planning while Baruch was advocating disarmament at the United Nations might lead to bad publicity. Spaatz won the support of War Department Plans and Operations for a compromise. The bomb would be mentioned in the PINCHER plans, with the proviso that it might be banned.[76]

---

[73] Extracts from Mins, JPS, Concept of Operations for "Pincher," Mar 6, 1946, Mar 13, 1946; Tentative Over-all Strategic Concept and Estimate of Initial Operations, Short Title "Pincher," Jun 18, 1946, both in RG 341, DCS/Ops, OPD, 381 Russia "Pincher" (Mar 2, 1946), Box 949; rprt, JWPC 486/1 to JPS, Strategic Guidance for Mobilization Planning, Dec 18, 1946, with Encl B: Joint Outline War Plan, RG 341, DCS/Ops, OPD, 381 Strat Guid (Feb 19, 1946), Box 382, all in MMB, NA.

[74] David A. Rosenberg, "American Atomic Strategy and the Hydrogen Bomb Decision," *Journal of American History*, 66 (Jun 1979), p 65; memo, Maj Gen G. C. McDonald, ACAS-2 (Intel), & Brig Gen J. A. Samford, Dep ACAS-2 (Intel), to Brig Gen W. L. Ritchie, Ch WPD ACAS-5 (Pl), subj: The Selection of Thirty Most Important Cities of the USSR Proper..., Oct 7, 1946, RG 341, DCS/Ops, OPD, P & O 381 (Sep 10, 1946), Box 380, MMB, NA.

[75] Rprt, JWPC 432/6, Tentative Over-all Strategic Concept and Estimate of Initial Operations, Short Title, "Pincher," Jun 10, 1946, RG 341, DCS/Ops, OPD, 381 Russia "Pincher" (Mar 2, 1946), Box 949, MMB, NA.

[76] Memo, Adm C. W. Nimitz, CNO, to Gen D. D. Eisenhower, CSA, Jun 13, 1946; draft memo, Gen C. A. Spaatz, CG AAF, to JCS, subj: Tentative Over-all Strategic Concept and Estimate of Initial Operations, Short Title "Pincher," n.d. [Jun 46]; rprt, JWPC 432/6 (Revised) to JPS, Tentative Over-all Strategic Concept and Estimate of Initial Operations, Short Title "Pincher," Jun 14, 1946, all in RG 341, DCS/Ops, OPD, 381 Russia "Pincher" (Mar 2, 1946), Box 949, MMB, NA; memo, Spaatz to JCS 1630/4, subj: Classification of General Assumptions for Joint Planning Purposes, Jul 1, 1946; memo, to Spaatz, subj: JCS 1630/4, n.d. [Jul 46]; memo, Brig Gen G. A. Lincoln, Ch Pl & Pol Gp, P & O, War Dept, to CSA, subj: Classification of General Assumptions for Joint Planning Purposes, Jul 11, 1946, all in RG 341, DCS/Ops, OPD, 381 Strat Guid (Feb 19, 1946), Box 382, MMB, NA.

Strategic Air Force

Elmendorf Field, later Air Force Base, near Anchorage, Alaska, in 1946 was part of the proposed U.S. Continental Defense Theater comprising Alaska and the islands of the North Atlantic from the Aleutians to Greenland.

Joint planners saw the atomic bomb as a means of intensifying the strategic air offensive and resolving it sooner. George Lincoln suggested that the weapon could be used against less accessible targets. On the other hand, AAF officers felt that an atomic "blitz," rapid strikes at key targets, might paralyze an aggressor and cause his defeat. The questions were: what are the key targets, and how does the force organize to attack them?[77]

With atomic weapons, just as with high explosives, the strategic air offensive required target lists and bases with secure access. Air intelligence officers had been collecting data about Soviet industry and geography since 1945. In the Air Intelligence Division a Strategic Vulnerability Branch had been established under the direct authority of the joint chiefs and was engaged in developing a worldwide "bombing encyclopedia" of potential strategic targets. Still, the services knew almost nothing about possible

---

[77] R & R Sheet, Maj Gen E. E. Partridge, ACAS-3 (Ops), to DCAS/R & D, Army Air Forces' concept of Strategic Bombing, Jun 7, 1946, RG 18, 1946–1947 AAG, 353.41 Bombing, Box 629; Extract from Mins, JPS, 245th Mtg, Apr 17, 1946, RG 341, DCS/Ops, OPD, 381 Russia (Mar 2, 1946), Box 949, both in MMB, NA.

targets in the Soviet Union. The rigid secrecy of a totalitarian society compounded the problem.[78] No air base could provide coverage of all the targets until the long-range B–36s became available in quantity. In April 1946 the Joint War Plans Committee focused on England and Egypt as the most promising areas for bases. B–29s could reach the oil facilities of the Caucasus region from Egypt. From Karachi and Lahore in British India they could strike most of the industrial complex that Stalin had built in the Urals. The joint committee believed that England and Egypt could be defended and that the Soviets could probably not cut sea communications except in the Mediterranean.[79]

Using the proposed bases required obtaining consent from the British, fortunately, a close ally of the United States. In Egypt the RAF's fields could serve as the nucleus of a strategic complex, and the United Kingdom's influence in the country seemed secure. On the other hand, civil disturbances in India could pose a security problem. Acquiring the existing RAF bases in England would be the logical first step, and the joint committee recommended sending a mission to London to negotiate for their use in wartime. At the time, PROJECT WONDERFUL was still alive, so the planners predicted that some of the B–29 groups might need to be stationed there in peacetime as well.[80]

When Spaatz visited England at the end of June and the beginning of July 1946, the subject of bases did arise. The Americans and the British had agreed to support international control of atomic weapons, but in the aftermath of two world wars, both were inclined to take precautions. The meeting between Spaatz and his British counterpart, Air Chief Marshal Sir Arthur Tedder, included symbolic gestures of Anglo-American solidarity, such as the visit to England of an AAF fighter squadron, but the two leaders did achieve real progress on a number of issues. They agreed to exchange material for use in their respective nations' debates over air

---

[78] John T. Greenwood, "The Emergence of the Postwar Strategic Air Force, 1945–1953," in Hurley & Ehrhart, eds, *Air Power and Warfare*, p 224; Air Intel Rprt 100–10/5/1–79,34, ACAS–2 (Intel), Estimate of the Capabilities of Potential Enemies to Conduct Air Attack Against the United States in the Period to 1955, Nov 5, 1946, RG 341, TS AAG File 26, Box 9, MMB, NA; Vance O. Mitchell, "The World War II Legacy and the Early Postwar Period, 1945–1948," Chapter I of draft CAFH study, *The United States Air Force and Intelligence, 1946–1953*, 1989, *passim*, CAFH.

[79] Rprt, JWPC to JPS 789/1, Staff Studies of Certain Military Problems Deriving from Concept of Operations for "Pincher," Apr 13, 1946, with App B: Appreciation of Air Base Areas Initially Required in Strategic Air Offensive against the USSR, RG 341, DCS/Ops, OPD 381, Russia (Mar 2, 1946), Box 949, MMB, NA.

[80] *Ibid.*

Strategic Air Force

power. The British appeared quite receptive to the use of their airfields in wartime and even before.[81] In addition, "Tedder agreed to insure that there would be certain physical facilities on two air fields adequate for the handling of some very special purpose VLR [very long range] aircraft."[82] Spaatz would send an officer knowledgeable in atomic operations to help with the construction. Col. Elmer E. Kirkpatrick, Jr., who had built the atomic site at Tinian, visited England later in the year under this agreement.[83] The air chiefs also discussed communications facilities on the air route across Africa. This route had proven critical during World War II in transporting air supplies and planes to Egypt and India, when the Germans had closed the Mediterranean.

As the PINCHER studies developed, the Air Staff produced its own strategic bombing plan for the early months of war. In September 1946 Maj. Gen. Otto P. Weyland, Norstad's successor as Assistant Chief of Air Staff for Plans, accepted this plan, known as MAKEFAST. When General Spaatz reviewed it, he directed that it be continually updated.[84] The plan drew heavily from the wartime experience with the B–29. Because the

---

[81] Memo, Maj Gen C. Bissell, Mil Att London, to Gen C. A. Spaatz, CG AAF, subj: Reminder on Decisions Taken during London Visit (Jun 25–28), Jun 28, 1946, RG 341, TS AAG File 23, Box 7, MMB, NA. For a discussion of the British atomic program, see Margaret Gowing and Lorna Arnold, *Independence and Deterrence: Britain and Atomic Energy, 1945–1952*, Vol I: *Policy-Making*, (NY: Saint Martin's, 1974), pp 63, 92–93, 183–185. The MacMahon Act had largely eliminated the chance for close Anglo-American cooperation in atomic energy. The British made the decision to manufacture an atomic bomb in January 1947, both the decision and the project being undertaken in the greatest secrecy. Tedder was acutely aware that the United Kingdom would be heavily dependent on the U.S. for any reliance on atomic deterrence that did not involve British-made weapons. There was in 1946 and 1947 no formal commitment from the United States to British security. An agreement with Spaatz on setting up atomic bases would clearly make American support easier in a crisis.

[82] Memo, Maj Gen C. Bissell, Mil Att London, to Gen C. A. Spaatz, CG AAF, subj: Reminder on Decisions Taken during London Visit (Jul 4–6), Jul 6, 1946, atch to R & R Sheet, Lt Gen I. C. Eaker, Dep CG AAF, to Air Staff, Decisions Reached in London between Gen Spaatz & Air Ministry (Jun 46), Jul 21, 1946, RG 341, TS AAG File 23, Box 7, MMB, NA.

[83] Ltr, Maj Gen C. Bissell, Mil Att London, to Gen C. A. Spaatz, CG AAF, Aug 16, 1946, Spaatz Coll, Aug 1–31, 1946, Box 250, MD, LC; Jones, *Manhattan*, pp 526–527.

[84] Memo, Brig Gen G. A. Lincoln, Ch Pl & Pol Gp, P & O, War Dept, to Brig Gen F. F. Everest, Dep ACAS–5 (Pl), subj: Plan for the Immediate Initiation of Strategic Air Operations, Sep 10, 1946, RG 341, DCS/Ops, OPD, P & O 381 (Sep 10, 1946), Box 380; memo, Gen H. S. Vandenberg, VCSAF, to Sec AF, subj: Status of Current Joint War and Mobilization Planning, Nov 6, 1947, RG 341, TS AAG File 28, Box 9, both in MMB, NA.

force available in the first six months of a war would be limited, the buildup thus far having proved painfully slow, the strategic air offensive could not hope to cripple the Soviet electric power net, steel industry, or transportation system. Instead, the planners turned to that sure winner in the European air war, oil. In fact, some of the POL [petroleum, oil, lubricants] targets listed in eastern Europe would be familiar to veterans of the Eighth Air Force.[85]

Based on the experience of the bombing of Japan, AAF planners envisioned night operations relying on radar for accuracy. The B-29s would fly singly, without escort. Some daylight attacks would go in, using a stream of squadron formations. The Air Staff used wartime figures to calculate probable bombing accuracies and aircraft losses. In the area of electronic defenses, the Soviets were using radars obtained from the United States under lend-lease or captured from the Germans—and similar to the equipment the Americans had acquired. Thus there was enough information to offer some hope for efforts at jamming Soviet defenses.[86] All the same, MAKEFAST could not be considered a capabilities plan, as an American strategic bombing capability did not exist. Rather, the plan presented the rationale for stating a series of requirements for the strategic air offensive. Essentially the airmen argued that a strategic air force was the one force that could be maintained in peacetime and allow America to strike effectively in the early months of a war.[87]

The atomic bomb therefore appeared the logical means of maximizing firepower in the face of the daunting task of achieving sufficient damage with conventional bombs. The fading prospect of international control made it easier for planners to assume the use of the bomb. And in the aftermath of the Bikini tests, the Air Staff was starting to think more seriously about atomic war. It was agreed that there was no defense against atomic attack. A nation could not afford to be unprepared, for atomic bombs could wipe out its means to fight before it could mobilize.[88] By the same token, a strong offensive force might allow victory to be

---

[85] Plan, ACAS-5 (Pl) to Dir P & O, War Dept, Air Plan for MAKEFAST, Oct 1, 1946, RG 341, DCS/Ops, OPD, P & O 381 (Sep 10, 1946), Box 380, MMB, NA.

[86] *Ibid.*

[87] Rprt, JWPC 486/1 to JPS, Strategic Guidance for Mobilization Planning, Dec 18, 1946, with Encl B: Joint Outline War Plan; memo, Lt Col R. C. Richardson III, Strat Br ACAS-5 (Pl), subj: Strategic Guidance for Mobilization Planning, n.d. [Dec 46], both in RG 341, DCS/Ops, OPD, 381 Strat Guid (Feb 19, 1946), Box 382, MMB, NA.

[88] Presentation by Brig Gen T. S. Power to Joint CROSSROADS Committee Symposium on the Scientific Aspects of Operation CROSSROADS, n.d., RG 341, DCS/Ops, OPD TS, Asst for AE, 1946, 373 Crossroads, Box 2, MMB, NA.

Strategic Air Force

gained by air power alone. And in the event that another country developed atomic weapons and "...neither the U.S. nor the potential enemy possesses adequate defenses, the Air Force may be employed as a retaliatory threat to aggression, and is the only force capable of being so employed."[89] This "retaliatory threat" then existed in SAC's Eighth Air Force. Despite the obvious strategic advantage, as Thomas Power cautioned the Operations staff, as long as bombs were scarce, careful planning and targeting were needed to give each strike the maximum effect.[90]

In July 1947 the Joint Chiefs of Staff Evaluation Board (the Compton Board) completed its long-awaited report on the Bikini tests. Many of the findings were no surprise to planners in the War and Navy Departments. The report's main contribution, however, lay in providing some common understanding of the technical facts and the potential of atomic weapons. The board concluded that atomic bombing could be decisive in a war and that it could "demolish [a nation's] social and economic structures." The only way to overcome this threat to civilization was to end war itself. Though the board did not cite the disappointing record thus far of attempts at international control under the auspices of the United Nations, those setbacks made their recommendations more persuasive. Other nations would have atomic weapons in due course. Failing peaceful solutions, the United States had to be ready to defend itself against a potential atomic threat.[91]

The Compton Board developed some longstanding themes of defense thinking of the time. The report repeated the call for adequate intelligence, including information on atomic programs abroad, and it recommended a strong program of research and development. Atomic testing had to continue. The development of weapons and their means of delivery had to be coordinated. Armies and navies were not obsolete, nor were overseas bases. The board also came to the support of the AAF. Excessive

---

[89] Rprt, Estimate of Potential Effects of Atomic Bomb On Air Forces Employment, Jan 23, 1947, atch to R & R Sheet, Cmt 3, Maj Gen C. E. LeMay, DCAS/R & D, to ACAS-3 (Ops), Technical Symposium, Operation CROSSROADS, Jan 27, 1947, RG 341, DCS/Ops, OPD S, Asst for AE, 1947, 373 Crossroads, Box 8, MMB, NA.

[90] See Note 88.

[91] Rprt, JCS 1691/10, Proposed Release of an Extracted Version of the Final Report of the JCS Evaluation Board on Operation Crossroads and the Related Proposed Press Release, Dec 29, 1947, RG 341, DCS/Ops, OPD TS, 384.3 (Aug 17, 1945), Sect 9, Box 450; memo, R. Dorfman, Ops An ACAS-3 (Ops), to Brig Gen T. S. Power, Dep ACAS-3 (Ops), subj: Brief of Evaluation Board Findings, Jul 25, 1947, RG 341, DCS/Ops, OPD TS, Asst for AE, 1947, 373 Crossroads, Box 4, both in MMB, NA.

secrecy, the report pointed out, was an obstacle to effective atomic forces. As for a real capability, this was said to consist of four things: "a) Of atomic weapons in adequate numbers, b) of suitable means for their delivery, c) of plans for their strategic use, d) of bases within range of enemy targets." Missiles and naval vessels would not be effective means of delivery for some years to come. The question of custody of the bombs was reopened as was the proposal of military representation on the AEC. The board also went into some planning for atomic war. Planners needed to assess what targets would be most destructive of the enemy's means and will to fight. They would have to consider the psychological effects of an atomic attack or of the threat of one. Perhaps the board's most striking proposal, however, concerned the danger of surprise attack. So devastating would such an event be that the United States ought to reconsider the meaning of aggression and allow the nation to strike first when necessary to prevent destruction.[92]

In general, AAF leaders received the Compton report favorably. LeMay noted the proposals on custody of the bombs, representation on the AEC, and the redefinition of aggression. He thought the board had in fact vindicated the AAF position and had called for a strategic striking force.[93] As Chief of the AAF's Atomic Energy Division, Kepner was perhaps less openly partisan in his comments on the report, preferring to focus on the weapon's capabilities:

> The Atom Bomb's possibilities for great destruction have increased the capacity of Air Power enormously. The variations in its use either alone or in conjunction with other forms of attack furnishes [*sic*] the greatest tool for the development of strategy and tactics ever conceived of to date. [A]tom bombs are in being and so is Air Power. Both are the product of science which even in its infancy has produced a terrifically destructive force. We must learn enough not to be destroyed by this weapon in the hands of an enemy.[94]

---

[92] See note above; Lilienthal, *Journals*, p 217. President Truman was reportedly disturbed by certain passages in the report. Perhaps this hint at preemption, if published during the conference in Paris on the Marshall Plan, might appear provocative. See Lilienthal, *Journals*, pp 233–234.

[93] Memo, Maj Gen C. E. LeMay, DCAS/R & D, to Gen C. A. Spaatz, CG AAF, subj: Operation CROSSROADS—Report of Joint Chiefs of Staff Evaluation Board, Jul 28, 1947, RG 341, DCS/Ops, OPD TS, Asst for AE, 1947, 373 Crossroads, Box 4, MMB, NA.

[94] Remarks by Maj Gen Kepner, Effect of Operation CROSSROADS on Air Force Materiel and Tactics, Jul 29, 1947, RG 341, DCS/Ops, OPD TS, Asst for AE, 1947, 373 Crossroads, Box 4, MMB, NA.

Kepner examined some of the technical data gathered at Bikini, especially concerning the possibility of detecting atomic blasts at a distance through the collection of radioactive air samples. He emphasized the need to coordinate the development of airplanes and bombs and for different agencies to cooperate on technical and planning matters. Concerning the question of security, he favored less stringent secrecy, repeating a statement he considered commonplace: "As has been said, 'Security of the bomb must not imperil security of the nation.' "[95]

Lilienthal, who attended one of the Evaluation Board's briefings, sensed that the services were interpreting the findings as confirming their traditional roles.[96] This may have been true to some extent, but in the War Department, including the AAF, there was a good deal of thought about the revolutionary implications of atomic weapons. The War Department's Plans and Operations Division, containing many officers well-versed in the traditional theories of warfare, had wrestled with the question of the bomb's effects. A paper prepared early in 1947 described the objective of war as overcoming the enemy's will to fight. Failing this, his means to fight had to be destroyed. Norstad, the Division Chief, passed the paper to Weyland with an endorsement. He commented especially on the psychological effects of the bomb. It might be able to produce fear, hopelessness, and even panic in an enemy country. This could either be exploited directly or treated as a bonus in a more conventional campaign to destroy the enemy's means to make war. Thus an atomic offensive might be used to blunt the advance of an aggressor over land, to paralyze him psychologically, or to destroy his industry. In any case, a balanced view held that the atomic bomb was quite obviously not "just another weapon;" on the other hand, "the way to understanding is not entirely unlighted by past experience."[97]

The limited capability of America to wage atomic war emerged clearly in the plans adopted during 1947. In February the Air Staff completed an update of its emergency plan. Covering the early months of a war that came without warning, EARSHOT went further than its predecessor, MAKEFAST. Nevertheless, it assumed that the atomic bomb would not be used. The plan provided for tactical forces as well as long range bombing. The B–29s would still operate mainly from England and Egypt, although the

---

[95] *Ibid.*
[96] Lilienthal, *Journals*, pp 217, 230, 233–234.
[97] Paper, The Theory of Atomic Bombing, Jun 16, 1947, atch to memo, Maj Gen L. Norstad, Dir P & O, WDGS, to Maj Gen O. P. Weyland, ACAS–5 (Pl), subj: Plans for Immediate Initiation of Atomic Warfare, Jun 18, 1947, RG 341, DCS/Ops, OPD TS, P & 0 381 (Sep 10, 1946), Box 380, MMB, NA.

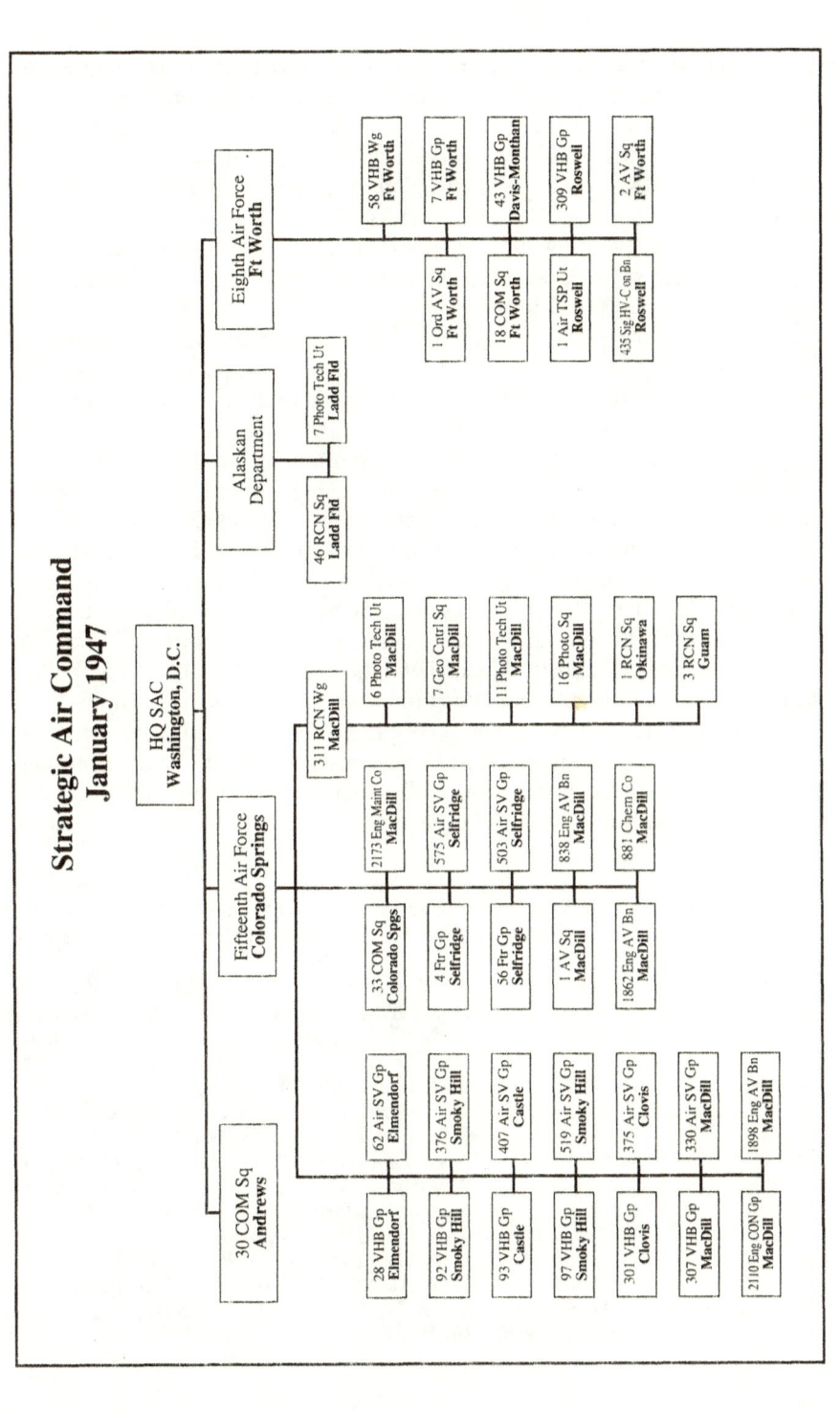

former might be in some danger from Soviet successes on the continent. As a result, the emphasis might shift to Egypt later on. The theater commander would control air operations, but AAF planners hoped that in due course the JCS might be persuaded to give control of all strategic operations to SAC. In any case, the main targets remained the oil and aviation fuel industries. The objectives of the strategic air offensive were defined as: first, blunting the aggressor's land offensive by weakening his logistical base; second, winning air superiority; and third, reducing the enemy potential to make war.[98]

Alongside the rather conventional Plan EARSHOT existed a tentative atomic war plan, which had been under consideration since December 1946. Eventually the plan became known as EARSHOT JUNIOR. It offered the hope that atomic bombs could win an early capitulation by the aggressor. Should this not occur, an atomic offensive would at least reduce the enemy's means to fight. Taking note of the limited resources of the Special Weapons Project and the 509th Bomb Group, EARSHOT JUNIOR anticipated that no more than one atomic bomb would be dropped each day. Up to eight bombs might be saved up and delivered in a one-day operation. Much of the plan, based as it was on inadequate data, was purely a guess, as Weyland openly admitted. Until more staff officers acquired clearances and the Special Weapons Project could be compelled to turn over data, the plan's major points would remain speculations.[99]

In April Lincoln advised the AAF planners to revise EARSHOT JUNIOR to account for a maximum effort. They were to assume that an atomic offensive would have priority over all other commitments and that "extraordinary measures" would be taken to drop the bombs.[100] In July

---

[98] Tab D, Air Force War Planning and Supporting Studies, n.d., to memo, Lt Gen H. S. Vandenberg, VCSAF, to Sec AF, subj: Status of Current Joint War and Mobilization Planning, Nov 6, 1947, RG 340, OSAF 1946–1950, 1 j(2), Box 3, MMB, NA; R & R Sheet, Brig Gen A. W. Kissner, Dep ACAS–5 (Pl), to Maj Gen S. E. Anderson, JSSC, AAF Short Range Emergency Plan, Mar 19, 1947, with atch: Outline Air Plan EARSHOT, Mar 15, 1947; memo, Maj Gen O. P. Weyland, ACAS–5 (Pl), to Gen C. A. Spaatz, CG AAF, May 9, 1947, all in RG 341, DCS/Ops, OPD TS, P & O 381 (Sep 10, 1946), Box 380, MMB, NA.

[99] Memo, Maj Gen O. P. Weyland, ACAS–5 (Pl), May 28, 1947; memo, Brig Gen A. W. Kissner, Actg ACAS–5 (Pl), to Brig Gen G. McDonald, ACAS–2 (Intel), subj: Revision of Short Range Emergency Plans, Jul 2, 1947; memo, Weyland to Brig Gen G. A. Lincoln, Ch Pl & Pol Gp, P & O Div WDGS, subj: Plans for Immediate Initiation of Atomic Warfare, Jun 5, 1947, all in RG 341, DCS/Ops, OPD TS, P & O 381 (Sep 10, 1946), Box 380, MMB, NA.

[100] Memo, Brig Gen G. A. Lincoln, Ch Pl & Pol Gp, P & O Div WDGS, to Brig Gen W. L. Ritchie, Ch War Pl Div, ACAS–5 (Pl), subj: Plans for Immediate Initiation of Atomic Air Operations, Apr 24, 1947, RG 341, DCS/Ops, OPD TS, P & O 381 (Sep 10, 1946), Box 380, MMB, NA.

LeMay asked the T & TLC to determine the requirements for an attack with ten or twenty-five bombs.[101] Such an operation might become possible under the AEC's 1948 production schedule. But if Lilienthal was not surprised at the reopening of the question of custody, he was also going to find pressure of another sort building up on Capitol Hill. When the Joint Committee on Atomic Energy, under the chairmanship of Senator Bourke B. Hickenlooper of Iowa, held hearings during the summer of 1947, Brereton testified for the Military Liaison Committee. He was informed that the Congressmen favored giving the highest priority in atomic matters to national defense, and that the armed services should be specific in the number of bombs they needed. Brereton reported to the Air Staff that the legislators "felt that a requirement which in effect says 'we need more than you can make' is inadequate and that such a statement would not exert sufficient pressure on the Atomic Energy Commission to produce what is needed."[102]

Brereton was told that the Air Staff was already working on a detailed plan.[103] This effort in the summer of 1947 produced a study of the number of bombs required in an atomic attack aimed at crippling Soviet industry. The planners, representing several agencies, agreed upon forty-nine cities which, if destroyed, would leave the country without military potential. By calculating probable bombing errors and the size of the cities, they determined that 100 bombs would be needed to do the job. Owing to the lack of fighter escort, losses would be heavy. Even night attacks and the use of decoy bombers with conventional bombs would not get more than fifty percent of the bombers through. As a result, 200 bombs would have to be deployed. Thus, tentatively, the AAF was starting to define its needs.[104]

The National Security Act, which passed on July 26, 1947, created a "National Military Establishment" headed by a Secretary of Defense. In addition to the War Department, renamed the Department of the Army, and the Navy Department, the Act created a new Department of the Air Force and directed that the AAF be transferred to it as the United States

---

[101] Ltr, Maj Gen C. E. LeMay, DCAS/R & D, to Chmn T & TLC, subj: Special Studies, Jun 27, 1947, RG 341, DCS/Ops, OPD TS, P & O 381 (Sep 10, 1946), Box 380, MMB, NA.

[102] Ltr, Lt Gen L. H. Brereton, Chmn MLC, to CG AAF, subj: Requirements for Stockpiling Bombs, Jul 7, 1947, RG 341, TS AAG File 29, Box 10, MMB, NA.

[103] Memo, Lt Gen H. S. Vandenberg, Dep Cmdr AAF, to Lt Gen L. H. Brereton, Chmn MLC, subj: Requirements for Stockpiling Bombs, Jul 30, 1947, RG 341, TS AAG File 29, Box 10, MMB, NA.

[104] Paper, Planning Factors for Atomic Bomb Requirements, n.d. [late 47], RG 341, DCS/Ops, OPD TS, Asst for AE, 1947, 471.6 Outline of Plng Factors for A-Bomb, Box 4, MMB, NA.

Strategic Air Force

Air Force, headed by a chief of staff co-equal with the Chief of Staff of the Army and the Chief of Naval Operations.[105] The airmen would no longer have to cope with attempts by the War Department to seek false economies in aircraft purchases, but they would have to accept responsibility for the planes they bought and win political support for adequate funding.

To develop a program for the new Air Force when the law took effect, General Spaatz convened a meeting of principal staff and major commanders, to be known as the Aircraft and Weapons Board. The first meeting took place on August 19 and was addressed by W. Stuart Symington, who was expected to become secretary of the new department. He spoke of the culmination of the years of effort to win autonomy for America's air arm. This effort had required taking the case to the people in a massive campaign of publicity. Now a new approach was needed. "[W]e are getting too much publicity," Symington said. Spaatz also addressed the group, emphasizing the Air Force would have to prove that it could do the job it had been given.[106]

Under existing budgets, the Air Force would have enough money to equip thirty groups with modern aircraft.[107] While the Aircraft and Weapons Board could wrestle with allocating these meager resources, the members would inevitably consider how to improve aircraft development and procurement. One alternative involved the manufacturers, who had failed to find new markets for their aircraft after the war. As Lt. Gen. George E. Stratemeyer, commanding the Air Defense Command, explained:

> I believe that in all this discussion, one of the things we have in the back of our minds—although we don't do it officially, I think it is a responsibility—is to keep the aircraft industry as healthy as possible.[108]

---

[105] Wolk, *Planning and Organizing*, pp 171–178.
[106] Verbatim mins, 1st Meeting—USAF Aircraft and Weapons Board, 1st Day: Aug 19, 1947, RG 341, DCS/Dev, Dir Rqmts, 1st AWB, 1947–1948, Box 181, MMB, NA.
[107] Memo, Maj Gen E. W. Rawlings, Air Comptr, to Civ Air Div, ACAS-5 (Pl), subj: Briefing of Mr Symington for Testimony before President's Air Policy Commission, Sep 5, 1947, RG 341, DCS/Comptr, Admin Div 1942–1953, 452.1 Acft Cmtes #63, Box 209, MMB, NA.
[108] Verbatim mins, 1st Meeting—USAF Aircraft and Weapons Board, 3d Day: Aug 21, 1947, p 435, RG 341, DCS/Dev, Rqmts Div, 1st AWB, 1947–1948, Box 181, MMB, NA.

With the number of jobs at stake, the size of some of the companies, and an election year coming up in 1948, the administration would not be able to escape the political aspects of the issue either.

Since 1946 Undersecretary of War Kenneth C. Royall had believed that a special presidential commission was needed to study the problems of the aircraft industry. On the recommendation of the Air Coordinating Committee, on July 18, 1947, President Truman named Thomas K. Finletter, an attorney who had served in the State Department during the war, to serve as chairman of a group of prominent civilians. This Presidential Air Policy Commission soon gained a parallel in Congress, when the Republicans in Congress set up a joint bipartisan board under the chairmanship of Senator R. Owen Brewster of Maine. Eventually both bodies would recommend actions to insure national security and help the industry.[109] The new Air Force would have two more forums within which to present its views.

---

[109] Verbatim rprt, 5th Meeting of the Air Board, Jun 5-6, 1947, RG 340, Bds & Cmtes, Mins of the Air Bd, Box 13, MMB, NA.

Part II

Austerity and Strategic Air Power 1947–1950

Chapter V

Decision for a Strategic Air Force

At the inception of the independent Air Force in September 1947, the strategic arm was still marginally effective at best. One group had achieved partial readiness for atomic operations, and SAC remained in essence a force of conventional U.S.-based B–29s, although these units were increasingly trained for operations overseas. But crucial decisions were in the making. A major public statement in favor of strategic air power might emerge from the proceedings of the Finletter Commission. In the near future, the atomic weapons program could increase dramatically, given the concerted efforts of the Atomic Energy Commission and congressional alarm at the current state of the atomic arsenal. The report of the Evaluation Board on the Bikini tests had shown that the new weapon played a vital role in deterrence, and other studies lent further support. The Air Force was more convinced than ever of the need to make SAC fully atomic-capable. War planning was reaching the point that the three-group program was clearly inadequate should general war come. And the development of new strategic aircraft was reaching a turning point. In particular, given the limited range of medium bombers, aerial refueling was emerging as a feasible means of extending the reach of the strategic force.

In terms of international relations, there were predictions of worsening conditions. However, the decisions related to the expansion of the atomic force responded to a situation that had existed for some time. The commitment to rebuild the armed forces after demobilization had been understood in the administration as a recognition that peaceful relations with the Soviet Union were far from certain. Given President Truman's fiscal caution, however, as well as the frugality of the Republican Congress elected in 1946, there were limits to how much rebuilding could be done.

Strategic Air Force

The crucial importance of an atomic air offensive made the strategic force one of the priority efforts within tight budgets.

As noted earlier, certain changes in military policy were inevitable simply because the National Security Act of 1947 created new positions and realignments. When Secretary of War Patterson turned down Truman's offer of the Secretaryship of Defense, the President chose James V. Forrestal, the Secretary of the Navy and a successful New York investment banker before the war. Forrestal had strenuously defended his department's position during the debate over unification. Patterson's deputy at the War Department, Kenneth C. Royall, became Secretary of the Army, and Forrestal likewise turned the Navy Department over to his undersecretary, John L. Sullivan. Despite Forrestal's misgivings, the Assistant Secretary of War for Air, W. Stuart Symington, became the new Secretary of the Air Force.[1]

Forrestal had been concerned for some time about the continuing failure of the United States to build up its military strength in the face of communist aggression. Nevertheless he was also sensitive to the "economic equation," the danger of wrecking the economy by excessive government spending.[2] Symington, devoted to the cause of air power since his War Department service, was an indefatigable administrator, determined to apply business methods to managing the Air Force. In this way he could provide the nation with a seventy-group air force at a reasonable cost. Both of these men could be expected to devote a great deal of effort to the budget.[3]

General Spaatz agreed to stay on for some months as the new Chief of Staff of the Air Force. He brought in Lt. Gen. Hoyt S. Vandenberg to replace Eaker as his deputy. Under Spaatz and Eaker, the Air Staff had developed a new organization for the headquarters, giving the Chief of Staff a vice chief and four deputies.[4] Vandenberg, previously in charge of the Central Intelligence Group, was a West Pointer, described by David E. Lilienthal of the AEC as "a slim young fellow—Gary Cooperish."[5] Forty-eight years old, he had risen during the war to command the Ninth Air Force in France. Arthur Vandenberg, Senator from Michigan and the Republican Chairman of the Foreign Relations Committee, was his uncle,

---

[1] Wolk, *Planning and Organizing*, pp 171–178; Lilienthal, *Atomic Energy*, p 231.
[2] Forrestal, *Diaries*, pp 412, 425, 429.
[3] Wolk, *Planning and Organizing*, pp 183–186.
[4] *Ibid*, pp 138–142.
[5] Lilienthal, *Atomic Energy*, p 104.

with whom he had been very close in boyhood. Chosen to be Vice Chief of Staff, Hoyt Vandenberg now held the rank of full general.[6]

The new Deputy Chiefs of Staff (DCS) were all lieutenant generals. Idwal H. Edwards, recently returned from command of U.S. Air Forces in Europe and with war service in the Mediterranean theater, took charge of personnel matters. The Deputy Chief of Staff for Operations would be responsible for a complex of matters, including intelligence, plans, requirements, and training. This important position went to Lauris Norstad, the youngest of the deputy chiefs. Another West Pointer, he had held vital staff positions in America and the Mediterranean, and as Chief of Staff of the Twentieth Air Force under Arnold, he had gained an intimate familiarity with worldwide strategic operations. Norstad had been the man in Washington who had kept in closest touch with LeMay in the Pacific during the B-29 campaign. In his postwar service as the War Department Director of Plans and Operations, he had played a leading role in the discussions with the Navy about unification. Howard A. Craig, the new DCS for Materiel, had commanded the Alaskan Theater after staff and command duties in Europe. The Comptroller of the AAF continued his duties under the new structure, with a higher grade. Now a lieutenant general, Edwin W. Rawlings held a business degree from Harvard and had worked at Wright Field. He was the man to apply the Symington approach of fiscal control to the Air Force.[7]

With an average age of forty-six, the six top officials in the headquarters brought the Air Force a variety of experience and background. This would compensate for the general youth and inexperience of the Air Force's leadership, a matter of concern to Forrestal, Marshall, and others.[8] This problem was exacerbated as the older generation of airmen—Arnold, Doolittle, and Eaker—turned over the power. A few senior leaders remained in key positions; besides Spaatz, Kenney was at SAC, Brereton with the Military Liaison Committee, and McNarney due to take over the Air Materiel Command. Supplementing the new faces in the Headquarters were bomber veterans such as LeMay and Twining, who had been given commands respectively in Europe and Alaska. Their broad experience would prove invaluable as the new Air Force expanded its global strategic power.[9]

---

[6] Fogerty, Study # 91, *passim*.
[7] *Ibid*.
[8] *Ibid*.; Forrestal Diary, IX:1999, Dec 31, 1947; 1919, Nov 8, 1947, in Forrestal Papers, OSD.
[9] See Note 6.

Strategic Air Force

Changes at the Top. *Left to right:* With the passage of the National Security Act of 1947 both a fully independent U.S. Air Force and a new civilian defense hierarchy were introduced. James V. Forrestal became Secretary of Defense; John L. Sullivan moved up from

Making the Case for Air Power: Finletter and Brewster

The formal creation of the independent Air Force in September of 1947 was a brief interruption in the normal routine of government. The fiscal 1949 budget was also in preparation. The new national security structure was to meet its immediate test in the upcoming defense debate. From that standpoint, both the Finletter Commission and the Brewster Board—the one answering to the Democratic White House and the other to the Republican Congress—might provide a coherent statement of the requirements for air power. Secretary Forrestal likewise faced the challenge of adjusting all the conflicting claims on the defense budget. Defense spending was now a single problem rather than a question of Army-AAF and Navy budgets considered separately. The Air Force's immediate future depended on the outcome of its first budget hearings. Prepared under War Department auspices, the U.S. Air Force budget provided $892 million for aircraft procurement, an increase over previous years, but not enough to make much progress toward building up a modern seventy-group force.[10]

---

[10] Hearings before the Committee on Appropriations, House of Representatives, *Military Functions, National Military Establishment Appropriations Bill for 1949*, 80th Cong. 2d sess, Pt 2, Mar 19, 1948, p 39; Rearden, *Formative Years*, pp 311–315, 331–333.

Decision for a Strategic Force

position; John L. Sullivan moved up from Undersecretary to Secretary of the Navy, replacing Forrestal; Kenneth C. Royall, a deputy in the old War Department, became Secretary of the Army; and W. Stuart Symington, Assistant Secretary of War for Air, became the first Secretary of the Air Force.

In any case, the service was going to have to present its case in virtual competition with the Army and the Navy.[11] Forrestal hoped to build a unified budget on the principle of "balanced forces." By this he meant that each service's spending would be on forces that fit into a larger strategic concept. He would have to resist a tendency for one service to acquire forces the other services could not support, and pressures for an equal three-way division of the budget without consideration of true balance. Forrestal also insisted on achieving a balance between defense spending and a strong economy. He defined the foundations of the U.S. defense posture in terms of the means to offset the "predominance of Russian land power in Europe and Asia." The United States had certain advantages that might avert pressure for excessive spending: "As long as we can outproduce the world, can control the sea, and can strike inland with the atomic bomb, we can assume certain risks...."[12]

The ability to "strike inland with the atomic bomb" was thus crucial to the Defense Secretary's strategic concept. Forrestal considered the question as to whether the Air Force could find targets in Russia, penetrate defenses to reach them, or obtain a decision, to be one of the most

---

[11] See Note 8.
[12] Forrestal, *Diaries*, pp 350–351; Gregg Herken, *The Winning Weapon: The Atomic Bomb in the Cold War, 1945–1950* (NY: Knopf, 1980), pp 235–239.

important facing the services.¹³ As the nation seemed ready to take a calculated risk on the decisiveness of atomic weapons, Air Force leaders fully understood the crucial role of the strategic air offensive. LeMay declared that "...if we fight in the next two years, we will put down an atomic attack first."¹⁴ A study at Air University reportedly concluded that a strategic offensive using only conventional bombs would not yield significant results. On the other hand, Kenney argued that an atomic offensive could win a decision in three weeks, if launched promptly. A study by Kepner's Special Weapons Group, now under the DCS for Materiel, argued that the destruction of only twenty key targets in the Soviet Union would either lead to capitulation or leave that country so weakened that the West would inevitably triumph through conventional means.¹⁵

The most determined opposition to the Air Force view was likely to be found in the Navy. A debate began within the sea service concerning its potential role in general war. Vice Adm. Forrest P. Sherman, the Deputy Chief of Naval Operations for Operations, who had worked well with Norstad in the unification talks, envisioned vigorous carrier-based operations against enemy naval facilities, especially submarine bases. This responded to recent improvements in submarine technology that undermined traditional methods. Others contended that the Navy could play an active role in the strategic air offensive.¹⁶ The three-engine (two prop and one jet) North American XAJ–1 Savage was designed to take off from a carrier and transport an atomic bomb. Three Midway-class carriers were to be modified to operate it. Kepner's staff was skeptical: "It is not apparent that the usefulness of this aircraft with its limited range can be proven, but the Navy is developing it just the same."¹⁷

---

[13] See Note 8.

[14] Verbatim mins, 2d Meeting—USAF Aircraft and Weapons Board, January 28–30, 1948, 2d Day, pp 191–194, RG 341, DCS/Dev, Dir Rqmts, 1st AWB, Box 183, MMB, NA.

[15] Rprt, Special Session Held after the Close of Day for Aircraft and Weapons Board, January 28, 1948, atch to ltr, Gen J. T. McNarney, CG AMC, to CSAF, subj: Atomic Weapons Program, Mar 1, 1948, RG 341, DCS/Ops, OPD TS, Asst for AE, 1948, 471.6 A-Weapons Prog, Box 11; Staff Study, United States Air Force and Atomic Warfare, atch to ASSS, Maj Gen W. E. Kepner, Ch SWG, to CSAF, Report on Air Force Atomic Energy Program, Jan 14, 1948, RG 341, DCS/Ops, OPD TS, Asst for AE, 1948, 381 A-Warfare, Box 10, both in MMB, NA.

[16] Michael A. Palmer, *Origins of the Maritime Strategy: American Naval Strategy in the First Postwar Decade* (Washington: Naval Historical Center, 1988), pp 24–32.

[17] See previous note; rprt, JSSC to JCS 1745/5, The Production of Fissionable Material, Dec 8, 1947, with Encl C, RG 341, DCS/Ops, Dir/Pl, TS OPD, 384.31 (Feb 3, 1947), Sect 1, Box 452, MMB, NA. Subsequently, the AJ went on to a brief career with the fleet as a nuclear-armed bomber.

Decision for a Strategic Force

The Finletter Commission would be a forum for an early round in this debate. Accordingly, one staff officer advised that in dealing with the commission "the Air Force should not ask questions. It should know the answers and should know where it is going."[18] In view of what the air leaders interpreted as traditionalist and self-serving pressures from the other services, an unbiased civilian body endorsing the concept of air power would be invaluable. To state its case, the Air Force had only to dust off its seventy-group program, which provided a clear statement of where the service wanted to go.[19]

Secretary Symington and the senior staff of the Air Force addressed the Finletter Commission in November 1947, and they spoke with the congressional group, the Brewster Board, in January 1948. Several officers met with John A. McCone, a member of the Finletter Commission, to explain their views further.[20] In general, their position was that the Air Force had two major missions in the event of war. General Spaatz said that "an immediate and paralyzing retaliatory offensive against the mainsprings of any attack launched against us, is our soundest defense."[21] But since the war might continue even after the atomic offensive, the Air Force also would be responsible for mobilizing combat forces for the next phase. For the retaliatory force, the Air Force needed an adequate number of trained men, up-to-date aircraft properly maintained, and bases within range of the targets. The service developed a full range of mobilization requirements: a defensive force to protect against air attack, cadres to be drawn from the regular, National Guard, and Reserve forces, a vigorous aircraft and weapons industry, and a plan for expansion. The core of the air program called for seventy groups on active duty.[22]

---

[18] Memo, Col P. M. Spicer, Ch Prog Monit Div, Air Comptr, to Air Comptr, subj: President's Air Policy Commission, Sep 4, 1947, RG 341, DCS/Comptr, Admin Div 1942–1953, 452–1 Acft Cmtes, File 63, Box 209, MMB, NA.

[19] Memo, Col R. S. Macrum, Ch Bud & Fisc Div, Air Comptr, to Air Comptr, subj: President's Air Policy Commission, Sep 5, 1947; memo, Maj Gen E. W. Rawlings, Air Comptr, to ACAS–5 (Pl), subj: Briefing of Mr. Symington for Testimony before President's Air Policy Commission, Nov 17, 1947, both in RG 341, DCS/Comptr, Admin Div 1942–1953, 452–1 Acft Cmtes, File 63, Box 209, MMB, NA.

[20] Memo, Lt Col E. J. Hopkins, Exec Ofc Air Comptr, to Hitchcock, subj: Air Policy Commission, Sep 10, 1947, RG 341, DCS/Comptr, Admin Div 1942–1953, 452–1 Acft Cmtes, File 63, Box 209, MMB, NA.

[21] Appearance of General Spaatz in a Public Hearing before the President's Air Policy Commission, Nov 17, 1947, RG 341, DCS/Comptr, Admin Div 1942–1953, 452–1 Acft Cmtes, File 63, Box 209, MMB, NA.

[22] Statement of Hon W. Stuart Symington, Secretary of the Air Force, before

Strategic Air Force

In the public sessions, witnesses before the Finletter Commission agreed on the decisive importance of air power as demonstrated in the Second World War. However, in the closed sessions an acrimonious debate arose between Air Force and Navy spokesmen. Admiral Nimitz argued in favor of larger aircraft carriers as an indispensable part of sea power. He insisted that command of the sea was essential and that reliance on land-based bombers alone would be dangerous. Carriers had played a major role in the air attacks against Japan, and sea power had proven its versatility. As the AAF's chief advocate, Spaatz called the use of carriers for deep penetration of enemy territory "a hopeless business." He assured the commission that land-based bombers had shown their ability to do the job. Forrestal, disturbed at the depth of the differences between the two services, did not take sides. He warned that as yet there was no general strategic concept on which to base force requirements for all the services. Attempting to place the debate in a broader perspective, he described the problems involved in maintaining occupation forces in Germany and Japan and suggested that a devastated Soviet Union would pose an even greater difficulty. The secretary also supported the President's call for limiting government spending, voicing the danger that a large defense establishment could do serious damage to the economy. On the issue of reliance on atomic forces, Forrestal pointed out that communist aggression, continuing on a limited scale, might require quite different forces, especially designed for local conflicts.[23]

In November the commission asked the joint chiefs for figures on the services' requirements for aircraft. Reluctantly, Forrestal agreed to the release of the information. The Finletter Commission then prepared its report, endorsing in general terms the procurement program the Air Force had recommended, urging a large program of naval aviation, and mentioning but not advocating the joint chiefs' qualification that "balanced" land, sea, and air forces were the foundation of a sound national defense.[24]

According to the Air Force presentation before the commission, the service needed to acquire 5,000 airplanes each year. This would maintain over 20,000 modern airplanes in the inventory, including a reserve supply

---

the President's Air Policy Commission, Nov 26, 1947, RG 341, DCS/Comptr, Admin Div 1942–1953, 452–1 Acft Cmtes, File 64, Box 209; transcript, Discussion following Air Force Presentation to the Combat Aviation Subcommittee, Congressional Aviation Policy Board, Jan 21, 1948, RG 341, TS AAG File 31, Box 10, both in MMB, NA; Futrell, *Ideas*, p 122.

[23] Rearden, *Formative Years*, pp 313–316.

[24] Ibid.; *Survival in the Air Age: A Report by the President's Air Policy Commission* [Finletter Report] (Washington: GPO, 1948), pp 31–36.

The New Air Force Team. *Clockwise from above:* Gen. Hoyt S. Vandenberg became Vice Chief of Staff under Gen. Carl A. Spaatz, who had agreed to stay on as Chief of Staff in the Air Force's adjustment to full independence; Lt. Gen. Idwal H. Edwards became DCS / Personnel and Administration; Lt. Gen. Lauris Norstad became DCS / Operations; Lt. Gen. Howard A. Craig became DCS / Materiel; and Lt. Gen. Edwin E. Rawlings became Air Comptroller.

of 8,000. SAC's very heavy bomber units would have 630 aircraft, with reconnaissance types and spares bringing the total to 988, plus a reserve of 2,500 in storage. Plans called for phasing out the B–29 by 1951, when the Air Force would rely on the B–36 and the B–50, with 4 groups of the former in place. The thousands of reserve aircraft were needed to equip units during the mobilization phase and to replace combat losses.[25]

In keeping with the intelligence estimate approved by the Joint Chiefs of Staff, the Finletter Commission reported that the Soviet Union could be ready to launch an atomic attack against the United States in 1953. For this reason, the commission established that year as the target for building the fully modern seventy-group air force. Although the budgetary proposals were not precise, the report implied that the Air Force budget for fiscal 1949 should exceed $5 billion.[26] Since the budget President Truman submitted to Congress on January 12, 1949, requested only $3 billion for the Air Force, the White House was reluctant to release the Finletter report. Nonetheless, on January 13 copies of "Survival in the Air Age" were placed in the hands of the national press.[27]

The President's Finletter Commission had expected to look for ways for the government to rescue and redirect the ailing aircraft industry. Instead, in a reversal of priorities, the members sought to revitalize the industry in order to support the urgent needs of national defense.[28] For its part, the Brewster Board, appointed by Congress to study air power, encountered a similar challenge. The representatives concentrated on readiness issues, asking pointed questions about the Air Force's ability to reach crucial targets. Spaatz testified that SAC bombers would go in under cover of darkness, as far as the season permitted (the polar route would of course be in daylight during the summer). Given the difficulty of penetrating Soviet airspace with fighter aircraft, the Air Force would probably not achieve real command of the air, and the Soviets' will to fight might persist

---

[25] Charts, Aircraft Inventory Requirements, Bombers, USAF 70 Combat Groups, Mar 48, all in RG 341, DCS/Comptr, Admin Div 1942–1953, 452.1 Acft Misc (Jan 1, 1948–Feb 1, 1949), Box 210, MMB, NA; Hearings before a Subcommittee of the Committee on Appropriations, Senate, *Supplemental National Defense Appropriation Bill, 1948*, 80th Cong, 2d sess, Pt 2, Mar 19, 1948, p 39; Rearden, *Formative Years*, pp 313–316.

[26] Finletter Report, pp 5–7, 19–21, 31–34.

[27] Rearden, *Formative Years*, pp 315–316.

[28] Statement of Hon W. Stuart Symington, Secretary of the Air Force, before the President's Air Policy Commission, Nov 26, 1947, RG 341, DCS/Comptr, Admin Div 1942–1953, 452.1 Acft Cmtes, File 64, Box 209, MMB, NA.

Decision for a Strategic Force

in spite of heavy atomic punishment. On the other hand, the Chief of Staff explained, Russia's vast size and its widespread industrial areas made the targets harder to defend. Radars would have to cover enormous territories. American intelligence staffs considered Soviet communications primitive, and Vandenberg discounted the value of Soviet-built "weather" stations recently detected in the Arctic. During the war the Soviets had been unable to control their interceptors effectively, and it would be five to seven years before the USSR possessed an adequate defensive system. Testifying before the Brewster Board, Air Force leaders admitted that they did not expect the strategic offensive to knock out the enemy immediately, but they did believe that it would blunt his offensive and ensure eventual victory for the West.[29]

The Brewster Board published its findings in March 1948. Although the congressional group was more critical of the administration than the Finletter Commission, the Brewster report received less public attention. The board's findings were basically the same as those of the Finletter Commission, and the congressional budgetary proposals, while more precise than those of the presidential group, were roughly similar, as both sets were largely based on the Air Forces's own recommendations. The Brewster report offered two alternatives: a full-scale Plan A and a more limited Plan B. Both options called for building up the Air Force to seventy fully modern groups by 1952 and then leveling off spending to keep this force up to date. At this point, under the first plan, the annual budget of the Air Force would be $7.5 billion. Plan B, somewhat less costly, eliminated the reserve airplanes in storage. The Brewster Board described the full-scale Plan A as providing "...the initial strength necessary to mount promptly an effective, continuing, and successful air offensive against a major enemy...." Plan B would sacrifice "sustained offensive action" and would gamble on the decisive power of the first blow. Thus, the nation would rely almost entirely on air power for deterrance. The congressional group reproved the Bureau of the Budget for a short-sighted policy of cutting expenditures for air power, which forced the Air Force to take obsolate wartime aircraft out of storage to supply new units.[30]

---

[29] Transcript, Discussion following Air Force Presentation to the Combat Aviation Subcommittee, Congressional Aviation Policy Board, Jan 21, 1948, RG 341, TS AAG File 31, Box 10, MMB, NA; Finletter Report, *passim*; Senate Rprt 949, *National Aviation Policy Report of Congressional Aviation Policy Board*, 80th Cong, 2d sess, Mar 1, 1948, *passim*.

[30] Senate Rprt 949, *National Aviation Policy Report of Congressional Aviation Policy Board*, 80th Cong, 2d sess, Mar 1, 1948, p 7 & *passim*.

Strategic Air Force

The Brewster Board further recommended that by 1953 the Air Force should be spending about one-sixth of the total national budget.[31] This figure, though somewhat arbitrary, emphasized Congress's support of air power and its belief that the economy could stand the expense of a major expansion of strategic forces. The Army and the Navy, however, had their own agendas. If Truman limited defense spending to 10 or 12 billion dollars a year, the seventy-group Air Force would require more than half of the total defense budget. To be sure, former Secretary of War Patterson had testified before the Finletter Commission that "...we will not need the strongest Army in the world or the strongest standing Navy in the world, but we will need the strongest Air Force in the world."[32] But the Army and the Navy were determined to resist any attempts to downgrade their forces. Given the modest defense spending of the period, members of the Air Board had reason to expect that any increase in the Air Force's budget would come at the expense of the other services.[33] Under the circumstances, as long as the service chiefs were convinced that the nation's security depended upon the adoption of their individual points of view, the controversy over defense priorities, already joined, would steadily intensify.

A Program for Atomic Readiness: JCS 1745 / 5

A critical dimension of the debate over American defense priorities centered on the Air Force's role in the national atomic energy program. During 1947, as more citizens became aware of the potential of the atomic bomb, a consensus was building that the new weapon represented an essential ingredient in the nation's long-term strategy. The American monopoly in the atomic field was emerging as a critical factor in national defense policy, and predictions as to when the monopoly would end were highly controversial. Many accepted Groves's view that it would take at least ten years for the Soviet Union to develop a bomb. Those who knew the true state of the American atomic arsenal also recognized that it would require more than a single test shot to produce Soviet atomic power. In December 1947 a report by the Central Intelligence Agency foresaw the

---

[31] *Ibid.*, pp 7–8.
[32] Hearings, President's Air Policy Commission, VI pp 2412–2414, cited in Futrell, *Ideas*, p 116.
[33] Verbatim rprt, 6th Meeting of the Air Board, Sep 9–10, 1947, p 220, RG 340, Air Bd, Mins of Mtgs, 1946–1948, Box 18, MMB, NA.

Decision for a Strategic Force

The Air Policy Commission presents its report, *Survival in the Air Age*, to President Harry S. Truman in January 1948. The commission had investigated a broad range of national aviation policy issues for the administration and endorsed the Air Force's goal of acquiring seventy groups. *Left to right:* **Palmer Hoyt; George Baker; John McCone; Truman; S. Paul Johnston; Thomas K. Finletter, Chairman of the commission; and Arthur Whiteside.**

development of a Soviet bomb in 1953, or in 1951 at the earliest. The Office of Naval Intelligence concurred. On the other hand, the Air Force's director of intelligence placed the date that the U.S. monopoly might end as early as 1949, though 1951 seemed more likely. The Finletter Commission more or less split the difference by predicting that atomic attacks on America would be possible by 1952 or 1953. By then, the seventy-group Air Force must be fully capable of retaliation, so as to deter the USSR from aggression against the United States or its allies.[34]

Rather than rely on speculation, some airmen favored an ambitious effort to gather intelligence on the Soviet atomic program. Crucial to this was the detection of atomic explosions, and early in September 1947 Eisenhower directed the AAF to develop a program to detect explosions at long range. The Air Force retained this mission after its independence. To

---

[34] Memo, Maj Gen G. C. McDonald, Dir Intel, to Sec AF, subj: CIA Report on the Status of Russian Atomic Energy Project, Jan 7, 1948, RG 341, DCS/Ops, Asst for AE, TS 1948, 350.09 Intel, Russian AE Prog, Box 8, MMB, NA.

Strategic Air Force

Maj. Gen. Albert F. Hegenberger went the task of organizing the program, as part of Kepner's Special Weapons Group.[35]

The call for an air force capable of delivering a retaliatory atomic strike followed logically from the widespread belief that the atomic bomb represented one of the mainstays of American power. As more policymakers accepted the view that a strategic air offensive using atomic weapons could be effective, or even decisive, against the Soviet Union, political pressure mounted in support of the Air Force's goals. Congress's Joint Committee on Atomic Energy began encouraging the Military Liaison Committee and the Air Force to demand action from the Atomic Energy Commission. War plans, meanwhile, were relying more heavily on an atomic capability that the nation did not yet fully possess. On August 29, 1947, the Joint Staff planners instructed the Joint War Plans Committee to prepare an emergency war plan called BROILER. In a directive that ran counter to the previous objections of Admiral Leahy, Chief of Staff to the President, the committee was told to assume that atomic weapons would be used. Given the availability of bases in England and Egypt, the drafters of BROILER concluded that the atomic offensive was both feasible and necessary.[36]

Despite these schemes, the actual capacity for atomic operations remained quite limited. By the end of 1947 the Air Force had acquired only thirty-two SADDLETREE-modified planes, many of them described as "quite weary."[37] These belonged primarily to the 509th Bombardment Group. In effect there were no spare aircraft. With an insufficient priority for supplies and spare parts, the 509th had all it could do to operate the planes on hand. Training for atomic bomber crews suffered from tight security restrictions, frustratingly cumbersome clearance procedures, and a

---

[35] Memo, Gen Army, D. D. Eisenhower, CSA, to Gen C. A. Spaatz, CG AAF, subj: Long Range Detection of Atomic Explosions, Sep 16, 1947, in Louis Galambos, ed, *The Papers of Dwight David Eisenhower: The Chief of Staff*, Vol IX (Baltimore: Johns Hopkins Univ Press, 1978), No. 1730, p 1918; rprt, Special Session Held after the Close of Day for Aircraft and Weapons Board, January 28, 1948, atch to ltr, Gen J. T. McNarney, CG AMC, to CSAF, subj: Atomic Weapons Program, Mar 1, 1948, RG 341, DCS/Ops, OPD TS, Asst for AE, 1948, 471.6 A-Weapons Prog, Box 11, MMB, NA.

[36] Kenneth W. Condit, *1947–1949*, Vol II of *The History of the Joint Chiefs of Staff: The Joint Chiefs of Staff and National Policy* (Washington: OSD, 1976), p 283; Herken, *Winning Weapon*, pp 226–229.

[37] Little, *Foundations*, Pt 1, pp 224–225; rprt, Special Session Held after the Close of Day for Aircraft and Weapons Board, January 28, 1948, atch to ltr, Gen J. T. McNarney, CG AMC, to CSAF, subj: Atomic Weapons Program, Mar 1, 1948, RG 341, DCS/Ops, OPD TS, Asst for AE, 1948, 471.6 A-Weapons Prog, Box 11, MMB, NA.

Decision for a Strategic Force

lack of training equipment. At the beginning of 1948 only six crews were fully qualified to drop the atomic bomb, although in an emergency enough trained people could be found to man another fourteen. Atomic units suffered a personnel turnover of nearly one hundred percent during 1947. But the most serious bottleneck involved the supply of weaponeers, attributable to the low caliber of many of the trainees as well as to delays by the Armed Forces Special Weapons Project, which trained them.[38]

The Air Force depended on the Special Weapons Project for much more than technical training; the project's responsibilities included setting up the bases, providing and assembling the weapons, and turning them over to the bomber crews. A study by the AAF Tactical and Technical Liaison Committee at Sandia in September 1947 revealed that the Special Weapons Project did not have the capability to assemble and load ten to twenty-five bombs in a few days' time. Although a new jacking mechanism allowed the 509th's ground crews to dispense with the pit method for loading the plane, a base still needed a lot of equipment, and no air bases had all the required equipment on hand for atomic operations. Estimates called for one thousand personnel to be ready to assemble the bombs, but the project fell far short with only two assembly teams.[39]

The Special Weapons Project answered directly to the Chiefs of Staff of the services. What disturbed the Air Force as much as its experience with Groves, the project director, was the influence of the Navy. While the Army expressed some interest in the possibility that increased production of bombs might eventually lead to their being available for tactical targets, the Navy was actively developing its own atomic program. Naval personnel were working on a project for nuclear propulsion for ships as well as plans to launch planes with atomic bombs from aircraft carriers.[40] Given the Navy's long-standing connection with the MANHATTAN District, the Atomic

---

[38] See note above; memo, Col H. J. Porter, SWG, to Col J. G. Armstrong, Dep Ch SWG, subj: 509th Composite Bomb Wing, Mar 10, 1948, RG 341, DCS/Ops, OPD TS, Asst for AE, 1948, 312.1 Corres. Box 15; memo, Lt Col L. D. Clay, Jr., Ch Security Br, SWG, to Ch SWG, subj: Summary of Trip, Mar 23, 1948, RG 341, DCS/Ops, OPD TS, Asst for AE, 1948, 314.7 Daily Diaries, Box 15; ltr, Brig Gen T. S. Power, Dep ACAS, to War Dept, subj: Supply Priority for the Eighth Air Force, Sep 8, 1947, RG 341, DCS/Ops, OPD TS, Asst for AE, TS 1947, 400.345 Supply Priority for 8 AF, Box 4, all in MMB, NA.

[39] Rprt, T & TLC, Requirements for Processing, Oct 1, 1947, in RG 341, DCS/Ops, OPD TS, 1947, 471.6 Assembly & Delivery of A-Weapons, Box 4, MMB, NA.

[40] See Note 17; Staff Study, United States Air Force and Atomic Warfare, n.d., atch to ASSS, Maj Gen W. E. Kepner, Ch SWG, to CSAF, Report on Air Force Atomic Energy Program, Jan 14, 1948, RG 341, DCS/Ops, OPD TS, Asst for AE, 1948, 381 A-Warfare, Box 10, MMB, NA.

Energy Commission, and Armed Forces Special Weapons Project, the large number of senior naval officers involved overshadowed the influence of the airmen in joint organizations, especially on the Military Liaison Committee to the AEC. The fact that one member of the commission, Lewis L. Strauss, was a reserve admiral did not allay suspicions on the Air Staff.[41] In spite of the Army's limited interest in atomic energy, however, the Air Force enjoyed support from Eisenhower, who believed in air power, as did Norstad's successor as the Army's Director of Plans and Operations, Lt. Gen. Albert C. Wedemeyer.

Interservice rivalries complicated the question of custody, from the Air Force's standpoint. Although the weapons were legally in the custody of the civilian Atomic Energy Commission, the Special Weapons Project guarded them and, if they were transferred to an armed service, would obtain custody. Thus, control would go to a joint organization and not to the Air Force. In fact, the Special Weapons Project claimed to act as the sole intermediary between the Air Force and the AEC. Under these circumstances, air leaders feared that delay-inducing red tape, confusion of lines of command, and breakdowns of communication might seriously hamper the opening of an atomic offensive. In Kenney's words:

> The VHB groups of the Strategic Air Command are now capable of taking off... within a few hours after an order to do so is received; but if the atomic bomb is used the takeoff might be delayed, by factors beyond the control of the Air Force....[42]

By now it had become evident that, to be successful, the atomic offensive must be delivered swiftly and on a large scale. A few bombs dropped one at a time over several weeks would produce neither the physical nor the psychological effect necessary to offset Soviet land power. Thus, Kenney's words had serious implications. To build an effective atomic force, the USAF needed to define ambitious goals and begin moving toward them. This effort must include stating the requirements for a strike force and establishing the most effective lines of control.

Whatever the problems, the situation was ripe for concerted action. The Atomic Energy Commission believed that it was on the verge of breaking the logjam in production and was developing a new design for the

---

[41] Briefing, Col J. G. Armstrong, Dep Ch SWG, to Lt Gen L. Norstad, DCS/Ops, Dec 30, 1947, RG 341, DCS/Ops, Asst for AE, S 1947, 350 Briefings, Box 8, MMB, NA.
[42] *Ibid.*; memo, Gen G. C. Kenney, CG SAC, to Gen C. A. Spaatz, CSAF, subj: SAC Participation in Atomic Bomb Offensive Operations, n.d., RG 341, DCS/Ops, Asst for AE, TS 1947, 381 National Defense, Box 4, MMB, NA.

Decision for a Strategic Force

bomb. If tests planned for the spring of 1948 at Eniwetok were successful, the Mark IV could be produced more rapidly than the Mark III, which was still a laboratory model. The Mark IV was also reportedly easier to assemble and less prone to erratic drops such as the one at Bikini.[43] Meanwhile, the Air Force managed to get its plans for an atomic strike force considered by the joint chiefs. This occurred because of Senator Hickenlooper's desire to pressure the Atomic Energy Commission into an ambitious production program. In frequent touch with Eisenhower and the Military Liaison Committee, Hickenlooper had received their assurances that they would give the AEC their genuine military requirements. In September 1947 one of Weyland's planners, Col. James B. Knapp, was appointed to a joint committee assisting the Joint Staff planners in a study of the number of atomic bombs needed. The efforts of the AAF planners on this issue began to bear fruit. The joint committee's report finally reached the joint chiefs in December as JCS 1745/5. Weyland, now reporting to Norstad as the Air Force Director of Plans and Operations, continued to receive support from Wedemeyer and his Army Plans and Operations staff.[44]

JCS 1745/5 showed much of the handiwork of the Air Staff group that had worked on weapons requirements in the summer of 1947. It proposed a production program and outlined a plan to enable the Air Force to build an atomic strike force. The AEC would be asked to produce bombs over a schedule running through 1953. At the time, the total number of bombs required, 400, was kept in the strictest secrecy, printed copies of the schedule appearing with blank spaces to be filled in with pencil for the few cleared personnel. Also by 1953 the Air Force would have eight groups of B-36s and B-50s modified to carry the weapons, all units fully manned and with spare aircraft available. The plan also imposed a schedule for the training of bomb commanders and weaponeers, as well as assembly teams. A number of C-97s would be equipped as mobile assembly facilities. Particularly ambitious were the interim steps on the way to a fully functional strike force. By the end of 1948 the Air Force

---

[43] Memo, subj: Present Status, atch to memo, Col J. G. Armstrong, Dep Ch SWG, to Lt Gen L. Norstad, DCS/Ops, subj: Atomic Warfare, Mar 25, 1948, in RG 341, DCS/Ops, Asst for AE, TS 1948, 381 A-Warfare, Box 10, MMB, NA; Little, *Foundations*, Pt III, pp 596-599.

[44] Ltr PM-587, Sec JPS to Capt T. B. Hill, USN, Col J. B. Knapp, Lt Col O. G. Haywood, subj: Proposed Study on the Production of Fissionable Material, Sep 15, 1947; memo, Brig Gen A. W. Kissner, Dep ACAS-5 (Pl), to Gen C. A. Spaatz, CG AAF, Sep 17, 1947; rprt, JSSC to JCS 1745/5, The Production of Fissionable Material, Dec 8, 1947, with encls, all in RG 341, DCS/Ops, Dir/Pl, TS OPD, 384.31 (Feb 3, 1947), Sect 1, Box 452, MMB, NA.

planned, according to the report, to have five atomic groups equipped with 225 modified bombers.[45] This meant that 1948 would be a very busy year, as only a fraction of the needed resources were on hand.

As it developed, the issue of requirements for the strike force became inseparable from that of control. On December 13 Admiral Nimitz submitted comments to the joint chiefs on 1745/5. The Joint Strategic Survey Committee had recommended that the JCS order the Air Force to proceed with the aircraft modifications and build a strike force for the atomic offensive. The Chief of Naval Operations proposed revising 1745/5 to authorize both the Air Force and Navy to develop atomic forces for strategic operations, until such time as the Air Force's planes had sufficient range to reach targets from the continental United States. At that point, the carrier forces could still supplement the Air Force's strategic capabilities.[46] Replying on December 19, 1947, Spaatz objected to the implication that the Air Force could not reach the potential target. He contended that plan CHARIOTEER, the draft JCS long-term war plan, acknowledged the primacy of the Air Force in the strategic air offensive. Carrier forces could assist, but they would not be essential. The Director of the Joint Staff, Maj. Gen. Alfred M. Gruenther, U.S. Army, urged approval of the current version, but Spaatz insisted on adding an explicit statement that the Chief of Staff of the Air Force was responsible for the strategic atomic offensive.[47] The Navy responded that bases would be an unknown factor in a future war, and carrier forces were uniquely suited for the strategic mission. Reviewing the joint chiefs' discussion, Colonel Knapp called these arguments "unacceptable to the Air Force."[48] Editing out the rather undiplomatic language his staff used in the draft reply, General

---

[45] Rprt, JSSC to JCS 1745/5, The Production of Fissionable Material, Dec 8, 1947, with encls; R & R Sheet, Cmt 1, Maj Gen O. P. Weyland, Dir P & O, to Dir Tng & Rqmts, Air Force Requirements for Implementation of the Atomic Bomb Program, Feb 10, 1948, both in RG 341, DCS/Ops, Dir/Pl, TS OPD, 384.31 (Feb 3, 1947), Sect 1, Box 452, MMB, NA.

[46] Memo, Col J. B. Knapp, Ofc of Dir P & O, to Gen H. S. Vandenberg, VCSAF, Dec 17, 1947, RG 341, DCS/Ops, Dir/Pl, TS OPD, 384.31 (Feb 3, 1947), Sect 1, Box 452, MMB, NA.

[47] Memo, CSAF to JCS, 1745/8, subj: Production of Fissionable Material, Dec 19, 1947; memo, SM–9372, Sec JCS to JCS, subj: Production of Fissionable Material, Dec 24, 1947; rprt, Dir Jt Staff to JCS 1745/9, Production of Fissionable Material, Dec 23, 1947; memo, CSAF to JCS 1745/10, subj: Production of Fissionable Material, Dec 31, 1947, all in RG 341, DCS/Ops, Dir/Pl, TS OPD, 384.31 (Feb 3, 1947), Sect 1, Box 452, MMB, NA.

[48] Memo, Col J. B. Knapp, P & O, to Gen C. A. Spaatz, CSAF, subj: Production of Fissionable Material (JCS 1745 Series), Jan 7, 1948, RG 341, DCS/Ops, Dir/Pl, TS OPD, 384.31 (Feb 3, 1947), Sect 1, Box 452, MMB, NA.

Decision for a Strategic Force

Spaatz finally signed a memorandum that emphasized the need to have one agency responsible for the strategic air offensive, not two. With progress in air refueling and improvements in jet engines, questions about the Air Force's long-range capabilities would cease. Carriers, in any case, were too vulnerable to sail close to shore, and their planes would otherwise lack enough range. Weyland meanwhile reported that the Army would probably support the Air Force position. He also predicted that Nimitz would say he only wanted his service to be free to develop an atomic capability. If the chiefs could not agree, Weyland advised Spaatz to pursue the matter at the secretarial level rather than give in.[49] Thus on January 21, 1948, after much discussion, the joint chiefs approved the Air Force plan. Gruenther had already passed on the proposed weapons requirements to the Atomic Energy Commission and sent a reassuring letter to Senator Hickenlooper.[50]

Implicit in the Air Force's insistence on primacy in the strategic air offensive was a right to more control over the atomic program. Kenney favored SAC stockpiling its own bombs and controlling the assembly teams —a clear infringement on the Special Weapons Project's functions. Although the Air Force did not formally present Kenney's proposal, the Air staff did support a major reshuffle of responsibilities. As Special Weapons Project's leading customer, the service argued that the project should be placed directly under its control. As the project was a joint agency, the Navy understandably objected to its control by a single service.[51] A resolution of the controversy, however, would have to wait until Secretary

---

[49] *Ibid.*; memo, subj: Brief of JCS 1945 Series, n.d.; memo, Maj Gen O. P. Weyland, Dir P & O, to Gen C. A. Spaatz, CSAF, subj: Production of Fissionable Material, Jan 21, 1948, RG 341, DCS/Ops, Dir/Pl, TS OPD, 384.31 (Feb 3, 1947), Sect 1, Box 452, MMB, NA.

[50] Rprt, JSSC to JCS 1745/5, The Production of Fissionable Material, Dec 8, 1947, with JCS Decision, Jan 21, 1948; memo, Maj Gen A. M. Gruenther, Dir Jt Staff, to JCS 1745/7, subj: Production of Fissionable Material, Dec 17, 1947, with JCS Decision, Dec 17, 1947, both in RG 341, DCS/Ops, Dir/Pl, TS OPD, 384.31 (Feb 3, 1947), Sect 1, Box 452, MMB, NA.

[51] Memo, Gen G. C. Kenney, CG SAC, to Gen C. A. Spaatz, CSAF, subj: SAC Participation in Atomic Bomb Offensive Operations, n.d.; memo, Col J. G. Armstrong, Dep Ch SWG, to Maj Gen W. E. Kepner, Ch SWG, subj: Comments of General Kenney's Atomic Bomb Operations Paper, n.d., both in RG 341, DCS/Ops, Asst for AE, TS 1947, 381 National Defense, Box 4; draft memo, Spaatz to W. S. Symington, Sec AF, subj: USAF Participation in Atomic Energy Matters, n.d., RG 341, DCS/Ops, Asst for AE, S 1947, 381 AAF Test Rqmts, Box 9; Daily Diary, Col G. Y. Jumper, Ch Pl & Intel, SWG, Meeting in AFSWP (Feb 19, 1948), Feb 24, 1948, RG 341, DCS/Ops, Asst for AE, S 1948, 314.7 Daily Diary, Pl & Intel, Box 16, all in MMB, NA.

Strategic Air Force

Forrestal answered the overall question of the military atomic program and its organization. The key problem involved the Military Liaison Committee to the AEC, over which Forrestal was trying to establish his authority. Should this happen, the Air Force expected to win equal representation. Col. Roscoe C. Wilson, the air deputy to Groves, served on the group studying the Military Liaison Committee. Some change in the committee might occur early in 1948 when Groves, the powerful chairman, was to retire.[52]

Even within the Air Staff itself, the question of organizational responsibility for atomic matters was not entirely settled. Kepner's Special Weapons Group, placed under the DCS for Materiel, continued to coordinate with the Special Weapons Project, mainly through its Tactical and Technical Liaison Committee, and to communicate directly with the Air Materiel Command. However, AMC had its own atomic energy officer; the Eighth Air Force and SAC had an interest in atomic matters, and Norstad's Operations staff was involved in war planning and preparations for the buildup of an atomic strike force. The main case for establishing a central office for atomic matters was that with so few people having access to reliable information, some agency had to monitor the interservice aspects of the question and spread the "gospel" within its own headquarters. By the end of 1947 the Special Weapons Group had assumed some of these responsibilities and was briefing key people on the basic role of the Air Force in atomic energy.[53]

Colonel Armstrong, Kepner's deputy, often presented the office's briefing. On these occasions, he outlined the problems of inadequate Air Force representation on the Military Liaison Committee and other groups, the service's lack of control over the Special Weapons Project, and the scarcity of information. On January 28, 1948, during the meeting of the Aircraft and Weapons Board, he gave the members a special after-hours briefing in which he introduced budgetary issues, in particular the funding of the long range detection project. McNarney, responsible as head of AMC for modifications of aircraft and procurement of equipment, took this opportunity to criticize the Special Weapons Group for its failure to pass on essential information. The only decisions emerging from these discussions were that a study of some kind should be conducted and the

---

[52] Memo, C. F. Brown, OSD, to M. Leva, Spec Asst to Sec Def, subj: Agencies Concerned with Atomic Warfare, Jan 6, 1948, RG 341, DCS/Ops, Asst for AE, S 1948, 334 Cmtes & Rprts, Box 18, MMB, NA; Little, *Foundations*, Pt I, pp 111–118.

[53] Little, *Foundations*, Pt I, pp 66–77.

Decision for a Strategic Force

Air Force's program for atomic warfare should be promoted as a major national priority.[54]

Aircraft for the Strategic Offensive

If those who lacked information about the atomic program were sometimes reluctant to express an opinion on the subject, many were willing to speak freely on questions of bomber design, although here, too, there was a certain amount of secrecy. For most airmen the question of whether the Air Force could deliver the bomb really came down to procuring the best possible design for an intercontinental bomber. With the B-29 and the B-50, the United States still needed overseas bases for a sustained offensive. Many doubted that bases in England and the Middle East could endure a Soviet land and air offensive, and at the outset of a war, the lack of aviation engineer battalions would long delay the preparation of new facilities. A solution to the problem of intercontinental reach became essential.[55]

By the end of 1947 experts agreed that a superbomber was probably not feasible. The Aircraft and Weapons Board had appointed a Heavy Bombardment Committee, mainly consisting of senior colonels, and they concurred in the von Kármán Committee's warning that the building of bigger and bigger bombers would not extend their range. The piston-powered B-36 was already dangerously slow by the time it reached the target. The controversial variable discharge turbine (VDT) engine might help, but the B-52 project was demonstrating the sterility of this line of approach. As the Heavy Bombardment Committee reported in November 1947: "...it will only serve to prove [the superbomber's] own fallacy and insure its own oblivion."[56] A plane weighing five hundred thousand pounds would cost so much and take so long to build that only a few could be

---

[54] Transcript, Special Session Held after the Close of Day for Aircraft & Weapons Board, (Jan 28, 1948), RG 341, DCS/Ops, Asst for AE, TS 1948, 471.6 A-Weapons Prog, Box 11, MMB, NA.

[55] Verbatim mins, 2d Meeting—USAF Aircraft and Weapons Board, January 27-30, 1948, 1st Day, Jan 27, 1948, pp 69-82, 2d Day, pp 191-194, RG 341, DCS/Dev, Dir/Rqmts, 1st AWB, Box 183, MMB, NA.

[56] Rprt, Heavy Bombardment Cmte to AWB, Report of Heavy Bombardment, n.d. [Nov 47], p 27, RG 341, DCS/Dev, Dir/Rqmts, Papers 1st AWB, Box 181, MMB, NA.

acquired. A tremendous expenditure of fuel would be required to bring it over the target at sufficient speed. Building airfields for such a huge aircraft would be a daunting task. And given progress in engine design and aerodynamics, it would be obsolete by the time it came off the assembly line.[57]

Rejecting the very heavy bomber, the Heavy Bombardment Committee examined more promising solutions, both for the long term and the short term. The short term solutions proposed involved mainly one-way missions, pilotless bombers, and air refueling. Each alternative had drawbacks, but all these measures would have to be tried.

Though one-way missions were generally regarded as an unpalatable solution, various types were proposed. If the aircraft had sufficient range (such as the B–50 with wing tanks), the crew could ditch at sea and be rescued by submarine. From certain targets, a plane could recover in a friendly country, ditching or even landing. Another option involved the bomber taking off without a crew. Unfortunately, with the incomplete maps and charts then available, a crew was needed to find the target, if only in a director plane accompanying the drone. But even a drone was preferable to a slow bomber like the B–36B.[58] Eventually, the B–36 was modified by four J47 turbojets to improve its dash speed over targets. It thus became an aeronautical behemoth with no fewer than ten engines.

Refueling during the mission was becoming SAC's preferred solution. Given the command's efforts to achieve a global reach and General Kenney's skepticism about the B–36, a project had been undertaken to extend the range of the B–29 and B–50. Tractor landing gear could eliminate the bomber's need for expensive airfields. Arctic research and training might demonstrate the feasibility of refueling at sites on the icecap. But refueling in the air turned out to be the technique with the best record of past performance.[59]

The airmen's interest in aerial refueling dated back to 1929, when Spaatz and Eaker set an endurance record of 150 hours in the air on board the *Question Mark* by using a primitive form of the technique. Since then a British firm, Flight Refueling, Ltd., had further developed refueling for transatlantic flight, and during the war the company had helped with tests at Eglin Field. With the Air Force now reviving its interest, late in 1947

---

[57] *Ibid.*, pp 1–18.
[58] *Ibid.*
[59] *Case History of Air-to-Air Refueling*, (Wright-Patterson AFB, Ohio: AMC, 1949), pp 11–18.

SAC began advocating tests of the B-29 as a tanker and a receiver. On October 14 the command headquarters sent Air Materiel Command a letter outlining its proposals and stating that the command "envisioned" heavy use of air refueling.[60] On October 23 the staff at AMC headquarters began to organize the development effort. The command planned to buy some equipment from Flight Refueling, Ltd, but it allocated $1 million of research and development money for fiscal 1948 to develop an American refueling system.[61] Brig. Gen. Thomas S. Power, the Air Force Acting Director of Training and Requirements, intervened for the Air Staff in November. He advised that SAC should provide two B-29s for the tests and develop the operational procedures, while the Materiel Command did the engineering.[62] The growing confidence of the airmen can be seen in Spaatz's reference to aerial refueling in refuting the Navy's skepticism and in the proposal by Maj. Gen. Laurence C. Craigie, Director of Research and Development (DCS for Materiel), to try refueling fighters as well.[63] By January 1948 Brig. Gen. Frederic H. Smith, Jr., Chief of the Requirements Division, Directorate of Training and Requirements, was examining the production program, "with preliminary studies indicating that this method of refueling is practicable." Drawing on 1948 funding, AMC would modify two B-29s as tankers for SAC, and in fiscal year 1949 another hundred would be so modified. At the same time, B-50s would undergo modification as receivers.[64] In a matter of a few months aerial refueling had progressed from a tentative testing program to a specific and ambitious requirement.

The Heavy Bombardment Committee had meanwhile added its support to the refueling program, endorsing it as the Air Force's number one priority. The members saw the effort as a means to convert the Arctic no-man's land into an American asset, where bombers could refuel in safety. The committee recommended that AMC "develop air-to-air, high

---

[60] Ltr, SAC to CG AMC, subj: B-52 Tanker Equipment, Oct 14, 1947, in *Case History of Air-to-Air Refueling*.

[61] *Case History of Air-to-Air Refueling*, pp 11–18.

[62] Ltr, Brig Gen T. S. Power, Actg Dir Tng & Rqmts, to CG SAC, subj: Air-to-Air Refueling Project, Nov 12, 1947, in *Case History of Air-to-Air Refueling*.

[63] Ltr, Maj Gen L. C. Craigie, Dir R & D, to CG AMC, subj: Air-to-Air Refueling for the Purpose of Extending Fighter Protection for Bombardment Aircraft, Dec 16, 1947, in *Case History of Air-to-Air Refueling*.

[64] Ltr, Brig Gen F. H. Smith, Ch Rqmts Div, DCS/Ops, to CG SAC, subj: Air-to-Air Refueling of Bombardment Aircraft, Jan 8, 1948, in *Case History of Air-to-Air Refueling*.

Aerial Refueling. First undertaken in 1923 and to more dramatic effect during the record-setting flight of the *Question Mark* in 1929, *above*, aerial refueling was renewed in 1947, largely because of British experience, and quickly perfected as a relatively inexpensive way for the Air Force to extend the range of its aircraft. In roughly twenty-five years two methods of aerial refueling had evolved—the American boom-type and British loop-type. Demonstrating the former method, *above, right*, a Boeing KC-97 Stratofreighter pumps fuel into a B-47 Stratojet. The tanker has flown a swiveling, telescopic flying boom, controlled by means of a vee-shaped "ruddevator," into a slipway coupling in the jet's nose before beginning a high speed transfer of fuel. Demonstrating the latter method by lowering a trailing hose, *below, right*, a B-29, refuels a B-50 (at the bottom left of the picture) by gravity. The B-50 has used a grapnel hook to catch, reel in, and connect itself to the hose before receiving its fuel. The British loop-type gravity-feed method transferred nearly 2,600 gallons of fuel at a rate of 90 to 100 gallons per minute. The American boom-type force-feed method allowed a greater flow of fuel, approximately 200 gallons per minute.

Strategic Air Force

capacity, single point, refueling systems and evolve a method of satisfactory rendezvous and refueling under all-weather conditions."[65] Both B–36s and B–29s could be used as tankers, while all types of bombers should be modified to receive fuel. The committee also favored work on other methods to extend the range of medium bombers. These options included devices for towing bombers, schemes for droppable landing gear that could save weight on one-way missions, and tractor landing gear for use on undeveloped fields in the Arctic.[66]

The Aircraft and Weapons Board endorsed the project at its January meeting. Kenney said: "Well I don't know any project that is more important than the refueling project right now."[67] McNarney supported it, but as an interim solution. As he told the board: "It seems we are rapidly reaching the point where we are willing to rest the security of the United States on the ability to refuel in the air."[68] Partridge, the Director of Training and Requirements, favored the concept especially because it eliminated the need for one-way missions.[69]

The Heavy Bombardment Committee embraced aerial refueling in part because of its doubts about the capabilities of the B–36. However, the variable discharge turbine engine did offer some hope for increasing the bomber's speed over the target.[70] And on September 4, Convair offered to put variable discharge turbine engines on thirty-four models, to be called the B–36C. The added cost of the engines would be offset by cutting total production to ninety-five (twenty-two A, thirty-nine B, and thirty-four C models). Kenney still opposed the B–36 and saw no need to waste money on a fancy new engine. He recognized that the B–36s being produced would be useful for auxiliary support, including sea search, reconnaissance, towing lighter aircraft, and as tankers. In SAC's view, thirty-four B–36s did not represent air power. Yet, when Vandenberg polled the members of the Aircraft and Weapons Board in November, SAC offered the lone dissent-

---

[65] Rprt, Heavy Bombardment Cmte to AWB, Report of Heavy Bombardment, n.d. [Nov 47], p 6, RG 341, DCS/Dev, Dir/Rqmts, Papers 1st AWB, Box 181, MMB, NA.

[66] *Ibid. & passim.*

[67] Verbatim mins, 2d Meeting—USAF Aircraft and Weapons Board, January 27–30, 1948, 1st Day, Jan 27, 1948, pp 113–119, RG 341, DCS/Dev, Dir/Rqmts, 1st AWB, 1947–1948, Box 183, MMB, NA.

[68] *Ibid.*, pp 190–191.

[69] *Ibid.*, pp 189–190.

[70] Rprt, Heavy Bombardment Cmte to AWB, Report of Heavy Bombardment, n.d. [Nov 47], RG 341, DCS/Dev, Dir/Rqmts, Papers 1st AWB, Box 181, MMB, NA.

ing vote on procuring the B-36, and on December 5 the Air Force agreed to the Convair proposal.[71]

Central to the Air Force's long-term plans was the B-52. In its current design with piston engines, the Stratofortress seemed likely to fulfill the gloomy predictions of the critics of the superbomber. The Heavy Bombardment Committee agreed that it would not be an effective long-range aircraft and recommended a radical change: the Air Force should develop a bomber with a range of 8,000 miles, which air refueling would extend. With Wright turboprop T35 engines and a serious effort at reducing weight, such a plane could attain a speed of 550 miles per hour over the target. The committee urged that the new approach be adopted at once, and no more money be poured into what could only be a lumbering, fuel-consuming giant.[72]

This recommendation raised a complicated issue for the Air Force. Earlier, LeMay had noted the likelihood of other companies wanting to compete with Boeing in this field. Norstad's and Craig's staffs generally favored canceling the Boeing contract and calling for a design competition with new specifications. Partridge wanted to examine the Flying Wing design, believing in any case that the Air Force should be free to choose the best design available. Furthermore, in view of the number of contracts awarded to Boeing, the Air Force might be open to charges of favoritism. Air Staff members reasoned that, if Boeing's B-52 really was the best design, it would win the competition anyway, and the Air Force would gain confidence in the aircraft, though at the cost of some time.[73]

But there were ample arguments to retain the Boeing contract. The Air Force probably could not afford to waste time on a new competition.

---

[71] Ltr, Col T. C. Doubleday, R & E Div, ACAS-4 (Mat), to CG AMC, subj: Proposed B-36 Production Schedule Submitted by Consolidated-Vultee, Sep 10, 1947, with atchs; ltr, Brig Gen F. H. Smith, Sec AWB, to CG AMC, *et al*, subj: Proposal to Improve Performance of the Last Thirty-Four (34) B-36 Type Aircraft, Oct 15, 1947, with 1st Ind: Gen G. C. Kenney, CG SAC, to Sec AWB, Nov 3, 1947; memo, Brig Gen F. H. Smith, Sec AWB, to VCSAF, subj: Proposal to Improve Performance of the Last Thirty-Four (34) B-36 Type Aircraft, Dec 5, 1947, all in RG 341, DCS/Dev, Dir/Rqmts, Papers 1st AWB, Box 181, MMB, NA.

[72] Rprt, Heavy Bombardment Cmte to AWB, Report of Heavy Bombardment, n.d. [Nov 47], RG 341, DCS/Dev, Dir/Rqmts, Papers 1st AWB, Box 181, MMB, NA.

[73] R & R Sheet, Cmt 1, Maj Gen L. C. Craigie, Dir R & D, to Ch Rqmts Div, DCS/Ops, XB-52, Nov 6, 1947, with Cmt 2, Maj Gen E. E. Partridge, Dir Tng & Rqmts, to Dir R & D, Nov 19, 1947; MR, Maj W. D. Brady, Ch Bbr Sect, Acft Br, DCS/Mat, XB-52 Conference, Dec 2, 1947; SSS, Lt Gen H. A. Craig, DCS/Mat, to VCSAF, Heavy Bombardment Aircraft, Dec 1947, with atchs & draft memo to Sec AF, all in Bagwell, *XB-52 Airplane*.

Col. Clarence S. Irvine, as a member of the Heavy Bombardment Committee, had met with Boeing officials and reported their confidence that they could meet new specifications. Writing to Craig "in some haste" on November 28, he urged that Boeing be given a change order and the contract not be canceled. He objected to the delays a competition would entail. General McNarney, agreeing with Irvine, pointed out that any firm getting the contract would have to duplicate a lot of the work Boeing had already done. Also, the Air Force would lose $2.8 million that would revert to the U.S. Treasury as a result of the cancellation.[74] Nevertheless, after reviewing the arguments, Vandenberg discussed the question with Arthur S. Barrows, Undersecretary of the Air Force, and with Barrows's concurrence, decided to cancel the contract. The new military characteristics were released on December 8, 1947, and the staff began preparations for a competition.[75]

But the issue was not resolved without a fight. On December 26 William M. Allen, President of Boeing, sent Secretary Symington a letter protesting the proposed cancellation. Allen assured Symington that his company could make the necessary changes. Besides dealing an "injustice" to Boeing, cancellation would not be in the best interest of the government. Citing the Air Force's official contracting goals, Allen wrote: "This Company has consistently advocated that the Air Force award its business on the basis of merit." Otherwise the quality of work done would decline. Boeing would have no other Air Force work in production at the time the B–52s were on the assembly line, so favoritism could not be the issue.[76] McNarney sent Craigie a message on December 30 also opposing cancellation.[77] The next day Headquarters USAF halted cancellation proceedings pending further review.[78]

Partridge and Craig urged the staff to stand firm, noting support from RAND and the National Advisory Committee for Aeronautics for the Flying Wing design. At Symington's urging, Allen agreed to give the Flying Wing due consideration. After further discussion, key members of the Air

---

[74] Ltr, Col C. S. Irvine, Asst CS, SAC, to Maj Gen L. C. Craigie, Dir R & D USAF, Nov 28, 1947; msg, CG AMC to Dir R & D USAF, Dec 30, 1947, AT 1016, both in Bagwell, *XB–52 Airplane*.

[75] Bagwell, *XB–52 Airplane*, pp 13–19.

[76] Ltr, W. M. Allen, Pres Boeing Airplane Co, to W. S. Symington, Sec AF, Dec 26, 1947, in Bagwell, *XB–52 Airplane*.

[77] Msg, CG AMC, to Maj Gen L. C. Craigie, Dir R & D USAF, Dec 30, 1947, AT 1016, in Bagwell, *XB–52 Airplane*.

[78] Memo, Maj Gen L. C. Craigie, Dir R & D USAF, to DCS/Mat, subj: Development of Heavy Bombardment Aircraft, Feb 13, 1948, in Bagwell, *XB–52 Airplane*.

Staff met on February 14, 1948, and decided to keep the Boeing contract and issue a change order. Undersecretary Barrows concurred in the action. Despite the painful experience, the B-52 program had been radically redirected and was now aimed at fulfilling a new concept of strategic air operations.[79]

Thus even before the Aircraft and Weapons Board met in January, two of the major proposals up for consideration had already been approved. Both the B-36 and the B-52 had received a new lease on life, as had, incidentally, the Northrop YB-49 Flying Wing. Also, the report of the Heavy Bombardment Committee had become a basic document for the Air Staff. Besides offering the recommendations on specific hardware, the committee's report established a concept of strategic operations and a set of priorities. Although vague on tactics, the document offered some general considerations. With air refueling, effective bombing results seemed more likely. The committee envisioned attacks at night at an altitude above 35,000 feet. This meant that the Air Force would have to work on improving the accuracy of bombsights. Also, large numbers of planes would be needed in order to saturate the defense. Not all would carry atomic bombs; those that did not would serve as decoys. Some of these would have ferret reconnaissance equipment capable of detecting enemy radars. Others would be equipped with jamming equipment or even guns. Thus the atomic bomb carriers could save weight by not transporting this equipment themselves, and they could fly faster. The principal tactical recommendation involved using a bomber stream similar to the one the Royal Air Force had employed against Germany.[80]

The Bombardment Committee did take a stand in the controversy over armament. In order to lighten the load, the members urged that future bombers be armed only with a tail gun. This decision had to be made soon with the B-52 in order to avoid the old problem of guns not being ready when the airplane came out of production. RAND had argued that at 35,000 feet a fast bomber could only be attacked from the rear.

---

[79] Memo, Maj Gen E. E. Partridge, Dir Tng & Rqmts, to DCS/Ops, subj: New Heavy Bomber Contracts, Jan 8, 1948, with atch: Reasons Why Competition is Desirable; memo, Lt Gen H. A. Craig, subj: XB-52 Development, Jan 15, 1948; ltr, W. M. Allen, Pres Boeing Airplane Co, to W. S. Symington, Sec AF, Feb 6, 1948; R & R Sheet, Cmt 1, Brig Gen D. L. Putt, Dep Ch Eng Div, AMC, Extracts from Daily Activity Reports of Headquarters USAF, Jan 14, 1948; msg, Hq USAF to Maj Gen A. R. Crawford, Ch Eng Div AMC, #1817, Feb 18, 1948, all in Bagwell, *XB-52 Airplane*.
[80] Rprt, Heavy Bombardment Cmte to AWB, Report of Heavy Bombardment, n.d. [Nov 47], RG 341, DCS/Dev, Dir/Rqmts, Papers 1st AWB, Box 181, MMB, NA.

Strategic Air Force

Advocates of Aerial Refueling. *Left to right:* Brig. Gen. Thomas S. Power, Acting Director of Air Force Training and Requirements; Maj. Gen. Laurence C. Craigie, Director of Research and Development for the Deputy Chief of Staff for Materiel; Brig. Gen.

Tests pitting P-80 against P-80 seemed to confirm this, but tests against bombers were pending.[81] Col. Pearl H. Robey of the Air University recognized that the implications were not easy to accept. As he told the Aircraft and Weapons Board:

> So it was with great reluctance that the [committee] said, "cast aside some of this armament;" because there were a lot of the boys on the Board [*sic*, the committee] who have been shot at. I can assure you that this was a last resort and was not taken lightly....[82]

Kenney bridled at suggestions of an evasive maneuver by a heavy bomber: "You get a bomber that just runs about 'G-ing' the crew to death all the time to keep from getting shot down." But amid the laughter the board accepted the committee's recommendation.[83]

In fact on many issues, the Aircraft and Weapons Board served merely as a sounding board for dissenters. Kenney's objections to the B-36

---

[81] *Ibid.*

[82] Verbatim mins, 2d Meeting—USAF Aircraft and Weapons Board, January 27-30, 1948, 1st Day, Jan 27, 1948, p 131, RG 341, DCS/Dev, Dir/Rqmts, Papers 1st AWB, Box 181, MMB, NA.

[83] *Ibid.*, p 138.

Decision for a Strategic Force

Frederic H. Smith, Jr., Chief of the Requirements Division of the Directorate of Training and Requirements; and Maj. Gen. Earle E. Partridge, the Assistant Chief of Air Staff for Operations, pushed hard for the acceptance of an aerial refueling program throughout the Air Force.

provided some comic relief, as did his reference to the planned purchase as "hundreds of marvelous tankers." But McNarney challenged Kenney to offer an alternative, and the committee's report stood.[84]

The Aircraft and Weapons Board confirmed the reorientation of the B-52 program, although it cut the required speed from 550 miles per hour to 500. Also at this meeting, LeMay reminded the members of the importance of strategic reconnaissance to the bombing of Japan. The Soviets would probably try harder to keep the target areas from being photographed, so the reconnaissance plane had to have good performance. Kenney concurred with the board's preference for the F-12 and approved funding it by cutting fifteen planes from the fiscal 1949 program for the B-50. For SAC and the Air Force as a whole, strategic reconnaissance had a higher priority than a new medium bomber. The board further proposed deferring funding for the medium aircraft until fiscal 1950. This would allow tests of both the B-47 and the Northrop B-49 Flying Wing.[85]

As finally approved, the total program for fiscal 1948 would consist of 664 aircraft. There would be no money for extra B-50s, for the F-12 (an acceptable cut since the project was behind schedule), or for the P-87. For fiscal 1949 the Bureau of the Budget had left the Air Force with $1,469 billion of direct appropriations, including $700 million for procuring air-

---

[84] *Ibid.*, pp 113–119 & *passim.*
[85] *Ibid.*, pp 192–195 & *passim.*

craft and $145 million for research and development. The program would buy 913 planes, including 91 B-50s and 20 F-12s. This was the third straight year of deep cuts in research and development, and the board agreed that if Congress appropriated more money, it should go for that purpose. The highest priority in development was air refueling, followed by the B-52, the F-12, medium bombers, armament, and an air-launched missile. A five-year purchasing program called for acquiring 186 B-50s per year until fiscal 1953, when the airmen hoped to begin buying a new bomber. Over the same period, the F-12 purchase would be 26 per year.[86]

By February 1948, the Air Force had charted a course for the next several years. An ambitious program to modernize the strategic bomber force had been approved, and goals existed for increasing the atomic stockpile and supporting elements. But implementation of this program would require money and effort. Whatever level of manning and funding was approved by Congress, it would be applied first to the development of the atomic force. Other missions of the Air Force would be served with any remaining resources. In developing this program, the service heeded the warnings of Spaatz and Symington and showed its determination to prove its ability to handle the critical atomic mission. The resources of the nation now were directed to building the atomic stockpile, developing the Special Weapons Project, modernizing the bomber force, and especially advancing air refueling technologies. The success of the agencies responsible for these activities would determine America's atomic capabilities for the foreseeable future.

---

[86] Rprt, Gen H. S. Vandenberg, VCSAF, *et al*, Summary Minutes of the 2d Meeting of the USAF Aircraft and Weapons Board (January 27, 28, 29, and 30, 1948), Feb 10, 1948, in RG 341, DCS/Dev, Dir/Rqmts, Mins 1st AWB, Box 183, MMB, NA.

Chapter VI

The Year of Crisis

Whether American leaders anticipated the critical international situation that developed during 1948 may be open to interpretation, but obviously the events had political repercussions during a presidential election year. Until 1948 Truman continued to hope that he could keep the budget under control. The White House had been reluctant to release the Finletter report in part because it would bring pressure to increase spending on the Air Force. However, the deepening Cold War irrevocably altered the assumptions underlying the administration's original budget and created urgent new problems. Late in February a coup in Prague brought the communists to power in Czechoslovakia. On March 5 a message from Gen. Lucius D. Clay, Commanding General, European Command, and U.S. Military Governor in Germany, noted "a subtle change in [the Soviet] attitude...which now gives me a feeling that [war] may come with dramatic suddenness,"[1] Evidently matters were more dangerous than had been thought. However exaggerated some of the fears may have been, and however much the warnings were motivated by the politics of the defense budget (and Clay's certainly were), the subsequent crisis over Berlin posed a genuine risk to world security. In Washington, fear of war would reach its peak in September.

As a result, Truman had to relax his budget limits somewhat. For Forrestal, this was encouraging, but the Defense Secretary still had to wrestle with continuing disputes among the services. For its part, the Air Force's effectiveness in the strategic air offensive would be limited by the degree of its control over the atomic weapons essential to that offensive.

---

[1] Msg, Gen L. D. Clay, US Mil Governor Germany, to Lt Gen S. J. Chamberlin, Dir Intel, Dept Army, Mar 5, 1948, in Jean E. Smith, ed, *The Papers of Lucius D. Clay,*. Vol II: *Germany, 1945–1949* (Bloomington, Ind: Univ of Indiana, 1974), pp 568–569.

Strategic Air Force

Twice during 1948, once at Key West, Florida, and again at Newport, Rhode Island, Forrestal tried to reach an interservice agreement and found this an elusive goal.

The Soviet blockade of Berlin in June brought American thinking sharply into focus. Even before, the joint chiefs were sufficiently concerned with the gravity of the situation to adopt, finally, a joint war plan. But given the general unreadiness of the armed forces, the chiefs also realized the true danger posed by the Berlin crisis. Fortunately, the airlift of provisions to the city, adopted as an expedient measure, proved a success and seemed likely to sustain the Western position for a long time. War did not erupt, and the Soviet plan to absorb Berlin failed. But deterrence of a world war rested on a slender reed. The relationship of force requirements to national policy was now easier to clarify, and an agreed policy of increasing military strength began to take hold.

In its deployments to Europe during the Berlin crisis, SAC was able to play a significant role in Western diplomacy. Yet despite this "show of force," there were reasons to doubt that the command was really ready for combat. As the modification finally began to provide SAC with an expanded atomic delivery capability, the operational readiness of the force became increasingly important. The result was closer attention to the actual state of affairs in SAC, and this in turn eventually led to a change in command.

Already new leadership had emerged at the top of the Air Force. On April 30 General Spaatz retired. Gen. Hoyt S. Vandenberg, the vice chief, became his successor, though both George C. Kenney, commanding SAC, and Joseph T. McNarney, at Air Materiel Command, were senior to him. For the new vice chief, Vandenberg called on Maj. Gen. Muir S. Fairchild, Commander of Air University. Fifty-three years old and a flyer since 1918, Fairchild had acquired extensive experience with the Joint Staff during the war.[2]

Toward A Crisis Budget

Under the budget submitted to Congress on January 12, 1948, the national military establishment would receive authorizations for $9.8 billion in fiscal year 1949. The Air Force share amounted to $3.3 billion, direct and indirect. The cut in aircraft procurement by the Bureau of the

---

[2] Fogerty, Study #91, pp 1917–1952.

Budget (from $892 to $700 million) accounted for a disproportionately larger cut in the number of airplanes (1,506 to 913) because the reduction especially affected trainers and other light, low-cost planes. Truman was determined to keep military spending down so that he could support the Marshall Plan and still balance the federal budget in an election year. Furthermore, this spending plan acknowledged Forrestal's belief that national strength required economic strength and would be undermined by excessive government spending. Though strongly supportive of the need for increases in the Air Force budget, the Finletter report did not lead to any change in the administration's plans. In fact, on February 2, when the House of Representatives passed a larger tax cut than the President had requested, increases in military spending became even less likely.[3]

Despite his fiscal conservatism, Truman did support a strong policy of deterrence. He took a broad view, attempting to balance several factors: a budget the country could afford, a strong Europe, and universal military training (UMT). The strongest advocates of these alternatives included the President himself and Secretary of State Marshall.[4] The Army largely supported UMT, and Forrestal had obtained assurances of support from the Air Force and the Navy, although Kenney feared that the Air Force would have to take an inordinate number of "half-wits" (presumably, men with low Army General Classification Test scores) under such a program.[5] In previous Congresses, UMT had not fared well, but Marshall believed that this reluctance to act would make the program a more effective deterrent when it was finally passed. Adopting such an unpleasant measure would show that Americans were determined to preserve world peace, even at a high personal cost. On the other hand, those who objected to the concept of universal military training found a technologically based alter-

---

[3] Verbatim mins, 2d Meeting—USAF Aircraft and Weapons Board, January 27–30, 1948, 3d Day, pp 405–407, in RG 341, DCS/Dev, Dir/Rqmts, Papers 1st AWB, Box 181, MMB, NA; hearings before the Committee on Appropriations, House, *Military Functions, National Military Establishment Appropriations Bill for 1949*, 80th Cong, 2d Sess, Pt 2, Mar 19, 1948, p 39; Rearden, *Formative Years*, pp 309–313. The federal appropriation historically had evolved into an *authorization* to "obligate" funds. This could be done through disbursing cash or by making a contract that committed the government to spend money. In any fiscal year an agency might not yet have spent or otherwise obligated funds voted in a previous year. What then counted was the authority to spend or contract for *new* funds; hence "new obligational authority" (NOA). The term "authorization" as used here refers to NOA.

[4] Rearden, *Formative Years*, pp 12–15.

[5] Forrestal, *Diaries*, pp 384–385; Verbatim rprt, 7th Meeting of the Air Board, January 6–7, 1948, pp 13–15, RG 340, Air Bd, Mins of Mtgs, 1946–1948, Box 18, MMB, NA.

native in the Finletter Commission report, which stressed the importance of air power in a future war[6] or as a deterrent.

The issues of air power and UMT, though significant, were suddenly overtaken by the international situation. Forrestal, always concerned with the link between armed strength and foreign policy, remained a supporter of the strategy of containment as outlined by George F. Kennan. While the Truman Doctrine and the Marshall Plan were the essential elements of this strategy, an important implication was that local incidents could lead to violence and thus trigger a world war. It might be necessary to bring American military force to bear at points where communist pressure was too strong or where fighting raised the risk of Soviet intervention. As he looked at the map, Forrestal saw several potential trouble spots. Disturbing reports on the civil war in Greece had been coming in all through the fall of 1947. The United States might have to send in troops or cede the country to Stalinist domination. Another group of foreign policy analysts foresaw a similar problem in China. Growing violence between Arabs and Jews in Palestine was proving to be more than the fifty-seven thousand British troops there could handle. Forrestal feared that the administration might be pressured into sending troops to replace the British, probably under the auspices of the United Nations. A critical period was approaching in Korea, where the U.S. occupation forces were already below strength. And many Americans feared that the communists might win a crucial election in Italy, possibly touching off civil war. With all the unrest overseas, precious few American fighting men were available should war come.[7]

As of February 1, 1948, the actual strength of the Army totaled 552,000, well under the budgeted figure, although the Marines had another 79,000 men. Recruiting was so slow that a continued decline could not be avoided. MacArthur, commanding in the Far East, said that his 140,000 men were 50,000 short of what he needed, even if Korea remained quiet. Fewer than 100,000 American personnel were stationed in Europe, and these were tied down with occupation duties in Germany and Austria. To back up its overseas forces, the Army at home had only two understrength divisions and an armored combat command of 2,000 men. Adding mobile support troops and eleven Marine battalion landing teams, the nation had a strategic reserve of 70,000 men in the continental United States. One trouble spot alone might require all the reserve forces. And besides personnel, there were shortages of critical equipment. Maj. Gen. Alfred M. Gruenther, U.S. Army, the Director of the Joint Staff, warned that

---

[6] Forrestal, *Diaries*, pp 369–388.
[7] *Ibid.*, pp 374–377 & *passim*; Rearden, *Formative Years*, pp 316–318.

deployment of more than a division (about 15,000 men) would require a partial mobilization, politically speaking a momentous step.[8]

In a meeting on February 12, 1948, the National Security Council discussed the civil strife in Greece. According to Forrestal, Secretary Marshall observed that "we are playing with fire while we have nothing with which to put it out." The Assistant Secretary of the Air Force for Materiel, Cornelius V. Whitney, representing Symington at the meeting, offered a proposal. Since the Air Force wanted to exercise its B-29 units in strategic areas, a few flights into Greek airfields by the bombers might serve the dual function of showing American strength and resolve while training the force. Thus strategic air power might be used in place of troops. Marshall agreed to consider the proposal, but both he and Forrestal appeared more interested in the problem of finding enough ground troops to deploy to Greece.[9] On February 18 the discussion turned to Palestine as the two leaders accompanied Army Secretary Royall and the joint chiefs to the White House. There Gruenther briefed the President on the military manpower crisis. Forrestal used personnel data to support his often repeated warning against allowing political pressure to force the United States to intervene in Palestine. He won Truman's approval for a discreet approach to Republican leaders for help in depoliticizing the Palestine issue by explaining the readiness problem.[10]

For the moment, this was all that Truman was willing to concede. But over the following week the news from Prague transformed the situation. The communist coup meant the elimination of the last vestiges of relative freedom in Czechoslovakia and dashed any hope of that country's shifting its allegiance away from the Soviet Union.[11] Although George F. Kennan at the State Department had warned of such a move, apparently in hopes of forestalling panic when it came, the Western leaders were stunned.[12] On March 10 Jan Masaryk, Czechoslovakia's foreign minister, much admired in the West as a liberal figure, was found dead in Prague under suspicious circumstances.[13] Meanwhile Clay's warning message had arrived, giving further confirmation to the growing Soviet threat and to a

---

[8] Forrestal, *Diaries*, pp 374-377.
[9] *Ibid.*, pp 370-373.
[10] *Ibid.*, pp 374-377.
[11] Msg, L. A. Steinhardt, U.S. Ambassador Czecho, to Sec State, Feb 26, 1948, no subj, in *FRUS*, 1948, Vol IV, pp 738-741, & 736n.
[12] *Ibid.*; rprt, Policy Planning Staff, State Dept, Resume of World Situation, Nov 6, 1947, in *FRUS*, 1947, Vol I, p 771; Rearden, *Formative Years*, pp 279-280.
[13] Rearden, *Formative Years*, p 280.

Strategic Air Force

George F. Kennan, State Department official and originator of the strategy of containment.

similar notice, some months earlier, from Gen. Ennis Whitehead, Commanding General of Far East Air Forces, that the Soviets were contemplating war.[14]

Directly involving the Soviet Union, the collapse of Czechoslovakia represented a crisis far worse than the Palestine unrest that had preoccupied Forrestal. The Strategic Air Command still had only one group ready for atomic operations. Its other forces were understrength and dependent on overseas bases if they had to strike at the USSR. Currently available bases in Europe were vulnerable to a westward sweep of powerful Soviet ground forces. And the Joint Chiefs of Staff had yet not approved a war plan.

In this time of extreme danger, the Secretary of Defense also saw an important opportunity for the services to resolve their rivalries. For some time, Forrestal had been planning to hold discussions to settle interservice differences, and on March 11 he took the joint chiefs to Key West, Florida, for a long weekend of meetings. Confronting a communist threat to world peace, the top military leaders appeared to reach agreement on several major issues:[15] the relationship of the Navy and the Air Force in strategic air operations; establishment of basic conditions for an agreed war plan

---

[14] Ltr, Lt Gen E. C. Whitehead, CG FEAF, to Gen C. A. Spaatz, CSAF, Dec 9, 1947, AFHRA 168.6008-3 Spaatz.

[15] Rearden, *Formative Years*, pp 282, 395-397; Forrestal, *Diaries*, pp 390-394.

and budget; a proposal for the reintroduction of the draft; and a call for increased military spending.[16]

On March 15 Forrestal brought the chiefs' proposals to the White House to win the President's support.[17] The next day he told a subcommittee of the House Appropriations Committee that Truman would probably seek a supplemental appropriation for fiscal 1949. The secretary warned against expecting mammoth increases, speaking in words that were to become a refrain: "Our defense organization...must be looked upon as but one factor. Among the others are high domestic production, a balanced budget, and a sound currency."[18] On March 17 the President addressed a joint special session of Congress. Condemning the bellicose policies of the USSR, he called on Americans to stand firm. He asked for full funding of the Marshall Plan program, enactment of universal military training, and the revival of selective service as a stopgap measure until UMT resolved the critical manpower problem.[19]

In the rapid pace of events, Forrestal and the military chiefs may not have fully understood Truman's agenda. Perhaps it would take time for the armed services to adjust to the complex issues involved in balancing foreign policy, domestic, and military requirements. In reality, there is ample reason to believe that the President, with Director of the Budget Webb at his side, had no intention of undertaking a major rearmament. By implementing selective service and some budget increases, Truman would attempt to correct the most glaring weaknesses in the nation's military power. These initiatives, along with universal military training, would increase preparedness for war and, by demonstrating national resolve, perhaps deter war. But for the President the surest defense lay in building a strong Europe, able to defend itself and immune to communist meddling. The European powers, meeting at Brussels, signed an alliance the same day that Truman addressed Congress. The formation of the Western European Union was a vital first step in rearming the West, both in military and moral strength.[20] A seventy-group air force had yet to win such an endorsement from the administration.

---

[16] *Ibid.*
[17] Forrestal, *Diaries*, pp 392–394.
[18] Hearings before the Committee on Appropriations, House, *Military Functions, National Military Establishment Appropriations Bill for 1949*, 80th Cong, 2d sess, Pt 1, Mar 16, 1948, p 13 & *passim.*
[19] Rearden, *Formative Years*, p 283.
[20] *Ibid.*, p 459. The Brussels Pact countries were the United Kingdom, France, Belgium, the Netherlands, and Luxembourg.

Strategic Air Force

Roles, Missions, and Budgets

The timing of the Berlin crisis, just before the joint chiefs' conference at Key West, was particularly fortuitous for Forrestal, as it showed the necessity for the services to agree on a war plan and defense program. The public quarreling between the Air Force and the Navy had placed the onus on the Secretary of Defense to achieve the true unification called for by the National Security Act of 1947. Shortly after Admiral Nimitz retired as Chief of Naval Operations, he issued a statement asserting, in part, that until the Air Force could develop a genuine intercontinental force at some future date, the Navy's carriers were prepared to conduct strategic operations. Similar observations and rejoinders appeared in a series of leaked newspaper stories and planted articles, which revealed the depth of the interservice rivalries. While Secretary of the Air Force Symington contended that the Navy was the worse offender, a full quota of ill-feeling existed on both sides. Many friends of the Navy believed that the Air Force wanted to absorb all aviation and virtually to abolish the aircraft carrier. On the Air Force side, the Navy was believed to be intent on wresting control of the strategic bombing mission. Also, although this was not a public issue, Air Force leaders saw proposals to allocate scarce atomic bombs to the Navy as a diversion from the proper use of the weapons.[21] The questions thus raised were at the heart of any discussion of budgets for the services, as they impinged directly on the plans and requirements each service could present to the administration and Congress as the basis of its funding. Defined under the heading of "roles and missions," these were the major issues considered at Key West.

The results of the conference appeared encouraging. The chiefs at Key West resolved several issues, clearing away obstacles to a joint war plan. Also, Forrestal obtained the draft of an agreement on the functions of the three services, which among other considerations, acknowledged the Air Force's primary responsibility for the strategic air offensive, although the Navy could assist in "the over-all air effort as directed by the Joint Chiefs of Staff." The Navy retained its sea-based atomic role; it could use "weapons and equipment" deemed suitable to do its job and could attack

---

[21] Ltr, W. S. Symington, Sec AF, to President Truman, May 24, 1948, with atch memo, subj: Naval Aviation Program; rprt, Adm C. W. Nimitz, The Future Employment of Naval Forces, Jan 7, 1948, both in RG 340, Spec File 4A, Roles & Missions Corres, MMB, NA; Rearden, *Formative Years*, pp 386–393.

any targets related to the fleet's mission. Conversely, the Navy was barred from developing a strategic air force.[22]

The most immediate result of the Key West agreements was a presidential endorsement of an increase in the defense budget, which Truman quickly approved. Forrestal had to allocate this money among the services and defend the revised budget before Congress. To settle interservice disputes by granting each side's request would create an enormous, politically unacceptable budget. And the Secretary of Defense, with his financial background, had strong views about the inflationary pressures that a large federal budget would impose on the economy. Forrestal's solution was "balanced forces," a sort of fair sharing of deficiencies. The argument, as advanced by Forrestal, Marshall, and others, began by acknowledging the primacy of air power in modern war. But the Air Force needed overseas bases in order to deliver the decisive blow in the event of war. This required a strong army to seize and hold base areas. One briefing prepared for Congress envisioned that a typical base complex supporting twenty air groups would require seven divisions and a total air and ground strength of 500,000 men. In addition, a strong navy would be needed to secure sea lanes and help obtain the bases. And the Navy asserted that the carrier task force was the most effective tool for these purposes. Adm. Louis E. Denfeld, the new Chief of Naval Operations, rejected the more extreme naval thesis, namely that the best bases for the strategic air offensive were floating ones. In any case, Forrestal argued that a seventy-group air force implied an army strong enough to support it and a navy that could operate on a comparable scale. Secretary Sullivan supported him by testifying that the Navy would need 550,000 men to support a seventy-group Air Force. While Forrestal considered seventy groups a desirable goal, he recognized that the country could not afford the ground and naval forces necessary to support them.[23]

The services backed Forrestal before Congress in March, albeit reluctantly. Spaatz did make vague references to the day when strategic air

---

[22] Memo, J. V. Forrestal, Sec Def, to Sec Army, Sec AF, et al, Apr 21, 1948, with atch: Functions of the Armed Forces and the Joint Chiefs of Staff; MR, Maj Gen A. M. Gruenther, Dir Jt Staff, Functions of the Armed Forces and the Joint Chiefs of Staff, Mar 26, 1948, both in Alice Cole, Alfred Goldberg, et al, eds, *The Department of Defense: Documents on Establishment and Organization, 1944–1978* (Washington: OSD, 1978), pp 274–289.

[23] Hearings before the Committee on Armed Services, Senate, 80th Cong, 2d sess, *Universal Military Training*, Mar 18, 1948, pp 31ff; Mar 25, 1948, pp 336, 351–352, 395–396; hearings before the Committee on Armed Services, House, 80th Cong, 2d sess, *Selective Service*, Apr 12, 1948, p 6098; Apr 13, 1948, pp 6204–6205.

forces could operate directly from the continental United States.[24] Ironically, the "balanced forces" concept faced its most serious opposition from Congress, not the service chiefs. There the request for a supplemental appropriation for defense, finally set at $3 billion, came under consideration at the same time as the bill for universal military training. Opposition to UMT was galvanizing, sparking a major debate on national strategy.

Most congressmen agreed with General Bradley's assessment of the Cold War. "...we are competing [with the Soviets] for the hearts and minds of men in Europe and Asia...."[25] Secretary Marshall, whose name would be forever linked to the plan for European recovery, emphasized the role of universal military training as a deterrent to aggression. He told the Senate Committee on Armed Services that UMT would demonstrate the resolve of the American people to defend freedom.[26] Though Senator Arthur Vandenberg and many of the Republicans were willing to forego their isolationist preconceptions and support aid to Europe, they could not resist the powerful tide of opposition to UMT. Under the circumstances, a widespread belief emerged that either the possession of the atomic bomb by itself or the existence of an effective atomic Air Force would suffice to deter the Soviet Union. The Finletter and Brewster reports had done much to promote this point of view. They thus gave the Republicans the basis for an alternative defense policy.[27] But members of both parties could identify with a demoncratic congressman from Arkansas who reported his constituents worries about the neglect of the Air Force.[28] Even Forrestal, in a measured statement on the atomic bomb, testified that:

> The mere possession of this undoubted asset would not necessarily turn the scale of war, if war should come. But its possession has undoubted power to dissuade from aggression any nation which believes we have sufficient military strength to put that weapon to effective use.[29]

---

[24] Hearings before the Committee on Armed Services, Senate, *Universal Military Training*, 80th Cong, 2d sess, Mar 25, 1948, pp 390–395.
[25] *Ibid.*, Mar 25, 1948, pp 351–352.
[26] *Ibid.*, Mar 17, 1948, pp 3–29.
[27] Forrestal, *Diaries*, pp 388, 413–414.
[28] Hearings before the Committee on Appropriations, House, *Military Functions, National Military Establishment Appropriation Bill for 1949*, 80th Cong, 2d sess, Mar 24, 1948, Pt 2, pp 99–100.
[29] Hearings before the Committee on Armed Services, Senate, *Universal Military Training*, 80th Cong, 2d sess, Mar 23, 1948, p 329.

For the Air Force, Symington described the atomic weapon as

> an active deterrent to any aggressor and...the force which envelops him in prompt and decisive retaliatory action if he risks war with the United States.[30]

As the sense of crisis receded somewhat, the debate on Capitol Hill continued through April and May 1948. The bill for reviving Selective Service passed, but universal military training died. Despite Forrestal's efforts, and thanks to judicious maneuvering by Symington, Congress voted the Air Force more funds than the President had requested. The Air Secretary indeed risked being removed for insubordination, testifying that if forced to choose between a seventy-group air force and universal military training, he would consider seventy groups more important to national security. To the President's request for $1.1 billion for aircraft, intended as a supplement in fiscal 1948 to allow the immediate letting of contracts, Congress added $822 million, to give a total just short of the Brewster Committee's recommendation. Spaatz agreed to an arrangement to raise the Air Force's personnel ceiling and to equip a total of sixty-six groups by the end of June 1949. This fell short of the full program by a few airlift and tactical air units. Strategic forces, under the current revision, would consist of twenty heavy and medium bomber groups and six for very long range reconnaissance.[31]

In spite of the setback, Truman continued to hold the line on defense spending. He had succeeded in getting a discretionary clause inserted in the supplemental appropriation that allowed him to refuse to spend the extra funds. When he signed the appropriation bills, he set ceilings on the services for 1949 as well. The Air Force limits of 400,000 personnel and 9,240 airplanes he later raised to 411,000 and 9,800 respectively, but at the same time the President released $1.3 billion to the Air Force to begin buying more airplanes. He also intended to set firm limits for the upcoming budget for 1950. On May 13 he told the military leaders that the ceiling for defense spending would be $15 billion.[32]

---

[30] Hearings before the Committee on Appropriations, House, *Military Functions, National Military Establishment Appropriation Bill for 1949*, 80th Cong, 2d sess, Pt 2, Mar 19, 1948, p 5.
[31] Hearings before the Committee on Armed Services, House, *Selective Service*, 80th Cong, 2d sess, Apr 13, 1948, pp 6136–6140; Rearden, *Formative Years*, pp 316–333.
[32] Rearden, *Formative Years*, pp 328–335; Mary R. Self, *History of the USAF Five-Year Aircraft Procurement Program, Jan 1, 1948–Jul 1, 1949* (Wright-Patterson AFB, Ohio: AMC, 1949), pp 11–14.

1949 Air Force Budget and Supplement

FY 49 Request	Aircraft Program	Voted for FY 49
$1.5 billion	$700 million	$897 million

For Aircraft	FY 49 Request	FY 48 Supplemental	
		Requested	Voted
Brewster Committee $2 billion	$700 million	$1.1 billion	$1.9 billion[a]
	(for tooling)	$108 million	$108 million
		$1.2 billion	$2 billion

Final Allocation, by Service, FY 48 Supplemental and FY 49

Army	Navy	Air Force
$5.8 billion	$4.4 billion	$3 billion
(approximately $1.8 billion for support of Air Force)		($2 billion for aircraft, $897 million for other)

[a] 100 million deleted for light aircraft. Aircraft procurment deleted from FY 49, placed in FY 48 so as not to have to wait for 1 July 1948.

The Air Force's plans for war, as has been noted, now included provisions for an atomic offensive, and SAC had written its own plans accordingly. However, at the beginning of 1948, the Joint Chiefs of Staff had approved no plan for joint action in the event of war. Committees had been working on BROILER as a plan for an emergency, but early in the year the joint chiefs called for a revision. The Air Force staff prepared plan HARROW as its contribution. Incorporated into the joint plan FROLIC, this concept came before the JCS in March. There both Admiral Leahy, still Chief of Staff to the President, and Admiral Denfeld attacked the heavy reliance on an atomic offensive, and although Spaatz defended the plan, it remained unapproved. In April, however, FROLIC served as the basis of the U.S. position in staff talks in Washington with the British and Canadians. The resulting allied plan, ABC (American-British-Canadian)–101, coordinated the British plan DOUBLEQUICK and a new American plan, HALF-MOON. On May 19, 1948, the JCS finally adopted "for planning purposes" the plans agreed upon with the British.[33]

HALFMOON outlined the initial actions the United States should take if attacked by USSR during the coming twelve months. It concentrated on the first phase, when the allies would evacuate such vulnerable areas as the European mainland, defend vital bases and lines of communications, and initiate a strategic air offensive "designed to exploit the destructive and psychological power of atomic weapons against the vital elements of the Soviet war-making capacity...."[34] In the second phase, the allies would build up bases in the Middle East and elsewhere in preparation for an ultimate counteroffensive. The objective of the war would be to cripple or destroy the Soviet Union's ability or will to make war, or at least to drive back the aggressor.[35]

For the strategic air offensive, SAC units were to deploy to England, Egypt, and Okinawa. If England proved untenable, the allies would shift their bases to Iceland. At the outset of the war, the Eighth Air Force's SADDLETREE-modified planes would start shuttling bombs from the Atomic Energy Commission's storage sites to England or the other bases. The assembly teams, still few in number, would go to England. As the atomic bombs were assembled, they would be dropped on targets, and the bombers would stage back to the continental United States for maintenance and more bombs. The targets were twenty major Soviet cities containing the largest share of the war-supporting industries. Meanwhile, conventional bombers would strike at oil targets and mine shipping lanes. Under HALFMOON, the Commanding General of SAC would control atomic operations, and theater commanders in England and the Middle East were to be Air Force officers. Naval carrier forces would "supplement and support the air offensive to the extent practical consistent with their primary task."[36]

With its atomic annex, plan HALFMOON, addressed the limitations under which the United States would be operating if war came in 1948. Atomic bombs remained disassembled and stored in the AEC's sites, and the few trained assembly teams and weaponeers were available to man the limited number of SADDLETREE bombers. Given the complexities of navi-

---

[33] K. Condit, *JCS, 1947-1949*, pp 283-289.
[34] Note, JCS 1844/4 Secs, Brief of Short-Range Emergency Plan HALFMOON, May 19, 1948, with encl, p 32, RG 341, DCS/Ops, OPD, Spec File HALFMOON, Sect 1, Box 1045, MMB, NA.
[35] *Ibid.*, pp 30ff.
[36] *Ibid.*; notes, Col G. Y. Jumper, Ch Pl & Intel Div, SWG, to Maj Gen D. M. Schlatter, Actg Ch SWG, n.d., RG 341, DCS/Ops, Asst for AE, TS 1948, 322 Spec Weapons Gp, Box 7, MMB, NA.

Strategic Air Force

DARKHORSE **War Planners.** *Clockwise from above:* Col. Wiley D. Ganey, Deputy Chief of the Operations in the Office of the Director of Plans and Operations; Col. James B. Knapp of the Office of the Director of Plans and Operations; and Cols. Paul Tibbets, George Y. Jumper, and Milton F. Summerfelt of the Special Weapons Group.

gating by radar over unknown territory, often snow-covered, finding the targets posed special problems.[37] Thus, cities made better targets than smaller industrial or transportation centers. Still, airmen were optimistic, even hoping that the atomic attack would knock Russia out of the war before the phase two counteroffensive plan had to be executed.[38]

With the sense of crisis in the spring of 1948, implementing HALF-MOON became an urgent priority. A crash program had started at the end of 1947 to prepare target folders by the beginning of June 1948. On the basis of ABC-101 the United States could approach the British about

---

[37] See note above; K. Condit, *JCS, 1947–1949,* pp 292–293; memo, Maj Gen G. C. McDonald, Dir Intel, to AAG, subj: Printing Requirements for Crash Program, Apr 21, 1948, RG 341, TS AAG File 33, Box 11, MMB, NA; memo, Col G. Y. Jumper, Ch Pl & Intel Div, SWG, subj: Daily Diary, Apr 6, 1948, RG 341, DCS/Ops, Asst for AE, TS 1948, 314.7 Daily Diary (Pl & Intel), Box 6, MMB, NA.

[38] Ltr, Col H. Bunker, Chmn T & TLC, to Col J. G. Armstrong, Dep Ch SWG, subj: Activities of Special Weapons Group, Apr 9, 1948, RG 341, DCS/Ops, Asst for AE, TS 1948, 314.7 Consolidated Diary, Box 6, MMB, NA.

bases, although LeMay had already sent officers from his headquarters in Wiesbaden to confer with the RAF. There were thought to be six fields in England that could handle B-29s. Okinawa was ready to support atomic operations, and Col. Robert O. Cork, Kenney's Assistant Chief of Staff for Plans, had investigated the possibility of using British bases in Egypt.[39]

Difficult as it had been to develop an acceptable joint emergency war plan, a longer-term plan, which would affect future budgets, was nearly impossible to negotiate. Early in 1948 the Air Staff began work on a medium-term war plan along lines suggested by General Spaatz. Known as DARKHORSE, this plan concentrated on an atomic offensive in a war taking place in 1951 or 1952, employing the kind of Air Force outlined in the Finletter and Brewster reports. The offensive would be a large blow delivered as rapidly as possible. In February, Col. Wiley D. Ganey, Deputy Chief of the Operations Division (Office of the Director of Plans and Operations), convened a panel to work on the details. Among the participants were Knapp from Plans, Paul Tibbets, and Cols. George Y. Jumper and Milton F. Summerfelt of the Special Weapons Group.[40]

The planners of DARKHORSE agreed that air refueling would be essential for an intercontinental effort. Jumper acknowledged that staging through forward bases left much to be desired. "As is well known to anyone who flies an airplane, every landing is an invitation to difficulties...." The operations of the B-29s through China during the previous war seemed to confirm this.[41] While overseas bases had value and were part of the plan, they "all present the same diplomatic inaccessibility. They are not operationally ready. They need construction and stockpiling.

---

[39] Notes, Col G. Y. Jumper, Ch Pl & Intel Div, SWG, to Maj Gen D. M. Schlatter, Actg Ch SWG, n.d., RG 341, DCS/Ops, Asst for AE, TS 1948, 322 Spec Weapons Gp, Box 7; ltr, Lt Gen C. E. LeMay, CG USAFE, to Gen H. S. Vandenberg, VCSAF, Feb 19, 1948, RG 341, TS AAG File 13, Box 5; Daily Diary, Col G. Y. Jumper, Ch Pl & Intel Div, SWG, Apr 20, 1948, RG 341, DCS/Ops, Asst for AE, TS 1948, 314.7 Daily Diary (Pl & Intel), Box 6; memo to Gen H. S. Vandenberg, CSAF, subj: Discussion of Advice to be Given to Planners on Emergency War Plan and Request for JCS Confirmation of Soundness Thereof, Oct 13, 1948, RG 341, DCS/Ops, OPD, Spec File HALFMOON, Sect 4, Box 1045; msg, Maj Gen C. Bissell, Mil Att London, to CSAF, # 72894, 061620Z Mar 1948, RG 341, Ofc Sec Air Staff, Msg Div, TS Msgs, Box 1, MC 318, all in MMB, NA.

[40] Little, *Foundations*, Pt I, pp 255-256; Daily Diary, Col G. Y. Jumper, Ch Pl & Intel Div, SWG, Apr 2, 1948, RG 341, DCS/Ops, Asst for AE, S 1948, 314.7 Daily Diary (Pl & Intel), Box 16, MMB, NA.

[41] Daily Diary, Col G. Y. Jumper, Ch Pl & Intel Div, SWG, Apr 5, 1948, RG 341, DCS/Ops, Asst for AE, TS 1948, 314.7 Daily Diary (Pl & Intel), Box 6, MMB, NA.

That brings in the State Department and interminable negotiations. No good."[42] The DARKHORSE planners considered Okinawa, then occupied by the United States, the best option. Karachi and fields in England were preferred on the basis of their relative security and proximity to Soviet targets. Among the possible locations in the Western hemisphere, the Alaska was considered too far from important targets, and its climate posed operational difficulties. This left bases in the continental United States, and much consideration had already been devoted to developing a field in the extreme northeast at Limestone, Maine. Also, if the Canadians concurred, tankers could be based in Newfoundland or Labrador.[43] All in all, this catalogue of difficulties in obtaining suitable bases reaffirmed the Air Force's need for extended bomber range, no matter how it was achieved.

The existing version of the seventy-group plan called for twenty groups of B-36s and B-50s, plus six groups of similar types for very long range reconnaissance, considered necessary because of the lack of intelligence about the target areas. The planned strategic force, including the complete SADDLETREE program and a modern reconnaissance force, would provide the strength needed to deliver the necessary massive strikes. Thus if the seventy-group force could be maintained in peacetime, it would have the means to strike the atomic blow early in a war. SAC's bomber units would consists of SADDLETREE planes, escort bombers armed with guns and radar jammers, and tankers for refueling in flight. The World War II concept of masses of bombers in formation, dropping on a single target, was no longer relevant. That earlier application of mass, a time-honored principle of war, now gave way to timing the force so that a large number of planes, though not all carrying atomic weapons, showed up on the enemy's radar screens all at once. The DARKHORSE planners also cited British tests that seemed to indicate that a reasonably fast bomber at high altitudes would have an advantage over interceptors. Provided the Air Force could solve the intelligence and navigation problems and ensure

---

[42] *Ibid.*, Apr 15, 1948.
[43] *Ibid.*, Apr 5, 15, & 20, 1948; R & R Sheet, Cmt 1, Maj Gen W. E. Kepner, Ch SWG, to Dir Air Installations, Acquisition of Land for Ammunition Storage Area—Limestone Army Air Field, Maine, Dec 2, 1947, with atchs, RG 341, DCS/Ops, Asst for AE, S 1948, 600 Buildings & Grounds, Box 21, MMB, NA. Talks on bases in Newfoundland and Labrador would have to wait until a plebiscite settled who had authority to negotiate on the other side. Then a British colony, Newfoundland was preparing to vote on whether to remain a colony, assume dominion status, or join Canada as a province.

accurate bombing from thirty thousand feet or more, the planners believed that the chances for success were good.[44]

Despite the apparent progress at Key West, interservice disagreements continued to hamper progress in postwar planning and readiness. During mid-July, Forrestal nearly asked for Symington's resignation after hearing news reports of a speech the Air Secretary gave in Los Angeles. In that speech, Symington continued to press for seventy groups and the primacy of strategic air power, though he had in fact rewritten the speech to tone down the attacks on Forrestal and the other services. Lt. Gen. Lauris Norstad, the Deputy Chief of Staff for Operations, called the earlier draft "beautiful," while acknowledging that it would have been Symington's "valedictory."[45] Unfortunately, the Defense Secretary obtained a copy of the first speech, but when Symington explained that he had given a different one, Forrestal accepted his version of events.

One of the Defense Secretary's goals involved obtaining a consensus on strategic principles as a basis for the military budget.[46] Since the services could not agree, and Truman warned Forrestal not to let this process interfere with developing the fiscal 1950 budget, the secretary's attempt at interservice negotiations largely failed. Budget Director James Webb took a more pragmatic approach. On July 16 he told Forrestal that the services would have a ceiling of $14.4 billion for fiscal 1950. Before long the Joint Chiefs of Staff reported that they were deadlocked on allocating this amount. Both Army and Air Force spokesmen agreed that the Navy's estimates far exceeded any reasonable requirements. For his part, Vandenberg held out for the procurement level called for in the seventy-group program. To overcome these obstacles, on August 12 the JCS agreed to form a Budget Advisory Committee, naming General McNarney chairman.[47]

---

[44] Daily Diary, Col G. Y. Jumper, Ch Pl & Intel Div, SWG, Apr 2, 1948, Apr 14, 1948, RG 341, DCS/Ops, Asst for AE, TS 1948, 314.7 Daily Diary (Pl & Intel), Box 6; notes, Jumper to Maj Gen D. M. Schlatter, Actg Ch SWG, n.d., NA 341, DCS/Ops, Asst for AE, TS 1948, 322 Spec Weapons Gp, Box 7, both in MMB, NA.

[45] Forrestal, *Diaries*, pp 462-463; Remarks by W. Stuart Symington, Secretary of the Air Force, at the Institute of Aeronautical Sciences, Jul 16, 1948, in *Public Statements & Speeches by W. Stuart Symington*, Vol IV, CAFH; MR, Col J. G. Armstrong, Ofc Asst DCS/Ops for AE, Staff Meeting, 0830, Jul 13, 1948, DCS/Ops, Jul 13, 1948, RG 341, DCS/Ops, Asst for AE, S 1948, 300.6 MR, Box 13, MMB, NA; USAF OHI, #K239.0512-1039, Herman S. Wolk & Hugh N. Ahmann, AFCHO & USAFHRC, with Sen W. Stuart Symington, May 2 and Dec 12, 1978, pp 85-88, AFHRA.

[46] See below, p. 33.

[47] Rearden, *Formative Years*, pp 336-342.

Strategic Air Force

Meanwhile Forrestal was experiencing no better luck reaching an agreement on the issue of roles and missions. At the end of July Vandenberg again explained to the Defense Secretary the importance of Air Force primacy in strategic air warfare, to include control of the atomic bomb, the main strategic air weapon.[48] The air chief made no objection to Forrestal's decision to call Spaatz out of retirement, along with Adm. John H. Towers, the naval aviation pioneer, to advise the Defense Secretary on the disputes between the Air Force and the Navy. On August 9 Forrestal instructed the two former aviators to explore the value of the Key West agreements, the role of carrier aviation, and the control of atomic weapons. Spaatz and Towers reported on August 18 that they too had failed to agree on some of the major issues. They did arrive at a definition of strategic warfare—"The general application of measures against the enemy designed to destroy his will and his capacity to continue war"—and strategic air operations—"the application of air power against targets of strategic significance to the enemy." And they urged a clarification of the Key West agreement that would in effect give the Air Force the right to define requirements for the strategic air offensive. On the other hand, Towers objected to Spaatz's reassertion of the Air Force's request to run the Special Weapons Project. Spaatz acknowledged that atomic weapons might be needed for naval operations and that the Navy could contribute to strategic air operations, but he contended that the supercarrier the Navy wanted to build could not be justified, as its primary rationale was its value for strategic operations. Towers supported the Navy's position.[49] In fact, the Navy was fighting to preserve its shipbuilding program, while the Air Force claimed the right to define the central requirements for the military budget because of the dominant importance of the strategic air offensive.

The overt divisions among the services undermined their positions even when they fundamentally agreed. On the issue of the custody of atomic weapons, for example, the services supported Forrestal in requesting transfer of custody from the Atomic Energy Commission to the military establishment. On July 21, 1948, Forrestal presented Truman with the formal request for transfer. Lilienthal voiced the AEC's objections, based largely on the need for civilian control of such a powerful weapon. But the President's advisers wondered whether the rival services would be able to agree on operational issues once they received the bombs. Admin-

---

[48] Forrestal, *Diaries*, pp 466–467.
[49] Memo, J. V. Forrestal, Sec Def, to Gen C. A. Spaatz (Ret), & Adm J. H. Towers (Ret), Aug 9, 1948; memo, Spaatz & Towers to Forrestal, subj: Your Memorandum (Aug 9, 1948), Aug 18, 1948, both in Air Force History Support Office.

istration officials also warned of the effect of such a seemingly bellicose move in a time of international crisis. In the end, Truman rejected Forrestal's request.[50] The President had already stated that he intended to reserve for himself the authority to decide on the use of the bomb, and he did not wish "to have some dashing lieutenant colonel decide when would be the proper time to drop one."[51]

Frustrated, Forrestal concluded that "the area of disagreement between the Air Force and Navy Air is not necessarily wide but it is quite deep."[52] Spaatz and Towers had clarified but not resolved the question of roles and missions. The secretary's next attempt at reconciliation was to sponsor a conference of the chiefs at Newport, Rhode Island, from August 20 to 22, 1948. There the services reached a compromise, agreeing that the Air Force would not exclude the Navy from strategic air operations, but that the Navy could not use its potential strategic role as a justification for its program or budget. The head of the Special Weapons Project was to report to the Chief of Staff of the Air Force on all matters pertaining to Plan HALFMOON (now renamed FLEETWOOD).[53] Harmony was restored, but since the essential issue was the defense budget, a recurring process with long-term implications, the rapport could not last.

The Berlin Crisis

The conference at Newport gained a sense of urgency from recent events in Europe. The forebodings of the winter of 1947 gave way to increased tension in early 1948, and in June the dissagreements between the Soviets and the Western powers over Germany came to a head. Since 1945 the Americans, the British, the Soviets, and the French had administered the four zones of postwar Germany. Berlin, an enclave within the Soviet Zone, was likewise split into four sectors. Through continued obstruction, the Soviets had brought the machinery of four-power government to a virtual breakdown. The United States and the United Kingdom had begun the economic integration of their zones in order to foster recovery. While the Soviets had no power to prevent this, they did control

---

[50] Rearden, *Formative Years*, pp 425–432.
[51] Forrestal, *Diaries*, p 458.
[52] *Ibid.*, p 464.
[53] Rearden, *Formative Years*, pp 401–402.

Strategic Air Force

The proposed supercarrier, USS *United States*, shown in an artist's rendering, was considered critical by the Navy, which was fearful of losing its air mission to the newly autonomous Air Force. Congress's decision to fund the B-36 instead of the *United States* followed a rancorous debate between the two services on the strategic air offensive, the future of carrier-based aviation, and control and delivery of the atomic bomb.

land and water access into the former capital. In April they had briefly closed the city to military transportation, and the Western countries had responded by airlifting supplies to their garrisons. When the Western powers initiated a reform of the currency on June 18, 1948, the Soviets again resorted to a blockade, finally sealing off all land and water routes. Starvation now threatened the two million inhabitants.[54]

The Western governments' response was inhibited by the awareness that they remained unprepared for war. Combat air forces in Germany, for example, consisted of the 86th Fighter Group at Neubiberg and one squadron of B-29s at Fürstenfeldbruck (in June 1948, the 353d from Smoky Hill Air Force Base). Clay anticipated the arrival of a jet fighter group in August, but he believed that the primary value of combat air forces in Germany was psychological. More important, with scarcely more than one bomber group equipped for atomic operations, and precious few

---

[54] *Ibid.*, pp 275–279.

other resources available, America lacked enough reserve forces to back up a strong diplomatic stand. Conventional B-29 groups could make a "show of force," however.[55]

In the event of war, Berlin would be extremely vulnerable. But if the Western powers gave in on their right to be in Berlin, the blow to their prestige could prove irreparable. To concede the currency question would be just as serious. For his part, Clay believed the USSR would make concessions if the West stood firm: "If the Soviets go to war, it will not be because of Berlin currency issue but only because they believe this [is] the right time. In such case they would use currency issue as an excuse."[56] Other Allied leaders were not so sure and wanted to avoid being provocative. For the moment, there was time to discuss the question, because Clay had directed an airlift in order to postpone the complete exhaustion of supplies in Berlin. Also, he reported that the German population was "remarkably steady."[57] On June 26 a C-47 took off from Wiesbaden for Berlin to begin the airlift. And if the transport planes on hand proved insufficient, the Air Force could send LeMay, the air commander in Europe, more planes for an expanded operation.[58]

The same day, British Foreign Secretary Ernest Bevin met in London with American Ambassador Lewis W. Douglas. Bevin agreed that the airlift would buy time for negotiations and for a military buildup. Further, as Douglas reported:

> Bevin believes that [the military chiefs] should examine the possibility of sending more heavy U.S. bomber planes to Europe. He does not suggest this as an operation which, in a military sense, would be particularly effective. It would, however, be evidence which the Soviet would construe as meaning that we are in earnest. It would accordingly tend to refute the view held by the Soviet that we are

---

[55] USAFE, *A Five-Year Summary of USAFE History, 1945–1950*, 1952, pp 68–79, 136–140; msg, Gen L. D. Clay, CINC, Europe 73179, to Lt Gen A. C. Wedemeyer, Dir P & O, Dept Army, Apr 27, 1948; msg, Clay, CC 4910, to W. H. Draper, USec Army, Jun 27, 1948, in Smith, *Papers of Lucius D. Clay*, Vol II, pp 641, 708.
[56] Telecon TT-9667, K. C. Royall, Sec Army, & Gen J. L. Collins, DCS Army, with Gen L. D. Clay, CINC Europe, Jun 25, 1948, in Smith, *Papers of Lucius D. Clay*, Vol II, p 702.
[57] Msg, Gen L. D. Clay, CINC Europe CC 4861, to K. C. Royall, Sec Army, 242124Z Jun 48, RG 341, Ofc Sec Air Staff, Msg Div, TS Msgs, Box 2, MC 1229, MMB, NA.
[58] A. Goldberg, *US Air Force*, p 235.

not determined—a view which HMG [His Majesty's Government] believes... is strongly held....[59]

On the 27th, Gen. Brian Robertson, the British Military Governor in Germany, learned of his government's interest in reinforcing the American bombers. He passed the word to Clay, who asked Washington to send additional B-29s and to speed up the movement of the jet fighter group he was expecting. Robertson further proposed basing one of the bomber groups in England.[60]

Ambassador Douglas radioed his report on the meeting with Bevin to the State Department on the evening of the 26th.[61] On Sunday, June 27, LeMay learned of the request and sent a message to Vandenberg stating that one B-29 group could go to Fürstenfeldbruck. Some existing plans could be used as a basis for moving bomber units to England. LeMay told Clay that England was preferable to Germany as a base for B-29s. From an operational standpoint, Clay agreed, but he continued to argue for the psychological value of basing combat air units in Germany.[62]

Also on the 27th, a delegation from the Air Staff traveled to Andrews Air Force Base to inform the SAC staff of these developments.[63] That afternoon, Norstad attended a meeting at which Forrestal and Lovett agreed to reinforce the bomber squadron in Germany and to sound out the British further.[64] With this apparent authorization, SAC went into action. Kenney ordered a squadron then at Goose Bay to return home, and the two squadrons of the 301st at Smoky Hill were sent there in its place. The whole command was alerted to be ready to move on 24 hours' notice. The 307th Bombardment Group at MacDill and the 28th at Rapid City were put on three and twelve hours' notice, respectively.[65]

---

[59] Msg, L. Douglas, Am Emb London 2822, to Sec State, Jun 26, 1948, no subj, in *FRUS*, 1948, Vol II, pp 923–924.

[60] Msg, Gen L. D. Clay, CINC Eur CC 4910, to W. H. Draper, Jr, USec Army, Jun 27, 1948, in Smith, *Papers of Lucius D. Clay*, Vol II, pp 707–708.

[61] See Note 59.

[62] Msg, Lt Gen C. E. LeMay, CG USAFE UA 8561, to Gen H. S. Vandenberg, CSAF, 271810Z Jun 48, RG 341, Ofc Sec Air Staff, Msg Div, TS Msgs, Box 2, MC 1253, NA; msg, Gen L. D. Clay, CINC Europe CC4914, to Gen O. N. Bradley, CSA, Jun 28, 1948, in Smith, *Papers of Lucius D. Clay*, Vol II, p 709.

[63] Hist, SAC, 1948, pp 146–148.

[64] Forrestal, *Diaries*, pp 452–455; Rearden, *Formative Years*, pp 290–291. Apparently, Forrestal's staff were unaware that the British had already expressed interest in the bombers, for Millis describes them as surprised by the easy acquiescence in the American proposal.

[65] See Note 63; msg, G. C. Marshall, Sec State 2429, to Am Emb London, Jun 27, 1948, in *FRUS*, 1948, Vol II, pp 926–928.

Apparently reassured, the British took a strong position on the Berlin question. On June 28 Bevin informed the Americans that the B-29s were cleared to enter the United Kingdom, and LeMay soon reported that RAF Stations Lakenheath and Sculthorpe were best suited for the B-29s. Meanwhile, President Truman approved the move to Germany, citing the United States' determination to stay in Berlin.[66] Lt. Gen. Albert C. Wedemeyer, the Army's Director of Plans and Operations, then on a visit to London, informed Washington of his belief that Berlin could be supplied indefinitely by air. He also recommended that Maj. Gen. William H. Tunner, who had managed the "Hump" airlift into China during the war, be assigned to direct the supply mission to Berlin. With such rapid and intense military cooperation, air power would clearly play a major role in the crisis.[67]

Finally ordered to Germany, the B-29s of the 301st at Goose Bay arrived at Fürstenfeldbruck by July 2. Meanwhile, arrangements were underway for the major deployment to England. The 28th and 307th Groups would take essential ground crews but would rely on the British for fuel, rations, and ammunition. LeMay was investigating what resources were available. The RAF offered Marham and Scampton, with support consisting of transportation, rations, fuel, and housing, including some tents. Scampton's runway was too short to accommodate a fully-loaded B-29, but the bombers could stage through other bases. LeMay would have operational control of the force, and he planned to establish a wing headquarters at Marham. The complexities of transatlantic coordination proved frustrating, with LeMay working through his representatives in London, who were in touch with the Air Ministry, while the Air staff met with the RAF delegation in Washington.[68] But, with all the operational problems, the primary delay in establishing the airlift involved diplomatic considerations. As the possibility of talks with the Soviets emerged, Bevin

---

[66] *FRUS*, 1948, Vol II, p 927n; msg, Lt Gen C. E. LeMay, CG USAFE UA 8570, to Gen H. S. Vandenberg, CSAF, & Gen O. N. Bradley, CSA, 281530Z Jun 48, RG 341, Ofc Sec Air Staff, Msg Div, TS Msgs, Box 2, MC 1273, MMB, NA; Forrestal, *Diaries*, pp 454–455.

[67] Msg, Lt Gen A. C. Wedemeyer, Dir P & O, Dept Army (Am Emb London 73558), to Maj Gen R. T. Maddox, P & O, Dept Army, 281020Z Jun 48, RG 341, Ofc Sec Air Stf, Msg Div, TS Msgs, Box 2, MC 1262, MMB, NA.

[68] Msg, Lt Gen L. Norstad, DCS/Ops, WARX 84854, to Lt Gen C. E. LeMay, CG USAFE, 291426Z Jun 48, RG 341, Ofc Sec Air Staff, Msg Div, TS Msgs, Box 2, MC 1279, MMB, NA; msg, LeMay, UAX 8592, to Norstad, 301635Z Jun 48, MC 1298; msg, LeMay, UA 8586, to Norstad, 301015Z Jun 48, MC 1296; msg, Norstad, WAR 84973, to LeMay, 302107Z Jun 48, MC 1304; msg, CSAF (OPO) WAR 84840, to CG SAC, (Jun 28) 290009Z Jun 48, MC 1276; hist, SAC, 1948, pp 146–148.

Strategic Air Force

on July 2 asked the United States to postpone the movement of the B-29s.[69]

It is necessary to ask what military purpose the B-29s were intended to serve. Bevin, as noted earlier, saw the movement of the bombers as purely political. Apparently, the foreign secretary's proposal did not mention atomic capability, either to request atomic carriers or to specify that he did not want modified bombers. Perhaps the foreign secretary did not understand the distinction. Certainly, the general public on both sides of the Atlantic recognized that the sole country armed with the atomic bomb was serving notice on the Russians. Perhaps when Secretary Marshall agreed to sound out the British on the "implications" of their request for the bombers, he may have had the atomic question in mind. As far as actual military use, however, LeMay later said that he and Clay had planned to use the European-based conventional bombers in the event fighting broke out in Germany. Clay further advocated sending an armed convoy to Berlin. If he received permission, the B-29s would be ready to provide air support for the convoy in the event the Soviets resisted.[70]

By July 10 the airlift was expanding, and operational plans were complete for moving the B-29s to England. Soon after, the British agreed to reactivate the depot at Burtonwood to service both the bombers and the cargo planes in the airlift. Col. Stanley T. Wray was selected to command the bombers.[71] On July 14 Bevin recommended that the B-29s deploy quickly in order to be in England before a meeting of the Brussels Pact countries on the 19th. However, some State Department officials thought that the British had delayed too long and "missed what we regarded as the psychological moment." In any case, the U.S. National Security Council agreed to the move on the 15th.[72] Forrestal outlined the reasons for the

---

[69] Msg, Maj Gen C. Bissell, US Mil Att London 73598, to USAFE, 021915Z Jul 48, RG 341, Ofc Sec Air Staff, Msg Div, TS Msgs, Box 2, MC 1321, MMB, NA; Rearden, *Formative Years*, pp 292-293.

[70] Forrestal, *Diaries*, pp 455-456; LeMay & Kantor, *Mission With LeMay*, pp 411-412.

[71] Msg, CG SAC, A3 B315014, to 307 BW, CG 15 AF, 022015Z Jul 48, RG 341, Ofc Sec Air Staff, Msg Div, TS Msgs, Box 2, MC 1325, MMB, NA; msg, CSAF, (MLP) WARX 85289, to CG SAC, CG AMC, *et al*, 070015Z Jul 48, MC 1325, MC 1339; msg, USAFE (Whitten), UAX 8745, to Lt Gen H. A. Craig, DCS/Mat, 130710Z Jul 48, MC 1390; hist, SAC, 1948, pp 146-148, 173-181.

[72] Memo of conversation, R. A. Lovett, USec State, Jul 14, 1948, with atch note, in *FRUS*, 1948, Vol II, pp 965-966; memo, C. E. Bohlen, Counsellor Dept State, to Sec State, Jul 14, 1948, in *FRUS*, 1948, Vol II, pp 966-967; msg, CG SAC, A3 B5111, to CG 15 AF, 141505Z Jul 48, RG 341, Ofc Sec Air Staff, Msg Div, TS Msgs, Box 2, MC 1401, MMB, NA; msg, CG SAC, A3 B5112, to MacDill AFB, 141503Z Jul 48, MC 1402.

bomber deployment in his diary:

1. It would be an action which would underline to the American people how seriously the government of the United States views the current sequence of events.
2. It would give the Air Force experience in this kind of operation; it would accustom the British to the necessary habits and routines that go into the accommodation of an alien, though an allied, power.
3. We have the opportunity *now* of sending these planes, and once sent they would become somewhat of an accepted fixture, whereas a deterioration of the situation in Europe might lead to a condition of mind under which the British would be compelled to reverse their present attitude.[73]

With President Truman's approval, the B–29s began the transatlantic move, and both groups were in England by July 17, the 28th at Scampton and the 307th at Marham (with one squadron at Waddington).[74]

As the buildup began, the international situation was growing more tense. The JCS ordered emergency plan HALFMOON distributed to the commands. Returning to Washington, Clay presented his case for an armed convoy to Berlin, and he received presidential permission to plan for one as a last resort. He also asked for a major increase in the size of the airlift so as to supply Berlin during the winter. This was not an easy question to settle, for Vandenberg resisted diverting the bulk of the Air Force's C–54 fleet to Germany. In the event of war, these planes would be needed to support SAC's movement overseas under HALFMOON. Nevertheless, the Air Force had been planning a reinforcement of the airlift in case it was ordered. Truman approved the reinforcement, and the Air Force sent Tunner and the C–54s to Germany.[75]

Though the major decisions had been made, one item remained unresolved: whether to retain some of the B–29 force in southern Germany. Norstad broached the subject of the bombers' vulnerability to LeMay on July 16.[76] But not until the 27th did Clay tell Wedemeyer that he wanted to keep one squadron in Germany. The next day the British

---

[73] Forrestal, *Diaries*, p 457.
[74] *Ibid.*; hist, SAC, 1948, pp 146–148, 173–181.
[75] Rearden, *Formative Years*, pp 292–295; K. Condit, *JCS, 1947–1949*, p 289; msg, Lt Gen L. Norstad, DCS/Ops, AFOPO 50306, to Lt Gen C. E. LeMay, CG USAFE, 221827Z Jul 48, RG 341, Ofc Sec Air Staff, Msg Div, TS Msgs, Box 2, MC 1496, MMB, NA.
[76] Msg, Lt Gen L. Norstad, DCS/Ops, AFODC 50194, to Lt Gen C. E. LeMay, CG USAFE, 162214Z Jul 48, RG 341, Ofc Sec Air Staff, Msg Div, TS Msgs, Box 2, MC 1423, MMB, NA.

Challenge in Berlin. *Clockwise from above, left:* **Douglas C–47s, lined up at Rhein-Main Air Base in Frankfurt, Germany, prepare to airlift thousands of tons of food, fuel, and other life-sustaining supplies to the western sectors of the city of Berlin, under Soviet blockade. To counter this and future Soviet provocations regarding the allied administration of Berlin, the United States reinforced its military presence in West Germany and England, deploying SAC B–29s to Fürstenfeldbruck and Lakenheath. Pictured is the 2d Bombardment Group being briefed at Labrador before take-off to Lakenheath in August 1948, readying itself for departure on the runway, being visited within a month of its arrival by Air Force Secretary W. Stuart Symington and 3d Air Division Commander Maj. Gen. Leon W. Johnson before conducting a maximum effort flight over England in September.**

Strategic Air Force

agreed to locate a B–29 group at Lakenheath.[77] The 301st Bombardment Group was recalled to the States, one B–29 making a record non-stop flight during the return movement. The 2d Bombardment Group deployed from Davis-Monthan Air Force Base, arriving at Lakenheath at the beginning of August.[78] Unlike the other groups, which LeMay was required to keep in England at all times, the 2d could be sent to Germany. On this basis, LeMay based one squadron at Fürstenfeldbruck. Meanwhile, all the bomber units in England were on alert.[79]

Allied leaders could reasonably hope that military deployments would deter the Soviets from interfering with the airlift to Berlin or attacking outright. Nevertheless, it would take considerable effort for the Air Force to convince skeptics that the airlift could sustain the city indefinitely. Talks with the Soviets began, but these discussions broke down on September 7. The Central Intelligence Agency reported no evidence of an actual Soviet mobilization for war. Still, presidential advisers suggested taking precautionary measures, and Truman felt that war was near. Even without actual conflict, a war scare would threaten his hopes for a balanced budget. Facing an uphill contest for re-election, Harry Truman was reluctant to risk a budget deficit. Still, he felt he had to stand firm on the question of Berlin.[80]

The only measures taken to increase atomic readiness were extremely discreet. The Atomic Energy Commission and the armed services began to review their procedures for transferring bombs from the commission's stockpile, now numbering over fifty. This action in itself helped to reveal weak spots. Col. John G. Armstrong of the Air Staff's Atomic Energy Office had the impression that the Eighth Air Force had no plans for an emergency transfer of weapons. In particular this reminded him of the days immediately after Pearl Harbor, with their confused atmosphere of

---

[77] Msg, Lt Gen A. C. Wedemeyer, Dir P & O, Dept Army, WARX 86521, to Gen L. D. Clay, CINC Europe, 272203Z Jul 48, RG 341, Ofc Sec Air Staff, Msg Div, TS Msgs, Box 2, MC 1563, MMB, NA; msg, Maj Gen J. W. Leonard, US Mil Att London 73727, to Lt Gen L. Norstad, DCS/Ops, 281213Z Jul 48, MC 1571; msg, Clay, CC 5342, to Wedemeyer, Jul 28, 1948, in Smith, *Papers of Lucius D. Clay*, Vol II, p 747.

[78] Hist, SAC, 1948, pp 173–181.

[79] *Ibid.*; msg, CSAF, OPO 50249, to Lt Gen C. E. LeMay, CG USAFE, 201450Z Jul 48, RG 341, Off Sec Air Staff, Msg Div, TS Msgs, Box 2, MC 1465, MMB, NA; msg, CSAF, OPO WARX 86604, to Col S. E. Wray, CO 3 AD (Prov), 282226Z Jul 48, MC 1581.

[80] Rearden, *Formative Years*, pp 296–298.

"orders and counterorders," and Armstrong hoped some of the turmoil could be avoided by more effective planning.[81]

The risk of war was further exacerbated by the small size of the force capable of delivering atomic weapons. The newly modified SADDLETREE bombers were "ready to roll off the lines," as the Air Staff reported, but it would be months before any units would be trained to deploy.[82] Until then, the 509th at Walker Air Force Base remained the only unit equipped for atomic operations. Any full-scale action by SAC would be impossible unless the airlift to Berlin were stopped and the transports made available to support the bomber force's overseas deployment.[83]

It soon became evident that war would not come. Although negotiations over the Berlin blockade did not reopen for months, the Soviets made no more threatening moves. The airlift continued, and starvation was averted in Berlin. Maj. Gen. Leon W. Johnson, then commanding the 3d Air Division in England, later recalled that operating the transports in Berlin's overcast skies depended on a radar beacon near Tempelhof Air Base that the Soviets could have eliminated with a few mortar rounds. Johnson told his staff to notify him at once if the Soviets fired on the beacon, as this would indicate that war was imminent.[84] That no action came was a sign that war would be avoided.

The Berlin crisis, though serious, did not monopolize the nation's attention, particularly during an election year. While making the decision to send the B–29s to England, Truman was accepting the Democratic nomination for president. He did this in the face of a serious split in the party. Henry A. Wallace was leading the Progressives and calling for a conciliatory policy toward the Soviet Union. The Southern wing formed the States' Rights Democratic Party and nominated J. Strom Thurmond, who protested the strong plank on civil rights adopted at the convention. With the Democrats in disarray, political observers freely predicted that

---

[81] Office of the Secretary of Defense, *A History of Strategic Arms Competition, 1945–1972*, USAF Supporting Studies, Vol I: *Description and Analysis* (Washington, Jun 1976), p 105; MR, Col J. G. Armstrong, Ofc Asst DCS/Ops for AE, National Emergency Procedures, Sep 8, 1948, with notes by "DMS" [Maj Gen David M Schlatter, Asst DCS/Ops for AE], RG 341, DCS/Ops, Asst for AE, S 1948, 300.6 MR, Box 13, MMB, NA; Rearden, *Formative Years*, p 297.

[82] Memo, Col W. L. Kennedy to Maj Gen D. M. Schlatter, Asst DCS/Ops for AE, Sep 27, 1948, RG 341, DCS/Ops, Asst for AE, TS 1948, 471.6 Bomb, General, Box 11, MMB, NA.

[83] Rearden, *Formative Years*, pp 296–300.

[84] USAF OHI, # 865, James C. Hasdorff, AFHRC, with Gen Leon W. Johnson, Ret, Aug 75, p 156, AFHRA.

Strategic Air Force

victory in the November election would go to the Republican challenger, Thomas E. Dewey.[85]

Containment, Deterrence, and NSC–20 / 4

America's success in averting war over Berlin did not entirely relieve the pressure on the nation's leaders. Indeed, the crisis raised alarm at the poor state of military preparation, particularly in the strategic bomber force. If the appearance of U.S. strength and resolve had deterred the Soviets, the bluff might be called next time. For Secretary Forrestal, this situation made formulating a coherent national security policy all the more urgent.

Previous work at the State Department and the National Security Council (NSC) staff had been directed toward this goal. The NSC staff had formulated a paper on the threat posed by "Soviet-directed world communism." This document, submitted in March 1948 as NSC–7, argued that the Russians were not likely to resort to war, at least so long as Cold War methods promised success. The true danger was a collapse from within of the free countries in Europe. To meet that threat, the council urged the restoration of Europe's economic and military strength. An immediate, broad-based effort would reinforce Western morale and also deter the Soviets from changing their minds about their chances in a war. The paper also proposed revitalizing U.S. forces and retaining atomic superiority. In reviewing the NSC's recommendations, the joint chiefs took a skeptical view, preferring more emphasis on the role of U.S. forces and warning against overcommitting the country to an overly ambitious program of European military and economic reform.[86]

In July 1948 Forrestal renewed his efforts to obtain a coordinated statement of national policy to guide military planners, initiating a series of papers circulated to the National Security Coucil under the designation of NSC–20. George F. Kennan's Policy Planning Staff at the State Department responded to Forrestal's initiative in August. In order to spell out some of the military implications of containment, the planners at State

---

[85] Robert J. Donovan, *Conflict and Crisis: The Presidency of Harry S. Truman, 1945–1948* (NY: Norton, 1977), pp 403–405, 416–439.

[86] Rprt, NSC–7, Report by the National Security Council on the Position of the United States with Respect to Soviet-Directed World Communism, Mar 30, 1948; memo, J. V. Forrestal, Sec Def, to NSC, Apr 17, 1948, both in *FRUS*, Vol I, Pt 2, pp 546–550, 561–564.

reviewed the likely objectives of the nation in peace or war. In either case, the main goals were the same: reducing Soviet power and changing Russian behavior toward the rest of the world. Should war come, Kennan's staff did not see how the allies could expect to invade and occupy Russia or demand unconditional surrender. The military power of the hostile nation, on the other hand, might be vulnerable to weakening "by extensive destruction of important industrial and economic targets from the air."[87] On the other hand, bombing might alienate the Soviet population.[88]

Kennan argued that American military strength was essential and had to be maintained for a long period of time. Such a defense posture would demonstrate American resolve, deter aggression, encourage free nations to resist Soviet encroachment, and enable the United States to fight if deterrence failed. The study concluded in the event of war, America would try to weaken Soviet military and economic power, but it fell short of an explicit sanction for a strategic air offensive.[89]

Once the planners at State had completed their paper, which was labeled NSC-20/1, the staff of the National Security Council started to revise it. Their conclusions clearly reflected the President's concerns. There were warnings against "[i]nadequate or excessive armament or foreign aid expenditures" and "an excessive or wasteful usage of our resources in time of peace."[90] Although the Joint Chiefs of Staff still voiced concern that military commitments exceeded capabilities, they concurred in the National Security Council study, which the President approved as NSC-20/4 on November 23, 1948.[91]

Meanwhile, a separate discussion covered the question of whether atomic weapons would be used in the event of war. Kenneth C. Royall, the Secretary of the Army, recognized that there was no clear policy in the

---

[87] Rprt, NSC-20/1, State Dept to NSC, US Objectives with Respect to Russia, Aug 18, 1948, in Thomas H. Etzold and John L. Gaddis, eds, *Containment: Documents on American Policy and Strategy, 1945–1950* (NY: Columbia Univ Press, 1978), pp 195, 173–203.

[88] *Ibid.*, p 191.

[89] Rearden, *Formative Years*, pp 340–350; rprt, NSC 20/2, State Dept to NSC, Factors Affecting the Nature of U.S. Defense Arrangements in the Light of Soviet Policies, Aug 25, 1948, in *FRUS*, 1948, Vol I, Pt 2, pp 615–624.

[90] Memo, RAdm S. W. Souers, Sec NSC, to President, no subj, Nov 23, 1948, with encl rprt NSC-20/4 to President, US Objectives with Respect to the USSR to Counter Soviet Threats to US Security, in *FRUS*, 1948, Vol I, Pt 2, p 667, pp 662–669.

[91] *Ibid.*; memo, RAdm S. W. Souers, Sec NSC, to NSC, subj: Existing International Commitments Involving the Possible Use of Armed Forces, Nov 17, 1948, with atch memo, NSC-35, JCS to Sec Def, Nov 2, 1948, in *FRUS*, 1948, Vol I, Pt 2, pp 656–662; Rearden, *Formative Years*, p 349.

administration on the use of atomic weapons.[92] However, not everyone agreed that a formal statement was necessarily desirable. In September, 1948, Maj. Gen. Samuel E. Anderson, the Air Force's Director of Plans and Operations, recommended caution: "If there is doubt that a policy permitting [atomic weapons'] use can be obtained at this time, it is better that we have no national policy at all on this subject."[93] Instead, he proposed advising Forrestal that the best means of employing the bomb in wartime was in a massed attack, as rapidly as possible, against enemy industrial concentrations. With the anticipation of as many as two hundred modified aircraft by the end of December 1948, this could mean an operation on quite a large scale.[94]

In fact, during September 1948 Truman received a paper called NSC–30, which urged a policy of being prepared to use atomic weapons "promptly and effectively" when the President ordered. He did not approve the report, but he assured Forrestal that he would authorize the use of atomic weapons should it be necessary. In any case, from the standpoint of policy, the cooperation between the Air Force and the Atomic Energy Commission was reaching the point that atomic operations on an increasing scale were now possible.[95]

Apparently, considerable public support existed in both America and Europe for some preparations to use atomic weapons. Forrestal had surmised this, and his meetings with members of the press confirmed his observations. Norstad, whom the secretary sent to England in the fall of 1948, returned with similar reports from across the Atlantic. His specific task was to prepare British air bases for atomic operations, but he also was expected to sound out British leaders on the question of actual use. After the November presidential election in the United States, Forrestal himself went to Europe. He and Norstad both agreed that the British were receptive to the use of atomic weapons if necessary. Leaders emphasized the role of air power and atomic weapons in their defense. Prime Minister Clement R. Attlee believed that the public favored this course. Winston Churchill, though in opposition, clearly reflected an important sentiment

---

[92] Rearden, *Formative Years*, pp 432–437.
[93] *Ibid.*, pp 434–435; memo, Maj Gen S. E. Anderson, Dir P & O, to CSAF, subj: Policy Questions with Respect to the Use of Atomic Weapons, Sep 20, 1948, with encls, RG 341, DCS/Ops, Asst for AE, TS 1948, 471.6 Employment and Effects of A-Bombs, Box 11, MMB, NA.
[94] See previous note.
[95] Memo, NSC–30, RAdm S. W. Souers, Sec NSC, to NSC, subj: United States Policy on Atomic Warfare, Sep 10, 1948, with atch draft rprt by NSC, in Etzold & Gaddis, *Containment*, pp 339–343; Forrestal Diary, Vol XII, p 2494, Sep 13, 1948, in Forrestal Papers, OSD.

when he warned that downplaying the power of the bomb would embolden the Soviets. Lord Tedder, the Chief of Air Staff, backed the effort to get bases ready to support SAC atomic units. For him, it was only a question of finding the money.[96]

The harsh realities of the Cold War confirmed Europeans in their views. In December 1948 talks began between the Western European governments of the Brussels Pact and the United States, with an eye to a formal alliance. The Europeans feared that a land force strong enough to stop a Soviet attack was simply beyond their means. And once the Soviets reached the English Channel, even England's fate was problematical. If the Americans then undertook to liberate Europe as they had in 1944, the devastation would probably exceed that of the previous war. Thus, the European nations sought an advance commitment from the United States that it would be involved from the start in any war with the Soviets, in hopes that this alliance would deter aggression. The American preponderance in atomic weapons would give that deterrent its persuasiveness.[97] Speaking in Boston in March 1949, just one month before the signing of the North Atlantic Treaty, Churchill expressed a widespread conviction: "It is certain ... that Europe would have been communized like Czechoslovakia and London under bombardment some time ago but for the atomic bomb in the hands of the United States."[98]

The "Hollow Threat" and General LeMay

In the aftermath of the the Berlin crisis, as American leaders assessed the potential of the atomic deterrent, they also began to focus on the instrument of atomic power—the Strategic Air Command. The view was not encouraging. Despite all the demands placed on SAC, Kenney and his Deputy Commander, McMullen, had stuck to their cross-training program. In a directive published in January 1948, Headquarters SAC reaffirmed its commitment in this regard. First priority in all training went to preparing for movements overseas. Next came cross-training, and only after that was

---

[96] Forrestal Diary, Vol XII, p 2482, Sep 9, 1948, p 2502, Sep 17, 1948, p 2598, Oct 23, 1948, pp 2642, 2644, Nov 12, 1948, in Forrestal Papers, OSD; memo, Sec Def, subj: Subjects on which Action by the Secretary of Defense is Required, Nov 17, 1948, PSF, Cabinet-Defense Misc (1), Box 156, HSTL; Rearden, *Formative Years*, p 347.
[97] K. Condit, *JCS, 1947–1949*, pp 355ff.
[98] *New York Times*, Apr 1, 1949, pp 1, 11.

provided for could units devote attention to routine training.[99] In view of the scarcity of resources, McMullen's personnel ceilings, shortages of men in key skills, and aging aircraft, the lowest priority suffered greatly. Yet McMullen was proposing to take the cross-training concept even further. Perhaps in a reflection of his own experience, he suggested that aircrew members should train for ground jobs as well as aircrew positions. To the commander of a fighter wing, he wrote: "[I]t takes a smarter officer to be a good supply officer than it does to be a good group commander. One of these days I may tell you to make one of your group commanders the supply officer."[100]

This adherence to an inflexible policy was only one of the obstacles to combat readiness. Groups making the transition to a new type of aircraft lost a good deal of training time, Davis-Monthan experiencing some technical problems after the arrival of the B–50, and the 7th Bombardment Group at Fort Worth canceling some flights in April to get ready for the B–36. Also, the tests of atomic weapons at Eniwetok borrowed many men from the Eighth Air Force, although this and other programs did offer long-term benefits as well.[101] All SAC units were liable to lose men ordered overseas, including those from the 509th who had finally received clearances from the Atomic Energy Commission. Manpower shortages were often compounded by poor management. In the critical 509th, for example, no attempt was made to keep crews together. In an emergency, it would take five days to get qualified bomb commanders out of staff positions, form aircrews, and do some familiarization flying.[102] Despite repeated protests, a staff officer observed that in both personnel and supply matters, the Eighth Air Force "is getting the same treatment as any other organization in the [U.S.] Air Force...."[103] Nor were the Eighth's aircrews able to get enough practice at flying in to the fields where the bombs were stored. Still, with all the limitations, Col. John D. Ryan, the

---

[99] Hist, SAC, 1948, pp 258–266. This history would have been compiled after the end of calendar year 1948, when LeMay was already in command and could be expected to speak with some candor about the previous regime.

[100] Ltr, Maj Gen C. McMullen, Dep CG SAC, to Col W. T. Hudnell, CO 56 Fighter Wing, Jan 9, 1948, SAC/HO.

[101] Hist, SAC, 1948, pp 327–330; Little, *Foundations*, Pt II, pp 472–487.

[102] Hist, SAC, 1948, pp 42–46; Daily Diary, Col G. Y. Jumper, Ch Pl & Intel, SWG, May 5, 1948, RG 341, DCS/Ops, Asst for AE, TS 1948, 314.7 Daily Diary (Pl & Intel), Box 6, MMB, NA.

[103] Daily Diary, Col G. Y. Jumper, Ch Pl & Intel, SWG, May 5, 1948, RG 341, DCS/Ops, Asst for AE, TS 1948, 314.7 Daily Diary (Pl & Intel), Box 6, MMB, NA.

Eighth's Director of Operations, considered it "better trained than any group overseas in World War Two."[104]

Despite this reassurance, the problems of the Strategic Air Command did attract attention. On March 2, 1948, Spaatz advised Kenney that the large number of planes out of commission indicated a low state of training.[105] Kenney himself was uneasy, especially at the poor results in bombing practice, and he ordered a competition to be held in June. Yet protests against rigorous enforcement of the standards in cross-training were seemingly ignored. When an officer from the Special Weapons Group on the Air Staff visited Fort Worth, Ryan took pains to make clear that his description of the Eighth Air Force's problems was not intended as a formal complaint.[106] Ironically, on March 17, at the height of the reverberations from Clay's telegram, McMullen wrote to Ramey, telling the Eighth Air Force Commander to train extra crews, drawing on noncommissioned officers for navigators and bombardiers if necessary, observing that: "The world situation indicates that we are rapidly moving towards the inception of the last great war."[107] Following such a dire prediction, the SAC Deputy Commander continued to defend policies that many considered real impediments to combat readiness.

At the same time, some more promising developments occurred. A SAC staff conference at Andrews in April agreed to support the concept of the "lead crew," which Headquarters SAC adopted. During the war, bomber groups organized a small number of crews with the best people available. These would train to the highest possible level of efficiency and would lead the rest of the group over the target, allowing the others to bomb after them. Three lead crews would now be organized in each group in SAC. Also under consideration was a plan to establish a board of officers in each group that would evaluate each crew's performance against a standard of proficiency. This process would identify problems in training and provide for continuing professional review of the force.[108] Also, Col.

---

[104] *Ibid.*

[105] Ltr, Maj Gen S. E. Anderson, Dir P & O, to CG SAC, subj: 509th BW, Very Heavy, May 4, 1948, SAC/HO; ltr, Gen C. A. Spaatz, CSAF, to Gen G. C. Kenney, CG SAC, Mar 2, 1948, Spaatz Coll, MD, LC.

[106] Hist, SAC, 1948, pp 258–266, 279–280; ltr, Brig Gen D. W. Hutchison, A–3 (Ops) SAC, to CG 8 AF, subj: Bombing and Gunnery Training, Jul 2, 1948; ltr, CG SAC to CG 8 AF, CG 15 AF, CO 307 BW, subj: Competitive Bombing Maneuvers, Castle AFB, May 27, 1948, both in AFHRA 416.01–48.

[107] Ltr, Maj Gen C. McMullen, Dep CG SAC, to Maj Gen R. M. Ramey, CG 8 AF, Mar 17, 1948, SAC/HO.

[108] Hist, SAC, 1948, pp 258–266, 278.

Clarence S. Irvine's efforts to improve cruise control were now extending the range of B–29s. SAC's fighter force was benefitting from the new P–82 Twin Mustang and the P–84 Thunderjet, the latter having much greater range than the P–80. And beyond the range of escort fighters, those who believed that the bomber could get through were heartened by the results of training exercises against the Air Defense Command.[109]

Because of SAC's mission as a worldwide striking force, Secretary Symington continued to press for the State Department's approval for a round-the-world flight, despite continuing rebuffs. Nevertheless, the regular rotation program proceeded. The 97th Bombardment Group spent the winter of 1947–1948 in Alaska, returning to a new base at Biggs Air Force Base, Texas (near El Paso). Headquarters SAC wanted to maintain a group in Germany all the time on ninety-day rotation, but Fürstenfeldbruck was not yet in condition to support an entire group. Failing that, the command managed to keep one squadron always in Europe during the early part of 1948. The 301st Bombardment Group from Smoky Hill crowded into Fürstenfeldbruck for a short visit in April, and the group then based one of its squadrons in Germany through June. In February flights to Japan resumed, with a squadron of the 509th visiting Yokota, and other units following. In the spring the P–51s of the 82d Fighter Group deployed to Alaska from Grenier Field, New Hampshire, making the trip across Canada both ways. Various units visited Shemya in the Aleutians and Goose Bay, Labrador, for short stays.[110]

Before the Berlin crisis, the most significant new commitment in the overseas program was in the western Pacific. For months, Kenney had been trying to get control of the B–29s assigned to MacArthur's Far East Command. He would then base all strategic bomber units in the continental United States, rotating them overseas. MacArthur, however, insisted that he needed his two groups permanently assigned. The Far East commander and his former chief airman found a compromise, agreeing to keep the 19th Bombardment Group at Guam and return the 22d from Okinawa to the States. One group from SAC would then always be on rotation to Kadena Air Base on Okinawa, under the operational control of the theater commander. In May the 93d Bombardment Group left Castle for the Far East and relieved the 22d. The latter group then returned to

---

[109] *Ibid.*, pp 182–202, 205–210, 284–285, 299–300; ltr, Gen H. S. Vandenberg, CSAF, to Gen G. C. Kenney, CG SAC, May 10, 1948, SAC/HO; Irvine OHI, pp 14–23.
[110] Hist, SAC, 1948, pp 149–224.

the United States, to be stationed at Smoky Hill. In all, nearly half of the units in SAC spent some time overseas in the first six months of 1948. For the newly manned groups, such deployments served as a kind of graduation exercise.[111]

To the Air Staff it was clear that the nature of atomic warfare demanded a new operational approach. Maj. Gen. Frederic H. Smith, Jr., now Assistant for Programming to the Operations Chief, expressed his views to Samuel Anderson, the Director of Plans and Operations: "Indications are that...the strategic bomber, when employed in the future will operate individually. If this is the case, it is necessary for the Air Force to train into all bomber crews the ability formerly associated with the so-called Lead Crew."[112] Smith noted that such conditions as unstable tours of duty kept crews from training to the required standard. He envisioned an elite force, proud of its accomplishments. A high state of readiness would be achieved through a combination of careful selection, a rigorous training program, and five-year tours of duty:

> If we are to have a force...with the esprit which must be an attribute of each member, we must accord to the personnel involved in the program, a degree of consideration beyond that normally accorded officers and men in a combat unit. The training schedules will be rigorous. Airplane commanders and crews will be under more strain than in other units. Maintenance standards of ground crews must be extremely high and work scheduled irregularly to match long flights originating and ending at various periods of the day.... The requirement for maintaining what approximates an alert status will tend to develop [high morale] if properly exploited.[113]

When asked to comment on Smith's observations, Maj. Gen. David W. Hutchison, SAC's Deputy Chief of Staff for Plans, replied that his command was already doing much of what was suggested. He objected to lengthening the tours of duty, because this would force the rest of the Air

---

[111] *Ibid.*, pp 182–202, 205–210, 284–285, 299–300; ltr, Gen H. S. Vandenberg, CSAF, to Gen G. C. Kenney, CG SAC, May 10, 1948, SAC/HO.

[112] Memo, Maj Gen F. H. Smith, Asst DCS/Ops for Prog, to Maj Gen S. E. Anderson, Dir P & O, subj: Strategic Striking Force, Increasing Current Capabilities of, May 14, 1948, atch to memo, Col O. S. Picher, Ch Ops Div, DCS/Ops, to Anderson, subj: Comments on Memorandum from Major General Smith, Jun 3, 1948, RG 341, DCS/Ops, Dir/Pl, P & O 322 (May 14, 1948), Box 137, MMB, NA.

[113] *Ibid.*

Force to spend more time overseas. Also, the program outlined for training would keep crew members away from their bases for long periods.[114]

Despite these reassurances, SAC had not yet attained such a level of effectiveness. On June 20, planes and crews from all the bomber groups except the 93d (then in Okinawa) assembled at Castle for the command's first bombing competition. The results of practice missions over the range at Wendover revealed a genuine difference between the command's two air forces. All units of the Eighth dropped their bombs within two thousand feet of the target, while the averages of the Fifteenth all exceeded that figure. The higher priority given the Eighth and its lighter overseas rotation schedule no doubt affected the results. However, even within the Eighth Air Force, overall performance was not all that good. The 509th reported some radar bombing missions with circular errors as high as four thousand feet, not satisfactory for atomic bombing. Whether it was reasonable to expect better performance could be argued. But a widespread feeling, not openly acknowledged at SAC Headquarters, had developed that the emphasis on cross-training and economy were serious impediments to any improvement. McMullen's response was simply to urge people to work harder.[115]

The Strategic Air Command's weaknesses should not obscure the fact that progress was taking place in a number of areas. The fact that as the results of the bombing competition were coming in, SAC was preparing to send units to Europe in response to the Berlin crisis points up the success Kenney had achieved in developing the command's ability to deploy. At the same time, while the B-29 remained the mainstay of the force, B-50s and B-36s began to enter the inventory early in 1948. And the expansion of the atomic force had begun. The 509th Bombardment Wing at Roswell (now renamed Walker Air Force Base), still the main unit with modified bombers, remained on station during the crisis. But by the end of September, seventy crews had been trained for atomic operations, and there would soon be bomb commanders and weaponeers for more crews. A

---

[114] Memo, Col O. S. Picher, Ch Ops Div, DCS/Ops, to Maj Gen S. E. Anderson, Dir P & O, subj: Comments on Memorandum for Major General Smith, Jun 3, 1948, RG 341, DCS/Ops, Dir/Pl, P & O 322 (May 14, 1948), Box 137, MMB, NA.

[115] Ltr, Maj Gen C. McMullen, Dep CG SAC, to Col W. T. Hudnell, CO 56 Fighter Wing, Jun 15, 1948, SAC/HO; USAF OHI, # 733, Robert M. Kipp, AFCHO, with Maj Gen W. C. Kingsbury, Ret, Dec 18, 1970, AFHRA; hist, SAC, 1948, pp 274–277.

Year of Crisis

fourth bomb assembly team was forming.[116] There was a foundation upon which to build.

The SAC Headquarters had designated the 43d and 2d Bomb Groups to be the next atomic-modified units and given them a 1-A priority for manning, the highest in the command. In the fall of 1948, the 2d Group was for the time being in England, but the 43d was ready to start receiving its B-50s at Davis-Monthan. At the same time, the 7th at Carswell was expected to replace its B-36As with atomic-capable B models. In addition, the 509th and 43d had recently formed tanker squadrons, which were soon to receive equipment and start training for air refueling operations.[117] A large part of SAC would remain a conventional bombing force. The Fifteenth Air Force would continue to provide conventional B-29 groups for overseas duty. In September half of its six groups were overseas, two in England and one in Okinawa.[118]

But whether atomic or conventional, SAC's bomber force had considerable limitations. The reconnaissance force possessed a few RB-29s and a number of shorter-range aircraft. Radar bomb sights needed to be brought up to date, and some experts feared that most sets could be jammed. The command's 5,100 officers and 39,500 airmen, with 420 bombers, looked less and less formidable as actual performance was examined. Practice bombing statistics did not look too bad, since few crews took their planes above 15,000 feet so as to avoid overtaxing the engines or freezing unprotected equipment. The targets used in most radar bombing practice were reflectors that showed up clearly on the screen. Furthermore, many traditional indicators of military fitness looked poor. In September SAC bases reported 408 men absent without leave, nearly one per cent of the force. About a third of the B-29s were out of commission at any given time. Crashes and minor accidents occurred at a rate of nearly sixty for every 100,000 hours flown. Injuries on the ground were also frequent, suggesting inattentiveness by maintenance crews.[119]

---

[116] Memo, Maj Gen D. M. Schlatter, Asst DCS/Ops for AE, to Lt Gen L. Norstad, DCS/Ops, subj: Air Force Capabilities for Atomic Warfare, Oct 22, 1948, RG 341, DCS/Ops, Asst for AE, TS 1948, 314.7 P & O Branch Diary items, Box 6, MMB, NA; hist, SAC, 1948, pp 1-12, 35-38; SAC Statistical Summary, Dec 1948, pp 24-25; Knaack, *Bombers*, pp 21, 169-170.

[117] See previous note.

[118] Hist, SAC, 1948, pp 153-200.

[119] SAC Statistical Summary, Dec 1948, pp 13-16, 24-49; LeMay & Kantor, *Mission with LeMay*, p 432; Borowski, *Hollow Threat*, p 167; SACM 11-3, SAC Statistical Data from 1946, Sep 8, 1970, p 22.

Strategic Air Force

These conditions were not new to the strategic bomber force. In the spring of 1948, Vandenberg had felt concerned enough to ask Charles A. Lindbergh to investigate the matter. As one of America's leading aviators and someone who might gain the confidence of flying crew members, Lindbergh could be expected to get beyond dry figures to the actual state of proficiency in SAC. After several months of travel, visiting, and flying with SAC units, he turned in a report on September 14.[120]

Lindbergh made the civilian airlines his basis of comparison. Arguing that the mass-production standards of training characteristic of the Second World War and its mass bomber attacks were inappropriate for atomic warfare, he considered SAC's crews inadequately trained:

> To be specific, accident rates are high, landings are too rough and fast, crew duties are not smoothly coordinated, equipment is not neatly stowed in flight, engine and accessory troubles are excessive, and there are not enough training missions which simulate the combat missions which would be required in event of war.[121]

Lindbergh mentioned some perennial grievances of SAC unit commanders:

> Numerous assignments to temporary duty, an intensive cross-training program, and extra-curricular flying activities have seriously interfered with training in the primary mission of the atomic squadrons. Resulting absences and frequent changes in home locations have had a bad effect on family relationships and over-all morale.[122]

The distinguished aviator blamed undermanning (a result of Maj. Gen. Clements McMullen's boast that he could cut manning without hurting efficiency) and the consequent overwork for much of the trouble. He recommended making service in the atomic force a separate career field, keeping crews together, and improving pay and living conditions so as to make SAC more competitive with private airlines. Most of all, he urged cutting back on cross-training and making peacetime bombing missions more realistic. Correcting these problems, Lindbergh wrote, would not be

---

[120] Rprt, C. A. Lindbergh to Gen H. S. Vandenberg, CSAF, Sep 14, 1948, atch to memo, Col F. M. Hoisington, Ch Pers & Admin Div, to Maj Gen D. M. Schlatter, Asst DCS/Ops for AE, subj: The Lindbergh Report, Oct 19, 1948, RG 341, DCS/Ops, Asst for AE, S 1948, 319.1 Rprts AEC, T & T Etc, Box 16, MMB, NA.
[121] Ibid.
[122] Ibid.

Year of Crisis

overly difficult, for "Most officers in the atomic forces are well aware of existing difficulties and are anxious to take steps which will overcome them."[123] This last comment, coming from an old friend of Gen. George C. Kenney's, could be considered a damning indictment of the SAC commander's leadership.

Supporting Lindbergh's view were the observations of Maj. Gen. Frederic H. Smith, Norstad's Assistant for Programming, who also visited some SAC bases. At Weaver Air Force Base, Rapid City, South Dakota, Smith found a vivid example of the toll of undermanning. When the 28th Bombardment Group left for England, most of the base staff accompanied it, leaving almost no one to run the airfield. Given the command's worldwide mission and the need to respond rapidly in time of crisis, this kind of situation was unsatisfactory.[124]

Kenney showed little sign that he saw a problem. Often absent from his headquarters, he gave frequent speeches throughout the country. As Symington's Director of Public Relations, Stephen F. Leo kept an eye on such activity. As Leo later recalled, Kenney liked to give speeches:

> in which he could forecast that as soon as the enemy bomber dropped a bomb on New York City, radioactive taxicab fenders would be found out beyond Danbury, Connecticut. Now if George could just get it out to Hartford, he'd make another speech.[125]

Later Kenney believed, incorrectly, that Leo had tried to warn him of his declining influence at the Pentagon.[126]

The SAC Commander obviously was becoming increasingly alienated from the Air Staff. In August he clashed with General Fairchild, Kenney claiming that the Training Command was not sending him graduates of the Technical Schools (a convenient way to explain the number of planes out of commission). Deputy Chief of Staff for Personnel Idwal H. Edwards, called this charge "not well founded," advising Fairchild that over four

---

[123] *Ibid.*

[124] Borowski, *Hollow Threat*, pp 146–147; memo, Maj Gen F. H. Smith, Jr., Dir Prog, to Lt Gen L. Norstad, DCS/Ops, subj: Orientation Visit to Strategic Air Command Medium Bomb, Aug 9, 1948, RG 341, DCS/Ops, Admin Ofc, 452.1 Programming General, MMB, NA.

[125] USAF OHI, #K239.0512–1558, George M. Watson, AFCHO, with Stephen F. Leo, Ret, Aug 18, 1982, p 77, AFHRA. See also Borowski, *Hollow Threat*, p 141; *New York Times*, Apr 7, 1948, p 4, May 20, 1948, p 10, Jun 13, 1948, p 31.

[126] Leo OHI, pp 78–79.

Strategic Air Force

At the request of Gen. Hoyt S. Vandenberg, world-renowned aviator Charles A. Lindbergh evaluated SAC's facilities and methods, citing poor living conditions, cross-training, and undermanning as the most serious of the command-wide problems he identified.

thousand such graduates had joined SAC over the past year. The vice chief accused Kenney of making "a lot of wild statements."[127]

One staff officer later recalled a briefing at which senior officers of all services had been present, as well as Symington and Forrestal. On this occasion Kenney had been poorly prepared and reportedly annoyed Symington.[128] It became clear that his stock was low on the Air Staff when in June 1948 Vandenberg ordered him to move his headquarters from Andrews to Offutt Air Force Base, near Omaha, Nebraska. Kenney had long vigorously protested such an action, citing his experience in GHQ Air Force in support of remaining in the Washington area. Nevertheless, the Air Staff had long wanted to reduce field activities near the Nation's capital, especially in view of increased commercial flying in the area. Offutt was one of several locations, mainly in the center of the continent, considered suitable for a major headquarters. It had sufficient office space (mainly in a disused bomber factory from the war), an airfield, access to communications, and reasonably good housing available in the local community. Political considerations may have played a role in its selection. Arthur C. Storz, a wealthy Omaha businessman, was an influential friend of the Air Force, and Senator Kenneth S. Wherry, Republican of Ne-

---

[127] Memo, Gen M. S. Fairchild, VCSAF, to Gen G. C. Kenney, CG SAC, Aug 25, 1948, with atch memo, Lt Gen I. H. Edwards, DCS/Pers, to Fairchild, Aug 23, 1948, Fairchild Coll, SAC 1948–1950, Box 3, MD, LC.

[128] Borowski, *Hollow Threat*, pp 148–149.

braska, would later be a powerful supporter of legislation on military housing. In any case, the Air Staff overruled Kenney, and the move was scheduled for November.[129]

Meanwhile, Vandenberg had Lindbergh's report in hand. The day before it was submitted, the air chief had briefed the President on measures needed to prepare for war.[130] Norstad apparently suggested that getting SAC ready would require new leadership. LeMay had the right kind of experience, with a record of taking over faltering organizations and getting them into shape. On September 21, Headquarters U.S. Air Force announced that LeMay was to take command of SAC, while Kenney would go to Maxwell Air Force Base, Alabama, as Commander of Air University.[131]

After hearing the news in Europe, LeMay took the opportunity to ask Leon Johnson, formerly a SAC Air Force Commander, about the actual situation in his new command. Johnson referred him to some young officers recently arrived from SAC. From them, LeMay learned, as Johnson phrased it, that SAC was "emphasizing the wrong things."[132] Returning to the States, LeMay took command as of October 19 and prepared to move west. Three weeks later he opened his headquarters at Offutt. Meanwhile, within days of assuming command, he had begun organizing a new staff. He drew on a group of officers who had served with him in the Marianas and had shown a grasp of bomber operations. Brig. Gen. Thomas S. Power, the Air Attache in London, became his Deputy Commander. Power, a voluble New Yorker, presented a contrast to his taciturn chief. LeMay's Chief of Staff in Europe, Brig. Gen. August W. Kissner, was soon assigned to the same post at SAC. To head his Operations and Plans Directorates, the new commander brought in two officers then serving in the Office of the Secretary of the Air Force: Brig. Gen. John B.

---

[129] Ltr, AFOTR to CG SAC, subj: Relocation of Headquarters, Strategic Air Command, Dec 11, 1947, Vandenberg Coll, Files 1947–1948, Box 32; memo, Gen H. S. Vandenberg, CSAF, to W. S. Symington, Sec AF, subj: Movement of Headquarters, Strategic Air Command, May 12, 1948, Vandenberg Coll, Files 1948, Box 32; ltr, Vandenberg to CG SAC, subj: Relocation of Headquarters, Strategic Air Command, Jan 3, 1948, with 1st Ind, Gen G. C. Kenney, CG SAC, to CSAF, Jan 15, 1948, Vandenberg Coll, Files 1948, Box 32; ltr, Gen M. S. Fairchild, VCSAF, to Kenney, May 28, 1948, Fairchild Coll, SAC 1948–1950, Box 3, all in MD, LC; Borowski, *Hollow Threat*, p 181, n 4; hist, SAC, 1948, pp 388–390.
[130] Rearden, *Formative Years*, pp 296–297.
[131] Borowski, *Hollow Threat*, pp 149, 159 n 39.
[132] Johnson OHI, # 865, pp 144–145.

Montgomery and Col. Walter C. Sweeney, Jr. Together, LeMay and these four officers had an average age of forty-one.[133]

Although there was much work to do, the young staff had to cope with being in the spotlight. The Joint Chiefs of Staff, recognizing the importance of SAC's mission, was taking an interest in whether it could be carried out. Within the Air Force, Vandenberg had scheduled a meeting of the top leaders at Maxwell Air Force Base, Alabama, on December 6. There, the plans and goals of all the commands would come under scrutiny. LeMay was not pleased with the current state of war planning in SAC, nor with the overall concept devised by the Air Staff.[134] Nevertheless, when he arrived at Maxwell, he was ready.

The results of "Dualism," as the conference was called, were striking. Many now recognized that the atomic offensive was the Air Force's number one job. Maj. Gen. Charles P. Cabell, the Director of Intelligence, gave the first briefing, in which he emphasized the deterrent effect of the bomb. He pointed out that the Soviet industrial system was vulnerable to air attack because of its high degree of concentration. "If a shooting war should come," Cabell emphasized, "we know that atomic destruction must be delivered to the heartland of the Soviet Union. Only *there* can Russia be stopped! The Russians know this...." Thus, the air offensive would be aimed at destroying Soviet industry and control centers and undermining morale.[135]

When LeMay's turn came, he introduced Montgomery, who had the room darkened to show slides of the deployment plan. One observer recalled hearing "the voice of doom" from the briefer.[136] The plan advocated, not the gradual expenditure of bombs as they were made ready, as

---

[133] Hopkins & Goldberg, *Development of SAC*, pp 11–12; LeMay & Kantor, *Mission with LeMay*, pp 429–432; Fogerty, Study # 91, "Kissner," "LeMay," "Montgomery," "Power," "Sweeney;" Remarks by Gen Jack Catton, at AFCHO, Bolling AFB, May 19, 1989. Catton reports that LeMay at the end of the first staff meeting instructed an assistant to arrange a telephone conversation with General Vandenberg. The next day he announced the changes that were to be made.

[134] Borowski, *Hollow Threat*, pp 167–168; remarks by Gen Jack Catton, at AFCHO, Bolling AFB, May 18, 1989.

[135] Transcript, *Operation Dualism*, USAF Commanders' Conference, Dec 6–8, 1948, Maxwell AFB, Ala, Vol I, p 22, AFHRA 168.15-10 [hereafter *Dualism*]. As with many code names and nicknames, the precise reason for the name Dualism is unclear.

[136] Briefing, Col J. G. Armstrong, Ofc Asst DCS/Ops for AE, Exercise Dualism, Dec 9, 1948, RG 341, DCS/Ops, Asst for AE, TS 1948, 360.2 Dev of AF for A-Warfare, Box 8, MMB, NA; *Dualism*, Vol II, pp 187–225.

in plan HARROW, but a single massive strike to initiate the atomic offensive. LeMay hoped SAC would ultimately be able to deliver the entire atomic stockpile in one mission, exploiting the principle of mass to the utmost. Furthermore, as McNarney emphasized, comparing SAC's plan with all the previous versions, LeMay had worked out the logistics of the deployment to England in great detail.[137]

The new SAC Commander addressed a number of problems, among them the lack of fighter units in England to help protect SAC's airfields and the uncertain state of plans for controlling the bomber force overseas. Norstad assured him of the Air Staff's support, making it clear that these issues had been raised at headquarters. Even the overseas commanders confirmed the belief that the atomic offensive and the Berlin airlift were the Air Force's highest priorities.[138] McNarney made the same point:

> I don't care what it is, there is nothing in all of our planning and all of our possibilities of reducing the length of the war which should take priority over the delivery of the atomic offensive.... I have recently given instructions to the Air Materiel Command that the first priority is seeing that the wherewithal to deliver the atomic bomb will be given first priority in funds, personnel, and... time.[139]

LeMay agreed that, in a time of tightening budgets, the Air Force needed to put first things (such as the SAC mission) first. He believed that neither American nor Soviet defensive forces could be effective; the offensive would get through. The SAC Commander estimated that the atomic offensive might cost the Soviets eight million dead. He also emphasized the need to develop intercontinental range through the deployment of the B-36 and the development of air refueling for the medium bombers. LeMay had also planned to station the conferees at the Maxwell runway to witness the landing of a B-36 and a B-50 returning from a simulated bombing mission to Hawaii. Unfortunately, because of schedule problems at the conference, the bombers were brought into Carswell instead.[140]

Dualism ended on December 8, and LeMay returned to Offutt to concentrate on preparing SAC to meet its high priority commitment. When Maj. Gen. Kenneth B. Wolfe, the Air Materiel Command's Director of Procurement and Industrial Planning, asked LeMay for a couple of good lieutenant colonels to help with procuring bombers, he replied that since "Dualism" he had readiness as his first mission and could spare no one. Likewise, he demanded that the Air Staff acknowledge SAC's priority,

---

[137] See previous note.
[138] *Dualism*, Vol II, pp 227, 258; Vol III, pp 322–329, 613–614.
[139] *Dualism*, Vol II, p 227.
[140] *Dualism*, Vol II, pp 322–329, 613–614.

A New Era at SAC. When Lt. Gen. Curtis E. LeMay, *center*, assumed command of SAC on October 19, 1948, he quickly assembled a capable new staff. Brig. Gen. Thomas S. Power, *above, left,* Air Attache in London, became his Deputy Commander. Brig. Gen. August W. Kissner, *above, right,* his Chief of Staff in Europe, became his Chief of Staff at SAC. Brig. Gen. John B. Montgomery, *below, left,* and Col. Walter C. Sweeney, *below, right,* were reassigned from the Office of the Secretary of the Air Force to head SAC Plans and Operations.

and he particularly resisted efforts to reduce the command's already undermanned headquarters units.[141]

Within SAC LeMay suspended cross-training so every crew member could concentrate on learning his primary job. As for overall training standards, he intended to make them more realistic, in keeping with Lindbergh's recommendation. In January 1949 he ordered a simulated radar bombing mission against Dayton, Ohio, in which the entire command would participate. Bombardiers and navigators received three-year-old photographs of the town. (They would be lucky to get anything that recent for the Soviet Union). The bombers were to fly at 30,000 feet. The results of the mission showed the effect of years of unrealistic training. Aside from the numerous aborts caused by failure to reach altitude, the bombing results were abysmal. Of 303 runs, nearly two-thirds were more than 7,000 feet off target. The average error was 10,090 feet. Such an error, even with an atomic bomb over Hiroshima would have left the target unscathed.[142] LeMay later called this episode "about the darkest night in American military aviation history."[143] A smaller-scale mission in May showed little improvement.[144]

Even granting equipment problems, LeMay considered the Dayton mission complete proof of SAC's low state of training. From then on he began to transform the command into a thoroughly professional organization. He planned to build the strategic bombing capability wing by wing. At the beginning of 1949, the 509th received first priority in all resources and training. Once that unit was ready, he intended to turn to another wing and build it in the same way. The SAC Developmental Program would outline the priorities. In addition, LeMay was determined not to add new demands on already over-burdened flying and ground crewmen. By paying attention to such morale-related issues as housing, he planned to emphasize both sides of a professional standard, to offer much and to expect much in return.[145] In this way, the new Commander of SAC would take the all-important final step in transforming the American strategic air force from a diplomatic bluff into a military reality.

---

[141] Ltr, Maj Gen K. B. Wolfe, Dir Proc & Indus Plng, AMC, to Lt Gen C. E. LeMay, CG SAC, Dec 13, 1948; ltr, LeMay to Wolfe, Dec 27, 1948, both in LeMay Coll, Wolfe, Box B61; ltr, LeMay to Lt Gen L. Norstad, DCS/Ops, May 28, 1949, LeMay Coll, Norstad, Box B56, all in MD, LC.

[142] Rprt, Springfield Evaluation Mission, Jul 7, 1952, LeMay Coll, Box B106, MD, LC; Borowski, *Hollow Threat*, pp 163–167.

[143] LeMay & Kantor, *Mission with LeMay*, p 433.

[144] Rprt, Springfield Evaluation Mission, Jul 7, 1952, LeMay Coll, Box B106, MD, LC.

[145] Borowski, *Hollow Threat*, pp 167–177.

Chapter VII

The Priority Mission

The receding of the international crisis after September 1948 allowed Truman to reassert his commitment to limit defense spending. But the basic problem of the Soviet threat remained, with Stalin's Russia as closed a society as ever, and efforts by U.S. intelligence services to develop information in their infancy, leaving policymakers susceptible to the most lurid reports. While most agencies tended to postpone the forecast date of a Soviet atomic weapon, the Air Force was proceeding with its program for detecting atomic explosions, based on early estimates. The Finletter Commission had concurred with intelligence reports stating that the Soviets were in no way ready for war, but the emergence of a Soviet atomic arsenal might well change these assessments. As for an early warning of an "atomic Pearl Harbor," the Nation's one air defense system had been largely dismantled by the end of the Second World War. The Polar frontier, most vulnerable to Soviet attack, lay completely open. With funds in short supply, the Finletter recommendation that an atomic striking force be built as a deterrent and the one means to strike back on the outset of a war took on driving importance.

Understandably, then, from the very beginning of LeMay's tenure as Commander of SAC, the Air Force placed great emphasis on building a combat-ready strategic force. The modification of medium bombers to constitute an atomic-capable, air-refuelable fleet was reaching a point where the hardware for a strategic force was on hand. Meanwhile, the Air Force's high hopes for the very heavy intercontinental B–36 were frustrated by continuing delays, making the medium bomber force all the more important. The increased appropriations voted in the spring of 1948 had demonstrated the nation's commitment to strategic air power, and the Air Force was giving it first priority. Decisions in 1948 to manufacture the B–36, to continue production of the B–50, and to redefine the B–52 as a jet heavy bomber all reflected this thinking.

Strategic Air Force

Ironically, subsequent budget reductions further emphasized the role of strategic air power. By the end of 1948, President Truman was setting rigid ceilings on defense spending. The Air Force began to fear that its seventy-group program would never be realized. In cutting back to forty-eight groups, SAC was left essentially untouched. Every other function of the service was subordinated to the strategic air offensive. A board of senior officers examined the budget and focused attention on the B–36, the B–47, and an improved reconnaissance force. Designs that seemed marginal had to be scrapped. Planners envisioned air refueling as the best way to give the force an intercontinental reach.

But the striking power of modern aircraft depended upon the performance of well-trained, disciplined air and ground crews. LeMay had found the state of the bomber force to be low in this respect. If SAC was to play the key role that Congress, the Air Force, and the public all seemed to envision, obviously, improvements were necessary. Accordingly, LeMay set a commandwide goal of reaching an unprecedented level of peacetime proficiency. At the heart of his plans was "standardization," a term which came to symbolize the "SAC way." Jobs were to be defined precisely, standards of proficiency outlined, and constant testing undertaken to see that standards were achieved.

This process reinforced itself. By rewarding the efficient, LeMay hoped to communicate his demand for high standards, as well as to improve the morale of the force. Spot promotions, for example, were valuable precisely because they were an exception to Air Force policy and unique to the Strategic Air Command. They demonstrated the command's special role in the Air Force and gave its personnel a sense of the rewards of being part of an elite organization. LeMay's efforts to improve living conditions in SAC also boosted morale while emphasizing the specialness of belonging to SAC.

In his continued efforts to build an efficient global striking force, then, LeMay was fulfilling the Air Force's commitment to provide the nation with an atomic deterrent. The role of the strategic force as an instrument of national policy had been already decided. But the strength of the deterrent and the combat readiness of the force would depend on the dedication of the new commander and his men.

Aircraft for Deterrence

The new budget voted in May 1948, at a time of growing international crisis, had given the Air Force the funds for a large aircraft procurement program. This might allow an acceleration of purchases to modernize and expand the atomic force. Also, sufficient funds might be available to equip tactical forces that otherwise would be squeezed by the priority given the strategic bombers. For the strategic program, the Air Force needed to modernize both the heavy and medium bombers and proceed with modifications to expand the atomic force. Basically, SAC was still a force of B–29s, now classed as medium bombers, so the heavy bomber then under development—the B–36—was a new system. Modernization of the force called for bringing the B–36 into service and deciding on a design for its successor, most likely the Boeing B–52. For the medium bomber fleet, the problem was more complicated, but it centered on achieving the maximum possible range. Modifications approved to expand the atomic force became an integral part of the medium bomber program. All these issues affected the allocation of the supplemental appropriation enacted in the spring of 1948.

As of April 1948 the B–36 program had been generally doing well. Tests showed good results, with one prototype plane staying in the air for thirty-two and a half hours in April and reaching a range of 8,500 miles in May.[1] On the other hand, problems arose with the variable discharge turbine (VDT) engine. McNarney warned the Air Staff that the engine would need a heavier cooling fan, which would add considerable weight to the airplane and thereby cut the speed of a plane already considered too slow. The Air Materiel Command recommended canceling the VDT, although this would leave thirty-four bombers without the engines they were designed to carry. McNarney made no recommendation, but he did point out that allowing Convair to manufacture all one hundred aircraft in the contract would yield the lowest unit cost and avoid the loss of money from a cancellation. Norstad proposed cancellation all the same. The Air Force could buy twenty-two B–36As and thirty-nine B models, enough of the latter to equip one group. The A models, not atomic-capable, might be used as tankers. Craig agreed, but Undersecretary of the Air Force Arthur S. Barrows continued to support the full purchase. He had the decision postponed, and by the time Symington, Fairchild, Kenney, and key members of the Air Staff met on June 24, 1948, to discuss the B–36's future, the Berlin crisis had erupted, altering the political environment.[2]

---

[1] Self, *Heavy Bombardment Aircraft*, p 90; ltr, Lt Col D. W. Graham, Actg Ch Acft & Msl Sect, Proc Div AMC, to Maj W. D. Brady, Proc & Indus Plng, DCS/Mat, subj: Preliminary Data on Long Range Flight of B–36 Airplane, May 20, 1948, RG 341, DCS/Comptr, Admin Div 1942–53, 452.1s Acft, B–36 Spec File, Box 212, MMB, NA.
[2] Ltr, Gen J. T. McNarney, CG AMC, to DCS/Mat, subj: B–36 Program, n.d. [Apr 48]; memo, Lt Gen L. Norstad, DCS/Ops, to Lt Gen H. A. Craig, DCS/Mat, subj: B–36 Program, Apr 24, 1948, with notations by Craig; MR, A. S. Barrows, USec AF, Re discussion May 22, May 24, 1948, all in RG 341, DCS/Comptr, Admin Div 1942–53, 452.1s Acft, B–36 Spec File, Box 212, MMB, NA.

If cancelling the B–36 was one of the choices, the consequences of termination became an issue. As Fairchild reported: "we would be left with a large bomber plant full of unusable cut-up material and partially fabricated and assembled parts." The resulting layoffs at Convair's Fort Worth plant would create disorder in the industry at a critical time. The group's recommendation, which Symington accepted, was to cancel the VDT engine and buy a total of ninety-five airplanes (twenty-two A models and seventy-three Bs), all with conventional engines.[3] The last fifty-four B models would come off the line modified to carry atomic weapons. As if to confirm this decision, one week later one B–36A dropped seventy-two thousand pounds of bombs in a practice run, and on July 8 the first B model flew.[4]

The proposed successor to the B–36 was the B–52. In early 1948 this aircraft existed only in a mockup of an early design. No sooner had Air Force officials agreed to one major redirection of the B–52 program then another one was proposed.[5] Research on jet engines was beginning to demonstrate that fuel consumption could be significantly reduced, allowing for greater range. Thus, in May 1948 the Air Staff suggested that Boeing consider jet propulsion for the B–52.[6]

The company submitted its first design for the jet version in July. Craig feared the risk involved in so radical a change and the delays that might ensue, even if the design were successful. All the same, the staff at Wright-Patterson Air Force Base, Ohio, headquarters of the Air Materiel Command, remained optimistic. On Thursday, October 21, a party of engineers from Boeing, visiting Wright-Patterson to discuss the B–52, learned of AMC's expectations. The command's representatives said that they needed a preliminary study for a plane equipped with Pratt and Whitney J–57 engines, not yet available. Some accounts in the press later reported that the Boeing engineers immediately went to a hotel room in Dayton and worked around the clock until they had completed a report and a hand-carved model. They drew on their knowledge of the existing Boeing designs and the B–47 project. On Monday morning, October 25, they turned in the results. By the end of 1948, a new design had been developed for a jet-powered B–52 with swept wings, a gross weight of 330,000 pounds, a range of about 8,000 miles, speeds of 520 to 570 miles

---

[3] MR, Gen M. S. Fairchild, VCSAF, Jun 25, 1948; Note, Maj Gen K. B. Wolfe, Dir Proc & Indus Prog, AMC, to 1st Ind, Lt Gen H. A. Craig, DCS/Mat, Jun 25, 1948, to ltr, AMC to CSAF, subj: B–36 Program, n.d., both in RG 341, DCS/Comptr, Admin Div 1942-53, 452.1s Acft, B–36 Spec File, Box 212, MMB, NA.
[4] Knaack, *Bombers*, pp 23–25.
[5] *Ibid.*, pp 23–25.
[6] *Ibid.*, pp 214–215.

per hour, and a service ceiling of 45,000 feet. Soon the new XB-52 model was under review in the Air Force.[7]

At the same time, the Air Force was considering several alternatives for new medium bombers to replace the wartime B-29. The early production models of the B-50 were performing well. Test reports, in the words of one staff officer, made the aircraft "look like a world-beater."[8] The first SAC unit to receive a B-50A was the 43d Bombardment Group at Davis-Monthan, which took delivery on February 20, 1948. Soon the B model would enter production and, starting with the twenty-fourth plane of the series, would leave the factory fully atomic-capable. The B-50C (subsequently redesignated the B-54) would be equipped with VDT engines. Among the experimental designs, the Northrop Company's B-49 Flying Wing might turn out to be an effective bomber, while the Boeing B-47 and the Martin B-48 would be jets of a more conventional type. By the middle of 1948, the Air Staff was most optimistic about the B-47. Although the model was not performing up to requirements, the Boeing test pilots liked it. Also, future models would be able to carry more powerful engines once they became available, and the plane's swept wings seemed to offer more aerodynamic potential than the Martin XB-48 design. The Northrop YB-49 Flying Wing also was testing well, but observers realized that the production aircraft could neither carry a large load of bombs nor be modified to carry atomic weapons. In flight the prototype revealed instabilities in pitch, roll, and yaw that seriously degraded any hope of its being an accurate bomber. A crash of one of the two YB-49s on June 5 not only delayed testing but also fueled the controversy surrounding the plane.[9]

A more realistic hope for the B-49 lay in reconnaissance. The Aircraft and Weapons Board, concerned about SAC's weakness in this function, had showed some interest in developing a reconnaissance version. In April 1948 a conference at AMC Headquarters brought together Maj. Gen. Earle E. Partridge, Director of Training and Requirements, Craigie, and key members of the staff at Wright-Patterson to discuss the problem of long-range, high-performance reconnaissance. These officers considered the potential of the B-49, the Republic F-12,[10] the Douglas DC-6, and the B-50. There were two prototype F-12s, which did not have the VDT engines that were thought to be essential for the job. The

---

[7] *Ibid.*; Bagwell, *XB-52 Airplane*, pp 19-22.
[8] Daily Diary, Col G. Y. Jumper, Ch Pl & Intel, SWG, Apr 2, 1948, RG 341, DCS/Ops, Asst for AE, S 1948, 314.7 Daily Diary (Pl & Intel), Box 16, MMB, NA.
[9] Self, *Heavy Bombardment Aircraft*, pp 70-74, 92-96; study, ARDC, *Air Force Developmental Aircraft*, 1957, pp 135-137, 183-191, 193-196.
[10] Before 1947, F stood for photographic.

conferees agreed to give Northrop a contract for thirty reconnaissance models of the B–49, subcontracting to Convair for twenty-nine of them, so as to direct some more business to the Fort Worth plant.[11]

The supplemental appropriation enacted in May 1948 led to a review of the Air Force's planned purchases. Anticipating the possibility of extra money for the seventy-group program, Maj. Gen. Kenneth B. Wolfe, AMC's Director of Procurement and Industrial Planning, had appointed a committee early in the year to study implementation. The resulting report initiated a series of procurement plans and revisions, the so-called "Finnster" (Finletter-Brewster) series. These were versions of a five-year program for building to seventy groups with modern aircraft. By May the plan called for the Air Force to buy 2,727 aircraft, with the fiscal 1948 supplemental appropriation then before Congress.[12] In Washington, the Air Staff made several changes, calling for more testing of some aircraft types. Headquarters officials agreed to defer the purchase of 300 planes, including the 30 B–49s. The rest of the program was endorsed, including 132 B–50Ds (featuring external fuel tanks and a new top turret), 43 B–50Cs, and 1,500 jet fighters.[13] But when Vandenberg and Symington met with Forrestal, they asked for all 2,727. The Secretary of Defense decided to postpone contracting for 526 planes, including 13 B–50Cs and 200 fighters. On May 28 Forrestal submitted his proposals to Truman, who authorized the program, releasing $1.3 billion for the Air Force and $600 million for the Navy.[14]

In July Forrestal's budget adviser, Wilfred J. McNeil, inquired what the Air Force wanted to do with the funds (about $200 million) allocated to the deferred aircraft. Undersecretary Barrows replied on August 6, with a request for $104 million for two hundred fighters plus the deferred

---

[11] Study, ARDC, *Air Force Developmental Aircraft*, 1957, pp 195–196; MR, Maj Gen L. C. Craigie, Dir R & D, to DCS/Mat, Procurement of Strategic Reconnaissance Aircraft, Apr 15, 1948; memo, subj: Determinations Favoring Procurement of the B–49 as a Photo-Reconnaissance Airplane, n.d., both in *Narrative History in Chronological Order of the B–35 and B–49 (and Variations)*, Tabs 61, 62, CAFH.

[12] Self, *Five-Year Aircraft Procurement Program*, pp 4–7.

[13] Memo, Col J. A. Brooks, Ch Prog An Div, Comptr, to Lt Gen E. M. Rawlings, DCS/Comptr, subj: Aircraft Procurement for Fiscal Year 1949, May 14, 1948, RG 341, DCS/Comptr, Admin Div 1942–53, 452.01 Acft, Jan 46–May 48, Box 202, MMB, NA.

[14] Ltr, J. V. Forrestal, Sec Def, to President, May 23, 1948; ltr, Forrestal to Sec Nav, Sec AF, May 28, 1948; memo, W. J. McNeil, Asst to Sec Def, to Brig Gen W. D. Eckert, Exec Off to USec AF, Jul 24, 1948, all in RG 341, DCS/Comptr, Admin Div 1942–53, 452.1s Acft, B–36 Spec File, Box 212, MMB, NA; memo, subj: USAF Supplement Fiscal Year 1948 Aircraft Program, Jun 1, 1948, RG 341, DCS/Dev, Dir Rqmts, Papers 1st AWB, Box 182, MMB, NA; Self, *Five-Year Aircraft Procurement Program*, pp 11–16.

Fiscal 1948 Supplemental Aircraft Program[a]

Model	AMC Plan	1st USAF Revision	Presidential Program	Quantity Deferred
B-50D	132	132	132	0
B-50C (B-54)	43	43	50	13
B-45C	68	68	51	17
Fighter & Tactical	1,605	1,605	1,405	200
Recon, Trainer & Transport, etc.	849	579	533	296
RB-49	30	0	30	0
TOTAL	2,727	2,427	2,201	526

[a]Ltr, J. V. Forrestal, Sec Def, to President, May 23, 1948; ltr, Forrestal to Sec Nav, Sec AF, May 28, 1948; memo, W. J. McNeil, Asst to Sec Def, to Brig Gen W. D. Eckert, Exec Off to USec AF, July 24, 1948, all in RG 341, DCS/Comptr, Admin Div 1942–53, 452.1s Acft, B-36 Spec File, Box 212, MMB, NA; memo, subj: USAF Supplement Fiscal Year 1948 Aircraft Program, Jun 1, 1948, RG 341, DCS/Dev, Dir Rqmts, Papers 1st AWB, Box 182, MMB, NA; Self, *Five-Year Aircraft Procurement Program*, pp 11–16.

B-50Cs. A month later Symington signed a memorandum to Forrestal, asking for the remainder of the program. However, there were some revisions to the list. By deleting some light bombers, transports, trainers, and helicopters, the Air Staff freed money for such projects as guided missiles and B-47s. The airmen planned to buy fifty-four of the jet bombers, but they funded only ten. By the end of October the President had released most of this remaining money. At the close of 1948, the Air Force had accepted more than one hundred bombers on all postwar contracts and had another three hundred on order.[15]

---

[15] Memo, W. M. McNeil, Asst to Sec Def, to Brig Gen W. D. Eckert, Exec Off to USec AF, Jul 24, 1948; memo, A. S. Barrows, USec AF, to J. V. Forrestal, Sec Def, subj: Utilization of Deferred Supplemental 1948 Procurement Funds, Aug 6, 1948; memo, W. S. Symington, Sec AF, to Forrestal, subj: Request for the Balance of Deferred Supplemental 1948 Aircraft Funds, Sep 7, 1948; ltr, Truman to Forrestal, Sep 16, 1948; ltr, Forrestal to President, Oct 1, 1948, with note, J. E. Webb, Dir Budget, Oct 1948, all in RG 341, DCS/Comptr, Admin Div 1942–53, 452.1s Acft, B-36 Spec File, Box 212, MMB, NA.

New Needs, New Aircraft. *Clockwise from above:* **The potential of the turbojet-powered version of the B–35 Flying Wing—the Northrop YB–49A, the Republic F–12, the Boeing B–50, and the Douglas DC–6 for long-range reconnaissance was carefully studied by the Aircraft and Weapons Board in its effort to improve intelligence gathering.**

Strategic Air Force

Bomber Programs (approximate)[a]

Manufacturer	Type	Total	Atomic Capable	SADDLETREE	Accepted
Convair	B-36A	22			21
Convair	B-36B	73	54	18	18
Boeing	B-50A	79		72	73
	B-50B	45	22	23	
	B-50D	140	140		
	B-54A	43	43		
	B-47A	10	10		
Northrop	RB-49	30			
TOTAL		442	269	113	112

[a]Knaack, *Bombers*, pp 21–23, 29, 174; Self, *Heavy Bombardment Aircraft*, pp 74, 92–96; study, ARDC, *Air Force Development Aircraft*, 1957, pp. 135ff.

While the larger appropriations affected many aircraft programs, the modification of bombers for the atomic force, considered high priority, would proceed with whatever funds were available. To the SADDLETREE modifications of the B-29 and other bombers, the Air Force added several more projects. These included winterization, a global electronics modification (GEM) to provide equipment for worldwide navigation, installation of equipment for air-to-air refueling, and the modification of some bombers to serve as tankers. All these efforts combined to form a single program, with the goal of creating a truly global atomic strike force.[16]

Because of the urgency of GEM/SADDLETREE, as the total modification program was called, the Air Staff proposed to bring additional B-29s out of storage rather than wait for production of newer models. During the early months of 1948, about one hundred bombers were to be returned to the active inventory in order to provide several of SAC's groups with a reserve of aircraft. As for other types, a project for SADDLETREE modifications on thirty-six B-50s fell behind schedule. In January AMC received instructions to start a large-scale, concerted effort on various aircraft. The B-29s would be modified in the field, the B-50As at Sacramento, the

---

[16] Little, *Foundations*, Pt 2, p 395.

Priority Mission

B–50Bs at the reopened Boeing plant at Wichita, and the B–36s at Fort Worth.[17] By March 1948 atomic modifications were authorized for eighty B–29s, ninety-five B–50s, and eighteen B–36s.

Besides the urgent SADDLETREE effort, the Air Staff was focusing attention on other modification projects. On February 26, the air refueling project had received a top priority, and on March 12 Boeing signed a contract to develop an air-to-air refueling system. Three days earlier, SAC representatives proposed the winterizing of half of the 509th's planes, the entire SADDLETREE force, and the F–80s. All of these projects combined to force a reassessment of schedules.[18] Craig especially insisted on careful planning, as AMC was already pressed for resources to provide routine support, considering all these top-priority projects. Finally, on April 16 Air Force Headquarters issued an integrated schedule. The deadline for all the modifications was December 15, 1948. The Materiel Command and the contractors had started tooling up.[19]

So urgent was the refueling project that it had been scheduled for testing and evaluation even before a workable design had been adopted. Boeing, the prime contractor, proposed developing an interim system right away, to be followed by a long-term solution. On March 28 the company held a successful demonstration of the looped-hose technique (using hoses and grapnel hooks to connect the tanker and the receiving aircraft). Over the next few weeks came a remarkable series of improvisations, and the first set of equipment, ready for installation, was delivered to the Air Force at the beginning of May. Obviously, the interim system was clumsy; planes had to drop below 10,000 feet and slow down to refuel. But even a makeshift solution offered important advantages. A B–29 that refueled before penetrating hostile air space could reach a target within a radius of 2,700 miles and return to base. With the increased range, basing in Iceland became feasible for strikes against the Soviet Union, and other targets were accessible from Alaska. Also in May, AMC selected a design for a

---

[17] Fenwick, *Saddletree Project*, pp 32–33; hist, SAC, 1948, p 327; R & R Sheet, Cmt 2, Maj Gen S. E. Anderson, Dir P & O, to Asst DCS/Ops for Prog, Acft Delivery and Mod Instructions, Apr 15, 1948, RG 341, DCS/Ops, Exec Ofc 452.1 (B–29), Box 1, MMB, NA.

[18] *Case History of Air-to-Air Refueling*, pp 13–15; Little, *Foundations*, Pt 2, pp 396–397.

[19] Memo, Lt Gen H. A. Craig, DCS/Mat, to Lt Gen L. Norstad, DCS/Ops, subj: AMC Aircraft Maintenance Workload, Apr 6, 1948, RG 341, DCS/Ops, Exec Ofc 452.1 (B–29), Box 1, MMB, NA; Little, *Foundations*, Pt 2, pp 399–400.

GEM/SADDLETREE Projects, 1948[a]

Quantity	Type	Source	Saddletree	GEM	Winterization	Ruralist
44	B–29	SAC	X	X[b]		
36	B–29	SAC	X	X[c]	X	X
40	B–29	Storage		X	X[b]	X
36	B–50A	Boeing	X	X	X[b]	
36	B–50A	Boeing	X	X	X[b]	X
23	B–50A	Boeing	X	X	X[b]	X
18	B–36B	Convair	X	X	X[b]	
48	P–80A	SAC		X	X	
6	YC–97	AMC			X[b]	

[a] Memo, Lt Gen H.A. Craig, DCS/Mat, to Lt Gen L. Norstad, DCS/Ops, subj: AMC Aircraft Maintenance Workload, Apr 6, 1948, RG 341, DCS/Ops, Exec Ofc 452.1 (B–29), Box 1, MMB, NA; Little, *Foundations*, Pt 2, pp 399–400.

[b] Added later

[c] To include a special modification for Alaskan conditions

SADDLETREE - the atomic modification
GEM - Global Electronic Modification
Ruralist - modification to receive refueling in the air
Superman - modification as tanker

permanent system, based on a "flying boom" technique, with the tanker carrying a boom containing a pipe.[20]

Complicating matters even more was the decision by Congress to allow the expansion of the Air Force to sixty-six groups by June 30, 1949. Such a rapid buildup would require withdrawing more B–29s from storage. Maj. Gen. Samuel E. Anderson, Weyland's successor as Director of Plans and Operations, had previously opposed deploying more obsolete aircraft. It cost $90,000 to make each plane combat ready.[21] But the approval of a sixty-six group program posed an irresistible need. Maj. Gen. Frederic H. Smith, the Assistant Deputy Chief of Staff for Operations (Programming), reported that to equip all strategic groups by June 1949 and provide a reserve, AMC would have to release 442 bombers. In June 1948 the Air Staff authorized the withdrawal of 300 B–29s from storage for assignment to SAC.[22]

By the summer of 1948 GEM/SADDLETREE was underway, funded by $25 million from the fiscal 1948 supplemental appropriation. In July another $15 million was allocated from fiscal 1949 money. Unfortunately, despite the infusion of funds, the program faltered. Boeing had fallen behind schedule as the result of a strike, which Air Force observers blamed on communist complicity.[23] Thus, at the outset of the Berlin crisis, the atomic force still consisted of the 509th Group, half of whose planes were old and probably unreliable. At least there were enough trained crews, and the Special Weapons Project could provide three assembly

---

[20] *Case History of Air-to-Air Refueling*, pp 15–32.

[21] Memo, Maj Gen S. E. Anderson, Dir P & O, to Asst DCS/Ops for Prog, subj: Aircraft Delivery and Modification Instructions, Apr 15, 1948, RG 341, DCS/Ops, Exec Ofc 1948–49, 452.1 (B–29), Box 1; memo, Brig Gen W. D. Eckert, Exec to USec AF, to Lt Gen H. A. Craig, DCS/Mat, Jan 24, 1949, RG 341, DCS/Ops, Exec Ofc 1948–49, 452.1 (B–29), Box 9, both in MMB, NA.

[22] Memo, Lt Gen L. Norstad, DCS/Ops, to Lt Gen H. A. Craig, DCS/Mat, subj: AMC Aircraft Maintenance Workload, Apr 27, 1948; memo, Maj Gen F. H. Smith, Asst DCS/Ops for Prog, to Dir P & O, subj: Aircraft Delivery and Modification Instructions, Apr 27, 1948, both in RG 341, DCS/Ops, Exec Ofc 452.1 (B–29), Box 1, MMB, NA; Dorothy Trester, *History of the AF Storage and Withdrawal Program, 1945–1952* (Wright-Patterson AFB, Ohio: AMC, 1954), pp 61–63.

[23] See previous note; Little, *Foundations*, Pt 2, pp 401–404; memo, Dir Pl to VCSAF, subj: Report on Air Force Capability and Program for Conduct of Atomic Warfare, Jun 30, 1948, RG 341, DCS/Ops, Asst for AE, TS 1948, 381 Current Ops Capabilities, Box 10; memo, for Gen H. S. Vandenberg, CSAF, subj: Availability of Modified Aircraft, Dec 13, 1948, RG 341, DCS/Ops, Dir/Pl, TS OPD, 384.31 (Dec 3, 1947), Sect 1, Box 452, both in MMB, NA.

teams.[24] Finally, on July 15, 1948, as the National Security Council decided to send two groups of unmodified B–29s to England, the Air Force took delivery of the first plane modified under GEM/SADDLETREE.[25] The revolution in American air power had finally, fitfully, begun.

Return to Austerity

With the Berlin crisis coinciding with the start of the atomic modernization project, administration and congressional leaders began to have an alternative to massive conventional rearmament as a response to an international threat. While the Air Force established the atomic offensive as its first priority, the administration's determination to minimize defense spending would insure that the nation would have little else to rely on at the outset of a war. Even after the critical moments of September 1948, President Truman continued to push for a firm ceiling on the defense budget, and the joint chiefs had to allocate the extremely limited resources.

During the summer of 1948 the President capped the armed services' expenditures at $14.4 billion in fiscal 1950. Even with the assistance of a Budget Advisory Committee under the chairmanship of McNarney, the joint chiefs at first could not agree on how to divide the amount. The Air Force alone estimated the cost of its seventy-group program at $8.8 billion. This included not only a strong tactical force but the beginnings of a modern air defense system. For Strategic Air Command, the planners requested twenty-eight groups (including five of fighters and four for reconnaissance). Two groups would have B–36s by mid-1950. A portion of the bomber units would operate as atomic carriers, while other planes would serve as decoys and jammers, as well as conventional bombers. But even this sizable strategic force alone could not guarantee victory in war. Long-term plans called for replacing all B–29s (except tankers) by 1952, the earliest target date possible without overexpanding the industry. By then, the planners hoped, Western Europe would be strong enough to contain a Soviet attack while the strategic air offensive did its work.[26]

---

[24] Memo, Dir Pl to VCSAF, subj: Report on Air Force Capability and Program for Conduct of Atomic Warfare, Jun 30, 1948, RG 341, DCS/Ops, Asst for AE, TS 1948, 381 Current Ops Capabilities, Box 10, MMB, NA.
[25] *Case History of Air-to-Air Refueling*, p 27.
[26] Department of the Air Force Presentation to JCS Committee on the Development of the Air Force During Fiscal Year 1950, Aug 25, 1948, Fairchild Coll, Dev of the AF During FY 1950, Box 2, MD, LC.

Accordingly, the Air Force trimmed its proposals to the Budget Advisory Committee to $7.6 billion. Any lower figure would mean cutting the number of groups. The other services also tried to protect what they considered vital capabilities. In October Bradley proposed deleting all funds for forces committed to holding the Mediterranean region. When he included large aircraft carriers in this category, the Navy objected. This proposal not only struck at a central component of the Navy's force plans, but it also implied a decision to rely entirely on strategic bombing—a position which the Navy would challenge over the coming year.[27]

At first, Forrestal hoped he could persuade the President to increase the funding limit. Both the continuing crisis in Europe and the fears of Republican attacks on the administration's defense program in an election year could be persuasive arguments for larger expenditures. In fact, the President did permit some planning for larger budgets. But Truman's surprising (except to himself) election victory in November weakened Forrestal's position. So did the President's determination to avoid appearing provocative to the Soviets (not to mention rumors that Forrestal had been trying to keep his job in a Dewey administration). In December 1948 Truman rejected all efforts to raise the ceiling beyond $14.4 billion.[28]

Meanwhile, the joint chiefs finally agreed on how to divide the $14.4 billion approved by the President for fiscal year 1950. The only remaining issue involved the number of large aircraft carriers to be kept in commission. The Air Force recommended four, the Army six, and the Navy nine. Forrestal settled on eight. Although larger alternative budgets were also prepared, the President never indicated that he would actually approve one. After the Bureau of the Budget made some adjustments, the President submitted to Congress an appropriations request which included $4.5 billion for the Air Force, to fund forty-eight groups and a strength of 412,000 personnel.[29]

Under this budget, the joint chiefs anticipated a major impact on U.S. military strategy. In the event of a Soviet attack, the British would be left

---

[27] Rearden, *Formative Years*, pp 340–345, 358–359; rprt, Aircraft Weapons Board Proceedings, Vol I, Jan 1949, pp 1–10, RG 341, DCS/Mat, Dir Prod & Proc, Prod Eng Div, Mins & Rprts, Dec 48–Jan 49, Box 4, MMB, NA. For an extended account of the development of the FY 50 budget, see Rearden, *Formative Years*, pp 335–360, and K. Condit, *JCS, 1947–1949*, pp 213–256.

[28] Rearden, *Formative Years*, pp 43 & n, 345–351; Robert J. Donovan, *Tumultuous Years: The Presidency of Harry S Truman, 1949–1953* (NY: Norton, 1982), p 60.

[29] Rearden, *Formative Years*, pp 345–347, 358–360.

Strategic Air Force

to secure the Middle East as best they could. America's mobilization base was severely weakened. Still, a strategic air offensive, somewhat reduced in weight and speed, could be launched from Okinawa and either England or Iceland. After a month, strikes might be launched from the Casablanca area. Given Forrestal's attempts to warn the President of the consequences of limiting defense spending, it may be presumed that Truman recognized that strategic air strikes would be the only offensive action available.[30]

The leaders of the Air Force understood that such restricted budgets were likely to continue for some years. The funds allocated for aircraft procurement totaled $1.48 billion, and this figure would probably not increase. By December 31 the Air Force-wide expansion begun earlier in 1948 had reached sixty groups. Now plans had to be made to cut back to forty-eight by the end of June. Ironically, SAC actually stood to gain some capability, for under the revised plan that command would have seventeen reconnaissance and bombardment groups, with another B–29 group in Far East Air Forces.[31] LeMay objected to the program on the grounds that he needed twenty bomber groups alone to carry out the strategic air offensive properly, especially operations were to be sustained after the initial blow.[32] Recognizing that the Air Force now had no choice but to defer the seventy-group program, Vandenberg convened a board consisting of Fairchild, McNarney, Norstad, and Craig to develop a long-term forty-eight-group program. At the end of December this body met, McNarney serving as chairman while Fairchild convalesced from an illness.[33]

The board concurred, with minor changes, with the forty-eight-group program as proposed by the Air Staff. The members did not intend to

---

[30] Rprt, Aircraft Weapons Board Proceedings, Vol I, Jan 1949, RG 341, DCS/Mat, Dir/Prod & Proc, Prod Eng Div, Mins & Rprts, Dec 48–Jan 49, Box 4, MMB, NA.

[31] *Ibid.*, pp 1–20. *Air Force Statistical Digest*, 1948, Vol I, p 3; Hopkins & Goldberg, *Development of SAC*, p 11; R & R Sheet, Cmt 1, Maj Gen F. H. Smith, Jr., Asst for Prog, DCS/Ops, to Dir P & O, Reduction to 48 Group Level, Dec 30, 1948, RG 341, DCS/Ops, Dir/Pl, Decimal File 1942–1954, Box 126, MMB, NA.

[32] Rprt, Aircraft Weapons Board Proceedings, Vol IV, Jan 1949, pp 398–447, RG 341, DCS/Mat, Dir/Prod & Proc, Prod Eng Div, Mins & Rprts, Dec 48–Jan 49, Box 4, MMB, NA.

[33] *Ibid.*, Vol I, Jan 1949, pp 1–20; R & R Sheet, Cmt 1, Maj Gen F. H. Smith, Jr, Asst for Prog, DCS/Ops, to Dir P & O, Reduction to 48 Group Level, Dec 30, 1948, RG 341, DCS/Ops, Dir/Pl, Decimal File 1942–1954, Box 126, MMB, NA.

overrule LeMay, whose central task they readily acknowledged. The question came down to politics and economics; McNarney observed that the SAC position ignored the "facts of life." And while LeMay and Norstad clashed on this issue when the SAC Commander met with the board, the members assured him that all secondary functions had been cut to the bone. The priorities established at the "Dualism" conference had not been forgotten.[34]

When the board turned to strategic aircraft programs, the big story was the success of the B-36. The first B models, now in testing with Convair and entering service in the 7th Bombardment Group at Carswell, had performed impressively. Pilots found the Peacemaker surprisingly responsive to the controls,[35] and engineers at the Air Materiel Command also liked it. One B model had already completed a mission of 8,000 miles, flying from Carswell to Hawaii and dropping a load of bombs and a B-36 had reached altitudes of 40,000 feet. The aircraft's main drawbacks were its low speed, at 319 miles per hour, and lack of armament, due to delays in production. This meant that altitude would be its main defense. In noting that the plane was underpowered, however, engineers commented that it was also lightly loaded; that is, the ratio of gross weight to the area of the wings was lower than with most aircraft. Therefore, more powerful engines would improve performance, and a proposal existed to hang two jet engines in a pod under each wing. Eventually, these jet pod modifications boosted its dash speed to 435 miles per hour. Maj. Gen. Edward M. Powers, Craig's Assistant Deputy Chief of Staff for Material, recalled that the B-36 had once been considered a "dud," but was now "a wonder."[36] Based on a group strength of eighteen planes, the ninety-five B-36s on order would outfit five groups, though virtually without spares. One of these groups could contain aircraft modified for reconnaissance. To increase the production order would require reducing funds for other programs, a matter for the McNarney Board to decide.[37]

---

[34] Rprt, Aircraft Weapons Board Proceedings, Vol II, Jan 1949, pp 158-161, Vol IV, Jan 49, pp 394-447, RG 341, DCS/Mat, Dir/Prod & Proc, Prod Eng Div, Mins & Rprts, Dec 48-Jan 49, Box 4, MMB, NA.

[35] *Ibid.*, Vol I, pp 63-69, Vol IV, pp 463-464; Harry E. Goldsworthy, "B-36 Peacemaker," *Aerospace Historian*, XXX (Dec 83), pp 261-267, Knaack, *Bombers*, pp 24-25.

[36] See previous note; rprt, Aircraft Weapons Board Proceedings, Vol IV, Jan 1949, p 470, RG 341, DCS/Mat, Dir/Prod & Proc, Prod Eng Div, Mins & Rprts, Dec 48-Jan 49, Box 4, MMB, NA.

[37] Rprt, Aircraft Weapons Board Proceedings, Vol I, Jan 1949, pp 52-55, 133, Vol IV, Jan 49, pp 393-394, 471, RG 341, DCS/Mat, Dir/Prod & Proc, Prod Eng Div, Mins & Rprts, Dec 48-Jan 49, Box 4, MMB, NA.

Strategic Air Force

Modernizing the medium bomber force was a less clear-cut proposition. The B-50 was now in full production, with the B-54 (a B-50 with VDT engines) on order. The B-49 Flying Wing jet and the B-47 jet seemed riskier investments, although the XB-47 performed well in tests.[38] The more conservative B-54 would probably attain a range of twenty-seven hundred to three thousand miles. On paper, it had shown the President and Congress that the Air Force could build a plane that would exceed current ranges. Considering the data now available, the intercontinental B-36 could safely play this role instead. Also, the B-54 would still require oversea bases or air refueling. Thus, the B-36 was by far the better buy.[39]

This line of reasoning put the B-54 into competition with the Flying Wing and the B-47. LeMay clearly favored the Stratojet, while the Flying Wing had yet to prove its potential as a bomb carrier. Given the uncertainties, the McNarney Board proposed a mixed force of medium bombers, eventually replacing all the YRB-29As. For a total of fourteen long-range bomber groups, the distribution would be as follows:[40]

B-36	4
B-50A	1
B-50D	4
B-54	3
B-47	2

LeMay's dissatisfaction with the existing reconnaissance force and McNarney's expressed concern combined to focus attention on the need for a more modern reconnaissance fleet. Few now backed the concept of an aircraft specifically designed for this role. Within SAC, planners preferred converted bomber types that could carry large amounts of sophisticated cameras and electronic equipment. The B-36, B-50, and B-47 each looked promising. As for the RB-49 Flying Wing, only the most advanced

---

[38] Knaack, *Bombers*, pp 104–105, 169–170, 181–182, 539–540.

[39] Rprt, Aircraft Weapons Board Proceedings, Vol IV, Jan 1949, pp 398–429, 439, 471, RG 341, DCS/Mat, Dir/Prod & Proc, Prod Eng Div, Mins & Rprts, Dec 48–Jan 49, Box 4; rprt, Report of Senior Board of Officers Convened to Consider the Production Program and the Research and Development Program for the USAF [hereafter Report of Board of Senior Officers], Vol I, Feb 1949, pp 16–18, RG 341, DCS/Mat, Dir/Prod & Proc, Prod Eng Div, Mins & Rprts, Jan–Feb 49, Box 5, both in MMB, NA.

[40] See previous note.

version seemed capable, and then only marginally. Until the B-49 showed more carrying capacity and stability in flight, the Air Force remained skeptical.[41]

The decision to buy additional B-36s also resolved one remaining question concerning the Flying Wing. During 1948, with considerable effort, the Air Force had obtained an agreement between Northrop and Convair for the RB-49 to be built at Convair's Fort Worth plant. This would keep the facility in business after B-36 production ended. In a public speech Secretary Symington had promised that the Fort Worth plant would remain open, so the board members felt obligated to ensure business for it. If the Air Force purchased more B-36s, the Flying Wing could be canceled.[42]

The McNarney Board thus decided to equip four strategic reconnaissance groups over the next few years. Each would have basically one type: RB-36, RB-50, RB-54, or RB-47. To fund additional purchases of B-36s and other types, the board recommended canceling further production of the disappointing B-45 jet light bomber and the RB-49 Flying Wing. Beyond the service life of the B-36, the B-52 jet would be the next heavy bomber, with LeMay's wholehearted endorsement. Considering a possible heavy bomber of still more advanced design, the board canceled Boeing's XB-55, proposing an industry-wide design competition instead.[43]

In the final analysis, the McNarney Board ratified many of LeMay's proposals, and in January 1949 submitted its report to Symington and Forrestal for approval. In the meantime, the debate continued. LeMay discovered still more reasons to endorse the B-36. Engineering studies showed impressive results in increased range and speed if jet engines were added. On February 2 the SAC Commander wrote Vandenberg suggesting a review of the B-54, in hopes that its cancellation might provide more funds for the B-36.[44] Nonetheless, others had doubts about the interconti-

---

[41] Rprt, Aircraft Weapons Board Proceedings, Vol I, Jan 1949, pp 52-62, Vol IV, Jan 49, pp 453-455, RG 341, DCS/Mat, Dir/Prod & Proc, Prod Eng Div, Mins & Rprts, Dec 48-Jan 49, Box 4, MMB, NA.

[42] *Ibid.*, Vol I, pp 63-68, Vol IV, pp 471-477; Final Report of Board of Officers In the Composition of the 48 Group Program, The Aircraft Production Program, and the Research and Development Program for the US Air Force, Dec 29, 1948-Jan 6, 1949, RG 341, DCS/Mat, Dir/Prod & Proc, Prod Eng Div, Mins & Rprts, MMB, NA.

[43] See previous note.

[44] Ltr, Lt Gen C. E. LeMay, CG SAC, to Gen H. S. Vandenberg, CSAF, Feb 2, 1949, RG 341, DCS/Dev, Dir/Rqmts, Gen Decimal Files, 1948-1951, 452.1 Bombardment 1948-1951, Box 33, MMB, NA.

nental bomber, notably Forrestal. The Secretary of Defense asked Symington for further information before approving the McNarney Board's recommendations. Late in February, Fairchild became board chairman and convened a session to examine the various choices.[45]

The issue was complicated, because the B-54, even if could not match the capabilities of the B-36 or even the B-47 medium, still represented a decided improvement on current medium types. Unfortunately, the development program was extremely expensive, all the more so since the aircraft's nose area needed redesigning. Also, the B-54's outrigger landing gear might necessitate widening taxiways on numerous airfields. LeMay disliked the 1941-era airframe design, arguing that more advanced types would become available over the same period of time. Thus, the B-54 was still limited in range and cost too much. Preferring to concentrate on the B-36, LeMay told the Fairchild Board that each of his squadrons could operate ten Peacemakers, rather than six, with no additional men. That is, four bomber groups and two reconnaissance groups could operate 180 planes plus spares, a requirement that would more than double the current 95-plane order. The board agreed to this plan, also proposing to accelerate the B-47 program. To fund the revised plan, the board recommended canceling the B-54 once and for all. On March 21 1949, Symington approved these proposals.[46]

In rejecting the B-54, the Air Force turned entirely to jet propulsion for the future bomber force. The B-36 and the B-50, the last propeller-driven models, continued to perform admirably. The huge Peacemaker was still making headlines and putting on air shows at Andrews Air Force Base. On March 2, 1949, *Lucky Lady II*, a B-50 in the 43d Bombardment Wing, landed at Carswell to complete the first nonstop flight around the world. This feat demonstrated the progress SAC was making with air refueling. Such national publicity at a time when the Air Force had canceled a number of programs in a troubled industry was likely to engender criticism. Norstad predicted that the Navy would inspire some letters to newspapers attacking the B-36, but the Air Force, he believed,

---

[45] Report of Board of Senior Officers, Vol I, Feb 1949, pp 1–8, 13–16, 114–122, Vol II, Feb 1949, p 298, Vol III, Feb 1949, p 451, RG 341, DCS/Mat, Dir/Prod & Proc, Prod Eng Div, Mins & Rprts, Jan–Feb 49, Box 5; rprt, Aircraft Weapons Board Proceedings, Vol IV, Jan 1949, pp 398–429, RG 341, DCS/Mat, Dir/Prod & Proc, Prod Eng Div, Mins & Rprts, Dec 48–Jan 49, Box 4, both in MMB, NA.
[46] See previous note; rprt, "Report of 2d Board of Officers," Feb 21–24, 1949, RG 341, DCS/Mat, Dir/Prod & Proc, Prod Eng Div, Mins & Rprts, Jan–Feb 49, Box 5, MMB, NA.

Priority Mission

Lucky Lady II, a B–50 of the 43d Bombardment Wing, successfully completed the first non-stop flight around the world in a spectacular demonstration of aerial refueling. She landed at Carswell Air Force Base in Ft. Worth, Texas, on March 2, 1949, after ninety-four hours of continuous flying. Her crew is shown being met by Secretary of the Air Force W. Stuart Symington and Chief of Staff Gen. Hoyt S. Vandenberg for an interview over local radio.

could deal with the repercussions.[47] In just a few months, Norstad's prophecy would come true with a vengeance.

Modernization and Standardization

An outgrowth of years of experience as a bomber commander, LeMay's approach to leadership revolved around three principles. First, people needed to believe in the importance of their jobs. Second, progress, however slight, toward an understandable goal had to take place. Third, the effort and the progress must be recognized. In practice, these fundamentals amounted to "standardization"—the watchword of SAC. Setting performance standards for each position in the command allowed the individual to see the relation of his job to others. Aside from the obvious importance of SAC to the nation's defense, this standardization and the sense of teamwork that it fostered gave importance to individual jobs. Of

---

[47] Leo OHI, p 87; hist, SAC, Jan–Jun 1950, Vol I, pp 53–63; rprt, Aircraft Weapons Board Proceedings, Vol IV, Jan 1949, pp 476–477, RG 341, DCS/Mat, Dir/Prod & Proc, Prod Eng Div, Mins & Rprts, Dec 48–Jan 49, Box 4, MMB, NA.

Strategic Air Force

course, standards also provided a means to measure progress. Some of the recognition was negative; merely allowing someone to keep his job indicated that he was progressing. On the other hand, LeMay considered acknowledgement essential on an organizational level, and he worked hard to improve career opportunities and living conditions as a means of recognizing his command's achievements.[48]

LeMay had arrived at SAC Headquarters during a period of high international tensions, but, for the new commander, readiness for war did not rise and fall with the diplomatic fever chart. In the air campaign against Germany, he observed that most bomber groups did badly on their first mission.[49] In a future war, the first SAC mission might be the decisive one, and the country could not afford wasted atomic bombs. Consequently, SAC came to require an unprecedented level of proficiency in its air crews.

The emphasis on high standards also resulted from the nature of the air offensive being planned. The formation flying that had posed such a challenge during World War II now seemed less important. With a limited number of bombers flying faster, at higher altitudes, and carrying more potent bombs, crews would no longer need to follow a lead aircraft. Every crew was in effect a lead crew.[50] It had to be able to navigate to its target, while evading or fighting off defensive forces, identify and bomb as planned, and then get away quickly. This tactic put a premium on a detailed plan assigning targets and adequate intelligence about the targets and their defenses. It also meant that each crew would have to study its target carefully and plan its own mission.

In atomic operations, the bomber force would rely on dispersion, massing in time rather than space and relying on darkness for protection.[51] Radar capabilities thus became crucial, and the work of the navigator-bombardier team grew increasingly complex. This is not to imply that SAC neglected visual bombing, for there were many missions to bombing ranges throughout the country. But radar bomb scoring now assumed added importance in the command.[52]

---

[48] USAF OHI, #239.0512-736, John T. Bohn, SAC/HO, with Gen Curtis E. LeMay (Ret), Mar 9, 1971, p 39, AFHRC; Borowski, *Hollow Threat*, pp 171-173; LeMay & Kantor, *Mission with LeMay*, pp 439-441.
[49] LeMay & Kantor, *Mission with LeMay*, pp 436-437; Borowski, *Hollow Threat*, p 165.
[50] LeMay & Kantor, *Mission with LeMay*, p 436.
[51] Hist, SAC, 1948, Vol I, p 256.
[52] *Ibid.*; rprt, Aircraft Weapons Board Proceedings, Vol II, Jan 1949, p 310, RG 341, DCS/Mat, Dir/Prod & Proc, Prod Eng Div, Mins & Rprts, Dec 48-Jan 49, Box 4, MMB, NA; memo, AF Bomb School, Mather AFB, subj: General Information on Bombing Techniques with APQ-13, APQ-23, and APQ-24 Radar Sets, Jul 49, LeMay Coll, Official Docs, Box B95, MD, LC.

Priority Mission

Realistic training did not involve actually flying to a practice target and dropping real bombs, but in learning to find and identify a wartime target. Crew members could train on the ground in a mockup of the bomber's cabin. The Air Force had obtained aerial photographs of Soviet cities, mostly from captured German records. The crews used drawings showing what the target would look like on the radar screen in "flying" countless indoor missions.[53] Another method was to study a city in the United States and then actually fly a radar bomb scoring mission. These techniques, plus a 4,000-mile mission required every three months, familiarized SAC crew members with their duties in the event of a real war.[54]

Besides training existing crews, SAC had to prepare to form new ones. As more of the wartime B–29 fliers left the active force, and personnel strength in the command increased, the Air Training Command had to produce more crewmen. When SAC received them, the pilots had flown two-engine planes but needed to be transitioned into the medium and heavy bombers.[55] The command also had to qualify its own gunners because the Air Force had decided that it could not afford a gunnery school. Among atomic crews, training schedules had to take into account the four to five months the Atomic Energy Commission required to provide security clearances.[56] On a more positive note, the commission was now supplying enough trained bomb commanders, weaponeers, and assembly teams.

As for training navigators, bombardiers, and radar operators, the increasing emphasis on radar made their work increasingly complex. The Air Force had initiated a new specialty—the "air observer"—with training in navigation, bombing, and radar. These "AOBs," as they were called,

---

[53] LeMay & Kantor, *Mission with LeMay*, p 436; Borowski, *Hollow Threat*, p 170; hist, SAC, Jan–Jun 1950, Vol I, pp 91–97.

[54] Borowski, *Hollow Threat*, pp 168–170; hist, SAC, 1948, Vol I, pp 279–282, Jan–Jun 1952, Vol I, p 64.

[55] Col Lawson S. Moseley, Jr, "Aircrew Training—Whose Responsibility?" *Air University Quarterly Review* IV (Summer 50), pp 43–48.

[56] Ltr, Lt Gen C. E. LeMay, CG SAC, to Gen H. S. Vandenberg, CSAF, Mar 12, 1949; ltr, Maj Gen W. F. McKee, Asst VCSAF, to LeMay, Apr 28, 1949, atch to R & R Sheet, Lt Gen I. H. Edwards, DCS/Pers, to CSAF, Letter from Chief of Staff to Commanding General, Strategic Air Command, Apr 21, 1949, both in Vandenberg Coll, SAC (4), Box 45, MD, LC; memo, Maj Gen H. J. Knerr, USAF IG, to CSAF, subj: Daily Activity Report—The Inspector General, Jun 16, 1949, atch to memo, Gen M. S. Fairchild, VCSAF, to DCS/Ops, subj: B–29 Bomber Gunnery, Jun 22, 1949, RG 341, DCS/Ops, P & O 353.4 (Feb 24, 1949), Box 183, MMB, NA; Robert D. Little, *Building an Atomic Air Force, 1949–1953*, Vol III of Bowen & Little, *The History of Air Force Participation in the Atomic Energy Program, 1943–1953* (Washington: USAF Hist Div, 1959), Pt 1, pp 193–205, Pt 2, 357–375.

were trained at a school at Mather Air Force Base, California, but production would be low until a new school at Houston, Texas, graduated its first class in the summer of 1950.[57] Until there were enough air observers, SAC would have to use the older, more specialized fields, who were also in short supply.

Once formed, air and ground crews alike began learning the "SAC way." Under LeMay, the staff wrote standing operating procedures (SOPs) for every position in the command.[58] Besides their obvious value for determining performance standards, the "SOPs" also contributed to flight safety. LeMay believed that inexperienced fliers, because they tended to rely on established procedures, had better safety records than pilots with more experience. The latter evidently often felt that they could dispense with rules. With the rigorous enforcement of standardization came a marked decline in the accident rate by early 1950.[59]

Enforcement of the standards was the next step. The Air Force Inspector General administered the Operational Readiness Test, in which individual units were evaluated on the basis of the number of aircraft they could get into the air, their scores in visual bombing and radar bomb scoring, and the general efficiency and safety of their operations. The staff at SAC headquarters used these readiness tests and the records of routine training to devise numerical performance scores. LeMay now had a rating system to rank units in terms of their ability to carry out a mission. A commander whose wing scored well stood high in the LeMay's estimation. Those with low scores faced scrutiny from SAC Headquarters.[60] Unless the numbers reflected that a commander was making progress in a difficult situation, LeMay was ready to replace him with someone who could produce better numbers. By the end of 1949, there had been enough changes among wing commanders to convince the others. Also, whenever a wing had a crash, its commander reported to LeMay in person to explain what he was doing to prevent a recurrence.[61]

Although every crew was expected to function like a lead crew, not all actually reached the highest standard. One form of standardization in-

---

[57] Little, *Building an Atomic Air Force*, Pt 1, pp 193–205, Pt 2, 357–375.

[58] Borowski, *Hollow Threat*, p 171; LeMay & Kantor, *Mission with LeMay*, pp 439–440.

[59] See note above; SACM 11–3, SAC Statistical Data from 1946, Sep 8, 1970, p 23.

[60] Hist, SAC, 1948, Vol I, pp 251–258; LeMay & Kantor, *Mission with LeMay*, pp 443–447; Borowski, *Hollow Threat*, pp 171–173.

[61] LeMay & Kantor, *Mission with LeMay*, pp 439–440; Charles A. Ravenstein, *Air Force Combat Wings: Lineage and Honors Histories, 1947–1977* (Washington: AFCHO, 1984), pp 7–9, 52–54, 70–73, 128–132, 138–141, 144–146, 151–156, 275–278.

volved recognizing the best crews as an example for the others. LeMay continued the existing policy of designating three lead crews in each squadron, but he also directed that these crews be kept intact, free from additional duties, and flying the unit's best planes.[62] A program of specialized training quickly developed for this elite force. In April 1949, SAC established schools for lead crews at Walker and Davis-Monthan Air Force Bases, with the standing operating procedures for aircrews as the curriculum. In October, the Combat Crew Standardization School opened at MacDill Air Force Base, replacing the other two. By the end of June 1950, the new school had graduated five classes, certifying thirty-six qualified lead crews, while Walker had produced two classes and Davis-Monthan one. To enter the course, a crew first had to fly together for thirty days. No substitutions were permitted. If one member demonstrated incompetence or deviated from the procedures, the whole crew would be sent home uncertified. Likewise, too many aborted missions or an uncooperative attitude could be grounds for sending a crew home without the coveted certificate.[63]

The recognition given lead crews tied in with larger issues. LeMay considered recognition a key factor in motivating people, but he also saw an application to the problem of retention. As long as Selective Service remained in force, the Air Force could rely on attracting plenty of recruits, but, once trained, these men saw opportunities in civilian life.[64] To retain as many of these mechanics and air crew members as possible for a full career, the Air Force could not hope to offer high pay. The most promising inducements were less tangible: a chance to start a family, with a stable career; challenging assignments, with hope for advancement, and perhaps sheer pride in serving one's country.

Lack of promotion potential adversely affected the ability to keep good officers on crew duty, as there were few authorizations for high grades on flight crews. LeMay's remedy involved special spot promotions for the most deserving individuals. On November 3, 1949, the SAC Commander addressed a letter to Lt. Gen. Idwal H. Edwards, the Air Force's Deputy Chief of Staff for Personnel, requesting the authority to promote officers temporarily, while keeping them with their crews.[65]

The Air Staff formally concurred on December 20, giving the Commanding General of SAC the prerogative to make temporary promotions to the grade of captain. The first lieutenants selected must have completed

---

[62] Hist, SAC, 1948, Vol I, pp 278–279, Jan–Jun 1950, Chap 6, pp 106–107.
[63] Hist, SAC, Jan–Jun 1950, Chap 6, pp 106–127.
[64] Borowski, *Hollow Threat*, pp 172–173.
[65] Ltr, Lt Gen C. E. LeMay, CG SAC, to Lt Gen I. H. Edwards, DCS/Pers, Nov 3, 1949, LeMay Coll, Edwards, Box B52, MD, LC.

four and a half years, including six months' service on a lead crew, and have demonstrated qualities of character and leadership. Unless the Air Force later approved the promotion in the normal cycle, LeMay could return the officer to his old grade. LeMay warned that this would occur automatically if he left his crew or his crew's performance declined.[66] As LeMay wrote: "...I intend to make an example of the first officer I find who has relaxed now that he has made temporary captain as a crew member."[67]

Everyone understood that spot promotions were an exception to policy, applying to SAC alone. LeMay promoted 237 officers under the authorization.[68] He was pleased with the results, and in February 1950, he asked for permission to continue the practice. The Air Staff displayed a predictable reluctance to continue a large-scale exception to Air Force-wide policy. Edwards replied that there would be a substantial number of routine promotions that spring, and SAC would receive its fair share. Unconvinced, LeMay continued to press his case. He now had further empirical evidence that crews with temporary captains on board achieved higher performance scores. In fact, LeMay favored extending the program to appoint some majors and lieutenant colonels. It appears that he discussed the matter with Vandenberg later that spring. In any case, the Air Staff approved the extension of the spot promotion program and its expansion to higher grades in mid-1950.[69]

Spot promotions doubtless improved the morale of the promotees and raised the hopes of other crew members. But this program did not address the retention problem among the non-flying officers and the enlisted force. Under LeMay's command, SAC paid some attention to leisure activities, such as hobby shops, but living conditions, especially housing, became a major issue. The SAC staff chose not to underrate the appeal of domesticity to the American male. Those who already had families or planned to start them were reluctant to embark on a career in which the prospect of obtaining adequate, affordable housing was so abysmal. This was a problem throughout the Air Force, but especially in SAC. Most of the command's bases had been built during the Second World War, with no provision for family housing. Generally, families had to live off-base, often

---

[66] *Ibid.*; hist, SAC, Jan–Jun 1951, Vol I, pp 98–99.
[67] Ltr, Lt Gen C. E. LeMay, CG SAC, to Lt Gen I. H. Edwards, DCS/Pers, Feb 2, 1950, LeMay Coll, Edwards, Box B52, MD, LC.
[68] Hopkins & Goldberg, *Development of SAC*, p 19.
[69] See Note 67; hist, SAC, Jan–Jun 1951, Vol I, pp 98–104; ltr, Lt Gen I. H. Edwards, DCS/Pers, to Lt Gen C. E. LeMay, CG SAC, Feb 24, 1950; memo, Maj Gen A. W. Kissner, CS SAC, to LeMay, Mar 3, 1950, both in LeMay Coll, Edwards, Box B52, MD, LC.

in small towns. In 1948 the nation was contending with a massive postwar housing shortage. Exorbitant rents and substandard quarters—LeMay claimed some married airmen had to live in converted chicken-coops—were the rule rather than the exception.[70] Rough living conditions for the troops were not the primary issue, although no one liked the dilapidated barracks. Lindbergh, on another tour of inspection for Vandenberg, reported conversations at the bases in England, where conditions were indeed rough. One airman worried: "I'm all right. It's my wife and children back at Smoky Hill I'm thinking about, in that tar-paper shack...." As Lindbergh phrased it:

> I find a general attitude to the effect that we've finished one war, that we may soon be in another, and that in this period between a man should have a chance to live with his wife and children in a reasonably good home.[71]

Compounding the problem, as the Air Force progressed toward racial integration, was the location of so many SAC bases in states where segregation was mandated by law or encouraged by custom. Since policy in SAC assumed that integration stopped at the installation's fence, off-base housing posed an even more serious problem for black airmen than for others. Desegregated housing did not represent a major policy issue, as strategic bomber units (historically all-white) were only beginning to tap this new source of talented men.[72] Still, any measure that alleviated the overall problem of family housing could prove especially beneficial to those least likely to obtain adequate housing.

Almost immediately on taking command, LeMay concluded that no remedy by Congress or the Pentagon was likely to be forthcoming soon. He learned of an Army project at Fort Bliss, Texas, called the "low-cost housing plan." Adapting this arrangement to SAC and extending it commandwide, LeMay's staff devised a "SAC Housing Association," which would build prefabricated housing on unused base land. The association would borrow the required funds from commercial institutions, the airmen would construct the quarters in their spare time, and the obligations would

---

[70] LeMay & Kantor, *Mission with LeMay*, pp 450–454, 468–470.
[71] Rprt, C. A. Lindbergh to Gen H. S. Vandenberg, CSAF, Feb 18, 1949, atch to cy, ltr, Vandenberg to Lindbergh, Apr 19, 1949, Vandenberg Coll, Vandenberg Files 1949, Box 32, MD, LC.
[72] Ltr, Lt Gen C. E. LeMay, CG SAC, to Lt Gen I. H. Edwards, DCS/Pers, Sep 27, 1949, LeMay Coll, Edwards, Box B52, MD, LC; Alan L. Gropman, *The Air Force Integrates, 1945–1964* (Washington: AFCHO, 1978), pp 86, 123–125.

SAC and Training. The high standards and intense rigor imposed by General LeMay in the training of SAC's bomber force became legendary as each crew was expected to function as independently as a lead crew. *Clockwise from above:* A typical SAC bomber crew plans its mission after a careful study of target intelligence. Navigators and radar observers work in the tight quarters of a B-36. A mobile Training Unit instructor explains B-36 components to crew trainees. Navigators, the "key men" in their crews, participate in a new and intensive forty-eight-week training regimen at Ellington Air Force Base in Houston, Texas, introduced by General LeMay in November 1949. The demands of their specialty were increasing as modern bombers and cargo planes traveled the vastness of SAC's higher-altitude, longer-range aerial routes.

be paid off using the men's quarters allowances.[73] Maj. Gen. William F. McKee, the Assistant Vice Chief of Staff of the Air Force, and General Fairchild, the vice chief, both heartily endorsed this self-help scheme.[74]

When SAC began to put the plan into effect, obstacles arose. The Air Force Comptroller's staff questioned the legality of paying quarters allowances to people living in what was in effect government housing. Also, as the Air Force reduced to forty-eight groups, no one knew for certain what bases SAC would retain and where to start building. The SAC plan was also in danger of being superseded by congressional action. Senator Kenneth S. Wherry of Nebraska introduced a bill to provide incentives for commercial builders to erect housing on or near military installations. LeMay considered the Wherry bill too expensive. Nevertheless, the bill did become law on August 8, 1949, and the SAC association, facing competition for financing and land, accordingly dissolved.[75]

As one historian observed: "SAC lost this battle but won its war."[76] The Wherry Act pioneered major improvements in military housing. In SAC, harried off-base residents started to believe that conditions would improve, and the highly publicized effort to solve the housing problem showed the families that their concerns were deemed important.[77] The payoff, a higher re-enlistment rate, might take time to materialize, however.

The attention paid to family housing did not detract from efforts to upgrade the living conditions of unmarried airmen. LeMay took innovative steps to improve their food and housing. A commandwide policy encouraged detailing a number of cooks to nearby hotels to learn a few tricks to make institutional food more palatable. Once objections from the civilian unions had been quieted, SAC could boast some of the best troop messes in the services.[78] As far as barracks were concerned, LeMay hoped to avoid replacing the wartime temporary buildings with the traditional Army open-bay structures. He considered them unsuitable for the round-the-clock operations of a war-ready air command. To the charge that two-per-

---

[73] LeMay & Kantor, *Mission with LeMay*, pp 469–472; Borowski, *Hollow Threat*, pp 173–175.
[74] Ltr, Lt Gen C. E. LeMay, CG SAC, to Gen H. S. Vandenberg, CSAF, Jan 14, 1949; memo, Lt Gen W. F. McKee, Asst VCSAF, to Gen M. S. Fairchild, VCSAF, Jan 24, 1949, with note signed "MSF," both in Vandenberg Coll, SAC (4), Box 45, MD, LC.
[75] Borowski, *Hollow Threat*, pp 175–176; LeMay & Kantor, *Mission with LeMay*, pp 471–472.
[76] Borowski, *Hollow Threat*, p 176.
[77] *Ibid.*, pp 176–177.
[78] *Ibid.*, pp 177–178; LeMay & Kantor, *Mission with LeMay*, pp 437–438.

son private rooms pampered unmarried airmen, he offered reasonably attractive cost figures and argued that the improvements would increase productivity and improve retention. A new model barracks building was constructed at Offutt, and citizens of Omaha donated money for furnishings. In time, LeMay hoped to extend this innovation to the other bases.[79]

LeMay's concept of a professional, highly skilled, extremely motivated career force harmonized with the priority the country seemed to accord the Strategic Air Command. A major modernization of equipment for the strategic force was now underway. In the same vein, SAC bulked ever larger in the Air Force. Early in 1949 overall group strength declined from sixty to forty-eight, while SAC remained constant at eighteen, later increasing to nineteen. Its personnel strength rose from 46,000 in January 1949 to over 60,000 by June 1950, its percentage of the total Air Force increasing from eleven to fifteen. Characteristically, the Air Force also approved equipping six medium bomber groups at a "war strength" of forty-five aircraft instead of the usual thirty.[80]

As noted previously, modernization of the bomber force entailed introducing a new medium bomber, the B–50, and atomic-modified (SADDLETREE) aircraft and taking the first halting steps toward an intercontinental striking force. The B–36 heavy bomber and the development of air refueling for the medium force promised to extend the range of the command and reduce the need for bases overseas.

The fact that the total number of bomber groups remained steady at fourteen obscures the extent of the change that took place. Units were subject to shifts in stations, due largely to the reductions resulting from the adoption of the forty-eight group program. The first conversions to atomic-modified equipment took place late in 1948. By the end of that year, over eighty SADDLETREE bombers had entered the force, in addition to the B–29s at Walker with the 509th, for a total of over 100 aircraft equipped to carry atomic weapons. By mid-1950, the figure exceeded 250, including the B–36Bs and B–50Ds coming off the assembly lines already atomic-capable.[81] While conversions ran behind schedule, there were by January 1949 three medium wings in the atomic force. Two more wings

---

[79] LeMay & Kantor, *Mission with LeMay*, pp 467–468.

[80] *Air Force Statistical Digest*, Jan 1949–Jun 1950, pp 3–7, 29–36; Summary of Strategic Air Command: Operational Data, Jun 1, 1950, in hist, SAC, Jan–Jun 1950, Vol V.

[81] Summary of Strategic Air Command: Operational Data, Jun 1, 1950, in hist, SAC, Jan–Jun 1950, Vol V, pp 25–37; Little, *Foundations*, Pt 2, pp 403–405; Little, *Building an Atomic Air Force*, Pt 1, pp 113–115.

Strategic Air Force

converted during the ensuing year, and two during the first months of 1950. Aging B-29s were now being retired or modified as tankers.[82]

Even after delivery, the modified bombers required additional maintenance. Many engines still had vintage World War II carburetors rather than the more modern fuel injection systems, and cylinders needed replacing. In the fall of 1949, General Fairchild intervened to expedite the necessary work.[83] The B-50 encountered similar problems, in spite of having a different engine. Because of difficulties with the turbo-supercharger, SAC was running out of spares. An altitude restriction of fifteen thousand feet interfered with training. Only during 1950 did necessary modifications take place to allow removal of the restrictions.[84]

A key element of the modernization effort involved the development and deployment of the B-36 Peacemaker. Under Kenney's command, the medium bomber force, handicapped by its limited range, had learned to be ready to deploy to oversea bases, in the event of an international crisis. Air strategists favored building an intercontinental force that would eliminate the requirement for large-scale deployments. Since 1941, the B-36 had seemed to be the means to this end. Though Kenney had been skeptical as to the Peacemaker's potential, LeMay vigorously supported making it an effective bomber.

Despite its unprecedented size, the B-36 presented a challenge the Air Force understood: a new airplane with teething problems. As had so often happened in wartime, improved versions were in testing as earlier models entered the force. In the original order of ninety-five planes, twenty-two appeared as A models. The B, though it featured improved engines and electronics, a larger payload, and an atomic capability, had its production curtailed in favor of the D, and only sixty-two were delivered. Subsequent orders would be restricted to reconnaissance types and the B-36Ds equipped with four jet engines in pods on the wings, for added power. Still, in June 1950 most Peacemakers in service were B models.[85]

The primary B-36 base from 1948 to 1950 was Carswell, where the 7th Bombardment Wing became a two-group organization in the fall of

---

[82] Strategic Air Command: Command Summary, Mar 1949–May 1950, in AFHRC; SAC Progress Analysis, 1953, p 73, LeMay Coll, Box B98, MD, LC; Ravenstein, *Combat Wings, passim.*

[83] Ltr, Gen M. S. Fairchild, VCSAF, to Lt Gen B. W. Chidlaw, CG AMC, subj: B-29 Accidents, Nov 17, 1949, LeMay Coll, Fairchild, Box B49, MD, LC; hist, SAC, Jan–Jun 1950, Vol I, pp 82–85; hist, Hq USAF, Jul 1, 1949–Jun 30, 1950, p 70.

[84] Memo, Capt F. K. Lane, Aide to Lt Gen LeMay, of phonecon, Lt Gen C. E. LeMay, CG SAC, with Maj Gen R. M. Ramey, CG-designate, 8 AF, Dec 15, 1949, LeMay Coll, Memos and R & Rs, 1949 and 1948, Box B64, MD, LC.

[85] Knaack, *Bombers*, pp 22–23, 29–34.

1948. Other B–36 groups began to form at Rapid City, South Dakota, and Fairfield-Suisun, California.[86] But this expansion was more apparent than real, for few of the aircraft were operational. Orders for spare parts had been limited during the early production, and the wing at Carswell began to experience shortages. Engine problems arose, and repairs fell behind schedule. Specialized equipment, such as dollies, jacks, and stands big enough to be used for the B–36, appeared slowly and in small quantities. Even maintenance docks had to be rebuilt to accommodate the huge plane. Given SAC's retention problem, the complexities of training mechanics almost escaped control. Even ground refueling, normally a routine process, proved cumbersome. Because of the height of the fuel tanks off the ground, the pumps had to work harder and failed faster. The gunnery system was not working, and this soon became one of the Air Force's major concerns. But for LeMay the parts shortage presented the most frustrating problem. The factory at Fort Worth agreed to make some by hand. Massive cannibalization kept a few planes flying, but most of the fleet remained grounded. Modification programs further reduced the size of the ready force. During 1949, SAC rarely had more than forty B–36s on hand, and of these perhaps five to eight were in commission at any one time. The 7th Bomb Wing became in essence a service test unit.[87] There was little opportunity to train crews extensively. Presumably the wing could have launched a few sorties in the event of war, but as of June 1950, the B–36 force could hardly be considered a major asset.

That LeMay was dissatisfied goes without saying. A supply conference in September representing major commands produced limited results.[88] In January 1950, the SAC Commander turned to Brig. Gen. Clarence S. Irvine, moving him from the high-priority 509th Wing to Carswell with orders to straighten out the situation. Irvine soon confirmed that the supply problem was still critical. He promised determined leadership and reported with pride that a flight engineer had found a method of dealing with engine fires in flight, a frequent problem, without having to feather the propeller.[89] Such improvisational skills would clearly be needed to make the B–36 fleet operational.

Even as the Peacemaker faltered, SAC was making progress with a more exotic technology for extending the command's reach. Air-to-air refueling became one of the Air Force's highest priorities. During 1948,

---

[86] Hist, SAC, Jul–Dec 1950, Vol I, pp 72–73, 81–85, 94–96.
[87] *Ibid.*, pp 72–116; Hopkins & Goldberg, *Development of SAC*, pp 11, 15; *Air Force Statistical Digest*, Jan 1949–Jun 1950, pp 232–241.
[88] Hist, SAC, Jul–Dec 1950, Vol I, pp 81–85.
[89] Irvine OHI, pp 23–32; ltr, Brig Gen C. S. Irvine, CG 7 BW, to Lt Gen C. E. LeMay, CG SAC, Feb 24, 1950, LeMay Coll, Irvine, Box B53, MD, LC.

Strategic Air Force

An aerial view of the Wherry Housing project at Bergstrom Air Force Base in Austin, Texas. By December 1951 eighty-three units were completed and ready for occupancy. Improved housing and other on-base amenities for Air Force families were pioneered at SAC at the insistence of General LeMay.

the Air Materiel Command had converted a number of B–29s to tankers and equipped bombers as "receivers." The Air Force rushed the British looped-hose design into production, while continuing work on the American flying-boom system.[90]

Tanker squadrons had been formed at Walker and Davis-Monthan, and by the end of 1948 the 509th Bomb Wing had made twelve successful hookups. Subsequently, two more bomb wings, at Castle and Biggs, activated tanker units. The inventory of tankers grew to thirty-seven in August 1949 and sixty-seven in December. The crews were mastering the techniques of transfering fuel. The biggest problem lay in the rendezvous of tanker and bomber. Crews were using a radar that was unreliable, and training suffered accordingly. Despite this difficulty, by June of 1950, there were nearly eighty tankers in the command, and a fifth squadron, at Barksdale, was forming to support reconnaissance units.[91]

---

[90] Hist, SAC, Jan–Jun 1950, Vol I, pp 51–53, 63–73.
[91] *Ibid.*; memo, Col H. T. Wheless, for Brig Gen J. B. Montgomery, Dir Pl SAC, to Lt Gen C. E. LeMay, subj: Air Refueling Brief, Aug 9, 1949, LeMay Coll, Memos and R & Rs, 1949 and 1948, Box B64, MD, LC; Knaack, *Bombers*, pp 490–493; Swanborough, *US Aircraft*, pp 102–103; hist, SAC, Jan–Jun 1950, Vol I, pp 63–74.

Two other elements of SAC, the reconnaissance force and the fighter force, suffered from a lack of technical direction: the Air Force had not yet defined the types of aircraft needed. LeMay considered reconnaissance a vital aspect of the strategic air offensive, but his command was equipped with a hodge-podge of converted bombers, RB-17s and RB-29s. Quantity presented no obstacle, as more RB-29s entered the inventory, some B-50s underwent modification for reconnaissance, and some RB-45 light jet bombers appeared—enough aircraft to form three wings. Meanwhile, the fighter wings were converting to jets, both the F-86 and F-84, neither one entirely satisfactory for long-range escort.[92]

Regarding the equipment requirements of the command, LeMay's views diverged from those of his predecessor. Unlike Kenney, the new commander emphasized the B-36 and the importance of making it an effective bomber. However, LeMay did have reservations about its future. In a few years the B-36 would be much too slow to contend with the next generation of fighter aircraft. By the late 1950s a five hundred-knot bomber would be needed to outrun Soviet fighters. Even if strategy emphasized night attacks, the long days of the northern summer could not be ignored. In the event of war, American bombers might be exposed to the large day fighter forces of the Soviet defense. Speed would also be valuable in helping the bomber escape the blast of a thermonuclear weapon. The SAC staff preferred modified bomber types for reconnaissance, but such aircraft would have to be fast to survive in Soviet air space. Yet for the near future, LeMay considered range, not speed, the crucial factor in his decsion to support the B-36. Likewise, he argued that a large airplane could carry not only bombs but also defensive guns and missiles, air-to-ground missiles, and electronic jamming equipment.[93]

The Air Staff, SAC, and RAND all looked further into the future, to the late 1950s. Studies of heavy bombers, medium bombers with extended range, and missiles all entered the equation. LeMay's partiality towards larger bombers gave rise to periodic disagreements over future designs.[94] Convair had been continuing its Generalized Bomber Study (GEBO), but the results were still on the drawing board. The Air Force's missile program focused on cruise types. The SAC staff recognized that long-range

---

[92] Hopkins & Goldberg, *Development of SAC*, pp 11-20; SAC Progress Analysis, [Oct] 1953, p 73, LeMay Coll, Box B98, MD, LC.
[93] Ltr, Lt Gen C. E. LeMay, CG SAC, to Lt Gen I. H. Edwards, Chmn, Sr Off Bd, subj: RAND Report No R-173S, May 2, 1950, in hist, SAC, Jan-Jun 1950, Vol IV, Chap V, Ex 15.
[94] *Ibid.*

missiles could be built, but it distrusted the new technology and favored a more conventional weapon system—the large, high-speed bomber.[95]

By 1949 Boeing's B-52 was emerging as a logical successor to the B-36. The mockup design was ready for inspection in April. Once again, range became the crucial concern, especially with the uncertainty of whether engines that could meet the specifications would be available in time.[96] At stake was the contract for the Air Force's next major production bomber, so other manufacturers continued to press their proposals. Fairchild Aircraft Corporation offered an unconventional design, while Convair argued for a swept-wing jet version of the B-36 (later designated the YB-60). For its part, Boeing altered the B-52 design to meet the Air Force's range requirements.[97] LeMay feared that further discussions of design would delay B-52 production and urged acceptance of the second Boeing model. Not until March 24, 1950, however, did the Senior Officers' Board approve a new Boeing design. Still, no definite decision on production occurred during the rest of the year, and the B-52 encountered still further delay.[98]

Meanwhile, the plans for the new medium bomber progressed more quickly. Boeing's six-engine jet B-47 would still require forward basing or air refueling to reach targets in the Soviet Union, but with its superior speed, it clearly outdistanced its nearest competitor—the non-jet B-50. In November 1949, the Air Force contracted for full production, ordering eighty-seven B models in addition to the ten then under contract. The first A model flew on June 25, 1950.[99]

The news of the Soviet atomic explosion in August 1949 highlighted all of the Air Force's concerns about bases overseas. As the operational commander, LeMay disliked the time it would take to deploy his force in an emergency.[100] A Soviet land offensive in Europe might succeed before

---

[95] *Ibid.*; Knaack, *Bombers*, pp 353-355; Neufeld, *Ballistic Missiles*, pp 27, 36-37.

[96] Knaack, *Bombers*, pp 215-217; graph, Milestones, B-52 Program, May 7, 1949, Vandenberg Coll, Budget 1949-50, Box 41, MD, LC.

[97] Knaack, *Bombers*, pp 215-217, 553-557.

[98] *Ibid.*, pp 217-218; Boeing Airplane Company, XB-52 and B-52 Implementation Program By Fiscal Years, May 9, 1949, Vandenberg Coll, Budget 1949-50, Box 41, MD, LC.

[99] Knaack, *Bombers*, pp 107-109.

[100] Ltr, Lt Gen C. E. LeMay, CG SAC, to Lt Gen K. B. Wolfe, DCS/Mat, Nov 16, 1949; ltr, LeMay to Gen M. S. Fairchild, VCSAF, Nov 16, 1949, both in LeMay Coll, Wolfe, Box B61, MD, LC; rprt, SAC, Immediate Strategic Air Command Base Requirements, Apr 15, 1949, atch to ltr, Maj Gen G. Gardner, Chmn AF Base Dev Bd, to LeMay, May 11, 1949, RG 341, DCS/Mat, Exec Ofc TS Corres, Box 1, MMB, NA.

the planned bombing campaign could take effect. And once they had reached the English Channel, the Soviets could try overrunning the bases there or bombing them conventionally, even before U.S. forces were mobilized for the defense. Now there also existed the possibility of an atomic attack on the English bases or even on the continental United States.

LeMay's staff studied possible solutions to the problem of basing. The northeastern region of North America was crucial, for a long-range air striking force based there could reach most of the potential targets. Some medium-range aircraft would have to land at bases overseas, and a few sorties launched from Alaska would complete the coverage. The principal northeast bases then available included Goose Bay, Labrador, and Ernest Harmon Air Base in western Newfoundland. Both had significant drawbacks. Goose Bay was ice-bound for half the year and inaccessible by land. Newfoundland (including Labrador) became a Canadian province in 1949, raising the prospect of political complications. Eventually, the planners' choice fell on Limestone, Maine, which SAC had considered a future B-36 base since the start of construction in 1947. LeMay envisioned an installation large enough to handle sixty B-36s permanently assigned and more staging through from the interior. Ultimately other fields might be added in that area. Also, weather permitting, Goose Bay might serve as a launching field for tankers and medium bombers deployed from the States.[101]

The Air Staff had some reservations about the plan. As Maj. Gen. Grandison Gardner, Chairman of the Air Force Base Development Board, commented to LeMay: "It appears to me that you may not have given sufficient weight to your own vulnerability if permanently concentrated in a relatively small area."[102] In fact, however, Gardner's warning about base security was overcome by the issue of cost. Both construction and operating costs at Limestone would be high, and expanding the base would entail still more expense. Despite these obstacles, Gardner told LeMay, SAC's concept offered a workable alternative to reliance on foreign bases.[103]

Meanwhile, construction at Limestone was proceeding too slowly to accommodate the growing B-36 force. As a result, the staff at SAC began

---

[101] Rprt, SAC, Immediate Strategic Air Command Base Requirements, Apr 15, 1949, atch to ltr, Maj Gen G. Gardner, Chmn AF Base Dev Bd, to Lt Gen C. E. LeMay, CG SAC, May 11, 1949, RG 341, DCS/Mat, Exec Ofc TS Corres, Box 1, MMB, NA.

[102] Ltr, Maj Gen G. Gardner, Chmn AF Base Dev Bd, to Lt Gen C. E. LeMay, CG SAC, May 11, 1949, RG 341, DCS/Mat, Exec Ofc TS Corres, Box 1, MMB, NA.

[103] *Ibid.*

Strategic Air Force

planning to base the Peacemakers at Carswell, Rapid City, and Fairfield-Suisun. Not until June 1950 was an Air Force unit stationed at Limestone, which still remained unfinished.[104]

Farther to the northeast, improvements at Goose Bay had come under consideration. Currently, the base belonged to the Military Air Transport Service. The war plan called for staging SAC bombers through Goose Bay on deployment. The installation was thus crucial in the existing plan as well as for the future. Early in 1948, a team of Army and Air Force officers visited the area and concluded that Goose Bay could serve as a staging field for B-36s. On taking command, LeMay argued more strongly for Limestone, but still saw uses for the Labrador base. He objected to proposals to use Pepperel Air Base in eastern Newfoundland. It was nearer the superior port facilities at St. John's and Torbay, to be sure, but the SAC Commander discounted its value as an airfield and noted that Goose Bay afforded better coverage of the targets.[105]

Recognition of SAC's increased role in the Northeast would make some knotty command problems. Besides MATS, the Navy was active in the area. To resolve the interservice conflict, in April 1949 the joint chiefs agreed to the establishment of a unified Northeast Command. The Canadians were uncertain what arrangements to support, and final concurrence was still pending in June 1950. The proposed command would support operations in the region by all services, but with an Air Force officer in charge. Thus SAC, MATS, and other commands would enter the area on equal footing with Army and Navy elements.[106]

---

[104] Memo, Gen C. A. Spaatz, CG AAF, to AS/WA, subj: Provision of a B-36 Air Base in Northern Maine, Feb 17, 1947, Spaatz Coll, Sec of the AF, Box 263, MD, LC; Robert Mueller, *Air Force Bases*, Vol I, *Active Bases within the United States of America on 17 September 1982* (Washington: AFCHO, 1989), pp 327-328; memo of phonecon, Lt Gen C. E. LeMay, CG SAC, with Maj Gen F. F. Everest, Asst DCS/Ops, Aug, 15, 1949, LeMay Coll, Memos and R & Rs 1949 and 1948, Box B64, MD, LC.

[105] Ltr, CG SAC to Cmdr MATS, subj: Strategic Air Command's Future Requirements at Goose Bay, Harmon, and Dhahran Air Force Bases, Aug 27, 1949, RG 341, DCS/Ops, P & O 686, SAC (Sep 1, 1949), Box 1; ASSS, Maj Gen S. E. Anderson, Dir P & O, to CSAF, Report of the Army-Air Force Base Planning Committee (Newfoundland Area), Mar 5, 1948, with atchs, RG 341, TS AAG File 32, Box 10, both in MMB, NA; ltr, Anderson to CSAF, subj: Joint Army-Air Force Action on Report of Army-Air Force Base Planning Committee (Newfoundland Area), Jun 8, 1948, Vandenberg Coll, Vandenberg Files 1948, Box 32, MD, LC; ltr, Lt Gen C. E. LeMay, CG SAC, to Lt Gen L. Norstad, DCS/Ops, n.d., LeMay Coll, Norstad, Box B56, MD, LC.

[106] Hist, JCS, *History of the Unified Command Plan*, pp 6-7. (See chap 8, note 19.)

Planners had also envisioned B–36s operating westward from Eielson Air Force Base, Alaska, and Okinawa. Although rotational training at these fields had ceased in 1948, they were still included in SAC's war plan.[107] Apparently, the expense of building hangars for B–36s to make Eielson usable in winter prompted reservations among Air Staff members. But in May 1950, Maj. Gen. Frank F. Everest, Assistant Deputy Chief of Staff for Operations, strongly maintained that the work was necessary.[108] On Okinawa a similar issue arose when a typhoon in July 1949 caused major damage. In this case, MacArthur himself, advocating a continued forceful American presence in the Far East, promoted the importance of repairing the airfields. In both Okinawa and Alaska, then, the installations could not yet fully support B–36 operations at the beginning of 1950. MacArthur, however, had his own B–29s, and medium bomber fields were available in the Far East.[109]

For the time being, the war plan focused mainly on England. There, although the country was subject to air attack, there were ways to improve the posture of the force. The bases in use by SAC bombers included Lakenheath, Marham, and Sculthorpe (which had replaced Scampton as the third field early in 1949). Located in East Anglia, all three sat near the east coast, exposed to attack out of the North Sea. Since 1948 bomber units had been rotating there for three-month tours. Beginning the following May, atomic-capable units joined the program. By the end of 1949, the rotational force was cut back to about two groups, but the current war plan envisioned the need to deploy a total of five medium bomber groups, a fighter group, and reconnaissance units to England within days.[110]

Late in 1948, soon after the first American bombers had arrived, the British Air Ministry began to consider making room for them at bases in the Midlands. There the B–29s would be protected by the air defense screen, and the RAF could station its own forces in East Anglia. The Commanding General of the 3d Air Division, Leon W. Johnson, opened talks with the Air Ministry to arrange the move. These conversations faltered on the issue of funding. Not only did the British and Americans differ on the extent and estimated cost of preparing the bases, but the

---

[107] Hist, SAC, 1948, Vol I, pp 201–220.
[108] Memo, Maj Gen F. F. Everest, Asst DCS/Ops, to DCS/Mat, subj: Plans of Development of Eielson Air Force Base, May 15, 1950, RG 341, DCS/Mat, Exec Ofc TS Corres, Box 1, MMB, NA.
[109] Borowski, *Hollow Threat*, pp 202–203.
[110] Vernon D. Burk, *The USAF in the United Kingdom, 1948–1973: Organization*, USAFE Hist Monograph (Ramstein Air Base, Germany: Hq USAFE, Nov 77), pp 15–17, 24–27; AF Emergency War Plan 1–50, Jun 1, 1950, RG 341, DCS/Ops, Dir/Pl, TS OPD, 381 (May 2, 1950), Sect 3, Box 327, MMB, NA.

SAC and Base Life. SAC became as concerned with the well-being of single as well as married airmen. General LeMay championed the replacement of traditional open-bay barracks, *above, right,* which housed over a dozen on bunk beds, with new models affording suites for two, *below, right and left,* and an unprecedented degree of privacy. An exterior view, *above, left,* of proposed airmen's barracks at Offutt Air Force Base, the site of SAC Headquarters, in Omaha, Nebraska, shows a typical dormitory-style housing unit—attractive, practical, and low cost.

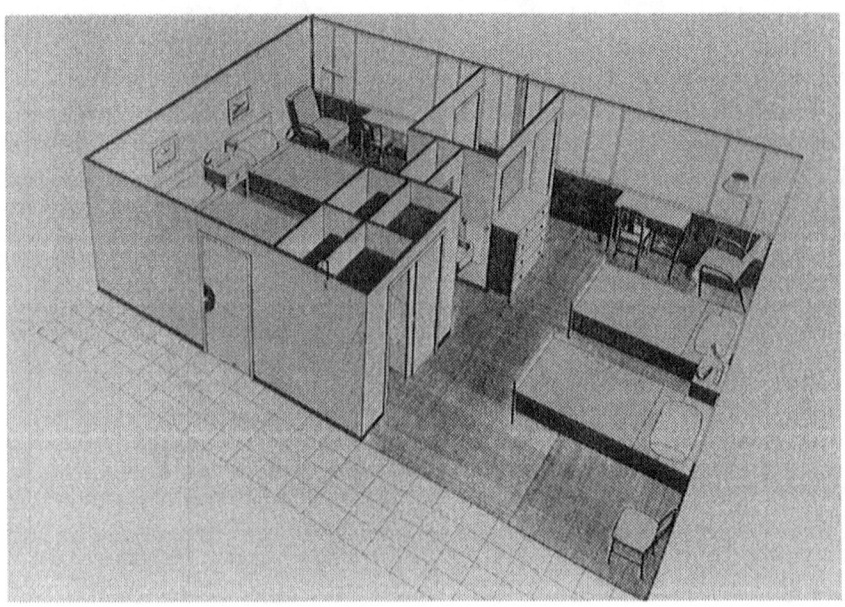

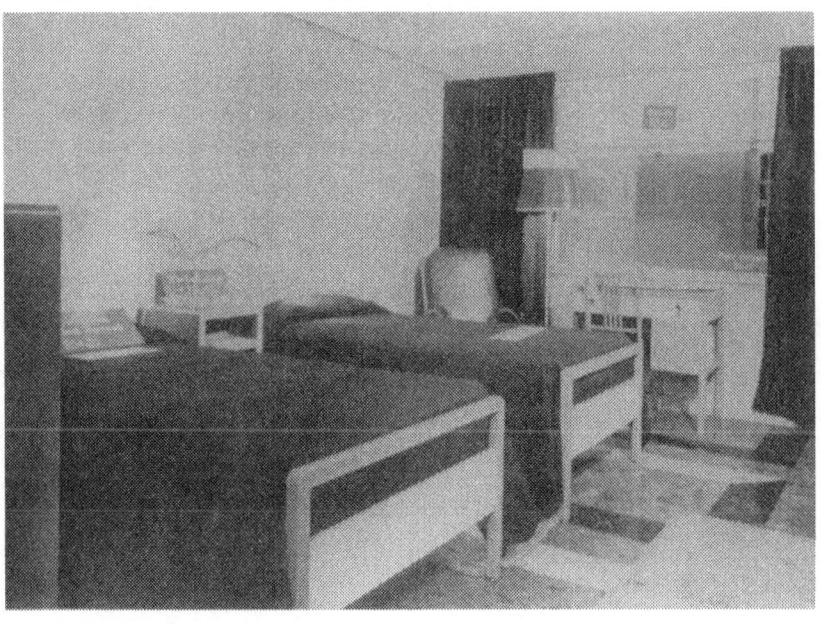

Strategic Air Force

Washington officials also disagreed among themselves on the source of the U.S. contribution. President Truman resolved the latter question by ordering the State Department to supply the funds. Further, the United States agreed to provide aviation engineer battalions to help with the work. In April 1950, the ambassadors in London and Washington approved the agreements for financing and scheduling construction of four B–29 bases situated north and west of Oxford: Upper Heyford, Brize Norton, Fairford, and one other field. (Greenham Common was named later.) By summer, planning had begun for the improvements to these fields.[111]

The emphasis on England as the principal base area for the strategic air offensive did not eliminate the need for Mediterranean bases. SAC still planned to use fields there for post-strike recovery. The British remained committed to improving the field at Abu Sueir, Egypt, and the United States retained rights at Dhahran, Saudi Arabia.[112] Planners also considered establishing a depot in French Morocco. In January 1950 a team from U.S. Air Forces, Europe, (USAFE) visited the Protectorate and selected Nouasseur as the preferred site. Generally, the U.S. Air Force in the Mediterranean region was pursuing a low-cost program to give more reach to the strategic force.[113]

Despite the apparent advantages of basing in England, the question of the vulnerability of these bases would not disappear. Should they not be available, the SAC staff thought medium bombers should operate from Morocco, while the B–36s and some of the medium bombers capable of refueling in the air operated from North America. Much of the force would then have to recover overseas. In December 1949, LeMay's deputy, Maj. Gen. Thomas S. Power, sent the Air Staff an alternate war plan discussing these concepts. In Washington, officials reacted almost immedi-

---

[111] Burk, *USAF in UK*, pp 15–18; rprt, NSC 45/1, to President, Airfield Construction in the United Kingdom and the Cairo-Suez Area, Apr 15, 1949, in *FRUS*, 1949, Vol I, pp 285–287; ASSS, Maj Gen S. E. Anderson, Dir P & O, to Sec AF, Base Utilization in the United Kingdom, Jan 24, 1949, with atchs, RG 341, TS AAG File 18, Box 6, MMB, NA.

[112] Ltr, CG SAC to Cmdr MATS, subj: Strategic Air Command's Future Requirements at Goose Bay, Harmon, and Dhahran Air Force Bases, Aug 27, 1949, RG 341, DCS/Ops, P & O 686, SAC (Sep 1, 1949), Box 1, MMB, NA; General Grussendorf's copy of Trip Book and Special Notes, n.d. [Oct–Nov 52], Vandenberg Coll, Box 84, MD, LC.

[113] Robert L. Swetzer, *USAF Operations in the Mediterranean, 1945–1975*, USAFE Hist Monograph (Ramstein Air Base, Germany: Hq USAFE, 1978), p 41.

ately to the increased cost. In the budget climate of the time, even the strategic force might be reaching the limit of what President Truman and Congress would be willing to provide.[114]

As oversea bases claimed a high priority, SAC's airfields in the continental United States were often in abysmal condition. Of the bomber bases, only Davis-Monthan had been in use before the war. Carswell, Rapid City, and Spokane had seen some postwar construction. Otherwise, paving and buildings constructed under wartime emergency conditions were deteriorating or were not designed for the needs of a modern bomber force. The housing situation was still far from satisfactory. For construction of operational facilities, LeMay had to assign strict priorities for the scarce dollars. He put the fields where the bombers went to pick up their bombs at the top of the list. He ranked Carswell and Limestone next, and then several of the B–29 and B–50 fields.[115]

Ironically, the forty-eight group program adopted in early 1949 helped alleviate SAC's basing problem. The Air Force-wide cutback meant that a number of bases would be closed. The Air Staff looked at location (availability of transportation, supplies, and housing) and condition (in terms of what necessary improvements would cost) in deciding which bases the Air Force could most readily do without. Doubtless, few in SAC were surprised when their bases were scheduled for closure. Both fighter fields, Grenier in New Hampshire and Kearney in Nebraska, appeared on the list. As units in other commands inactivated, their stations opened up for SAC to take. Among these locations were Barksdale Air Force Base, Louisiana, and Fairfield-Suisun and March Air Force Bases, both in California. Given the political sensitivities that always accompanied the question of closing bases, it is worth noting that Secretary Symington

---

[114] Ltr, Maj Gen T. S. Power, Dep Cmdr SAC, to Dir P & O, USAF, subj: Alternate Emergency War Plan, Dec 1, 1949; memo, Maj Gen S. E. Anderson, Dir P & O, to Gen H. S. Vandenberg, CSAF, subj: Strategic Air Command Alternate Emergency War Plan Study, Dec 23, 1949, with encl: Plan Digest; R & R Sheet, Col P. E. Ruestow, Asst for Log Pl, DCS/Mat, to Ch Ops Div, DCS/Ops, Strategic Air Command Alternate Emergency War Plan Study, Feb 2, 1950, all in RG 341, DCS/Ops, OPD, 381, SAC (Dec 1, 1949), Sect 1, Box 1027, MMB, NA.
[115] Rprt, SAC, Immediate Strategic Air Command Base Requirements, Apr 15, 1949, atch to ltr, Maj Gen G. Gardner, Chmn AF Base Dev Bd, to Lt Gen C. E. LeMay, CG SAC, May 11, 1949, RG 341, DCS/Mat, Exec Ofc TS Corres, Box 1, MMB, NA; Mueller, *Air Force Bases*, Vol I, pp 63–70, 149–156, 171–178, 327–330 & ff; ltr, LeMay to Gen H. S. Vandenberg, CSAF, Dec 4, 1948, with encl: SAC Station Priority List, Vandenberg Coll, SAC (4), Box 45, MD, LC.

SAC and Maintenance. B–36s and B–50s of SAC's strategic bomber fleet, on constant alert, demanded frequent maintenance by skilled technicians. *Clockwise from above:* A line of B–36s awaiting checkups in their maintenance docks seems to go on forever. The trucks, cranes, and moving platforms essential to B–50 propeller installations and repairs or engine replacements were, in a time of decreasing budgets and increasing work, often in short supply. These remote-control turret repairmen face a daunting thicket of wires and other components in a highly complex system.

concurred in these actions. This gave him the opportunity to link the basing structure to the reductions Congress had voted.[116]

Further realignments followed, with SAC giving up Smoky Hill Air Force Base, Kansas (where the expense of needed construction was excessive), McGuire Air Force Base, New Jersey (housing considered "deplorable"), and Topeka, Kansas. The headquarters of Fifteenth Air Force moved from Colorado Springs to March Air Force Base, California, and Maj. Gen. Joseph H. ("Hamp") Atkinson moved the staff of his 311th Air Division from Topeka to Barksdale.[117] These headquarters moves, late in 1949, suggested some restructuring of the command. Atkinson thought that SAC might signal a new emphasis on reconnaissance by upgrading his division to an air force. For this reason, Atkinson's headquarters, on leaving Topeka, opened for business at Barksdale on November 1, 1949, as Headquarters, Second Air Force.[118]

This reorganization gave SAC three air forces. For years, the Eighth had been regarded as the atomic strike force, while Fifteenth represented the worldwide conventional capability. Now the Second Air Force would specialize in reconnaissance. But the distinction had never been perfect, and by the middle of 1950, the Fifteenth was becoming atomic capable. In addition, the Fifteenth Air Force had stations stretching from California to Florida, and the Second was almost as widely dispersed. Early in 1950, staff studies suggested a new pattern of geographical realignment. A new RB–36 unit would be based at Rapid City instead of Fairfield Suisun, and the air forces would be assigned more compact areas of responsibility. The changes took effect on April 1, with Second Air Force at Barksdale covering the Southeast, the Eighth at Carswell responsible for the central

---

[116] 1st Ind, (ltr, Lt Gen W. F. McKee, Asst VCSAF, to CG SAC, subj: Strategic Air Command Base Utilization Plan, Feb 24, 1949), Lt Gen C. E. LeMay, CG SAC, to CSAF, Mar 12, 1949, LeMay Coll, McKee, Box B56; memo of phonecon, Maj Gen F. F. Everest, Asst DCS/Ops, to LeMay, Aug 15, 1949, LeMay Coll, Memos and R & Rs, 1949 and 1948, Box B64; R & R Sheet, Maj Gen F. H. Smith, Jr, Asst for Prog, DCS/Ops, to VCSAF, Strategic Air Command Base Utilization Proposals, n.d., with atch ltr, Gen M. S. Fairchild, VCSAF, to LeMay, same subj, Aug 30, 1949, Fairchild Coll, SAC 1948–1950, Box 3, all in MD, LC; memo, Gen H. S. Vandenberg, CSAF, to Sec AF, subj: Reduced Installation Program, Jan 13, 1949, Symington Papers, Corres File 1946–1950, Vandenberg, Box 13, HSTL.
[117] See previous note.
[118] Ltr, Maj Gen W. F. McKee, Asst VCSAF, to Senator E. D. Millikin, Aug 31, 1949, LeMay Coll, McKee, Box B56; ltr, Lt Gen C. E. LeMay, CG SAC, to Lt Gen L. Norstad, DCS/Ops, Sep 10, 1949, LeMay Coll, Norstad, Box B56, both in MD, LC; Maurer, *AF Combat Units*, pp 420, 458, 470.

states, and the Fifteenth at March Air Force Base, positioned to deploy from the Far West.[119]

Organizational realignments, like other actions designed to increase the effectiveness of the strategic force, contributed to the national goal of creating a strategic deterrent in the face of rising Soviet power. LeMay had made a personal commitment to ensuring that SAC was combat ready in every respect. Under his leadership, the command's capacity to meet its worldwide obligations gradually improved. However, the decision to build a powerful bomber fleet was not LeMay's to make. Soon critics once again questioned the emphasis on the strategic air force, and challenges to the national strategy were increasingly raised.

---

[119] Staff Study 4–50, 15 AF, DCS/Ops, Pl Sect, LeMay Coll, Box B106, MD, LC; hist, SAC, Jan–Jun 1950, Vol I, pp 1–8.

Chapter VIII

Challenges to Strategy

The role of the strategic air force in the nation's defense had essentially been established in the JCS 1745 series and by the budget reductions after the Berlin crisis. LeMay's progress in making the force effective gave it some degree of credibility. But not everyone was entirely satisfied. Opponents of the Air Force's priority mission raised a series of challenges. In the end, the Air Force made its case, and the decision for a strategic force was confirmed. Likewise, the news of the end of the American atomic monopoly, while it raised again the spectre of an "atomic Pearl Harbor" and altered the terms of the national debate, did not in fact change the basic strategy. In that September of 1949, the Atomic Energy Commission was fully engaged in producing the four hundred weapons planned for in 1947, and the prospect of meeting this goal by the end of 1950 appeared good.[1] Furthermore, the fiscal 1950 force reductions, in effect by July 1949, placed such extreme limits on other categories of forces that the strategic air offensive became more than ever the core of the joint war plan. The national debate, as a result, did not focus on what strategy to pursue but whether the Air Force had properly executed its stewardship of strategic air resources.

The major internal challenge came from the Navy. A critique of the strategic air offensive, questioning both its feasibility and its desirability underlay several attempts by naval advocates to weaken, divert, or dismiss altogether the strength of the Air Force role. The strategic air offensive, so long as Cairo-Suez was one of its major base areas, served as a rationale for strong naval forces to secure the Mediterranean. The new emphasis on bases in England and North America vitiated such an argument. Likewise,

---

[1] OSD, *Strategic Arms Competition*, USAF Supporting Studies, Vol I: *Description and Analysis*, p 105.

the Navy countered the airmen's efforts to ensure centralized control of the strategic air force in the event of war and to protect it against diversions to other tasks. The same issue, the independence of air power, seemed to be present in any commitment to an allied strategy in Europe.

At the beginning of 1949, some of the participants in the debate changed. Admiral Leahy, who had presided over the JCS virtually since its inception in 1942, decided to retire. Forrestal, hoping to help the chiefs to reach agreement, asked Gen. of the Army Dwight D. Eisenhower, now President of Columbia University, to return to Washington to advise him on war planning and budget matters and to chair the joint chiefs. For years an advocate of air power, Eisenhower believed that in a restricted budget the strategic air force had to be a priority commitment.[2]

Forrestal himself was unable to benefit from Eisenhower's leadership in the JCS. At the end of February 1949, President Truman, disturbed at continuing budget quarrels and doubts as to Forrestal's loyalty, was ready to ask for the Defense Secretary's resignation. This he did, and Forrestal resigned effective March 28. His sense of frustration heightened and mental health deteriorating, the former secretary took his own life at the end of May. The new Defense chief was Louis A. Johnson, a prominent lawyer, past president of the American Legion, and former Assistant Secretary of War under Roosevelt. Secretary Johnson had been instrumental in starting the buildup of American forces before the Second World War. Having been the principal fund raiser for Truman's campaign in 1948, however, he now considered himself to have a mandate from the President to cut defense spending.[3]

Budget considerations aside, the strategic air offensive faced the all-important question—whether it could succeed as planned. Here the Air Force could not oppose an objective investigation, and in late 1949 and early 1950, several individuals and groups debated the issue. Ironically, the more the potential of the strategic air offensive came into question, the more evident its importance became. After the Berlin crisis waned, the return to limited budgets ensured that the forces would not be adequate to any other military task. Only a strong atomic attack could stave off disaster in the event of war.

Throughout the national debate, the Air Force continued to argue the case for the approved strategy. An opportunity arose to defend the service's position before Congress and the public when opponents, disgruntled at Johnson's cancellation of the Navy's supercarrier, chose to present the B–36 as the symbol of a failed strategy. The hearings that followed

---

[2] K. Condit, *JCS, 1947–1949*, pp 294–296.
[3] Rearden, *Formative Years*, pp 43–47.

actually reinforced the decisions already made and established the strategic air force as a virtually unassailable component of national strength. Public attention turned more and more to the inadequacies of other elements of the nation's military. The Army, concerned at the danger that it would have to assist pitifully weak European forces, hoped that the strategic air force could help to "retard" any Soviet land offensive. The Air Force's resistance to diverting funds to land and naval forces, while relatively successful in protecting the strategic air offensive, guaranteed that questions along this line would continue to arise.

The report confirming that the Soviets had exploded an atomic bomb caught the West by surprise. The Air Force had considered it a reasonable precaution to rush an interim detection system into operation, but few had really expected the weapon so soon.[4] In the wake of such a startling development, assessing the next step took time. Meanwhile, Secretary of Defense Louis Johnson's proposed fiscal 1951 budget continued the trend toward austerity. When Truman finally reacted to the apparent new threat, he authorized both expanded atomic bomb production and the development of a hydrogen weapon.

The administration's commitment to controlling military spending left many officials in the State and Defense Departments uneasy at the fact that the United States had a strategic force of limited size and a bare skeleton of any other military capacity. One outgrowth of this uneasiness was a major study the National Security Council prepared early in 1950, known as NSC-68. The immediate outcome of the document was a tentative look at possible increases in spending, but the long-term impact was uncertain.

Analysts agreed that more funds were necessary to bolster Air Force programs in air defense and tactical air power, given the increased threat of a Soviet atomic attack. And whether or not the coming Soviet atomic arsenal undermined deterrence, the call for ground forces and tactical air forces to help the western Europeans defend themselves grew stronger.

Under the circumstances, the strategic air force remained central to the nation's deterrent strength. Some individuals doubted SAC's ability to accomplish the mission. The command might not yet have the resources to do so, but its effectiveness with the available personnel and equipment was less and less open to question. It was LeMay's success in overcoming SAC's growing pains and his reputation as an effective combat leader that gave the Air Force confidence that the deterrent could work.

---

[4] Little, *Foundations*, Pt I, pp 288–291.

Strategic Air Force

The propeller-driven Northrop XB–35 Flying Wing, a futuristic and evocative, though seriously flawed, design.

The Challenge at Home

Concerned that budgetary restraint would force serious reductions in carrier forces, the Navy feared it would be unable to secure the sea lanes in the event of war. The emerging Soviet submarine technology seemed to pose a threat that could only be overcome by powerful air attacks on naval facilities. Naval spokesmen challenged the Air Force's predominance in several ways. They questioned the emphasis on the strategic air offensive in the joint war plans. They sought to insure the ability of theater commanders to divert bomber forces from the strategic role. They challenged the money being spent on the strategic force. Ultimately they attacked the B–36 as the symbol of the strategic air offensive. The Army also voiced some reservations, but it was the naval challenge that quickly claimed the time of government leaders and the attention of the public.

The Air Force's leadership in turn needed to ensure that the air offensive could achieve results, and that the joint chiefs, the Secretary of Defense, and the President all understood this. The budget situation did help in this respect, as it became apparent that the existing strategic air force, now marginally effective, could be improved, while no other forces could be made reasonably effective with the funds available.

Challenges to Strategy

By late in 1948, planners recognized that budget forecasts for fiscal 1950 would require reductions of forces in all services. These cuts would make the existing war plan HALFMOON (renamed FLEETWOOD in August) obsolete.[5] Nor was the plan entirely practical as written. Col. Robert O. Cork of the SAC staff reported that the British bases in the Cairo-Suez area intended for the strategic force could not be used in the opening phase of a potential conflict. Expensive construction would be needed first. Until that work was done, aviation engineer units, already in short supply, would have to be prepared for immediate deployment to get the bases ready.[6]

Shortages of personnel and equipment were only part of the problem. Everything needed for support of the strike force in Cairo-Suez would have to come through the Mediterranean by sea. The British were as aware as the Americans that these waters could be dominated by land-based air.[7] The allies predicted that the Soviets would be able to bring strong air forces to bear to prevent supply and to attack the bases heavily. Thus plan FLEETWOOD called for conducting a major part of the strategic air offensive from a base area of doubtful tenability.[8]

The Air Staff anticipated the Navy's argument that a strong naval force could keep the Mediterranean open. Naval strategists described the Middle East as vital both as a base area and a wartime source of oil. Airmen referred to studies indicating that the oil supply in question was

---

[5] K. Condit, *JCS, 1947–1949*, pp 293–296.

[6] Rprt, JSPC to JCS, Revision of Fleetwood, n.d. [Oct 48]; memo (unsigned), Col J. B. Cary, AF Mem JSPC, to Gen H. S. Vandenberg, CSAF, subj: Discussion of Advice to be given to Planners on Emergency War Plan and Request for JCS Confirmation of Soundness Thereof, Oct 13, 1948, both in RG 341, DCS/Ops, Dir/Pl, OPD, Spec File HALFMOON, Sect 4, Box 1045, MMB, NA; rprt, JLPG to FLPC 416/32, The Logistic Feasibility of ABC 101, Nov 12, 1948, RG 341, DCS/Ops, Dir/Pl, OPD, Spec File HALFMOON, Sect 5, Box 1046, MMB, NA.

[7] Ch Marshal RAF Arthur, Lord Tedder, *Air Power in War* (London: Hodder & Stoughton, n.d. [1948]), pp 63–70, 72–79.

[8] Memo, subj: Revision of Fleetwood, n.d. [1949], RG 341, DCS/Ops, Dir/Pl, OPD, Spec File HALFMOON, Sect 6, Box 1046; memo, Maj Gen S. E. Anderson, Dir P & O, to Gen H. S. Vandenberg, CSAF, subj: Revision of Joint Outline Emergency War Plan (JCS 1844/32), Jan 18, 1949, RG 341, DCS/Ops, Dir/Pl, OPD, Spec File HALFMOON, Sect 6, Box 1046; memo, RAdm W. F. Boone, Navy Mem JSPC, to RAdm C. D. Glover, Brig Gen C. Van R. Schuyler, Col J. B. Cary, subj: Brief of Joint Outline Emergency War Plan—Short Title ORACLE, n.d. [1949], with marginal notations, RG 341, DCS/Ops, Dir/Pl, OPD, Spec File HALFMOON, Sect 7, Box 1047, all in MMB, NA.

Strategic Air Force

not essential in a war.⁹ The Army's spokesmen, recalling the strategic debates of 1943 and 1944, when advocates of a Mediterranean strategy seemed to be opposed to striking at the heart of Germany, still considered the Middle East unacceptable as a major base area. Both the Air Force and the Army contended that the British Isles needed to be secured first, and remained in any case a priority for basing.¹⁰

By late 1948 joint planners were at work on a revision to the existing plan, the new one to be named TROJAN. This plan would have an annex for the atomic offensive. By this time SAC had decided not to use Cairo-Suez for launching bombers, although a commitment still existed to secure the Cairo-Suez area.¹¹

Instead, TROJAN called for England and Okinawa as the main strategic air base areas for the medium bomber force. Any available B-36s would launch from North America. Like the new SAC plan, TROJAN emphasized a powerful initial atomic strike, exploiting the weaknesses of an untested Soviet air defense system. In general, TROJAN retained the timing used in earlier plans. In the first phase of a war, it called for mounting defensive operations in Europe and the strategic air offensive, although some operations envisioned in previous plans would have to be curtailed because of budget reductions. The next phases would entail mobilization for the final offensive, a longer process under TROJAN be-

---

⁹ Memo, RAdm W. F. Boone, Navy Mem JSPC, to RAdm C. D. Glover, Brig Gen C. Van R. Schuyler, Col J. B. Cary, subj: Brief of Joint Outline Emergency War Plan—Short Title ORACLE, n.d. [1949], with marginal notations; memo, Col J. B. Cary, AF Mem JSPC, to Maj Gen S. E. Anderson, Dir P & O, subj: JSPC Work on New Short-Range Emergency Plan, Jan 28, 1949, both in RG 341, DCS/Ops, Dir/Pl, OPD, Spec File HALFMOON, Sect 7, Box 1047; memo, subj: Revision of Fleetwood, n.d. [1949], RG 341, DCS/Ops, Dir/Pl, OPD, Spec File HALFMOON, Sect 6, Box 1046; memo, Col T. C. Rogers to Cary, subj: Plans ORACLE and PINECREST (JSPC 877/43 and JSPC 877/44), Feb 23, 1949, with atch tabs, RG 341, DCS/Ops, Dir/Pl, OPD, Spec File HALFMOON, Sect 8, Box 1047, all in MMB, NA.

¹⁰ MR, Brig Gen W. L. Ritchie, AF Mem JSPC, Meeting of the Operations Deputies with the JSPC (Oct 12, 1948), Oct 12, 1948, with atchs; memo (unsigned), Col J. B. Cary, AF Mem JSPC, to Gen H. S. Vandenberg, CSAF, subj: Discussion of Advice Given to Planners on Emergency War Plan and Request for JCS Confirmation of Soundness Thereof, Oct 13, 1948, both in RG 341, DCS/Ops, Dir/Pl, OPD, Spec File HALFMOON, Sect 4, Box 1045, MMB, NA.

¹¹ US Air Force Initial Strike Plan, atch to memo, Col Haywood to Brig Gen W. L. Ritchie, AF Mem JSPC, subj: Atomic Supplement to TROJAN (JSPC 877/32), Nov 29, 1948; rprt, JSPC to JCS, & JCS Decision, JCS 1974, Atomic Weapons Supplement to TROJAN, Dec 23, 1948; ltr, Brig Gen W. C. Sweeney, Jr, Dir Pl SAC, to Col J. B. Cary, Pl Div, DCS/Ops USAF, Jan 18, 1948, all in RG 341, DCS/Ops, Dir/Pl, OPD, Spec File HALFMOON, Sect 6, Box 1046, MMB, NA; K. Condit, *JCS, 1947-1949*, pp 293-294.

cause so little could be done in peacetime to prepare. Although air planners had hoped to include the possibility of an early Soviet surrender after the initial air offensive, the chiefs would only agree to a mandatory review of plans after three months of war. With this provision, TROJAN was approved in January 1949.[12]

The influence of the upcoming budget on the war plan was pervasive. Eisenhower had begun work with the joint chiefs on both. Looking at the budget reductions then in prospect and hoping to update existing plans accordingly, he outlined a strategy intended to stop the Soviet offensive on the Rhine. Considering the lack of resources, Eisenhower recognized that this might not be possible. In that case the only alternative was to prepare for an ultimate allied counteroffensive. The essential tasks were three-fold: to hold the United Kingdom, the western entry into the Mediterranean, and the Middle East.[13]

The budget developed for fiscal 1950 provided no forces for the Middle East at the outset of a war and left the British to bear the burden of defending that region. As far as the American airmen were concerned, holding the Middle East would not "permit achievement of any worthwhile strategic objective."[14] Nonetheless, Col. John B. Cary, the Air Force member of the Joint Strategic Planning Committee, found that the Navy was still advocating a commitment to the region, budget or no budget.[15]

In line with Eisenhower's proposals, the joint chiefs ordered a new plan prepared. Accordingly, the Joint Strategic Planning Committee began to look at Northwest Africa as a potential base area, either in addition to or in place of the British Isles. Arguments over the role of carrier aircraft and of the importance of the strategic air offensive held up progress, and

---

[12] See previous note; memo, CSAF to JCS 1844/34, subj: Revision of Joint Outline Emergency War Plan, Jan 18, 1949, RG 341, DCS/Ops, Dir/Pl, OPD, Spec File, HALFMOON, Sect 7, Box 1047, MMB, NA.

[13] Memo, Maj Gen S. E. Anderson, Dir P & O, to Lt Gen L. Norstad, DCS/Ops, subj: Force Requirements for Implementation of the Three Tasks Proposed by General Eisenhower, Feb 27, 1949, RG 341, DCS/Ops, Dir/Pl, OPD, Spec File HALFMOON, Sect 8, Box 1047, MMB, NA; K. Condit, *JCS, 1947–1949*, pp 294–296.

[14] Memo, subj: Revision of Fleetwood, n.d. [1949], RG 341, DCS/Ops, Dir/Pl, OPD, Spec File HALFMOON, Sect 6, Box 1046, MMB, NA.

[15] Memo, Col J. B. Cary, AF Mem JSPC, to Maj Gen S. E. Anderson, Dir P & O, subj: JSPC Work on New Short-Range Emergency Plan, Jan 28, 1949; rprt, JSPC 877/43, Feb 15, 1949 (both in RG 341, DCS/Ops, Dir Pl, OPD, Spec File HALFMOON, Sect 7, Box 1047, MMB, NA).

Strategic Air Force

not until late summer of 1949 did plan OFFTACKLE approach its final form.[16]

To the Air Staff, command of the strategic air offensive was possibly an even more important issue than the Mediterrean bases. Dating back to the wartime campaign of the Twentieth Air Force, a precedent existed for undivided control of the strategic force, free from interference by the theater commanders. The joint chiefs were willing to ratify LeMay's appointment to command SAC as a specified command and to designate the Chief of Staff of the Air Force as executive agent for SAC. These actions were generally in keeping with the Unified Command Plan as it developed since 1946.[17] However, the control of naval forces engaged in strategic operations and the status of "exempt units"—the atomic force not available to theater commanders—proved far more controversial elements of the joint plan.

The conferences at Key West and Newport in 1948 had seemingly confirmed the Air Force as the service primarily responsible for strategic air warfare. Nevertheless, Maj. Gen. Samuel E. Anderson, Director of Plans and Operations, reported in October 1948: "The three services are developing weapons and are organizing forces which are capable of conducting strategic air warfare." Guided missiles were among the weapons that all services were working on.[18] Obviously, one way to insure effective central control involved placing the strategic forces of all services under a unified command. Early in 1949 the Air Force made an abortive effort to have SAC declared a "unified" rather than a "specified" command. This would create a rationale for eventually giving it control over naval forces committed to the strategic role. While the Navy was prepared to concede to the Commanding General of SAC some control over selecting targets and timing the attacks, command of the forces in question had to remain with the fleets. Accordingly, on April 11, 1949, the joint chiefs issued a

---

[16] See note above; K. Condit, *JCS, 1947–1949*, pp 294–302.

[17] Memo, CSAF to JCS, & Decision JCS 1259/104, subj: Unified Command Plan, Dec 13, 1948; memo, CSAF to JCS & Decision JCS 1259/110, subj: Unified Command Plan, Jan 4, 1949, both in RG 341, DCS/Ops, Dir/Pl, OPD, 323.361 (Nov 8, 1943), Case 13, SAC, Box 151, MMB, NA.

[18] Memo, Maj Gen S. E. Anderson, Dir P & O, to Lt Gen L. Norstad, DCS/Ops, subj: Implementing Amendment to Joint Chiefs of Staff Unifed Command Plan Implementing the Strategic Air Command, n.d. [Oct 48], RG 341, DCS/Ops, Dir/Pl, OPD, 323.361 (Nov 8, 1943), Case 13, SAC, Box 151, MMB, NA.

formal directive to SAC, outlining its commander's responsibility to "conduct strategic air operations," but not to command them.[19]

Even SAC units themselves were at risk. Under the Unified Command Plan, theater commanders had the authority to take command of all forces in their areas in an emergency. The joint chiefs had exempted SADDLETREE-modified units from this provision so that they would always be available for atomic operations.[20] At "Dualism" LeMay had expressed concern that the wording of the provision was inadequate, and Norstad had outlined a proposal to exempt all units involved in any way with the atomic offensive. LeMay observed: "Then I gather that no Strategic Air Command units are available to theater commanders." This would not be the precise wording, Norstad indicated, but the effect would be similar.[21]

On December 27, 1948, Vandenberg submitted the Air Force's plan to the joint chiefs. Wings currently receiving modified aircraft were to be added to the 509th, already on the exempt list. In addition, other aircraft were used for reconnaissance to support the atomic offensive, as decoys, electronic jammers, and for fighter escort. Air planners speculated that if theater commanders took these forces, the atomic offensive would be seriously impeded. This was especially so because of the close timing involved in LeMay's deployment plan. Instead, Vandenberg requested a blanket exemption of affected units, with the list revised from time to time as units were reorganized and re-equipped.[22]

Both the Chief of Staff of the Army and the Chief of Naval Operations objected to the plan. Though in basic agreement with the need for an independent strategic air force, the Army continued to fear that all long-range air reconnaissance would be centrally controlled and vital information denied to the theater commanders. Vandenberg acknowledged SAC's obligation to support other JCS commanders and agreed to

---

[19] Rprt, JSPC to JCS 1259/117, The Unified Command Plan, Jan 6, 1949; memo, Maj Gen S. E. Anderson, Dir P & O, to Lt Gen L. Norstad, DCS/Ops, subj: The Unified Command Plan, Feb 9, 1949; memo, CS Army to JCS & Decision JCS 1259/129, subj: Unified Command Plan, Mar 3, 1949, all in RG 341, DCS/Ops, Dir/Pl, OPD, 323.361 (Nov 8, 1943), Case 13, SAC, Box 151, MMB, NA.

[20] *Dualism*, Vol II, p 258.

[21] *Ibid*.

[22] Memo, Gen H. S. Vandenberg, CSAF, to Sec JCS, subj: Designation of Units Exempt from Operational Control of Theater Commanders, Dec 27, 1948, with atch memo, CSAF to JCS, subj: Unified Command Plan; memo, Maj Gen S. E. Anderson, Dir P & O, to Vandenberg, subj: Designation of Units Exempt from Operational Control of Theater Commanders (Unified Command Plan JCS 1259/115), Jan 12, 1949, both in RG 341, DCS/Ops, Dir/Pl, OPD, 323.361 (Nov 8, 1943), Case 14, Cont of Atom Units, Box 152, MMB, NA.

Louis A. Johnson succeeded James V. Forrestal in 1949 as Secretary of Defense.

provide that support when it was needed.[23] The Navy's objection was that the original concept had been to husband the scarce resources of atomic-capable bombers. Vandenberg pointed out that even though these aircraft were no longer so scarce, they were intended for use in the strategic air offensive, which enjoyed a high priority in all war plans. Accordingly, all units committed to that offensive had to be exempted. His views prevailed, and the joint chiefs approved his proposal on January 19, 1949.[24]

The creation of the North Atlantic Alliance added to the controversy surrounding the control of the strategic force. The treaty signed on April 4, 1949, provided in Article V "that an armed attack against one or more of [the members] shall be considered an attack against them all...."[25] When ratifications were completed in August, the United States was thus com-

---

[23] Memo, CS Army to JCS, subj: Unified Command Plan—Designation of Units for Atomic Operations, n.d.; memo, Maj Gen J. Smith, Dep Dir P & O, to Gen H. S. Vandenberg, CSAF, subj: Unified Command Plan—Designation of Units for Atomic Operations (JCS 1259/172), Sep 21, 1949; memo, CSAF to JCS, 1259/166, Unified Command Plan—Designation of Units for Atomic Operations, Aug 22, 1949, & Decision, May 9, 1950, all in RG 341, DCS/Ops, Dir/Pl, OPD, 323.361 (Nov 8, 1943), Case 14, Cont of Atom Units, Box 152, MMB, NA.

[24] Memo, CNO to JCS, 1259/120, subj: Unified Command Plan—Designation of Units for Atomic Operations, Jan 14, 1949; memo, CSAF to JCS, 1259/121, subj: Unified Commands—Designation of Units for Atomic Operations, Jan 19, 1949; memo, CSAF to JCS, 1259/115, subj: Unified Command Plan—Designation of Units for Atomic Operations, Dec 28, 1948 & Decision, Jan 19, 1949, all in RG 341, DCS/Ops, Dir/Pl, OPD, 323.361 (Nov 8, 1943), Case 14, Cont of Atom Units, Box 152, MMB, NA.

[25] NATO Information Service, *NATO Facts and Figures* (Brussels, 1976), p 301.

Challenges to Strategy

mitted to regard a Soviet attack on Western Europe in the same light as an attack upon itself. This language did not guarantee any specific action, but it did indicate that the resources of the United States, including its atomic force, might enter the balance. This brought atomic deterrence clearly into America's relations with Europe.

The problem of allied command relationships had received serious thought long before the North Atlantic Treaty actually took effect. At Newport the joint chiefs had agreed that in time of war, the allies should have an American commander under direction of the Anglo-American Combined Chiefs of Staff. This officer would have three major subordinate commanders, one for Western Europe, one for the Mediterranean and Middle East, and one for strategic air forces. In the interim, the Americans suggested that the Brussels Pact countries appoint a British or French commander. Clearly, any future allied strategic air force would be mainly American in composition. Only the British possessed a force of this type, and it was small and equipped only for conventional bombing.[26]

Vandenberg may have harbored doubts about this arrangement. He proposed measures that would preclude creating an allied strategic command.[27] As for placing SAC under an allied command at all, opinions diverged. Cary thought that in an inter-allied forum, where Lord Tedder or a successor of comparable stature would have influence, there would be less obstruction than in a purely American one. Nevertheless, the Air Force increasingly favored keeping SAC under exclusively American control, even in war. As matters were to develop, the NATO forces in Europe became committed to a land defense, and the allied commander was likely to seek the diversion of strategic air forces to support the ground operations. Staff papers prepared by joint committees increasingly tended to include diagrams placing SAC under the U.S. joint chiefs in both peace and war.[28]

---

[26] MR, Ofc of Sec Def, Newport Conference Decisions with Respect to Command, Aug 23, 1948, RG 341, DCS/Ops, Dir Pl, OPD, 323.361 (Apr 22, 1948), Box 146, MMB, NA.

[27] Paper, ... extract views of the Chiefs of the Services ..., n.d. [1949], RG 341, DCS/Ops, Dir/Pl, OPD, 323.361 (Nov 8, 1943), Case 1, Anx A, Box 148, MMB, NA.

[28] Memo, Col J. B. Cary, Asst Ch Pl Div, DCS/Ops, to Maj Gen S. E. Anderson, Dir P & O, subj: Allied Higher Direction and Command for FLEETWOOD, Sep 17, 1948; MR, Capt G. W. Lalor, USN, Sec JCS, (a) Command Plan for FLEETWOOD. (b) FLEETWOOD Planning for Mediterranean-Middle East Area, Sep 16, 1948, both in RG 341, DCS/Ops, Dir/Pl, OPD, 323.361 (Apr 22, 1948), Box 146; R & R Sheet, Anderson to Dir Tng & Rqmts, Strategic Air Warfare Command Relationships, Mar 15, 1949, RG 341, DCS/Ops, Dir/Pl, OPD, 323.361 (Apr 22, 1948), Sect 3, Box 146.

Strategic Air Force

Disturbed at the rising tide of acrimony in the discussion of strategy, Forrestal had written to the service secretaries on November 8, 1948, establishing ground rules for congressional testimony. He hoped that witnesses would refrain from any "attack upon, or criticism of, the competence, equipment or weapons of another service." These attacks and criticisms were going on in private and would continue, but the Secretary of Defense hoped the services could resist the temptation to make public attacks on each other's alleged pet weapons.[29]

Forrestal was also troubled by the substance of the disagreements, especially because he recognized how much the country was coming to rely on the strategic force. Symington told him of Vandenberg's repeated assurances that "he was absolutely certain [the bomb] could be dropped..." wherever required.[30] Nevertheless, late in 1948 Forrestal asked the joint chiefs to study the feasibility of an atomic offensive and its potential effectiveness.

Vandenberg responded to the first question—whether the offensive could be carried out—by submitting a description of SAC's existing plan. He noted the command's progress in building an effective force and argued that it could penetrate Soviet air space. According to intelligence sources, Soviet air defenses were weak, with a radar net totally inadequate for protecting a vast extent of territory. The enemy possessed no fighters capable of nighttime operations, and its antiaircraft guns could not be expected to hit targets above thirty thousand feet. Estimating twenty-five percent losses to the attacking force, Vandenberg reported that SAC could deliver the entire atomic stockpile.[31]

Admiral Louis E. Denfeld, the Chief of Naval Operations, objected to the Air Force report, primarily on the grounds that the intelligence about Soviet air defenses was too uncertain. Although the joint chiefs might reach a partial agreement, major issues remained unresolved. In due course, the question of the air offensive's feasibility was referred to the new Weapons Systems Evaluation Group (WSEG), then being organized under a JCS agreement made at the Newport Conference to deal with precisely this kind of question.[32]

However, the WSEG would not consider the problem of what the atomic offensive would actually achieve if the bombers got through. The

---

[29] Memo, J. V. Forrestal, Sec Def, to Secs Army, Navy, AF, Nov 8, 1948, Forrestal Diary, Vol XIII, p 2629, in Forrestal Papers, OSD.
[30] *Ibid.*, p 2539 (Oct 5, 1948).
[31] Rprt, Gen H. S. Vandenberg, CSAF, to JCS, JCS 1952/1, Dec 21, 1948, in Etzold & Gaddis, *Containment*.
[32] Rearden, *Formative Years*, pp 403–405.

chiefs referred that matter to a committee headed by Lt. Gen. Hubert R. Harmon of the Air Force. A classmate of Eisenhower and Bradley at West Point, Harmon had attended the Army War College and served on the Army Staff before a brief wartime tour in command of Thirteenth Air Force in the South Pacific. He was on the military staff at the United Nations, an assignment suggesting a reputation for fairmindedness.[33]

The Harmon Committee did not submit its report until May 1949. It estimated that a successful strategic air offensive would temporarily reduce Soviet industrial capacity by thirty or forty percent and severely damage the oil industry. A Soviet attack on Western Europe could not be stopped, but over time the enemy's military strength would be undermined. Offering a conservative assessment of casualties, the committee estimated the probable dead at nearly three million, in addition to millions of homeless. The commitee admitted that the psychological reaction among Soviet civilians the the international community might not serve American interests, and that the air offensive in itself would not be enough to "win the war." Nevertheless,

> the atomic bomb...would constitute the only means of rapidly inflicting shock and serious damage to vital elements of the Soviet war-making capacity. In particular, an early atomic offensive will facilitate greatly the application of other Allied military power....

In sum, "the advantages of its early use would be transcending."[34]

Vandenberg reacted to the Harmon report by insisting that it be changed before its submission to the Secretary of Defense. The Air Force's assistant for atomic energy, among others, objected to the report, noting that it neglected any consideration of damage from fires started by the bombing. The Air Force's dissent was acknowledged in the final report the JCS sent to Secretary Johnson.[35]

The controversy over the effectiveness of the strategic air offensive highlighted the same issues that perennially arose during the budget negotiations. In early 1949 these discussions resumed. As the Air force was

---

[33] Fogerty, Study # 91, "Harmon, Hubert R.;" John Ponturo, *Analytical Support for the Joint Chiefs of Staff: The WSEG Experience, 1948–1976* (Institute for Defense Analyses Study S–507, Washington, Defense Technical Information Center, 1979), pp 52–55.

[34] Rprt, Evaluation of Effect on Soviet War Effort Resulting from the Strategic Air Offensive, May 49, in Etzold & Gaddis, *Containment*, pp 363–364, 360–364; memo, subj: The Harmon Board Report, Oct 14, 1949, RG 340, OSAF Numeric-Subject Files 46–50, 1j (2), Box 3, MMB, NA.

[35] Little, *Building an Atomic Air Force*, Pt II, pp 343–348.

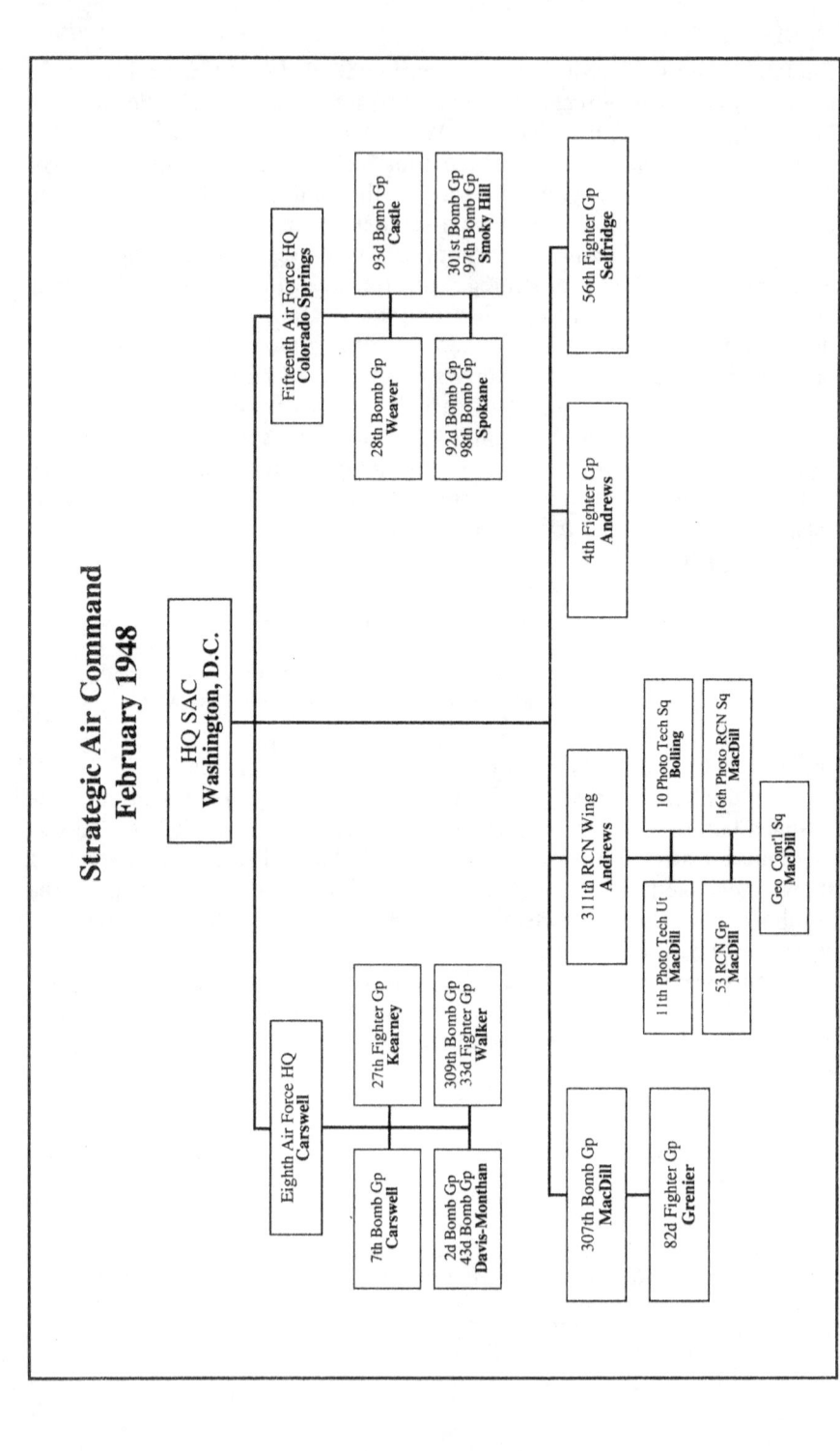

cutting back to forty-eight groups before the end of June, Congress was considering the 1950 budget and the joint chiefs were turning to the plans for fiscal 1951. In the congressional debate on fiscal 1950, the greatest controversy involved the size of the Air Force. In April 1949, citing the need for an atomic striking force that could deter Soviet aggression, the House added nearly $800 million to the defense budget, earmarked for more air groups.[36] Should an increase be approved, the Air Staff intended to build four new groups of long range bombers. This would especially strengthen the second phase of the offensive, a sustained effort "policing" targets previously hit. However, the additional money would also fund three new fighter groups and one each of light bombers and troop carrier aircraft. These would largely augment the air defense and tactical forces. In fact, the number of groups approved at "Dualism" and the McNarney-Fairchild Boards had already ensured that the strategic striking force would be strong. With any extra money, the Air Force would try to repair the damage resulting from the stripping of the other forces. Despite these positive signs, however, the defense establishment entered fiscal year 1950 dependent on continuing resolutions to pay its bills, while the Senate debated the regular budget.[37]

When Eisenhower began his work with the joint chiefs on fiscal 1950, he understood that the budget ceiling would again be in the neighborhood of $15 billion. He told Forrestal that the top priorities for defense centered on a strategic air force, a Navy to fight submarines, and an Army to mobilize for defensive operations. Eisenhower recognized that the biggest disagreement lay between the Navy and the Air Force. Meeting with naval leaders, he concluded that they were emphasizing air power as their contribution in a future war. The argument that Sherman had earlier advanced, that carrier aviation should be used to attack submarine yards, was apparently getting short shrift in the Navy. The sailors contended that the long range bomber was too vulnerable; only carrier-based planes could reach defended targets. Eisenhower believed that if Air Force bombers could not get through, neither could Navy planes. To resolve this disagree-

---

[36] Warner R. Schilling, "The Politics of National Defense: Fiscal 1950," in Warner R. Schilling, Paul Y. Hammond, & Glenn H. Snyder, *Strategy, Politics, and Defense Budgets* (NY: Columbia Univ Press, 1962), pp 71–79.
[37] Memo, Maj Gen S. E. Anderson, Dir P & O, to Gen H. S. Vandenberg, CSAF, subj: Composition of the 9 Groups Which May Be Added to a 48-Group Air Force, Feb 4, 1949, RG 341, DCS/Ops, Dir/Pl, OPD, 320.2 (Dec 31, 1948), Box 126, MMB, NA; Rearden, *Formative Years*, pp 354–356.

Strategic Air Force

ment, he favored an objective evaluation of the bomber's ability to penetrate.[38]

As the cost-conscious Louis Johnson assumed direction of the defense program, Eisenhower recognized that pressure on the budget would not abate. He needed to get the military chiefs to agree on plans for fiscal 1951. He devised what he called the "red brick" plan, under which each service defined the minimum size for each of the other two. Any addition to the minimum for each service would then be open to debate. The Air Force asked for seventy-one groups and proposed that the Navy retain no large carriers, only escort carriers for anti-submarine work. The Navy, in turn, recommended limiting the Air Force to forty-eight groups and requested ten large carriers in commission. While skeptical of the Navy's demands, Eisenhower believed that at least one carrier task force would be needed at the onset of a war.[39] The chiefs were starting to work toward agreement when Eisenhower learned to his frustration that the President had lowered the ceiling by nearly $2 billion, to $13 billion. The Bureau of the Budget, fearing inflationary pressures, was insisting on rigorous economies in government spending.[40]

Given the new fiscal reality, by July 1949, Eisenhower could submit a budget plan proposal calling for forty-eight groups in the Air Force and four large carriers.[41] Vandenberg had been reluctant to concur. In May he wrote Eisenhower that:

> ...it has become apparent to me that an increase in the retaliatory striking power of the Air Force and an increase in the mobile striking power of the Army are needed. It has become equally apparent to me that in Fiscal Year 1950 [sic] there will be maintained in the Navy forces which are not essential to the maintenance of an acceptable degree of national security.[42]

Although the Air Force failed in its attempt to eliminate large carriers from the active fleet, the new secretary did decide to cancel construction of the Navy's first new flushdeck supercarrier. Work was scheduled to

---

[38] Rearden, *Formative Years*, pp 364–366; Dwight D. Eisenhower, *The Eisenhower Diaries*, ed Robert H. Ferrell (NY: Norton, 1981), Dec 13, 1948, p 150, Jan 8, 1949, pp 152–153, Jan 27, 1949, pp 154–156, Feb 4, 1949, pp 156–157; Palmer, *Origins of Maritime Strategy*, pp 22–29, 46–52.

[39] Rearden, *Formative Years*, pp 365–372; K. Condit, *JCS, 1947–1949*, pp 262–264.

[40] Eisenhower, *Eisenhower Diaries*, Feb 9, 1949, p 157, Jun 4, 1949, p 159.

[41] Rearden, *Formative Years*, pp 378–379.

[42] Ltr, Gen H. S. Vandenberg, CSAF, to Gen Army D. D. Eisenhower, May 23, 1949, Vandenberg Coll, Files 1947–1948, Box 32, MD, LC.

Challenges to Strategy

begin in April 1949, and Johnson asked Eisenhower and the chiefs whether it should proceed. Everyone except Denfeld opposed the carrier.[43] Vandenberg restated his position that no requirement existed for the carrier in strategic operations, nor could it serve any real function against a negligible Soviet surface navy.

> The Military Establishment does not possess the resources, nor is there a need, to prepare military forces for all possible types of wars against all possible types of enemies. We have only one potential enemy and we know his military characteristics.[44]

On April 23, without further consultation with the Navy, Johnson cancelled the supercarrier. Secretary of the Navy John L. Sullivan issued a strong protest, and angry naval officers sought ways to attack the B-36 program.[45]

Others also challenged the Air Force's reliance on the strategic air force. In April 1949 Frank Pace, Jr., Director of the Bureau of the Budget, warned the President of the implications of plans for the atomic offensive. In essence he feared that the President's options would be limited if war plans committed him to use atomic weapons at the start of a war.[46] Undeterred, Truman declared publicly in a speech on April 6 his willingness to employ atomic weapons if necessary.[47]

The President did indeed appear to be concerned primarily with the effectiveness of the atomic strategy. Recalling the wartime charge that a band of "battleship admirals" had impeded the Navy in adapting to the conditions of modern war, he worried that the Air Force was fixated on bombers, with the same potential result. Brig. Gen. Robert B. Landry, Truman's air aide, arranged to have the SAC staff send a representative to brief the President on the war plan. Landry further explained to his chief that the Air Force's rationale for supporting the B-36 was based on a clearly defined mission. In a future conflict, the three primary tasks of the armed forces would be the defense of the United States, the destruction of the enemy's industrial capacity, and the occupation of bases for the

---

[43] Rearden, *Formative Years*, pp 410-413.
[44] Memo, Gen H. S. Vandenberg, CSAF, to Sec Def, subj: CVA-58 Project, Apr 23, 1949, Vandenberg Coll, Navy vs Air Force, Box 52, MD, LC.
[45] Rearden, *Formative Years*, pp 412-413.
[46] Memo, Frank Pace, Jr, Dir Bureau of the Budget, to President, Apr 5, 1949, PSF, NSC-Atomic, AE Budget, Box 200, HSTL.
[47] Remarks to a Group of New Democratic Senators and Representatives, Apr 6, 1949, *Public Papers of the Presidents of the United States: Harry S. Truman, 1949*, p 200.

eventual counter-offensive. The Air Force was responsible for the first two tasks, while all three services would implement the third. Landry advised Truman that the Peacemaker represented the best weapon then available for the second function. Either a better bomber or guided missiles would be the next developmental step for the strategic mission.[48] On April 20, at the air aide's request, a SAC representative briefed Truman. Following this, the President asked Johnson what had been done to determine if the air offensive would succeed. Meanwhile, Landry made sure that Truman was aware of the controversy between the services. But even though he still had doubts, on May 4, 1949, the President approved the additional B–36 orders recommended by the McNarney-Fairchild Boards.[49]

With the cancellation of the supercarrier by Secretary of Defense and the President's approval of the B–36 order, a symbolic as well as substantive decision had been made to rely on the strategic air offensive. However, Truman did foster continued debate among the services by encouraging further study. Unfortunately, the discussions were becoming more rancorous. The previous January Eisenhower had written in his diary: "God help us if ever we go before a congressional committee to argue our professional fights as each service struggles to get the lion's share of the money."[50] By May 1949 that very prospect was coming closer to reality.

Facing the Challenge

The challenge to the Air Force's priority mission ultimately came down to a question of national strategy. The joint chiefs had approved a war plan in which the strategic air offensive was the central feature. They had likewise sanctioned the development of an atomic strike force to carry out that offensive. If opponents questioned the Air Force's strategic role, that challenge went to the very rationale of the JCS decisions. If critics contended the Air Force could not provide enough resources for any other functions, such as tactical support of ground forces, the reply in essence admitted that this was true, given the budget limitations on all the services. The 1949 congressional hearings on the B–36 bomber and the debate

---

[48] Memo, Brig Gen R. B. Landry, AF ADC, to President, Apr 16, 1949, Symington Coll, Corres File 1946–1950, L-general, Box 7; Cross-ref sheet, memo, Landry to President, Apr 19, 1949, CF 1285–D, 1949, Box 1638, both in HSTL.
[49] Rearden, *Formative Years*, pp 406–407.
[50] Eisenhower, *Eisenhower Diaries*, Jan 8, 1949, p 152.

Secretary of Defense James V. Forrestal with the Joint Chiefs of Staff and their advisers outside the Naval War College at the Newport Conference in Rhode Island, August 1948. *Left to right:* Gen. Lauris Norstad, USAF; Gen. Hoyt S. Vandenberg, USAF; Lt. Gen. Albert C. Wedemeyer, USA; Gen. Omar N. Bradley, USA; Forrestal; Adm. Louis E. Denfeld, USN; Vice Adm. Arthur W. Radford, USN; and Maj. Gen. Alfred M. Gruenther, USA.

within the JCS on a tactical mission for the strategic force illustrated two distinct national defense issues.

The public dispute between the Navy and the Air Force over the B-36 is an oft-told tale.[51] Indeed, the controversy was a dramatic event, although it focused on decisions that had already been made. At center stage, the Air Force found itself forced to defend its hard-won position in the nation's strategy.

In the aftermath of Johnson's order in April 1949 canceling the Navy's supercarrier, the press portrayed the defense debate as a contest in which the Air Force had beaten the Navy. Now the Navy was prepared to retaliate.[52] Late in 1948, the Deputy Chief of Naval Operations for

---

[51] See especially Paul Y. Hammond, "Super Carriers and B-36 Bombers: Appropriations Strategy, and Politics," in Harold Stein, ed, *American Civil-Military Decisions: A Book of Case Studies* (Tuscaloosa, Ala: Univ of Ala Press, 1963), pp 465-568; George M. Watson Jr., The Office of the Secretary of the Air Force, 1947-1965 (Washington: CAFH, 1993), pp 83-101; Murray Green, "Stuart Symington and the B-36," (Ph.D. Dissertation: American Univ, 1960); K. Condit, *JCS, 1947-1949*, pp 330-351; Rearden, *Formative Years*, pp 412-422; Futrell, *Ideas*, pp 129-134.

[52] G. Watson, *Secretaries*, pp 83-101; Rearden, *Formative Years*, pp 412-413.

Administration had approved the creation of a research and policy office called "Op–23." In charge of the office was Capt. Arleigh A. Burke, who took on the job of building the Navy's case for the supercarrier and against the B–36. Others within the Navy Department acted on their own, with more initiative than discretion, to argue the service's case. One unofficial advocate was Cedric R. Worth, a former Hollywood scriptwriter with war service in the Navy and now an assistant to Undersecretary of the Navy Dan A. Kimball. Worth privately assembled a document detailing various rumors of corruption in the B–36 program. Glenn L. Martin, whose XB–48 and XB–51 bombers had not been accepted by the Air Force for production, circulated this paper without attribution.[53]

The contents of the "anonymous document" became public knowledge on May 26, 1949, when James E. Van Zandt, a Republican Congressman from Pennsylvania with wartime naval service, delivered a speech on the House floor. According to the rumors, Symington, Secretary of Defense Johnson, and Floyd B. Odlum, Chairman of the Board of Convair, had pressured Air Force leaders to order more B–36s in spite of the bomber's known deficiencies. Van Zandt called for a congressional investigation. Symington immediately denied the charges and also asked for an investigation. In June, Congressman Carl Vinson of Georgia, Chairman of the House Armed Services Committee, agreed to the hearings, which he scheduled for August. During the summer, the press learned of the existence of the "anonymous document," as the source of Van Zandt's allegations. Symington invited Col. W. Barton Leach, a law professor at Harvard and an Air Force reservist, to organize the Air Force's defense in the hearings and assigned the Air Force's Director of Special Investigations, Brig. Gen. Joseph F. Carroll, to inquire into the origins of the document. Leach proceeded to construct a carefully researched historical account of the B–36 program. Meanwhile Carroll's investigators traced the path to Cedric Worth.[54]

When the hearings began on August 9, Vinson declared the purpose of the first part of the investigation to be an assessment of the charges against the Air Force. Only later would the committee discuss the question of strategy. Nevertheless, the Air Force's defense was that the decision to

---

[53] Rearden, *Formative Years*, pp 412–414; study, ARDC, *Air Force Developmental Aircraft*, 1957, pp 135–138, AFCHO. Burke had commanded a destroyer squadron in the Pacific with great distinction. His nickname, "thirty-one knot" Burke, referred to a sardonic message of his referring to the effect of maintenance problems on the squadron's operational capability.

[54] Rearden, *Formative Years*, pp 413–414; Symington OHI, pp 33–36; Hammond, "Super Carriers," pp 498–500, 505–506; G. Watson, *Secretaries*, pp 83–101.

order more B-36s had been based on technical and strategic grounds, not in response to pressure motivated by greed. Maj. Gen. Frederic Smith presented the documentary evidence.[55] But perhaps one of the most effective witnesses was LeMay. Preceding testimony served to foreshadow his appearance by emphasizing his qualifications as an authority on strategic operations. Vandenberg, for example, noted that:

> General LeMay has participated in more strategic bombing in time of war than any other man in the world. He knows more about it. He constantly keeps in touch with the latest developments both here and abroad.[56]

Fairchild, McNarney, and others reinforced this by testifying to the importance they had attached to LeMay's recommendations.[57] Thus, when LeMay himself took the stand, his observations on the B-36 carried considerable weight with the committee:[58] "I expect that if I am called upon to fight I will order my crews out in those airplanes, and I expect to be in the first one myself." Van Zandt and other critics cross-examined him thoroughly, but LeMay never wavered and continued to argue that the B-36 was the only plane that could perform the intercontinental mission.[59]

As noted earlier, the Air Force's case required a discussion of strategy, and Vandenberg's testimony provided this. But larger questions of policy and strategy were soon overshadowed by the climactic testimony of Cedric Worth. The revelation that Worth was the culprit behind the "anonymous document" essentially brought the hearings to an end. The attack on the Air Force had backfired on the Navy, forcing the creation of a court of inquiry to examine Worth's behavior. Vinson and his committee concluded that the charges of corruption were unfounded.[60]

If knavery could not be proved in the purchase of the B-36, it would be necessary to demonstrate folly. The rationale for producing the Peacemaker would be the issue when the hearings reconvened in October 1949. By then, the news of the Soviet atomic explosion had captured public attention, making any debate over strategy better press than might have been expected.

---

[55] Hearings before the Committee on Armed Services, House, *Investigation of the B-36 Bomber Program*, 81st Cong, 1st sess, Aug, Oct 49, pp 42–90.
[56] Ibid., p 177.
[57] Ibid., pp 402–441.
[58] Ibid., p 148.
[59] Ibid., pp 139–163.
[60] Ibid., pp 165–173, 524ff; Rearden, *Formative Years*, pp 414–415.

Adding to the excitement was the "Revolt of the Admirals." In fact, the "revolt" was started by a captain, a flier named John G. Crommelin who told the press that there was a move in the works to eliminate the Navy. The Secretary of the Navy, Francis P. Matthews, (who had succeeded Sullivan on the latter's resignation), told the congressional hearing that the service's morale was good, only to be followed by a succession of naval leaders, led by Adm. Arthur W. Radford, Commander in Chief, Pacific, who contradicted the secretary.[61] Besides embarrassing Matthews, this immediately created a forum for any uniformed Navy witness to express his dissatisfaction with defense decisions. As for the question of strategy, Radford maintained that the heavy bomber's "day is largely past." The Navy witnesses dismissed the theory of the "atomic blitz" as a false promise of a cheap and easy victory. The B-36 could not bomb accurately from high altitudes, could not survive without escort, and would produce mass slaughter of civilians with no significant strategic result. Meanwhile, the naval leadership contended, the money poured into the B-36 could have been spent for the tactical aviation so vitally needed for the defense of western Europe.[62] Rear Adm. Ralph A. Ofstie, who had tangled with Orvil Anderson on the Strategic Bombing Survey, testified as the Navy member of the Military Liaison Committee to the AEC. He forcefully challenged the very concept of strategic air warfare: "Must the Italian Douhet continue as our prophet because certain zealots grasped his doctrine many years ago and refuse to relinquish this discredited theory in the face of vast, costly experience?"[63] This thrust at a straw man, suggesting the intemperate tone of much of the Navy's argument, detracted from the positive case the Navy sought to make for its own role. The service's credibility was further weakened by its failure to use a statement submitted by Admiral Sherman, serving in the Mediterranean, which outlined the role of a balanced Navy in a unified strategy. As for the Air Force, Sherman wrote:

> We need long range air force elements ready for action in forward positions such as the bomber groups now in England, and if the B-36 is not a good bomber the Air Force should get a better one.

---

[61] Rearden, *Formative Years*, pp 415–416. Successor to Sullivan after the latter's resignation, Matthews had little standing in the serving Navy, where the allegation that he had never been in anything larger than a rowboat led to his nickname, "Rowboat" Matthews.

[62] Hearings before the Committee on Armed Services, House, *The National Defense Program—Unification and Strategy*, 81st Cong, 1st sess, Oct 49, pp 45, 39–132.

[63] *Ibid.*, pp 189–193; MacIsaac, *Strategic Bombing*, pp 119–135.

Challenges to Strategy

The need for maintaining a Navy does not depend on the merits or defects of any particular bomber.[64]

Sherman's statement was out of step with the position of many of the Navy witnesses, and moderation lost out.

As in August, it fell to Vandenberg to outline the Air Force's larger views on national defense. The Air Force Chief of Staff denied that the strategic air offensive was intended to win the war by itself, or that victory would be cheap and easy. What the Air Force did believe, he argued, was that there could be only one possible enemy in a future war: the Soviet Union. Only long range bombers could strike at its industrial heartland, especially if the United States lost its oversea bases. Vandenberg assured the congressional committee that the Air Force was acting vigorously to make the B-36 effective. He also pointed out that the strategic air offensive was part of a plan approved by the Joint Chiefs of Staff, and SAC was under the direction of the joint chiefs. While denying that the Air Force was neglecting tactical air and air defense, Vandenberg maintained that cutting the strategic force would condemn the allies to a grueling, costly, and far more uncertain effort against huge ground and air forces in Europe.[65]

Vandenberg found considerable support from outside the uniformed Air Force. Secretary Symington gave him forceful support, especially by introducing a letter from General Harmon denying charges that he had been pressured to make his report more favorable to air power.[66] But the most eloquent voices in favor of the Air Force were those of Eisenhower, Bradley, and Marshall. All reiterated the point that the air offensive was a legitimate part of a JCS-approved war plan. Bradley, as Chairman of the Joint Chiefs of Staff, added his own remarks attacking the Navy as poor losers who resisted true unification of the services.[67]

Much of the press described the hearings as a victory for the Air Force, and apparently many naval officers agreed. In the aftermath, Admiral Denfeld was relieved as Chief of Naval Operations, and Burke (a future Chief of Naval Operations) was briefly removed from the promotion list. Some congressmen objected to these actions as "reprisals" against Navy witnesses, but no change in policy resulted. In approving the final report on the hearings, and in increasing the defense appropriation in the

---

[64] Palmer, *Origins of Maritime Strategy*, p 52.
[65] Hearings before the Committee on Armed Services, House, *The National Defense Program—Unification and Strategy*, 81st Cong, 1st sess, Oct 49, pp 451–515.
[66] *Ibid.*, pp 401, 404, 397–451.
[67] *Ibid.*, pp 562–567, 597–606, 515–543.

fiscal 1950 budget passed that October, the members of Congress demonstrated their continued confidence in the leadership of the Air Force.[68]

Critics of the B-36 often saw the intercontinenal bomber as a symbol of the strategic air offensive, against which in reality many of the attacks were directed. Objections to the Peacemaker were in essence attempts to criticize the plans for the offensive at different levels. The B-36 represented a wrong concept of war, or it was designed for an impossible task, or it could not do what it was designed to do. Implicit in the first argument was the belief that strategic bombing, and by implication, atomic war, was immoral and should not be undertaken. Any money committed to it ought to be assigned to other types of forces. Given the weakness of the West's defenses against Soviet land power in Europe, this view had few adherents in the Defense Department or even in Congress. In the pages of *The Air University Quarterly Review*, the moral question was generally seen in terms of necessity: a war with the Soviet Union would jeopardize the survival of the free nations, and only strategic bombing offered any chance of turning the tide. Also, the threat of atomic attack constituted a deterrent that could prevent war altogether.[69]

Critics claiming that strategic bombing simply could not accomplish its purpose found themselves on increasingly weak ground. The Harmon Committee, despite its reservations, maintained that the air offensive could inflict real damage. Though not charged to consider the effectiveness of strategic bombing, the Weapons Systems Evaluation Group did conclude that the advertised number of bombs could be delivered on target. The WSEG report, briefed to President Truman on January 23, 1950, did raise questions of the third category: whether the existing force, including the B-36, could carry out the strategic air offensive. On this topic, however, all the observations agreed with the views of LeMay and other airmen. The parts shortages and mechanical problems plaguing the B-36 were facts of life, of which SAC was all too aware. The WSEG report merely noted the small number of serviceable heavy bombers. Though its capabilities were well short of the miraculous, the B-36 would be able to strike assigned targets. In a broader context, the WSEG cataloged the inadequate bases and fuel stocks overseas, weaknesses in airlift support for the war plan, and related logistical problems. The group also expressed apprehension about air attacks on overseas bases and cited uncertainties about the strength of Soviet air defense, raising the spectre of heavy losses

---

[68] Rearden, *Formative Years*, pp 415–422, 351–360.
[69] Maj Gen Orvil A. Anderson, "Air Warfare and Immorality," *AUQR* III (Winter 49), pp 5–14; Chap John W. Wood, "The Morality of War," *AUQR* IV (Summer 50), pp 31–42.

Challenges to Strategy

Lt. Gen. Hubert H. Harmon, whose committee appointed by the Weapons Systems Evaluation Group conducted an in-depth analysis of the probable effects of an atomic offensive on the Soviet Union's war-supporting industries.

in the attacking force. While analysts believed Soviet night fighters to be primitive and few in number and considered antiaircraft artillery to be ineffective against high-altitude bombers, none of these claims were entirely certain. Further, an attack in summer could not avoid some daytime exposure to Soviet fighters, and the B-36s, which could fly above fighter cover, were not yet available in large numbers. Much of the enemy's defense might be susceptible to electronic jamming, but SAC's electronics countermeasures capability remained underdeveloped. In short, the WSEG report concluded that, if the logistical problems were corrected, SAC could deliver the required number of weapons, though possibly with heavy losses.[70]

Again, Air Force planning had generally acknowledged the risks inherent in the strategic air offensive. A year earlier, LeMay had gone on record with the Senior Officers' Board as believing that fourteen bombardment groups were insufficient.[71] In view of the priority the nation gave to SAC's mission, the answer to criticism seemed to lie in building the force up to the level required to do the job.

In FLEETWOOD and TROJAN, the first joint plans of the Cold War era, it was assumed that periodic updates would occur. The scope of the

---

[70] A valuable account of the WSEG report is in Rearden, *Formative Years*, pp 407-410. See also Ponturo, *Analytical Support*, pp 52-55, 74. An "advance copy" of the summary report is attached to Memo, Lt Gen J. E. Hull, USA, Dir WSEG, to JCS, Jan 21, 1950, in OSD Historical Office. The ten-volume full report is in RG 330, WSEG Spec File, MMB, NA.

[71] See Chapter VII.

307

Strategic Air Force

revisions, however, went beyond expectations, because budget cuts required major changes in the forces available. Updating the plans also gave services the chance to revive earlier controversies and to introduce new ones. This was especially the case with OFFTACKLE, the draft plan under discussion beginning early in 1949.[72] Besides long-standing Air Force-Navy differences, a new issue arose between the Air Force and the Army concerning the role of bombers in support of ground forces. The Joint Strategic Plans Committee failed to resolve these questions, thus becoming, in the view of Col. John B. Cary, the Air Force member, "a useless organization." Indeed, Cary considered his own behavior symptomatic; the Army and Navy members' efforts to weaken the strategic air offensive compelled him to adopt arguments that he himself described as "extreme."[73]

Through the summer of 1949, major issues in OFFTACKLE remained unsettled, though much of the detail work was finished. In August, when the joint chiefs visited Europe, there was still no agreed proposal. The next month Secretary Johnson settled a number of questions about the plan, but not all.[74] The B-36 congressional hearing, which absorbed much staff effort, doubtless caused further delays.

In May, Eisenhower had decided against a major commitment to hold the Eastern Mediterranean, but the Navy continued to argue in favor of the Cairo-Suez base area. SAC now was planning to use the bases there only for recovery of bombers after their strikes. Cary expected the Navy to oppose any plan that did not call for launching strategic missions from Egypt. It was, in fact, somewhat of a surprise to Cary later in the year when the Navy gave in on this point. So in October 1949, when the British Chiefs of Staff visited Washington, their American counterparts could tell them not to expect help in trying to hold the Eastern Mediterranean-Middle East region.[75]

---

[72] K. Condit, *JCS, 1947-1949*, p 295.

[73] Memo, Col J. B. Cary, AF Mem JSPC, to Maj Gen S. E. Anderson, Dir P & O, May 13, 1949; memo, Cary to Brig Gen J. Smith, Ch WPD, DCS/Ops, subj: Plan OFF TACKLE [*sic*], Jun 2, 1949, both in RG 341, DCS/Ops, OPD, Spec File HALFMOON, Sect 9, Box 1047, MMB, NA.

[74] K. Condit, *JCS, 1947-1949*, pp 297, 388-389.

[75] MR, Col J. B. Cary, AF Mem JSPC, JSPC Appearance Before the JCS and Subsequent JSPC Meeting of May 13, 1949, May 16, 1949; memo, Cary to Maj Gen S. E. Anderson, Dir P & O, subj: Progress on Plan OFFTACKLE, Jun 7, 1949, both in RG 341, DCS/Ops, OPD, Spec File HALFMOON, Sect 9, Box 1047; memo, Anderson to Gen H. S. Vandenberg, CSAF, subj: Joint Outline Emergency War Plan OFFTACKLE (JCS 1844/46), Nov 29, 1949, RG 341, DCS/Ops, OPD, Spec File SREP, Sect 14, Box 1056, all in MMB, NA.

Challenges to Strategy

The North Atlantic Pact contributed to reviving a historic dispute between the Air Force and the Army, namely, the issue of strategic bombers in a tactical role. Before the signing of the treaty in April 1949, U.S. planners had anticipated the problem of defending Western Europe. In the European Command (then an Army organization), existing plans called for withdrawal to England in the event of a full-scale Soviet attack. Eisenhower noted the shift when he advocated holding the line at the Rhine in OFFTACKLE. Given the weakness of allied forces in Europe, this appeared to be a monumental task, and many doubted it could be done at all. In any case, a defending ground force would need massive support from air power. Realizing the weaknesses of tactical air power throughout the alliance, Army planners examined SAC and its atomic capability. Atomic weapons seemed especially useful for deep interdiction strikes at the Soviet lines of communication. These operations would retard the advance of the aggressor's armies. The Air Force naturally feared the diversion of scarce bombers and weapons from the strategic air offensive. Thus, each service had views on "retardation."[76]

In previous years, the Air Staff's Plans Division had considered the possibility of using conventionally armed B-29s against the rear areas of a Soviet advance. The concept bore the name OPERATION STRANGLE—evocative of the major effort at air interdiction in Italy in 1944.[77] A similar plan, using atomic weapons, was outlined at a meeting of the Joint Strategic Plans Committee on May 12 and 13, 1949. On the 13th, the committee briefed the joint chiefs, and a discussion followed on the use of strategic bombers "in retarding the Russian advance into Western Eurasia." The services concurred on this wording, and Eisenhower consented to have it included as an element of OFFTACKLE.[78]

At this point, the services actually seemed to be in agreement. The Air Force was preparing to meet the new commitment in its own planning and in its own way. Vandenberg had the task of providing the joint chiefs with the detailed plan for the strategic air offensive.[79] On August 31 he submitted an Air Staff proposal, which envisioned "maximum exploitation of the power of the atomic bomb, at the earliest practicable date." Already

---

[76] MR, Lt Col J. J. Kruzel, Red Tm WPD, DCS/Ops, Jan 24, 1950, RG 341, DCS/Ops, OPD, Spec File SREP Impl Dir, Sect 3, Box 1052, MMB, NA.

[77] Memo, Col C. B. Dougher, Actg Ch AWPD, DCS/Ops, to Maj Gen S. E. Anderson, Dir P & O, subj: Operation STRANGLE, Jun 13, 1949, RG 341, DCS/Ops, OPD, Spec File SAO, Sect 1, Box 1057, MMB, NA.

[78] MR, Col J. B. Cary, AF Mem JSPC, JSPC Appearance Before the JCS and Subsequent JSPC Meeting of May 13, 1949, May 16, 1949, RG 341, DCS/Ops, OPD, Spec File HALFMOON, Sect 9, Box 1047, MMB, NA.

[79] K. Condit, *JCS, 1947-1949*, p 299.

this was growing more feasible, as the atomic force continued to expand. The objectives of the strategic air offensive were defined as "the destruction of the vital elements of the enemy war-making capacity and the retardation of enemy advances in western Eurasia." Industrial targets had the first priority, followed by other traditional target categories such as oil and electric power. The planners intended to achieve retardation by striking at the transportation net, arms factories, and the oil industry. In all, the plan required 292 atomic bombs, allocated to specific targets within groupings.[80]

Following study by the Joint Staff agencies, the joint chiefs approved the plan in December 1949. On the 8th, they ratified the overall plan OFFTACKLE as well. In doing so, the chiefs reaffirmed the strategic air offensive as the sole offensive operation the U.S. could undertake at the beginning of a war. The joint chiefs had also authorized expanding the scope of the offensive by directing that strategic air power was intended not merely to be "sent against" the enemy's war economy. Now the bombers were to "destroy" it.[81]

The Air Force leaders had apparently accepted retardation as one of the objectives. Cary, for one, had reservations about another service simply assuming that the Air Force could take on an additional task. The previous June, he had warned that should war come, ground and naval forces would be left idle because no air forces existed to support them. He saw danger in the Army and Navy being encouraged to accept this premise:

> Any acceptance by the Air Force of...falsely optimistic estimates as to Air Force capabilities would be most prejudicial to the Air Force and to the United States, immediately during budgetary proceedings, and in the long run through the acceptance of the fact that woefully inadequate air power will be able to insure the national security.[82]

In spite of the wording of the joint plan, Army officials had reason to doubt the Air Force's true commitment to retardation. This skepticism emerged when SAC, after a prolonged exchange with the Air Staff, submitted its Emergency War Plan to the JCS for review. (This was a

---

[80] Rprt, CSAF to JCS 2056, Target System for Implementation of Joint Emergency War Plan (short title OFFTACKLE), Aug 31, 1949, RG 341, DCS/Ops, OPD, Spec File SAO, Sect 1, Box 1057, MMB, NA.

[81] K. Condit, *JCS, 1947–1949*, pp 297, 300n.

[82] Memo, Col J. B. Cary, AF Mem JSPC, to Maj Gen S. E. Anderson, Dir P & O, subj: Relationship of Plan OFFTACKLE to Budgetary Procedures, Jun 8, 1949, RG 341, DCS/Ops, OPD, Spec File HALFMOON, Sect 9, Box 1047, MMB, NA.

requirement for SAC as a specified command).[83] In December 1949, when the Joint Strategic Planning Group discussed the SAC plan, Col. C.V.R. Schuyler, the Army member, wanted to write in a strong commitment to retardation, along with procedures for close coordination in an emergency with the Commander in Chief, Europe.[84] Another Army staff officer objected to SAC's stated intention of being able to deliver all atomic weapons in a single strike. As the stockpile grew, this obviously would require a larger force and thus mandated continuing expansion of the Air Force.[85] By the end of the year, the Air Force agreed to compromise wording that insured that SAC operations would be coordinated with the theater commanders to accomplish retardation. The joint chiefs then approved SAC's plan on January 18, 1950. Power, LeMay's deputy, had in the meantime defended the single-strike concept, declaring that it might not always be feasible, but that SAC needed to plan around the idea.[86]

Despite the overt assurances, the Army still had doubts. In March 1950, Schuyler warned: "I do not concur in the exclusive commitment of the Strategic Air Command to a large scale bombardment of Soviet industry during the initial stages of hostilities when ominous events will be taking place in Western Europe."[87] While the Army staff withdrew its proposal to assign some SAC units to theater commanders, it did not

---

[83] Ltr, Col J. B. Cary, AF Mem JSPC, to Brig Gen W. C. Sweeney, Jr, Dir Pl SAC, May 25, 1949, RG 341, DCS/Ops, OPD, 381 SAC (Mar 23, 1949), Box 1027, MMB, NA.

[84] Memo, Col G. F. McGuire, Ch Ops Div, DCS/Ops, subj: Strategic Air Command Emergency War Plan 1–49 (JSPC 934/3), Dec 21, 1949; memo, Brig Gen C. Van R. Schuyler, Army Mem JSPC, to Maj Gen R. C. Lindsay, AF Mem JSPC, et al, subj: Strategic Air Command Emergency War Plan 1–49 (JSPC 934/3), Dec 21, 1949, both in RG 341, DCS/Ops, OPD, 381 SAC (Mar 23, 1949), Box 1027, MMB, NA.

[85] Ltr, Maj Gen R. E. Duff, Actg Dir P & O, Army, to CSAF (AFOOP), subj: Strategic Air Command Emergency War Plan 1–49, Sep 12, 1949, RG 341, DCS/Ops, OPD, 381 SAC (Mar 23, 1949), Sect 1, Box 1027, MMB, NA.

[86] Memo, Capt W. G. Lalor, USN, Sec JCS, to Gen O. N. Bradley, Chmn JCS, Gen H. S. Vandenberg, CSAF, et al, subj: Strategic Air Command Emergency War Plan 1–49, Dec 30, 1949, with atch rprt, JCS 2057/3, same subj, Dec 29, 1949; memo, Lalor to CSAF, subj: Strategic Air Command Emergency War Plan 1–49, Jan 18, 1950, both in RG 341, DCS/Ops, OPD, 381 SAC (Mar 23, 1949), Box 1027; ltr, Maj Gen T. S. Power, Dep CG SAC, to CSAF, subj: Revision of the Strategic Air Command Emergency War Plan 1–49, Apr 1, 1950, RG 341, DCS/Ops, OPD, 381 SAC (Mar 23, 1949), Sect 2, Box 1028, all in MMB, NA.

[87] Memo, Brig Gen C. Van R. Schuyler, Army Mem JSPC, to JSPC, subj: Employment of Units of the Strategic Air Command in Support of CINCEUR and CINCFE, Mar 8, 1950, RG 341, DCS/Ops, OPD, Spec File SAO, Sect 1, Box 1057, MMB, NA.

concede the principle of direct Air Force support of the land battle. For his part, LeMay argued that in a plan for implementing the strategic air offensive, support of theater forces was out of place, no matter how legitimate the goal.[88]

The Air Force's Emergency War Plan in June 1950 put OFFTACKLE into effect. Clearly, the strategic air offensive remained the service's first priority. The plan assumed that the European continent would be overrun and that SAC would function as NATO's strategic air force, in keeping with OFFTACKLE. The command's mission remained the bombing offensive and long range reconnaissance. The authors of the plan expected heavy losses, especially if the attack had to be launched in summer, when the hours of darkness were short. By the end of the three-month first phase of the war, SAC would have largely expended itself. All other commands were to give "priority to SAC operations." The command would base its selection of targets on the objective of disrupting Soviet industry and political control, undermining the will to fight, and disarming enemy forces. For the retardation mission, the bombers were to hit some arms factories and the petroleum industry. A few weapons would remain in reserve to be used against the Soviet atomic program, as targets were discovered. The reconnaissance forces were to assess bomb damage and look for atomic targets, including factories and airfields. Only after the first three months would SAC be expected to consider such missions as aerial mining or hauling freight.[89]

Although the retardation question had been settled for the time being, the Army's concerns persisted. Doubt surfaced, for example, in some particularly pointed observations from Vannevar Bush, a consultant for the Army then with the Carnegie Institution. In April 1950 Bush wrote Bradley that he was "appalled" at the condition of the nation's defenses. Bush believed that the United States could no longer hope to win a war with atomic weapons alone, if indeed there had ever been a chance of doing so. By this time, of course, the existence of a Soviet atomic arsenal had to be given serious consideration. Given poor allied intelligence concerning strategic targets and the state of Soviet air defenses, he wondered if the Air Force could carry out an offensive and suggested

---

[88] Memo, Col W. S. Steele, Dep AF Mem JSPC, to Maj Gen S. E. Anderson, Dir P & O, subj: Diversion of the Strategic Air Offensive, Apr 20, 1950, RG 341, DCS/Ops, OPD, Spec File SAO, Sect 1, Box 1057, MMB, NA.
[89] AF Emergency War Plan 1–50, Jun 1, 1950, RG 341, DCS/Ops, Dir/Pl, TS OPD, 381 (May 2, 1950), Sect 3, Box 327; Air Intel Div, Suppl to Intel App-USAF SREP Based on OFFTACKLE, "Intelligence Requirements for Reconnaissance," Feb 14, 1950, RG 341, DCS/Ops, Dir/Pl, TS OPD, 381 (May 2, 1950), Sect 1, Box 325, both in MMB, NA.

Challenges to Strategy

greater emphasis on retardation. He considered the tactical air forces needed for the defense of Western Europe desperately weak.[90] He then called for an unbiased assessment of the services:

> This applies to every Service, of course. But it applies particularly to the Air Force, for, in their enthusiasm, which is an indispensable and invaluable asset, I feel that they have been drawn down a single line of reasoning much too long.[91]

For a reply to Bush's letter, Vandenberg turned to the new Assistant Deputy Chief of Staff for Operations, formerly the Air Force member of the Joint Strategic Studies Committee, Maj. Gen. Truman H. Landon. It was Landon who, as a young major on December 7, 1941, had landed a squadron of B–17s in Oahu during the Japanese attack. Landon denied that the Air Force was over-emphasizing strategic bombing. He did agree with Bush's observation that the West lacked a "tactical air force worthy of the name."[92] But, Landon pointed out, the strategic air offensive, though it would not necessarily result in a Soviet collapse, was an essential part of the nation's effort in the event of war. The Air Force therefore had to build up its strategic forces. As for the other commitments, the Air Force had "continually maintained that it cannot meet all its requirements under a 48 group ceiling"—hence the need to put first things, namely strategic and air defense forces, first. The equal three-way split of budgets among the services guaranteed ineffective allocation of strength. For this reason, Landon heartily endorsed Bush's argument that large aircraft carriers had no economically justifiable role. He also agreed that improved anti-tank weapons offered an opportunity for the Army. As for an impartial review of the Air Force's role, Landon felt his service "certainly has nothing to fear from such an inquiry."[93]

The External Challenge: The Soviet Bomb

One of the factors that disturbed observers about the open disputes among the armed services was the fear that their programs might soon be tested by actual war. The temporary anxiety of September 1948 was

---

[90] Ltr, V. Bush to Gen O. N. Bradley, Chmn JCS, Apr 13, 1950, in *FRUS*, 1950, Vol I, pp 227–234.
[91] *Ibid.*, pp 229–230.
[92] *Ibid.*, p 229; memo, Maj Gen T. S. Landon, Asst to DCS/Ops, to Gen H. S. Vandenberg, CSAF, subj: Letter from Dr V. Bush to General Bradley, Jun 13, 1950, Vandenberg Coll, 1. File here Miscellaneous, Box 83, MD, LC.
[93] See previous note.

alleviated for a time by the realization that the Soviets probably did not want a war. This may have reinforced a tendency to put off the day when the United States had to face the significance of possible Soviet nuclear weapons. The sudden revelation that the Soviets possessed atomic weapons upset these assumptions, raising questions as to the nature of deterrence and whether sole reliance on the strategic air force was enough to counter the threat. The Air Force tended toward the view that the best response to Soviet atomic strength lay in the ability to retaliate swiftly. Nonetheless, political pressure to protect the U.S. population through air defense along with concerns for the vulnerability of the strike force itself further complicated Air Force planning.

A futher major source of controversy resulted from Truman's and Secretary of Defense Johnson's continued commitment to cuts in the defense budget. Opponents of these reductions would need a great deal of effort, including a major government study, to begin redirecting policy. Building more and bigger bombs seemed one plausible solution, but only a partial one, as it would make demands on the delivery force. In any case, the growing public sense of danger also raised popular concern about possible communist subversion, producing a politically explosive atmosphere. Under the circumstances, the role of strategic air power would never be far from the center of the debate.

The actual discovery of the Soviet atomic bomb was the product of an Air Force effort. When the service gained responsibility for long-range detection of atomic explosions in September 1947, it began to develop a permanent system, but it also put an interim arrangement into service. In December 1947, Maj. Gen. Albert F. Hegenberger, an aeronautical engineer and pilot, who had flown the first nonstop flight from California to Hawaii in 1927, took charge of the project. His Long Range Detection Division was part of the Air Staff Special Weapons Group, then under the Deputy Chief of Staff for Materiel.[94] Hegenberger found the division already at work preparing to study methods of detection during the atomic tests at Eniwetok. Those tests in April and May 1948 showed that the best method was to mount geiger counters and air filters in an airplane. Radioactive air samples could then be collected for laboratory analysis.[95]

The resulting interim program involved collecting samples from air currents coming out of the Soviet Union. Having established a few ground stations, the Air Weather Service equipped aircraft and flew them on routine weather missions. A contract laboratory analyzed the samples and

---

[94] Little, *Foundations*, Pt I, pp 288–291.
[95] Little, *Foundations*, Pt I, pp 288–302.

The Soviet Threat. In 1949 the Soviet Union detonated its first series atomic bomb, a disarmed version of which is shown, *above*. A product of wartime and postwar atomic espionage as well as indigenous research, this test weapon galvanized the West and altered forever the postwar world. The Mikoyan-Gurevich MiG–15 jet fighter, *below*, designed to shoot down atomic-armed B–29s, blended British engine technology, acquired through ill-considered sales of Nene jet engines, and German-inspired sweptwing design.

Strategic Air Force

notified the Long Range Detection Division of the results. After the first flights, the Air Force opened Shemya Air Force Base in the Aleutians, allowing for better coverage. By the end of 1948, the system was in full operation. Nearly seventy alerts had taken place, all "cancelled as negative."[96]

Hegenberger meanwhile, was directing plans for a permanent system. Unfortunately, disagreements over the project's priority affected his timing. In March 1948, the Joint Nuclear Energy Committee, an interdepartmental group linked to the National Security Council, estimated that the Soviets could develop a bomb as early as the middle of 1950, although 1953 seemed a more likely date. The Air Force then sought funding to have a full permanent detection system operating by the middle of 1950.[97] Although the joint chiefs in general supported the plan, they weakened the emphasis, particularly on the aspects concerning seismic stations. By early 1949, planning was complete, but there had been several delays. Much of the credit for keeping the program alive belonged to Lewis L. Strauss of the Atomic Energy Commission.[98]

On September 3, 1949, a WB-29 passing east of the Kamchatka Peninsula collected a radioactive air sample. Laboratory findings triggered another alert, and the Air Weather Service scheduled more flights to monitor the apparent cloud. This time there was no cancellation. The Long Range Detection Division notified the Atomic Energy Commission, which in turn convened a panel headed by Vannevar Bush and including J. Robert Oppenheimer and other scientists. The group reported on September 19 that the air samples carried products of nuclear fission "consistent with" an atomic explosion in the Soviet Union late in August. That evening the joint chiefs urged President Truman to announce the news to the public. Although Secretary Johnson remained skeptical, virtually all scientific opinion held that the Soviets had exploded an atomic bomb. The President made a public announcement to this effect on September 23.[99]

The initial concern of the administration was to avoid any sign of panic. In an interview quoted in the *Saturday Evening Post*, General Bradley discounted any immediate significance of the Soviet weapon.[100] The question, however, was what to do next. One group concluded that the

---

[96] *Ibid.*, pp 302–309.
[97] *Ibid.*, pp 309–319; K. Condit, *JCS, 1947–1949*, pp 525–529.
[98] See previous note.
[99] Little, *Building an Atomic Air Force*, pp 279–286; Hewlett & Duncan, *Atomic Shield*, pp 362–368.
[100] Futrell, *Ideas*, p 140; draft memo, W. S. Symington, Sec AF, to L. A. Johnson, Sec Def, (Nov 8, 1949), Jan 9, 1950, Symington Papers, Corres File 1946–1950, Johnson, Louis, Box 6, HSTL.

country had anticipated the end of the atomic monopoly, and thus existing programs would suffice. On the other hand, many no doubt agreed with the Chairman of the Atomic Energy Commission, David E. Lilienthal, who believed that the idea that business as usual would suffice ". . . is the bunk."[101] The on-going congressional hearings on the B–36 and national strategy added to the sense of urgency.

Among those hoping to continue on the same course was Louis Johnson. He had become Secretary of Defense convinced of his presidential mandate to cut or at least control defense spending. Johnson had told Congress and the joint chiefs that he expected to achieve an annual rate of savings of a billion dollars by the end of 1949. In August, about the time of the Soviet explosion, he was trimming expenditures for the current fiscal year (1950) although the appropriation bill was still in Congress. He had concurred in the President's ceiling of $13 billion for fiscal 1951. Politically, Johnson would have faced severe problems had he acknowledged that immediate increases were required in the wake of the Soviet bomb.[102]

In fact, after Congress finally approved the 1950 budget in October 1949, Johnson went beyond cutting actual current expenditures. He had already agreed with Truman to impound the extra $736 million that Congress had appropriated for the Air Force. Clearly, Johnson's efforts to reduce military spending sharply had succeeded.[103]

The defense budget for 1951 would continue the trend toward austerity. The President's ceiling of $13 billion had led during the summer of 1949 to a series of revisions directed by Eisenhower, working with the joint chiefs. The original proposal of fifty-seven air groups would have cost $6 billion, nearly half the budget. Eisenhower trimmed the number of groups to fifty and then forty-eight. He managed to keep the strategic forces stable, cutting tactical air units in tandem with reductions in the Army. When Johnson sliced another $200 million off the Air Force total, Eisenhower warned against interfering with strategic air power.[104] It was now August 1949, and Eisenhower was finally able to return to New York, as Bradley took over as the first statutory Chairman of the Joint Chiefs of Staff under the new amendments to the National Security Act. Eisenhower would be heard from again on the subject of defense budgets.

---

[101] Lilienthal, *Journals*, p. 580.
[102] Rearden, *Formative Years*, pp 372–377; hearings before the Committee on Armed Services, House, *The National Defense Program: Unification and Strategy*, 81st Cong, 1st sess, Oct 21, 1949, pp 624–625; memo, L. Johnson, Sec Def, to Sec AF, Nov 16, 1949, with atch, Vandenberg Coll, Sec of National Defense (1), Box 62, MD, LC.
[103] See previous note.
[104] Rearden, *Formative Years*, pp 372–379.

Strategic Air Force

Symington and the Air Staff lodged strong protests against the allocations. The Air Secretary noted the $1.1 billion for procurement of aircraft, and pointing to estimates that the Soviet Air Force would reach a peak strength in 1956, he predicted that a continuation of funding at the proposed level would leave the U.S. Air Force with thirty-four modern groups in that year.[105] (In the event, fiscal 1951 aircraft procurement was set at $1.2 billion). The Air Staff particularly objected to starving the Air Force when the Navy was spending so much money on fleet carriers. The Directorate of Plans and Operations argued that these were not the best ships for anti-submarine warfare and that the war plan had no mission for them at the outset of a war. Such ships, the planners stated, should best be laid up in peacetime.[106] Along similar lines, an officer writing in the *Air University Quarterly Review* at the end of 1949 attacked the prevalent view of "balanced forces." He contended that there was no inherent reason why an increase for the Air Force should require additions to the Army and the Navy.[107]

But in fact there was little chance of overturning Truman's decision even after the news of the Soviet bomb. The budget presented to Congress in January 1950 was close to the presidential ceiling. It provided the Air Force with $4.4 billion for forty-eight groups. The Bureau of the Budget had shifted some funds around to increase the strength of B-36 groups at the expense of reductions in the manning levels of some units, including medium bombers.[108] Congress responded with the usual move to add funds for the Air Force. Meanwhile, pressure was mounting both within the administration and in public debate to increase defense spending. In March Eisenhower, speaking as a private citizen, stated publicly that defense reductions had gone far enough. Truman finally authorized Johnson to mitigate some of the pressure by asking Congress to make some spending adjustments, including an additional $300 million for the Air Force. The adminstration's request went to the House in April 1950, where members voted some increases and sent the entire appropriation to the

---

[105] Memo, W. S. Symington, Sec AF, to L. A. Johnson, Sec Def, Jul 21, 1949, Vandenberg Coll, Budget 1949–1950, Box 41, MD, LC.
[106] ASSS, S. E. Anderson, Dir P & O, to CSAF, Preparation of Fiscal Year 1951 Budget, Aug 10, 1949, Vandenberg Coll, Budget 1949–1950, Box 41, MD, LC.
[107] John J. Daunt, "In My Opinion: The Balance in Our Armed Forces," *AUQR* III (Winter 49), pp 66–69.
[108] Memo, W. J. McNeil, Comptr ASD, to Sec Army, Sec Nav, Sec AF, Jan 18, 1950, with charts, Vandenberg Coll, Budget 1949–1950, Box 41, MD, LC.

Senate, where it was under consideration when the previous fiscal year ended in June.[109]

Austerity in the defense budget thus survived the initial reaction to the detection of the Soviet bomb. But within the Air Force establishment, the sense of urgency continued to build. The service's response to the news gradually emerged from discussions initiated by General Fairchild on September 30, 1949. The principal members of the Air Staff agreed in conference that Vandenberg should be prepared to testify in favor of a fifty-eight group program then being considered in the House for fiscal 1950. (This revision to the budget would have allowed the Air Force to organize ten new groups during the first half of 1950). The service should take the opportunity to request enough funds to carry out the air defense program envisioned for the seventy-group Air Force. Vandenberg, Fairchild, and Maj. Gen. Samuel E. Anderson, Director of Plans and Operations, met to examine the possibility of a major study of air defense needs.[110]

This emphasis on air defense made sense to the extent that it acknowledged public concern about the danger of an atomic attack on the United States. Within the Air Force, however, most thinking followed the doctrinal emphasis on the offensive. It was considered far more effective to destroy enemy bombers at their home bases with a determined attack than to attempt to shoot them down individually as they approached their targets. At the same time, the bomber offensive, by threatening to undermine the enemy's war potential, could deny his hope for victory and thus deter him from attacking in the first place. LeMay not surprisingly recognized the advantages accruing to the side that struck first in an atomic war.[111] But Maj. Gen. Gordon Saville, an expert on air defense, also pointed that it was essential for SAC to be able to attack an enemy's atomic striking force. The problem with the theory was that under the forty-eight group program, the strategic striking force was marginally adequate to the task of hitting the industrial base, without having to contend with the hostile atomic force.[112]

---

[109] Rearden, *Formative Years*, pp 372–382.

[110] MR, Gen M. S. Fairchild, VCSAF, Sep 30, 1949; memo, Fairchild to Gen H. S. Vandenberg, CSAF, Sep 30, 1949; draft memo, Vandenberg, Nov 10, 1949, with marginal notes, all in Fairchild Coll, Sep–Dec 1949, Box 1, MD, LC.

[111] Ltr, Lt Gen C. E. LeMay, CG SAC, to Gen H. S. Vandenberg, CSAF, Dec 12, 1949, RG 341, DCS/Ops, OPD, 600.96 SAC (Feb 10, 1950), Box 1029, MMB, NA.

[112] Futrell, *Ideas*, pp 140–144; draft memo, atch to memo, W. S. Symington, Sec AF, to L. A. Johnson, Sec Def, Mar 21, 1950, Symington Papers, Corres File 1946–1950, Johnson, Louis, Box 6, HSTL; Lt Col Harry M. Pike, "In My Opinion: Limitations of an Air Defense System," *AUQR* III (Fall 49), pp 46–48.

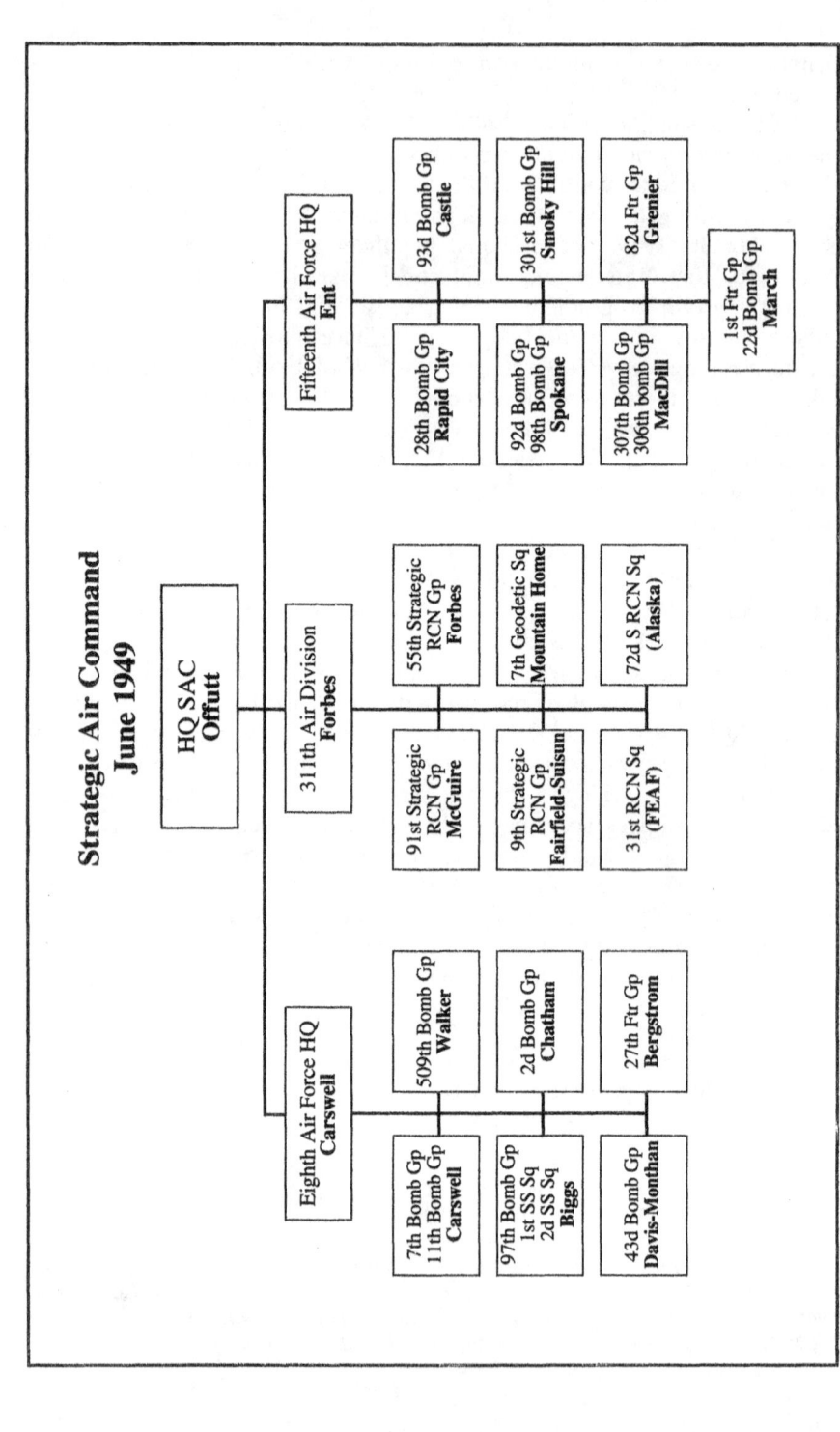

Challenges to Strategy

In any case, the need was clear, according to an editorial in the *Air University Quarterly Review*:

> It is a matter of history that we have refrained from striking the first blow. Hence it is vital that we be capable of immediate and decisive reprisal. No longer can we depend upon time as an ally to prepare the return blow. It must be struck in hours.[113]

Others might have read the historical record differently, but nevertheless, the rationale here existed for maintaining a strike force in being, ready to go. As for preventive war, airmen hastened to reject the idea in public, Saville citing the sheer risk involved.[114]

Further, even when both potential enemies had atomic weapons, deterrence was not necessarily undermined. Barton Leach outlined the idea to Symington:

> ...the effect of a deterrent is not lost by the fact that the other fellow has a deterrent too. The Soviets have heretofore professed to believe that we are preparing war against them.... Now they have the A-bomb and should feel much happier.... We do not begrudge this sense of security to the Soviets; and we trust that they will not begrudge the same to us.[115]

News of the atomic bomb stimulated a variety of proposals. These included increasing the production of atomic weapons, developing a "Super" (hydrogen) bomb, strengthening the European allies, increasing defense spending generally, or a combination of these. Given the failure of efforts to stop the Soviet atomic program through international control, further negotiations on the subject attracted little enthusiasm in the administration.

Since early 1949, the Atomic Energy Commission and the military establishment had been considering the expanded production of bombs. The commission developed plans to build more facilities, and the Military Liaison Committee was studying whether or not to put additional pressure on the AEC by asking for more weapons than the existing capacity could produce. The Secretary of Defense pushed strongly for an increase, and when Truman appointed him to a committee with Secretary of State Dean Acheson and AEC Chairman Lilienthal, Secretary Johnson made sure that

---

[113] Maj R. J. Seabolt, "Prize Editorial: Why Emphasize Air Power?" *AUQR* III (Winter 49), p 3.

[114] Futrell, *Ideas*, p 142.

[115] Memo, W. B. Leach, Feb 15, 1950, Symington Papers, Corres Files 1946–1950, Leach, Box 7, HSTL.

arguments in favor of expansion were included in their report. Similar pressures came from Congress, especially the Joint Committee on Atomic Energy. Since the Democratic victory in 1948, the chairman of that committee had been Senator Brien McMahon of Connecticut, the author of the 1946 Atomic Energy Act. His executive director was a recent graduate of Yale Law School and a former B–24 pilot named William L. Borden, who had written *There Will Be No Time*, a book calling for the nation to prepare for modern war.[116]

For Johnson's efforts to boost atomic bomb production, the detection of the Soviet atomic test proved fortuitous. The Johnson-Acheson-Lilienthal report reached the President in October 1949, and Truman agreed to seek an appropriation to support expanded production. In December, the joint chiefs stated their postion on the matter. They advised the President that the increase in weapons production would not affect current war planning, but it was necessary to deter the Soviets as their production expanded and would provide a more versatile stockpile. For the Air Force, the issue revolved around its consistent opposition to developing weapons for use by the Army and Navy. An expanded stockpile might allow other services to obtain bombs more easily, without having to impose a limit on those available for the strategic air offensive. When Secretary Johnson presented the services' views to the President in January, however, the decision had in reality already been made to expand production.[117]

Scientists had recognized the possibility of developing a thermonuclear weapon (i.e. employing the principle of fusion) since 1942. The Atomic Energy Commission had given first priority to the production of fission (atomic) weapons, but research into fusion continued. In the summer of 1949, the Air Staff's Atomic Energy Office and the Directorate of Intelligence had examined the military value of a very large bomb, with a yield of 1,000 kilotons. They concluded that such a weapon would permit execution of the current war plan with fewer sorties.[118]

Among the supporters of the "Super" fusion device were Lewis L. Strauss, a member of the Atomic Energy Commission, and Senator Mc-

---

[116] Rearden, *Formative Years*, pp 439–446; Hewlett & Duncan, *Atomic Shield*, pp 178–184.

[117] K. Condit, *JCS, 1947–1949*, pp 535–536; Rearden, *Formative Years*, pp 444–446; Lee Bowen, *The Development of Weapons*, Vol IV of Bowen & Little, *The History of Air Force Participation in the Atomic Energy Program, 1943–1953* (Washington: USAF Historical Division), Pt 1, pp 101–124.

[118] Bowen, *Development of Weapons*, Pt 1, pp 176–180, 188–189; Little, *Building an Atomic Air Force*, Pt 2, pp 357–359.

Mahon. As a flag officer in the naval reserve, Strauss had no objection to atomic weapons for the Navy, but he also favored national strength in all categories. Because the hydrogen bomb needed an atomic explosion to trigger the thermonuclear reaction, the program would compete with the expansion of atomic bomb production. Still, Senator McMahon considered that both efforts were needed. While there was no absolute certainty that the hydrogen bomb was feasible, the Soviets were certain to develop one if it was. Consequently, atomic energy experts found it difficult to oppose at least a study of this new technology.[119]

In October, General Vandenberg testified in favor of the Super before the McMahon Committee.[120] However, Strauss was in the minority in the Atomic Energy Commission, where opposition was strongly supported by J. Robert Oppenheimer and the other scientists on the General Advisory Committee. The joint chiefs turned to the Joint Strategic Studies Committee for advice. Supported by Landon, the Air Force representative issued a report to the JCS on November 17, confirming the Air Staff belief that the hydrogen bomb would make the strategic air offensive more efficient. The report also noted the tremendous psychological importance, both at home and abroad, should the United States not have the weapon when the Russians did. The joint chiefs supported this finding, viewing the weapon mainly as a deterrent and doubting that the American refusal to develop it would stop the Soviets. These arguments certainly reflected Bradley's opinion, as he had expressed it before the Oppenheimer Committee.[121]

To resolve this controversy, Truman once again turned to Johnson, Acheson, and Lilienthal. The three convened a working group, which included Norstad, Maj. Gen. Kenneth D. Nichols of the Armed Forces Special Weapons Project, and representatives of other agencies. By the time the study was completed, the committee found itself split two to one, with Lilienthal dissenting. Truman heard him out sympathetically, but approved the majority recommendation for a feasibility study. Full-scale development of a hydrogen bomb was deferred so as to keep from tying up fissionable material.[122] Clearly, both in the matter of expanded atomic bomb production and in the decision on the hydrogen bomb, the growing

---

[119] Hewlett & Duncan, *Atomic Shield*, pp 373–399.
[120] Bowen, *Development of Weapons*, Pt 1, p 188.
[121] K. Condit, *JCS, 1947–1949*, pp 543–549; Hewlett & Duncan, *Atomic Shield*, p 382.
[122] K. Condit, *JCS, 1947–1949*, pp 549–557; Rearden, *Formative Years*, pp 446–453; David A. Rosenberg, "American Atomic Strategy and the Hydrogen Bomb Decision," *Journal of American History* 66 (Jun 79), pp 79–87.

Strategic Air Force

First, Gen. Muir S. Fairchild, Air Force Vice Chief of Staff, *left*, and then, Gen. Joseph T. McNarney, Commander, Air Materiel Command, *right*, chaired a special board charged by General Vandenberg with designing a forty-eight group service while weighing the needs of SAC. Generals Norstad and Craig also served on the McNarney-Fairchild Board.

sense of national danger had been an influential factor. Lilienthal, overruled on both questions, observed: "More and better bombs.... We keep saying, 'We have no other course;' what we should say is 'We are not bright enough to see any other course.' "[123]

The case for the hydrogen bomb as a deterrent to Soviet aggression acquired special significance in the eyes of many Europeans, who were convinced that a Soviet attack spelled inevitable disaster. For them, the question was not whether to defend themselves or be overrun. A war would entail a "liberation" even more devastating than the one in 1944. In that view only deterrence made sense. Leach told Symington that Europe's true defense lay not in the underfunded tactical forces but in the power of America's atomic strike force. He noted Churchill's repeated endorsement of atomic air power and also the views of Gen. Pierre Billotte, formerly the French representative on the United Nations Military Staff Committee, who had been advocating the immediate development of the hydrogen bomb by the United States.[124]

---

[123] Lilienthal, *Journals*, p 577.
[124] See note 115; ltr, W. B. Leach to W. S. Symington, Sec AF, Feb 10, 1950, both in Symington Papers, Corres Files 1946–1950, Leach, Box 7, HSTL.

Challenges to Strategy

Compounding the shock of the Soviet explosion, on October 1, 1949, the Chinese communists declared the formation of the People's Republic. Nanking had fallen earlier in the year, and in December the Nationalists under Chiang Kai-Shek gave up their position on the mainland of China and established themselves in Taiwan. Although this development was less surprising in official circles than the Soviet bomb, the strong interest of the American public in Chinese matters made it a comparable trauma.[125]

Bad news continued into the new year. On February 2, 1950, confirmation was received that Klaus Fuchs, a German-born scientist active in both the British and American atomic projects, had been arraigned in London on espionage charges. He had already confessed, and the information he was suspected of passing on to the Soviets, which concerned the fusing mechanism of the bomb and suggested a means of counteracting it, was valuable indeed. Lilienthal informed Congress that there was no way the story could be sugar-coated. If there was any doubt of the detrimental effect of these events on the national mood, it was dispelled several days later by the intense public reaction to a speech by Senator Joseph R. McCarthy (Republican of Wisconsin), which blamed espionage and treason for the danger to America's security. The tremendous success of political rhetoric about communist subversion could only reflect considerable public unease at the international situation.[126]

Still, Truman seemed determined to hold the line on the defense budget. In his view, the need to spend money on military and economic aid to the European allies made economies in the U.S. military budget all the more important. The joint chiefs warned that further cuts posed a serious danger to military capabilities. But even they tempered their warning, emphasizing that the economy could not support increases in defense spending.[127] Symington had expressed similar views, and he once again predicted the long-term dangers posed by limiting the Air Force's program. He learned from Doolittle of reports that the Soviets were working on air refueling and heavy bombers. For the near future, their jet fighters would

---

[125] Rearden, *Formative Years*, pp 230–232; Robert A. Divine, *Since 1945: Politics and Diplomacy in Recent American History* (NY: John Wiley, 1975), pp 27–28.
[126] Hewlett & Duncan, *Atomic Shield*, pp 412–415; Lilienthal, *Journals*, pp 634–635. See note #98
[127] Walter S. Poole, *1950–1952*, Vol IV, *The History of the Joint Chiefs of Staff: The Joint Chiefs of Staff and National Policy* (Washington: Historical Division, JCS, 1976), pp 25–35; memo, W. S. Symington, Sec AF, to L. A. Johnson, Sec Def, Mar 21, 1950, Symington Papers, Corres Files 1946–1950, Johnson, Louis, Box 6, HSTL.

furnish a powerful air defense, and their large numbers of conventional bombers would be a powerful support for the ground forces, should they attack westward in Europe. To the east, the Soviets might also attack Alaska to get a base. Intelligence sources early in 1950 estimated the Soviet air defense force at eighteen hundred fighters, while medium bombers numbered fifteen hundred. Few analysts expected war in the near future, but at some point the Soviets' rising power might tempt them into aggression.[128] Urging more emphasis on research and development, Doolittle also suggested to Symington that, "...with the approval of the President, the Secretary of State and the Secretary of Defense [should] advise the American people of the true state of affairs as regards our relative air strength."[129]

A similar alarm was sounded by Lt. Gen. Ennis C. Whitehead, formerly air commander in the Far East and now in charge of Continental Air Command (the consolidation of Tactical Air Command and Air Defense Command). Based on current briefings, Whitehead concluded that by 1952 the Soviets would be able to destroy the United States. The current budget restrictions would not allow the Air Force to match the enemy's capabilities. Thus it was imperative that concerted efforts be made to strengthen the strategic air force and continental air defense. Convinced that the nation faced a crisis on the scale of the American Revolution, Whitehead urged Vandenberg to brief the Secretary of Defense and "the highest authority of our country."[130]

In a larger context, the Soviet military threat had already captured presidential attention. In January 1950, Truman authorized a study by the State and Defense Departments of the implications of the latest international developments. When he decided at the end of that month to proceed with development of the hydrogen bomb, he gave the study a broader mandate. A ten-member Program Review Group took on the task of drafting the report. Paul H. Nitze, Kennan's successor at the Policy

---

[128] Draft memo, W. S. Symington, Sec AF, to L. A. Johnson, Sec Def, (Nov 8, 1949) Jan 9, 1950, Symington Papers, Corres Files, 1946–1950, Johnson, Louis, Box 6, HSTL; memo, J. H. Doolittle to Sec AF, subj: Report, Jan 3, 1950, Symington Papers, Corres Files, 1946–1950, Johnson, Louis, Declas Docs, Box 4, HSTL.

[129] Memo, J. H. Doolittle to Sec AF, subj: Report, Jan 3, 1950, Symington Papers, Corres Files, 1946–1950, Johnson, Louis, Declas Docs, Box 4, HSTL; Rearden, *Formative Years*, pp 522–526; Poole, *JCS, 1950–1952*, pp 4–9.

[130] Ltr, Lt Gen E. C. Whitehead, CG CONAC, to CSAF, subj: Capability of the United States Air Force to Meet Its Responsibilities, May 1, 1950, RG 341, DCS/Ops, Dir/Pl TS, P & O, 381 (Jun 9, 1950), Box 324, MMB, NA.

Planning Staff, assumed the lead for the State Department, and Landon represented the joint chiefs. The Defense Department members all believed that Secretary Johnson was keeping them on a tight leash, and they accordingly confined their role to providing information. Nitze, on the other hand, oversaw the preparation of a lengthy, detailed analysis of the world situation, making a case for a major buildup of American military strength. His draft report entered the National Security Council papermill as "NSC-68" and soon became recognized as one of the major state papers of the Cold War.[131]

The estimate supplied by NSC-68 was indeed sobering. The document described the world as engaged in a political struggle between two opposing camps. From twenty atomic bombs in the middle of 1950, the Soviet stockpile would expand to 200 by 1954. Land and air forces could overrun most of Europe more or less at will, and the atomic arsenal could nullify any chance of American intervention. This military strength was subordinated to a larger "Kremlin design" of communist expansion through political means. While Soviet leaders were unlikely to resort to war, a weak free world might tempt them into one.[132]

As conditions stood, in the event of war it was still possible for the United States to offer some resistance. American forces could:

> provide a reasonable measure of protection to the Western Hemisphere, bases in the Western Pacific, and essential military lines of communication; and an inadequate measure of protection to vital military bases in the United Kingdom and in the Near and Middle East. We will have the capability of conducting powerful offensive air operations against vital elements of the Soviet war-making capacity.[133]

Unfortunately, the paper went on to explain, continuation of present policies would lead to deterioration of the American position: "From the military point of view, the actual and potential capabilities of the United

---

[131] Rearden, *Formative Years*, pp 522–526; Poole, *JCS, 1950–1952*, pp 4–9; Paul H. Nitze, with Ann M. Smith & Steven L. Rearden, *From Hiroshima to Glasnost: At the Center of Decision—A Memoir* (NY: Grove Weidenfeld, 1989), pp 87–99.
[132] A Report to the President Pursuant to the Presidential Directive of January 31, 1950, Apr 7, 1950, encl to note, J. S. Lay, Jr, Exec Sec NSC, to NSC, NSC–68, Apr 14, 1950, in *FRUS*, 1950, Vol I, pp 239–244, 249–252, 287.
[133] *Ibid.*, p 262.

States . . . will become less and less effective as a war deterrent." A major Soviet atomic attack would even prevent U.S. forces from mobilizing and recovering lost ground.[134]

Nitze and the other drafters of the report agreed that there were four possible courses of action: preventive war, continuing on the present course, isolation, and "a Rapid Build-up of Political, Economic, and Military Strength in the Free World." The first was deemed unacceptable. Besides being risky, preventive war would be repugnant to many Americans. Following the current program would lead to the deterioration previously described. In the drafters' view, isolation meant abandoning allies, including the inhabitants of the major industrial areas of Europe. The argument thus led to a call to strengthen the forces of freedom.[135]

While NSC–68 considered military aspects in a larger context, it held them to be crucial. The free countries had to be able to hold key areas and defend the American mobilization base until new strength could be built up. The study group maintained that the strategic air offensive was important as a means "to destroy vital elements of the Soviet war-making capacity and to keep the enemy off balance until the full offensive strength of the United States and its allies can be brought to bear."[136] Defense of specific local positions was also needed in order to avoid "the dilemma of reacting totally to a limited extension of Soviet control or of not reacting at all (except with ineffectual protests and half measures)."[137]

NSC–68 did not contain any specific estimates of costs of the proposed defense buildup. Still, the drafters made two essential points on that subject. The added burden to the economy was justified because the survival of the free world was at stake. The other statement challenged directly the usual economic reasoning that had held budgets down. That is, the effects of large increases might be less harmful to the economy than had been feared.[138]

During the drafting of NSC–68, Secretary of State Acheson had kept himself abreast of the work. Defense Secretary Johnson's involvement, by contrast, remained limited. Indeed, at a meeting on March 22, 1950, to discuss progress on the report, Johnson said he had not had time to read it. He reacted angrily to what he perceived as an attempt to railroad the

---

[134] *Ibid.*, p 277.
[135] *Ibid.*, pp 272, 279–287.
[136] *Ibid.*, p 283.
[137] *Ibid.*, p 278.
[138] *Ibid.*, pp 286–287.

paper through, and he then left the meeting. This contributed to the extension of Johnson's and Acheson's political conflict into a personal one. Nonetheless, Truman assured the Secretary of State, the study would continue. In the end, when Johnson realized that Pentagon officials were perceptibly cheered by the report, he endorsed it. On April 12 Truman asked for cost figures for the recommended long-term defense buildup. As noted, at the same time Johnson was asking Congress for more money.[139] Both actions signaled a possible departure from the tight fiscal policies of the Truman administration.

Symington's was among the welcoming voices:

> The report is strong....We believe that under current world conditions this country has gone too far in disarmament...and believe this disarmament trend should be reversed immediately.... Despite the serious and far-reaching consequences of this Report to the President, the Air Force respectfully recommends that it be approved and forwarded....[140]

So far, however, all the discussion had produced little more than a potential addition of $300 million for the Air Force. These were difficult times. Looking ahead to fiscal 1952, Maj. Gen. Frederic Smith, Director of Programs, began outlining plans for a forty-two group force.[141] Lt. Gen. Benjamin W. Chidlaw, commanding Air Materiel Command, described the aircraft procurement problem as cutting the suit to fit the cloth and having to decide "what part of our anatomy we want covered."[142] In the light of the increasingly unstable international situation, it is tempting to speculate that there was a rising level of anxiety among American leaders. What contribution this made to General Fairchild's death on March 17, 1950, following a heart attack, would be hard to say, but Symington said Fairchild had "literally worked himself to death."[143]

---

[139] Rearden, *Formative Years*, pp 525–527.
[140] Memo, W. S. Symington, Sec AF, to L. A. Johnson, Sec Def, Apr 6, 1950, Symington Papers, Corres Files 1946–1950, Johnson, Louis, Box 6, HSTL.
[141] Memo, Maj Gen F. H. Smith, Asst for Prog, DCS/Ops, to CSAF, subj: Tentative 42 Group Program for FY 1952, Apr 5, 1950, Vandenberg Coll, Budget 1949–1950, Box 41, MD, LC.
[142] Briefing, AMC Presentation on Materiel Deficiencies, Dec 30, 1949, LeMay Coll, Official Docs, Misc, Box B105, MD, LC.
[143] *New York Times*, Mar 18, 1950, p 13; memo, W. S. Symington, Sec AF, to L. A. Johnson, Sec Def, Mar 22, 1950, Vandenberg Coll, Sec of AF, 1950, Box 61, MD, LC. Symington was arguing for more senior general officer authorizations for the Air Force.

Strategic Air Force

The Air Force Secretary himself had decided that prospects for real rearmament were not encouraging. In addition, for a man of Symington's ambition, following the 1949 amendments to the National Security Act, a post in which he was no longer a statutory member of the National Security Council and yet subordinate to Louis Johnson was not one to stay in. Early in 1950, he told Truman he did not wish to remain responsible for the condition of the Air Force, which he considered inadequate to its mission. In April he resigned to become Chairman of the National Security Resources Board. There his familiarity with business and with industrial mobilization could be put to good use, independent of the Secretary of Defense, and he would gain a seat on the National Security Council. If the long-range buildup advocated in NSC-68 were implemented, this would be an important position. Meanwhile, Truman named Thomas K. Finletter as Symington's successor. Having chaired the President's Air Policy Commission, Finletter had served as Chief of the Economic Cooperation Administration mission in London. He took office as Secretary of the Air Force on April 24, 1950.[144]

By early 1950 the strategy of deterrence had weathered major challenges. The long-range atomic striking force at the ready now clearly was central to national strategy. Challenges had included criticism of the strike force because it was not strong enough to achieve decisive results, proposals to divert or weaken the strike in order to support ground forces, attacks on the decision to procure the B-36 as the mainstay of the intercontinental force, and charges that the Air Force was neglecting tactical air forces or continental defense. The result tended to be a reinforcement of the strategic force's role. Its alleged inadequacy merely highlighted the need for more spending to strengthen it. That the Air Force's ability to accomplish such other missions as support for ground forces and air defense was limited, the service was only too ready to admit. The danger posed by Soviet atomic weapons merely buttressed the argument for the strike force. And the public attacks on the strategy merely confirmed the fact that the central role of the strategic air offensive had already been decided. Central to the nation's faith in the strategic air force as a deterrent to world war was the knowledge that the resources were being ably managed, and that the strategic air offensive, should it fail, would not do so for lack of competent effort on the part of the force itself. General

---

[144] Symington OHI, pp 60–63; Cole, *et al, Department of Defense,* pp 84–86.

Challenges to Strategy

From THE HERBLOCK BOOK (Beacon Press, 1952)

Political cartoons such as this one by Herblock for the *Washington Post* on the detonation of the first atomic bomb by the Soviet Union in 1949 provided only a little comic relief to an American public alarmed by the Cold War and, by 1952, the ever intensifying military rivalry between the United States and the Soviet Union.

Strategic Air Force

LeMay's achievements in this respect insured confidence in the priority mission.

The Strategic Force at the Ready: SAC in 1950

Recognition of LeMay's success at SAC was not slow in coming. When Lindbergh visited Air Force units in 1949 he singled out SAC for special praise, and Vandenberg made a point of passing on his comments to LeMay.[145] In administrative matters, LeMay was beginning to enjoy the prerogatives of a successful field commander. A draft letter criticizing the rates of crime and disciplinary infractions in SAC and instructing LeMay to make improvements reached Vandenberg's desk in March 1950, and the Chief of Staff immediately ordered it rewritten to soften the tone.[146] About the same time, Idwal Edwards, Acting Deputy Chief of Staff for Operations (while Norstad was acting vice chief after Fairchild's death), vetoed an Air Staff plan for upgrading navigator training on the grounds that SAC did not need any supervision on matters of crew training.[147] No doubt cases of overregulation occurred, but the senior leadership of the Air Force recognized a successful command and tried not to interfere.

In October 1949 LeMay held a bombing competition. For SAC, the rules set demanding standards that would involve ground crews and entire units, as equipment failures would not excuse poor performance. Bombing was to be from 25,000 feet. The results provided the SAC staff with data for assessing where the command stood. Curiously, the two winning units had both recently re-equipped. The number one crew, from Rapid City, flew a new B–36, scoring a visual bombing average error of 441 feet and an average error in radar bombing of 1,053 feet. The 93d Bombardment Wing at Castle was recognized as the best overall unit. Having recently con-

---

[145] Ltr, Gen H. S. Vandenberg, CSAF, to Lt Gen C. E. LeMay, CG SAC, Sep 21, 1949, Vandenberg Coll, V. Files 1949, Box 32, MD, LC.

[146] Ltr, Gen H. S. Vandenberg, CSAF, to Lt Gen C. E. LeMay, CG SAC, Mar 27, 1950, Vandenburg Coll, SAC (3), Box 45, MD, LC.

[147] Memo, Lt Gen I. H. Edwards, Actg DCS/Ops, to Maj Gen S. E. Anderson, Dir P & O, Apr 1, 1950, atch to ASSS, Anderson to CCS/Ops, Capabilities of SAC Navigators, Mar 27, 1950; ASSS, Maj Gen J. Smith, Dep Dir P & O, Capabilities of Strategic Air Command Navigators, Apr 25, 1950, RG 341, DCS/Ops, Dir/Pl, P & O, 211, SAC (Mar 27, 1950), Box 1027, MMB, NA.

Challenges to Strategy

verted to B-50s, the wing had to use B-29s because of fuel leaks in its new planes.[148]

As 1950 opened, LeMay was reporting progress and stating urgent needs. SAC's ability to implement the war plan had much improved under his leadership. With eighteen atomic assembly teams, an expanding stockpile of weapons, and over two hundred aircraft modified to carry them, the United States was well ahead of its position eighteen months before. Crews had target materials on hand for about half of the objectives in the plan, and for the others LeMay believed reconnaissance would be needed just before the offensive anyway, although the weaknesses of the reconnaissance units continued to trouble him.[149]

While the training of crews progressed, SAC did experience shortages. Until the school at Houston started graduating air observers in July 1950, more specialized crew members were needed for navigator, bombardier, and radar positions. Radar repairmen and engine mechanics were also in short supply.[150]

Improvements in materiel could be expected, but problems with the new B-36 still seemed to be defying solution. Late in 1949, serious leaks began to develop in fuel tanks. The guns, still totally unsatisfactory, raised doubts about the B-36's chances in a fight. Vandenberg had called on Air Materiel Command to mobilize its expertise to get an improved armament system into service. With the B-50, engine malfunctions persisted, but repairs were finally completed late in the spring of 1950. For the moment it appeared that the B-29 engine problem was solved. Despite these achievements in major systems, the Air Force was still plagued by shortages of spare parts. Chidlaw and his Air Materiel Command understood that the supply system had trouble keeping up with numerous modifications and that many parts had to be diverted to the production line. This

---

[148] Ltr, Lt Gen C. E. LeMay, CG SAC, to Gen H. S. Vandenberg, CSAF, Oct 11, 1949, atch to memo, Maj Gen S. E. Anderson, Dir P & O, to CSAF, subj: SAC Bombing Competition, Oct 27, 1949, Vandenberg Coll, SAC (4), Box 45, MD, LC.)
[149] Rprt, Materiel Deficiencies Which Limit the Combat Capabilities of the Strategic Air Command, Jan 4, 1950, LeMay Coll, Official Docs, Misc, Box B105, MD, LC; according to David A. Rosenberg, "U.S. Nuclear Stockpile, 1945 to 1950," *The Bulletin of the Atomic Scientists* 38 (May 82), pp 26, 29-30, a study in February 1950 asserted that plans calling for the delivery of 292 atomic weapons "could be executed" on May 1, 1950.
[150] See previous note; ltr, Maj Gen W. F. McKee, Asst VCSAF, to Lt Gen C. E. LeMay, CG SAC, Apr 28, 1949, Vandenberg Coll, SAC (4), Box 45, MD, LC.

Strategic Air Force

would require a painful choice between meeting delivery schedules for new aircraft or keeping the existing force flying. Chidlaw also foresaw similar difficulties with the B–47. From the point of view of materiel, he felt the weak areas were the lack of a service test program for new aircraft and insufficient planning for spares.[151]

Whatever the limitations, and whatever doubts the Weapons Systems Evaluation Group might raise about SAC's ability to fight its way to the targets, LeMay intended to undertake a demonstration of his command's abilities. The exercise he planned had to be postponed for a number of reasons. Until the end of the Berlin airlift in September 1949, MATS was unavailable to provide the needed airlift. Other delays followed, but finally in June 1950, SAC was ready to carry out Exercise BECALM.[152]

This was to be an exercise of the entire medium bomber force, including reconnaissance, tanker, fighter, and transport units. Crews were warned ahead of time, but no one on temporary duty was to be called home for the exercise. The 301st Bombardment Group, then in England, was the only medium unit excused. First, in the deployment phase, each unit would load for overseas and fly a long-distance mission, simulating the move overseas. Some units would practice air-to-air refueling. The exercise was then to conclude with a full-scale simulated atomic bombing mission.[153]

On June 4 at 2224 hours, Central Standard Time, Headquarters USAF sent out the message ordering execution of BECALM and establishing June 5 as E-Day (Execution Day).[154] Headquarters SAC set up a control room and in little over two hours issued the order to its air forces. Eighth Air Force prepared to deploy an advanced echelon. SAC's major units began to move on E + 1, and over the following days 314 of the 395 bombers on hand launched long-distance missions. An exercise with the Atomic Energy Commission gave the atomic wings practice in picking up the weapons from storage depots. On E + 6 (June 11) the command flew a

---

[151] See previous note; transcript, Conference held January 6, 1950, Vandenberg Coll, Files 1950 (3), Box 33; briefing, AMC Presentation on Materiel Deficiencies, Dec 30, 1949, LeMay Coll, Official Docs, Misc, Box B105, both in MD, LC; rprt, Summary of Deficiencies Which Impair the Execution of the SAC Emergency War Plan, Apr 1, 1950, RG 341, DCS/Ops, Dir/Pl, OPD, 381 SAC (Mar 23, 1949), Sect 2, Box 1028, MMB, NA.

[152] Ltr, Lt Gen C. E. LeMay, CG SAC, to Gen H. S. Vandenberg, CSAF, Oct 4, 1949, atch to ltr, Vandenberg to LeMay, Nov 8, 1949, RG 341, DCS/Ops, Dir/Pl, OPD, 381 SAC (Mar 23, 1949), Box 1027, MMB, NA.

[153] Hist, SAC, Jan–Jun 1950, Vol II, Chap 7.

[154] *Ibid.*; msg, Hq USAF/OOP-C to CG SAC, CG CONAC, Cmdr MATS, *et al*, 050425Z Jun 50, subj: Execution Order for SAC OPSORD 15-50; msg, CG SAC to Hq USAF, AFSWP, *et al*, 050505Z Jun 50, RG 341, DCS/Ops, Dir/Pl, OPD, 381 SAC (Mar 23, 1949), Sect 2, Box 1028, MMB, NA.

Challenges to Strategy

concerted attack against sites representing groups of targets in the Soviet Union. Sixty aircraft simulated atomic sorties, while 104 other bombers flew as decoys or jammers, and 19 reconnaissance planes and 22 tankers provided specialized support. The report of Exercise BECALM estimated that 58 bombers struck their targets, an impressive achievement.[155]

Although the exercise did not test the bases overseas or the staging fields, and MATS did not exercise its entire plan, BECALM appeared to be a success overall. The SAC staff believed that the command had shown its ability to launch the atomic attack as planned, while nonatomic units had also proved their effectiveness. For the future, they could envision increasing the scale of the attack. Though the weary crewmen at Biggs, Castle, March, and Spokane did not know it, in less than a month they would be loading out again, and the ones at March and Spokane would not be bombing for practice.[156]

---

[155] Hist, SAC, Jan–Jun 1950, Vol II, Chap 7.
[156] *Ibid.*; msg, CG SAC to CSAF, 122300Z Jun 50, subj: SAC-MATS Mobility Test, Flash Report, RG 341, DCS/Ops, Dir/Pl, OPD, 381 SAC (Mar 23, 1949), Sect 2, Box 1028, MMB, NA.

Part III

Expansion of the Strategic Force 1950–1953

Chapter IX

Limited War, Atomic Plenty, and Rearmament

Sunday, June 25, 1950, was an important day for the U.S. Air Force. The first Boeing B-47A, intended as the initial production model of the Stratojet, completed its first flight. Meanwhile the newspapers and radio offered the usual catalogue of misfortune; the lead story was the crash of an airliner in Lake Michigan with heavy loss of life, and there were reports of armed clashes in a country called Korea. As the day went on, it became clear to those who followed foreign news that the hostilities were not mere repetitions of the frequent incidents on the border between North and South Korea. In point of fact, the forces of the communist North Korean regime had launched an all-out offensive against the United Nations-backed, pro-American Republic of Korea to the south. Accordingly, late Sunday the Security Council of the United Nations called upon the North Koreans to cease and desist.[1]

The three-year conflict that erupted that day on the 38th parallel was in its roots a Korean civil war, in which the People's Democratic Republic of Korea, headed by Kim Il-Sung, attempted to unify the peninsula by force. It also marked a major East-West confrontation, raising fears of general war between the United States and the Soviet Union. While the North Koreans achieved surprise (evidence suggests that even the Soviets were surprised by the timing, although not by the attack itself), key American observers had been expecting a communist move somewhere in the world for months.[2]

---

[1] Knaack, *Bombers*, pp 108-109; Glenn D. Paige, *The Korean Decision, June 24-30, 1950* (NY: Free Press, 1968), pp 108, 145-147.
[2] Steven L. Rearden, *The Evolution of American Strategic Doctrine: Paul H. Nitze and the Soviet Challenge* [SAIS Papers, No.4] (Boulder, Colo: Westview, 1984), pp 27-28; Paige, *Korean Decision*, pp 116-121.

Strategic Air Force

The apparent failure of the United States to deter local aggression in Korea seemed for a time to presage a much larger failure of the policy of deterrence. In the unstable situation brought on by the war, the preservation and expansion of the strategic air force became more crucial than ever to national policy. Even with the decision to keep the war in the Far East limited, it proved necessary to deploy some of SAC's conventional B-29s. The policy of limited war was itself partly motivated by the desire to maintain the Air Force's ability to deter general war.

Besides the Korean war, another factor influencing the expansion of strategic forces was the predicted onset of an age of atomic plenty. This led to speculation concerning the availability of various weapon types as an alternative to reliance on strategic bombardment. The ensuing debate became a recurring theme in disputes among the armed services as to the importance of the strategic air offensive in defense planning.

In ordering a partial mobilization for Korea, the Truman administration intended to expand SAC as well as other forces. This challenge to the command affected all aspects of its operational activities. At the same time, SAC faced the broader issues of organization and the threat of Soviet atomic capabilities. Coping with all these pressures, the command asserted its dominance in the U.S. defense establishment, a destiny confirmed in the national budget by the end of 1951.

Deterrence at Risk

The global implications of the Korean war were evident from the outset. Not only did Kim's regime bear all the earmarks of a Soviet satellite with a Soviet-trained army, but the attack probably had at least Stalin's tacit approval. In the anxious atmosphere of the time, observers in the West were inclined to assume that the Soviet leader had ordered it directly. Given the American role in establishing Korea's southern regime in 1948 and its assistance to the Republic's armed forces, as well as the involvement of the United Nations, from the first there was strong pressure for the Truman administration to react.[3]

---

[3] Robert F. Futrell, *The United States Air Force in Korea, 1950–1953*, rev ed (Washington: AFCHO, 1983), pp 14–20; Nikita S. Khrushchev, *Khrushchev Remembers*, ed by Edward Crankshaw (Boston: Little, Brown, 1970), pp 367–368. See also Robert R. Simmons, *The Strained Alliance; Peking, P'yongyang, Moscow, and the Politics of the Korean Civil War* (NY: Free Press, 1975) for an interesting thesis about the outbreak of the war. For a survey of the most recent literature on the Korean war, see Michael Schaller, "U.S. Policy in the Korean War," *International Security* 11 (Winter 86–87), pp 162–166.

War and Rearmament

When Secretary Finletter arrived in Washington from his vacation home at Bar Harbor, Maine, early on June 25, he joined a number of weekending officials congregating on the capital. Attention focused on Korea, but over the next few days the State Department raised the prospect of another incident in Germany, Yugoslavia, or Iran. Should any incident lead to general war, the allies had only ten divisions on the continent in Western Europe, facing at least twenty Soviet divisions in East Germany alone. French forces were committed in Indochina and the British in Malaya.[4]

On the other hand, perhaps the Soviets realized the risk of more serious provocations. Brig. Gen. Richard C. Lindsay, USAF, the Deputy Director for Strategic Plans of the Joint Staff, argued that the Soviets would not initiate a general war without major attacks on NATO forces and the continental United States. Since they were probably not yet strong enough to attack the United States, such a widening of the war seemed unlikely. In fact Moscow's note on of June 29 on Korea, while blaming the South for the war, made no threats.[5] On July 1 the National Security Council staff concluded that the Soviet goal in Korea was to embarrass the United States, either by liquidating an American client or by tying down the forces sent to save it. While the Chinese communists might take action, the Soviets' intent appeared to be to divert and distract, not to attack directly.[6]

Consequently, as the North Koreans captured Seoul, the southern capital, on June 28 and swept southward, the risk of sending U.S. troops to salvage the situation did not seem excessive. The initial decision to intervene with air and naval units proving insufficient to stop the invaders, Truman ordered the deployment of American ground forces.

Even as the first units arrived in the peninsula on July 1, the Truman administration could not ignore the broader implications of the Soviet threat in the light of the move on Korea.[7] Symington, the Chairman of the National Security Resources Board, persuaded the National Security

---

[4] Paige, *Korean Decision*, p 109; memo, NSC Consultants Meeting, Jun 29, 1950, in *FRUS*, 1950, Vol I, pp 327–330.

[5] Memo, NSC Consultants Meeting, Jun 29, 1950, in *FRUS*, 1950, Vol I, pp 327–330.

[6] Draft rprt, NSC-73, The Position and Actions of the United States With Respect to Possible Further Soviet Moves in the Light of the Korean Situation, Jul 1, 1950, in *FRUS*, 1950, Vol I, pp 332–333.

[7] Roy E. Appleman, *South to the Naktong, North to the Yalu (June–November 1950)* [The United States Army in the Korean War] (Washington: GPO, 1961), pp 30–35; Paige, *Korean Decision*, pp 143, 174–176, 214–216, 253–261.

Strategic Air Force

Council to discuss the possibility of at least a partial mobilization.[8] NSC-68[9] contained a program for a military buildup, and one of the State Department officials who had worked with Nitze on that paper, Charles E. Bohlen, urged that the government:

> Initiate measures to bring about a rapid build-up of the United States military position both in manpower and in production in order to place us as speedily as possible in a military situation commensurate with the present state of international affairs.[10]

Bohlen outlined several diplomatic and military objectives, among them improving the state of defense, deterring potential enemies, offsetting any loss of prestige resulting from Korea, and encouraging friends.[11]

While discounting the risk of general war, the administration realized that the only ready force available as a hedge against that risk was the Strategic Air Command. The Air Force was already drawing on SAC forces to bolster readiness in the Far East, and on July 7 the joint chiefs formally recommended the deployment of bomber and fighter units to the United Kingdom, "[i]n light of the international situation . . . and in order to improve our immediate military posture."[12]

Within hours Headquarters USAF had notified SAC to ready two B-29 groups for England.[13] With the 301st Bombardment Group on normal rotation at Lakenheath, this action would triple the medium bomber force in the country. Vandenberg sent word of the order to Maj. Gen. Leon W. Johnson, Commander of the 3d Air Division in the United Kingdom. By this time it was Saturday, July 8, and when Johnson realized that British approval of the deployment of the two bomber groups would not be a matter of routine, he knew he faced a diplomatic challenge. Even the Chief of Air Staff, Marshal of the Royal Air Force Sir John Slessor, needed higher authorization before agreeing to accept the two groups.[14]

---

[8] Statement, W. S. Symington, Chmn NSRB, to NSC, Jul 6, 1950, in *FRUS*, 1950, Vol I, pp 338–341 & 338n.

[9] See pp 327–329.

[10] Memo, C. E. Bohlen, Jul 13, 1950, in *FRUS*, 1950, Vol I, p 343.

[11] *Ibid.*

[12] Rprt, JSSC to JCS, *Record of Actions Taken by the Joint Chiefs of Staff Relative to the United Nations Operations in Korea from Jun 25, 1950 to April 11, 1951*, Apr 27, 1951, p 20, RG 341, DCS/Ops, Dir/Pl, OPD, 333.5 (May 17, 1951), MMB, NA. Hereafter referred to as *Record of Actions*.

[13] Hq SAC Command Section Journal, Jul 8–10, 1950, in SAC/HO.

[14] Burk, *USAF in UK*, pp 26–27; Johnson OHI (with Hasdorff), p 155, in AFHRC; msg, Maj Gen L. W. Johnson, CG 3 AD, to Lt Gen L. Norstad, Actg VCSAF, 101340Z Jul 50, Vandenberg Coll, Jul 1950 (1), Box 86, MD, LC.

War and Rearmament

Thomas K. Finletter, second Secretary of the Air Force.

Complicating matters further was LeMay's request that certain nonnuclear components of atomic weapons accompany the units. These were the casings of the bombs, with the high explosives and wiring, but without the fissionable core. The SAC Commander argued that this would speed up operations in the event of war and economize on airlift, now at a premium with so many transports committed to the Far East.[15] Here was a sensitive matter for the American commander to clear with the British authorities.

Johnson succeeded in obtaining Air Ministry approval and even discussed the matter with Churchill, leader of the opposition. Accompanying Ambassador Lewis Douglas, Johnson called Prime Minister Clement R. Attlee out of a cabinet meeting on Monday morning to obtain his approval. Despite his concern that the show of strength might provoke a Soviet reaction, Attlee agreed to the move. British Chief of Air Staff Slessor insisted that no official statements link the bomber deployment to the war in Korea.[16]

At the same time, Vandenberg was consulting with Army Chief of Staff J. Lawton Collins and the Chief of Naval Operations, Adm. Forrest

---

[15] Msg, Lt Gen C. E. LeMay, CG SAC, to Gen H. S. Vandenberg, CSAF, Redline 081300Z Jul 50, in SAC/HO.
[16] Johnson OHI, pp 157–158; Burk, *USAF in UK*, p 22; msg, CG 3 AD to Lt Gen L. Norstad, Actg VCSAF, 101340Z Jul 50; msg, Norstad to Lt Gen C. E. LeMay, CG SAC, Jul 9, 1950; msg, Maj Gen L. W. Johnson, CG 3 AD, to Norstad, 101440Z Jul 50, all in Vandenberg Coll, Jul 1950 (1), Box 86, MD, LC.

343

P. Sherman, and on Monday, July 10, the joint chiefs gave their formal approval to the shipment of the atomic bomb casings. The same day the Atomic Energy Commission agreed to transfer custody of the casings, and on the eleventh President Truman gave his approval.[17] Official news releases linked the bomber movements to routine training, and crews were briefed on the importance of security. The British had objected to plans that would have virtually quarantined the crews, arguing that this would merely increase the chance of public attention.[18]

The two units alerted for England were the 93d Bomb Wing at Castle and the 97th at Biggs, both equipped with B-29s. Individual squadrons deployed during the period July 15 to 20, the 93d reforming at Mildenhall and the 97th at Sculthorpe. Meanwhile, the Tactical Air Command's 20th Fighter Group moved to Manston. The vulnerability of the bomber groups concentrated at Mildenhall, Sculthorpe, and Lakenheath concerned LeMay because they were vulnerable to air attack. British air defenses offered no protection against night attack, while the radar system could not be operated around the clock without mobilization, which the British were unwilling to order.[19]

W. Barton Leach, the Harvard law professor and air reservist, confirmed the vulnerability of the bases in East Anglia during a trip in July. He also observed that the units from the States had arrived with a sense of urgency, heightened by their having to subsist for the first week on canned rations. Thus, the airmen felt a letdown when they discovered that their British hosts were conducting business as usual. Vandenberg rejected LeMay's implication that the allies be pressured into mobilizing their air defense. Despite their disagreements, both parties recognized the risk

---

[17] Msg, Lt Gen L. Norstad, Actg VCSAF, to Lt Gen C. E. LeMay, CG SAC, Jul 9, 1950, Vandenberg Coll, July 1950 (1), Box 86, MD, LC; Hewlett & Duncan, *Atomic Shield*, pp 521-522. See also Roger Dingman, "Atomic Diplomacy During the Korean War," *International Security* 13 (Winter 88-89), p 63; according to Dingman, casings were also sent to Guam at about this time. See also Poole, *JCS, 1950-1952*, pp 153-154; R & R Sheet, Col Putnam, Psychological Warfare Div, Dir Pl, to Pol Div, Dir Pl, Crash Deployment of SAC Units, Jul 18, 1950, RG 341, DCS/Ops, Dir/Pl, P & O, 686 SAC (Jul 18, 1950), Box 1030, MMB, NA.

[18] SAC Cmd Sect Journal, Jul 10 & 12, 1950, in SAC/HO; msg, Lt Gen L. Norstad, Actg VCSAF, to Maj Gen L. W. Johnson, CG 3 AD, Jul 12, 1950, Vandenberg Coll, July 1950 (1), Box 86, MD, LC.

[19] Burk, *USAF in UK*, pp 22-23; msg, Gen H. S. Vandenberg, CSAF, to Maj Gen L. W. Johnson, CG 3 AD, Aug 9, 1950, Vandenberg Coll, Aug 1950 (2), Box 86; msg, Johnson to Lt Gen C. E. LeMay, CG SAC, 061209Z Sep 1950, Vandenberg Coll, Sep 1950 (3), Box 86, both in MD, LC.

involved in having over a third of America's atomic strike force concentrated on three fields near the North Sea.[20]

Though Air Ministry was fully cooperative about providing fields for dispersal, it also took the threat of sabotage seriously and required security guards at the fields. Johnson accommodated his hosts by obtaining some security units from the States to supplement the British effort. Ironically, the only act of "sabotage" involved the slashing of B-29 tires with bayonets by two drunken British soldiers with no political motive, only pique at their sergeant. However, lax security allowed a London reporter to walk onto the hardstand unchallenged, and he reported the incident in the *Daily Express*.[21]

By the end of August the British had provided another six airfields for dispersal of aircraft in an emergency. Paratroops had replaced the unit involved in the tire-slashing, and Air Chief Marshal Sir George Pirie informed Vandenberg that fencing would soon be available, and "In meantime heaven help the next reporter who tries to get near one of these aircraft." As a further precaution against air attack, Johnson experimented with smoke generators, camouflage, and dummy bases and planes. He also recommended that the United States send an F-86 wing to reinforce the RAF.[22]

As part of the American effort to keep the fighting limited to Korea, the deployment of strategic forces to Europe was intended to deter Soviet actions to expand the war. The joint chiefs, however, also envisioned the

---

[20] Ltr, Maj Gen A. J. Old, Dep CG 8 AF, to Lt Gen C. E. LeMay, CG SAC, Aug 15, 1950, with atch ltr, Col D. Flickinger, Hq 3 AD, to Old, Aug 7, 1950, LeMay Coll, Old (8th AF & 7th AD), Box B57; msg, Gen H. S. Vandenberg, CSAF, to LeMay, Redline, Aug 9, 1950, Vandenberg Coll, Messages, Aug 50 (2), Box 86, both in MD, LC; Burk, *USAF in UK*, p 22; ltr, Maj. Gen. L. W. Johnson, CG 3 AD, to Vandenberg, Oct 2, 1950, RG 341, DCS/Ops, Dir/Pl, OPD, 330.1 (Sep 7, 1950), Case 6, 3 AD, Box 163, MMB, NA; encl, Preliminary Memorandum, Vulnerability of SAC Bases in the UK and Outline of Defensive Measures Taken, Planned, and Feasible, Aug 7, 1950, to memo, Brig Gen W. B. Leach, Spec Asst to Sec AF, to LeMay, Aug 10, 1950, in SAC/HO.

[21] Msg, CG SAC to CSAF, DIA9533, 262246Z Jul 50; msg, Maj Gen L. W. Johnson, CG 3 AD, to Lt Gen L. Norstad, Actg VCSAF, 271805Z Jul 50, both in Vandenberg Coll, Jul 1950 (1), Box 86, MD, LC; msg, Johnson to Lt Gen C. E. LeMay, CG SAC, 061209Z Sep 50; msg, Johnson to Gen H. S. Vandenberg, CSAF, & LeMay, 141725Z Sep 1950, Vandenberg Coll, Sep 1950 (3), Box 86, MD, LC.

[22] Ltr, ACM G. Pirie to Gen H. S. Vandenberg, CSAF, Sep 15, 1950, Vandenberg Coll, Classified, Box 53; msg, Maj Gen L. W. Johnson, CG 3 AD, to Lt Gen L. Norstad, Actg VCSAF, 271805Z Jul 50, Vandenberg Coll, Jul 1950 (1), Box 86, both in MD, LC; Burk, *USAF in UK*, p 22; encl, Preliminary Memorandum, Vulnerability of SAC Bases in the UK and Outline of Defensive Measures Taken, Planned, and Feasible, Aug 7, 1950, to memo, Brig Gen W. B. Leach, Spec Asst to Sec AF, to Lt Gen C. E. LeMay, CG SAC, Aug 10, 1950, in SAC/HO.

Strategic Air Force

possibility that deterrence might fail. On July 8, while the England-bound groups were being alerted, the JCS recommended a course of action should the Soviets intervene in Korea. Plans called for the United States to pull all of its troops off the peninsula, begin mobilization, and execute the emergency war plan.[23] In short, direct Soviet involvement would prompt general war.

It was precisely the worldwide peril that encouraged U.S. leaders to attempt to limit the scope of the Korean War. Still, with forces being sent to the Far East to reinforce General of the Army Douglas MacArthur's United Nations Command, SAC was not exempt from the pressure to deplete America's strategic reserve for a local conflict. With a number of nonatomic B–29 units, the command had a well-trained conventional force usable in Korea. On July 3 Vandenberg alerted the 22d Bomb Wing at March and the 92d at Fairchild to prepare their combat groups for deployment. On the 8th, Headquarters Far East Air Forces organized FEAF Bomber Command to incorporate these two units with the theater's own Bomb Group, the 19th. Headquarters Air Force assigned Maj. Gen. Emmett O'Donnell, Jr., then commanding Fifteenth Air Force, to take over the new organization.[24]

On July 13, 1950, ten days after the alert, the 22d Bomb Group was in place at Kadena Air Base, Okinawa, and the 92d at Yokota, Japan, both ready to fly their first combat mission. The American ground forces already on hand in Korea were still too weak to do more than slow the enemy's advance. MacArthur needed a maximum air effort to support the sagging front line and interdict the advance of the North Koreans. Accordingly, FEAF Bomber Command flew a variety of missions. The first was directed against the railroad yards and oil refineries at Wonsan. That night O'Donnell learned of an emergency at the front, and so on the 14th B–29s, directed by controllers in the Fifth Air Force, hit strictly tactical targets.[25] Thus, in the first two days of bombing, the group's missions illustrated the nature of their work over the next three years, against targets of every kind.

At the same time, Headquarters, SAC, had begun to review North Korean industrial targets, drawing on material collected when they were Japanese industrial targets. To be sure, the real production base of the North Korean war machine was in Soviet territory and thus inviolate under the policy of limited war. Still, SAC planners concluded that incendiary attacks on the North Korean strategic targets could weaken the aggressor's

---

[23] *Record of Actions*, p 20.
[24] Futrell, *Korea*, pp 46–47.
[25] *Ibid.*, pp 91–92.

warmaking capacity and deprive the Soviet Union of a source of manufactured goods. O'Donnell accordingly recommended a campaign against these facilities. Although the joint chiefs rejected the technique of firebombing, on July 31 they approved the targets and authorized the deployment of two more B-29 groups.[26] Accordingly, SAC alerted the 98th Bomb Wing at Fairchild and the 307th at MacDill. By August 7 the 98th had a group in position to launch a mission from Yokota, and the 307th at Kadena flew its first attack the next day. For nearly two months, while busy with other types of targets, the FEAF Bomber Command struck at North Korean industry. Meeting virtually no opposition, the B-29s made short work of the plants, reducing them to rubble.[27] Meanwhile, hammered by superior American air power, the North Koreans proved unable to break the Pusan perimeter during August 1950. Likewise, they proved no match for the counteroffensive MacArthur opened on September 15. By the time the United Nations forces approached the 38th parallel and prepared to enter North Korea, the strategic campaign had come to an end. The 22d and 92d Bomb Groups returned home, leaving FEAF with three medium bomber groups.[28]

In order to prevent an expansion of fighting, the Truman administration essentially improvised a concept of limited war. Though this policy met considerable resistance, the free world's overall military weakness forced decision makers to conserve the critical elements of strength in the hope of deterring the Soviet Union from more serious action. Defense Secretary Johnson did raise the possibility of conducting a preventive war, but he did recognize the need to prepare the public for such a step. The administration, however, rejected any open discussion of an American first strike, and when Secretary of the Navy Matthews overstepped these bounds in a speech on August 25, Truman made him retract his statement.[29]

Maj. Gen. Orvil A. Anderson, Commandant of the Air War College, had frequently discussed the case for preventive war. With singularly poor timing, he gave an interview to a reporter for the *Montgomery Advertiser* late in August, just when Matthews's speech was in the press and bad news from Korea was harming public morale. Apparently misunderstanding the ground rules for the interview, Anderson stated his views. He argued that since the American lead in atomic weapons was ephemeral, the potential

---

[26] *Ibid.*, pp 183–187.
[27] Hopkins & Goldberg, *Development of SAC*, pp 22–23; Futrell, *Korea*, pp 193–198.
[28] Hopkins & Goldberg, *Development of SAC*, p 23; Futrell, *Korea*, pp 157–175.
[29] Poole, *JCS, 1950–1952*, pp 74–75; Futrell, *Ideas*, p 148.

Maj. Gen. Emmett O'Donnell, Commander, Fifteenth Air Force, at the outbreak of the conflict in Korea, was assigned to build and lead FEAF's new Bomber Command in Yokota, Japan.

Soviet threat should be dealt with sooner rather than later. He could identify "Russia's five A-bomb nests," and believed they could be attacked. For Anderson, the situation required a direct response: "[T]o assume that Russia won't use their A-bombs if we sit by and watch them build them is a dangerous assumption." In light of Truman's displeasure, Vandenberg had no alternative but to relieve Anderson from the War College on September 1.[30]

Another casualty of the uncertain times was Secretary Johnson himself. Identified with the stringent budgets of the recent past, he was vulnerable to any criticism of the state of preparedness of U.S. forces as well as the larger questions of national strategy. Accordingly, Truman asked the secretary for his resignation, which was submitted on September 12. To succeed him, the President recalled General Marshall to serve once more. Marshall's deputy secretary would be Robert A. Lovett, who had served with the Royal Naval Air Service long-range force in 1918 and as Assistant Secretary of War for Air during the Second World War. Few could match Lovett's experience in mobilization for an air war.[31]

Unofficial criticism of the administration's strategy of limited war continued, however, even when the news from Korea improved. Editors of

---

[30] *New York Times*, Sep 2, 1950, p 1.

[31] Poole, *JCS, 1950–1952*, pp 74–75. Johnson's departure continued a long-standing practice in which Presidents usually sought a new Secretary of War early in a wartime mobilization. Richard H. Kohn, *Eagle and Sword: The Federalists and the Creation of the Military Establishment in America, 1783–1802* (NY: Free Press, 1975), p 243.

War and Rearmament

the magazine *Air Force*, for instance, agreed that General Anderson's remarks were inappropriate, but only because of the timing and his official position. The Soviet threat was too serious, an editorial argued, to ignore the possibility that Anderson was right.[32]

On November 1 American aircraft in Korea encountered communist MiG-15 jet-propelled sweptwing fighters. MacArthur remained optimistic that the fighting was nearly over. Then on November 26 the Chinese struck in force, and one of the worst disasters in American military history began to unfold. Those forces unable to retreat were surrounded and had to fight their way out with heavy loss. By the end of the year North Korea was again in communist hands and the chance of stabilizing the front did not appear great.[33]

The end of November 1950 until about May of 1951 was a critical period. American leaders could no longer dismiss the possibility of general war between the West and the Soviet Union. If the United Nations forces were driven out of Korea altogether, the blow to U.S. prestige would create an extremely dangerous situation. In order to retain a foothold, MacArthur argued at first, it would be necessary to take action directly against mainland China. On December 6, 1950, the joint chiefs advised commanders to look at their war plans. A series of most unattractive options seemed to face U.S. decision makers.[34]

The atmosphere of danger was keenly felt in Europe. When Truman revealed in a news conference on November 30, 1950, that the atomic bomb was always under "active consideration" for use in Korea, the publicity prompted a strong international reaction. The White House issued an immediate "clarification" that the President had not authorized the use of atomic weapons. Still, Prime Minister Attlee flew at once to Washington to confer with Truman. A joint communique followed, promising consultation between the British and Americans before any decision to use atomic weapons.[35]

The growing anxiety among European nations was evident at the NATO meeting on December 18-19 in Brussels. Overcoming their usual

---

[32] Editorial, *Air Force*, Oct 50, p 5.

[33] Futrell, *Korea*, pp 157-168, 214-237. Recent evidence indicates that there were, indeed, Soviet aircraft engaged.

[34] *Record of Actions*, p 91; *Public Papers: Truman*, 1950, pp 746-747; Dean Acheson, *Present at the Creation: My Years in the State Department* (NY: W. W. Norton, 1969), pp 485-488; James F. Schnabel & Robert J. Watson, *The History of the Joint Chiefs of Staff: The Joint Chiefs of Staff and National Policy*, Vol III: *The Korean War*, Pt I (Washington: Historical Division, JCS, 1978), pp 394-406; Futrell, *Korea*, p 241.

[35] *Public Papers: Truman*, 1950, p 727; Futrell, *Ideas*, p 150.

differences, the representatives agreed to accept the American terms for strengthening Europe's defenses against a land attack. These included establishing an American supreme allied commander, Europe (SACEUR), a position to which Truman named General Eisenhower on December 19. The assignment of American ground troops and tactical air forces to Europe would soon follow.[36]

As the news from the Far East grew more discouraging, Truman faced tremendous pressure to prepare for the worst. Symington submitted a report to the National Security Council in January recommending forceful action. He proposed evacuating Korea, attacking the Chinese mainland, and making an explicit atomic threat against the Soviets.

> Atomic bombing by itself cannot win a war against Soviet Russia, but today it is the most powerful military weapon. In this world of power politics, therefore it should be further utilized in political negotiation.[37]

Symington also called for a more rapid mobilization, focusing heavily on air power.[38] He addressed a memorandum to the President, in which he condemned containment as a failure. Truman apparently confined his response to recording a visceral reaction in the margins of his copy of the memorandum. Words such as "bunk!" were inscribed frequently, and at the end he annotated: "[as] big a lot of Top Secret malarkey [sic] as I've ever read."[39] The President's considered, more restrained, reaction can be seen in the policy he chose to pursue.

The public controversy centered on what action to take toward China. MacArthur especially wanted to attack Chinese supply lines and airfields in Manchuria, but he also favored operations directly against the centers of the communists' power in East Asia. The joint chiefs discussed possible actions, but showed a strong reluctance to consider strategic air operations.[40] As for a major war with China, Bradley later described such a development as "the wrong war, at the wrong place, at the wrong time, and with the wrong enemy."[41]

---

[36] Poole, *JCS, 1950–1952*, pp 213–220.
[37] Rprt, Chmn NSRB to NSC, Recommended Policies and Actions in Light of the Grave World Situation, Jan 11, 1951, in *FRUS*, 1951, Vol I, p 12.
[38] *Ibid.*, pp 7–18.
[39] Memo, W. S. Symington, Chmn NSRB, to President, subj: Current History of National Planning Policy, n.d., in *FRUS*, 1951, Vol I, pp 21–33 & 33n.
[40] Schnabel & R. Watson, *JCS: Korean War*, pp 394–406, 417–421.
[41] *Ibid.*, p 542.

On Target. Marshalling yards, *above*, in the Kaenson-Chunchon sector of North Korea are visually struck by B–29s of the 92d Bombardment Group, July 1951. Bombs, *below*, are loaded onto the hardstands beside waiting B–29s of FEAF Bomber Command.

In the end, the United States gambled on its ability to hold the line in Korea. By the end of February the United Nations forces had stopped the communist advance, and a counteroffensive in March brought the front to the vicinity of the 38th parallel. Reports of an impending communist offensive included accounts of Chinese or Soviet forces massing in Manchuria. Truman warned congressional leaders that the United States might widen the war if necessary and authorized transfer of some complete atomic weapons to military custody. Over the next few months, the front in Korea held.[42]

The public controversy over strategy embroiled military men. O'Donnell had favored hitting the bases in Manchuria, and when he returned from the Far East in January 1951 to resume command of Fifteenth Air Force he was misquoted on the matter in the press.[43] More significant, of course, was MacArthur's outspoken disagreement with the administration's decision not to attack Manchuria. His direct challenge to Truman's policies finally led to his relief on April 11, 1951, and to congressional hearings in which the administration and the joint chiefs stated their case.[44]

The period of crisis that subsided in May and June 1951 finally led the administration to seek a negotiated settlement of the war. Talks between the opposing military commands in Korea began on July 8, ushering in a two-year period of negotiating and fighting.[45] This situation, as well as the strategy of limited war, gave rise to exacerbated criticism of Truman's policy. The public controversy in turn damaged the standing of the Democratic administration as the election year of 1952 drew near.

In supporting the decision to keep the Korean War limited, Vandenberg repeatedly argued that the Air Force simply could not fight an expanded war in the Far East and still have forces available in the event of a general war. The nation could not afford to expend its limited stock of atomic weapons in Korea or China. Nonetheless, the Chief of Staff acknowledged the frustrations involved, telling the British and French military chiefs that ". . . there must be a limit as to how far we can extend this fighting against satellites."[46]

---

[42] Poole, *JCS, 1950–1952*, p 152 & 152n.
[43] *New York Times*, Jan 19, 1951, p 7.
[44] Poole, *JCS, 1950–1952*, p 152 & 152n; Schnabel & R. Watson, *JCS: Korean War*, pp 542–558.
[45] Walter G. Hermes, *Truce Tent and Fighting Front* [*The United States Army in the Korean War*] (Washington: GPO, 1966), pp 20–21 & *passim.*
[46] Notes, Sec JCS, US-UK-French Chiefs of Staff Talks, Jan 11, 1952, RG 341, DCS/Ops, Dir/Pl, OPD, 323.361, Sect 6, Anx (Aug 16, 1950), Box 142, MMB, NA.

Rearmament Begins

Secretary of Defense Marshall and Deputy Secretary Lovett began their terms of office as MacArthur was launching his offensive in September 1950. The two officials took charge of the short-term rearmament program that had been initiated after alarming news from the Korean front. However, the blueprint for the expansion, NSC-68, argued that the need for military strength was continuous. President Truman had requested that Congress add nearly $12 billion to the $13 billion already budgeted for fiscal 1951, and this proposal was faring well. The legislators had also removed all manpower ceilings for the armed forces. The President had approved specific increases, including 10 more wings for the Air Force by June 1951. Reserve forces were starting to go on active duty, and planners in the services were considering long-term increases that would entail a partial mobilization. The Air Force alone was asking for an increase to 130 wings.[47]

The President had made his first request for a supplemental appropriation for fiscal year 1951 on July 24. At that time the war was still being financed under continuing resolution. (Congress adopted the 1951 regular appropriation only on August 24, already aware that it would be superseded).[48] In presenting his case to Congress, Truman explained his rationale for the increases as well as for further programs he intended to propose:

> First, we need to send more men, equipment, and supplies to General MacArthur.
>
> Second, in view of the world situation, we need to build up our own Army, Navy, and Air Force over and above what is needed in Korea.
>
> Third, we need to speed up our work with other countries in strengthening our common defenses.[49]

These three goals—sustaining the fighting forces, general rearmament, and aid to allies—would remain the focus of Truman's defense policy for the rest of his presidency.

---

[47] Poole, *JCS, 1950-1952*, pp 38-57; Rearden, *Formative Years*, p 382.
[48] Rearden, *Formative Years*, p 382, Poole, *JCS, 1950-1952*, p 46.
[49] Radio and Television Address to the American People on the Situation in Korea, Jul 19, 1950, in *Public Papers: Truman*, 1950, p 540.

Strategic Air Force

Although NSC-68 had not been formally approved, it now served as the basis for plans for the long-term rearmament under way. The joint chiefs were unable to agree on the size of the Air Force in the program until late in September 1950, when they recommended a goal of seventy wings by June 1951 and ninety-five wings by 1954. However, the sense of crisis brought on by the Chinese intervention on the Korean peninsula prompted Congress to vote more money than the Defense Department was requesting. Supplemental appropriations now pushed the fiscal 1951 defense budget to more than $40 billion. The services agreed to accelerate the buildup, and the Air Force would have its ninety-five wings two years earlier, by June 1952. Thirty-four of the wings would be allocated to the strategic force.[50]

Indeed, one rationale for the ninety-five wing program involved the proposed size of the strategic force. Calculations showed that twenty-six bomber wings were needed in order to drop 330 atomic bombs in fifteen days, sustain the anticipated heavy losses, and still have a force in condition to "police" targets where rebuilding might occur, support ground forces, and start training the mobilization force. Six of the bomber wings would be heavy, equipped with B-36s, and the other twenty medium wings would consist of B-50s and B-47s. Eight reconnaissance wings would be divided into four heavy (RB-36) and four medium wings. The remaining sixty-one wings represented a considerable buildup in tactical and air defense forces, but given the seriousness of the global threat, even these resources might prove insufficient.[51]

The Role of Nuclear Weapons

Even as Defense officials planned a major expansion of the nation's strategic air force, developments in atomic weapons technology also pointed to considerable growth in the stockpile and advancements in the means of delivery. Yet, the likelihood of atomic plenty and the advent of small "tactical" weapons raised controversies. Some strategists hoped that if

---

[50] Poole, *JCS, 1950–1952*, pp 38–57, 63–64, 66–71; memo, R. A. Lovett, Dep Sec Def, to Sec AF, Jan 12, 1951, Vandenberg Coll, Classified, Box 61, MD, LC; mins, 75th Mtg NSC, Dec 14, 1950, PSF, NSC Mtg # 75, Box 210, HSTL.
[51] Memo for Maj Gen T. D. White, Dir Pl, subj: Increase in Wings Above the 95 Wing Program, May 22, 1951; memo for Gen H. S. Vandenberg, CSAF, subj: Strategic Air Force, n.d., both in RG 341, DCS/Ops, Dir/Pl, Decimal 1942–1954, 320.2 (Jul 24, 1950), Sect 2, Box 123, MMB, NA.

atomic weapons could enable the outnumbered forces of NATO to defend Western Europe, a strategic air offensive against the Soviet Union would not be necessary. Likewise, the Army and the Navy envisioned having nuclear weapons available for a variety of tasks, not merely the strategic ones.

By 1951 the Atomic Energy Commission had production in full swing, with construction of more facilities at Hanford and Oak Ridge already in progress. President Truman had approved the building of new heavy-water reactors for the hydrogen bomb project. The era of atomic scarcity was coming to an end. The laboratory at Los Alamos was developing designs for new weapons, both atomic and thermonuclear, ranging in yield from a few kilotons to megatons.[52] Planners could anticipate a variety of weapons for different purposes.[53]

The armed services faced new decisions concerning the potential uses of the smaller, more powerful bombs. These decisions in turn would affect the larger questions of organization, control, and targeting. Air doctrine, as the Air University was inclined to point out, stressed the versatility of air forces. However, the Air Staff continued to maintain that the forces designated for the strategic air offensive needed to be preserved for that essential task. Under the circumstances, the primacy of the strategic air offensive and SAC's role as the centerpiece of atomic deterrence were more and more subject to debate.[54]

The Atomic Energy Commission's achievements involved success on several fronts. More deposits of uranium were being discovered in the United States. New bomb designs, as previously mentioned, allowed for varied yields. In addition, "boosted" weapons, using some nuclear fusion to increase efficiency and yield, were awaiting tests. Small, compact weapons, soon to be on the production line, could be delivered by smaller planes, guided missiles, or even cannon. Thus both improved strategic and new "tactical" weapons were becoming available.[55]

As knowledge of these developments grew, pressure on the commission from the armed forces and Congress increased dramatically. McMahon's Atomic Energy Committee began to challenge Secretary Johnson's initial reluctance to support a larger weapons program. Calling on General Bradley to testify, the committee obtained a statement from the joint

---

[52] One megaton is equivalent to a million tons of TNT.
[53] Rosenberg, "U.S. Nuclear Stockpile, 1945 to 1950," *The Bulletin of the Atomic Scientists* 38 (May 1982), p 26; Bowen, *Development of Weapons*, Pt I, p 21, Pt II pp 37ff, 407; Hewlett & Duncan, *Atomic Shield*, pp 430, 669.
[54] Futrell, *Ideas*, pp 191–192.
[55] Bowen, *Development of Weapons*, Pt I, pp 21ff, Pt II, pp 370ff.

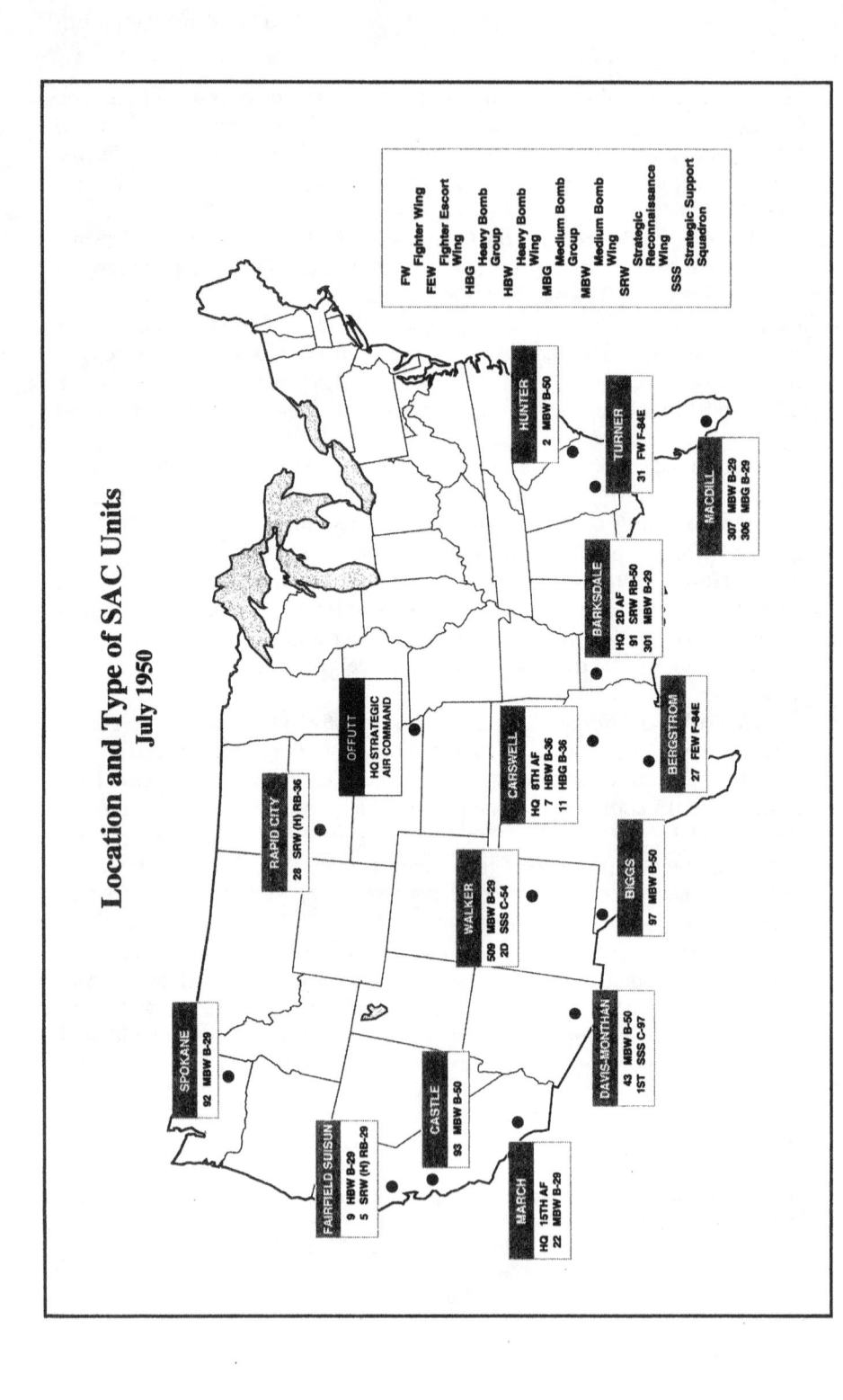

chiefs on August 9, 1950, in favor of expansion. Johnson now regarded the question favorably, and the chiefs soon supplied the AEC's Military Liaison Committee with a formal statement of requirements. This led to a production program approved by President Truman on October 9.[56]

The armed forces' requirements for weapons were increasing in number and scope. Up to 1950 the AEC's production capacity determined the services' priorities. Now that the commission was preparing to expand its facilities, the continuing requirement for weapons for the strategic air offensive was open to discussion. Both the Air Staff and LeMay considered the existing stockpile inadequate for destroying the Soviet industrial base. But the strategic bombing capability was not the only issue. Fears of a mounting Soviet atomic stockpile raised the question of countermeasures. Logic seemed to suggest that defensive measures alone could not prevent serious damage to the United States, and doctrine told Air Force planners that the answer was to attack the hostile atomic striking force. In addition, there were those who advocated retardation, using atomic weapons for the interdiction of the Soviet land offensive in Europe.

In August 1950, the Joint Strategic Plans Committee defined three tasks for atomic-capable forces. Attacking Soviet atomic targets was known as "blunting" the offensive (later called "counterforce"). Industrial targets would be struck to achieve "disruption" of the hostile war economy. To these strategic tasks, the committee added retardation. (These three tasks were subsequently named in accordance with the new NATO phonetic alphabet, BRAVO, DELTA, and ROMEO). A few additional weapons could be justified for a reserve and for post-attack policing of targets.[57]

Once targets had been identified, an ad hoc committee under the joint chiefs, with an Air Force officer as chairman, applied a sophisticated methodology to compute the actual number of weapons needed. The Air Staff and experts at RAND had developed formulae to determine the specific number and yield of weapons that would give the desired probability of destroying a target. Industrial plants of modern construction, for example, would require considerable yields to produce the necessary blast effect. As intelligence about the targets improved, estimates of how many

---

[56] *Ibid.*, Pt II, pp 419-421.

[57] *Ibid.*, pp 422-423; Futrell, *Ideas*, pp 142-144; ltr, Col J. F. Bird, XO, National War College, to Lt Gen C. E. LeMay, CG SAC, Aug 19, 1952, with atch lecture, Strategic Air Operations, Mar 6, 1952, LeMay Coll, Semi-Official # 15, 1952, Box B80, MD, LC; David A. Rosenberg, "The Origins of Overkill: Nuclear Weapons and American Strategy, 1945-1960," *International Security* 7 (Spring 83), pp 16-19.

weapons would actually get through the defenses produced the needed number and type of weapons. By December 1950 the joint chiefs could submit a proposal for a thirty percent increase over the production plan approved in the October program, based on these calculations.[58]

Still further gains in weapons production soon became likely. The commission's efforts to increase capacity had entered a new phase with the approval by the President late in 1950 of construction of new facilities. These included a plant near Paducah, Kentucky, and reactors for the hydrogen bomb project at the Savannah River site, near Aiken, South Carolina. Meanwhile, an extensive series of tests, some at Eniwetok and some at a new site in Nevada, scheduled during 1951, would validate new designs and probably affect the armed forces' requirements.[59]

The ensuing debate over nuclear roles and missions arose in part from the idea that smaller weapons might be used on the battlefield to offset the superior numbers of the Soviet ground forces. The Army hoped to develop such a concept and had the support of Oppenheimer, who was Chairman of the Atomic Energy Commission's General Advisory Committee.[60] Specifically, the Army leadership was interested in atomic-armed tactical air forces as well as developing a 280-millimeter gun, the "atomic cannon." The Navy in turn wanted to expand the potential of carrier-based aircraft to strike naval targets or support strategic operations. The Air Force did not in principle reject these claims. Instead, it argued that true nuclear plenty would not exist for a number of years, and until then the strategic air offensive should have priority for all nuclear weapons. Another, more technical view claimed that large bombs made the most efficient use of fissionable material. Behind these discussions lay the question of whether an effective defense on the battlefield would eliminate the need for the strategic air offensive.[61]

The Air Force was prepared to make a major concession and support weaponry for tactical aircraft—a move which would benefit both the Army and the Air Force. Since 1949, work had proceeded on the technical problems of delivery by fighters and light bombers. Col. John D. Stevenson in the Air Staff's atomic energy office outlined a plan for an air division equipped with atomic-capable B–45s and F–84s. Stationed in England, such an organization could play a role in the task of retardation.[62]

---

[58] Bowen, *Development of Weapons*, Pt I, pp 421–427.
[59] Hewlett & Duncan, *Atomic Shield*, pp 531–532, 669, 672–673.
[60] Kaplan, *Wizards of Armageddon*, p 81.
[61] Bowen, *Development of Weapons*, Pt II, pp 427–433.
[62] *Ibid.*, p 428; Futrell, *Ideas*, pp 156–157.

It took several months to reach an agreement on the issues of weapon design or quantities. When Vandenberg submitted a proposal for requirements to the joint chiefs on September 15, 1951, they passed the matter to the Joint Strategic Plans Committee, which negotiated without success. Then the chiefs took up the matter themselves, and with further Air Force concessions, new requirements emerged in January 1952.[63]

At the end of 1951 Truman approved yet another construction program for the Atomic Energy Commission, and progress continued over the next year. Successful weapons tests, in addition to the discovery of a major deposit of uranium in Canada confirmed that the age of plentiful and varied weapons was approaching. Then on October 31, 1952, a major breakthrough occurred. The commission detonated its first thermonuclear device in the IVY test series at Eniwetok.[64] The "21-ton cryogenically-cooled, liquid-fueled monster,"[65] as one historian has called it, yielded a ten megaton explosion. A "dry" and lighter device was known to be on the way, and with it the prospect of an operational hydrogen bomb.[66]

Having new, more sophisticated atomic weapons in prospect, the armed forces had to plan for their use in the event of war. However, such decisions reflected back to the question of establishing requirements. The basic joint emergency war plan, OFFTACKLE, remained in effect, although its name changed from time to time. This plan continued to give the central role at the onset of a war to the strategic air offensive, while the other forces held their ground and the nation mobilized. True, the Korean War and the expansion of the armed forces led to some changes, but the basic plan remained the same. The arrangements for targeting atomic weapons, however, was subject to change.[67] The approved target list in the summer of 1950 was JCS 2056. Despite his reservations about the document, LeMay did use it as a basis for the SAC bombing plan. The Army was dissatisfied, believing that the list failed to provide for the interdiction role. The controversy came to a head among the joint chiefs in August 1950 over what revisions to make in the list.[68]

---

[63] Bowen, *Development of Weapons*, Pt II, pp 429–436; Hewlett & Duncan, *Atomic Shield*, pp 561–567.

[64] Hewlett & Duncan, *Atomic Shield*, pp 576–578, 669, 672–673.

[65] Rosenberg, "Origins of Overkill," p 24.

[66] *Ibid.*; Bowen, *Development of Weapons*, Pt I, p 29.

[67] Poole, *JCS, 1950–1952*, pp 167–169.

[68] ASSS, Maj Gen T. H. Landon, Dir Pl, to DCS/Ops, Target Destruction Annex for SHAKEDOWN, Jan 5, 1951, RG 341, DCS/Ops, Dir/Pl, OPD, Spec File SAO, Sect 3, Box 1058, MMB, NA.

Strategic Air Force

Previously, the Air Targets Division of the Air Staff's Directorate of Intelligence had set to work to develop a new list. Appearing on June 30, 1950, this list reflected the experience of the Second World War. It emphasized the oil industry—including synthetic fuels—and electric power. The study also recommended assigning some weapons against the Soviet atomic energy industry and holding back some weapons for use against enemy military forces, including bomber bases. It was in its review of this study that the Joint Strategic Planning Committee identified the three tasks of blunting, disruption, and retardation.[69]

On August 15, 1950, the joint chiefs approved the three tasks but failed to reach an agreement on the rest of the review.[70] The Air Force supported the Air Targets Division study, with some revisions. On November 30 Vandenberg submitted that study as JCS 2056/9—called SLANT NINE in Joint Staff parlance. The wrangling went on. The Army and the Air Force could not agree on procedures for controling retardation operations. For its part, the Navy sought a role in the strategic air offensive without being subjected to central control.[71]

By the beginning of 1951, the joint chiefs had progressed to the point of allocating sixty weapons for retardation.[72] Also, although they had not adopted SLANT NINE, Vandenberg appeared to believe that there was enough consensus for him to tell SAC to start using the new target list.

---

[69] Memo, Col G. H. Tibbets, Ch Blue Team, WPD, DCS/Ops, to Maj Gen T. H. Landon, Dir Pl, subj: Target Systems Submitted for Consideration for the Strategic Air Offensive in Support of the Objectives of the Joint Outline Emergency War Plan, Fiscal Year 1951 (DI/USAF-ONI Study No. 245), Jul 4, 1950, with encl; rprt, JSPC 877/128 to JCS, Responsibility for the Continuing Selection of Targets and Target Systems for the Strategic Air Offensive, Aug 8, 1950, with atch, all in RG 341, DCS/Ops, Dir/Pl, OPD, Spec File SAO, Sect 2, Box 1057, MMB, NA.

[70] Rprt, JSPC to JCS, 2056/7, Target Selections for the Strategic Air Offensive, Aug 12, 1950, with JCS Decision 2056/7, Aug 15, 1950, RG 341, DCS/Ops, Dir/Pl, OPD, Spec File SAO, Sect 2, Box 1057, MMB, NA.

[71] Memo, Brig Gen D. Hale, Ch WPD, DCS/Ops, to Maj Gen J. Smith, Dep Dir Pl, subj: Target Selection for Strategic Air Offensive (JSPC 902/72), Sep 28, 1950; memo, CSAF to JCS, 2056/9, subj: Target Destruction Annex for Plan SHAKEDOWN, Nov 30, 1950; memo, Maj Gen T. H. Landon, Dir Pl, to Gen H. S. Vandenberg, CSAF, subj: Target Selection for Strategic Air Offensive (JCS 2057/10), Nov 4, 1950, all in RG 341, DCS/Ops, Dir/Pl, OPD, Spec File SAO, Sect 2, Box 1057, MMB, NA.

[72] Msg, Maj Gen T. H. Landon, Dir Pl, to Lt Gen J. K. Cannon, CINC USAFE, Maj Gen L. W. Johnson, CG 3 AD, Jan 6, 1951, RG 341, DCS/Ops, Dir/Pl, TS OPD, 384.5 (Aug 28, 1950), Box 452, MMB, NA.

However, LeMay had serious objections to SLANT NINE and visited Washington on January 22, 1951, to present his case. As later outlined, the SAC Commander's reservations were based on the limited stockpile of weapons and on practical operational considerations.[73]

The problem with both retardation and blunting was that no one knew where the targets were. Once the offensive began, reconnaissance would have to identify elements of the Soviet atomic force.[74] Although LeMay had no objection to attacking retardation targets, he suspected that many would turn out to be disruption targets already on the list, "strategic in the classical sense of the word."[75] Further, he insisted on SAC control of retardation operations, coordinating with theater commanders at the discretion of the joint chiefs.[76]

As far as the industrial targets were concerned, SAC planners considered many electric power plants too difficult to find and remote from other targets. Thus there was no "bonus" in a strike, destroying more than one target with a single weapon. In fact, no information existed for many of the power plants in SLANT NINE. The SAC Headquarters staff planners still preferred the oil industry as a target, while government centers (thought to be crucial in a rigidly centralized economy), atomic plants, and other factories followed on the list. A city, seen as an aggregation of industrial targets, including the labor force, was the most promising objective overall.[77] For LeMay, a veteran of the costly campaign against the German ball bearing industry, focusing on a single type of target was suspect. In LeMay's own words, "disruption" should give way to an absolute goal: "Destroying that [industrial] base means blasting it down, plant by plant."[78]

---

[73] ASSS, Maj Gen T. H. Landon, Dir Pl, to CSAF, Target Destruction Annex for SHAKEDOWN, Jan 5, 1951; ltr, Gen H. S. Vandenberg, CSAF, to CG SAC, subj: Target Destruction Annex for SHAKEDOWN, Jan 12, 1951, both in RG 341, DCS/Ops, Dir/Pl, OPD, Spec File SAO, Sect 3, Box 1058, MMB, NA.

[74] Briefing, Brig Gen W. C. Sweeney, Jr, Dir Pl SAC, to Sec AF, Jan 17, 1951, RG 340, OSAF/OOA Numeric-Subject File 51, 1j(2), Box 16, MMB, NA.

[75] Ltr, Lt Gen C. E. LeMay, CG SAC, to Maj Gen T. D. White, Dir Pl, May 7, 1951, in SAC/HO, 0rganization, Mission & Command.

[76] *Ibid.*

[77] *Ibid.*; Briefing, Brig Gen W. C. Sweeney, Jr, Dir Pl SAC, to Sec AF, Jan 17, 1951, RG 340, OSAF/OOA, Numeric-Subject File 51, 1j(2), Box 16; ltr, Maj Gen T. S. Power, Dep CG SAC, to CSAF, subj: JCS 2056/9, Mar 27, 1951, with encl: SAC Comments and Recommendations on the Target Destruction Annex for Plan CROSSPIECE [*sic*] (encl to JCS 2056/9), Mar 23, 1951, RG 341, DCS/Ops, Dir/Pl, OPD, Spec File SAO, Sect 3, Box 1058, all in MMB, NA.

[78] Briefing, Strategic Air Command Presentation for Secretary Finletter and Gen Vandenberg, Sep 4, 1951, SAC/HO HA-0086.

On January 23, the day after LeMay's meeting with the Air Staff, the Vice Chief of Staff, Gen. Nathan F. Twining, advised the SAC Commander to continue using JCS 2056. With the Chinese communists still advancing in Korea, Air Staff officials expressed doubt that the target list could be revised in time. In any case, given the joint chiefs' general support for SLANT NINE, a team chief in the War Plans Division warned of serious repercussions about SAC's not complying with it. However, Maj. Gen. Thomas D. White, Special Assistant to Maj. Gen. Truman H. Landon, the Director of Plans, argued that both JCS 2056 and SLANT NINE were out of date, and that with new weapons and new intelligence another major revision was due. Lt. Gen. Idwal H. Edwards, the DCS for Operations, essentially agreed and advised LeMay to develop proposals for a revision to SLANT NINE. Considering the time needed for SAC to change target folders and plan missions, LeMay would actually be using JCS 2056 for some time. Meanwhile, on February 26, 1951, the Army and the Air Force were able to force the issue and win approval of SLANT NINE.[79]

Faced with conflicting views from two groups of planners, Vandenberg was looking for new insights. Bernard Brodie of Yale University had written an article that appeared in August 1950, calling for more analytical thinking about atomic targeting. Acquainted with Orvil Anderson, Brodie attracted the notice of Norstad, at the time acting vice chief, and of Lt. Gen. Howard A. Craig, the Inspector General. When asked for his view, LeMay had suggested that Brodie might be useful to the target experts in Washington.[80] Vandenberg asked the professor to look at the plans and give him his thoughts. After receiving Brodie's initial report, the Chief of Staff intended to organize a talented outside panel with Brodie as chairman. However, this effort proved abortive. Norstad, Brodie's chief supporter, was now in Europe, and the civilian scientist failed to establish a good working relationship with the Air Force targeting staff. Apparently,

---

[79] ASSS, Maj Gen T. D. White, Dir Pl, to DCS/Ops, Target Destruction Annex for SHAKEDOWN, Mar 10, 1951; memo, Col R. E. Applegate, Ch Red Team, WPD, DCS/Ops, to Brig Gen D. D. Hale, Ch WPD, DCS/Ops, subj: Target Destruction Plan for SHAKEDOWN, Feb 7, 1951; ltr, Lt Gen I. H. Edwards, DCS/Ops, to CG SAC, Mar 13, 1951, RG 341, DCS/Ops, Dir/Pl, OPD, Spec File SAO, Sect 3, Box 1058; memo, CSAF to JCS, 2056/9, subj: Target Destruction Annex for Plan SHAKEDOWN, Nov 30, 1950, with Decision, JCS 2056/9, Feb 26, 1951, RG 341, DCS/Ops, Dir/Pl, OPD, Spec File SAO, Sect 2, Box 1057, both in MMB, NA.
[80] Ltr, Lt Gen H. A. Craig, IG, to Lt Gen C. E. LeMay, CG SAC, Aug 21, 1950; ltr, LeMay to Craig, Aug 28, 1950, both in LeMay Coll, Craig, Box B52, MD, LC; Kaplan, *Wizards of Armageddon*, pp 38–40.

Secretary Finletter also disapproved of Brodie's selection.[81] In any case, a new panel convened under the chairmanship of Henry C. Alexander, the executive Vice President of J. P. Morgan and former Vice Chairman of the U.S. Strategic Bombing Survey at the end of World War II. Alexander's committee submitted its report on July 20, 1951.[82]

The Alexander Panel favored an emphasis on targeting electric power. However, it conceded that operational problems might prevent an effective attack. Further, although it considered limiting the number of human casualties a desirable goal, the panel did not think that striking power plants would achieve this. Still, if it could be done, hitting the electrical system would prove the most economical means to achieve disruption of the Soviet industrial base. The panel also favored a reserve of weapons to be held for use against targets that had escaped damage in the first onslaught.[83]

Maj. Gen. Charles P. Cabell, the Director of Intelligence, found the panel's report "constructive," and especially liked the idea of a reserve of weapons. The SAC staff, however, gave the report a cooler reception. The arguments against the electrical program persisted. As for the reserve, the command's planners argued that, under existing conditions, the length of time required to deliver the stockpile of atomic weapons would allow for any adjustments for new targets or undamaged old ones.[84]

Meanwhile, on July 16, the joint chiefs gave SAC permission to use JCS 2056 as the target list, as opposed to SLANT NINE. The JCS remained deadlocked over approval of a new list.[85] In effect, with JCS 2056 largely

---

[81] Memo, Gen H. S. Vandenberg, CSAF, to Bernard Brodie, subj: Formation of Special Advisory Panel on Strategic Bombing Objectives, Mar 23, 1951, Vandenberg Coll, 1. File here—Misc, Box 83, MD, LC; Kaplan, *Wizards of Armageddon*, pp 45–49 & 49n. According to Kaplan's account, Brodie clashed with the Targeting Division and the Director of Intelligence, Maj. Gen. C. P. Cabell. Finletter's concern, according to Kaplan, probably resulted from a meeting the secretary had on May 7, 1951, with the historian Edward Meade Earle, long a critic of Brodie. Brodie's report has been the object of at least two unsuccessful searches in the National Archives.

[82] Rprt, Panel of Consultants to Sec AF, CSAF, Dir Intel, Target Systems for a Strategic Air Offensive, Jul 20, 1951, RG 340, OSAF/OAA Numeric-Subject File 51, 1j(2), Box 16, MMB, NA.

[83] *Ibid*.

[84] Memo, Maj Gen C. P. Cabell, Dir Intel, to T. K. Finletter, Sec AF, Gen N. F. Twining, VCSAF, Jul 3, 1951; ltr, Maj Gen T. S. Power, Dep CG SAC, to Dir Intel, USAF, subj: Report of Panel of Consultants to Secretary of the Air Force, Chief of Staff, USAF, and Director of Intelligence, Headquarters USAF, Oct 1, 1951, both in RG 340, OSAF/OAA Numeric-Subject File 51, 1j(2), Box 16, MMB, NA.

[85] Poole, *JCS, 1950–1952*, p 172.

Strategic Air Force

out of date, LeMay was targeting his own force, at least for disruption and blunting tasks.

Control of the retardation task raised controversies on an even broader scale. Support of ground forces with nuclear weapons was intimately connected to the issues of command structure in the European theater and the rearmament of NATO being pursued with renewed vigor as a result of the outbreak of the Korean War. The structure of SAC in Europe had to serve not merely to control its forces but also to insure effective cooperation with the allied command. This was a special and complicated case of the problem of SAC's role as a worldwide specialized force dealing with theater commanders.[86]

Even before Truman had selected Eisenhower for the supreme command in Europe, the joint chiefs had begun to reorganize American forces in the area. In particular they detached United States Air Forces, Europe, from the European Command to create a third co-equal specified command (along with Army and Navy commands), over all of which Eisenhower had authority as the JCS representative.[87]

The Air Force's own leadership was realigned in connection with these changes. In the interim structure Vandenberg had created after Fairchild's death, Norstad acted as Vice Chief of Staff, Edwards headed Operations, and Twining came in from Alaska to replace Edwards in Personnel. Now that the air command in Europe was to be a critical position, Norstad took it, becoming Eisenhower's air chief. He replaced Lt. Gen. John K. Cannon, who returned to the States to preside over the revival of the Tactical Air Command. Twining became Vice Chief of Staff.[88]

Norstad's new position was ambiguous, for while Eisenhower had authority in the theater, Vandenberg was the joint chiefs' executive agent for U.S. Air Forces, Europe. Furthermore, Eisenhower made Norstad the NATO air commander on the central front. Landon moved to Wiesbaden as Norstad's American deputy, while the latter ran his international headquarters at Fontainebleau.[89]

---

[86] Staff Study (draft), Col H. C. Huglin, NATO Stdg Gp, Relationship of Strategic Air Command to NATO, Feb 3, 1951, atch to memo, VAdm J. Wright, Dep US Rep Stdg Gp NATO, to Gen H. S. Vandenberg, CSAF, subj: Relationship of the Strategic Air Command to the North Atlantic Treaty Organization, 26 A 51, RG 341, DCS/Ops, Dir/Pl, OPD, 323.361 (Aug 16, 1950), Sect 4, Box 141, MMB, NA.
[87] Spec Study, JCS Hist Div, *History of the Unified Command Plan*, 1977, pp 7–8; Poole, *JCS, 1950–1952*, p 225.
[88] Fogerty, Study # 91, "Edwards," "Fairchild," "Norstad," "Twining."
[89] *Ibid.*; Poole, *JCS, 1950–1952*, p 231.

War and Rearmament

Gen. Nathan F. Twining became Air Force Vice Chief of Staff in October 1950. As head of Fifteenth Air Force during World War II, he was one of the service's most experienced commanders of strategic air forces. He succeeded Gen. Hoyt S. Vandenberg as Air Force Chief of Staff in 1953.

The arrangements to coordinate this structure with SAC were inadequate. At the time, Maj. Gen. Samuel E. Anderson was in England at the head of Eighth Air Force Advanced Echelon (ADVON), leaving a deputy at Carswell to control his air force. In April 1951 Headquarters SAC developed a plan for "Command Elements," to be headed by senior officers provided by the headquarters of the numbered air forces. These would deploy or prepare to deploy to specific theaters overseas to coordinate SAC operations with the theater commands. The chiefs of these elements would be agents of LeMay himself. LeMay had been concerned at the possibility of atomic operations in Korea as well as the debates over retardation. These command elements would enable him to control strategic operations everywhere and arrange any support for the theaters directed by the JCS. Elements were identified by phonetic alphabet designations, SAC X-Ray and SAC Zebra being the first.[90]

It remained to reach agreement with the theater commands to set up these elements. Even as the risk of escalation in Korea was fading, the first liaison agreement SAC got was with the Far East Command. General

---

[90] Study, Col J. S. Samuel, Red Team, WPD, DCS/Ops, The Atomic Aspects of Retardation and Associated Problems, Jul 18, 1951, RG 341, DCS/Ops, Dir/Pl, OPD, Spec File SAO, Sect 4, Box 1058; ltr, Maj Gen T. S. Power, Dep CG SAC, to CG 2 AF, subj: Organization and Deployment of Headquarters Strategic Air Command, Apr 19 (altered to 20), 1951, RG 341, DCS/Ops, Dir/Pl, OPD, 323.36, SAC (Apr 19, 1951), Box 1027, both in MMB, NA; msg, Power to Lt Gen C. E. LeMay, CG SAC, 011620Z May 51; ltr, Power to CG 8 AF, subj: Headquarters SAC Command Elements, Aug 19, 1952, both in SAC/HO, Organization, Mission, & Command.

Strategic Air Force

Power signed the text in May. SAC X-RAY would operate in the theater, and in the event of general war FEAF Bomber Command would come under it.[91] Arrangements in Europe, closely tied as they were to the issue of retardation, proved more complex. The staff at Supreme Headquarters, Allied Powers, Europe (SHAPE), had developed the so-called "Eisenhower Plan" for the defense of Western Europe. Eisenhower himself calculated that at the outbreak of a war in the region, the first thirty days would be critical. Ground forces would have to hold a defensive zone east of the Rhine while a maximum air effort, using atomic and conventional weapons, was launched against the aggressor's forces. Allied planners proposed to have SAC units allocated and on call to bomb targets identified by SHAPE.[92]

The Air Staff considered the provisions for retardation to threaten SAC's ability to do its other tasks.[93] Indeed, the plans in NATO fitted well with the proposals being offered from other quarters. The whole question of the relation of strategic forces to local commands and the procedures to use them in a tactical role was involved in the debate. The availability of tactical atomic weapons was only part of the equation.

The proposal to designate specific bomber units for retardation missions might be objectionable, but some on the Air Staff recognized that some action would be necessary. Norstad certainly shared such views.[94] Col. J. S. Samuel of the War Plans Division urged in July 1951 that SAC be encouraged to move in such a direction. He anticipated the need to modify more B–29s for the purpose. The Army's atomic cannon and the Navy's carrier-borne planes enabled those services to address the need for tactical operations. Samuel felt that the Air Force's failure to deal with tactical air issues had given rise to this. In the long run, he believed tactical atomic air units would have to be assigned to theater commanders. He noted "SAC's general tendency to minimize the problems associated with retardation in

---

[91] Msg, Maj Gen T. S. Power, Dep CG SAC, to Lt Gen C. E. LeMay, CG SAC, 011620Z May 51; MR, M. S. Oldham, Ops An, SAC, Conference with General Stratemeyer, May 5, 1951, May 11, 1951, both in SAC/HO, Organization, Mission, & Command.

[92] Memo, subj: Air Force Comments on Plan "Headstone," Sep 24, 1951, with atch memo, subj: A Specific Example to Show How Plan "Headstone" is Incompatible with Air Force Planning, n.d., RG 341, DCS/Ops, Dir/Pl, TS OPD, 381 (Feb 7, 1950), Case 3, Sect 8, Box 338, MMB, NA; Poole, *JCS, 1950–1952*, p 254.

[93] See previous note.

[94] Msg, Lt Gen L. Norstad, CINC AAFCE, to Gen H. S. Vandenberg, CSAF, 251210Z Aug 51, Vandenberg Coll, Redlines Jun 1951–, Box 86, MD, LC.

spite of the positive steps taken to meet the responsibility." In that context, the role of the atomic 49th Air Division then forming at Langley was clearer.[95]

The lobbying for tactical atomic weapons continued, with both the Army and Navy developing concepts. Navy planners late in 1951 recommended allocating all new weapons production to the theater and fleet commanders. They also recommended joint policies for tactical atomic operations.[96]

The Air Staff had meanwhile initiated a study of tactical air power, to be conducted by the California Institute of Technology under the chairmanship of its President, the physicist Lee A. DuBridge, who was a former member of the USAF Scientific Advisory Board. The Army agreed to join the Air Force in sponsoring the study, called VISTA. Approved in April 1951, PROJECT VISTA soon started to shift its focus. The potential of small nuclear weapons in the tactical role soon overshadowed other aspects of the problem. And the European land battle, as the potential scene for testing tactical air power, drew special attention from the Caltech group.[97]

Late in 1951 Robert F. Bacher, who was head of the VISTA group working on tactical atomic weapons, brought J. Robert Oppenheimer in to help write his report. Oppenheimer accompanied DuBridge and others of the VISTA group that visited Europe soon after.[98] Vandenberg had been following VISTA and kept Norstad informed. On December 5 and 6 the study group met with Norstad at Fontainebleau. The allied air chief discussed the group's report and was disturbed to learn that it carried the implication that tactical atomic weapons were to be considered as an alternative to a strong strategic air offensive. This was precisely Oppenheimer's view, of course, but DuBridge readily agreed to revise the report so as to eliminate the implication that there was an opposition between tactical and strategic weapons. Completed in January 1952, the VISTA report advocated expanding the stockpile of tactical atomic weapons

---

[95] Study, Col J. S. Samuel, Red Team WPD, DCS/Ops, The Atomic Aspects of Retardation and Associated Problems, Jul 18, 1951, RG 341, DCS/Ops, Dir/Pl, OPD, Spec File SAO, Sect 4, Box 1058, MMB, NA.

[96] Memo, Maj Gen R. M. Lee, Dep Dir Pl, subj: Target Systems Which Could Be Destroyed by the Strategic Air Offensive in Support of the JOEWP (JCS 2056/21 and /22), Nov 30, 1951, RG 341, DCS/Ops, Dir/Pl, OPD, Spec File SAO, Sect 4, Box 1058, MMB, NA.

[97] David C. Elliot, "Project Vista and Nuclear Weapons in Europe," *International Security* 11 (Summer 86), pp 163–183.

[98] Futrell, *Ideas*, p 167; Hewlett & Duncan, *Atomic Shield*, p 580.

without being a vehicle for Oppenheimer's view.[99] Nonetheless, when Secretary Finletter received the report, he took no further action on it, not even circulating it in spite of protests from DuBridge and leaks to the press of some of its contents.[100]

During 1952 the Army further developed its own concepts for tactical atomic weapons. Unlike VISTA, Air Force observers noted, they failed to consider the problem of overcoming Soviet air power in Europe and neglected much of the real retardation task. In any case, the joint chiefs authorized continuing plans for tactical atomic weapons.[101]

While the Army and the Air Force looked at the European land battle during 1951, SAC and SHAPE were concluding an agreement. In October, at Vandenberg's suggestion, LeMay had visited Europe to confer with Eisenhower and Norstad. An accord similar to that in the Far East resulted, with a command element called SAC ZEBRA to be stationed in Europe. This agency was to control the SAC forces located in the theater and coordinate any atomic missions flown in support of the allied command.[102]

While SAC was working with SHAPE to coordinate their possible wartime operations, the joint chiefs formed an ad hoc committee to study how to control atomic forces. Maj. Gen. Walter C. Sweeney, SAC's Director of Plans, was the Air Force member. He was committed to an uncompromising defense of Air Force and SAC control of the strategic air offensive. In fact, the Air Force position was essentially adopted by the joint chiefs and an agreement finally concluded. True, this required conceding that SAC's atomic monopoly would end. The joint chiefs would

---

[99] See previous note; msg, Lt Gen L. Norstad, CINC AAFCE, to Gen H. S. Vandenberg, CSAF, 081245Z Dec 51, Vandenberg Coll, Redline Messages May–Dec 1951 (2), Box 86, MD, LC; USAF OHI, #K239.0512–1116, Hugh N. Ahmann, with Gen Lauris Norstad, Feb 13–16 & Oct 22–25, 1979, pp 433–434, in AFHRA.

[100] Elliot, "Project Vista," pp 170ff.

[101] Ibid.; memo, Maj Gen R. M. Lee, Dir Pl, to Lt Gen T. D. White, DCS/Ops, subj: Outline of Presentation of Army Concept Given to Joint Chiefs of Staff, Jul 7, 1952, Jul 15, 1952, with atch briefing notes, RG 341, DCS/Ops, Dir/Pl, TS OPD, 381 (Jan 19, 1952), Box 319, MMB, NA.

[102] Msg, CINC AAFCE to Gen H. S. Vandenberg, CSAF, Lt Gen C. E. LeMay, CG SAC, Redline 1005, 271337Z Sep 51, RG 341, DCS/Ops, Dir/Pl, OPD, 323.361 (Aug 16, 1950), Sect 5, Box 141; ltr, LeMay to Lt Gen T. D. White, DCS/Ops, USAF, Dec 19, 1951, RG 341, DCS/Ops, Dir/Pl, OPD, Spec File SAO, Sect 4, Box 1058, both in MMB, NA; msg, Vandenberg to Lt Gen L. Norstad, CINC AAFCE, Redline 344, 081710Z Oct 51, Vandenberg Coll, May–Dec 1951 (8), Box 86; msg, Norstad to Vandenberg, Redline 393, 071742Z Dec 51, Vandenberg Coll, Redline Messages, May–Dec 1951 (2), Box 86, both in MD, LC; ltr, Gen A. M. Gruenther (USA), CS SHAPE, to LeMay, Dec 29, 1951, with atch, in SAC/HO, HA-0104.

allocate the weapons to be used for retardation. On the other hand, Norstad would select the targets in his theater that required atomic attack, and then he and SAC ZEBRA would consult on methods and suitability. Eisenhower would then ask the joint chiefs to authorize the strikes. If SAC received direction to fly the missions, SAC ZEBRA would control the operations.[103] This still failed to address the question of what the joint chiefs would decide to do, but at least the question would be handled at the level where plans for the strategic air offensive were also approved.

For the time being, SAC's cooperation was in fact essential for any tactical atomic mission. The 49th Air Division did arrive in England in June 1952. It became part of U.S. Air Forces, Europe, and the NATO command, but its effectiveness was limited. Its B-45s were grounded late in the year and SHAPE canceled an exercise in which they were to have taken part. Still, the atomic air division was a beginning of a new chapter in the story of atomic weaponry.[104]

The effort to preserve the integrity of the strategic air offensive largely succeeded, at the price of conceding its monopoly of atomic weapons. LeMay was skeptical of the potential for tactical atomic warfare, arguing that it would destroy the battlefield.[105] Norstad believed a few weapons could have a powerful effect in the NATO area. Noting the concern that the Soviets could overrun Europe while SAC was attacking Russia, Norstad saw these few weapons as serving a useful purpose. In his view, the strategic air offensive and the defensive battle on the Rhine were "complementary and not alternative."

> It is my firm belief that strength in Western Europe fixes a horizon against which the strategic air offensive can operate, and without which we would continue to have, as we have had during the last

---

[103] Briefing, Brig. Gen. W. C. Sweeney, Dir Pl SAC, Presentation at Hq TAC, Langly [sic] AFB, Va, on Jan 8, 1952, in SAC/HO, HA-0135, Tab 2; memo (T/R & D), Sweeney to Lt Gen T. D. White, DCS/Ops, n.d., in SAC/HO, HA-0135, Tab 14; rprt, Ad Hoc Cmte (Maj Gen R. E. Jenkins, USA, RAdm S. H. Ingersoll, Brig Gen W. C. Sweeney, USAF) to JCS, 2056/24, Procedures for Control and Coordination of all the Forces Possessing an Atomic Delivery Capability, & JCS Decision, Feb 29, 1952, in SAC/HO, Organization, Mission, & Command; msg, Gen H. S. Vandenberg, CSAF, to Lt Gen L. Norstad, CINC AAFCE, Redline 443, Mar 28, 1952, Vandenberg Coll, Redlines, Nov to...(OUT), Box 87; msg, Vandenberg to Norstad, Lt Gen C. E. LeMay, CG SAC, Redline 327, Aug 23, 1951, Vandenberg Coll, Messages Jun-Oct 1951 (9), Box 86, both in MD, LC.

[104] Msg, Lt Gen L. Norstad, CINC AAFCE, to Lt Gen T. D. White, DCS/Ops, 011055Z Feb 53, Vandenberg Coll, Redlines, Dec 52, Box 87, MD, LC.

[105] Briefing, Strategic Air Command Presentation for Secretary Finletter and Gen Vandenberg, Sep 4, 1951, in SAC/HO, HA-0086.

seven years, considerable difficulty in answering questions relative to the time and space factors involved.[106]

At the end of May 1952 Eisenhower left Europe to take up his candidacy for President of the United States Gen. Matthew B. Ridgway succeeded him as SACEUR. In August, Ridgway also became U.S. Commander in Chief, Europe, with three component commands. This clarified the position of Norstad to some extent. He was now clearly subordinate to Ridgway in most cases, but he retained authority in Morocco, not as a component commander in a unified command, but as a specified commander directly under the JCS.[107]

Another aspect of the relations between SAC and the theaters revolved around the "exempt units." The atomic force was not subject to seizure by theater commanders in the event of an emergency. Clearly, should the United States launch a strategic air offensive, it would be at precisely a time when theater commanders might be facing emergencies. From SAC's standpoint this was clearly no time to allow disruption of the war plan.[108]

Moreover, the prospect of nuclear plenty provided a rationale for attacking the concept of exempt units. The Chief of Naval Operations advised the joint chiefs early in 1952 that atomic units had been exempted from seizure in order to protect scarce weapons, but that this justification no longer applied. At that time the JCS and the Joint Strategic Plans Committee were deadlocked over the Air Force's proposal to exempt new atomic units from seizure. This condition remained until October 1952.[109]

In part the controversy dealt with the question of "functional" commands, such as those in the Air Force, SAC and the Air Defense Command, as well as the Military Air Transport Service, which would be largely supporting SAC at the onset of a war. The Army and the Navy presented

---

[106] Msg, Lt Gen L. Norstad, CINC AAFCE, to Gen N. F. Twining, VCSAF, 021131Z Aug 52, Vandenberg Coll, Redlines, Jul 1, 1952, Box 87, MD, LC.

[107] Spec Study, JCS Hist Div, *History of the Unified Command Plan*, 1977, pp 7-8.

[108] Memo, Maj Gen J. Smith, Dir Pl, to Gen H. S, Vandenberg, CSAF, subj: Command Relationship Between SAC and Other JCS Commands, Aug 18, 1951; memo, Vandenberg to T. K. Finletter, Sec AF, Aug 22, 1951, both in RG 341, DCS/Ops, Dir/Pl, OPD, 323.361 (Nov 8, 1943), Case 14, Cont of Atom Units, Box 152; memo, Finletter to Vandenberg, Jul 31, 1951, RG 341, DCS/Ops, Dir/Pl, OPD, 323.361 (Nov 8, 1943), Case 13, SAC, Box 151, all in MMB, NA.

[109] Rprt, JSPC 757/134 to JCS, Composition of Major Commands, Including Exempt Units, Jul 31, 1952; memo, CNO to JCS, 1259/229, subj: Units to Be Exempt Under the Provisions of Paragraph 13 of the Unified Command Plan, Feb 28, 1952, with JCS Decision, Feb 29, 1952, all in RG 341, DCS/Ops, Dir/Pl, OPD, 323.361 (Nov 8, 1943), Case 14, Cont of Atom Units, Sect 2, Box 152, MMB, NA.

themselves as advocates of the theater commanders. By the fall of 1952 there was in fact an Army-Navy proposal to do away with exempt units altogether.

Maj. Gen. Robert M. Lee, Director of Plans, advised Twining:

> This is a matter of vital concern to the Air Force. No compromise, other than [minor deletions], should be accepted at the JCS level. Approval of the Army-Navy view would be the first step toward dismemberment of SAC and MATS.... The Air Force must work toward strengthening the functional command concept and must, if necessary, split this issue to the President.[110]

Yet it was shortly after this that an agreement began to emerge. In essence, it barred theater commanders from seizing any forces engaged in carrying out a JCS-approved plan. It was conceivable that the theater commander could define what constituted such a plan, but the Air Staff seemed confident that the strategic air offensive obviously qualified. Vandenberg in turn agreed not to have the exempt units specified in advance.[111] Still, Lt. Gen. Thomas D. White, Deputy Chief of Staff for Operations, wrote to both LeMay and the commander of the Military Air Transport Service telling them to designate exempt units in their war plans and to be prepared to advise theater commanders that these were not subject to seizure.[112]

---

[110] Memo, Maj Gen R. M. Lee, Dir Pl, to Gen N. F. Twining, VCSAF, subj: Composition of Major Commands, Including Exempt Units—JCS 1259/246, Sep 2, 1952, RG 341, DCS/Ops, Dir/Pl, OPD, 323.361 (Nov 8, 1943), Case 14, Cont of Atom Units, Sect 2, Box 152, MMB, NA.

[111] Memo, Col L. H. Dalton, Asst Ch WPD, DCS/Ops, to Maj Gen H. B. Thatcher, Dep Dir Pl, subj: Composition of Major Commands—JSPC 757/142, Dec 10, 1952, RG 341, DCS/Ops, Dir/Pl, OPD, 323.361 (Nov 8, 1943), Case 14, Cont of Atom Units, Sec 3, Box 152; memo, Maj Gen R. M. Lee, Dir Pl, to Gen H. S. Vandenberg, CSAF, subj: Composition of Major Commands, Including Exempt Units (SM-2325-52), Oct 8, 1952, RG 341, DCS/Ops, Dir/Pl, OPD, 323.361 (Nov 8, 1943), Case 14, Cont of Atom Units, Sect 2, Box 152 (Besides Lee's signature, the memo has radical revisions in his handwriting); memo, Lee to Vandenberg, subj: Supplement to Brief dated Oct 13, 1952 on Composition of Major Commands, Including Exempt Units (JCS 1259/252), Oct 29, 1952, RG 341, DCS/Ops, Dir/Pl, OPD, 323.361 (Nov 8, 1943), Case 14, Cont of Atom Units, Sect 2, Box 152 (Here also Lee revised the draft by hand and signed); memo, Col J. F. Whisenand, Asst Dep Dir Pl, to Lee, subj: JCS 1259/274, Jan 30, 1953, RG 341, DCS/Ops, Dir/Pl, OPD, 323.361 (Nov 8, 1943), Case 14, Cont of Atom Units, Sect 3, Box 152, all in MMB, NA.

[112] ASSS, Col W. C. Barrett, XO, Dir Pl, to DCS/Ops, Operational Control of SAC and MATS Units by JCS Commanders, Mar 13, 1953, with atch ltr, Lt Gen T. D. White, DCS/Ops, to CG SAC, Mar 27, 1953, RG 341, DCS/Ops, Dir/Pl, OPD, 323.361 (Nov 8, 1943), Case 14, Cont of Atom Units, Sect 3, Box 152, MMB, NA.

Strategic Air Force

Expanding the Strategic Force

The inclusion of a major expansion of SAC in the Air Force's rearmament program reflects as much as anything the extent of the nation's commitment to atomic deterrence. By the time Deputy Secretary Lovett approved the ninety-five-wing program in January 1951, SAC was fully aware that it faced the challenging task of building an expanded force while at the same time maintaining the existing force in a high state of readiness. Vandenberg emphasized this, saying that SAC had "a much longer hill to climb" than the other commands.[113]

The new program called for a near doubling in the size of the command. It involved conversions to new equipment, training new men, and adjusting organization. At the same time, SAC had to revise its plans for overseas bases, especially in light of the growth of the Soviet atomic stockpile. And all of this had to go on simultaneously.

Vandenberg considered the most important problem to be that facing the aircraft industry. After five years of starvation budgets, its ability to expand was limited.[114] Until new planes came off the production line, then, the service's capacity to receive and train men would exceed its power to provide them with aircraft.

The effect of the creation of the new units required under the ninety-five-wing program was to accentuate the division of SAC into two commands, or three if one counted FEAF Bomber Command. First was the atomic force, together with the reconnaissance and other elements having critical roles in the war plan. This had become the larger part of SAC by June 1950, and continued to grow in size as new bombers entered the inventory. Secondly, the wings with the unmodified B-29s constituted a potential addition to the atomic force, but for the time being their major mission was to train toward the day when they could convert to new types of equipment. As SAC expanded, more of these units formed, using B-29s taken out of storage. They were to train and to serve as pools for replacements for the B-29 groups in the Far East.

As of June 1950 SAC was still building up the planned bomber force of fourteen wings. Four of these were to have B-36s, and two at Carswell

---

[113] Commanders Conference, Hq USAF, Jan 22, 1951, LeMay Coll, Box B100, MD, LC.
[114] *Ibid.*

War and Rearmament

were equipping and trying to get their bombers operational. The ten medium wings were to include five of B-50s. The progress of the jet B-47 program seemed to justify ending B-50 production and planning to convert all remaining B-29 wings to the jets. Four reconnaissance wings were planned. Two were starting to equip with RB-36s at Rapid City and Fairfield-Suisun. Another was getting RB-50s. The fourth was using B-45s and RB-45s and waiting to see the progress of a B-47 reconnaissance model. The B-36s and B-50s were coming off the assembly lines. There were now fewer than one hundred atomic-capable B-29s.[115]

During the fall of 1950, as the services' manpower ceilings were removed, terms of enlistment extended, and draft calls increased to meet the Army's needs, the Air Force found its recruiting offices swarming with volunteers. Tent cities went up at Lackland Air Force Base, Texas, to shelter the trainees. But it would take time to turn out pilots and mechanics. The only ready supply of qualified men was the reserve forces. Beginning in October 1950 the Air Force started calling up units and individuals of the Air National Guard and Air Force Reserve.[116]

The SAC staff would have preferred graduates of the Air Training Command's schools to reservists.[117] The turbulence of the call-up, compounded by inadequate records, tended to add to the bitterness many reservists felt. The morale problems were easy to anticipate. But in the short term, SAC had no choice. During the first six months of 1951 the command took in 7,000 officers, mainly reservists, and 42,000 noncommissioned officers and airmen, little more than half from the Air Training Command. Reservists experienced in multi-seated aircraft were to be found in the light bomber and troop carrier units, besides men who had been in B-29 units in the previous war. Early in the year the Air Force assigned SAC two National Guard light bombardment wings: the 106th from New York and the 111th from Pennsylvania. Four fighter-bomber units were also added.[118]

---

[115] *Ibid.*; Knaack, *Bombers*, pp 28-30, 36-37, 88-89, 169-172; Hopkins & Goldberg, *Development of SAC*, pp 15, 20; *Air Force Statistical Digest*, Jan 1949-Jun 1950, pp 164-181; Little, *Building an Atomic Air Force*, Vol III, Pt II, pp 309-316.

[116] Rprt, Sec Def, *Semi-Annual Report of the Secretary of Defense, 1 Jan to 30 Jun 1951*, pp 228-234.

[117] Ltr, Maj Gen T. S. Power, Dep CG SAC, to Lt Gen R. E. Nugent, DCS/Pers, Jan 4, 1951, LeMay Coll, Nugent, Box B58; Notes for Commanders Conference, Jul 24, 1951, LeMay Coll, Box B101, both in MD, LC; Gerald W. Cantwell, draft, *History of the Air Force Reserve*, CAFH; hist, SAC, Jan-Jun 1951, Vol I, pp 22-39; rprt, Col A. J. Russell, Dir Pers, SAC, to CS SAC, Report of Staff Visit, Jan 8, 1951, in hist, SAC, Jan-Jun 1951, Vol III, Chap I, Ex 3.

[118] Hist, SAC, Jan-Jun 1951, Vol I, pp 22-39.

Strategic Air Force

The North American B-45 was part of SAC's aircraft inventory in June 1950 when the command's force expansion for Korea and deterrent backup for England were ordered.

Additional units were activated to be built from scratch. All operating units were liable to have men pulled out to form cadres for new units. However, SAC insisted that no transfers be allowed if they reduced the effectiveness of the atomic force. In other units strength could be cut to ninety per cent. Reservists and recruits would man the new units and replace those drawn off for cadres. Meanwhile, the two light bomber units were to convert to B-29s. Units were also to send men to schools as these expanded, and thus train replacements for men being drawn off.[119]

The Strategic Air Command was also the logical source for replacement crews for FEAF Bomber Command. By establishing a six-month rotation cycle, SAC could receive combat experienced crews in return, not to mention commanders—O'Donnell returned to Fifteenth Air Force in January 1951. The Air Training Command formed a B-29 Combat Crew Training School at Randolph Air Force Base, Texas. From this school, crew members would go to further training at an Operational Training

---

[119] *Ibid.*

War and Rearmament

Unit (OTU) in SAC. These were set up at Forbes and at Lake Charles, Louisiana, when that field was reopened. Crews trained by the OTUs went to the Far East, to one of the existing SAC units, or to form one of the newly-activated wings. But it took time to get this system working, and until it was, the operational units had to provide replacement crews for the Far East.[120]

Based on his experiences in 1941 and 1942, LeMay was certainly aware of the challenge of organizing a bombardment unit from scratch. He also knew experienced officers to whom he could turn. He described the job of wing commander as the most complex and challenging in SAC. Any colonel being considered for promotion had to hold this position. LeMay also asked for a number of officers to be transferred to SAC to take over wings. This list, including such names as Burchinal, Compton, Holzapple, Martin, Nazzaro, and Preston, could be considered the decisive turn in a number of distinguished careers.[121] One promising career that had ended abruptly shortly before was that of Brig. Gen. Robert F. Travis, who was killed in a crash at his own base, Fairfield-Suisun (subsequently known as Travis Air Force Base), in August 1950.[122]

While the new units these officers were to command were beginning to form and train on old B-29s from storage, the aircraft industry was preparing to provide them with modern bombers. The ninety-five-wing program provided authority to order more B-36s and RB-36s and to expand orders for the B-47. But to reactivate factory space and tool up would take time and money. Bottlenecks would certainly appear. It would doubtless help that the Deputy Secretary of Defense, Robert A. Lovett, had presided over the industry's expansion in the Second World War. But now the mobilization was only partial and was to limit its interference with civilian needs. Thus while the peak monthly output for the AAF in 1944 had been 6,800 planes, the Air Force now planned an increase from 200

---

[120] *Ibid.*; memo, Col D. D. Hale, Ch WPD, DCS/Ops, to Ops Div *et al*, subj: Air Force Policy on Flying Training, Nov 20, 1950, with atch study, RG 341, DCS/Ops, Dir Pl, OPD 353 (Aug 30, 1950), Box 250, MMB, NA.

[121] Ltr, Lt Gen C. E. LeMay, CG SAC, to Lt Gen R. E. Nugent, DCS/Pers, Jan 30, 1951, LeMay Coll, Nugent, Box B58, MD, LC. David A. Burchinal retired as Deputy Commander in Chief, Europe; Keith K. Compton as Vice Commander in Chief, SAC; Joseph R. Holzapple, Commander in Chief, USAFE; Glen W. Martin, Vice Commander in Chief, SAC; Joseph J. Nazzaro, Commander-in-Chief, SAC; and Maurice A. Preston, Commander in Chief, USAFE.

[122] Mueller, *Air Force Bases*, Vol I, p 553; Hopkins & Goldberg, *Development of SAC*, p 26.

per month to 1,100 by the end of 1952. This level would drop after an adequate reserve of modern aircraft had been built up.[123]

At the outbreak of the Korean War, the Air Force had not yet ordered its planned full complement of B–36s. Some 80 were on hand, with 40 in the active inventory. The expansion approved in January 1951 gave authority to order enough for four more wings at 30 each, plus spares. During fiscal 1951 the Air Force accepted 55 more planes from Convair, most of them D models with the added jet engines. The next fiscal year added over 100 more, with still more on order. By that time three bombardment wings—two of them at Carswell—had been equipped and two reconnaissance wings. That is to say, SAC was halfway to the complete ten-wing program.[124]

Medium bombers on order in June 1950 were B–50s and RB–50s to equip six wings, and 97 B–47s. By a year later all B–50 units were equipped. Boeing was now producing the B–47 as its primary bomber. The new budgets called for production in the hundreds. In the ninety-five-wing program there were to be twenty medium bombardment wings. Subtracting the five B–50 wings, this meant fifteen wings at 45 planes per wing. Likewise, the program called for three wings of the reconnaissance model, or 810 of all types of Stratojet, plus spares. As will be seen, the B–47 encountered serious delays, and by June 1952 only 124 had been received. And by then the program had expanded still more.[125]

The bomber force in 1951 was thus still strongly a B–29 and B–50 organization. It was manned in part with fresh trainees and recalled reservists. LeMay, meanwhile, was concerned to keep up its readiness. The deployments in July 1950 showed that the wing and base organization was still unsatisfactory. Although nothing occurred like the situation in 1948, the separation of the functions of the combat unit and the air base remained unclear. LeMay ordered revisions, laying down the principles he believed important. The officer responsible for dropping the bombs should have full authority over all his units, including those directly supporting him. Just because he transferred some legal functions to the commander of the air base group, he did not lose any responsibility or authority. That

---

[123] Memo, J. A. McCone, USec AF, to Sec Def, Apr 19, 1951, Vandenberg Coll, Asst Sec of the AF, Box 38, MD, LC.

[124] Knaack, *Bombers*, pp 29, 34; *Air Force Statistical Digest*, Jan 1949–Jun 1950, pp 164–181; Ravenstein, *Combat Wings*, pp 16–18, 112–113, 128–130, 133–134; Futrell, *Ideas*, pp 126–127, 145.

[125] See previous note.

transfer was made so that if the wing commander took his unit overseas, someone at the base was still legally empowered to run it.[126]

The new arrangement worked out in the SAC staff took advantage of the increase in the number of units, creating more two-wing bases. Early in 1951 the command established several air divisions. At a base, the division commander was normally placed over the two wing commanders as well as the air base group.[127]

As for the wings themselves, the four-group (combat, maintenance and supply, air base, and medical) scheme gave way to a simpler one. In January 1951 the Air Staff approved a service test of the concept, and by the end of the year a slightly revised version was approved for all of SAC. The combat group existed now only in name, and the maintenance and supply group disappeared altogether. Each wing had flying squadrons, an aviation squadron trained to handle atomic weapons (if the wing was in the atomic bombing force), and three specialized maintenance squadrons which embodied LeMay's concepts about their duties. These three squadrons centrally provided for field (repair shops), periodic (routine inspection), and armament and electronic maintenance. Each wing then included an air base group, including the medical unit, to operate the base. Overseas bases had air base groups on the spot ready to receive a deploying wing. The flying squadrons still did flight line maintenance, but all activities were directed by the wing's maintenance control officer.[128]

The uneasiness of the units deploying to England in the summer of 1950 at the danger of air attack came as no surprise to LeMay. Although estimates of the Soviets' atomic stockpile did not attribute large numbers to it, the five hundred Tu–4s the Soviets were reported to have could strike with conventional weapons at bases in England and North Africa. From East Germany they could reach the Azores. In January 1951 the Air Staff's Directorate of Intelligence estimated that the Soviets could keep ten

---

[126] R & R Sheet, Col E. B. Broadhurst, Dir Pl, SAC, to CS SAC, Notes from Air Force and Wing Commanders' Conference, Jan 15, 1951, LeMay Coll, Official Docs, SAC Commanders Conference, Box B100, MD, LC.

[127] *Ibid.*; Hopkins & Goldberg, *Development of SAC*, pp 31–32.

[128] Hopkins & Goldberg, *Development of SAC*, pp 31, 38; ltr, Maj Gen A. W. Kissner, CS SAC, to Dir Manpower & Orgn, USAF, subj: Revised Combat Wing Organization, Oct 13, 1951, RG 341, DCS/Ops, Dir/Pl, P & O, 323.3 SAC (Jun 21, 1949), Box 1027, MMB, NA; hist, SAC, Jul–Dec 1950, Vol I, pp 131–149, Jul–Dec 1951, Vol I, p 182. The combat groups continued to exist on paper, but their headquarters were absorbed in the wing headquarters. On June 16, 1952, the groups were formally inactivated, and their lineages and honors were subsequently "temporarily bestowed" on the parent wings. Ravenstein, *Combat Wings*, p xxiii.

General LeMay's new wing commanders were destined for high rank and responsibility. *Clockwise from above, left:* **Joseph R. Holzapple** of the 47th Bombardment Wing became CINCUSAFE; **Maurice A. Preston** of the 308th Bombardment Wing became CINCUSAFE; **Joseph J. Nazzaro** of the 68th Bombardment Wing became CINCSAC; **Glen W. Martin** of the 6th Bombardment Wing became Vice CINCSAC; **Keith K. Compton** of the 97th Bombardment Wing became Vice CINCSAC; **David A. Burchinal** of the 43d Bombardment Wing became Deputy USCINCEUR; **Robert F. Travis** of the 9th Bombardment Wing was killed in the crash of a B-29 on August 6, 1950, at Fairfield-Suisun Air Force Base, which was subsequently named in his honor.

War and Rearmament

airfields out of action with those numbers. And behind their advancing land forces they could put new airfields in even closer.[129]

When the Korean War broke out, the Air Staff was studying a plan submitted by SAC to deal with this vulnerability. Called the Outline Alternate Emergency War Plan, it envisioned airfields ranging from Newfoundland to Morocco to which the medium bomber force would deploy.[130]

By the time the SAC representatives reached Washington to brief their latest revisions of the plan on July 18, groups were arriving in England. The new plan called for routine rotations to forward bases. Units there would thus be able to strike more rapidly if the order came to do so. The overburdened airlift force would get some relief, and the forward positioning had value as a demonstration to the Soviets.[131]

The Air Staff was generally favorable. In Edwards's words, "We all seem to be in favor of this scheme—what is the next step?"[132] Landon pointed up the real problem. Many of the bases lacked the necessary supplies, and negotiations would have to begin with the Portuguese for the Azores and the French for Morocco. Perhaps, though, the United States had some leverage in NATO channels with both countries.[133]

---

[129] R & R Sheet, Brig Gen E. Moore, Actg Dir Intel, to Dir Pl, SAC OAEWP 2-50 (Revised), Jan 30, 1951, with Appendix, Soviet Threat to SAC Bases in the Azores and Northwest Africa, Jan 30, 1951, RG 341, DCS/Ops, Dir/Pl, OPD, 381 SAC (Dec 1, 1949), Sect 2, Box 1027; AF Emergency War Plan 1-52, as of Jan 1, 1952, RG 341, DCS/Ops, Dir/Pl, TS OPD, 381 (May 2, 1950), Sect 3, Box 328, all in MMB, NA.

[130] Ltr, Maj Gen T. H. Landon, Dir Pl, to CG SAC, subj: SAC Outline Emergency War Plan 2-50, Aug 8, 1950, with atch ltr, Maj Gen A. W. Kissner, CS SAC, to CSAF, subj: SAC Outline Alternate Emergency War Plan 2-50, Jul 27, 1950, RG 341, DCS/Ops, Dir/Pl, OPD, 381 SAC (Dec 1, 1949), Sect 1, Box 1027; memo, Col H. O. Bordelon, Dir Ops, to Maj Gen R. M. Ramey, Dir Ops, subj: Strategic Air Command Alternate Emergency War Plan, Jul 19, 1950, RG 341, DCS/Ops, Dir/Pl, P & O, 686 SAC (Jul 18, 1950), Box 1029; memo, Landon to Gen H. S. Vandenberg, CSAF, SAC Outline Alternate Emergency War Plan 2-50, Aug 15, 1950, RG 341, DCS/Ops, Dir/Pl, OPD, 381 SAC (Dec 1, 1949), Sect 1, Box 1027, all in MMB, NA.

[131] See previous note.

[132] Memo, Lt Gen I. H. Edwards, Actg DCS/Ops, to Maj Gen F. F. Everest, Asst DCS/Ops, Maj Gen T. H. Landon, Dir Pl, Maj Gen R. M. Ramey, Dir Ops, Jul 22, 1950, RG 341, DCS/Ops, Dir/Pl, P & O, 686 SAC (Jul 18, 1950), Box 1029, MMB, NA.

[133] Memo, Maj Gen T. H. Landon, Dir Pl, to Lt Gen I. H. Edwards, Actg DCS/Ops, subj: SAC's Outline Emergency War Plan, n.d.; memo, Landon to Edwards, subj: Base Rights for SAC Plan, Jul 19, 1950, atch to memo, Brig Gen P. M. Hamilton, Ch Pol Div, DCS/Ops, to Landon, subj: SAC Crash Plan, Jul 25 [1950], all in RG 341, DCS/Ops, Dir/Pl, P & O, 686 SAC (Jul 18, 1950), Box 1029, MMB, NA.

Another problem arose when Vandenberg tried to get the plan through the joint chiefs.[134] He finally withdrew it but, as Twining advised SAC in November, "The Chief of Staff believes, even though the plan has now been withdrawn, that it has served a useful purpose in that its submission is responsible for action now under way...."[135] In fact, approval by the joint chiefs soon followed for talks with the French about Morocco and for the Air Force's efforts to upgrade communications, stock supplies, and arrange for air defense. Meanwhile, at the end of November, Twining sent the plan back to SAC for revision.[136]

A further difficulty throughout the effort to develop this plan finally became clear as the Air Staff went over SAC's revision in January 1951. Feeling that the plan was still not ready to go to the joint chiefs, Edwards had Sweeney bring a group of his planners to Washington to work on further revisions with the Air Staff. It was essential for the staff of a specified command to learn the requirements involved in putting together material for presentation to the Joint Chiefs of Staff.[137]

The revisions were complete by March 1. By now it was no longer an alternate plan but a complete revision and updating of the SAC Emergency War Plan. As such it attracted the interest of Finletter, who shared the concern about the threat to SAC bases. He received a briefing on the plan on March 12, and it soon had gone to the joint chiefs.[138]

There it still did not secure immediate approval. For one thing it tied in with the other controversies then swirling around the strategic air offensive. The chiefs finally approved the plan on October 22, 1951.[139] But

---

[134] Memo, CSAF to JCS, 2057/7, subj: Strategic Air Command Outline Alternate Emergency War Plan 2–50 (SAC OAEWP 2–50), Aug 24, 1950, with note by Secs, Aug 31, 1950, RG 341, DCS/Ops, Dir/Pl, OPD, 381 SAC (Dec 1, 1949), Sect 1, Box 1027, MMB, NA.

[135] Ltr, Gen N. F. Twining, VCSAF, to CG SAC, subj: SAC OAEWP 2–50, Nov 28, 1950, with atchs, RG 341, DCS/Ops, Dir/Pl, OPD, 381 SAC (Dec 1, 1949), Sect 1, Box 1027, MMB, NA.

[136] *Ibid.*

[137] SAC Emergency War Plan 1–51, Mar 1, 1951, atch to memo, Maj Gen T. D. White, Dir Pl, to Gen H. S. Vandenberg, CSAF, subj: SAC Emergency War Plan 1–51, Mar 10, 1951, RG 341, DCS/Ops, Dir/Pl, OPD, 381 SAC (Mar 23, 1949), Sect 3, Box 1028; memo, T. K. Finletter, Sec AF, to Vandenberg, Feb 23, 1951, with marginal note, Meeting held in Secretary's office, 0950, March 12, RG 341, DCS/Ops, Dir/Pl, TS P & O, 384.5 (Jul 10, 1950), Box 452, all in MMB, NA; memo, Finletter to Vandenberg, Nov 23, 1951, Twining Coll, AFCVC Reading File Nov 1951, Box 55, MD, LC.

[138] See previous note.

[139] Memo, RAdm Lalor, Sec JCS, to JCS, SM–2462–51, subj: Strategic Air Command Emergency War Plan 1–51, Oct 12, 1951, with atch JCS 2057/26, Oct 11, 1951, with JCS Decision, RG 341, DCS/Ops, Dir/Pl, OPD, 381 SAC (Mar 23, 1949), Sect 4, Box 1028, MMB, NA.

War and Rearmament

in the meantime, the reassessment of the situation of SAC bases overseas had led to important action with important consequences. The coming years were to see a major leap overseas by the Strategic Air Command.[140]

An Investment in Air Power

In spite of the seemingly interminable disputes among the services over the strategic air offensive, agreement on the budget was possible even when air power was the issue. During 1951 the Air Force mounted a major effort to go beyond the ninety-five-wing program. This effort was to a considerable degree successful and reflected an understanding of the depth of the nation's commitment to strategic deterrence.

Based on the Harmon report,[141] air planners were confident that the strategic air offensive could do serious damage to Soviet industry. Even the appearance of the MiG-15 in Korea, where it showed it could take on strategic bombers, did not betoken a major improvement in night defenses in the Soviet Union. It was easy to assume that the Russians were undertaking major improvements in this area, but the offensive threat was taken more seriously.[142]

Predictions of the growth of the Soviet atomic stockpile grew gloomier and influenced thinking about the scale of the strategic air offensive. In 1950 an estimate foresaw 200 weapons by 1954, but at the beginning of 1952 the Air Staff was predicting 320 by the same date. It was thought the Tu-4 fleet had reached 700 planes by then. To this, Finletter was not the only one to add the threat of conventional attacks on SAC bases.[143] Under such circumstances, the Air Force estimated the requirements for the blunting as well as the disruption task. Given all the commitments in the strategic air offensive, the ninety-five-wing program seemed far from adequate. Just as an example, eight reconnaissance wings were not enough to meet such commitments as going in search of the Soviet atomic force.[144]

---

[140] See Chapter X.
[141] See Chapter VIII.
[142] ASSS, Col J. F. Pinckney, for Dir Est, Dir Intel, to CSAF, Revision of Air Intelligence Study: Aircraft of the US and the USSR, May 19, 1952, with encl, Vandenberg Coll, 13. Acft of the US & the USSR, Box 84, MD, LC.
[143] A Report to the President Pursuant to the Presidential Directive of January 31, 1950, Apr 7, 1950, encl to Note, NSC-68, J. S. Lay Jr, Exec Sec to NSC, Apr 14, 1950, in *FRUS*, 1950, Vol I, p 251.
[144] Memo to Maj Gen T. D. White, Dir Pl, subj: Increase in Wings Above the 95 Wing Program, May 22, 1951; memo to Gen H. S. Vandenberg, CSAF, subj: Strategic Air Force, n.d., RG 341, DCS/Ops, Dir/Pl, OPD, 320.2 (Jul 24, 1950), Sect 2, Box 123, MMB, NA.

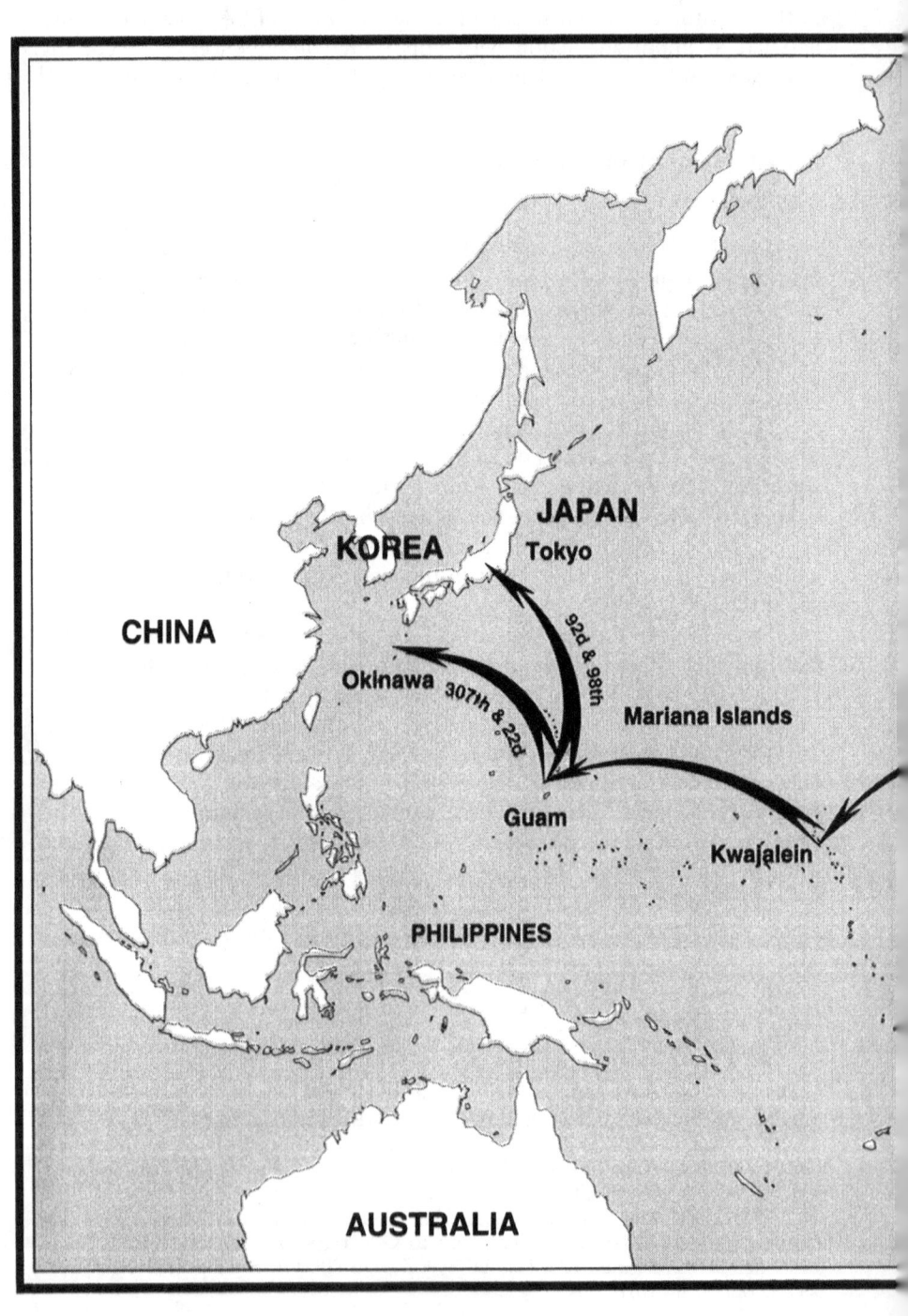

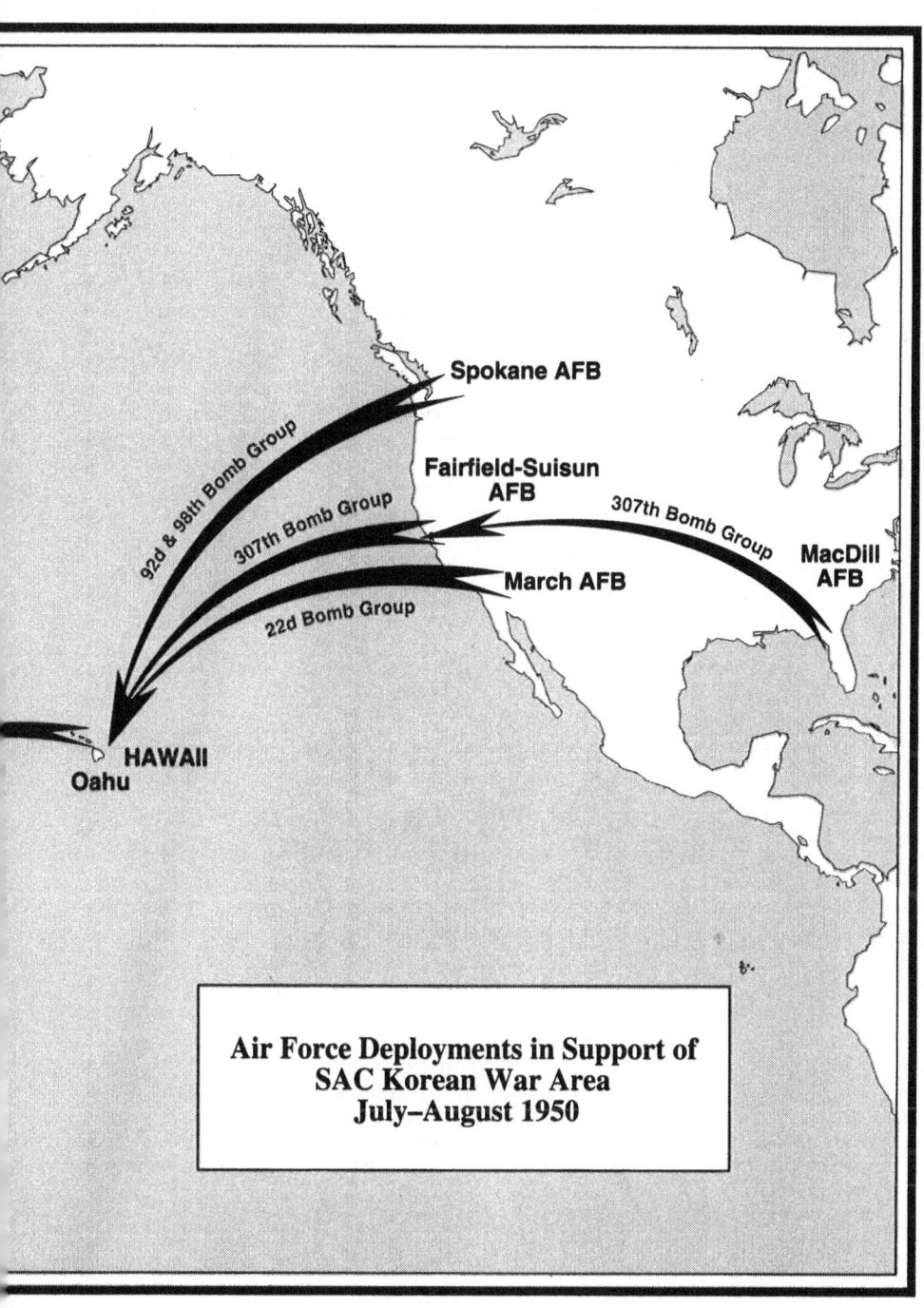

Strategic Air Force

It was Secretary Finletter and Professor Leach who worked out much of the political line for the Air Force in advocating further expansion. Influenced perhaps by briefings on the target lists and the three atomic "tasks," Finletter discussed with Leach the possibility of defining all the tasks of the armed forces in the event of a war. This, both of them came to believe, would reveal that the Army and Navy had not clearly justified their programs in the light of their specific missions. In Finletter's words, "the concept theoretically should produce the maximum defense for any given budget...."[145]

Early in October 1950 Leach outlined the military tasks the United States would have to accomplish at the outset of a war. In a memorandum to the secretary, he put the strategic air offensive first:

> We can build and maintain, for decades if necessary, an atomic air offensive as a deterrent to the USSR. It must be kept at combat readiness with increasingly effective aircraft types. It must grow in size and in ability to penetrate. Some growth in size is necessary because it can be anticipated that Soviet ability to attack SAC installations will grow; and we must increase the size of SAC to whatever extent is required to permit it fully to perform its mission after absorbing the expectable losses from Soviet counter-air-force operations.[146]

Leach likewise expected Soviet air defenses to improve, necessitating a continuing evolution in SAC's ability to penetrate.[147]

With regard to other Air Force missions, Leach favored the formation of a mobile strike force of ground and tactical air units to deal with local trouble spots like Korea. He hoped that until technology could make for an effective air defense force, the Air Force could resist political pressures to build up that component. As for NATO, he argued, "We cannot defend Western Europe on the ground." He believed that a large land force for defending Europe would be too expensive over time and would have to be cut back, or there would be a temptation to use it in a war.[148]

---

[145] Paper, Comments on Memo to Mr Finletter, n.d., atch to memo, W. B. Leach to T. K. Finletter, Sec AF, subj: The "Task" Concept in Planning Forces in Being, Oct 50, RG 341, DCS/Ops, Dir/Pl, OPD, 381 (Feb 7, 1950), Case 3, Sect 6, Box 336, MMB, NA. The "Comments" appear to have been typed from Finletter's dictation.
[146] *Ibid.*
[147] *Ibid.*
[148] *Ibid.*

Politically, the goal was to "turn Russia's energies inward upon its own people." Leach favored a strong Anglo-American alliance. What he feared was that pressure was building in NATO to build massive land forces. Churchill, in spite of his endorsement of the atomic deterrent, seemed to be aiding in this kind of pressure.[149]

Reacting to these arguments, Finletter was less optimistic that the "task concept" would appeal politically. He feared that there would be no limit to the expansion of SAC. He was also sensitive to the Europeans' concerns as they were still trying to rebuild from the last war: "To [them] liberation has little appeal." A realistic strategy would contain a Soviet land offensive while SAC struck at the aggressor's heartland.[150]

Still, both the secretary and the professor were agreed on the centrality of the deterrent role of SAC. With the "task concept" they could use the Air Force's commitment to that role to make a case for the Air Force's expansion program. In a similar vein, Landon's Directorate of Plans had developed a program with specific links to tasks outlined in NSC-68. The results showed that the 95-wing program was insufficient. Air defense forces and tactical air units to fight in the European land battle needed to be larger, bringing the total in one study to 163 wings, without even expanding the strategic force.[151]

Nor did the strategic forces look all that awesome when new intelligence estimates appeared. While NSC-68 had predicted that the Soviets would have 200 atomic bombs by 1954, new information pointed to 1953 for this event.[152] The increasing stockpile, the commitment to the blunting, disruption, and retardation tasks, and the need to survive a Soviet attack made an expansion of SAC feasible and necessary.

The calculations now being used in the Air Staff envisioned an Air Force far exceeding anything that had existed since 1945. Still, the political prospects for expansion seemed to be improving during the early months of 1951. The public debate was focusing more on air power and deterrence. In February Republican Senator Kenneth Wherry of Nebraska started hearings to challenge the sending of troops to Europe. In the

---

[149] *Ibid.*
[150] *Ibid.*
[151] Plan WEEKEND, n.d., RG 341, DCS/Ops, Dir Pl, OPD, 381 (Oct 16, 1950), Box 324, MMB, NA.
[152] NSC-114/1, Status and Timing of Current US Programs for National Security, Aug 8, 1951, in *FRUS*, 1951, Vol I, p 132; Poole, *JCS, 1950-1952*, p 94.

so-called "great debate" that followed, the "isolationist" congressional bloc led by Republican Senator Robert A. Taft, emboldened by their party's gains in the elections the previous November, advanced air power as the alternative to entanglement in NATO. General Vandenberg testified in support of the administration, describing the need for a force to shield NATO Europe until the strategic air offensive had weakened the Soviets. It was Senator Henry Cabot Lodge, Jr., Republican of Massachusetts, who led the successful effort to block a bill that would have limited further deployments.[153]

This may have been what led one of Lodge's constituents, Professor Leach of Harvard, to write the senator to discuss national strategy. The result was to make Lodge one of the Senate's leading advocates of expansion for the Air Force. Citing Leach, Lodge delivered a speech on the floor on April 30 in favor of a 150-wing program.[154]

Similarly, such advocates as Seversky and General Spaatz appeared in the press to promote air power. Spaatz condemned the "wall of flesh" strategy he considered implicit in the administration's plans for NATO.[155] Vandenberg's opportunity to enter the debate came in May, when the Senate investigated the relief of General MacArthur. On May 28 and 29 the air chief took the stand before the committee. He adopted a pragmatic defense of administration policy in the Far East. A wider war in the region would cause losses the Air Force could not afford if it was to remain a deterrent force.

> The fact is that the United States is operating a shoestring air force in view of its global responsibilities.
>
> Starting from a forty-odd-group Air Force, the aircraft industry is unable until almost 1953 to do much of a job toward supplying the airplanes that we would lose in war against any major opposition.
>
> In my opinion, the United States Air Force is the single potential that has kept the balance of power in our favor. It is the one thing that has, up to date, kept the Russians from deciding to go to war.

---

[153] Futrell, *Ideas*, pp 162–163.
[154] *Ibid.*
[155] *Ibid.*

> In my opinion, we cannot afford to... peck at the periphery as long as we have a shoestring air force....
>
> Today the United States is relatively safe from air attack. Tomorrow in my opinion we will not be....
>
> Today we have only one job that we would have to do if we got into a major war with Russia, and that is to lay waste the industrial potential of that country. Tomorrow when they have developed their long-range air force and they have more atomic weapons, we have two jobs.
>
> We would have to put into first place the job of destroying the Russian air potential that could utilize atomic bombs against the United States, and lay waste the industrial potential....
>
> [W]e have to have an Air Force that can take the attrition that would be necessary to destroy that [Russian] air force....[156]

The Air Force was now heavily engaged in promoting a major expansion. From March to May 1951 a task group in the Air Staff developed a program going well beyond 95 wings. By June, when they briefed Finletter, Vandenberg, and the Air Force Council, this group had the main features in place for an Air Force of 163 wings. Subtracting 25 airlift wings, this produced the so-called "138 combat wing" program.[157] In July the Air Force presented this to the joint chiefs, an earlier version of it having been agreed to by the Joint Strategic Planning Committee in May. The 163-wing plan called for a strategic force with 45 bomber wings (12 of them heavy) and 14 for reconnaissance—a recognition of the crucial need for target intelligence. Also, for support of NATO forces, the planners included not only fighter-bombers but also 7 wings of medium bombers, so as to free SAC for its primary mission.[158]

General Vandenberg proposed this 163-wing goal for fiscal 1952, but it would be difficult not only to get it approved but also to produce the

---

[156] Hearings before the Committee on Armed Services and Committee on Foreign Relations, Senate, *Military Situation in the Far East*, 82d Cong, 1st sess, Pt 2, May 28–29, 1951, pp 1379–1380, 1425.

[157] Table, Unit Aircraft Assigned the 80 and 138 Combat Wing Programs, Sep 19, 1951, Vandenberg Coll, 2A. Memos Re 138 Wings, Box 83, MD, LC; hist, Hq USAF, Jul 1950–Jun 1951, p 18; Poole, *JCS, 1950–1952*, pp 96–103, 100n.

[158] See previous note.

aircraft. By April 1951 total appropriations to the Air Force for the current fiscal year were $16 billion, while the 1952 budget then in Congress asked for $20 billion for 95 wings.[159] To go beyond this would require a supplemental appropriation, which the Army and Navy would not be likely to favor.

Indeed the joint chiefs did prove unable to agree on the Air Force program. The idea of "balanced forces" still prevailed. Specifically, the Army and Navy chiefs asked for cost figures before they could agree to anything, while Vandenberg was trying to get a commitment in principle to the 163-wing goal before submitting costs.[160] On June 11, 1951, the other chiefs conceded a willingness to expand the Air Force to 102 wings by June 1952 and to discuss further growth later, but Twining (acting for Vandenberg while the latter was in Europe) rejected this proposal. The next day Lovett informed the services of rising pressure in Congress to expand the Air Force.[161]

In fact Senator Lodge had returned to the charge. In July he testified in budget hearings, calling again for 150 wings. Although he emphasized the weak condition of U.S. tactical air, he also recommended a strategic force of 62 wings. To the economic argument he offered the rejoinder that existing plans called for forces that were both costly and ineffectual. Besides this, deterrence was cheaper than war.[162] Other members of Congress were not as easily convinced. Chairman Vinson doubted that the industry could produce the planes. However, Finletter met with Vinson at the end of August and was able to win his support for the Air Force's program.[163]

Before reaching Congress, however, the Air Force needed to go through the joint chiefs. Bradley arranged for them to meet with Lovett on August 9. The deputy secretary believed that the services could meet their manpower and production goals for fiscal 1952. To expand the Air Force to 163 wings would require a supplemental appropriation of $4.3 billion. Soon after this meeting, Vandenberg came to an agreement with the chiefs

---

[159] *Air Force Statistical Digest*, FY 1951, p 312: Poole, *JCS, 1950–1952*, p 85.
[160] Poole, *JCS, 1950–1952*, pp 96–100.
[161] *Ibid.*, p 98; msg, Gen N. F. Twining, VCSAF, for J. A. McCone, USec AF, to Lt Gen O. P. Weyland, CG FEAF, for T. K. Finletter, Sec AF, Redline 263, 112231Z Jun 51, Vandenberg Coll, Messages Jun–Oct 1951 (9), Box 86, MD, LC.
[162] Statement of Sen H. C. Lodge, Jr, Senate Committee on Appropriations, Jul 13, 1951, Vandenberg Coll, Sec of AF (2) [1951], Box 61, MD, LC.
[163] Memo, T. K. Finletter, Sec AF, to Gen H. S. Vandenberg, CSAF, Jul 28, 1951, Vandenberg Coll, 8. Selected Memos, Box 84, MD, LC.

that he would seek the supplemental with their approval of a "possible expansion" beyond the 1952 goals. A final decision would be made in September.[164]

Anticipating a detailed discussion, Finletter and Vandenberg prepared their arguments carefully. The Air Secretary considered it likely that the Secretary of Defense would have to resolve the question. He decided to make sure that, if civilian consultants were called in, they would include DuBridge and other experts who had worked well with the Air Force.[165]

Meanwhile, the services were preparing their proposals for fiscal 1953 and 1954. In these and the comments exchanged over them during September 1951, the debate over strategic forces began to assume a characteristic form. Collins, for the Army, proposed that the Air Force expansion not be so great. He recommended cutting down on strategic air power and airlift and deletion of the seven medium bomb wings included in tactical forces, in favor of fighter-bombers. As rationale he argued that it was important to stop the Soviet attack on Western Europe because the strategic air offensive could not do that. Adm. William M. Fechteler, Chief of Naval Operations after Sherman's fatal heart attack on July 22, favored even stronger limits on strategic air forces. He argued that tactical forces were more flexible and able to respond to a variety of threats.[166]

The Air Staff could hardly have been surprised by these arguments. Finletter emphasized the point that the first task of the armed forces was to deter an attack on the United States. If war came it would be necessary to destroy the atomic force that could make such an attack and to dismantle Soviet industry. Although he favored strong air forces in support of the European land battle, the Air Secretary opposed trying to meet aggression everywhere. "We are not able to create a force in being to take care of local wars." He hoped to cast the Navy's argument in such a light as to make it appear that such a force was in fact their objective. From the economic standpoint, the Air Force program should be presented, he

---

[164] Poole, *JCS, 1950–1952*, pp 99–102.
[165] Memo, subj: Presentation Support of 138-Wing Program, atch to memo, T. K. Finletter, Sec AF, to CSAF, n.d. [Aug 51], Vandenberg Coll, 2A, Memos Re 138 Wings, Box 83, MD, LC.
[166] Tab B, Views of the Chief of Staff, US Army, to draft memo for Sec Def, subj: United States Programs for National Security, Sep 12, 1951; memo, Adm W. M. Fechteler, CNO, to JCS, n.d., atch to draft memo for Sec Def, subj: United States Programs for National Security, Sep 12, 1951, all in Vandenberg Coll, Classified, Box 83, MD, LC; Poole, *JCS, 1950–1952*, pp 99, 103n.

Strategic Air Force

argued, as part of a national defense program that could be sustained for years.[167]

One line of argument that also concerned Finletter arose from the recognition that atomic plenty lay in the future. Rather than making a reduced strategic force possible, he believed the future stockpile called for a redoubled effort.

> The air power atomic strike force against industry must be maintained. There is nothing in the new wealth of weapons which justifies in any way the diminution of this striking weapon. On the contrary, the increase in weapons should increase the volume of the strategic strike against industry.[168]

General Vandenberg recognized the need to present the Air Force's case soon. Tooling up industry, placing orders, and taking delivery of equipment, especially a large number of bombers, as well as building airfields and training men, would take time. He had assurances from Assistant Secretary of Defense Anna Rosenberg that the manpower would be available. A study by Air Staff and outside experts showed that an Air Force of 1,200,000 men could operate 163 wings, a reduction from previous estimates. Thus a variety of arguments would show that the Air Force could meet its goals at a manageable cost to the nation.[169]

In mid-September the joint chiefs reported that they could not agree on the defense program. Robert Lovett, now Secretary of Defense since Marshall's retirement on September 12, withheld final decision pending other studies under way. In particular, a scientific panel questioned the idea that tactical atomic weapons could replace strategic ones, the very issue that would arise in PROJECT VISTA. Nonetheless, it proposed a cut in the heavy bomber program.[170]

With this information, Lovett and the chiefs arrived at agreement, although Vandenberg concurred under protest, to set the goal for the Air

---

[167] Memo, subj: Presentation Support of 138–Wing Program, atch to memo, T. K. Finletter, Sec AF, to CSAF, n.d. [Aug 51], Vandenberg Coll, 2A. Memos Re 138 Wings, Box 83; memo, Finletter to Lt Gen T. D. White, Dir Pl, Sep 10, 1951; memo, Finletter to Gen H. S. Vandenberg, CSAF, Aug 28, 1951, Vandenberg Coll, 8. Selected Memos, Box 84, all in MD, LC.

[168] See previous note.

[169] Poole, *JCS, 1950–1952*, pp 96–103; Doris Condit, *The Test of War, 1950–1953*, Vol 2 [*History of the Office of the Secretary of Defense*] (Washington: Office of the Secretary of Defense, 1988), pp 261–268.

[170] See previous note.

War and Rearmament

Force at 143 wings. These were all to be activated by June 1953, but not all would be combat ready until the next year. The heavy bomber force was to increase little beyond that planned for the 95-wing force. The other serious reductions affected airlift. The medium bomber units for the European theater were largely eliminated in favor of other tactical forces.[171] To recapitulate:[172]

Wings	Programmed June 1950	Approved for FY 52	Air Force Proposed July 1951	Approved for FY 53
Heavy Bombardment	4	6	12	7
Medium Bombardment	10	20	33	30
Strategic Reconnaissance				
Heavy	2	4	6	4
Medium	3	4	8	6
Fighter Escort	1	7	10	10
Total Strategic	20	41	69	57
Air Defense	12	20	31	29
Medium Bombardment	1		7	2
Other Tactical	9	19	31	38
Total Tactical	10	19	38	40
Troop Carrier	6	15	25	17
Grand Total	48	95	163	143

A historian for the Joint Chiefs of Staff rightly calls this debate and its outcome "momentous."[173] Although President Truman's approval was only "tentative," the Secretary of Defense had decreed that one service—the Air Force—should get well over one-third of future defense budgets.[174] A new era of air power had begun in the history of American defense policy.

---

[171] D. Condit, *The Test of War*, pp 267-269; memo, W. C. Foster, Actg Sec Def, to Sec Army, Sec Nav, *et al*, Oct 15, 1951, Vandenberg Coll, 4A. FY 53 Budget, Box 88, MD, LC.
[172] *Air Force Statistical Digest*, Jan 1949-Jun 1950, pp 3-5; table, Unit Aircraft Assigned to the 80 and 138 Combat Wing Programs, Sep 19, 1951, Vandenberg Coll, 2A. Memos Re 138 Wings, Box 83; memo, W. C. Foster, Actg Sec Def, to Sec Army, Sec Nav, *et al.*, Oct 15, 1951, Vandenberg Coll, 4A. FY 53 Budget, Box 88, both in MD, LC.
[173] Poole, *JCS, 1950-1952*, p 103.
[174] D. Condit, *The Test of War*, pp 267-269.

Strategic Air Force

Previously, the defense program had given a central role to air power, and especially strategic air power. But when the budget had been allocated, the other services got rough parity. Now the Air Force would be funded without a commitment to keep the other services on a comparable budget level. No longer would the size of the Air Force be limited because the country could not afford to bring the other services' budgets up to the same amount. Nevertheless, part of what reconciled the Army and the Navy to such an increase was the fact that they too were expanding, even if to a lesser degree. This meant annual defense budgets exceeding $50 billion. As the sense of emergency subsided, as well it might, it would be increasingly difficult to sustain such levels. Then the controversy might once again be joined.

Chapter X

"Never Before Surpassed"

The military stalemate and truce talks in Korea, though frustrating to the nation, did not divert the Air Force from the important task of building up its strength overall. Expanding SAC remained a high priority, and by 1952 LeMay's contribution in this regard had made him virtually identifiable with the command itself. Even as the Korean War was approaching its climax, Secretary Finletter personally assured him of his continued interest in the command.[1] In January 1952, Thomas D. White (since July 1951 a lieutenant general and DCS for Operations) wrote to LeMay, "I am personally well aware that you have, without any qualification, the most vital military mission of any man in the world...."[2] The commitment to building SAC went beyond words. Previously, while commanding the Military Air Transport Service, Kuter had initiated an arrangement to transfer to SAC all his pilots with four thousand hours in four-engined planes, in return for all of SAC's pilots with two thousand hours.[3]

LeMay's promotion to full general came on October 29, 1951. He had been SAC's commanding general for three years, and in the normal pattern of military service he could expect to rotate to another position in the coming year. Vandenberg's term as chief of staff would expire on April 30, 1952. However, both Twining and McNarney were senior to LeMay, who shared the same date of rank with John K. Cannon at the Tactical Air

---

[1] Ltr, T. K. Finletter, Sec AF, to Lt Gen C. E. LeMay, CG SAC, Nov 8, 1950, LeMay Coll, Finletter, Box 53, MD, LC.
[2] Ltr, Lt Gen T. D. White, DCS/Ops, to Lt Gen C. E. LeMay, CG SAC, Jan 21, 1952, LeMay Coll, White, Thomas, Box B61, MD, LC.
[3] Ltr, Lt Gen L. S. Kuter, Cmdr MATS, to Lt Gen C. E. LeMay, CG SAC, Sep 13, 1951; ltr, Maj Gen A. W. Kissner, CS SAC, to Kuter, Sep 22, 1951, both in LeMay Coll, Kuter, Box B55, MD, LC.

Command and Benjamin W. Chidlaw of the Air Materiel Command. In view of LeMay's aversion to duty in Washington—in which he was not alone—and his belief in the importance of SAC, he would have reason to prefer to remain in Omaha. Norstad proposed that Vandenberg's term be extended, resolving the question of a successor.[4] With congressional approval, an extension of fourteen months was announced in March 1952. In spite of a growing personal estrangement between Vandenberg and Secretary Finletter, both continued in office. At the same time as the announcement of Vandenberg's extension, the Air Force also reported that Twining would assume command of SAC, with LeMay succeeding him as vice chief of staff. What happened next is not clear, but the switch never took place. Vandenberg was not well, having learned that he needed surgery for cancer.[5] The vice chief would have to act for him, and recent experience on the Air Staff may have been considered a key asset. In any case, LeMay remained at SAC, and the identification of command and commander became even more pronounced.

Meanwhile, the acceptance of the 143-wing program by Congress marked a new phase in the history of the independent Air Force. From September 1947 to June 1950 the Air Staff's advocacy of a seventy-group force had only produced continued frustration. The outbreak of the Korean War had altered the political climate, leading to the adoption of the 95-wing program as the Air Force's share of a general program of rearmament. The significance of the larger program adopted in 1952 was that the Army and Navy would remain stable while the Air Force expanded to 143 wings. The nation's leaders had decided to rely on air power for defense.

The military and political situations in Korea and Europe continued to exert a major influence on the U.S. defense program. With the stabilization of the front in Korea in the spring of 1951, it was clear that United Nations forces would not be driven from the peninsula. At the same time, reconquest of North Korea was becoming an increasingly elusive goal. Truce talks between the opposing forces began in July, though the fighting persisted as both sides hoped to improve their negotiating position. Superior American air power counterbalanced the Chinese advantage in num-

---

[4] Msg, Lt Gen L. Norstad, CINC AAFCE, to Gen H. S. Vandenberg, CSAF, 221330Z Jun 51, Vandenberg Coll, Redline Messages (May–Dec 51) (2), Box 86, MD, LC; Fogerty, Study # 91, "LeMay" & *passim*.

[5] *New York Times*, Mar 7, 1952, p 3; LeMay & Kantor, *Mission with LeMay*, p 395; USAF OHI, # 744, James C. Hasdorff, AFHRA, with Brig Gen Noel F. Parrish (Ret), Jun 74, p 225, in AFHRA. For a discussion of the personal difficulties between Finletter and Vandenberg, see G. Watson, "Secretaries," pp 111–112

bers of ground troops. A concerted air interdiction campaign failed to weaken the communists to the point of allowing a major advance by United Nations forces. Thus in 1952 the strategic goal for Far East Air Forces shifted from interdiction to "air pressure," an effort to inflict enough damage on the enemy to encourage him to come to an agreement in the truce talks. The terrible fear of a widening war and an even greater catastrophe, so evident at the beginning of 1951, gave way to frustration at the continued bloodshed and financial drain of an indecisive conflict.[6]

In Europe, as American forces began to arrive in the summer of 1951, the allies gradually regained confidence. The high point of cooperation was reached in the NATO meeting at Lisbon in February 1952, when the allies agreed to ambitious force goals, which eventually included a plan to have ninety divisions and ten thousand combat aircraft available in Europe on thirty days' notice. But increased confidence in Europe, as in Korea, detracted from the sense of urgency, creating what Secretary of State Dean G. Acheson later termed a "receding tide of political will."[7] Added to the malaise was the growing economic crisis in the United Kingdom and the general unwillingness to sustain huge military budgets on both sides of the Atlantic.

The possibility of a stretchout, a decrease in planned force levels, or even an actual reduction, especially strong once the war ended in Korea, concentrated the Air Staff's attention. So many American officials considered the concept of "balanced forces" as a rationalization for dividing the defense budget into equal thirds that the Air Force could be forced to cut back with the rest. This would straightjacket the Air Force within an inadequate budget and allow the spending of vast sums on land and naval forces with a strategic function hardly discernible to the airmen.[8] The nation could ill afford to reduce SAC; nor, the air leaders argued, would the public be assured by reductions in air defense. And the Army would be equally handicapped by cuts in tactical air forces.

Finletter had originally constructed the case for the 143-wing Air Force on the "task concept," which required justifying programmed forces in terms of the specific wartime task they were to perform. Meanwhile, the

---

[6] Futrell, *Korea*, pp 63–372, 433–474, 605–629.
[7] Acheson, *Present at the Creation*, p 625. Ironically, there has been speculation that Stalin, beginning early in 1951, was actively preparing the Soviet bloc for an attack on the West. No Western intelligence agency at the time seems to have had any information on this. See Mikhail Heller and Aleksandr Nekrich, *Utopia in Power: The History of the Soviet Union from 1917 to the Present*, trans by Phyllis B. Carlos (NY: Summit, 1986), pp 504–505.
[8] See for example, John J. Daunt, "In My Opinion: The Balance in Our Armed Forces," *AUQR* III (Winter 49), pp 66–69.

Strategic Air Force

Air Staff during 1951 and 1952 developed what came to be called the "Air Concept" to define the way the service proposed to make its case. This focused on the strategic air offensive as the crucial operation in the event of war, with forces for other tasks in a supporting role. Deterrence would be assured by the services' being able to undertake operations at once.

Public discontent with the stalemate in Korea and large budgets, together with the widespread fear of communism and an image of a scandal-ridden Democratic administration, placed the Air Force in a difficult position. It was, after all, Secretary Lovett who had approved the 143-wing program. At the same time, many Republican critics advocated an increased emphasis on air power as the solution to the problem of defense spending. The platform of the Republicans in the upcoming presidential election campaign, stressing what came to be called the "K and two C's"—Korea, communism, and corruption—promised an effective defense at less cost.[9] The airmen only hoped that their service would not become a political football in the course of the debate. If this did not materialize, the Air Force was likely to be in a strong situation whoever won. In the meantime, the Air Force would continue to provide forces for the war in the Far East and to build up under the 95-wing program and then the 143-wing program.

Medium Bombers in Korea

The three years of FEAF Bomber Command operations in Korea were rich in ironies. A plane designed to carry all-out war to the industrial heart of enemy nations served in a limited, localized, peripheral conflict. In that war the strategic bomber was used against a variety of targets. The obsolescent, second-line segment of SAC did the actual fighting, though the B–29 showed a good deal of versatility. These circumstances came about precisely because the true industrial base of the communist forces lay within the Soviet Union, and off limits to allied bombers. As a result, the Superfortresses were not used in their primary mission.

After the return of the 22d and 92d Bomb Groups to SAC in October 1950, Far East Air Forces normally had a little more than one hundred B–29s and some twenty-five reconnaissance and weather types. Although Bomber Command was part of the theater forces, it drew its crews,

---

[9] Herbert S. Parmet, *Eisenhower and the American Crusades* (NY: MacMillan, 1972), p 141.

"Never Before Surpassed"

commanders, and methods from SAC. The commanding generals of FEAF Bomber Command normally served tours of four to six months before returning to SAC. Beginning in March 1951 crews rotated back to SAC after their tours.[10] The stateside command thus built up a new generation of combat-tested aircrew members. In addition, operations provided lessons in new techniques, particularly against Soviet-built air defenses.

In 20,000 sorties Bomber Command lost 24 aircraft to enemy action. All operational losses accounted for 627 aircrew members killed or missing and 96 wounded. In contrast, 5,800 completed tours unscathed. This was a far cry from "Black Thursday" perhaps,[11] but losses did at times inhibit operations, and combat flying remained a hazardous enterprise.[12]

Much was made at the time of the age of the B-29s. They no doubt posed a headache for maintenance. A faster, more modern aircraft might have been better prepared to contend with MiGs and flak. On the other hand, the Superfortresses were fitted with new equipment such as Shoran to enhance their survivability and bombing accuracy. And there was no doubt of the value of a plane that could carry such a large bomb load.[13]

Of the more than 20,000 total sorties flown by FEAF Bomber Command in Korea, 12,000 were directed against the transportation network—roads, railroads, bridges, marshaling yards, and supply centers. Other targets included troop areas (over 700 sorties), industrial areas (about 1,400), and airfields (approximately 1,250). Besides interdiction missions, the command flew 2,800 sorties in support of United Nations ground units. The bombers dropped leaflets, and the RB-29s of the reconnaissance squadron provided essential photographic coverage.[14] Furthermore, SAC sent some KB-29 tankers to the Far East to refuel fighters. The first combat refueling took place on July 6, 1951, when an Air Materiel Command tanker and a SAC crew refueled four RF-80s.[15]

When Bomber Command went into action in July 1950, a controversy immediately arose concerning the control of its operations. Responding to the emergency of the North Korean advance, FEAF found it difficult to refuse calls for support missions at the front line. Subsequent experience showed the difficulty of planning and flying B-29 missions from bases in

---

[10] This account is drawn primarily from Futrell, *Korea*; see pp 93–94.

[11] On Thursday, October 14, 1943, Eighth Air Force launched 291 bombers in an unescorted daylight attack on the ball-bearing facilities at Schweinfurt, Germany. Of these 60 were lost, and, from then until escort fighters were available, no major deep penetrations of Germany were attempted.

[12] *Air Force Statistical Digest*, FY 1953, pp 58, 59, 90, 92, 110–111.

[13] *Ibid.*, p 32; Futrell, *Korea*, pp 93–94, 773, 387.

[14] *Air Force Statistical Digest*, FY 1953, p 77.

[15] Hopkins & Goldberg, *Development of SAC*, p 34.

Strategic Air Force

Japan and Okinawa to operate in a volatile situation. So Lt. Gen. George E. Stratemeyer, the Commanding General of Far East Air Forces, managed to convince MacArthur and his staff that the B–29s were better suited for interdiction missions, which could be planned some time ahead. From that point on, although political considerations intervened, and overall arrangements for control of air operations in Korea remained unsatisfactory throughout the war, FEAF itself selected most of the targets for the B–29s.[16]

Until the Chinese with their MiG–15s entered the war in November 1950, Bomber Command encountered negligible oppposition. The 19th Bomb Group lost one bomber in the early days of the war. The next loss occurred several months later, on November 10. That month incendiary attacks on supply centers were authorized and went ahead successfully. The bridges on the Yalu, where Chinese forces were entering Korea, proved tougher to handle, especially since the attacking bombers had to avoid entering Chinese air space.[17]

Once the Chinese offensive started in November 1950, FEAF concentrated all its efforts to help the United Nations ground forces stem the tide. As the communists' supply lines lengthened, they came under continuing air attack until the enemy's drive south came to a halt. In April 1951 Bomber Command became involved in a grueling air battle near the Yalu. The bridge and supply center at Sinuiju were circled with heavy air defenses, and the 27th Fighter Escort Wing's F–84s proved unequal to the task of keeping the MiGs away. On April 12 three of the thirty-nine bombers dispatched against the bridge at Sinuiju were lost. Stratemeyer at once suspended Bomber Command operations in the far north until a solution to the air defense problem could be found. Even so, bomber losses continued.[18]

The answer was not long in coming. First, the ground radar that Fifth Air Force used for close support at night was found to be workable with the B–29. Further, in June Bomber Command began installing Shoran sets on a few B–29s, which could then use the Fifth Air Force's beacon for night operations. These developments made Bomber Command an increasingly effective night bombing force.[19]

Late in 1951 the command engaged in two major operations, one for interdiction and the other counter-air. Its participation in a major interdiction campaign, inaptly named STRANGLE, began in June. As this operation began, the communist air forces made a strong bid to gain air superiority

---

[16] Futrell, *Korea*, pp 50–55, 92–94, 501–504.
[17] *Ibid.*, pp 220–230, *Air Force Statistical Digest*, FY 1953, p 59.
[18] Futrell, *Korea*, pp 293–300.
[19] *Ibid.*, pp 355–359, 408–409.

by setting up important bases within Korea. The B-29 was the prime weapon to use against airfields, and Bomber Command thus played a major role in this new air battle. The daylight attacks that followed brought the heaviest aircraft losses yet. During October the enemy shot down five B-29s and two more in November. Still, the U.S. effort kept the bases from becoming operational, and by the end of 1951 the communist airmen had been forced back into their sanctuary in Manchuria.[20]

In the early months of 1952, as STRANGLE failed to produce satisfactory results, the United Nations Command began to formulate the concept of "air pressure." To overcome the political stalemate at the truce talks, the allies decided to use concerted air attacks to maximize the cost to the enemy of continuing the war. Operating at night, the B-29s brought their massive bomb tonnages to bear against rear area targets. The enemy resorted to a number of ruses to defend against the Superforts. For example, fighters at high altitude dropped flares to guide searchlights onto the bomber stream. U.S. losses increased, with three B-29s shot down in January 1953. This, however, represented the enemy's last stand. The crucial weapon in night defense, the radar-equipped fighter, never appeared in the communist order of battle. From February to the end of the fighting, not a single B-29 was lost to enemy action thanks in large measure to the heroic efforts of U.S. Air Force, Marine Corps, and Navy radar-equipped F-94 and F3D air crews which fought grueling night dogfights over Korea's rugged hills against communist MiGs.[21] Air pressure continued up to the armistice in July 1953. In May the B-29s struck at irrigation dams, while continuing their interdiction and close support missions. On July 27 an RB-29 on a photographic mission had the distinction of flying FEAF Bomber Command's last combat sortie of the war. Over the next year, although they now no longer flew combat missions, the crews of the command still constituted a major conventional bombing force in the Far East. Not until June and July 1954 was FEAF Bomber Command inactivated and its units reincorporated into SAC.[22]

Expansion and Professionalism

There existed a basic tension between rapidly expanding the atomic force and maintaining the existing deterrent force intact. In deciding not to draw heavily on the older atomic units for experienced personnel, SAC

---

[20] *Ibid.*, pp 401–413, 471–474.
[21] *Ibid.*, pp 475–482, 613–616.
[22] *Ibid.*, pp 666–672; Hopkins & Goldberg, *Development of SAC*, p 43.

SAC and the Korean War. Elements of SAC's non-atomic strategic reserve were hurriedly deployed to the Far East in July 1950 to bolster FEAF Bomber Command and begin missions in Korea. Members of the 307th Bombardment Wing, *above,* line up before departing for Japan. One, *center, left,* bids goodbye to his family. A C–97, *center, right,* of the 307th from MacDill Air Force Base in Florida is well-loaded for takeoff. Piles of empty boxes, *below,* attest to the haste with which the 307th left for the Korean battle zone. Arriving at Kadena Air Base on Okinawa from March Air Force Base in California, the 22d Bombardment Wing turned an open field into a tent city, *left, below.* A tent serves as the 22d's interrogation room, *left, center.* B–29s of the 22d, *left, above,* unload their bombs on communist targets in North Korea.

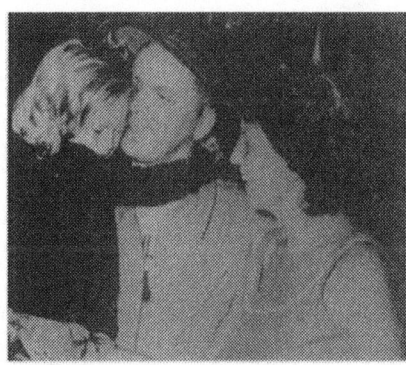

Strategic Air Force

posed a challenge for the newly formed wings to use their resources efficiently in training to a wartime level of ability. These wings, equipped with unmodified B–29s from storage, also had to support the program of sending replacement crews to the Far East.

SAC expected the new units to make significant progress toward full readiness, as measured by the rating system. In August 1950 Col. Robert O. Cork, the SAC Comptroller, assured LeMay that the rating system worked. For example, such events as the arrival of new crews or a rotation to England, which could be expected to lower performance, usually had the predicted effect on the ratings. On the other hand, units that had long been the command's highest priority, such as the 509th Bomb Wing, looked excellent in the ratings.[23] Thus SAC's staff could hold up a credible standard for the newer units.

But a look at the SAC manpower and strength figures suggested that commanders would be hard pressed to keep their units effective. During the three years of the Korean War, SAC's strength grew from 58,000 to 162,000, the number of officers increasing from 9,000 to 19,000 in the same period. Medium bomber wings expanded from ten to nineteen, those of heavy bombers from two to four, and heavy reconnaissance also from two to four. Much of this increase was in untrained or partially trained men. To cope with the shortage of experienced people, the command utilized more military women and civilian employees in support roles. Reservists also provided a leavening of wartime experience. But these solutions were short lived. The enlistments extended by Congress at the outbreak of the war in Korea began to expire in July 1951. By November 5,000 men in SAC had taken their discharges. Late the next year the reservists would start to go home, and in due time the officers and enlisted men who had joined in the wake of rising draft calls would reach the ends of their terms.[24] LeMay's long-standing interest in the issues of morale, incentives, and reenlistment had prepared SAC for this challenge, but it would be a difficult situation all the same.

The SAC rating system was indeed a valuable way to note the command's progress. It covered all aspects of a unit's activities. In addition, regular missions, especially those against radar bomb scoring sites, as

---

[23] Ltr, Col R. O. Cork, Comptr SAC, to CG SAC, subj: Analysis of the SAC Rating System, Aug 4, 1950, LeMay Coll, Multiple Addressees (1), Box B62, MD, LC.
[24] *Air Force Statistical Digest*, Jan 1949–Jun 1950, pp 29, 35, FY 1953, pp 364, 367; hist, SAC, Jul–Dec 1952, Vol I, p 3, Jul–Dec 1952, Vol I, pp 9–10; Ravenstein, *Combat Wings*, pp 141–142, 170–172.

well as the annual bombing competition, evaluated the end result—the command's ability to deliver weapons on target. LeMay affirmed the rating system's real purpose; it was designed to reveal a unit's strong and weak points, not to decide who was in first place.[25] Nevertheless, certain units consistently performed well. Irvine's B-36 units regularly ranked high, especially in radar missions. Considering the problems they faced, this was commendable indeed.[26] But then LeMay had said that these units had the toughest mission in the war plan, since they had to reach the deepest targets. The pioneering 509th, 43d, and 2d Wings did well, the 509th most consistently.[27] When the 2d Bomb Wing's B-50s began to enter the depot at Sacramento in the summer of 1952 for modification of some electronics, the Air Materiel Command informed LeMay that the aircraft were in outstanding shape, the sign of superior maintenance.[28]

Bombing accuracy had improved dramatically from the dismal days of 1949. By May of 1950 the radar bombing average error was cut to 4,500 feet (from 10,000 feet in the Dayton mission) and gross errors halved. A year later, missions against the radar bomb scoring site, then at Binghamton, New York, using seven-year-old photographs of the city, produced an average error of 3,000 feet and only fourteen percent gross errors. The best crews scored a remarkable 2,500 feet. But by late 1951, the average SAC crew's circular error probable declined to 1,840 feet.[29]

The competitions showed similar results. The critical situation in Korea in late 1950 prompted the cancellation of that year's meet, but in August 1951 SAC renewed the event. The 97th Bomb Wing, the B-50 unit at Biggs, proved the best overall unit, a real recovery from earlier problems. To emphasize the importance of reconnaissance units, a separate navigation event had been added, for which a trophy, donated by the Hughes Aircraft Company, had been named in honor of Muir Fairchild. The 97th won that contest as well. Taking part in the meet were Royal Air

---

[25] Notes for Commanders Conference, Jul 24, 1951, LeMay Coll, Box B101, MD, LC.

[26] See below, p. 19.

[27] Ltr, Lt Col Miller, Asst AG SAC, to AFs, et al, subj: SAC Rating System—Operations Section (April 1951), May 12, 1951; ltr, Lt Col H. N. Moore, Asst AG SAC, to AFs, et al, subj: SAC Bombardment Wing Rating System—January 1952, Feb 27, 1952; ltr, Moore to AFs, et al, subj: SAC Bombardment Wing Ratings—March 1952, Apr 25, 1952, all in LeMay Coll, Box B96, MD, LC.

[28] 1st Ind, (ltr, Lt Gen E. W. Rawlings, CG AMC, to CSAF, CG SAC, subj: Commendation, Jul 11, 1952), Gen N. F. Twining, VCSAF, to CG SAC, Jul 31, 1952, Twining Coll, AFCVC Reading File, Jul 52 (2), Box 57, MD, LC.

[29] Rprt, Springfield Evaluation Mission, Jul 7, 1952, LeMay Coll, Box B106; SAC Progress Analysis, Oct 53, LeMay Coll, Box B98, both in MD, LC.

Strategic Air Force

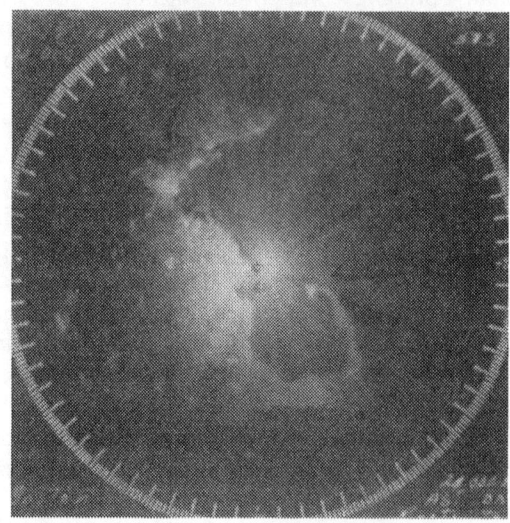

New and improved radar allowed SAC to tighten its bombing accuracy by impressive percentages during test runs and simulations from 1949 through 1952. Pictured is a radar scope image of Massachusetts that highlights the contrast between land and water from the Boston area to the tip of Cape Cod.

Force Washington bombers (B-29s), while SAC B-29s won the British bombing competition.[30] After the October 1952 competition LeMay described the performance of the navigators as "phenomenal." The overall best crew, from the 2d Wing, consisted entirely of men with spot promotions. The 97th had to share the Fairchild Trophy with the 93d (Castle Air Force Base). The B-36s had an incredibly low radar error of 465 feet. In a separate reconnaissance competition the Paul T. Cullen Trophy[31] went to the 28th Strategic Reconnaissance Wing (RB-36s) which two years earlier

---

[30] Memo to Lt Gen T. D. White, Dir Pl, subj: SAC Bombing Capability, n.d. [Aug 51], Vandenberg Coll, 2A Memos Re 138 Wings, Box 83; ltr, Maj Gen S. E. Anderson, CG 8 AF, to CO 97 BW (Med), subj: RBS Scores, n.d. [Jan 11, 1951], LeMay Coll, Anderson, S. E., Box B49, both in MD, LC. Over the years, SAC press releases invariably referred to the "coveted [or even 'Coveted'] Fairchild Trophy."

[31] See below, p. 432.

"Never Before Surpassed"

had been lambasted by the Eighth Air Force commander for general sloppiness.[32]

The unit ratings vindicated the commandwide programs to improve proficiency. Standardization of training and performance criteria still ruled, as did the lead crew system. The standardization school at MacDill was in full operation, evolving in May 1951 into the 3908th Strategic Evaluation Squadron. Fourteen crews entered the course every three weeks, each one required to fly four missions with a total of thirty-six hours. The command's long-term objective was to provide most squadrons in the war plan with five lead crews.[33]

As indicated by the results of the 1952 competition, spot promotions were an important factor in developing first-rate crews. During 1950 LeMay obtained authority to promote captains and majors as well as lieutenants. Boards of flying officers were to screen candidates, whom LeMay or his deputy would then interview before selecting. Candidates had to be members of lead crews and possess personal qualities suitable to their new rank. On January 23, 1951, SAC was allowed to make the system permanent, and three days later the authority was extended to promote enlisted crew members. By the end of June SAC had promoted 321 officers, and 9 of these had lost their new grade through failure to perform. Of 554 promotions of noncommissioned officers, only 20 were later revoked.[34]

Though SAC made progress toward improving promotion opportunities and recognition of aircrew members, other morale issues, often imponderable, claimed the command's attention. The talk of "one-way missions" could resurface, and the careful planning for assigned targets focused the attention of the crews on the dangers they would likely face. They might not see the report by the Weapons Systems Evaluation Group, but common sense suggested the degree of risk. Little could be done directly except to emphasize the overriding importance of the task for the nation's defense. Gradually training could increase the crews' confidence

---

[32] Ltr, Gen C. E. LeMay, CG SAC, to Gen H. S. Vandenberg, CSAF, Oct 31, 1952, Vandenberg Coll, SAC 6, Box 45; ltr, Maj Gen S. E. Anderson, CG 8 AF, to Col A. T. Wilson, Jr, CO 28 Strat RW (Heavy), Sep 11, 1950, LeMay Coll, S. E. Anderson, Box B49, both in MD, LC; Hopkins & Goldberg, *Development of SAC*, pp 38–39.

[33] Hist, SAC, Jan–Jun 51, Vol I, pp 86–94; ltr, Lt Gen C. E. LeMay, CG SAC, to Lt Gen R. E. Nugent, DCS/Pers, May 14, 1951, LeMay Coll, Nugent, Box B58, MD, LC.

[34] Ltr, Lt Gen R. E. Nugent, DCS/Pers, to CG SAC, subj: Spot Promotions for Lead Aircrew Members, Jan 23, 1951, LeMay Coll, Nugent, Box B58, MD, LC; hist, SAC, Jan–Jun 1951, Vol I, pp 98–119.

Strategic Air Force

in their ability to complete the mission. The command survival school established first at Camp Carson, Colorado, and later at Reno Army Air Base (renamed Stead Air Force Base), Nevada, taught crewmen that should they come down in hostile territory, they were not totally without resources. Danger and anxiety posed difficult problems, no doubt, but young Americans had responded to good leadership before, and there was growing reason to believe that this was happening again.[35]

So a proficient crew member had many reasons to continue flying. When he returned to the ground, however, he shared the same concerns as the mechanics and other support personnel. The SAC staff had long been aware that the heavy workload, frequent travel, possible hazardous duty, combined with inadequate base facilities, made airmen fear assignment to the command. Also, there was a sense that commanders were not good at communicating with their men. Finally, with only ten percent of the married officers and men living on base, the availability of suitable family housing remained a crucial issue.[36]

A report prepared for General LeMay early in 1952 indicated that even though many "irritants" could be eliminated, SAC would continue to demand long working hours and frequent disruptions. A major factor in the command's success then would have to be the ability to instill a different attitude in the force. Besides appeals to patriotism, adventure, and comradeship, SAC should emphasize pride in belonging to an elite force. The command's emblem had been approved in January 1952 and it provided a means to symbolize that pride. Signs and equipment could bear it, and it could appear on personal items for sale in the base exchange. The report recommended other ways to emphasize the special role of the command, such as LeMay wearing a flight suit when he visited bases or encouraging units to send letters of congratulations to the parents of newly assigned airmen.[37]

None of these efforts were intended to downplay the arduous task of improving conditions on the bases. Commanders needed to keep people informed. LeMay insisted that every base have a Personal Affairs Officer to help families deal with the disruptions of service life, and he resisted attempts to eliminate such support positions. Meanwhile progress was being achieved in an important morale-building program: family housing

---

[35] Remarks by Gen. Jack Catton, Office of Air Force History, May 18, 1989.
[36] Memo, Lt Col Reade Tilley, Spec Asst to CG, SAC, to Gen C. E. LeMay, CG SAC, subj: Development of Incentive in the Strategic Air Command, May 1, 1952, with atch, Item Project: A Program to Raise and Maintain Incentive Levels, LeMay Coll, Box B106, MD, LC.
[37] Ibid.

authorized by the Wherry Act housing was under construction and soon occupied.[38]

The chance to raise a family in a decent house was an obvious inducement to reenlist, but for the unmarried personnel, representing sixty percent of the enlisted force, the condition of the barracks was crucial. In 1951 the new SAC barracks with their furnished two-person rooms were being built at Offutt and elsewhere. LeMay was determined to expedite the construction. When he encountered opposition from the Directorate of Installations on the Air Staff, he included in his next Washington trip a call on the chief of materiel, in which he "discussed, in strong language, his unhappiness over the resistance on the part of [the Installations Directorate]" to the new barracks design.[39] The Senate Preparedness Committee judged the new-style barracks too expensive and luxurious, but in December 1951 Kissner replied that the old designs were a false economy:

> The services have passed the point when they can afford a constant turnover of highly-trained non-commissioned officers in technical specialties....YMCA's and even third-class rooming houses [afford some privacy]. We no longer operate on the principle that a company or battalion will rise each morning to reveille and turn out lights at taps.[40]

Kissner emphasized that SAC's round-the-clock operations made open-bay barracks even less livable. Besides, SAC hoped to attract personnel who would study to qualify for advanced training: "Open bay barracks do not afford this opportunity."[41]

In reality, a majority of the SAC enlisted force continued to live in old-style barracks, and change came slowly. But at least the SAC staff could resist reactionary proposals. After the Air Force abolished "kitchen police" (KP) duty, someone in Eighth Air Force became disturbed by high absenteeism and discipline problems in the food service squadrons (with their generally low-skilled personnel). The proposed solution involved reestablishing KP—or rather a "food service rostering system." The SAC staff was not misled by the change of name, and LeMay turned down the

---

[38] *Ibid.*; ltr, Gen C. E. LeMay, CG SAC, to Gen H. S. Vandenberg, Nov 20, 1952, Vandenberg Coll, SAC (6), Box 45, MD, LC.

[39] Memo, Lt Col P. K. Carlton, Air Defense Command, to CG SAC & CS SAC, subj: Movement of Commanding General, Nov 19, 1951, LeMay Coll, Trip Rprts 1951, Box B74, MD, LC.

[40] 1st Ind, Maj Gen A. W. Kissner, CS SAC, to Dir L & L, USAF, Dec 28, 1951, to 34th Rprt, Preparedness Subcommittee, US Senate, LeMay Coll, Multiple Addresees (1), Box B62, MD, LC.

[41] *Ibid.*

proposal. There were not enough trained enlisted personnel, and they could not be diverted to such low-level tasks.[42]

A new kind of military organization was emerging. When young airmen no longer slept in open bays or "pulled KP"; when they were encouraged to start families and study for advanced schooling, SAC would be far removed from the traditional American pattern of peacetime soldiering. Nor did one find in SAC the proverbial leisurely pace of the interwar years. Perhaps one of the reasons for the changes was that, however remote from the war zone, this was not peacetime. Deterrence of an atomic war imposed demands that threw many traditions out the window.

Although the reenlistment statistics highlighted SAC's morale problems, the most spectacular episode concerned reserve officers. Most of the pilots and observers recalled to active duty during the buildup had flown in the Second World War. Many had volunteered for recall under the misapprehension that their rank and age would entitle them to administrative and staff jobs rather than aircrew duty. They thus soon shared the bitterness of the involuntary recallees at the prospect of being sent to fly combat missions in Korea. As a result, these officers assiduously searched for loopholes in the regulations.[43]

They quickly came across a provision entitled "Fear of Flying," which gave unit commanders the discretion to deal with aircrew members who had psychological problems. By late 1951 hundreds of officers had obtained suspension from flying under this provision with relatively slight repercussions, as they waited for final rulings from Headquarters U.S. Air Force.[44]

Whatever emotions may have motivated the recallees, the situation inspired very different feelings among the Air Force's leadership. In one of the SAC B-29 squadrons alerted for the Far East in July 1950, a navigator had requested suspension due to fear of flying and had accordingly been grounded. On his crew's first mission over Korea the substitute navigator was killed. When Kuter became Deputy Chief of Staff for Personnel, he

---

[42] Ltr, Maj Gen S. E. Anderson, CG 8 AF, to Gen C. E. LeMay, CG SAC, Nov 14, 1952; ltr, LeMay to Anderson, Dec 3, 1952, both in LeMay Coll, Anderson # 2, Box B49, MD, LC.
[43] Hist, ATC, Jan-Jun 1952, pp 105-110, 118-121. The author is indebted to Lt Col Vance O. Mitchell of the Office of Air Force History for material concerning this episode; see his draft study, *The USAF and Intelligence*.
[44] Hist, ATC, Jan-Jun 1952, pp 105-110, 118-121.

had occasion to comment on the officer who had been grounded: "I am convinced we have no place in the service for [him]."[45]

LeMay was less diplomatic on the subject. He considered any aircrew member who requested relief from flying duties on such grounds a "contaminating influence." He had long favored their summary dismissal from service. In any case, the Air Force leadership regarded the recallees as having entered knowingly into a contract to serve when needed. Those who tried to avoid flying were breaking the contract.[46]

Although the Air Force as a whole was slow to recognize the scope of the problem, SAC took strong action from the start. Applicants for suspension were removed from their units until a final ruling could be made. By November 1951 some twenty-eight pilots and seventy-two observers had been grounded.[47] More worrisome were the cases in the Air Training Command. At the B-29 Combat Crew Training School at Randolph Air Force Base, fear-of-flying applications multiplied. In January 1952 there were 134 cases in the command. The training command officials recommended that future applications be rigorously screened to excuse only those with real psychological problems, with the option of court-martial action against anyone who still refused to fly after the suspension was revoked.[48] Having a definite interest in the B-29 school at Randolph, LeMay felt strongly about the Air Force's policy on this question and favored court-martial action. In April 1952 charges were brought against twelve officers at Randolph. Six of them then issued a statement and received sympathetic coverage in the news media.[49]

In view of the publicity and the impression that would be created by prosecuting decorated combat veterans, Finletter and Vandenberg were reluctant to proceed. Secretary Finletter dismissed the charges but ordered that all further applicants pleading fear of flying be expelled from service. On April 16 the Air Staff issued a firm policy exempting only those with

---

[45] Memo, Lt Gen L. S. Kuter, DCS/Pers, to VCSAF, subj: Retroactive Application of Fear of Flying Policy, May 16, 1952, Twining Coll, AFCWC Reading File, Jun 52 (2), Box 56, MD, LC. This memorandum, signed by Kuter, also contains the memorandum of disapproval, signed by Kuter as Acting Vice Chief of Staff and dated June 27, 1952 (during Vandenberg's hospitalization). Those recalling the case of the pre-civil war officer who arrested himself need to note that Kuter's two opposing positions were consecutive, not simultaneous.
[46] Mitchell, draft, *The USAF and Intelligence*.
[47] Notes for Commanders Conference, Jul 24, 1951; Notes for Commanders Conference, Nov 7, 1951, both in LeMay Coll, Box B1O1, MD, LC.
[48] Hist, ATC, Jan-Jun 1952, pp 112-117.
[49] Mitchell, draft, *The USAF and Intelligence*.

ten years' service and a critically needed skill in a ground job.[50] This left unresolved the fate of the 570 fliers suspended before the announcement of the policy. LeMay and Kuter urged full retroactivity, but the Air Staff turned this down. The episode was soon closed, but it reaffirmed SAC's reluctance to rely on reserve call-ups. Even though most of the fear-of-flying cases did not come from involuntary recalls, the staff was convinced that the flying force should be all-volunteer.[51]

Planes and Weapons, 1950–1953

Effective modern aircraft remained, along with trained air and ground crews, the most effective aircraft, and suitable bases, one of the essential components of air power. The Air Force continued to pursue its historic commitment to advancing the technology of flight. As SAC expanded, considerable progress was made in upgrading current bombers and equipment. Meanwhile, Air Force planners focused their attention on new bomber designs for the middle and late 1950s. As the debate began over the direction of the future bomber program, LeMay's staff voiced a commitment to the large intercontinental bomber that was not universally shared by Air Force decision makers.

Throughout the period of the Korean War, SAC relied primarily on the B-36 and the B-50 for the capability to deliver the atomic blow. After years of development, the B-36 itself was finally coming into its own. The large number of B-29s—exceeding four hundred in 1952—was deceptive.[52] Few of the Superforts were atomic-modified. Many of the newly established B-29 units were not yet operational, and much of the training concentrated on preparing for deployment to Korea. But the World War II vintage bombers still represented a valuable conventional bombing potential and might contribute to the American strategy of deterrence.

Accompanying the dramatic increase in the atomic weapons stockpile was an accelerated expansion of the strike force. The latter was almost entirely due to new production of the B-36. The Peacemaker was now becoming an effective part of the force in large numbers. With production

---

[50] *Ibid.*
[51] Memo, Lt Gen L. S. Kuter, DCS/Pers, to VCSAF, subj: Retroactive Application of Fear of Flying Policy, May 16, 1952, Twining Coll, AFCWC Reading File, Jun 52 (2), Box 56; Notes for Commanders Conference, Nov 7, 1951, LeMay Coll, Box B101, both in MD, LC; G. Watson, p 118.
[52] Hopkins & Goldberg, *Development of SAC*, p 37.

"Never Before Surpassed"

in full swing, the active inventory grew from 42 in June 1950 to 271 three years later.[53] Meanwhile, the modernization of the medium bomber force encountered delays as production of the B-47 fell behind schedule and those produced experienced numerous problems. Still, as 1953 began, the prospect of a large force of jet bombers with nuclear weapons ready to be loaded on fairly short notice, was a virtual certainty. As for the weapons, the expanding supply demanded the construction of new storage facilities, which, if properly located, would ease the logistical problem of transferring the weapons to the operational bases. And with more bombs stored overseas as well as the newer, more convenient sites in prospect, the Air Force was gaining more control over its most powerful weapon.

The same period saw a major improvement in SAC's reconnaissance force. LeMay took a great interest in this perennial stepchild of the strategic program. Again, growth was primarily attributable to the large-scale production of the RB-36. The progress was encouraging because the RB-36's range and carrying capacity made it ideal for the many powerful cameras needed for high-altitude, intercontinental missions.[54]

In just a few years, the characteristics of a strategic bomber—range, speed, and capacity—had taken on new dimensions. Besides the approach to the range problem epitomized by the massive B-36s and B-52s, another option, air-to-air refueling, offered a highly practical means of extending the reach of a smaller plane. However, the development of forward bases remained crucial to the existing medium force. In the new era, speed was only one means of defense against enemy fighters. High-altitude flying, evasive courses, improved armament, use of darkness, escort fighters, and increasingly, electronic countermeasures all were part of the formula. Bomber aircraft also needed an effective radar bombing system, and it was no coincidence that training so heavily emphasized the latest bombing techniques. Unfortunately, this complex mix of new requirements allowed no easy technological solutions.

By the end of 1950, Convair had begun full production of the B-36 and the RB-36. If SAC had not altogether resolved its problems with the Peacemaker, at least the in-commission rate was vastly increased by 1952. The availability of spare parts improved, while the mechanics learned to keep up with the workload. In a new modification program, Convair converted the B models to Ds by installing jet engines and other new

---

[53] *Air Force Statistical Digest*, Jan 1949–Jun 1950, p 179, FY 53, p 211.
[54] Hopkins & Goldberg, *Development of SAC*, pp 21, 30, 37; Knaack, *Bombers*, pp 36, 112–119.

equipment. Newer models began to arrive in 1951, with the last production model—the J—flying in 1953.[55]

Solutions to the B-36s teething problems appeared at irregular intervals. In 1950 the fuel leaks seemed to subside, but at the end of the year there was an outbreak at Rapid City. Not until the production of the H and J models, with their improved tanks and sealants, was the problem overcome. Earlier aircraft continued to be affected; for example, the D model B-36s still had numerous fuel leaks every winter. Deficiencies in the gunnery system proved even more intractable. Although gunners and mechanics benefitted from more training and experience, as of 1953 the situation remained unsatisfactory.[56]

The gunnery system's troubles had a further impact on the problems of altitude and navigation. With inadequate armament, the Peacemaker would need all of its climbing ability to reach forty thousand feet and escape enemy fighters. Even then, the MiG-15 could reach it. And at high altitudes accurate bombing required good sights and radars. The serious inadequacies with the bombing and navigation system were in some measure resolved when SAC was able to replace the sets beginning in 1952. Though the B-36 fleet was grounded briefly early in the year after a landing gear failed, the overall development was encouraging. SAC was finally acquiring a fairly reliable operational heavy bomber force.[57]

More time in commission meant more time to train the crews. The B-36 bomber carried a crew of fifteen, largely because extra men were required for long flights. (There were three pilots, for example.) Reconnaissance crews numbered twenty-two. The operational concept for the bombers involved staging through Limestone, Maine, or Alaska. As part of their training in long-range flights, six B-36 crews deployed to England in January 1951, and six more flew nonstop to Morocco in December.[58]

Ironically, the most serious setback to the readiness of the B-36 force occurred at a high point in the program. On Labor Day, September 1, 1952, the weather forecast at Carswell Air Force Base called for thunderstorms and gusting winds. At about 1800 hours a few people observed heavy clouds moving toward the base, and within moments the base was engulfed in cloud and high winds. The anemometer climbed to ninety-one

---

[55] Knaack, *Bombers*, pp 29–37, 49; *Air Force Statistical Digest*, FY 1951, pp 190–197, FY 52, pp 202–222, FY 53, pp 230–232.

[56] Knaack, *Bombers*, pp 28–33.

[57] *Ibid.*, pp 32–33; ASSS, Col J. F. Pinckney, for Dir Est, Dir Intel, to CSAF, Revision of Air Intelligence Study "Aircraft of the US and the USSR," May 19, 1952, Vandenberg Coll, 13. Acft of the US & the USSR, Box 84, MD, LC.

[58] Knaack, *Bombers*, p 55; Hopkins & Goldberg, *Development of SAC*, p 35.

"Never Before Surpassed"

A crew of the 6th Bombardment Wing works on an RB–36 in the remoteness and cold of Greenland at Thule Air Base, a staging stop on SAC's arduous long-range training flights.

miles per hour before breaking. It became impossible to move about in the open. The storm tossed B–36s about as if they were made of paper. Fuel tanks burst. The duty officer of the 7th Bombardment Wing saw that power lines were down and broken near the fuel spills and hurried to turn off the electricity, possibly averting a disastrous fire. As the storm subsided, an estimated two-thirds of America's heavy bomber force was out of action.[59]

One B–36 was reported "demolished" by the storm, and out of a total of eighty-two damaged, including ten at the Convair plant, twenty-four were seriously damaged. On receiving the news, General LeMay had no choice but to remove the 19th Air Division from the war plan. The base went on an eighty-four-hour week until the repairs were completed. Brig. Gen. Kingston B. Tibbetts, SAC's Director of Materiel, arrived the day after the storm to observe the work. Within ten days one of the wings was

---

[59] Hist, 7 BW, Sep 1952, & Ex I; Summary Rprt, Bd Sr Offs to CSAF, Investigation of Tornado Damage at Carswell Air Force Base, Dec 10, 1952, atch to ltr, Gen N. F. Twining, VCSAF, to Gen C. E. LeMay, CG SAC, Dec 22, 1952, Twining Coll, AFCVC Reading File, Dec 52 (2), Box 58, MD, LC.

Strategic Air Force

operational, and by the end of the month, with help from Air Materiel Command, the base was operating more airplanes than before the storm. Undersecretary of the Air Force Roswell L. Gilpatric called the achievement "remarkable." The initial cost estimates proved to be exaggerated.[60]

Secretary Finletter and the Air Staff found the news of the storm "disturbing," to say the least. Finletter worried about a possible Soviet reaction to the news that America's premier atomic bomber was nearly out of action.[61] Yet a press release would probably have to be issued. However, by the time of the announcement on September 12, the situation had greatly improved. Meanwhile, Lt. Gen. Bryant L. Boatner, the Inspector General of the Air Force, conducted an investigation and determined that the storm, probably a full tornado, could not have been predicted. A Board of Senior Officers was content to recommend some procedural changes.[62]

The question that remained was what so many bombers were doing on one base. The Air Staff tended to believe that, in the case of Carswell, concentration had been unavoidable. The problems in materiel associated with the new aircraft would have been far more complicated had the force been widely dispersed. Lt. Gen. William F. McKee, the Assistant Vice Chief of Staff, assured the secretary that the Air Force favored greater dispersion, but the complexities of building the 143-wing program had prevented action thus far. All agreed that the issue was not closed.[63]

Medium bombers reached intercontinental ranges by the use of forward bases and air refueling. This enabled designers to provide a smaller aircraft with superior performance. Such was the Boeing B–47

---

[60] Msg, Gen H. S. Vandenberg, CSAF, to Gen C. E. LeMay, CG SAC, Sep 11, 1952, Vandenberg Coll, SAC (6), Box 45; memo, Maj Gen W. D. Eckert, Asst DCS/Mat, to CSAF, subj: Status of Repair Program on B–36 Aircraft Damaged at Carswell AFB, Sep 18, 1952, Vandenberg Coll, Aircraft, Box 34; msg, LeMay to Vandenberg, 032145Z Sep 52, Vandenberg Coll, Redlines, Jul 1, 1952, Box 87; ltr, R. L. Gilpatric, USec AF, to Sen L. B. Johnson, Chmn, Preparedness Investigation Subcommittee, Dec 20, 1952, Twining Coll, AFCVC Reading File, Dec 52 (1), Box 58, all in MD, LC; hist, 11 BW, Sep 1952, pp 20–24

[61] Ltr, T. K. Finletter, Sec AF, to Rep C. Vinson, Chmn, House Armed Services Cmte, Sep 9, 1952, Vandenberg Coll, Sec AF (2), Box 62; memo, Finletter, to CSAF, Sep 5, 1952, Vandenberg Coll, 8. Selected Memos, Box 84, both in MD, LC.

[62] *Facts on File*, 1952, p 305F; msg, Gen H. S. Vandenberg, CSAF, to Gen C. E. LeMay, CG SAC, Sep 11, 1952, Vandenberg Coll, SAC (6), Box 45; Summary Rprt, Bd Sr Offs, to CSAF, Investigation of Tornado Damage at Carswell Air Force Base, Dec 10, 1952, atch to ltr, Gen N. F. Twining, VCSAF, to LeMay, Dec 22, 1952, Twining Coll, AFCVC Reading File, Dec 52 (2), Box 58, all in MD, LC.

[63] Memo, Lt Gen W. F. McKee, Asst VCSAF, to T. K. Finletter, Sec AF, Oct 31, 1952, atch to ltr, Finletter to Sen A. Wiley, Nov 5, 1952, Vandenberg Coll, Sec AF (2), Box 62, MD, LC.

"Never Before Surpassed"

Stratojet. The symbolic date marking the entry of the bomber force into the jet age was October 23, 1951, when Col. N. W. McCoy, Commanding Officer of the 306th Bombardment Wing, flew a B–47B from the Boeing plant at Wichita, Kansas, to MacDill Air Force Base. Soon nicknamed *The Real McCoy*, this plane represented more a promise than an actual combat capability. It would be more than a year before SAC had an operational B–47 unit.[64] The very month that McCoy brought the first B model to MacDill, a high-level Air Force conference discussed the future of the entire B–47 program. The complexities of producing a high-speed jet bomber combined with the troubles plaguing an expanding aircraft industry endangered the program. The service's plans for the bomber had proven overly ambitious.[65]

The test program with the B–47A that began in June 1950 ran concurrently with production of the B model. Unfortunately, the latest version encountered many delays, caused by design uncertainties, scheduling difficulties, and unsatisfactory equipment. Boeing had difficulties tooling up because the Air Force insisted on manufacturing the plane at Wichita, as well as other reasons. Anticipating that extensive testing of the product would be required, the Air Force instituted Project WIBAC (Wichita Boeing Airplane Company). Beginning in April 1950, representatives from SAC and the Air Proving Ground Command went to Wichita to do the testing. But even before any B models were ready, serious problems arose. Obviously, many design questions had been settled with inadequate data.[66]

The first B model flew in February 1951, confirming that the production model was in unsatisfactory condition. The General Electric engines lacked sufficient power. Numerous subcontractors had not recognized the need for sophisticated component design. In particular, the navigation radar and the armament system had fallen behind schedule, so the B–47 would have to use the same unreliable sets as the B–36. Design changes had added weight, affecting handling, and yet another problem, fuel boil-off at high altitude, reduced the aircraft's range. Even the ejection seat, which the Air Force considered essential for escaping from the plane at high speeds, had been delayed.[67]

While SAC had planned for the conversion of B–29 units to B–47s, the staff had kept itself informed of the production difficulties and postponed much of the conversion program. Only two B–29 wings, the 305th

---

[64] Knaack, *Bombers*, pp 115n, 120.
[65] *Ibid.*, pp 115–117.
[66] *Ibid.*, pp 108–116.
[67] *Ibid.*, pp 115–118.

Strategic Air Force

and 306th, both at MacDill and the former only recently activated, stood down to convert. The 306th began training on A models in May 1951 but had too few aircraft for a serious program. The wing had little enough time to train its own crews, let alone serve as SAC's transition school.[68]

Throughout 1951 Boeing and the Air Force wrestled with the continuing unsatisfactory performance of the B–47 program. Participants in an October meeting of top Air Force officers recognized that the 143-wing program called for at least 25 wings of Stratojets, and a contract for 445 planes was under discussion. The outcome of the meeting was an order by Twining to the Air Staff to develop a "refinement" program to start in January 1952. All of the necessary fixes would be applied on the production line, while completed items would undergo modification. At first the Grand Central Depot of Air Materiel Command assumed the task of modifying 310 B–47Bs for SAC. But the depot lacked enough workers and plant capacity to meet the schedule, and soon the Air Force had to contract with Boeing and Douglas to get the work done. Finally, after all these delays, the first modified bombers reached SAC in October 1952. By the end of the year the command had 62 B–47s and had almost equipped both wings at MacDill up to operational levels.[69]

The basic B–47B delivered to SAC, with a takeoff weight of 185,000 pounds, used six General Electric engines of the improved J47 type. It could climb to more than 40,000 feet and cruise at 433 knots. Its top speed exceeded 500 knots, and its radius of operation was 1,700 nautical miles. Two .50-caliber machine guns were mounted in the tail and the bomb bay could accommodate up to 25,000 pounds. With its swept-back wings, the Stratojet had the look of a new style of bomber.[70]

The plane's newness affected the training of crews. Carrying modern radar and electronic gear, the B–47 was far less labor-intensive than earlier bombers, using a highly skilled crew of only three. The pilot and co-pilot sat in tandem in the cockpit, while the observer's compartment was in the nose of the plane. Ideally all crew members were to be pilot-observers: that is, qualified multi-jet engine pilots would go to observer school to master navigation, bombing, and radar. But because of the production and modification delays, pilots duly finished observer school only to become surplus. To ease the problem, SAC made an interim change. Only one pilot-observer would be assigned to each B–47 crew. The rest would go to B–29 or B–50 units to fill navigator or bombardier seats and replace

---

[68] *Ibid.*, pp 109–110, 109n; hist, SAC, Jul–Dec 1951, Vol I, pp 29, 203–205.
[69] Knaack, *Bombers*, pp 113–120, 124; Hopkins & Goldberg, *Development of SAC*, p 37.
[70] Knaack, *Bombers*, p 156.

departing reservists. In the B–47, a pilot without observer training would sit in the second seat, and an observer without pilot's wings manned the navigator's station. Meanwhile training imbalances persisted; although there were surpluses in aircrew, mechanics were in short supply.[71]

Despite these obstacles, by the beginning of 1953 the B–47 program was well under way, with 1,760 aircraft ordered for the 143-wing program. In April 1953 the 303d Bomb Wing at Davis-Monthan, one of the B–29 expansion units, was the first to receive the E model, which incorporated a number of changes. Also that month, on the reconnaissance front, the first RB–47Bs arrived at Lockbourne Air Force Base, Ohio, to replace the B–45s. A conference at Wichita agreed on a final standard for all B–47s remaining to be produced, while requiring the modification of those aircraft still in the plant.[72]

The 306th Bomb Wing put its Stratojets through an extensive combat exercise, and on April 6 Colonel McCoy flew from Limestone to Fairford, England, one of the new United Kingdom bases, in a record time of 3,120 miles in five hours and thirty-eight minutes. McCoy's record lasted less than two months. In June the entire wing staged to Fairford through Limestone in three days. Nine planes beat the colonel's time, the last one to arrive taking first place with five hours and twenty-two minutes.[73]

Even when its deficiencies were corrected, the B-47 had several drawbacks. Its abbreviated range could be mitigated by air-to-air refueling and staging through overseas bases. However, the bomber's small size limited the amount of electronic equipment or cameras it could carry. Also, with a crew of only three in cramped quarters, a long-distance mission would be grueling. Its speed and altitude characteristics, though, made it a promising addition to the force, and, considering the large numbers in production, defending against the Stratojet would be a costly problem for a potential enemy.[74]

Ever since the appearance of the first jet fighter, designing an effective long-range escort had proved challenging. The SAC fighter force by June 1950 consisted of two wings of Republic F–84E Thunderjets. These aircraft soon found themselves diverted to other tasks than strategic escort. The 27th Fighter Escort Wing at Bergstrom Air Force Base, Texas, was tapped during the fall to ferry nearly 180 F–84s to Europe to reequip U.S. units there. For this operation, known as FOX ABLE III, the wing received the Mackay Trophy. In November the 27th and its planes went by

---

[71] *Ibid.*; hist, SAC, Jul–Dec 1951, Vol I, pp 29, 203–205.
[72] Knaack, *Bombers*, pp 120–121, 133–134, 155.
[73] Hopkins & Goldberg, *Development of SAC*, p 45.
[74] Knaack, *Bombers*, pp 147–148; hist, SAC, Jul–Dec 1951, Vol I, pp 29, 203–205.

Strategic Air Force

Force of Nature. B-36s, lie strewn like toys and battered, many beyond salvage, at Carswell Air Force Base in Ft. Worth, Texas, home of the 7th Bombardment Wing, after a disastrous storm on September 1, 1952. The cataclysm destroyed equipment, buildings, and approximately two-thirds of SAC's heavy bomber force.

ship to the Far East. There, in combat over Korea, the Thunderjet's limitations as an escort fighter were obvious; the F–84 performed best as a low-level fighter-bomber. The 27th returned to the U.S. in mid–1951 and reequipped with F–84Gs.[75]

The new model Thunderjet had been designed to carry atomic weapons and be refueled in the air. The latter feature could be attributed to the efforts by Col. David C. Schilling of the Air Staff to develop air refueling for fighters. By January 1953 SAC had five wings of the Gs either operational or forming. Meanwhile, the diversion to other tasks continued, with two wings deploying to Japan to augment the air defenses. The first deployment, Fox Peter I, led by Schilling himself, consisted of a mass, tanker-supported flight to Japan. This occurred in July 1952, and Fox Peter II followed later that year.[76]

Given the limitations of the F–84 in air combat, the atomic-capable fighter-bomber seemed to have a different role from that of the traditional escort fighter. The Air Staff gave the matter much study, and as a result in January 1953 SAC's fighter units became "Strategic Fighter" Wings. The F-84s would operate as atomic intruders, both for reconnaissance and escort patrols and to attack air defense positions. Two years earlier, in search of a better plane for these roles, SAC had secured the revival of the McDonnell XF–88 project, which ultimately led to the development of the much more advanced F–101 Voodoo.[77] In the 143-wing program SAC was to have 10 fighter wings. Given that the F-84 force would constitute only one-seventh of the total SAC force and one-seventh of the total Air Force fighter needs, it would prove difficult to maintain a priority to secure adequate equipment for this force in the coming years. In the strategic bomber program, the emphasis on speed, dispersal, overwhelming numbers, night, and jamming seemed to outweigh the importance of fighter escort as means to insure penetration by the bombers.

Air-to-air refueling of bombers, fighters, and reconnaissance aircraft would obviously be essential to maintaining SAC's intercontinental reach for the forseeable future. The operation itself, from the days of George

---

[75] Ravenstein, *Combat Wings*, pp 27–29, 49–52, 54–57; Hopkins & Goldberg, *Development of SAC*, pp 23–26.

[76] Marcelle Size Knaack, *Post World War II Fighters, 1945–1973* [Vol I of *Encyclopedia of U.S. Air Force Aircraft and Missile Systems*] (Washington: AFCHO, 1978), pp 36–38; Hopkins & Goldberg, *Development of SAC*, pp 37, 39–40.

[77] Memo, Col R. Taylor, Actg Dir Ops, 8 AF, to CG 8 AF, subj: Potential Capabilities of SAC Fighter Units, Oct 17, 1952SAC/HO, HA-0227; Hopkins & Goldberg, *Development of SAC*, pp 37, 43; Knaack, *Fighters*, pp 35–138.

Strategic Air Force

Kenney's "stunt," had become almost a matter of routine. In September 1950 the boom-fitted KB-29P tanker entered the command's inventory. This brought the "American" system into operation. Like the M, looped-hose (British) type, however, the model was already obsolescent. The tanker's performance was compatible with some bombers, but a B-47 Stratojet would have to sacrifice speed and altitude to position itself below a KB-29. Boeing proposed to modify the C-97 Stratofreighter to meet the requirement. The Air Force ordered sixty KC-97Es, the first of which joined a unit on July 14, 1951. There were subsequent F and G models. By the end of 1952 SAC had 179 KB-29s and 139 KC-97s in nineteen squadrons.[78]

The KC-97 program, though promising, experienced some early operational difficulties. The tanker had a crew of five: pilot, co-pilot, flight engineer, navigator, and boom operator. SAC soon established a Combat Crew Training School for tankers at MacDill Air Force Base. Newly trained crews found that the nozzles on the booms often broke during a mission. The most serious equipment problem, however, involved the radar beacon necessary for the bomber and tanker to rendezvous. In fact, the only reliable procedure was for bomber and tanker to fly out together to the refueling point. The SAC staff therefore endorsed a continuing effort to come up with more accurate beacons.[79] The total purchase of KC-97s fell short. According to the standard organization, a squadron of twenty tankers supported a medium bomb wing of forty-five bombers. Though the SAC staff wanted a one-to-one ratio between tankers and bombers in order to ensure a full intercontinental capability, the Air Staff continued to authorize only one squadron per bomber wing in the 143-wing program.[80]

The B-47 program absorbed a major part of the Air Force's procurement effort during 1951 and 1952, and the development and production delays were no doubt a factor in the congressional criticism of September 1952. At the same time, longer term developmental programs suffered from the high priority given the current production. Of particular importance was the development of the B-52 as a successor to the B-36.[81] B-52

---

[78] Hist, SAC, Jan-Jun 1950, pp 53-63, Jul-Dec 1952, pp 102-122; Swanborough, *US Aircraft*, pp 127-129; Hopkins & Goldberg, *Development of SAC*, pp 26, 34-37.

[79] Hist, SAC, Jul-Dec 1952, pp 102-122. To rendezvous, the tanker's navigator generated a pulse on a radar beacon or transponder. The receiving airplane received the pulse on its radar and homed in on it.

[80] *Ibid.*; Paper, with marginal notes "Discussed with CG LeMay, Feb 29, 1952 after transmittal to Col Van Sickle," Mar 13, 1952, SAC/HO.

[81] Knaack, *Bombers*, pp 115-120, 205-207.

"Never Before Surpassed"

prototype models were under construction at the start of the Korean War, and a decision was pending on quantity manufacture. Alternatives under consideration included a new Boeing design called the B–47Z and the Convair YB–36G, a sweptwing jet version of the B–36. Later known as the YB–60, the modified B-36 prototype was already scheduled for flight testing.[82]

In November 1950, Secretary Finletter received briefings on the various options. The B–36 itself was now clearly obsolescent. Convair acknowledged that the B–60 had little potential for further design growth; its real promise lay in a new application—as a carrier for a small, high-performance "parasite" bomber which could be launched near the target. The Air Force was already planning to test the parasite concept with a B–36 and an F–84. As for the B–47Z, although the basic Stratojet design was sound, it held little further potential. The newer B–52 design, drawing on Boeing's experience with the B–47, offered more possibilities for the future. Experts at Air Materiel Command doubted that the B–36 could actually carry the eight jet engines needed to boost its performance and calculated that the B–52 would be faster than the B–60.[83]

Accepting this rationale, Finletter supported the B–52, and the Air Force on February 14, 1951, contracted with Boeing for thirteen B–52As. The program was soon extended to include B models, and work proceeded with little delay. A controversy arose over whether the pilot and co-pilot should be seated in tandem or side-by-side. LeMay favored side-by-side seating, and at his insistence Boeing changed the design accordingly. For the first flight, a YB–52 took off from Boeing's Renton, Washington, plant on April 15, 1952, and performed well. Under the 143-wing program, plans called for the last one of seven heavy bombardment wings to equip with B–52s, after the first six wings all had acquired B–36s.[84]

Despite Finletter's approval, the B–52's future remained uncertain. The Air Staff and the secretary recognized that if the words "Maginot Line" symbolized hidebound reaction in a ground soldier, and admirals were accused of a "battleship fixation," big bombers might evoke the same image for airmen. Besides, by the summer of 1952 the B–47 program was finally getting under way and any attempt to reduce it in favor of developing the B–52 might lead to congressional inquiries. The Air Force's top

---

[82] *Ibid.*; briefing transcript, Hq USAF to T. K. Finletter, Sec AF, Nov 1, 1950; briefing transcript, Hq USAF to Finletter, Nov 15, 1950, both in RG 341, DCS/Mat Exec Ofc, Gen File 1949–1951, Box 1, MMB, NA.
[83] Knaack, *Bombers*, pp 38, 132, 228, 228n, 553–555.
[84] *Ibid.*, pp 218–223.

leadership were inclined to expect the B-52 to make its own case.[85] LeMay, for one, believed that the Stratofortress could win funding on its own merits. Though its large size might make the bomber conspicuous on a radar screen, it could carry a lot of electronic gear and jam the enemy's radar. Or, depending on the mission, it might employ sophisticated reconnaissance cameras. By the end of 1952 the Air Force had sixty-three of the mammoth jet bombers on order.[86]

The question of the big bomber extended beyond the development of the B-52. The Air Force and industry began to debate the relative merits of large versus small bombers. One sponsor of reduced sizes was Col. Bernard A. Schriever, Assistant for Development Planning to the Deputy Chief of Staff for Development, and sponsor of a Development Planning Objective for strategic aircraft in the period 1955-1960. Issued on May 29, 1952, with Air Staff approval, the Planning Objective favored teaming a small, fast, high-altitude bomber with a tanker to offset the bomber's limited range. Both Boeing and Convair had been working on an advanced medium bomber. Boeing relied on its experience with the B-47 and B-52 for its effort, while Convair looked at a delta-wing design for a supersonic plane that could be launched from the bomb bay of a B-36. With the Air Force's growing confidence in air refueling, however, the "parasite" concept was abandoned.[87] Convair's second general bomber study (GEBO II) confirmed the refueling approach, and a RAND study concurred.[88]

LeMay's staff did not share this enthusiasm for the small bomber. While acknowledging that the B-52 would probably need air refueling to reach some targets, SAC officials pointed out that the big bomber was not dependent on the tanker in intercontinental operations. On the other hand, even using forward bases, a small bomber would require refueling. Limited size, as in the B-47, meant confining the crew to cramped quarters for a long mission. And, however small or fast, smaller bombers could not carry the load of radar and electronic gear the B-52 could. Finally, the SAC staff worried about the technological risk of producing a supersonic bomber, arguing that there were too many unanswered questions.[89]

---

[85] Paper, The New Phase—A Statement of Air Force Policy, Aug 2, 1952, Twining Coll, TS File (1), Box 122, MD, LC.
[86] Knaack, *Bombers*, pp 217-220, 223-229.
[87] *Ibid.*, pp 357-358, 363-364.
[88] *Ibid.*, pp 356-357.
[89] *Ibid.*, pp 357-364.

"Never Before Surpassed"

Republic F–84E Thunderjets delivered by the 27th Fighter-Escort Wing via SAC's North Atlantic flight route are arrayed at a USAFE air unit in Fürstenfeldbruck, Germany during the Fox Able III ferrying mission of September 1950. The 27th deployed to FEAF later that year and escorted B–29s over Korea. There, F–84s proved more effective as low-level fighter-bombers than as high-altitude bomber-escorts.

In September 1952 the Wright Air Development Center ruled in favor of the Convair design, stating that the company had the best chance of actually producing a supersonic bomber. The report went to the center's parent headquarters, the Air Research and Development Command, where the Commander, Lt. Gen. Earle E. Partridge, although worried about the potential costs, approved it. At the Pentagon, Vandenberg ratified the selection of the Convair design, later designated the B–58 Hustler, on November 18, and the first contract for a mockup was signed on February 12, 1953. The Air Staff anticipated the production of 244 planes, with deliveries to begin in January 1956.[90]

If the Air Force was tolerant of technical risk in designing bombers, it was perhaps less so in the matter of guided missiles. The service's view could be summed up in the words of a briefing sheet presented to General Vandenberg on the 163-wing program: "Pilotless Bomber (Strat) will

---

[90] *Ibid.*, pp 361–367.

replace Piloted Bombardment Units when operationally proven."[91] In the early 1950s missiles emerged from a purely experimental state to the status of testing possible combat types. Among those with strategic possibilities were the Rascal, the Snark, the Navaho, and the Atlas. The Rascal would be launched from a bomber within one hundred miles of the target. The Snark and the Navaho were ground-launched, jet-powered cruise missiles of intercontinental range. For years Convair's Atlas ballistic missile had been a developmental stepchild. But in December 1952 the Air Force's Scientific Advisory Board noted that new designs for nuclear weapons made a smaller, more powerful warhead possible. Suddenly the lower accuracy of the ballistic missile was not such a significant drawback, and the Atlas began to attract more attention.[92]

The Air Force's interest in the atomic stockpile was as much organizational as technical. As the stockpile expanded, the service's relationship with the Atomic Energy Commission would inevitably change. Meanwhile, the Air Force's own approach to atomic weapons was evolving. The service was consciously moving toward handling atomic weapons as a normal part of its arsenal and administering the effort through regular organizational channels. The Air Materiel Command managed the logistics of the weapons allocated for the Air Force, maintaining the weapons and ancillary gear. The Special Weapons Command at Kirtland Air Force Base, New Mexico, worked with the Armed Forces Special Weapons Project and handled the specialized training and technical data. And though the Strategic Air Command remained the primary element preparing to use the weapons, the Tactical Air Command was developing its own program. The Armed Forces Special Weapons Project included Air Force personnel, and the service had representation on the AEC's Military Liaison Committee. Maj. Gen. Howard G. Bunker, who succeeded Roscoe Wilson as Assistant for Atomic Energy on the Air Staff in October 1951, anticipated that his office could soon be eliminated. Already the Special Weapons Command had been absorbed by the Air Research and Development Command, becoming the Special Weapons Center.[93]

The Air Staff also wanted the authority to deal directly with the Atomic Energy Commission, without having to go through the Armed

---

[91] Memo, subj: Force Composition and Deployment, Vandenberg Coll, 2A Memos Re 138 Wings, Box 83, MD, LC.
[92] Futrell, *Ideas*, pp 240–245; Neufeld, *Ballistic Missiles*, pp 61–76.
[93] Little, *Building an Atomic Air Force*, Vol III, Pt 1, pp 11–33; Fogerty, Study # 91, "Bunker;" Charles A. Ravenstein, *The Organization and Lineage of the United States Air Force* [USAF Warrior Studies] (Washington: AFCHO, 1986), p 19.

"Never Before Surpassed"

Forces Special Weapons Project. Unfortunately for the service, Secretaries of Defense tended to rely more and more on the Special Weapons project to control the expanding nuclear program and manage the stockpile.[94] While the Air Force did inherit some of the training functions, the project's units continued to guard the storage sites and maintain the weapons. In November 1951 the Defense Department and the Atomic Energy Commission agreed to terms that increased the project's control over the weapons, especially in some of the storage sites then scheduled to be built. In many cases, legal "custody," which the commission still retained over most weapons, had become a mere formality.[95]

The Air Force scored one gain in February 1951. Under the agreements leading to construction of new storage sites, the Air Force would administer them under the project's overall supervision. Air Materiel Command would in effect operate the sites and would be able to insure rapid transfer of weapons to combat units in an emergency.[96] In April 1951, when some weapons were transferred from the commission's custody (in addition to the casings already stored overseas), the Military Liaison Committee tried to raise the question of transferring custody of the whole stockpile. Committee members argued that, while the world situation was deteriorating, the stockpile was outgrowing the commission, and the armed services' expertise, aided by standardized weapon designs, was increasing.[97]

In November Secretary Lovett raised the matter with the joint chiefs. Replying on December 11, the JCS recommended transfer of enough weapons "to assure Operational flexibility and Military readiness."[98] The next month, President Truman referred the matter to Acheson, Lovett, and Gordon Dean, Chairman of the Atomic Energy Commission. The three officials submitted a report in August 1952 on "Agreed Concepts Regarding Atomic Weapons," which basically supported the joint chiefs' recommendations. In approving the report on September 10, the President appeared to have taken the momentous step of giving the armed services full custody of the weapons in the stockpile. But in fact no executive order effecting this transfer followed, despite the joint chiefs' request. Truman decided to defer the matter for the next administration. In March 1953 the question did in fact come before the new Secretary of Defense, Charles E.

---

[94] Little, *Building an Atomic Air Force*, Vol III, Pt 1, pp 33–48.
[95] Ibid., pp 57–67.
[96] Ibid., pp 20–21.
[97] Ibid., pp 60–61.
[98] Ibid., pp 63–64; Poole, *JCS, 1950–1952*, pp 152–154.

Strategic Air Force

Wilson. He, too, deferred action on an executive order, and the custody question remained unsettled throughout 1953.[99]

If 1953 was not destined to be the year of decision in the question of custody, it proved to be the year the Air Force developed an "emergency" delivery capability with the hydrogen bomb. Truman had approved the construction of facilities in 1950, and work had progressed to the point of testing a device and designing a workable bomb. Though this was still an experimental program, enough B–36s were available to allow an allocation for the thermonuclear project.[100]

Basing for a Global Strike Force

The subject of bomber design, as it dealt with matters of range and payload, touched directly on the location of bases for the strategic force. With the bulk of the medium bomber force committed to deploy overseas in the event of an emergency, SAC had to think in global terms about the basing structure. In the states the medium forces needed home bases to train. The heavy bombers would operate from their bases, staging through more northerly fields. Overseas, bases served as strike launching areas, or as alternate fields or recovery bases for those missions in which the bomber could not return straight home from the target. Besides having adequate facilities, bases had to be dispersed, secure against ground attack, and capable of an effective air defense and dispersing their aircraft.

Because basing requirements involved large-scale construction work, they attracted considerable congressional interest. It must be noted that the Corps of Engineers and thus the Secretary of the Army were directly responsible for the actual construction. And since the bases overseas required negotiations with the host country, the Air Force found itself immersed in a brew of strange and varied ingredients.

Since 1945 the condition of the stateside bases had varied considerably. One of the few benefits to arise from the budget cuts in 1949 was that SAC inherited older, better-built bases such as Barksdale and March. The command still had some of the wartime fields where the "temporary" facilities were deteriorating. There was little money to refurbish them, let alone build more permanent structures. And the new bombers, the B–36

---

[99] Little, *Building an Atomic Air Force*, Vol III, Pt 1, pp 64–67; Poole, *JCS, 1950–1952*, p 159.
[100] Bowen, *Development of Weapons*, p 174–233.

and B-47, both required extensive facilities that were not available on all bases.[101]

After June 1950, as the drive for rearmament led to major budget increases, LeMay outlined an agenda for base construction. The work planned included new facilities, base reopenings, more family housing, and new-style barracks. Despite the new funding, construction could not keep pace with the expansion of the force, and most of SAC's bases were crowded.[102] The Air Force Installations Board (established in July 1950 to replace the Air Force Base Development Board) assigned twenty bases to SAC, including Ramey in Puerto Rico, listed as overseas. These came from a list of eighty-five "permanent" Air Force bases in the continental United States and twelve overseas. One purpose of this list was to identify those bases where the Air Force intended to justify construction designed to last twenty-five years, as opposed to the ten years considered normal for temporary construction.[103]

LeMay wanted another base from the Installations Board's "permanent" list, so he could have twenty wing bases plus Offutt for his headquarters. This would allow him one wing per base if there were another force reduction. Also, the SAC commander emphasized that long-term construction plans should include provisions for B-52 bases. Permanent construction, he maintained, would encourage real estate developers to build housing nearby. In any case, closing bases during a force reduction was a false economy:[104] "This saving of a million dollars per year in operating cost per station, and then spending twenty to forty million dollars per base to put them back in minimum usable condition, needs no further discussion."[105]

Under the 95-wing program, SAC would have to find new bases anyway. At the end of 1950 the command had sixteen main bases to accommodate twenty wings. The new program would require enough

---

[101] Ltr, Lt Gen C. E. LeMay, CG SAC, to CSAF, subj: Permanent Peacetime Bases Under the 48 Wing Program, Feb 5, 1951, in hist, SAC, Jan-Jun 1951, Vol III, Chap II, Ex 35; hist, SAC, Jan-Jun 1951, Vol I, pp 42-47.

[102] See previous note.

[103] Memo, Lt Gen L. S. Kuter, Actg Chmn, AF Council, to CSAF, subj: Procedures for Approving Additions to the Permanent Base Structure of the Air Force, n.d. [Dec 52], with atchs, Twining Coll, AFCVC Reading File, Dec 52 (2), Box 58, MD, LC.

[104] *Ibid.*; ltr, Lt Gen C. E. LeMay, CG SAC, to CSAF, subj: Permanent Peacetime Bases Under the 48 Wing Program, Feb 5, 1951, in hist, SAC, Jan-Jun 51, Vol III, Chap II, Ex 35; ltr, LeMay to Maj Gen P. W. Timberlake, Dir Instal, USAF, May 25, 1951, in hist, SAC, Jan-Jun 1951, Vol III, Chap II, Ex 34.

[105] Ltr, Lt Gen C. E. LeMay, CG SAC, to Maj Gen P. W. Timberlake, Dir Instal, USAF, May 25, 1951, in hist, SAC, Jan-Jun 1951, Vol III, Chap II, Ex 34.

The Jet Age. **The high speed Boeing B-47 Stratojet,** *left,* **and Boeing B-52 Stratofortress,** *right,* **joined the Consolidated Vultee B-36 Peacemaker, whose D version was fitted with jet pods, in the Air Force's growing atomic armada. The B-47 was America's first large jet aircraft that featured swept wings.**

stations for twenty-one additional wings. LeMay considered the doubling up to be inevitable, a necessary evil. Still, because the new units would be essentially training wings, it would be possible to disperse the operational units, the war plan force, somewhat.[106]

The B-36 force posed the biggest problem on this score. Indeed, the disastrous storm of September 1, 1952, highlighted the reasons why the war plan bombers should not be so concentrated, and why SAC had for so long attempted to acquire more bases for the heavy bombers. The parking ramp at Carswell was failing from poor construction well before the storm, a highly visible reason for LeMay's concern over the basing issue. Before the storm Brig. Gen. Clarence S. Irvine, commanding at Carswell had worried that dispersal would compound the massive logistical problem he faced, and some of the Eighth Air Force staff supported this view. On the Air Staff, Lt. Gen. Kenneth B. Wolfe, the Deputy Chief of Staff for Materiel, tended to agree. Wolfe also advocated moving the RB-36 wing

---

[106] *Ibid.*; msg, Maj Gen S. E. Anderson, CG 8 AF, 3524, to Gen C. E. LeMay, CG SAC, Oct 11, 1952, LeMay Coll, Anderson # 2, Box B49, MD, LC.

"Never Before Surpassed"

at Rapid City (the 28th Reconnaissance Wing) to a warmer location, but Maj. Gen. Samuel E. Anderson, commanding the Eighth Air Force, resisted what he considered overconcentration at southern bases, and LeMay himself opposed the move. The SAC commander anticipated easing the crowding at Carswell by transferring the 11th Bomb Wing to Limestone Air Force Base, Maine, once the new base was ready. However, work there went too slowly to allow a movement in the near future. Naturally, the SAC leadership agreed that Travis, one of the few suitable bases for B–36s, could not be ceded to the Military Air Transport Service.[107]

The ninety-five-wing program required fields for ten wings of B–36 aircraft. When the program was adopted at the end of 1950, the only bases available were Carswell, Rapid City, and Travis. Work was in progress at Limestone, though stop-and-start funding created many delays at the

---

[107] Draft ltr, Lt Gen C. E. LeMay, CG SAC, to Maj Gen S. E. Anderson, CG 8 AF (ADVON), n.d. [Mar 51]; ltr, Maj Gen A. J. Old, Actg CG 8 AF, to LeMay, Jul 7, 1950; ltr, Old to LeMay, Mar 20, 51, all in LeMay Coll, Old (7AF & 7th AD), Box B57; memo, Anderson to CG SAC, subj: Limestone Air Force Base, Apr 26, 1951, LeMay Coll, Anderson, S. E., Box B49; ltr, LeMay to Gen N. F. Twining, VCSAF, Jun 7, 1951, Twining Coll, Jun 51 (2), Box 55, all in MD, LC.

429

Strategic Air Force

Maine base. The difficulties were compounded by the field's isolation in the Maine north woods (population of the town was 1,213) and the extreme winters. These factors affected transportation, supply, and the availability of labor. In December 1950 SAC anticipated completion by the next October, but that month came and went with the project delayed indefinitely. In particular, Congress had balked at spending a large sum for family housing, but LeMay countered that no developer would want to build even Wherry housing in such an unpromising area. Clearing up the funding issue took time.[108]

By March 1952 the construction at Limestone was nearly finished, although the family housing would not be ready for another year. Twining agreed not to move the 11th Bomb Wing from Carswell. Meanwhile, SAC did establish an air base group and started using the field as a staging base for overseas deployments. Then the heating system began to fail, and basing a unit there over the winter of 1952–1953 would have posed a health hazard. Thus Carswell remained a two-wing base. Finally, when Limestone was ready, a new wing was activated there on February 25, 1953. Conditions were still rough, with inadequate housing and only partial facilities for personnel. There was no service club, library, chapel, or exchange, and of course, unless one hunted or fished, there were no recreational opportunities off base.[109]

In fact, B–36 production in the early fifties had outstripped the preparation of facilities. Work at Walker Air Force Base, New Mexico, (formerly Roswell Field) and Fairchild began later than at Limestone. As these bases became ready during 1951 and 1952 some of the bombers went there. As of 1952 construction was scheduled to begin soon for Biggs Air Force Base, near El Paso, Texas.[110]

During 1951 SAC acquired three bases with specific functions. Lake Charles, Louisiana, and Forbes Air Force Base, Kansas, were to hold the B–29 training units, and Lockbourne Air Force Base, Ohio, received

---

[108] Ltr, Lt Gen C. E. LeMay, CG SAC, to Maj Gen S. E. Anderson, CG 8 AF, Dec 9, 1950, LeMay Coll, Anderson, S. E., Box B49; ltr, Gen N. F. Twining, VCSAF, to LeMay, Mar 20, 1952, Twining Coll, AFCVC Reading File, Mar 52, Box 56; ltr, LeMay to Twining, May 10, 1951, Twining Coll, AFCVC Reading File, May 51 (2), Box 54, all in MD, LC; hist, SAC, Jul–Dec 1951, Vol I, pp 16–18.

[109] Ltr, Gen N. F. Twining, VCSAF, to Gen C. E. LeMay, CG SAC, Mar 20, 1952, Twining Coll, AFCVC Reading File, Mar 52, Box 56; memo, LeMay to Lt Gen T. D. White, DCS/Ops, subj: Limestone Air Force Base, Dec 16, 1952, LeMay Coll, White, Thomas, Box B61, both in MD, LC; Mueller, *Air Force Bases*, Vol I, pp 324–329.

[110] Msg, Maj Gen S. E. Anderson, CG 8 AF, 3524, to Gen C. E. LeMay, CG SAC, Oct 11, 1952, LeMay Coll, Anderson #2, Box B49, MD, LC.

reconnaissance units, relieving crowding at Barksdale. This left Offutt and Travis as SAC's most crowded bases as of mid-1951. LeMay hoped to ease the situation at Offutt with a new headquarters building. Travis was suited for the B-36, but a medium bomb wing was also shoehorned in. Also serving as home to the Military Air Transport Service's west coast aerial port, the base was bound to be busy as long as there was a war in the Far East.[111]

At Offutt SAC had established its headquarters in an aircraft factory operated by the Martin Company during the Second World War. Mobilization planners on the Air Staff continued to envision reopening the plant in any wartime expansion. So, to allow for this contingency, the Air Force sought funds to construct a permanent headquarters building and command center at Offutt. Senator Wherry and the prominent Omaha brewer Arthur Storz helped keep the proposal moving in Congress, but money was slow in coming.[112] In August 1950, when the possibility of mobilization seemed real, Kissner was pessimistic: "It looks as though someone will have to admit that it was wrong to move this headquarters here in the first place."[113]

In spite of increased defense appropriations, funds for SAC headquarters were still delayed, while Air Materiel Command eyed taking over the factory. Finally, Edwards, as Deputy Chief of Staff for Operations, assured SAC in October 1950 that the headquarters would stay in the building "until suitable facilities have been provided."[114] But the threat of displacing SAC remained alive. In September 1951 Lt. Gen. Edwin W. Rawlings, commanding Air Materiel Command, tried to raise the issue again. LeMay's reaction was blistering as he pointed out that many seemed unaware that

---

[111] Hist, SAC, Jan-Jun 1951, Vol I, pp 42-47; Mueller, *Air Force Bases*, Vol I, pp 553-559.

[112] MR, Maj Gen A. W. Kissner, CS SAC, Aug 8, 1950, LeMay Coll, Memos, R-Rs, 1950, Box B64; SSS, Brig Gen Troup Miller, Jr, Dir Indus Resources, DCS/Mat, to VCSAF, Reactivation of Air Force Plant No 1, Omaha, Nebraska, Oct 22, 1951, Twining Coll, AFCVC Reading File, Feb 52, Box 95; ltr, Arthur C. Storz, to Lt Gen C. E. LeMay, CG SAC, Oct 19, 1951, LeMay Coll, Storz (1948-1951), Box A5; ltr, Storz to Gen N. F. Twining, VCSAF, Dec 13, 1951, Twining Coll, AFCVC Reading File, Dec 51, Box 55; ltr, Twining to Storz, Oct 14, 1952, Twining Coll, AFCVC Reading File, Oct 52 (1), Box 57, all in MD, LC.

[113] MR, Maj Gen A. W. Kissner, CS SAC, Aug 8, 1950, LeMay Coll, Memos, R-Rs, 1950, Box B64, MD, LC.

[114] Memo, Col Troup Miller, Jr, XO, DCS/Mat, to Maj Gen R. M. Ramsy, Dir Ops, DCS/Ops, Sep 28, 1950, with atch ltr, Lt Gen I. H. Edwards, DCS/Ops, to CG AMC, subj: Joint Occupancy and Utilization of Facilities of GAP # 1, Offutt Air Force Base, Omaha, Nebraska, Oct 17, 1950, RG 341, DCS/Mat, Exec Ofc TS Corres, Box 1, MMB, NA.

the headquarters was actually in the plant, or perhaps they thought a major command organization could function while factory production went on.[115] This settled the matter for the time being. The next year Twining once again had to affirm that the headquarters would remain in the former plant.[116]

Late in 1952 Secretary Finletter approved a new list of permanent bases, adding six more for SAC. This was essential if the command were to continue to expand. By the end of the year some new bases were already occupied. SAC units returned to Smoky Hill, having given up the base in 1949, but Sedalia, Missouri, a disused wartime base now refurbished, was a new location for the command. Expansion and construction work had now reached the point of "bursting at the seams."[117]

From their home bases, most medium bomber units cited in the war plan were to deploy to England on short notice. The expansion of the medium bomber force had little immediate impact on foreign-based forces, but with an eye to future contingencies, LeMay wanted to acquire more bases, not only in England, but also in other areas, particularly French Morocco. The alternate war plan developed at SAC guided the planning and preparations to extend the command's base area.[118]

To command the forward-based forces, LeMay created two new air divisions early in 1951. The 5th Air Division headquarters under Maj. Gen. Archie J. Old, Jr., was to organize at Offutt and then travel to French Morocco. The 7th, under Brig. Gen. Paul T. Cullen, would deploy to England. On March 23 Cullen and some fifty members of his staff departed on board a C–124. The plane went down, without a trace, somewhere in the North Atlantic. Immediately, Old and his staff were rushed to the planned headquarters at South Ruislip, near London, remaining there for a month while Maj. Gen. John P. McConnell organized a new staff. McConnell reached South Ruislip late in May, and Old then proceeded to Rabat, Morocco, with his staff.[119]

---

[115] Ltr, Lt Gen E. W. Rawlings, CG AMC, to Lt Gen C. E. LeMay, CG SAC, Oct 9, 1951, with atch ltr, LeMay to Rawlings, Sep 28, 1951, LeMay Coll, Rawlings, Box B58, MD, LC.

[116] Msg, Gen N. F. Twining, VCSAF, to Gen C. E. LeMay, CG SAC, Sep 29, 1952, Twining Coll, AFCVC Reading File, Oct 52 (1), Box 57, MD, LC.

[117] Memo, Lt Gen L. S. Kuter, Actg Chmn, AF Council, to CSAF, subj: Procedures for Approving Additions to the Permanent Base Structure of the Air Force, n.d. [Dec 52], with atch Tabs A, B, C, D, Twining Coll, AFCVC Reading File, Dec 52 (2), Box 58, MD, LC.

[118] See Chapter IX.

[119] Hopkins & Goldberg, *Development of SAC*, pp 32–33.

"Never Before Surpassed"

Maj. Gen. Archie J. Old, Jr., Commander, 5th Air Division Headquarters in Rabat, Morocco, one of the forward-based facilities created by General LeMay in 1951.

One reason for establishing a new SAC air division in the United Kingdom was to keep command lines to the strategic force clear. Plans for expanding U.S. forces in NATO called for a tactical force under U.S. Air Forces in Europe to operate from fields in both France and England. Leon Johnson, commanding 3d Air Division, was the person best situated to work with the British and command the base area. On May 1, 1951, his division was replaced by Third Air Force, which would be the tactical force and support the SAC 7th Air Division bases. McConnell would then be directly responsible to LeMay for SAC operations.[120]

McConnell later described the poor conditions he found at the bases in East Anglia:

> Lack of hardstands resulted in bombers having to be parked in neat rows on closed runways. Aircraft maintenance had to be conducted in the open. Hangars were too small for medium bombers and they were unheated. Maintenance control was non-existent. Vehicles were World War II types requiring extensive maintenance. Power and water supplies were critical. Housing was crowded and recreation facilities were undeveloped....Messing facilities were bad.[121]

---

[120] Burk, *USAF in UK*, pp 25–31.
[121] Encl, Summary of Seventh Air Division Deployment from May 1951 to February 1953, to memo, Maj Gen J. P. McConnell, Dep Dir Pl, SAC, to Maj Gen T. S. Power, Dep CG SAC, Mar 16, 1953, in SAC/HO.

Strategic Air Force

The new bases to the west were being upgraded under a bilateral agreement of April 1950. The British, with the help of four battalions of American aviation engineers, were preparing four fields to the north and west of Oxford for B-47 operations. Work had started during the summer of 1950, but bad weather and shortages of materiel caused delays. Besides monitoring the construction, McConnell had to manage the rotational program. After the 93d and 97th wings returned home in October 1950, SAC resumed the normal one-wing rotation force. Later, in response to the crisis in Korea during January 1951, B-36s visited Lakenheath.[122]

Also in 1951 General Johnson approached the British about a much more extensive program of base construction. To expedite the work, the Third Air Force commander reached an agreement with the Air Ministry on an interim cost-sharing arrangement. A long-term agreement was postponed because the British were coming to grips with their severe balance-of-payments problem. Further, the elections in October 1951 brought Churchill and the Conservatives back to power and once again raised the overall question of American bases. In January 1952 Churchill and Truman issued a joint statement that use of the bases in war would be a matter for joint decision by the two governments. Talks continued, although the final signature of an agreement at the ambassadorial level did not come until September 1953.[123]

During the negotiations, the four bases were nearing completion. The 7th Air Division took over Upper Heyford in January 1952, but it was not actually ready until later in the year. Fairford, Brize Norton, and Greenham Common were turned over to the SAC units late in 1952, again unfinished.[124]

The move to French Morocco had been under consideration since early 1950, when planning began for a depot at Nouasseur, twenty miles

---

[122] Ltr, Maj Gen L. W. Johnson, CG 3 AD, to Gen H. S. Vandenberg, CSAF, Oct 2, 1950, RG 341, DCS/Ops, Dir/Pl, OPD, 330.1 (Sep 7, 1950), Case 6, 3 AD, Box 163, MMB, NA; inder, General Grussendorf's copy of Trip Book and Special Notes, n.d. [Oct-Nov 52], Vandenberg Coll, Box 84, MD, LC; hist, 3 AD, Jul-Dec 1950, pp 62-85, 140-142.

[123] Ltr, Maj Gen L. W. Johnson, CG 3 AD, to A/M W. F. Dickson, RAF, Aug 31, 1950, atch to ltr, Johnson to Gen H. S. Vandenberg, CSAF, Oct 2, 1950, RG 341, DCS/Ops, Dir/Pl, OPD, 330.1 (Sep 7, 1950), Case 6, 3 AD, Box 163, MMB, NA; Burk, *USAF in UK*, p 23.

[124] *SAC Operations in the United Kingdom, 1948-1956*, 7 AD Historical Monograph, p 10; Burk, *USAF in UK*, pp 38-39; ltr, Maj Gen J. P. McConnell, CG 7 AD, to Gen C. E. LeMay, CG SAC, Aug 26, 1952, LeMay Coll, McConnell, Box B55, MD, LC.

from Casablanca. In August, as SAC developed its alternate war plan, officials advocated basing up to three wings on the existing airfields at Meknes and Casablanca. It appeared that some construction would be needed to improve the airfields and provide ground transportation and air defense. The planners at SAC and the Air Staff initiated a "crash program" to get bombers in operation in Morocco as soon as possible.[125]

What seemed a fairly simple process became incredibly complicated as the Air Force entered this relatively unfamiliar area. Yet so important was the extension of the strategic basing complex that the airmen persisted. The negotiations involved diverse groups, not only the French in Morocco but those in Paris, as well as the Moroccans and the Army Corps of Engineers, not to mention contractors and Congress.

Late in 1950 a party of Air Force officers and Army engineers visited Morocco under the leadership of Col. Stanley T. Wray, USAF. The group identified five airfields, then in use by the French, which could be put into shape for SAC operations in six months. Meanwhile, the American Embassy in Paris approached the French Foreign Ministry.[126] Although Morocco was outside the North Atlantic Treaty area, the United States stressed the important contribution the bases could make to the defense of the alliance. On December 22, 1950, the two governments concluded an agreement for the United States to use the existing bases. The United States would do the necessary construction, subject to a provision for hiring some French subcontractors and, significantly, a limit on American purchases on the underdeveloped Moroccan economy. By this point, the Air Force had prepared the necessary construction directive to the Corps of Engineers. Issued on November 29, this directive required that there be

---

[125] Memo, G. A. Brownell, Spec Asst to Sec AF, to Gen H. S. Vandenberg, CSAF, Nov 21, 1950, RG 341, DCS/Ops, Dir/Pl, TS OPD, 381 (Feb 7, 1950), Case 6, Sect 1, Box 334; R & R Sheet, Maj Gen T. H. Landon, Dir Pl, to Dir Ops USAF, Deficiencies in Major Air Force Commands, Nov 17, 1950, RG 341, DCS/Ops, Dir/Pl, OPD, 330.1 (Sep 7, 1950), SAC Case 2, Box 163, both in MMB, NA; Study, Log Pl Div, DCS/Mat, Logistics Data and Policies for Use in Planning Development of USAF Base Complex in Morocco, Jun 8, 1951, in SAC/HO; hist, Hq USAF, Jul 1, 1950–Jun 30, 1951, p 91; R & R Sheet, Col Broadhurst, Dir Pl SAC, to CS SAC, Notes from Air Force and Wing Commanders' Conference, Jan 15, 1951, LeMay Coll, Official Docs, SAC Commanders Conference, Box B100, MD, LC.

[126] Ltr, Col E. Vandevanter, Dir Pl SAC, to CS SAC, subj: Report on Visit to USAFE and French Morocco by SAC Party, Oct 27, 1950, in SAC/HO; hist, Hq USAF, Jul 1, 1950–Jun 30, 1951, p 92.

Strategic Air Force

facilities for limited bomber operations within six months of the day the workers entered Morocco.[127]

The French had reason to be uneasy about turning Morocco into an American base area. Their position in the country was based on a complex political foundation in which France was the "Protector" of the nominal sovereign, the Sultan Mohammed ben Youssef. In effect, the French Resident-General in Morocco governed the country (except for the Spanish Zone and Tangier to the north), frequently bypassing the native government. What disturbed the French was the rising nationalist agitation among the Moroccans. Arab countries in the United Nations were supporting this agitation, and France hoped that strategic interests would induce the United States to suppress its urge to sympathize with emerging colonial peoples.[128]

The implications of this quickly became clear in the airman-to-airman negotiations on the details of the agreement. The head of the U.S. Air Force mission to Morocco, Brig. Gen. Pierpont M. Hamilton, had recommended presenting the American needs piecemeal.[129] The technical agreement concluded on April 14, 1951, offered only half a loaf for the United States. The Resident-General, Alphonse Juin (who had commanded the French Corps in the Italian campaign) drove a hard bargain. The list of bases, numbering four with a fifth to be named later, was almost entirely new. All except Nouasseur lay in remote areas of the coastal plain or the plateau and would have to be built from scratch. There was a peacetime ceiling of two wings of aircraft and seventy-four hundred U.S. military personnel, with few or no dependents. While the Americans foresaw

---

[127] Study, Log Pl Div, DCS/Mat, Logistics Data and Policies for Use in Planning Development of USAF Base Complex in Morocco, Jun 8, 1951; memo, Col W. E. Creer, USAF Msn Rabat, to Col Broadhurst, Dir Pl SAC, subj: Periodic Report Number 3 Regarding Negotiations for French Moroccan Air Bases, Mar 1, 1951, both in SAC/HO; memcon, Leo G. Cyr, OIC N African Affairs, Dept of State, Morocco, Apr 23, 1951, in *FRUS*, 1951, Vol V, pp 1381–1383; rprt, Preparedness Investigating Subcommittee, Committee on Armed Services, Senate, *Investigation of the Preparedness Program: Interim Report on Moroccan Air Base Construction* (Washington, 1952), pp 2–3.

[128] Richard F. Nyrop, Beryl Lieff Benderly, et al, *Area Handbook for Morocco*, DA Pamphlet 550–49 (Washington: Dept of Army, 1972), pp 49–57; paper, Dept of State, Morocco, Aug 29, 1951, in *FRUS*, 1951, Vol V, pp 1384–1386.

[129] Memo, Col W. E. Creer, USAF Msn Rabat, to Col Broadhurst, Dir Pl SAC, subj: Periodic Report Number 3 Regarding Negotiations for French Moroccan Air Bases, Mar 1, 1951; msg, Brig Gen P. M. Hamilton, Ch USAF Msn Rabat, to Col H. L. Maddux, Asst Air Base Prog, DCS/Ops, USAF, 272252Z Jan 51; ltr, Hamilton to Maddux, Jan 20, 1951, all in SAC/HO.

morale problems, Norstad, commanding in the area, approved the agreement in order to expedite work on the bases.[130]

The Air Force secured $62 million from Congress for the Morocco program. The Corps of Engineers retained the firms of Porter-Urquhart and Skidmore, Owings, Merrill as architect-engineers and contracted with a consortium of building companies called Atlas Constructors to do the work. The contractors were ready to begin at the signing of the technical agreement, but completing a major project by July 1951 would be a challenge.[131]

General Old's arrival at Rabat was delayed in the aftermath of the loss of the Cullen party, but when he arrived late in May 1951 work had already begun. The District Engineer, Col. George T. Derby, was well aware of the pressure to get results. At a meeting of Old, Norstad, and Derby, it was agreed that one usable runway would be finished by July 14, Bastille Day.[132] Old was conscious of his role as customer of a project in the hands of others, although with LeMay as his superior he understood he could not remain passive. He did demand and obtain what he knew were costly changes. By July work was under way at Ben Guerir, Sidi Slimane, and Nouasseur, and by the 13th the latter two had operational airstrips but little else. Old flew from Rabat to Sidi Slimane with a party of French dignitaries to greet a flight of F–84s. The next day, with great ceremony, a similar group at Nouasseur witnessed a flyover and landing of eighteen B–50s and KB–29s sent from England, followed by a demonstration by the American fighters. The bombers left the next day, and no more came until December. Nouasseur's capabilities were still mostly symbolic.[133]

---

[130] Hearings before the Subcommittee on Military Public Works, Committee on Appropriations, House, *Moroccan Air Base Construction*, 82d Cong, 2d sess (pub info), Pt 4, pp 280–281; Technical Agreement Number One Between the French Air Force and the USAF Regarding the Occupancy of the Moroccan Air Bases, Mar 26, 1951 (copy approved by USAF Mission & French AF in Morocco, not final copy signed Apr 14, 1951 in Paris, but substantially the same), in SAC/HO; ltr, Maj Gen S. E. Anderson, CG 8 AF, to Lt Gen C. E. LeMay, CG SAC, Mar 13, 1951, LeMay Coll, Anderson, S. E., Box B49; ltr, Gen N. F. Twining, VCSAF, to LeMay, Jul 9, 1951, Twining Coll, AFCVC Reading File, Jul 51, Box 55, both in MD, LC.

[131] Hist, Hq USAF, Jul 1, 1950–Jun 30, 1951, p 92; Hearings before the Preparedness Subcommittee, Committee on Armed Services, Senate, *Hiring for Work at Overseas Bases*, 82d Cong, 2d sess, Pt 2, pp 217–240, 290.

[132] See previous note; Hopkins & Goldberg, *Development of SAC*, pp 30–31.

[133] Ltr, Maj Gen A. J. Old, CG 5 AD, to Lt Gen C. E. LeMay, CG SAC, Jun 23, 1951; ltr, Old to LeMay, Jul 8, 1951, both in LeMay Coll, Old (5th AD), Box B57, MD, LC; Hearings before the Preparedness Subcommittee, Committee on Armed Services, Senate, *Hiring for Work at Overseas Bases*, 82d Cong, 2d sess, Pt 2, p 261; hist, 5 AD, Jul–Dec 1951, pp 68–69; ltr, Lt Gen T. D. White, DCS/Ops, to LeMay, Aug 9, 1951, LeMay Coll, White, Thomas, Box B61, MD, LC.

Strategic Air Force

On the coastal plain of Morocco, the rainy season begins in October. By November 1951 General Old was growing uneasy at the condition of the pavement at Sidi Slimane and Nouasseur. He believed Derby had lost control over Atlas, which had spent a lot of money on camps for the American workers. The architect-engineers had reported unsatisfactory work, but the chief engineer had refused to call a halt. Should the pavement be inadequately supported, water would get in and start washing away the ground underneath. Old's cooperative relations with Derby began to turn sour. Then the apron at Nouasseur and the runway at Sidi Slimane began to fail.[134]

The six B-36s that visited Sidi Slimane on December 3, 1951, stayed six days and left. Old was too worried about the state of the airfields to put the bombers at risk. The architect-engineers shared his doubts. By this time Vandenberg was informed, but the problem was soon out of his hands. Early in 1952 the Preparedness Subcommittee of the Senate Armed Services Committee, under the chairmanship of Lyndon B. Johnson of Texas, began to investigate the Morocco project.[135]

The Johnson Subcommittee hearings began in February 1952, and the next month the Army recalled Derby, ostensibly to testify. Lt. Gen. Lewis A. Pick, USA, the Chief of Engineers (and builder of the Ledo Road in Burma), endured much of the subcommittee's criticism. On the whole, the senators were sympathetic to the Air Force and its problems. As members of the SAC staff agreed, the Air Force and SAC had avoided the political repercussions, even if the Moroccan airfields remained only marginally useful.[136]

---

[134] Ltr, Maj Gen A. J. Old, CG 5 AD, to Gen C. E. LeMay, CG SAC, Nov 30, 51; ltr, Old to LeMay, Feb 9, 1952, with atch ltr, Old to Lt Gen L. Norstad, CINC AAFCE, Feb 8, 1952; ltr, Old to LeMay, Dec 11, 1952, all in LeMay Coll, Old (5th AD), Box B57, MLD, LC; Hearings before the Preparedness Subcommittee, Committee of Armed Services, Senate, *Hiring for Work at Overseas Bases*, 82d Cong, 2d sess, Pt 2, pp 219-248.

[135] Ltr, Maj Gen A. J. Old, CG 5 AD, to Gen C. E. LeMay, CG SAC, Dec 11, 1951; ltr, Old to Lt Gen L. Norstad, CINC AAFCE, Feb 8, 1952, atch to ltr, Old to LeMay, Feb 9, 1952, both in LeMay Coll, Old (5th AD), Box B57; msg, Norstad to Gen H. S. Vandenberg, CSAF, 151031Z Dec 51, Vandenberg Coll, Redlines, Nov to-, IN, Box 87, all in MD, LC; hist, Dir Ops, DCS/Ops, Hq USAF, Jul 1-Dec 31, 1951, p 2.

[136] Msg, Lt Gen L. Norstad, CINC AAFCE, to Gen H. S. Vandenberg, CSAF, 151031Z Dec 51, Vandenberg Coll, Redlines, Nov 1951, IN, Box 87, MD, LC; Hearings before the Preparedness Subcommittee, Committee on Armed Services, Senate, *Hiring for Work at Overseas Bases*, 82d Cong, 2d sess, Pt 2, Pt 5 *Investigation of Overseas Air Force Bases*; ltr, Maj Gen A. J. Old, CG 5 AD, to Norstad, Feb 8, 1952, atch to ltr, Old to Gen C. E. LeMay, CG SAC, Feb 9, 1952; ltr, Old to LeMay, Mar 28, 1952, both in LeMay Coll, Old (5th AD), Box B57, MD, LC.

"Never Before Surpassed"

Estimates for the repair bill ran from $4 million to $30 million, and satisfactory repairs would have to wait until 1953. In the meantime SAC used the Moroccan bases for limited operations. During 1952 only two B-29 wings spent time there. With such a minor mission, morale in the air base units was impaired. At Nouasseur the contractors had not built a water tower, so there was no running water. No money was available to repair boilers, so there was no hot water either. Without paved walkways, men had to cross seas of mud during the rains. The huts leaked, and recreational facilities were limited. Moroccan nationalist agitation led to rioting in the towns, rendering them off limits, not to say that the recreation they offered was especially wholesome. In September 1952 the venereal disease rate at Nouasseur was two hundred per thousand.[137] Finletter called the lack of recreational facilities in Morocco a "national disgrace."[138] Anna Rosenberg, Assistant Secretary of Defense for Manpower and Reserve Affairs, on a worldwide tour of U.S. facilities, called Nouasseur the worst overseas base she had seen.[139]

Ironically, for an as yet marginal strategic benefit, the United States was taking a significant political risk. Determined to retain their influence in Morocco, at the end of 1952 the French were arresting nationalists and communists alike, professing to see a link between the two. The United States was ambivalent about the issue in the United Nations, aware of the risk that the rising tide of Arab nationalism would take an anti-American stance. The State Department believed that the threat to stability in Morocco had increased in direct proportion to the strength of the American interest there.[140]

---

[137] Ltr, Maj Gen A. J. Old, CG 5 AD, to Gen C. E. LeMay, CG SAC, Jul 29, 1952; DF, Brig Gen C. J. Bondley, Jr, Dir Mat SAC, to CG SAC, Construction Problems in North Africa, Jan 20, 1953; msg, Old to LeMay, Gen L. Norstad, CINC USAFE, Maj Gen T. H. Landon, VCINC USAFE, 131315Z Dec 52, all in LeMay Coll, Old (5th AD) # 2, Box B57, MD, LC; msg, R. L. Gilpatric, USec AF, E. V. Huggins, Asst Sec AF/Mat, to T. K. Finletter, Sec AF, Sep 23, 1952; msg, Huggins to Old, Sep 19, 1952, both in Vandenberg Coll, Redlines, Jul 1, 1952, Box 87, MD, LC; msg, CINC USAFE to CSAF, 291300Z Sep 52, RG 341, DCS/Ops, Dir/Pl, OPD, 330.1 SAC, Case 2, Sect 2, Box 163; memo, A. Rosenberg, Asst Sec Def (M & RA), to Sec AF, Aug 23, 1952, RG 341, OPD 333.1, AF Pl (Jan 15, 1952), Sect 1, Box 165, both in MMB, NA; hist, Dir Ops, DCS/Ops, Hq USAF, Jan 1–Jun 30, 1952, p 99, Jul 1–Dec 30, 1952, p 144.

[138] Msg, T. K. Finletter, Sec AF, to R. L. Gilpatric, USec AF, 211350Z Sep 52, Vandenberg Coll, Redlines Jul 1, 1952, Box 87, MD, LC.

[139] Memo, A. Rosenberg, Asst Sec Def (M & RA), to Sec AF, Aug 23, 1952, RG 341, OPD 333.1, AF Pl (Jan 15, 1952), Sect 1, Box 165, MMB, NA.

[140] Policy paper, Dept of State, United States Policy in Morocco, Nov 21, 1951, in *FRUS*, 1951, Vol V, pp 1392–1395; msg, J. C. Vincent, Dip Agt Tangier, to Sec State, Dec 14, 1952, in *FRUS*, 1952–1954, Vol XI, Pt 2, pp 604–606.

Strategic Air Force

In contrast, a better-controlled but still costly overseas project was undertaken at Thule, Greenland. Extremely interested in the strategic potential of the Arctic, Secretary Finletter conferred with the Air Force's leading expert on the region, Col. Bernt Balchen. The Norwegian-born explorer and aviator was then commanding the 10th Rescue Squadron at Elmendorf Air Force Base, Alaska. Years before, the explorer Knut Rasmussen had told Balchen about a harbor that was open during the summer, along the northwest coast of Greenland. During the Second World War Balchen had occasion to fly over Thule to confirm the report. The AAF had subsequently established an emergency airstrip at Thule, calling the station Bluie West Six. Balchen continued to believe that the site could be a major base, and eventually Finletter agreed. On October 2, 1950, the secretary instructed the Air Staff to study the possibilities of bases in the Arctic.[141]

Col. George E. Glober of the War Plans Division led the study, consulting with Balchen and other experts. His report recommended Thule as the best site. Situated six hundred miles north of the Arctic Circle, it was near enough to the Soviet Union that a B–36 could reach eighty-five percent of the targets, and a B–47 with one in-flight refueling could reach half of them. But neither the Air Staff nor SAC was enthusiastic about Arctic bases on the proposed scale. The Glober Committee's cost estimates ranged from $75 million to $125 million. This funding would have gone much further in more hospitable climates. SAC operations analysts stressed that should the project be approved, it needed to be pressed with vigor.[142]

On learning that a base at Thule was feasible, Finletter had no further reservations and he initiated PROJECT BLUEJAY. The secretary had obtained Congressman Vinson's concurrence, and in January 1951 he asked Deputy Secretary Lovett to approve the major construction project. After some consultation with Congress, Lovett gave his consent.[143]

---

[141] Bernt Balchen, *Come North with Me: An Autobiography* (NY: Dutton, 1958), pp 235–236, 298, 305–306; paper, Brief Chronology of Thule, n.d., Vandenberg Coll, 27. Papers Used by CS Before Senate, Box 85, MD, LC.

[142] Staff study, Glober Cmte, Dec 50; msg, CG SAC to CSAF, 202355Z Dec 50; R & R Sheet, C. L. Zimmerman, Ch Ops An SAC, to Dir Ops, SAC, SAC Bases in Greenland, Jan 3, 1951, all in SAC/HO; paper, Brief Chronology of Thule, n.d., Vandenberg Coll, 27. Papers Used by CS Before Senate, Box 85, MD, LC; hist, Hq USAF, Jul 1950–Jun 1951, pp 93–94.

[143] Memo, G. A. Brownell, Spec Asst to Sec AF, to J. A. McCone, USec AF, subj: Thule, Jan 11, 1951; memo, T. K. Finletter, Sec AF, to R. A. Lovett, Dep Sec Def, Jan 13, 1951; memo, Gen N. F. Twining, VCSAF, to CSAF, Mar 30, 1951; memo, Lovett to Sec AF, subj: Construction of a Bomber Staging Base at Thule, Greenland, Feb 16, 1951, all in Vandenberg Coll, 27. Papers Used by CS Before Senate, Box 85, MD, LC.

"Never Before Surpassed"

Lt. Gen. George E. Stratemeyer, Commander, Far East Air Forces.

Establishing a major base in the Arctic obviously demanded a strenuous effort. Items that might be considered luxuries elsewhere would be necessities in northern Greenland. LeMay insisted on a heated shelter for bomber maintenance. A logistician pointed out that without skilled mechanics, equipment failures could cost lives. And when the Army Engineers toured the site, they increased the cost estimates to $168 million.[144] Construction would be limited to a few summer months each year. The first party flew to the site in March 1951. The engineers set up an office in a suburb of Saint Paul, Minnesota, which recruited 8,500 men for a construction job somewhere overseas in a cold climate. These work conditions required making offers of up to $4.20 an hour, then a large sum for construction work. The work force reached Thule by ship in July. By September the crews had completed a 7,500-foot runway and facilities for limited operations. The main body returned to the States for the winter, leaving a caretaker force behind.[145]

LeMay continued to urge speed in completing the project. He was especially concerned that the base be well equipped with navigation aids

---

[144] Memo, Gen N. F. Twining, VCSAF, to CSAF, Mar 30, 1951, Vandenberg Coll, 27. Papers Used by CS Before Senate, Box 85, MD, LC; MR, Lt Gen O. R. Cook, DCS/Mat, Sep 28, 1951, RG 341, DCS/Mat, Exec Ofc TS Corres, Box 1, MMB, NA.

[145] *Air Force Times*, Sep 27, 1952, p 1; monograph, Project BLUE JAY, NEAC Hist Br, Nov 52, pp 6, 9, 61.

Strategic Air Force

for Arctic flying. The SAC commander envisioned using Thule primarily for staging B-47s. The Northeast Air Command, selected to operate the base, took possession in January 1952. The 1952 construction season rendered the base virtually operational, and most work was done by late 1953. Costs had exceeded all estimates, going over $200 million. But in marked contrast to Sidi Slimane or Nouasseur, Thule was finished on time and did not have to be rebuilt.[146]

In other areas, base construction was a simpler process, although few proposed installations were free of political complexities. Okinawa was in fact the only war plan base solidly in U.S. hands at the time. Most fields were to be used as recovery bases or for staging. Basing rights for Wheelus in Libya depended on talks with the government of King Idris, to whom the British and French had turned over power. British work on Abu Sueir in Egypt proceeded irregularly, being finally finished in 1952. However, that same year saw the overthrow of King Farouk II in a military coup, and foreign bases in Egypt suddenly were in jeopardy. While Dhahran, Saudi Arabia was probably more secure, the regime there requested economic aid. Obtaining rights to Lajes, in the Portuguese Azores, and Keflavik, Iceland, required continual negotiations, but both countries were members of NATO and thus gave the United States a good hearing. In general, SAC did not operate these bases, nor were they exclusively committed to the strategic air offensive. Still, they had various uses in the command's war plan.[147]

Secretary Finletter was also interested in what he called "bargain alternates." Spain, Portugal, and Northern Ireland appeared from time to time in his correspondence.[148] Spain was promising strategically, being closer to the targets than Morocco but shielded by the Pyrenees from a rapid Soviet conquest. Once again, the problems were political. The

---

[146] Hist, NEAC, Jan-Jun 1952, pp 156-157; hist, 8 AF, Jul-Dec 1952, pp 339-340, Jan-Jun 1957, pp 5-6.

[147] Rprt, USAF Requirements, Deployments, Activations, and Public Works Program and Status of Negotiations for Military Rights, Nov 10, 1952, Vandenberg Coll, Classified, Box 34; General Grussendorf's copy of Trip Book and Special Notes, n.d. [Oct-Nov 52], Vandenberg Coll, Box 84; ltr, Maj Gen T. S. Power, Dep CG SAC, to DCS/Ops USAF, subj: Designation of Facilities at Keflavik for Strategic Air Command, Apr 22, 1952, Vandenberg Coll, SAC (6), Box 45; MR, J. Wise, Asst Dep Sec AF/Instal, Feb 9, 1953, Twining Coll, AFCVC Reading File, Feb 53, Box 58; memo, T. K. Finletter, Sec AF, to Gen H. S. Vandenberg, CSAF, Nov 23, 1951, Vandenberg Coll, AFCVC Reading File Nov 51, Box 55, all in MD, LC.

[148] Msg, R. L. Gilpatric, USec AF, to T. K. Finletter, Sec AF, Sep 20, 1952, Vandenberg Coll, Redlines, Jul 1, 1952—, Box 87, MD, LC.

regime of Francisco Franco seemed stable enough, but until late 1950 the United States had had no diplomatic relations with it, in keeping with a ban on the government by the United Nations. The Spanish regime was unpopular in many circles in the United States. Nevertheless, as the Cold War developed, the United States had maintained some contacts, including a visit by LeMay during his tour in Europe. Soon after the Korean War began, the United Nations lifted its ban and relations resumed. During 1951 the United States broached the question of bases, and in July the Chief of Naval Operations, Admiral Forrest Sherman, visited Madrid.[149]

The Air Force hoped eventually to be able to base five B-47 wings in Spain. In the short term, emergency landing rights would help.[150] In April 1952 Maj. Gen. August W. Kissner, until then LeMay's chief of staff, arrived in Madrid with a negotiating team. He began talks with Lt. Gen. Juan Vigon, Chief of the High General Staff. The Spanish drove a hard bargain, and no agreement was reached until September 1953.[151]

The bases overseas raised domestic political controversies as well. Late in 1952 two members of the Senate Armed Services Committee, Russell B. Long, Democrat of Louisiana, and Wayne L. Morse, Republican of Oregon, questioned the need to station so many men overseas. In fact, the Air Force did not entirely disagree. SAC policy called for limiting the size of the permanent parties as much as possible.[152] During his travels, Secretary Finletter was disturbed by the frequent hostility of local populations and the questions raised by foreign officials. He also wondered about "the effect on the men themselves" of these overseas tours.[153]

In February 1953 Senators Long and Morse released a report critical of the costs, fiscal and political, of large-scale overseas basing. Their report and the committee hearings reflected a widespread public concern. Finletter and Twining both sought to reassure the senators, arguing that the forward bases, with a widely dispersed force, were currently essential to the strategic air offensive. Twining noted the Air Force's efforts to keep

---

[149] Swetzer, *Operations in the Mediterranean*, pp 33-34.
[150] Ltr, Col H. R. Maddux, Asst DCS/Ops for Air Bases, to Gen N. F. Twining, VCSAF, subj: USAF Requirements in Spain, Jul 9, 1951, Twining Coll, Jul 51, Box 55, MD, LC.
[151] Swetzer, *Operations in the Mediterranean*, p 34.
[152] Msg, E. V. Huggins, Asst Sec AF/Mat, to T. K. Finletter, Sec AF, Sep 23, 1952; msg, Finletter to Huggins, 011114Z Oct 52, both in Vandenberg Coll, Redlines, Jul 1, 1952, Box 87, MD, LC; memo, Finletter to CSAF, Oct 21, 1952, RG 341, DCS/Ops, Dir/Pl, OPD, 320.2 (Jul 24, 1950), Sect 3, Box 126, MMB, NA.
[153] Memo for file, T. K. Finletter, Sec AF, Oct. 23, 1952, RG 341, DCS/Ops, Dir/Pl, OPD, 320.2 (Jul 24, 1952), Sect 3, Box 126, MMB, NA.

Strategic Air Force

overseas manning down. Apparently, the question of overseas basing was not closed.[154]

In planning the construction of bases both overseas and within the continental United States, dispersal of air resources to reduce vulnerability to air attack was a recognized goal. Secretary Finletter continued "to be worried about the security of SAC bases," and concentration was viewed as a necessary evil.[155] The wider implications of dispersal at a time when the Soviet atomic threat was increasing had begun to interest the staff at RAND. A young researcher there named Albert Wohlstetter was studying the matter thoroughly and beginning to attract an audience for his concerns.[156] Other factors were involved in protecting the strategic force. For one, the sheer size of the force planned in the 143-wing program would pose a challenge to an attacker. And although the Air Force held the view that no level of defense against air attack could prevent serious damage to the United States, the service was successful in having the Army allocate a number of anti-aircraft artillery battalions to key SAC bases.[157]

Besides the threat from the air, LeMay devoted attention to protecting the bases against attackers on the ground, especially saboteurs. He had instituted a plan to improve base security in November 1949, proposing to build up the Air Police in quality and quantity. On each base, the commander was to set apart critical areas, fence and light them, and strictly control entry. Although SAC approved the basic plan in May 1950, manning ceilings and limited budgets prevented action. Nor was the Army in any better position to provide men for the ground defense units.[158]

---

[154] MR, J. Wise, Asst Dep Sec AF/Instal, Feb 9, 1953, Twining Coll, AFCVC Reading File, Feb 53 (1), Box 58; MR, Col A. J. Cox, Jr, Ch, Senate & White House Liaison, General Bradley's Testimony—Military Public Works Hearing, Senate Armed Services Committee, Feb 10, 1953, Vandenberg Coll, 27. Papers Used by CS Before Senate, Box 85, both MD, LC; msg, Sec AF to Asst Sec AF/Mat, 011114Z Oct 52; memo, Gen N. F. Twining, VCSAF, to T. K. Finletter, Sec AF, subj: Air Force Personnel in Overseas Areas, Nov 12, 1952, both in RG 341, DCS/Ops, Dir/Pl, OPD, 320.2 (Jul 24, 1950), Sect 3, Box 126, MMB, NA.

[155] Memo, T. K. Finletter, Sec AF, to Gen H. S. Vandenberg, CSAF, Nov 23, 1951, Twining Coll, AFCVC Reading File, Nov 51, Box 55, MD, LC.

[156] *The Cost of Decreasing Vulnerability of Air Bases by Dispersal: Dispersinq a B-36 Wing*, RAND Rprt R-235, Jun 1, 1952.

[157] SAC Proqress Analysis, Oct 53, LeMay Coll, Box B98, MD, LC.

[158] *Ibid.*; encl 1, IG SAC, to ltr, Lt Gen C. E. LeMay, CG SAC, to CSAF, Jan 27, 1950; draft memo, Dir Pl, DCS/Ops, to Gen H. S. Vandenberg, CSAF, subj: Security of Bases of the Strategic Air Command, May 29, 1950, with atch memo, Maj Gen F. H. Smith, Jr, Asst to DCS/Ops for Prog, subj: Nonconcurrence in Proposed Memorandum for General Vandenberg Re Security of Space of the Strategic Air Command, Jun 1, 1950, all in RG 341, DCS/Ops, Dir/Pl, OPD, 600.96 SAC (Feb 10, 1950), Box 1029, MMB, NA; SAC Proqress Analysis, Oct 1953, LeMay Coll, Box B98, MD, LC.

"Never Before Surpassed"

With increased funding after the Korean War broke out, manning ceilings could be lifted, and Air Police squadrons were beefed up. A SAC school at Camp Carson, Colorado, trained officers and noncommissioned officers destined for the command's Air Police units. In addition, J. Edgar Hoover, the Director of the Federal Bureau of Investigation, detailed fifteen of his agents to SAC bases as instructors. At the same time, the command undertook the needed construction, and by May 1951 LeMay could report that most of the fencing, lighting, and towers were in place. Routine procedures were in effect for screening people and controlling entry to restricted areas. Armed reaction teams were on duty. Only the more expensive security measures remained: the construction of dispersed and revetted parking for the planes and underground storage for fuel.[159]

Having established the apparatus for base security, SAC needed to know that it worked. By arrangement between SAC and the Air Force Office of Special Investigations (OSI) in 1951, agents of the latter began covert penetrations of SAC stations to test their security. These activities provided a continuing program to evaluate and correct weaknesses. According to one account, during an exercise in 1952 ten agents attempted to perform simulated acts of sabotage. One succeeded in reaching a parked B–36, but eight were captured.[160] In other words, acts of sabotage could produce losses, but SAC had a pretty good score in trying to prevent them.

From New Phase to New Look

The decision by the Secretary of Defense to halt the expansion of the Army and Navy in 1952, while the Air Force would continue to grow, did not of course guarantee that this would happen. But in fact President Truman and Congress concurred. In the current political atmosphere, no service was going to grow larger and faster than the Defense Department requested. The question was how fast the Air Force would grow, as well as how large. The general diminishing of the sense of danger, both in Europe

---

[159] Memo, Maj Gen W. F. McKee, Asst VCSAF, to Gen H. S. Vandenberg, CSAF, Lt Gen L. Norstad, DCS/Ops, Aug 14, 1950, Vandenberg Coll, SAC (3), Box 45; ltr, J. E. Hoover, Dir FBI, to T. K. Finletter, Sec AF, Jul 13, 1950, Vandenberg Coll, Sec of the AF-1950, Box 61; ltr, Lt Gen C. E. LeMay, to Gen N. F. Twining, VCSAF, May 10, 1951, Twining Coll, May 51 (2), Box 54; Security folder, Strategic Air Command, Feb 3, 1953, LeMay Coll, Box B106, all in MD, LC.

[160] SAC Progress Analysis, Oct 1953, LeMay Coll, Box B98, MD, LC; LeMay & Kantor, *Mission with LeMay*, pp 479–480.

Strategic Air Force

and in the United States, meant that the pressure to limit the defense budget would be strong. On December 28, 1951, President Truman set ceilings on defense spending both for the current year and the next. The Joint Strategic Plans Group told the Joint Chiefs of Staff that these ceilings would actually lower the Army's and Navy's force goals and slow the Air Force's expansion, 143 wings to be attained only in 1956.[161] The Air Force found the budget cutbacks disturbing because the "task concept" was still not being applied to justify expenditures, and there were land and naval forces programmed for no particular strategic function. Col. James F. Whisenand in the Directorate of Plans agreed, "That Army and Navy programs are not only over on forces but have a tremendous fat for expansion and war reserves."[162] The strategy of mobilization still had its proponents.

President Truman's budget request for fiscal 1953 included $48 billion for defense, $21 billion of that for the Air Force. Congress seemed to be in a strong mood to cut these amounts. Lovett intended in his congressional testimony to highlight the danger facing the country, asserting that 1954 was still the year of maximum peril, as well as defend all programs while stressing that cuts would limit the Air Force. Vandenberg testified about the increasing strength of the Soviet air force. The potential enemy was thought to have one hundred heavy bombers and fifteen hundred mediums, a quarter of them jets, while its air defenses were improving. Only the U.S. Air Force, the Air Force chief said, was "charged with striking from enemy hands the weapon most dangerous to this nation."[163] Senator Taft, a presidential candidate, was not alone in calling for cuts, and in favoring air power as a means to economize, he foreshadowed congressional action. The final appropriation increased the Air Force share from $20.7 billion to $21.2 billion, trimming $2 billion from the Army budget.[164]

The congressional debates thus perpetuated the political argument concerning the Truman administration's defense policy. The U.S. ground

---

[161] Poole, *JCS, 1950–1952*, pp 109–111.

[162] Memo, Col J. F. Whisenand, to Maj Gen R. M. Lee, Dir Pl, DCS/Ops (and passed to Gen H. S. Vandenberg, CSAF), subj: Comparison of Strategic Requirements for Service Programs, Dec 14, 1951, Vandenberg Coll, Z. Memos from Col Whisenand on Strat Rqmts, Box 83, MD, LC.

[163] Hearings before the Committee on Appropriations, Senate, *Department of Defense Appropriation for 1953*, 82d Cong, 2d sess, pp 3–11, 143–161, 197–221; Hearings before the Committee on Appropriations, House of Representatives, *Air Force Appropriation for 1953*, 82d Cong, 2d sess, p 72; memo, Col J. V. Murphy, to Gen H. S. Vandenberg, CSAF, Apr 4, 1952, with atch draft statement for O'Mahoney Committee, Vandenberg Coll, 14. Proposed Statement, Box 84, MD, LC.

[164] Poole, *JCS, 1950–1952*, pp 111–113.

and tactical air units that began arriving in Europe during the last half of 1951 were one focus of the debate. In February 1952 at Lisbon, the NATO allies agreed to have ninety divisions available on thirty days' notice, supported by ten thousand aircraft.[165] To many this seemed to symbolize the commitment to the futile effort to defeat Soviet land armies should they attack. Another sign of the times seemed to be the change in the allied command. Eisenhower, although he had advocated strong land forces in Western Europe, was a strong proponent of air power as well. On Eisenhower's resignation in April to begin his candidacy for President, Gen. Matthew B. Ridgway succeeded him as supreme commander. Although highly respected in the Army, Ridgway was less known as a supporter of air power than Eisenhower had been.[166]

Despite these trends, the Air Staff was taking steps to defend the 143-wing program by articulating an air power strategy for the nation. By the end of 1951 some work was under way, with Finletter's assistance. No doubt this effort played a part in the congressional testimony, but it also had long-term significance. The "Air Concept," as its authors called it, represented an interweaving of basic ideas on airpower with current strategic and budgetary realities. Its central elements concerned geography, technology, budgets, and strategy.[167]

The geographical argument held that the Soviet Union was not vulnerable to naval or land forces. Though it had limited access to the sea, it had become a major power. Its vast expanse of territory, including the satellite countries of Eastern Europe, together with its enormous manpower and industrial capacity, made invasion or occupation by land forces infeasible. By the same token, it could strike with great strength across Western Europe. Only air power, by penetrating and neutralizing targets, could defeat the Soviets.[168]

It was now technically possible for the U.S. Air Force to do just that. New weapons, bombers with intercontinental reach (albeit with forward basing and tankers) and equipped with nuclear weapons, would be able to destroy the Soviet Union's ability to make war. At the very least, the

---

[165] *Ibid.*, pp 297–301.
[166] Briefing, Military Philosophy as a Basis for Strategic Decision, n.d., RG 341, DCS/Ops, Dir/Pl, TS OPD, 381 (Jan 19, 1952), Box 319, MMB, NA; paper, The New Phase—A Statement of Air Force Policy, Aug 2, 1952, Twining Coll, TS File (1), Box 122, MD, LC; Poole, *JCS, 1950–1952*, pp 307–308.
[167] Briefing, Military Philisophy as a Basis for Strategic Decision, n.d., RG 341, DCS/Ops, Dir/Pl, TS OPD, 381 (Jan 19, 1952), Box 319, MMB, NA.
[168] *Ibid.*; plan, Mob Div, Dir Pl, DCS/Ops, US Air Force Planned Wartime Activity, CUMULO–NIMBUS, FY–54 Budget Guidance, Apr 52, RG 341, DCS/Ops, Dir/Pl, TS OPD, 381 (Aug 10, 1951), Box 321, MMB, NA.

strategic air offensive would prevent disaster. The entire force would have to be ready on D-day. Losses would be heavy, but the stakes were high. The Air Staff estimated that in 1954 Soviet attacks on SAC could inflict twenty percent losses on the command in the continental United States and thirty percent overseas. Attrition to the attacking SAC forces during the first month could approach fifty percent, although this depended on the timing. But, according to the Air Concept, the planned force would be equal to the task. Nuclear weapons would be in short supply until 1956, which meant that the strategic force should have priority in allocation.[169]

The budget argument proposed that spending reflect political realities. Money allocated to a costly and ineffective effort to defeat the Soviet Union on land or by sea would be wasted. For the United States to maintain the kind of forces needed for such a strategy would disrupt the economy and turn the country into a garrison state. Spending had to be for essentials, and the first priority was the strategic air force.[170]

Soviet atomic weapons would soon be numerous enough to threaten serious damage to the United States. A modern air defense could weaken but not stop an atomic attack, so the strategic force should devote a serious effort to the blunting task. The atomic threat also meant that mobilization at the outbreak of a war would be impossible, and the country really needed a ready D-day force. Besides continental air defense, the United States needed forces to support the Europeans in holding back the Soviets until the air campaign had taken effect. Ground forces thus had a role, along with tactical air forces, in winning the air battle. Naval forces were needed to keep the sea lanes open.[171]

The air planners did not entirely agree about the need for forces to fight local wars. The frustrations of the Korean situation suggested that such conflicts should be avoided. Many agreed with Finletter that the United States could not afford to maintain enough forces to oppose local aggression. As long as the real adversary was the Soviet Union, local forces were not really necessary. Instead, the nation needed a diplomatic approach that translated strategic air power into deterrence of all aggression.[172]

The Europeans had a similar strategic problem. W. Barton Leach, Finletter's special adviser, described the widespread desire to prevent war in Europe. A deterrent that kept the Soviets at bay was preferable to a war by the United States to liberate an occupied Europe. Writing from

---

[169] See previous note; paper, The New Phase—A Statement of Air Force Policy, Aug 2, 1952, Twining Coll, TS File (1), Box 122, MMB, NA.
[170] See Notes 167–169.
[171] See Notes 167–169.
[172] See Notes 167–169.

"Never Before Surpassed"

Europe, Leach also noted another dimension, similar to the American budgetary issue: "Can you imagine any French premier coming to power on a program of increase in the period of military service, higher taxation, more land devoted to U.S. air bases, and more U.S. troops quartered in France?"[173] Leach did not see much chance of holding anywhere on the continent north of the Alps. Under the circumstances, an air-oriented strategy to deter war or end it quickly would have definite appeal. Leach did emphasize, however, that the Air Force could contribute to European security by developing sound strategy and assigning effective staff officers to SHAPE.[174]

The Air Concept presented the case for the 143-wing program. It also, as Leach anticipated, offered a strategic solution when European enthusiasm for the Lisbon program waned. Leach believed that Churchill would support something along the lines of the Air Force's proposed strategy. Indeed, soon after his government took office in October 1951, Churchill had to deal with Great Britain's massive international exchange deficit. The British would have to devote as much industrial plant as possible to production for export rather than armaments. Reductions in the armed forces were necessary, and this meant a cut in the British contribution under the Lisbon accords. Before broaching this to the allies, the British chiefs of staff decided in July 1952 to prepare the arguments for a reorientation of strategy.[175]

Among the chiefs, Admiral of the Fleet Sir Rhoderick McGrigor, Field Marshal Sir William Slim, and Marshal of the Royal Air Force Sir John Slessor, it was Slessor who most strongly influenced the white paper prepared.[176] The chiefs agreed that the American atomic strike force formed the primary deterrent to war. Massive land forces on the continent could not be the basis of allied strategy. Also, an effective defense against atomic air attack was unlikely. Thus the primary reliance for the United

---

[173] Ltr, W. B. Leach to Gen H. S. Vandenberg, CSAF, Apr 30, 1952, Vandenberg Coll, 6. Bart Leach Memos, Box 83, MD, LC.
[174] *Ibid.*
[175] See Note 173; msg, Gen L. Norstad, CINC AAFCE, to Gen N. F. Twining, VCSAF, RL 1065, 311152Z Jul 52, Vandenberg Coll, Redlines, Jul 1, 1952 to Dec 1952, Box 87, MD, LC; memo, JSPC to JCS, subj: Report by the United Kingdom Chiefs of Staff on United Kingdom Defense Policies and Global Strategy, Jul 24, 1952, encl to memo, RAdm W. G. Lalor, Sec JCS, to Gen Army O. N. Bradley, Chmn JCS, Gen H. S. Vandenberg, CSAF, *et al*, same subj, Jul 28, 1952, RG 341, DCS/Ops, Dir/Pl, OPD, 323.361, Sect 6, Anx (Aug 16, 1950), Box 142, MMB, NA; Ronald Lewin, *Slim: The Standardbearer* (London: Leo Cooper, 1976), pp 278–280.
[176] Lewin, *Slim*, pp 278–280.

Strategic Air Force

President-elect Dwight D. Eisenhower, *center,* **with John Foster Dulles, his Secretary of State-designee, and Charles E. Wilson, his choice for Secretary of Defense. Both were active in his New Look initiative.**

Kingdom had to be on the deterrent power of the American strategic air force. The British were much impressed by that force.[177]

> The strength of the American long-range bomber force is steadily increasing, and the training of its specialised crews has reached a point never before surpassed by any air force in peace, and only equalled by the best crews of our own Bomber Command.[178]

The British saw their own role as contributing a portion of the allied strategic air force, as soon as they developed their own atomic capability. Other than that, all existing forces had to be reduced.[179]

---

[177] Study, Dir Pl, DCS/Ops, Defense Policy and Global Strategy, Jul 52, atch to memo, Maj Gen H. B. Thatcher, Dep Dir Pl, to Gen N. F. Twining, VCSAF, subj: Report by the United Kingdom Chiefs of Staff on United Kingdom Defense Policy and Global Strategy, Jul 25, 1952, RG 341, DCS/Ops, Dir/Pl, OPD, 323.36, Sect 6, Anx (Aug 16, 1950), Box 142, MMB, NA.

[178] Rprt, COS UK, Defence Policy and Global Strategy, Jul 9, 1952, p 6, RG 341, DCS/Ops, Dir/Pl, OPD, 323.36, Sect 6, Anx (Aug 16, 1950), Box 142, MMB, NA.

[179] Study, Dir Pl, DCS/Ops, *Defense Policy and Global Strategy*, Jul 52, atch to memo, Maj Gen H. B. Thatcher, Dep Dir Pl, to Gen N. F. Twining, VCSAF, Report by the United Kingdom Chiefs of Staff on United Kingdom Defense Policy and Global Strategy, Jul 25, 1952, RG 341, DCS/Ops, Dir/Pl, OPD, 323.36, Sect 6, Anx (Aug 16, 1950), Box 142, MMB, NA.

"Never Before Surpassed"

Unlike some of their American counterparts, the British chiefs rejected the idea that there was a year of maximum danger and expected that the Cold War would continue for years. Thus allied forces had to be maintained at a steady, affordable level. This could only be assured by reliance on air power. A "1914-1918" strategy, that is maintaining large armies on the continent of Europe, would require forces so large that no European nation could afford them without American aid.[180]

At the end of July Slessor and Slim visited Washington to begin discussion of their plan to reduce the Lisbon force goals. During the meetings with the top leaders of the American services—at which the U.S. Navy was heavily represented—Bradley and Collins were skeptical. The British had dismissed the importance of carrier task forces, a position the American naval officers protested. Twining and White, however, sought to assure the British that the strategic air offensive had a good chance of success.[181] Slessor offered his own perspective: "I would say 20,000 U.S. airmen in Norfolk [England] might be a better guarantee than the number of ground troops that we have now in Germany."[182] The upshot of the discussions was a U.S. agreement that NATO should study possible reductions in long-term force goals. This allowed Bradley to keep emphasizing the idea of 1954 as an especially critical year in the Cold War.[183]

The Air Staff naturally welcomed a British white paper which was so close to its own position.[184] On June 26 the Air Force Council (established in 1951 as representing the top echelon of the Air Staff) approved a statement proposed by the Director of Plans, that in the event of war with the Soviet Union: "The war objectives of the United States and her Allies will be imposed on the USSR by the application of military air force,

---

[180] *Ibid.*

[181] Note, Lt Gen T. D. White, DCS/Ops, Jul 29, 1952, handwritten in Copy 9, rprt, COS UK, Defence Policy and Global Strategy, Jul 1952; MR, Maj Gen H. B. Thatcher, Actg Dir Pl, DCS/Ops, Minutes of the Meeting with Air Chief Marshal Slessor and Air Chief Marshal Elliot on the British Concept Paper, Aug 1, 1952; summary of notes, Sec JCS, Meeting of Jul 29, 1952; summary of notes, Sec JCS, Politico-Military Meeting, Jul 13, 1954 [*sic*, 1952], all in RG 341, DCS/Ops, Dir/Pl, OPD, 323.36, Sect 6, Anx (Aug 16, 1950), Box 142, MMB, NA.

[182] Summary of notes, Sec JCS, Meeting with CMRAF Slessor, Jul 29, 1952, RG 341, DCS/Ops, Dir/Pl, OPD, 323.36, Sect 6, Anx (Aug 16, 1950), Box 142, MMB, NA.

[183] *Ibid.*

[184] Draft msg, Gen N. F. Twining, VCSAF, to Gen L. Norstad, CINC AAFCE, Redline, n.d. [Jul 31, 1952], not sent, RG 341, DCS/Ops, Dir/Pl, OPD, 323.36, Sect 6, Anx (Aug 16, 1950), Box 142, MMB, NA.

properly supported by essential land and sea forces."[185] In short, the Air Force was officially advocating reliance on an airpower strategy.

After the meetings with the British, Finletter, Gilpatric, Twining, and Kuter (Vandenberg was convalescing from cancer surgery) went to Finletter's summer home in Bar Harbor, Maine. There they prepared a memorandum outlining the approach to take in furthering the Air Concept. The Air Force officials gave their paper the title "The New Phase." In the history of the independent Air Force, the first phase had been the unsuccessful struggle for seventy groups. The next phase encompassed the buildup to ninety-five wings. That expansion was virtually complete, and the first funds were available for the 143-wing program. The Air Force was ready to lead in the nation's defense.[186]

The conferees at Bar Harbor proposed to end once and for all America's reliance on a strategy of mobilization. Instead, the United States would maintain as a deterrent a permanent military establishment, ready to go into action on D-day. Once again, they made the point that with unessential forces eliminated, the country could afford a strong defense, without becoming a garrison state. Specifically, if the Air Force received Congress's budgetary support and operated the 143-wing force efficiently, and the Army and Navy were maintained at appropriate levels, an adequate defense was attainable for ten percent ($34.5 billion at 1952 levels) of the gross national product.[187]

As a planning document, the memorandum constructed the pillars of what it considered a sound American military strategy, to include air defense, NATO forces of reasonable size, tactical air capabilities, and the strategic air offensive. It reiterated the need to devote the scarce nuclear arsenal to the primary tasks. And it rejected maintaining forces for local wars. Instead, its authors advocated maximizing the deterrent power of the strategic force. In short, the Bar Harbor Memorandum outlined the views that had been developing in the Air Staff for some time.[188]

After Kuter and Twining had returned to Washington, Kuter discussed what further action was needed. The Air Force should, he believed, present its views as part of the public debate on the best military strategy for the country, one in which the Air Force could and should play the

---

[185] Memo, Col D. A. Burchinal, Sec AF Council, to Dir Pl, subj: Development of a Military Strategic Concept, Jul 1, 1952, RG 341, DCS/Ops, Dir/Pl, OPD, 381 (Jan 19, 1952), Box 319, MMB, NA.

[186] Paper, The New Phase—A Statement of Air Force Policy, Aug 2, 1952, Twining Coll, TS File (1), Box 122, MD, LC.

[187] Ibid.

[188] Ibid.

leading role. The service's argument should focus on national priorities and avoid giving the impression that "the Air Force is feeling its oats." He also suggested that the Air Force redefine the idea of "balanced forces" rather than attack it.[189] And when General Vandenberg returned from convalescent leave late in August, Kuter advised the chief that the Air Concept was one of the small number of major issues requiring immediate attention. Kuter anticipated a test of the Air Force's position.[190]

That challenge came in just a few weeks, and it largely concerned the Lisbon force goals. The NATO Standing Group (representing the American, British, and French military staffs in Washington) gave the joint chiefs their proposed update to the NATO Strategic Guidance on July 28. The review of that document revealed a major split among the American services. The Army, Navy, and Marine Corps generally approved the Strategic Guidance, with the exception of the limited role it assigned to carrier task forces.[191] The Air Force wanted the whole document rewritten. In the words of Maj. Gen. Robert M. Lee, Jr., the proposed guidance would produce:

> a strategy that calls for a blend of maritime air and land operations which includes large scale offensive naval operations, a land defense and counteroffensive, and, in general, subdues [sic] the effect of the strategic air offensive. In other words, it is a modernized 1914–1918 concept—an attempt to superimpose a new atomic strategy upon the old traditional strategy, mixed with a philosophy which grew out of U.S. Naval operations of World War II in the Pacific.[192]

The Air Staff recommended that the chiefs ask the Standing Group to revise the proposal. The strategic air offensive ought to be regarded as a central operation of NATO, and the guidance should emphasize the deterrent effect of the strategic force.[193]

---

[189] Memo, Lt Gen L. S. Kuter, Actg VCSAF, to T. K. Finletter, Sec AF, R. L. Gilpatric, USec AF, Gen N. F. Twining, Actg CSAF, Aug 11, 1952, Twining Coll, TS File (1), Box 122, MD, LC.
[190] Ltr, Lt Gen L. S. Kuter, DCS/Pers, to Gen H. S. Vandenberg, CSAF, Aug 20, 1952, Twining Coll, AFCVC Reading File, Aug 52, Box 57, MD, LC.
[191] Rprt, JSPC to JCS, 2073/408, Strategic Guidance, Aug 25, 1952, RG 341, DCS/Ops, Dir/Pl, OPD, 381 (Feb 7, 1950), Case 2, Sect 2, Box 334, MMB, NA.
[192] Memo, Maj Gen R. M. Lee, Dir Pl, DCS/Ops, to Gen H. S. Vandenberg, CSAF, subj: Strategic Guidance (JCS 2073/408), Aug 26, 1952, RG 341, DCS/Ops, Dir/Pl, OPD, 381 (Feb 7, 1950), Case 2, Sect 2, Box 334, MMB, NA.
[193] *Ibid.*; memo, Maj Gen R. M. Lee, Dir Pl, DCS/Ops, subj: Strategic Guidance (JCS 2073/408), Sep 2, 1952, RG 341, DCS/Ops, Dir/Pl, OPD, 381 (Feb 7, 1950), Case 2, Sect 2, Box 334, MMB, NA.

Strategic Air Force

Lee was prepared for another interservice wrangle, proposing that the Air Force carry the matter to Secretary Lovett if necessary. In fact this did not prove necessary. On September 3 the joint chiefs agreed to most of the changes the Air Force had recommended, particularly those stressing the contribution the strategic air offensive made to NATO. Lee could no doubt expect that the British would support this position. By the end of 1952 a reexamination of NATO strategy had begun.[194]

The debate on U.S. strategy gained a wide audience during the 1952 presidential campaign. The two leading Republican candidates brought differing perspectives to the question of national defense. Eisenhower, of course, would be seen by the public as uniquely qualified on the subject. But he was also identified with the buildup of American forces in Europe, a sore subject with many in the Taft bloc. Senator Taft himself stressed the importance of air power as the means to an economical defense policy. His position strongly appealed to isolationist voters.[195]

Leach in fact saw a political problem in the Taft embrace. The Democratic platform endorsed "balanced forces," clearly a defense of Truman administration defense policy. Emphasis on strategic air power over land and naval forces might thus be attacked by the Democrats as isolationism. The secretary's adviser maintained:

> Taft favors a strong Air Force policy because it will "keep war out of America" (an isolationist reason) instead of because it is the most effective deterrent to war and the decisive military factor if war comes (the Churchill-Eisenhower reason).[196]

---

[194] Rprt, JSPC to JCS, 2073/408, Strategic Guidance, Aug 25, 1952; memo, RAdm W. G. Lalor, Sec JCS, to US Rep, Stdy Gp NATO, subj: Strategic Guidance (SM-2079-52), Sep 3, 1952, encl on note, Lalor & Col E. H. Carns, & JCS Decision 2073/413, Strategic Guidance, Sep 3, 1952, both in RG 341, DCS/Ops, Dir/Pl, OPD, 381 (Feb 7, 1950), Case 2, Sect 2, Box 334, MMB, NA.

[195] Memo, W. B. Leach, subj: Danger to the USAF if Taft is Nominated—Preventive Measures, Jun 28, 1952, atch to memo, Capt M. Berry to Col W. F. Hipps, XO to Sec AF, Jul 1, 1952, Twining Coll, AFCVC Reading File, Jul 52 (1), Box 57; memo, Lt Gen L. S. Kuter, Actg VCSAF, to T. K. Finletter, Sec AF, R. L. Gilpatric, USec AF, Gen N. F. Twining, Actg CSAF, Aug 11, 1952, Twining Coll, TS File (1), Box 122, both in MD, LC.

[196] Memo, W. B. Leach, subj: Danger to the USAF if Taft is Nominated—Preventive Measures, Jun 28, 1952, atch to memo, Capt M. Berry to Col W. F. Hipps, XO to Sec AF, Jul 1, 1952, Twining Coll, AFCVC Reading File, Jul 52 (1), Box 57, MD, LC.

Leach suggested that if Taft were nominated Finletter should advise the President to lead the Democrats in an attack on the politicization of defense rather than on the strategy proposed.[197]

At the Republican convention in July, former President Herbert C. Hoover denounced the administration for bankrupting the nation to arm Europe, arguing that "The sure defense of London, New York, and Paris is the fear of counterattack on Moscow from the air."[198] But with Eisenhower's nomination, a somewhat different tone could be expected. In the Republican platform, the general had insisted on the deletion of the word "retaliation" from the plank on defense. On the other hand, the leading Republican spokesman on foreign policy, John Foster Dulles, saw a clear value for the concept of retaliation. Indeed he specifically advocated using the threat of retaliation to deter general or local aggression.[199] This in Dulles's view was precisely the key to the diplomacy of deterrence.

The Democratic nominee, Adlai E. Stevenson, faced long odds from the start. The November voting gave Eisenhower the presidency, and planning began for a revision of the defense program. The incoming administration was committed to take a "New Look" at defense. Evocative as this term was of Christian Dior's "New Look" of 1946 in women's clothing, it was natural, in the words of one historian, "to extend [the term] from the activity to the results."[200] After a visit to Korea in fulfillment of a campaign promise, the President-elect returned to the United States on the cruiser USS *Helena*. On board he conferred with Dulles, his designee as Secretary of State, and his Secretary of Defense-designate, Charles E. Wilson. Eisenhower also consulted, among others, Admiral Arthur W. Radford, Commander in Chief, Pacific.[201]

The New Look evolved in two phases. First, it was necessary to revise the Truman budget for fiscal 1954 and to organize the administration's

---

[197] *Ibid.*

[198] Quoted in Parmet, *Eisenhower*, p 95.

[199] *Ibid.*, pp 120–123; John Foster Dulles, "A Policy of Boldness," *Life* (May 19, 1952), p 151.

[200] Robert J. Watson, *The History of the Joint Chiefs of Staff*, Vol V: *The Joint Chiefs of Staff and National Policy, 1953–1954* (Washington: Hist Div, JCS, 1986), p 35; William Manchester, *The Glory and the Dream: A Narrative History of America, 1932–1972* (Boston: Little, Brown, 1974), p 422.

[201] Glenn H. Snyder, "The 'New Look' of 1953," in Schilling, et al, *Strategy, Politics, and Defense Budgets*, pp 191–193. Wilson was at the time of his nomination President of General Motors. He was called "Engine Charlie" to distinguish him from Charles E. Wilson, President of General Electric ("Electric Charlie"), who had served in the Truman administration.

new defense team. This done, a formal policy evaluation produced the concepts that were to guide future defense policy. The concept that emerged was not altogether new. Ending the Korean War and reducing defense spending responded to the political pressures that had brought the previous administration down. Key elements of the New Look—a reliance on America's lead in nuclear weapons, an emphasis on air power, especially strategic forces, support of NATO, and a strong nuclear deterrence —were already part of the national strategy. The Eisenhower adminstration's particular contribution lay in the doctrine of so-called "massive retaliation," the threat that the United States might not limit its response to aggression as it had in Korea. This was a matter of making the underlying deterrent threat more explicit to potential adversaries.[202]

The first initiative of the New Look, then, focused on the defense budget. Submitted by the previous administration before Eisenhower's inauguration on January 20, 1953, this document allocated $16 billion for the Air Force for fiscal 1954. Because of the backlogs in B–47 production and other aircraft programs, the service had considerable unobligated money available, so this was not as serious a cut as might have appeared. The issue of excess funds had indeed already aroused criticism of the Air Force, and the Bar Harbor Memorandum addressed improved financial management as a means of maintaining the service's credibility with Congress. Though the budget situation seemed workable for the time being, the Air Force's Comptroller, Lt. Gen. Charles B. Stone III, warned that the 143-wing program faced trouble if downward pressure on the budget continued.[203]

On February 7 the new Deputy Secretary of Defense, Roger M. Kyes, instructed the services to review their budgets. The joint chiefs took the position that reductions were out of the question, and the Secretary of the Air Force, Harold E. Talbott, defended his service's programs.[204] The crucial development came, however, on March 9, when Kyes, having received word from the Bureau of the Budget on the cuts required under the new spending ceilings, assigned each service its share. The Air Force

---

[202] R. Watson, *JCS, 1953–1954*, pp 1–3, 35–37.

[203] Ltr, A. H. Berding, Dir PIO, DoD, to R. A. Lovett, Sec Def, subj: Notes on Newsmens' Luncheon, Aug 28, 1952, Vandenberg Coll, Class, Box 62; memo, Lt Gen C. B. Stone III, DCS/Compt, to CSAF, Jan 5, 1953, with note, Gen N. F. Twining, VCSAF, to CSAF, Jan 5, 1953, Twining Coll, AFCVC Reading File, Jan 53 (2), Box 58, all in MD, LC; Poole, *JCS, 1950–1952*, pp 117–131.

[204] R. Watson, *JCS, 1953–1954*, p 5; memo, H. E. Talbott, Sec AF, to Sec Def, Feb 12, 1953; memo, Lt Gen T. D. White, Actg Chmn, AF Council, to CSAF, subj: Re-examination of the USAF FY 1954 Budget Program, Feb 16, 1953, both in Twining Coll, AFCVC Reading Files, Feb 53 (1), Box 58, MD, LC.

would receive $14.4 billion in 1954. The next fiscal year would see a balanced federal budget, under which the Air Force would receive $11.6 billion and aircraft procurement would shrink to $5.3 billion and strength to 850,000.[205] General Vandenberg was in Europe at the time, but when Twining saw the figures he immediately cabled the chief, informing him of cuts "so substantial as to warrant your personal consideration."[206]

According to Air Staff estimates, the new budget would provide sufficient funds for only seventy-nine wings. This would render the Air Force unable to meet any commitment at all. Talbott warned of the probable effect on the aircraft industry. He calculated that two airframe plants would close in 1953, nine in 1954, and one the year after that, while the situation with engines would be even worse.[207] The protests were for the most part unavailing. Defense Secretary Wilson insisted that the Air Force could manage its programs better. On April 29, 1953, he presented the proposed budget to the National Security Council. Vandenberg was present as acting chairman of the JCS and lodged a formal protest. Despite the bleak outlook, the Air Force was able to salvage part of its program; the service would expand to 114 wings in June 1954 and to an "interim" goal of 120 the year after.[208]

In the normal budgetary process, Vandenberg had used up his last opportunity for open opposition. However, certain factors altered the situation. The Air Force chief's extended term would expire on June 30, 1953, and a further extension seemed unlikely. Vandenberg also knew that his cancer surgery of the year before had been unsuccessful. On May 7 the White House announced that Twining would succeed him, and within a few days the successors of the other chiefs, whose terms were to expire in August, had also been named. Admiral Radford would be the new Chairman of the Joint Chiefs of Staff. At this point, Vandenberg concluded that he was in a position to make his objections known during the congressional budget hearings.[209]

---

[205] Memo, R. M. Kyes, Dep Sec Def, to Sec Army, Sec Nav, *et al*, Mar 9, 1953, Vandenberg Coll, Budget (FY 54), Box 41, MD, LC.
[206] Msg, Brig Gen R. A. Grussendorf, XO to CSAF, to Gen H. S. Vandenberg, CSAF, Mar 13, 1953, Vandenberg Coll, Redlines Dec 52, Box 87, MD, LC.
[207] Statement, Gen H. S. Vandenberg, CSAF, to NSC, Reasoning and Procedures Used by the Air Force in Calculating the Impact of Budget Levels as Indicated in Sec Def Memo of March 9, 1953, Mar 25, 1953; memo, H. E. Talbott, Sec AF, to Sec Def, Mar 16, 1953, both in Vandenberg Coll, 31. Impact of Reduced Budget, Box 85, MD, LC.
[208] R. Watson, *JCS, 1953–1954*, pp 7–9, 61–63.
[209] Parrish OHI, p 229: R. Watson, *JCS, 1953–1954*, p 15.

Strategic Air Force

The decision to do so was made with extreme reluctance. Symington, now a Democratic Senator from Missouri, met with Vandenberg and Leach to discuss the issue. Twining and the Air Staff were also providing much assistance. At a prolonged evening discussion in his quarters at Fort Myer, Virginia, Vandenberg explained how unwilling he was to oppose the Commander in Chief. In the end, he agreed to attack the budget and had his special assistant, Col. Noel F. Parrish, prepare his statement.[210]

Appearing before the Senate Committee on Appropriations from June 3 to 5, the air chief gave his views forthrightly:

> No sound military reason has been advanced to explain why the Air Force build-up to the agreed force level is again to be delayed. Once again the growth of American air power is threatened with start-and-stop planning, and at a time when we face an enemy who has more modern jet fighters than we have and enough long-range bombers to attack this country in a sudden all-out effort. Rather than reduce our efforts to attain air superiority over the Communists, we should now increase those efforts.[211]

Although Vandenberg's testimony won much public sympathy, the President's budget prevailed. Former Secretary Finletter denounced the resurgence of the idea of balanced forces. However, the Air Concept was stronger than may have appeared at the time. The fiscal year 1954 budget was easier on the Army and the Navy, but eventually the formal policy evaluation under the New Look would bring a clearer understanding to the new administration of the importance of air power.[212]

Making sharp reductions in the military budget presupposed that the war in Korea would soon end. In the face of a continuing deadlock in the truce talks at Panmunjom, the administration had to consider whether to extend the war. NSC–147 outlined several courses of action, which included the use of atomic weapons and striking at China.[213] In addition, the death of Stalin in March 1953 had raised the prospect of a change in the Soviet position. On May 21, 1953, meeting with India's Prime Minister

---

[210] Parrish OHI, pp 227–230; memo, Brig Gen R. A. Grussendorf, XO to CSAF, to Maj Gen M. J. Asensio, Dir Budget, DCS/Compt, & Maj Gen O. S. Picher, Asst DCS/Ops for Prog, May 26, 1953, Vandenberg Coll, Budget (FY 54–2), Box 41, MD, LC.

[211] Hearings before the Committee on Appropriations, House of Representatives, *Department of Defense Appropriations for 1954*, 83d Cong, 1st sess, p 474.

[212] Futrell, *Ideas*, p 210. Vandenberg died on April 2, 1954.

[213] Note, James S. Lay, Exec Sec NSC, to NSC, NSC–147, Analysis of Possible Courses of Action in Korea, with encl, Apr 2, 1953, in *FRUS, 1952–1954*, Vol XV, Pt 1, pp 839–857.

"Never Before Surpassed"

Air Force Chief of Staff Gen. Hoyt S. Vandenberg, although mortally ill, continued to carry heavy professional burdens, testifying before Congress in June 1953 to protest the administration's severe budget cuts on the service. Exhausted and strained, he is shown resting briefly during a recess.

Jawaharlal Nehru at New Delhi, Dulles warned that the United States was contemplating stronger action.

> I [stated] that if the armistice negotiations collapsed, the United States would probably make a stronger rather than a lesser military exertion, and that this might well extend the area of conflict. (Note: I assumed this would be relayed [to the Chinese].).[214]

Eisenhower subsequently attributed the conclusion of the armistice to this warning.[215] When the fighting ended on July 27, the administration had witnessed a successful outcome of its policy of deterrence, particularly when explicitly stated.

The formal development of the New Look policy took place in a series of conferences in the summer of 1953. In PROJECT SOLARIUM, an undertak-

---

[214] Memcon, Sec of State, May 21, 1953, in *FRUS, 1952–1954*, Vol XV, Pt 1, pp 1068–1069.

[215] Dwight D. Eisenhower, *The White House Years: Mandate for Change, 1953–1956* (NY: Doubleday, 1963), p 181.

ing devised by Eisenhower and his advisers during a meeting in the White House solarium, prominent military and civilian officials conferred at the National War College in June. The conferees sought to outline alternative strategies for the United States in the Cold War. The results generally confirmed containment of communism and Soviet influence as the preferred course. The new members of the JCS met in August, at Quantico, Virginia, and on board the yacht assigned to the Secretary of the Navy, the USS *Sequoia*. From these discussions emerged the concepts for the force levels to be sought in fiscal 1955 and after.[216]

The culmination of the process was a speech Dulles gave in New York on January 12, 1954. In it he outlined the concept subsequently known as "massive retaliation." The United States had decided to extend the concept of deterrence by declaring that it would no longer be bound by artificial limits in local conflicts:

> Local defense must be reinforced by the further deterrent of massive retaliatory power.... We need allies and collective security. Our purpose is to make these relations more effective and less costly. This can be done by placing more reliance on deterrent power and less dependence on local defensive power.[217]

Here was the declaratory policy, the coercive diplomacy envisioned by Eisenhower and Dulles. Under the New Look, the defense establishment built up forces to support this diplomacy. In reality, "massive retaliation" and extended deterrence were not altogether new concepts; rather they confirmed existing tendencies among the armed forces, as seen in the Air Concept and the 143-wing program. These trends had been obscured by the costs of the war in Korea and the periodic resurgence of the idea of "balanced forces." Also, the first instinct of the Eisenhower administration, as seen in the budget for fiscal 1954, involved maintaining such balanced forces. As for the declaratory policy, both Dulles's writings earlier in his career and his "message" to the Chinese via Nehru foreshadowed the New York speech.[218]

For his part, Admiral Radford saw that the outcome of the New Look implied a reinvigorated strategy of air power. Late in 1953 the Air Force concurred in a minor reduction of its long-term development program, a total of 137 wings to be reached in 1957. Air defense forces would be augmented, and SAC was to lose only three wings from its final program. Despite these cutbacks, the Air Force would become the lead service in

---

[216] R. Watson, *JCS, 1953–1954*, pp 11–21.
[217] *New York Times*, Jan 13, 1954, p 2.
[218] R. Watson, *JCS, 1953–1954*, pp 36–37.

the New Look. Its budget was the largest of the three services. When Dulles spoke of deterrent forces, he clearly had SAC, and its atomic capabilities, first and foremost in mind. The link between the diplomacy of a deterrent threat and the forces necessary to support it had been made.[219]

By the end of 1953 SAC had achieved an unprecedented level of striking power. Of seventeen wings in the atomic force, eleven were equipped. The B-47 force had grown during the year from 62 to 329 planes, the B-36 force reached 185, and the reconnaissance RB-36 component numbered 137. Supporting the bomber force were more than 500 tankers and 200 fighters. The unmodified B-29s were being phased out. Personnel strength stood at nearly 160,000, based at twenty-nine bases in the states and ten overseas. Of course, the figures did not tell the whole story. Indeed the numbers that indicated the precise ability of the command to deliver a decisive blow were often preserved in the strictest secrecy. But LeMay's achievement in building a combat-ready force with a high state of discipline was open knowledge. The prestige of the Strategic Air Command bespoke assurance that whatever the numbers of personnel and aircraft, if determination and training could deliver the atomic blow, the threat of atomic retaliation was real. The deterrent force was in this sense beyond question.[220]

---

[219] *Ibid.*, pp 35–37.
[220] Hopkins & Goldberg, *Development of SAC*, pp 37, 42.

Conclusion

As the authors of the Bar Harbor Memorandum presented their views on future defense priorities, they looked back over the five years since the signing of the National Security Act of 1947.[1] The airmen who met at Secretary Finletter's summer home in July 1952 had a unique vantage point, and they presented an interpretative framework for the history of the Air Force in the immediate postwar period. The first phase began at the independence of the Air Force in 1947 and encompassed the consolidation of independence as well as the unsuccessful struggle to obtain adequate funding for air power. It was a period of austerity, ending at the outbreak of war in Korea in 1950. According to the memorandum, the second phase consisted of the buildup of air power in connection with the general rearmament of the nation. The New Phase to which the airmen referred would be an outgrowth of the reexamination of defense strategy due to the stalemate in Korea and the unpopularity of high defense budgets. In this phase, the Air Force was well positioned to lead the realignment of the armed forces for a strategy of nuclear deterrence. Thus, as matters developed, the New Phase envisioned by the air leadership bore a great similarity to the New Look of the Eisenhower administration.

The immediate postwar years up to 1947 had been a period of reorganization. It had brought America's leaders to the conviction that it was both necessary and feasible for the nation to build a strategic air force. The perception of necessity arose from the experience of the past war, and in particular from the painful experiences of Munich and Pearl Harbor. It also derived from the strength of ideas about air power, international tensions, and the perceived nature of the Soviet threat. Obstacles and uncertainties plagued the effort to build a strategic air force, but as these were overcome it became clear that the project was feasible. Ambiguities and secrecy surrounding the atomic bomb itself were among the most

---

[1] See p 452.

important problems facing the fledgling Air Force. Political barriers tended to give way to the awareness that more than diplomacy and monetary aid to foreign countries were needed to meet the Soviet challenge to world security. And the existence of a force capable of global air operations under a single command assured that the personnel and organization were in place to serve as a true strategic air force.

Past experience had taught that mere preparedness was not enough. Only ready forces would deter aggression and prevent crippling surprise. Further, airmen found many of their beliefs confirmed or only partially modified by the experiences of the war. Unity of command in the air was vital. Air forces were flexible but primarily offensive in nature. A powerful bombing offensive could break down the industrial war machine of an enemy country. Arnold's call for continued technological advance also affected their thinking about the needs of a deterrent force.

The emergence of a plausible enemy in the form of the Soviet Union took these ideas out of the abstract. It seemed that in Stalin another aggressive dictator had emerged who had to be deterred by the threat of force. The failure of efforts to achieve international control of atomic weapons exacerbated the perception of a Soviet threat. As Truman reluctantly conceded the need for the United States to arm with atomic weapons, he also came to recognize the value of being able to deliver the bomb. At the same time, the West, vulnerable to attack by Soviet ground and tactical air forces, could scarcely afford the burden of maintaining strength sufficient to meet this threat. The strategic air offensive seemed to be the only way to offset enemy superiority at the front line.

Still, several obstacles had to be overcome before the strategic force could be built. The armed forces were engaged in demobilization and the occupation of former enemy countries, and there were few resources of troops or money for anything else. American military leaders became preoccupied with the inevitable postwar reorganization. The airmen were particularly absorbed in the quest for an independent service. Only with the creation of the new military establishment could other matters receive attention.

Atomic weapons, of course, posed the knottiest conceptual problem. The tests at Bikini and new developments in design suggested that strategically important numbers of weapons could be built. Reorganization of the atomic program finally led to a program to build weapons. Recognizing the bomb as a potential strategic air weapon, the AAF developed a plan for three atomic bombing groups. Secrecy on the part of the Manhattan Project and the Atomic Energy Commission was overcome sufficiently for the AAF to develop concepts for employing the weapon. This progress demonstrated the real possibility of building a striking force centered around the atomic bomb.

Conclusion

The actual design of the atomic force posed fewer problems than the development of the bombs themselves. It was a matter of directing and intensifying an already existing technological effort. Some naval planners were prepared to argue that carrier-based forces could carry out the mission of hitting strategic targets. But design work for B-29s, B-50s, and B-36s to carry the bomb was more advanced, and the Air Force was better positioned in the short run to carry out the mission. In the long term, an effective intercontinental capability would be essential to the Air Force's plans for the strategic air offensive. In any case, the Strategic Air Command was increasingly able to operate over long distances. The Unified Command Plan gave the Air Force a charter for a global strike force, and the joint war plan clearly acknowledged the importance of the strategic air offensive. As far as extending range was concerned, the B-36 showed promise as an intercontinental bomber. Pending its appearance in large numbers, such technological devices as air-to-air refueling or tractor landing gear for undeveloped Arctic airfields remained relatively unexplored. One-way missions might prove a necessary evil. But bases, especially in England, were likely to become available, and air refueling was mainly a matter of engineering refinements. As the building of a strategic air force seemed increasingly necessary, planners became convinced that it could be done.

The decision to build an atomic air force of some size was reached at the end of 1947 and the beginning of 1948. It was accompanied by the appearance of public reports by the Finletter Commission and the Brewster Committee endorsing a major role for air power in the nation's defense. The decision itself involved approval by the joint chiefs of a series of important intiatives: a war plan in which the strategic air offensive played a critical part, requirements for the production of atomic weapons, and a plan for modifying bombers for an expanded atomic force. At the same time the Air Force decided on various equipment modifications and the development of new air-to-air refueling techniques.[2] These actions would secure a role for the Air Force in strategic air warfare.

The planned atomic force might seem an adequate deterrent, but even before the marked rise in international tension during 1948, Secretary of Defense Forrestal had been worried about the condition of the rest of the armed forces as well. Unsure of the potential of a strategic air force not yet built, he saw the need for forces to serve in those local crises in which the policy of containment was likely to involve the United States.

---

[2] See Chapter V.

Forrestal's concept of "balanced forces" likewise stressed the interrelationship of the strategic force with other elements of national strength. More parochial minds than his would make "balanced forces" a code term for an equal division of funds among the services regardless of strategic rationale. In any case, Forrestal secured agreement on the Air Force's leading role in the strategic air offensive and supported the slowly emerging strategic air force.

The crises of 1948, particularly the confrontation over Berlin, had significant impacts on the strategic air force. International tensions stimulated defense budget increases, which, while not concentrated on an already approved program like the strategic force, did generally improve the condition of the armed forces and may have lessened competition for funds. The Berlin crisis also improved the positioning of the force. Bomber units were now deployed and based in England, and an organization, the 3d Air Division, was committed to improving this base area. But perhaps the most important development occurred as the chief of staff became concerned that the slowly emerging strategic force was not receiving the leadership necessary to make it into an effective, combat-ready force. As a result, in October the Air Force called in Curtis E. LeMay to head the Strategic Air Command.

LeMay articulated a growing consensus within the service that its primary mission was strategic air offensive operations. As the crises of 1948 subsided (largely because of the success of the Berlin airlift), budget austerity returned. Forrestal's tenure ended with more funding reductions and the failure to develop balanced forces as the defense secretary had intended. Now the strategic air force stood as the one ready element capable of taking the offensive at the outbreak of war. Forces for local wars were starved. At the same time, the tight allocation of funds within the Air Force only allowed the service to maintain certain strategic forces and little else in any strength.

The Harmon and WSEG reports highlighted the problem.[3] Initiated in response to challenges to the role of the strategic air offensive, ironically these studies demonstrated that a stronger atomic blow than was possible at the time might achieve valuable results. In short, the strategic force was inadequate, but the only plausible weapon. Here was an implicit mandate to increase strategic air power. In September 1949 the discovery that the Soviets possessed an atomic capability heightened public concerns about national defense. In the atmosphere of growing threat, new initiatives seemed likely.

---

[3] See pp 294–297.

Conclusion

Truman's decision to proceed with the thermonuclear effort and the related NSC-68 study, examining possible expansions in all armed forces, arose from the widespread sense of national danger. When war broke out in Korea and the president decided to intervene, about all the nation had available were run-down occupation forces and the strategic air force. Though the bomber units could assist in the allied intervention and deter any wider aggression, the United States essentially faced a military challenge for which it was unprepared. The one consolation was that the strategic force itself had achieved a high pitch of combat readiness, whatever its material limitations.

The war in Korea affected the strategic air force in a number of ways. As medium bomber units became involved in supporting ground forces and flying interdiction missions, aircrews gained valuable combat experience. The American decision to confine the fighting to the Korean peninsula, even after the Chinese intervention, no doubt helped avert a confrontation with the Soviets, but it limited the direct role strategic air forces could play in the fighting. On the other hand, the fear that the fighting would expand into general war led to increased funding and major improvements in the strategic force itself. More units were stationed overseas, and the effort to expand the armed forces overall included a major emphasis on the atomic deterrent.

The rearmament itself began slowly, but the expansion of the atomic stockpile planned before the outbreak of war in Korea allowed for the possibility of increased forces to deliver the weapons. In particular, increased appropriations funded the acquisition of large numbers of the new B-47 jet for the atomic force, although the modernization effort encountered delays. New units were formed and trained on unmodified B-29s until the Stratojets became available. The expansion of the strategic force had begun, although the process was not always neat and orderly.

The increasing number of atomic weapons available also raised questions of control and use. The Air Force managed to defend the integrity of the strategic force as a single specified command with a worldwide mission. However, the use of atomic weapons in a tactical role proved more controversial. In the end, SAC had to prepare for operations in support of theater commanders, while tactical nuclear forces began to develop in the other services. As commander of the allied forces in central Europe, Lauris Norstad, for one, welcomed the strengthening of theater forces, with both atomic and conventional weapons, as a complement to the strategic air offensive.

The strategic force soon expanded overseas. More bases became available in England, but concern at the vulnerability of these new fields led to a search for alternative basing areas. Morocco and Spain proved

Strategic Air Force

especially attractive in this respect, though both posed bewildering political complications. When construction began in Morocco, problems soon arose with the Army engineers as well. But the urgency of acquiring a more secure group of bases led the Air Force to persevere. Meanwhile in the continental United States, the vulnerability of bases was becoming a concern for the long term as Soviet stockpiles were expected to increase. If a tornado could nearly eliminate the heavy bomber force at Carswell Air Force Base for a time, SAC had a definite problem, and a future issue was emerging.[4]

What made such matters especially sensitive was the growing emphasis on the role of strategic air forces and air power in general. At the end of 1951 Secretary of Defense Lovett approved programs that set new limits on the expansion of the Army and Navy, while directing continued growth in the Air Force. In the past, although its preeminent role had been recognized, the strategic force had been obliged to compete for funds with other elements of the armed forces. Now air power would be funded to a level approaching what could be considered politically feasible, while ground and naval forces would be forced to accept lower levels.

If the rearmament in the wake of the North Korean attack heralded an expansion of the strategic force, ironically the defense cutbacks that began during 1952 supported the development of strategic air power even further. It was the Europeans, and especially the British, who first reacted to the high cost of arming. The decision by the Churchill government to reduce naval and ground forces and emphasize atomic weapons and air power seemed to promise a more rational and economical strategy. The example was not lost on the Air Force leaders as they drew up the Bar Harbor Memorandum. As public discontent at huge budgets helped bring Eisenhower to the White House, the Air Force leaders decided to develop their own approach to the challenge of retaining the preeminence of their service.

The New Phase conceived at Bar Harbor in fact dovetailed easily into the New Look. The SAC expansion program endured some budget cuts during 1953, but as the new administration formulated its defense strategies, it became clear that the deterrent power of SAC was to be a central instrument of national policy and would be funded accordingly. The command faced some difficult questions, such as the best choice for future weapon systems and how to reduce vulnerability to hostile atomic attack. Yet, with the renewed emphasis on strategic air power, the leaders of the

---

[4] See pp 412–414.

Conclusion

Air Force had confidence that their needs would receive serious attention at the highest levels.

An important strand throughout the early postwar period had been the increasing combat readiness of SAC. What LeMay achieved can be seen as both traditional and innovative. Standardization created a highly disciplined, capable organization. Commanders who demanded and received top performance were nothing new in the nation's history. In fact, one could predict that Americans in uniform would respond to a challenge and take pride in their special status. Yet maintaining air forces at such a high state of readiness, especially during peacetime or at home, was unprecedented—and so were some of LeMay's solutions. The new style barracks he promoted, with their two-man rooms, were far more suitable housing than open bays for a force emphasizing round-the-clock operations and technical training. The same focus on retaining skilled personnel also affected the strong emphasis on family housing. Likewise the pressures of maintaining readiness produced a new heightening of the inherent tension of deterrence—training to fight a war so that it would not happen.

In any case, SAC earned a reputation for almost fanatical devotion to high performance: "To err is human; to forgive is not SAC policy."[5] The crews had few illusions about the dangers they faced if they actually had to fly to those targets so assiduously studied. Yet there is little on record to suggest that they would have failed to respond to the call. Perhaps the very gravity of the challenge led SAC personnel to welcome demanding leadership. Surrounding the command were numerous secrets concerning numbers of weapons, units, and the like. But the world saw SAC's open dedication to its mission. This intangible was a large part of what made the deterrent "credible," to use a word soon to appear in the strategic lexicon.

A look at the 143-wing program reveals that airpower strategy involved more than the strategic force. The United States was prepared to rely heavily on air power to stop a Soviet onslaught in Europe, to sustain its position in the Pacific, and to intervene in trouble spots. Airlift would be an important part of the strategy. In addition, a large program was being undertaken to defend the nation against air attack. Nevertheless, SAC obviously would play the lead role. When commentators referred to Dulles's speech of January 1954, they quoted the term "massive retaliation" and usually had in mind the threat of a full-scale strategic air

---

[5] This tag, like so many unofficial mottoes, has proved exceedingly difficult to document. The author can personally attest to its authenticity, and a telephone conversation with Mr. J. C. Hopkins of the SAC Historian's Office on February 10, 1989, did establish that it remains part of the lore of the command to this day. In any case, the actual origins of the expression will probably always be obsure.

offensive against the Soviet Union. In his various clarifications of that address, the Secretary of State did not altogether rule out the ultimate threat. And the sheer size of the planned strategic force indicated its importance in the administration's policy of deterrence.

Thus by early 1954 the strategy of nuclear deterrence was in place. At the end of the Second World War, the Truman administration had understood the potential of the bomb as a deterrent. Eisenhower and Dulles took this strategy one step farther by being more explicit and trying to prevent indecisive limited wars. The strategic force constituted a threat in peacetime, and in war it would serve two functions, retaliation against an attack and disruption of an enemy's war economy. In either case, its effects could be devastating. A naval officer visiting SAC Headquarters in 1954 described the war plan, perhaps with some hyperbole, as one that envisioned turning the Soviet Union into "a smoking, radiating ruin at the end of two hours...."[6] At the least, the strategic air offensive would help prevent disaster to the free world.

Born of an invention, a simple flying machine, the American air arm emerged from the World War II with a second revolutionary invention, the atomic bomb. Arnold's enduring legacy became an awareness that in the technology of warfare, change is the constant. From this standpoint the challenge was to preserve America's technological preeminence.

In this light, the appearance of Soviet atomic weapons posed a very real threat. Since MAKEFAST, the first atomic war plan, the American armed forces had envisioned a situation in which they might use atomic weapons in a war with the Soviet Union. At the time, the Soviets themselves did not possess an atomic capability. This did not fit the normal definition later given to the word "preemption," which referred to launching a nuclear attack in anticipation of one by the other side. But the early postwar plans did establish that the United States would not necessarily be limited to a non-atomic response to a non-atomic attack. When the Soviets themselves acquired nuclear weapons, the issue took on a new dimension. Still, for the United States, deterrence in 1953 was still largely a question of a warning as to the consequences of aggression in general, and not just a way to deter a nuclear attack.

Since it could be assumed that the potential enemy was building a striking force of his own, SAC's stateside bases would soon be vulnerable. The Air Force was receiving a lot of advice on this matter, and as of 1953 a clear answer had not emerged. Nevertheless, the service intended to defend its bases, protect the aircraft, and build an offensive force large

---

[6] David A. Rosenberg, ed, "A Smoking, Radiating, Ruin at the End of Two Hours," *International Security*, 6 (Winter 81–82), p 25.

enough to sustain heavy losses—both on the ground and during penetration—and still deliver a crushing blow. Developing this capability would obviously be expensive. In the long term then, it was not certain that the new administration had solved the problem of a strong affordable defense. But for the time being, the Air Force had a well-defined mission—to be ready to deliver global strategic power in the event of war—and it had the means to do so well in hand. For a military organization charged with defending a democratic society, such was welcome news.

Glossary

Glossary

Glossary

AAG File	Air Adjutant General File
ACAS	Assistant Chief of Air Staff
AFB	Air Force Base
AFCHO	Office of Air Force History
AFHRC	Air Force Historical Research Agency
AFM	Air Force Manual
AFR	Air Force Regulation
AFSHRC	Albert F. Simpson Historical Research Center, predecessor organization of the Air Force Historical Research Agency
AHR	*American Historical Review*
AU	Air University
Bd	board
Bx	box
CMH	U.S. Army Center for Military History
DCAS	Deputy Chief of Air Staff
FRUS	U.S. Department of State, *Foreign Relations of the United States*

Strategic Air Force

GPO	Government Printing Office
Hist	historical
JCS	Joint Chiefs of Staff
Mtg	meeting
NA	National Archives
Ofc	office
Pl	plans
Pub	publication
SAC	Strategic Air Command
TS	Top Secret classification
Univ	university
USAF	United States Air Force
USAF Hist Div	USAF Historical Division

Bibliography

Biography

Bibliography

Governmental Sources

National Archives and Records Administration

The records of the United States Air Force and the predecessor Army Air Forces for the period 1945–1953 are to be found in the Military Reference Branch (formerly the Modern Military Branch) of the National Archives, Washington, D.C. Because of the wide-ranging scope of the subject (the strategic force being a major focus of Air Staff attention and a major element of all Air Force planning) and the condition of the records, location of the most important material is always difficult. Because of the lack of detailed finding aids and the fact that material is often filed under seemingly unrelated subjects, a great deal of inspired searching on the part of the researcher and the archivist is required. An additional difficulty is that, at this writing, much of the material remains classified.

Nonetheless, the record groups at the National Archives that contain the pertinent material are easy to identify. They are RG 18, records of Headquarters Army Air Forces; RG 165, records of the War Department General and Special Staffs; RG 218, records of the U.S. Joint Chiefs of Staff; RG 319, records of the Army Staff; RG 330, records of the Office of the Secretary of Defense; RG 340, records of the Office of the Secretary of the Air Force; and RG 341, records of Headquarters, United States Air Force. The record groups most heavily used for this volume are 341, 18, and 340.

In record group 18 the Air Adjutant General File, notably under decimal file 320, contains a wealth of material concerning the immediate postwar period. Under the records of the Office of the Chief of Air Staff is material concerning the Scientific Advisory Group.

Record group 340 contains valuable material under a number of headings. Most important for this volume were the proceedings of the Air Board and correspondence found in the Office of the Secretary of the Air Force Numeric Subject Files.

Strategic Air Force

In record Group 341 are vast collections of material, much of it hard to locate. The most important heading for this volume was under the Deputy Chief of Staff for Operations, Director of Plans. The so-called "OPD" decimal files under this were of surpassing importance. Decimal files 320, 322, 323, 330, 353, 381, 384, and 686 were the most heavily used. The British white paper of 1952 and its related material is in file 323. The files of the Assistant for Atomic Energy (AFOAT) are indispensable for a study of this nature. There are also special files for war plan HALFMOON, the Short-Range Emergency Plan (SREP), and the Strategic Air Offensive (SAO). Also under the Deputy Chief of Staff for Operations is the Executive Office File, especially decimal file 452.

Also valuable in RG 341 is the Office of the Secretary of the Air Staff Message File. The Deputy Chief of Staff-Comptroller file 452 is useful on aircraft programs, as is the same designation in the files of the Deputy Chief of Staff for Materiel. The proceedings of the Aircraft and Weapons Board and the Senior Officers' Board that replaced it are found in two places. The records of the board itself are in the files of the Deputy Chief of Staff for Development, while later meetings are in the records of the Deputy Chief of Staff for Materiel under the Directorate of Production and Procurement.

Library of Congress

The Manuscript Division, Library of Congress, holds the collections of the papers of the Chiefs of Staff, United States Air Force.

Both of the chiefs for the greater part of the period under consideration, Carl A. Spaatz and Hoyt S. Vandenberg, provide in their collections a rich body of material. These collections contain a wealth of material covering every aspect of the evolution of the Air Force. Since they deal with large questions of national defense, the budget, and procurement of weapon systems, as well as correspondence with SAC and other commands, there is little that is not in some way pertinent to the subject of this study. Of particular interest to the later phases is the correspondence of Secretaries Symington and Finletter, and General Vandenberg, with W. Barton Leach, who served as a semi-official advisor to the Air Force during these years. A reservist and a law professor at Harvard, Leach served as counsel for the 1949 B–36 hearings and then became a regular consultant to the leadership.

The Curtis E. LeMay Collection is of value in this case for the material from the years as commander of SAC. Some correspondence

Bibliography

from the period when LeMay was DCAS/RD and in Europe is also included. But again the wealth of material, well-organized and diverse, makes this an extremely important collection. Among the wealth of documents here is the file of regular SAC Progress Analyses.

Both the vice chiefs from the period, Muir S. Fairchild and Nathan F. Twining, have material of value. The Bar Harbor Memorandum and related material are in the Twining Collection.

Harry S. Truman Library

Holdings in the Harry S. Truman Library, Independence, Missouri, cover the entire period of this volume. The President's Secretary's file and the papers of W. Stuart Symington are full of useful material. Papers from the National Security Council as well as the Joint Chiefs of Staff appear in these collections.

Office of the Secretary of Defense

Besides its publication effort, the Office of the Historian of the Office of the Secretary of Defense, Washington, D.C., houses some useful records, notably the papers of James V. Forrestal, which contains material that was not included in the published edition by Walter Millis.

Office of Secretary of Defense. *History of Strategic Arms Competition, 1945–1972.* 3 volumes plus supporting studies. Washington: Office of the Secretary of Defense, 1974.

Defense Technical Information Center

Ponturo, John. *Analytical Support for the Joint Chiefs of Staff: The WSEG Experience, 1948–1976.* IDA Study S–507. Washington: Institute for Defense Analyses, 1979.

Air Force Historical Research Agency

The massive records housed at the Air Force Historical Research Agency (formerly the Albert F. Simpson Historical Research Center), Maxwell Air Force Base, Alabama, contain an immense collection valuable

Strategic Air Force

material. Much of this is on microfilm at the Air Force History Support Office in Washington, D.C.

In preparing a major study of a large institution, the historian is inevitably dependent on the work of others within the organization. The histories prepared in wings and groups, air forces, and major commands, especially, in this case, the Strategic Air Command, for the period in question have been a major source. These are some of the main features in the records at Maxwell, and many have been declassified.

Historical Studies

Fogerty, Robert P. *Biographical Data on Air Force General Officers, 1917–1952.* USAF Historical Study 91. Maxwell Air Force Base, Ala.: USAF Historical Division, Air University, 1953.

Gleckner, Robert F. *The Development of the Heavy Bomber.* USAF Historical Study 6. Maxwell Air Force Base, Ala.: USAF Historical Division, Air University, 1951.

Greer, Thomas H. *The Development of Air Doctrine in the Army Air Arm, 1917–1941.* USAF Historical Study 89. Maxwell Air Force Base, Ala.: USAF Historical Division, Air University, 1951.

Sanders, Chauncey E. *Redeployment and Demobilization.* USAF Historical Study 77. Maxwell Air Force Base, Ala.: USAF Historical Division, Air University, 1952.

Air Materiel Command
(Air Force Logistics Command) Historical Studies

Bagwell, Margaret C. *The XB–52 Airplane.* Wright-Patterson Air Force Base, Ohio: Air Materiel Command, 1949.

Case History of XB–36 Airplane Project. Wright-Patterson Air Force Base, Ohio: Air Materiel Command, 1946.

Case History of the XB–36, YB–36, and B–36 Airplanes. Wright-Patterson Air Force Base, Ohio: Air Materiel Command, 1948.

Case History of Air-to-Air Refueling. Wright-Patterson Air Force Base, Ohio: Air Materiel Command, 1949.

Fenwick, Amy C. *History of Saddletree Project.* Wright-Patterson Air Force Base, Ohio; Air Materiel Command, 1953.

Self, Mary R. *History of the Development and Production of U.S. Heavy Bombardment Aircraft, 1917–1949.* Wright-Patterson Air Force Base, Ohio: Air Materiel Command, 1950.

———. *History of the USAF Five-Year Aircraft Procurement Program, 1 January 1948–1 July 1949.* Wright-Patterson Air Force Base, Ohio: Air Materiel Command, 1949.

Trester, Dorothy. *History of the AF Storage and Withdrawal Program.* Wright-Patterson Air Force Base, Ohio: Air Materiel Command, 1954.

Bibliography

Other Studies and Monographs

Air Force Developmental Aircraft. ARDC Study. Baltimore, Md.: Air Research and Development Command, 1957.
Bowen, Lee, and Robert D. Little. *The History of Air Force Participation in the Atomic Energy Program, 1943–1953.* 5 volumes. Washington: Office of Air Force History, 1959.

    I. Bowen, Lee. *Project Silverplate, 1943–1946.*
    II. Little, Robert D. *Foundations of an Atomic Air Force and Operation Sandstone, 1946–1948.* Parts 1 and 2.
    III. Little, Robert D. *Building an Atomic Air Force, 1949–1953.* Parts 1 and 2.
    IV. Bowen, Lee. *The Development of Weapons.* Parts 1 and 2.
    V. Alling, Frederick A., et al. *Atomic Weapon Delivery Systems.* Parts 1 and 2.

Burk, Vernon D. *The USAF in the United Kingdom, 1948–1973: Organization.* USAFE Historical Monograph. Ramstein Air Base, Germany: Headquarters, United States Air Forces, Europe, 1977.
Lemmer, George F. *The Air Force and the Concept of Deterrence, 1945–1950.* Washington: Office of Air Force History, 1963.
———. *The Air Force and Strategic Deterrence, 1951–1960.* Washington: Office of Air Force History, 1968.
Swetzer, Robert L. *USAF Operations in the Mediterranean, 1945–1975.* USAFE Historical Monograph. Ramstein Air Base, Germany: Headquarters, United States Air Forces, Europe, 1976.

Reports

Annual Report of the Secretary of the Air Force, Fiscal Year 1948. Washington: Government Printing Office, 1948.
Arnold, Henry H. *Third Report of the Commanding General of the Army Air Forces to the Secretary Of War.* Washington: War Department, 1945.
Second Annual Report of the Secretary of Defense. Fiscal Year 1949. Washington: Government Printing Office, 1949.
Semi-Annual Report of the Secretary of Defense. Fiscal Years 1950–1953. Washington: Government Printing Office, 1950–1953.
Survival in the Air Age: A Report by the President's Air Policy Commission. Washington: Government Printing Office, 1948.
The United States Strategic Bombing Surveys (European War) (Pacific War). Reprint. Maxwell Air Force Base, Ala.: Air University Press, 1987.

Statistical Information

Air Force Statistical Digest, 1948–1953.
Army Air Forces Statistical Digest, World War II, 1946, 1947.

Strategic Air Force

Interviews

The Oral History Program at the Air Force Historical Research Agency has undertaken an ambitious effort over the years to interview important participants in the history of the Air Force, including those involved in the events described in this volume. The author has depended heavily on the achievements of the interviewers and transcribers who have produced these.

Gen. Curtis E. LeMay, USAF, Ret., was most courteous in granting time to the author to clear up a number of points. Brig. Gen. William G. Hipps also consented to an interview by the author and other members of the staff of the Air Force History Support Office.

The following interviews were used and are available at the Air Force Historical Research Agency and the Air Force History Support Office:

Lt. Gen. Ira C. Eaker
Brig. Gen. William G. Hipps
Brig. Gen. Clarence S. Irvine
Gen. Leon W. Johnson
Gen. George C. Kenney
Gen. Curtis E. LeMay
Stephen R. Leo
Gen. Lauris Norstad
Brig. Gen. Noel F. Parrish
Gen. Earle E. Partridge
W. Stuart Symington

Strategic Air Command

In the Office of the Historian at Headquarters, Strategic Air Command, Offutt Air Force Base, Nebraska, there is an extensive collection of material concerning the development of the command, its operations and plans. Much of this is classified, but all of it is well-organized and usable finding aids exist. Much of it supplements material in other collections and was indispensable for this volume.

Department of State

The international scope of the issues covered in this volume required that the published documentary series *Foreign Relations of the United States* be consulted.

Bibliography

Foreign Relations of the United States. Volumes covering the period 1946–1954. Washington: Government Printing Office, 1972–1985.

Congress

The importance of strategic air power in national policy inevitably brought the Air Force into the legislative arena. Of particular importance were the budget hearings, the annual ritual by which all federal agencies present their case. These hearings took place before the appropriate subcommittee (initially for the AAF the military appropriations subcommittee, and then one for all defense spending) of the Committees on Appropriations of the House of Representatives and the Senate, respectively. The Military Affairs Committee and later the Armed Services Committee in each house was not so heavily involved in the resources question. However, on certain occasions, basic issues of strategy actually came before the latter committees. Such was the case for example in 1949, when the Committee on Armed Services of the House of Representatives held the hearings on the B–36 and subsequently on "unification and strategy."

House. Hearings before a House Subcommittee on Appropriations. Military Appropriations. Annual volumes, fiscal years 1946–1954. Washington: Government Printing Office, 1945–1953.

House. Hearings before the House Committee on Armed Services. *Investigation of the B–36 Bomber Program.* 81st Cong, 1st sess. Washington: Government Printing Office, 1949.

House. Hearings before the House Committee on Armed Services. *The National Defense Program: Unification and Strategy.* 81st Cong, 1st sess. Washington: Government Printing Office, 1949.

Senate. Hearings before a Senate Subcommittee on Appropriations. Military Appropriations. Annual volumes, fiscal years 1946–1954. Washington: Government Printing Office, 1945–1953.

Presidential Papers

Public Papers of the Presidents of the United States: Harry S. Truman. 1945–1953. Washington: Office of the Federal Register, National Archives and Records Service, 1961–1966.

Books

Appleman, Roy E. *South to the Naktong, North to the Yalu (June–November 1950).* [The United States Army in the Korean War] Washington: Government Printing Office, 1961.

Army, Department of the. *The Army Almanac: A Book of Facts Concerning the Army of the United States.* Washington: Government Printing Office, 1950.

Cantwell, Gerald T. *History of the Air Force Reserve.* Unpublished Manuscript. Washington: Air Force History and Museums Program.

Cole, Alice C., Alfred Goldberg, Samuel A. Tucker, Rudolph A. Winnacker, eds. *The Department of Defense: Documents on Establishment and Organization, 1944–1978.* Washington: Office of the Secretary of Defense, 1978.

Condit, Doris M. *The Test of War, 1950–1953.* Vol II of *History of the Office of the Secretary of Defense.* Washington: Historical Office, Office of the Secretary of Defense, 1988.

Condit, Kenneth W. *1947–1949.* Volume II of *The History of the Joint Chiefs of Staff: The Joint Chiefs of Staff and National Policy.* Washington: Historical Division, Joint Chiefs of Staff, 1976.

Craven, Wesley Frank, and James Lea Cate, eds. *The Army Air Forces in World War II.* 7 volumes. Chicago: University of Chicago Press, 1948–1958. New imprint, Washington: Office of Air Force History, 1983.

Douhet, Giulio. *The Command of the Air.* Translated by Dino Ferrari. New York: Coward-McCann, Inc., 1942. New imprint. [USAF Warrior Studies] Washington: Office of Air Force History, 1983.

Frisbee, John L., ed. *Makers of the United States Air Force.* [USAF Warrior Studies] Washington: Office of Air Force History, 1987.

Futrell, Robert F. *Ideas, Concepts, Doctrine: Basic Thinking in the United States Air Force, 1907–1984.* 2 volumes. Maxwell Air Force Base, Ala.: Air University, 1971. New imprint, 1989.

———. *The United States Air Force in Korea, 1950–1953.* Revised edition. Washington: Office of Air Force History, 1983.

Goldberg, Alfred, ed. *A History of the United States Air Force, 1907–1957.* Princeton, N.J.: Van Nostrand, 1957.

Gropman, Alan L. *The Air Force Integrates, 1945–1964.* Washington: Office of Air Force History, 1978.

Hansell, Haywood S. *The Strategic Air War against Germany and Japan: A Memoir.* [USAF Warrior Studies] Washington: Office of Air Force History, 1986.

Hennessy, Juliette A. *The United States Army Air Arm, April 1861 to April 1917.* Washington: USAF Historical Division, 1958. New imprint. Washington: Office of Air Force History, 1985.

Hermes, Walter G. *Truce Tent and Fighting Front.* [*The United States Army in the Korean War*] Washington: Government Printing Office, 1966.

Hewlett, Richard G., and Oscar E. Anderson, Jr. *The New World, 1939–1946.* Vol I of *A History of the United States Atomic Energy Commission.* University Park, Pa.: Pennsylvania State University Press, 1962.

——— and Francis Duncan. *Atomic Shield, 1947–1952.* Vol II of *A History of the United States Atomic Energy Commission.* University Park, Pa.: Pennsylvania State University Press, 1969.

Holley, Irving B. *Ideas and Weapons.* New imprint. [USAF Warrior Studies] Washington: Office of Air Force History, 1985.

Hopkins, J. C., and Sheldon A. Goldberg. *The Development of Strategic Air Command, 1946–1986 (The Fortieth Anniversary History).* Offutt Air Force Base, Neb.: Office of the Historian, Headquarters, Strategic Air Command, 1986.

Bibliography

Jones, Vincent C. *Manhattan: The Army and the Atomic Bomb.* [*The United States Army in World War II: Special Studies*] Washington: U.S. Army Center for Military History, 1985.

Knaack, Marcelle S. *Post-World War II Bombers, 1945–1973.* Volume II of *Encyclopedia of U.S. Air Force Aircraft and Missile Systems.* Washington: Office of Air Force History, 1988.

――――. *Post-World War II Fighters, 1945–1973.* Volume I of *Encyclopedia of U.S. Air Force Aircraft and Missile Systems.* Washington: Office of Air Force History, 1978. New imprint, 1986.

Kohn, Richard H. and Joseph P. Harahan, eds. *Strategic Air Warfare: An Interview with Generals Curtis E. LeMay, Leon W. Johnson, David A. Burchinal, and Jack J. Catton.* [USAF Warrior Studies] Washington: Office of Air Force History, 1988.

Matloff, Maurice, and Edwin M. Snell. *Strategic Planning for Coalition Warfare, 1941–1942,* in [*United States Army in World War II: The War Department*] Washington: Office of the Chief of Military History, 1953..

Maurer, Maurer. *Aviation in the U.S. Army, 1919–1939.* Washington: Office of Air Force History, 1987.

――――, ed. *Air Force Combat Units of World War II.* Washington: U.S. Government Printing Office, 1961. New imprint. Washington: Office of Air Force History, 1983.

――――, ed. *Combat Squadrons of the Air Force, World War II.* Maxwell Air Force Base, Ala.: Air Force Historical Division, Air University, 1969.

――――, ed. *The U.S. Air Service in World War I.* 4 volumes. Maxwell Air Force Base, Ala.: Albert F. Simpson Historical Research Center, 1978.

Mitchell, Vance O. *History of the Air Force Officer Corps.* Unpublished Manuscript. Washington: Air Force History and Museums Program.

Mueller, Robert. *Active Air Force Bases Within the United States of America on 17 September 1982.* Volume I of *Air Force Bases.* Washington: Office of Air Force History, 1989.

Murray, Williamson. *Strategy for Defeat: The Luftwaffe, 1933–1945.* Maxwell Air Force Base, Ala.: Air University Press, 1983.

Neufeld, Jacob. *The Development of Ballistic Missiles in the United States Air Force, 1945–1960.* Washington: Office of Air Force History, 1990.

Nyrop, Richard F., Beryl Lieff Benderly, et al. *Area Handbook for Morocco.* Department of the Army Pamphlet 550-49. Washington: Department of the Army, 1972.

Palmer, Michael A. *Origins of the Maritime Strategy: American Naval Strategy in the First Postwar Decade.* Contributions in Naval History, No. 1. Washington: Naval Historical Center, 1988.

Poole, Walter S. *1950–1952.* Volume IV of *History of the Joint Chiefs of Staff: The Joint Chiefs of Staff and National Policy.* Washington: Historical Division, Joint Chiefs of Staff, 1976.

Ravenstein, Charles A. *Air Force Combat Wings.* Washington, Office of Air Force History, 1984.

――――. *The Organization and Lineage of the United States Air Force.* [USAF Warrior Studies] Washington: Office of Air Force History, 1986.

Rearden, Steven L. *The Formative Years.* Volume I of *History of the Office of the Secretary of Defense.* Washington: Historical Office, Office of the Secretary of Defense, 1984.

Strategic Air Force

Schnabel, James F. *1945–1947*. Volume I of *History of the Joint Chiefs of Staff: The Joint Chiefs of Staff and National Policy*. Washington: Historical Division, Joint Chiefs of Staff, 1979.

——— and Robert J. Watson. *The Korean War*. Volume III of *History of the Joint Chiefs of Staff: The Joint Chiefs of Staff and National Policy*. Washington: Historical Division, Joint Chiefs of Staff, 1978.

Sparrow, John C. *History of Personnel Demobilization in the United States Army*. Washington: Office of Chief of Military History, 1951.

Watson, George M. *History of the Office of the Secretary of the Air Force, 1947–1965*. Washington: Air Force History and Museums Program, 1993.

Watson, Mark S. *The Chief of Staff: Prewar Plans and Operation* [The United States Army in World War II: The War Department] Washington: Government Printing Office, 1950.

Watson, Robert J. *1953–1954*. Volume V of *History of the Joint Chiefs of Staff: The Joint Chiefs of Staff and National Policy*. Washington: Historical Division, Joint Chiefs of Staff, 1986.

Wolk, Herman S. *Planning and Organizing the Postwar Air Force, 1943–1947*. Washington: Office of Air Force History, 1984.

Articles

Anderson, Orval A. "Air Warfare and Immorality." *Air University Quarterly Review* III (Winter 1949).

Daunt, John J. "In My Opinion: The Balance in Our Armed Forces." *Air University Quarterly Review* III (Winter 1949).

Greenwood, John T. "The Emergence of the Postwar Strategic Air Force, 1945–1953." Alfred F. Hurley and Robert C. Ehrhart, eds. *Air Power and Warfare*. Proceedings of the 8th Military History Symposium, USAF Academy, October 18–20, 1978. Washington: Office of Air Force History, 1979.

LeMay, Curtis E., O. P. Weyland, and William I. Martin. "The Perceptions of Three Makers of Air Power History." Alfred F. Hurley and Robert C. Ehrhart, eds. *Air Power and Warfare*. Proceedings of the 8th Military History Symposium, USAF Academy, October 18–20, 1978. Washington: Office of Air Force History, 1979.

Pike, Harry M. "In My Opinion: Limitations of an Air Defense System." *Air University Quarterly Review* III (Fall 1949).

Seabolt, R. J. "Prize Editorial: Why Emphasize Air Power?" *Air University Quarterly Review* III (Winter 1949).

Smith, Dale O. "One-Way Combat." *Air University Quarterly Review* I (Fall 1947).

Wood, John J. "The Morality of War." *Air University Quarterly Review* IV (Summer 1950).

Non-Governmental Sources

Books

Acheson, Dean. *Present at the Creation: My Years at the State Department*. New York: W. W. Norton, 1969.

Bibliography

Alperowitz, Gar. *Atomic Diplomacy: Hiroshima and Potsdam—The Use of the Atomic Bomb and the American Confrontation with Soviet Power.* New York: Simon & Schuster, 1965. New edition. New York: Penguin, 1985.

Ambrose, Stephen. *Rise to Globalism: American Foreign Policy, 1938–1980.* 2d rev. ed. New York: Penguin, 1980.

Arnold, Henry H. *Global Mission.* New York: Harper & Brothers, 1949.

Aron, Raymond. *The Imperial Republic: The United States and the World, 1945–1973.* Translated by Frank Jellinek. Englewood Cliffs, N.J.: Prentice-Hall, 1974.

Balchen, Bernt. *Come North With Me: An Autobiography.* New York: Dutton, 1958.

Berger, Carl. *B-29: The Superfortress.* New York: Ballantine, 1970.

Blackett, P. M. S. *Fear, War, and the Bomb: Military and Political Consequences of Atomic Energy.* New York: Whittlesey House, 1949.

Borden, William L. *There Will Be No Time: The Revolution in Strategy.* New York: MacMillan, 1946.

Borowski, Harry R. *A Hollow Threat: Strategic Air Power and Containment Before Korea.* Westport, Conn.: Greenwood, 1982.

Bradley, David. *No Place to Hide.* Boston: Little, Brown, 1948.

Brodie, Bernard. *The Absolute Weapon: Atomic Power and World Order.* New York: Harcourt Brace, 1946.

Bundy, McGeorge. *Danger and Survival: Choices about the Bomb in the First Fifty Years.* New York: Random House, 1988.

Bush, Vannevar. *Modern Arms and Free Men: A Discussion of the Role of Science in Preserving Democracy.* New York: Simon & Schuster, 1949.

Clay, Lucius D. *The Papers of General Lucius D. Clay: Germany 1945–1949.* Jean Edward Smith, ed. 2 volumes. Bloomington, Ind.: Indiana University Press, 1974.

Coffey, Thomas M. *Iron Eagle: The Turbulent Life of General Curtis LeMay.* New York: Crown, 1986.

Coletta, Paulo E. *The United States Navy and Defense Unification, 1917–1953.* Newark, Del.: University of Delaware Press, 1981.

Copp, DeWitt S. *A Few Great Captains: The Men and Events That Shaped the Development of U.S. Air Power.* Garden City, N. Y.: Doubleday, 1980.

_____. *Forged in Fire: Strategy and Decisions in the Air War over Europe, 1940–1945.* Garden City, N.Y.: Doubleday, 1982.

Davis, Vincent. *Postwar Defense Policy and the U.S. Navy, 1943–1946.* Chapel Hill, N.C.: University of North Carolina Press, 1966.

Divine, Robert A. *Since 1945: Politics and Diplomacy in Recent American History.* New York: John Wiley, 1975.

Donovan, Robert J. *Conflict and Crisis: The Presidency of Harry S Truman, 1945–1948.* New York: W. W. Norton, 1977.

_____. *Tumultuous Years: The Presidency of Harry S Truman, 1949–1953.* New York: W. W. Norton, 1982.

Eisenhower, Dwight D. *The Eisenhower Diaries.* Robert H. Ferrell, ed. New York: W. W. Norton, 1981.

_____. *The White House Years: Mandate for Change, 1953–1956.* Garden City, N.Y.: Doubleday, 1963.

Emme, Eugene M., ed. *The Impact of Air Power: National Security and World Politics.* Princeton, N.J.: Van Nostrand, 1959.

Foot, Rosemary. *The Wrong War: American Policy and the Dimensions of the Korean Conflict, 1950–1953.* Ithaca, N.Y.: Cornell University Press, 1985.

Forrestal, James V. *The Forrestal Diaries.* Walter Millis & E. S. Duffield, eds. New York: Viking, 1951.

Frankland, Noble. *The Bombing Offensive Against Germany: Outlines and Perspectives.* London: Faber & Faber, 1965.
Gaddis, John L. *The Long Peace: Inquiries Into the History of the Cold War.* New York: Oxford University Press, 1987.
_____. *Strategies of Containment: A Critical Reappraisal of Postwar American National Security Policy.* New York: Oxford University Press, 1982.
_____. *The United States and the Origins of the Cold War, 1941–1947.* New York: Columbia University Press, 1972.
_____ and Thomas H. Etzold, eds. *Containment: Documents of American Policy and Strategy, 1945–1950.* New York: Columbia University Press, 1978.
Gardner, Lloyd C. *Architects of Illusion: Men and Ideas in American Foreign Policy, 1941–1949.* Chicago: Quadrangle, 1970.
George, Alexander L. and Richard Smoke. *Deterrence in American Foreign Policy: Theory and Practice.* New York: Columbia University Press, 1974.
Gowing, Margaret and Lorna Arnold. *Independence and Deterrence: Britain and Atomic Energy, 1945–1952.* Volume I: *Policy–Making.* Volume II: *Policy Execution.* New York: Saint Martin's, 1974.
Graebner, Norman A. *Cold War Diplomacy: American Foreign Policy, 1945–1960.* Princeton, N.J.: Van Nostrand, 1962.
Groves, Leslie R. *Now It Can Be Told: The Story of the Manhattan Project.* New York: Harper & Row, 1962.
Halle, Louis J. *The Cold War As History.* New York: Harper & Row, 1967.
Hammond, Paul Y. *Organizing for Defense: The American Military Establishment in the Twentieth Century.* Princeton, N.J.: Princeton University Press, 1961.
Haynes, Richard F. *The Awesome Power: Harry S. Truman as Commander in Chief.* Baton Rouge, La.: Louisiana State University Press, 1973.
Heller, Mikhail and Aleksandr Nekrich. *Utopia in Power: The History of the Soviet Union from 1917 to the Present.* Translated by Phyllis B. Carlos. New York: Summit, 1986.
Herken, Gregg. *The Winning Weapon: The Atomic Bomb in the Cold War, 1945–1950.* New York: Knopf, 1980.
Howard, Michael. *The Franco-Prussian War: The German Invasion of France, 1870–1871.* New York: MacMillan, 1961.
Huntington, Samuel P. *The Common Defense: Strategic Programs in National Politics.* New York: Columbia University Press, 1961.
Hurley, Alfred F. *Billy Mitchell: Crusader for Air Power.* New York: Franklin Watts, 1964.
Huzar, Elias. *The Purse and the Sword: Control of the Army by Congress Through Military Appropriations, 1933–1950.* Ithaca, N.Y.: Cornell University Press, 1950.
Kaplan, Fred. *The Wizards of Armageddon.* New York: Simon and Schuster, 1983.
Kennett, Lee. *A History of Strategic Bombing.* New York: Scribner's, 1982.
Kenney, George C. *General Kenney Reports.* New York: Duell, Sloan and Pearce, 1949.
Khrushchev, Nikita S. *Khrushchev Remembers.* Ed. Edward Crankshaw. Boston: Little, Brown, 1970.
Kohn, Richard H. *Eagle and Sword: The Federalists and the Creation of the Military Establishment in America, 1783–1802.* New York: Free Press, 1975.
Kolko, Gabriel, and Joyce Kolko. *The Limits of Power: The World and United States Foreign Policy, 1945–1954.* New York: Harper & Row, 1972.

Bibliography

Kolodziej, Edward A. *The Uncommon Defense and Congress, 1945–1963.* Columbus, Ohio: Ohio State University Press, 1966.
LaFeber, Walter. *America, Russia and the Cold War, 1945–1975.* 3d ed. New York: John Wiley, 1976.
Laurence, William L. *Dawn Over Zero: The Story of the Atomic Bomb.* 2d ed. enl. Westport, Conn.: Greenwood, 1977.
LeMay, Curtis E. and MacKinlay Kantor. *Mission With LeMay: My Story.* Garden City, N.Y.: Doubleday, 1965.
Lewin, Ronald. *Slim: The Standardbearer.* London: Leo Cooper, 1976.
Lieberman, Joseph I. *The Scorpion and the Tarantula: The Struggle to Control Atomic Weapons, 1945–1949.* Boston: Houghton Mifflin, 1970.
Lilienthal, David E. *The Atomic Energy Years.* Volume II of *The Journals of David E. Lilienthal.* New York: Harper & Row, 1964.
MacIsaac, David. *Strategic Bombing in World War II: The Story of the United States Strategic Bombing Survey.* New York: Garland, 1976.
McNeil, William H. *America, Britain, & Russia: Their Co-operation and Conflict, 1941–1946.* London: Oxford University Press, 1953. Reprint. New York: Johnson Reprint Corp., 1970.
Mahan, Alfred Thayer. *The Influence of Sea Power Upon History, 1660-1783.* Boston: Little, Brown, 1918.
Manchester, William. *The Glory and the Dream: A Narrative History of America, 1932–1972.* Boston: Little, Brown, 1974.
Mandelbaum, Michael. *The Nuclear Question: The United States and Nuclear Weapons, 1946–1976.* New York: Cambridge University Press, 1979.
———. *The Nuclear Revolution: International Politics before and after Hiroshima.* New York: Cambridge University Press, 1981.
Mierzejewski, Alfred C. *The Collapse of the German War Economy, 1944–1945: Allied Air Power and the German National Railway.* Chapel Hill, N.C.: University of North Carolina Press, 1988.
Allan R. Millett and Peter Maslowski. *For the Common Defense: A Military History of the United States of America.* New York: Free Press, 1984.
North Atlantic Treaty Organization. *NATO Facts and Figures.* Brussels: NATO Information Service, 1976.
Paige, Glenn D. *The Korean Decision, June 24–30, 1950.* New York: Free Press, 1968.
Parmet, Herbert S. *Eisenhower and the American Crusades.* New York: MacMillan, 1972.
Parrish, Noel F. *Behind the Sheltering Bomb: Military Indecision from Alamogordo to Korea.* New York: Arno, 1979.
Paterson, Thomas G. *Soviet-American Confrontation: Postwar Reconstruction and the Origins of the Cold War.* Baltimore, Md.: Johns Hopkins University Press, 1973.
Pogue, Forrest C. *George C. Marshall.* Volume IV: *Statesman, 1945–1959.* New York: Viking, 1987.
Prados, John. *The Soviet Estimate: U.S. Intelligence Analysis and Russian Military Strength.* New York: Dial Press, 1982.
Quester, George H. *Deterrence before Hiroshima: The Airpower Background of Modern Strategy.* New York: John Wiley, 1966.
Raleigh, Walter and H. A. James. *The War in the Air: Being the Story of The Part played in the Great War by the Royal Air Force.* 6 volumes. Oxford: Clarendon Press, 1922–1937.

Rearden, Steven L. *The Evolution of American Strategic Doctrine: Paul H. Nitze and the Soviet Challenge.* Boulder, Colo.: Westview Press, 1984.

Rhodes, Richard. *The Making of the Atomic Bomb.* New York: Simon & Schuster, 1986.

Rogow, Arnold A. *James Forrestal: A Study of Personality, Politics, and Policy.* New York: MacMillan, 1963.

Rose, Lisle. A. *Dubious Victory: The United States and the End of World War II.* Kent, Ohio: Kent State University Press, 1973.

Ross, Steven T. *American War Plans, 1945–1950.* New York: Garland, 1988.

Schaffer, Ronald. *Wings of Judgement: American Bombing in World War II.* New York: Oxford University Press, 1985.

Schilling, Warner R., Paul Y. Hammond and Glenn H. Snyder. *Strategy, Politics, and Defense Budgets.* New York: Columbia University Press, 1962.

Schratz, Paul R., ed. *Evolution of the American Military Establishment Since World War II.* Lexington, Va.: George C. Marshall Research Foundation, 1978.

Sherry, Michael S. *Preparing for the Next War: American Plans for Postwar Defense, 1941–1945.* New Haven, Conn.: Yale University Press, 1977.

———. *The Rise of American Air Power: The Creation of Armageddon.* New Haven, Conn.: Yale University Press, 1987.

Sherwin, Martin J. *A World Destroyed: The Atomic Bomb and the Grand Alliance.* New York: Knopf, 1975.

Simmons, Robert R. *The Strained Alliance: Peking, P'yongyang, Moscow, and the Politics of the Korean Civil War.* New York: Free Press, 1975.

Smith, Malcolm. *British Air Strategy Between the Wars.* Oxford: Clarendon Press, 1984.

Smith, Perry McCoy. *The Air Force Plans for Peace, 1943–1945.* Baltimore, Md.: Johns Hopkins University Press, 1984.

Stein, Harold, ed. *American Civil-Military Decisions: A Book of Case Studies.* Tuscaloosa, Ala.: University of Alabama Press, 1963.

Tedder, Arthur, Lord. *Air Power in War.* Reprint. Westport, Conn.: Greenwood, 1975.

Thomas, Gordon and Max Morgan Witts. *Enola Gay.* New York: Stein & Day, 1977.

Truman, Harry S. *Memoirs.* Volume I: *Year of Decisions.* Volume II: *Years of Trial and Hope.* Garden City, N.Y.: Doubleday, 1955–1956.

Truman, Margaret. *Harry S. Truman.* New York: Morrow, 1973.

Ulam, Adam B. *The Rivals: America and Russia Since World War II.* New York: Viking, 1971.

Webster, Charles and Noble Frankland. *The Strategic Air Offensive Against Germany, 1939–1945.* 4 volumes. London: HMSO, 1961.

Weigley, Russell F. *The American Way of War: A History of United States Military Strategy and Policy.* New York: MacMillan, 1973.

Yergin, Daniel. *Shattered Peace: The Origins of the Cold War and the National Security State.* Boston: Houghton Mifflin, 1977.

York, Herbert. *The Advisors: Oppenheimer, Teller, and the Superbomb.* San Francisco: W. H. Freeman, 1976.

Zimmerman, Carroll L. *Insider at SAC: Operations Analysis Under General LeMay.* Manhattan, Kans.: Sunflower University Press, 1988.

Bibliography

Articles

Boyle, James M. "This Dreamboat Can Fly." *Aerospace Historian* 14 (Summer 1967).

Dingman, Roger. "Atomic Diplomacy During the Korean War." *International Security* 13 (Winter 1988–1989).

Dulles, John Foster. "A Policy of Boldness." *Life* (May 19, 1952).

Elliot, David C. "Project Vista and Nuclear Weapons in Europe." *International Security* 11 (Summer 1986).

Foot, Rosemary J. "Nuclear Coercion and the Ending of the Korean War." *International Security* 13 (Winter 1988–1989).

Gaddis, John L. "The Long Peace: Elements of Stability in the Postwar International System." *International Security* 10 (Spring 1986).

Goldsworthy, Harry E. "B–36 Peacemaker." *Aerospace Historian* 30 (December 1983).

Hansell, Haywood S. "B–29 Superfortress." Robin Higham and Abigail T. Siddall, eds. *Flying Combat Aircraft of the USAAF-USAF*. Ames, Iowa.: Iowa State University Press, 1975.

Lundestad, Geir. "Moralism, Presentism, Exceptionalism, Provincialism, and Other Extravagances in American Writings on the Early Cold War Years." *Diplomatic History* 13 (Fall 1989).

MacIsaac, David. "Voices from the Central Blue: The Air Power Theorists." Peter Paret, ed. *Makers of Modern Strategy from Machiavelli to the Nuclear Age*. Princeton: N.J.: Princeton University Press, 1986.

Mark, Eduard. "October or Thermidor? Interpretations of Stalinism and the Perception of Soviet Foreign Policy in the United States, 1927–1947." *American Historical Review* 94 (October 1989).

Resis, Albert. "The Churchill-Stalin 'Percentages' Agreement on the Balkans, October 1944." *American Historical Review* 83 (April 1978).

Rosenberg, David A. "American Atomic Strategy and the Hydrogen Bomb Decision." *Journal of American History* 66 (June 1979).

———. "The Origins of Overkill: Nuclear Weapons and American Strategy, 1945–1960." *International Security* 7 (Spring 1983).

———. "U.S. Nuclear Stockpile, 1945 to 1950." *The Bulletin of the Atomic Scientists* 38 (May 1982).

———, ed. "A Smoking, Radiating Ruin at the End of Two Hours." *International Security* 6 (Winter 1981–1982).

Schaller, Michael. "U.S. Policy in the Korean War." *International Security* 11 (Winter 1986–1987).

Spaatz, Carl A. "Strategic Air Power: Fulfillment of a Concept." *Foreign Affairs* 24 (April 1946).

———. "The Airpower Odds Against the Free World." *Air Force Magazine* (April 1951).

Trachtenberg, Marc. "A 'Wasting Asset': American Strategy and the Shifting Nuclear Balance, 1949–1954." *International Security* 13 (Winter 1988–1989).

Wolk, Herman S. "Building the Peacetime Air Force." *Air Force Magazine* (September 1980).

Strategic Air Force

———. "Roots of Strategic Deterrence." *Aerospace Historian* (September–October 1972).
———. "The Strategic World of 1946." *Air Force Magazine* (February 1971).
"X" [Kennan, George F.]. "The Sources of Soviet Conduct." *Foreign Affairs* 25 (July 1947).

Ph.D. Dissertations

Converse, Elliot V. "United States Plans for a Postwar Overseas Base System, 1942–1948." Princeton University, 1984.
Fanton, Jonathan F. "Robert A. Lovett: The War Years." Yale University, 1978.
Green, Murray. "Stuart Symington and the B–36." American University, 1960.

Index

Index

ABC-101: 198-201
Abu Sueir, Egypt: 276, 442
Acheson, Dean G.: 46, 425
    and NSC-68: 328
Acheson-Lilienthal Report: 46
Aerial refueling: 176-186, 201, 245, 247, 267-268, 419-420, 422, 465
Africa
    as basing area: 289
Air Coordinating Committee: 70
Air Corps Tactical School: 15, 20
Aircraft industry: 150-151, 254, 388
    competition and favoritism: 181-183
    and defense needs: 164-165
    and SAC buildup: 375-376
    See also names of companies
Aircraft, Soviet. *See under* model number
Aircraft, U.S. *See under* model number
Aircraft and Weapons Board: 10-12, 150, 242
    approves B-36: 181
    and B-52: 185
    endorses aerial refueling: 180
    Heavy Bombardment Committee: 175-177, 181-185
    and reconnaissance aircraft: 239
Air Defense Command (ADC)
    responsibility of: 61, 63
    strength: 65
Air Divisions
    3d: 273, 466
    5th: 432, 433
    7th: 432, 433, 434
    19th: 413
    49th: 367, 369
Air Force: 349
Air Force Council: 387, 451

Air Force Installations Board: 427
Air Force Reserve: 373
Airlifts: 206, 207, 469
Air Materiel Command (AMC): 92, 93
    on atomic energy: 174
Air National Guard: 373
Air observers: 257-258
Air Police: 444-445
Air Staff
    Air Targets Division: 360
    articulates national air power strategy, Air Concept: 396, 447-449, 452-453, 458
    Atomic Energy Division: 128
    and B-52 contract: 181-183
    DARKHORSE: 201-202
    and design of atomic strike force: 59-60
    emergency war plan (EARSHOT): 146-147
    meets on B-36: 237
    and postwar force issues: 55
    strategic bombing plan (MAKEFAST): 142-143
    study of tactical air power (VISTA): 367-368, 390
    wants direct relationship to AEC: 424-425
Air Training Command: 373-374
    and fear of flying: 409
Air University: 355
Air University Quarterly Review: 109, 306, 318, 321
Air War Plans Division (AWPD)
    AWPD-1: 20-22, 24, 25, 97
Alamogordo, New Mexico: 6
Alaskan Air Command: 85, 108-109

497

Aluminum Company of America: 100
Allen, William M.: 182
AN/APQ-13 radar equipment: 89
Anderson, Frederick L.: 84
Anderson, Orvil A.: 304, 347–349, 362
Anderson, Samuel E.: 218, 223, 247, 290, 319, 365, 429
Andrews Air Force Base, Maryland: 84, 208, 254
   as SAC headquarters: 63
Alexander, Henry C.: 363
Alexander Panel: 363
American Expeditionary Force (AEF): 15, 16
Appeasement: 10
Arctic operations: 67, 80, 439–441
   command for: 133–134
   importance in strategic plan: 106, 108
   refueling: 177, 180
Armed Forces Special Weapons Project (AFSWP), 201, 204–205
   becomes Special Weapons Center: 424
   and Berlin crisis: 247–248
   control of: 173–174
   guarding of bombs: 126–127
   and interservice rivalry: 169–170
   as priority: 186
   tension with AEC: 128
   training: 129, 169
   in war plan: 148
Armed Services Committee: 75
Armstrong, Frank A.: 95, 97, 174
Armstrong, John G.: 124–125, 214–215
Armstrong Committee: 125
Army Air Forces (AAF)
   CAF position in command structure: 61
   FY 1947 budget effect on strength: 70–73
   FY 1948 budget: 75–76
   Hobson reorganization plan: 92–93
   and Manhattan Project: 7
   Peripheral Basing Plan: 49, 53, 79
   planning strategic air offensive for atomic war: 137–149
   postwar shortages: 68
   proposed 70-group size: 54, 57, 73, 76
   R&D budget: 72–73
   role of atomic weapons in: 55–57
Army Corps of Engineers: 426, 435, 438, 441
Army General Classification Test (AGCT): 81, 83, 189
Arnold, Henry H. ("Hap"): 10, 36
   and air power: 17, 28, 34
   and atomic weapons: 7–8, 56
   and basing plan: 47
   commands of: 50
   forms AWPD: 20–21
   on morale bombing: 16
   and organization of strategic bombing of Japan: 26
   and preparedness: 13
   and separate air force: 27, 34–35, 38
   and 70-group size: 54
   and UMT: 27
Ashworth, Frederick L.: 6
Atkinson, Joseph H. ("Hamp"): 280
Atomic Energy Act of 1946: 48, 322
Atomic Energy Commission (AEC): 48, 113, 124, 126–127, 464
   Air Force relation to: 424–425
   bomb transfer procedures: 214
   custody of bombs: 126, 170
   and detection of Soviet atomic detonation: 314–316
   and hydrogen bomb: 322–323
   and Korean War: 344
   military control of: 204–205
   Military Liaison Committee: 124, 127–129, 132, 168–170, 174, 321
   production levels: 170–171, 321–322
   and security: 128–129, 257
Atomic Energy Committee: 355, 357
Atomic weapons: viii, 24, 26, 464
   ability to strike inland, Air Force case for: 159–160
   aircraft designed to carry: 104–105
   and AAF: 56–58
   change to administration through normal channels: 424
   development of American program

Index

for: 39–48
first use: 3–8, *9*
increases, buildup: 357–359, 467
and New Look: 456
planned uses in emergency war
  plan: 309–310
public support for use: 218–219
size of arsenal needed to attack
  Soviets: 149
Soviet use: 270, *331*
stockpile issues: 321–322, 354–371,
  390, 467
storage sites: 425
as strategic weapon: 55
tactical: 366–368
targets: 360–363
testing: 115–122
thermonuclear: 322–324, 326, 467
war plans and policy: 216–219
Atlas Constructors: 437–438
Atlas missile: 424
Attlee, Clement R.: 218, 343, 349

B–17: 14, 16, 20, 79, 94, *96*, 97
B–24: 16, 27, *96*, 97
B–29: 4, 13–14, 16, 23, 24, 26, 29, 49,
  54, 60, 67, 71, 80, 106, *107*, 109,
  111, 224, 273, *315*, *351*, 372,
  375–376, 410, 465
  aerial refueling: 176–177, *178*, 180
  "air pressure:" 399
  in atomic testing: 119–120
  basing needs: 141, 430
  combat crew training school: 374
  conventional force for use in Korea:
    346
  crews: 95
  and cruise control: 222
  demonstrations of: 90
  deployment in Berlin Crisis: 209–212,
    213
  deployment in England during
    Korean War: 342–345
  Dreamboat: 95
  European basing of: 146, 148
  in Korea: 347, *401*

modifications to: 93, 123, 125–126
Pacusan Dreamboat: 95
phaseout: 164
postwar inventory: 97
qualities of: 94–97
record flights: 95, 97, 214
SADDLETREE modifications: 244–245,
  247–248
and STRANGLE: 309
B–29D: 54
B–35: 99
B–36: 16, 27, 61, 68, 97, 99–102, 104,
  106, 108–109, 111–112, *131*, *206*,
  224, 273, 354, 372, 373, 375–376,
  410–411, 427, 438, 465
  Arctic basing: 440
  basing needs: 141
  capabilities and uses: 180–181
  crew size: 412
  in England: 434
  force in 1953: 461
  inventory, 1948: 164
  maintenance: *279*
  modifications: 126, 130, 132, 171
  Navy challenge to program: 283–295,
    300–306
  obsolescence: 421
  overconcentration: 428–429
  procurement and modifications:
    235–238, 244, 245
  production exceeds facilities: 430
  shortages and mechanical problems:
    266–267, 306, 333–334
  storm damage to: 412–414, *418*, 428
B–36B: 176
B–36C: 180
B–45: 130, 358, 369, 373, *374*
B–47: 110, 130, *131*, *178*, 185, 239, 252,
  270, 354, 373, 375–376, 420–422,
  427, *428–429*
  Arctic operations: 440, 442
  characteristics: 416, 417
  crews: 416–417
  in England: 434
  force in 1953: 461
  testing, problems: 414–416
B–47A: 339

499

Strategic Air Force

B–48: 239
B–49 Flying Wing: 182–185, 239–240, 252–253
B–50: 55, 97, 103, 104, 106, 109–111, 224, 239, *242*, 245, 252, 254, *255*, 265, 270, 354, 372, 373, 376, 410, 437, 465
   aerial refueling: 177, 178
   extended range: 176
   maintenance: *279*
   modification for atomic bomb: 130, 132, 171
   nonstop flight around world: *255*, 266
   procurement: 186
B–52: 101–105, 108, 111, *131*, 175, 270, 411, 420–422, 427
   armament: 183–184
   atomic bomb accommodations: 130
   development: 238–239
   program redirection: 181–183, 186
B–54: 252–254
B–58: 423
B–60
   "parasite" concept: 21, 422
Bacher, Robert F.: 367
Baker, George: 167
Balchen, Bernt: 440
Bar Harbor Memorandum: 452, 456, 463, 468
Barksdale Air Force Base, Louisiana: 277, 268, 280–281, 426, 431
Barrows, Arthur S.: 182, 237, 240
Baruch, Bernard M.: 46, 47, 139
Bases
   conditions of in U.S.: 277–278
   in England: 433–434
   global: 426–445
   in Mediterranean: 276
   need for European: 114, 141
   in North American: 270–272
   overseas: 142, 273, 276, 283–284, 287–288, 377, 467
   security of: 444
   for Soviet attack: 201–202, 208
   vulnerability of: 271, 276
BECALM: 334–335

Bergstrom Air Force Base, Texas: *268*, 417
Berlin crisis: 187, 205–216
Beser, Jacob: 4, 6, *11*
Bevin, Ernest: 207, 209–210
Biggs Air Force Base, Texas: 222, 268, 335, 403, 430
Bikini Atoll bombing tests: 67, 78, 113–114, 117–122, 144, 146, 464
Billotte, Pierre: 324
Binghamton, New York: 403
Blanchard, William H.: 122
Blandy, William H. P.: 118, *119*
Boatner, Bryant L.: 414
Bock, Frederick C.: 6
Bock's Car: 6, *107*
Boeing Aircraft Company: 98, 99, 102, 421, 422
   B–47 problems: 416
   B–52: 238, 247
   competition controversy: 181–183
Bohlen, Charles E.: 342
Bolling Field, D.C.: 49
   as SAC headquarters: 63, 65, 84
Bombardment Groups
   2d: *213*, 214, 225
   7th: 92, 220, 225, 251
   19th: 222, 346, 398
   22d: 222–223, 346, 347, 396
   28th: 80, 108, 133, 208, 209, 227
   43d: 88, 90, 105, 225, 239
   92d: 347, *351*, 396
   93d: 222, 224
   97th: 91, 222
   301st: 209, 214, 222, 342
   305th: 17
   307th: 208, 209
   449th: 65
Bombardment Squadrons
   340th: 91
   393d: 6
Bombardment Wings
   2d: 403, 404
   6th: *377*, 413, *413*
   7th: 266–267, 412–414, *418*
   9th: *377*
   11th: 429, 430

Index

22d: 346, *401*
43d: 254, *255*, *377*, 403
58th: 60, 81–82, 117, 125
68th: *377*
92d: 346
93d: 332, 344, 404, 434
97th: 344, *377*, 403, 434
98th: 347
303d: 417
305th: 415–416
306th: 415–416
307th: 347, *401*
308th: *377*
Bombing accuracy: 403, *404*
Bombing competitions: 224, 332, 403–405
Bong, Richard I.: 64n92
Borden, William L.: 322
Born, Charles F.: 80
Bradley, Omar N.: 196, 249, *301*, 305, 310, 316, 350, 355, 451
Brereton, Lewis H.: 121–122, 124, 149, 157
Brewster, R. Owen: 151
Brewster Board: 158, 161, 164–166, 465
Brewster Report: 196, 197
British Independent Air Force: 15
Brodie, Bernard: 39–41, 362–363
Bunker, Howard G.: 128, 424
Burchinal, David A.: 375, *377*
Burke, Arleigh: 302
Bush, Vannevar: 41–42, *51*, 312–313, 316
Byrnes, James F.: 35, 52

C–47: 90, *213*
C–54: 93, 211
C–97: 60, 171, *401*
   KC–97 program:
Cabell, Charles P.: 230, 363
California Institute of Technology: 367
Camp Carson, Colorado: 406
   SAC school: 445
Cannon, John K.: 364, 393
Career fields
   atomic force service: 26

Carnegie Institution: 312
Caron, George R.: 5, *11*
Carroll, Joseph F.: 302
Cary, John B.: 289, 293, 308
   on Air Force capabilities in war plans: 310
   on joint emergency war plans: 308
Carswell Air Force Base, Texas: 225, 231, 251, 253, 254, *255*, 265, 266, 271, 277, 280, 365, 372, 376, 412–414, *418*, 428, 429, 430
Castle Air Force Base, California: 71, 222, 224, 268, 332, 335, 404
Central Intelligence Agency: 166–167, 214
Chauncey, C. C.: 76–77, 87
Chiang Kai-Shek: 325
Chidlaw, Benjamin W.: 329, 334, 394
China: 190, 458
   controversy over action against: 350–351
   basing Superfortresses in: 23–24
Churchill, Winston S.: 8–9, *28*, 218–219
   and American bases: 434
   and atomic air power: 324
   and Korean War: 343
   and land force buildup: 385
   and U.S. strategy: 449
CINCSAC: *377*
CINCUSAFE: *377*
Clay, Lucius D.: 187, 191, 207, 208, 211
Collins, J. Lawton: 343, 389
Collins Plan: 34
Columbia University: 284
Combat Crew Standardization School: 259
Communism
   economic aid as weapon against: 74
   and need for military buildup: 156
Compton, Karl T.: 121
Compton, Keith K.: 375, *377*
Compton Board: 114, 144–145
Consolidated Vultee Aircraft (Convair) Corporation: 98–100, 102, 180–181, 269, 270, 422, 423
   and B–36 congressional hearings: 302

501

ballistic missiles: 424
B-36 production: 411-412
general bomber study (GEBO II): 422
Containment: 190, 216
Continental Air Forces
  becomes SAC: vii
  groups in: 61-62
  and occupation forces: 49, 54
Cork, Robert O.: 201, 287, 402
Craig, Howard A.: 157, *163*, 362
  and B-52: 181-183
Craigie, Laurence C.: 177, *184*
  and experimental aircraft: 99-100
Crawford, Alden R.: 103
Crommelin, John G.: 304
Cross-training: 219-221, 226, 233
Cullen, Paul T.: 432
Cullen Trophy: 404
Currency reform, Germany: 206, 207
Czechoslovakia: 10, 45
  Soviet invasion of: 187, 191-192

Dave's Dream: 119-120
Davis-Monthan Air Force Base, Arizona: 88, 90, 105, 214, 220, 225, 259, 268, 277, 417
Dayton, Ohio
  simulated bombing mission: 233, 403
DC-6: *242*
Dean, Gordon: 425
Demobilization: 50-52
Denfeld, Louis E.: 195, 198, 294, *301*, 305
Denmark
  U.S. basing rights in: 53
Derby, George T.: 437, 438
Deterrence: viii, xii, 41, 47, 321, 448-450
  bomb seen as: viii, 470
  European economy and: 216-217
  and hydrogen bomb: 324
  joint chiefs meeting on: 230
  Korean War as failure of: 340
  and massive retaliation: 455-456, 469
  SAC effectiveness and confidence in: 285

strategy, 1950: 330
  Truman and: 189
Dewey, Thomas E.: 216
Dhahran, Saudi Arabia: 276, 442
Dior, Christian: 455
Doolittle, James H.
  on air power: 34
  on Soviet threat and U.S. defense: 325-326
DOUBLEQUICK: 199
Douglas, Lewis W.: 207, 343
Douglas Aircraft Company: 98
Douhet, Giulio: 15, 16
Dresden, Germany: 23
DuBridge, Lee A.: 367, 368, 389
Dulles, John Foster: *450*, 455, 459-460, 469

Eaker, Ira C.: 21, 25, *57*
  and aerial refueling: 176
  on atomic bomb: 55
  and planning for atomic strike force: 58-59
Earle, Edward Meade: 363n81
EARSHOT: 146-147, 148
EARSHOT JUNIOR: 148
Eberstadt Report: 34
Edwards, Idwal H.: *163*, 259, 332, 364, 379, 380
  and SAC headquarters: 431
  and SAC staffing: 227
  and SLANT NINE: 362
Eglin Field, Florida: 176
Egypt
  as basing site, 114, 141, 146, 148, 168, 201
Eielson Air Force Base, Alaska: 273
Eighth Air Force: 25, 63, 82, 85, 280, 428
  aircraft: 125
  as atomic force: 125, 214
  bombing competition: 224
  mobility plan testing: 92
  as retaliatory threat: 144
  and security clearance for: 128-129
  size: 87

Index

training: 90, 220–221
Eighth Air Force Advanced Echelon (ADVON): 365
Eisenhower, Dwight D.: 364, 368, *450*, 454–455, 459
   and Air Force/Navy budget disagreements: 297–300
   and air power: 63
   as Army Chief of Staff: 31, *37*
   and atomic strategy: 43, 47, 55–56
   authority in Europe: 364
   begins presidential campaign: 370, 447
   and budget effects on war plans: 289
   chairs JCS: 284
   command of: 25–26
   emergency war plan of: 308–309
   named SACEUR: 350
   and national defense strategies: 459–460
   and 1951 defense budget: 317, 318
   and occupation force: 53
   postwar budget cutting: 72, 73
   as pro Air Force: 305
Eisenhower Plan: 366
Elmendorf Air Force Base, Alaska: 80, 133, *140*, 440
Engineer Battalion (Special) 2761st: 122
Engines
   in experimental aircraft: 239
   General Electric: 415–416
   jet: 98, 105, 425–416
   Pratt and Whitney J47: 415, 416
   Pratt and Whitney J57: 238
   T–35–3: 104
   variable discharge turbine (VDT): 102–103, 108, 110–111, 175, 180, 237–238
   Wright R–3350: 94
   Wright R–3350–23: *107*
   Wright R–4360: 102
   Wright turboprop T–35: 181
Eniwetok: 314, 358
   bombing tests: 220, 359
England. *See* United Kingdom
Enola Gay: 4, *11*, *107*, 127

Ernest Harmon Air Base, Newfoundland: 271
Europe
   emergency war/defense plans for: 309–310
   and hydrogen bomb: 324
   U.S. atomic defense of: 292–293
Everest, Frank F.: 138, 273

F3D: 399
F–12: 110–111, 185–186, 239, *242*
F–13: 71, 97
F–84: 269, 358, 398, 437
F–84E: 417, *423*
F–84G: 419
F–86: 269, 345
F–94: 399
F–101: 419
Fairchild, Muir S.: 227, *324*
   and austere defense budget: 319
   on B–36: 237–238
   death of: 329
   as Air Force vice chief of staff: 188
Fairchild Air Force Base, Washington: 430
Fairchild Board: 254
Fairchild Trophy: 403–404
Fairfield-Suisun Air Force Base (Travis Air Force Base), California: 271–272, 277, 375, *378*
Far East Air Forces (FEAF): 68, 91–92, 22, 346
   "air pressure" program: 395, 399
   Bomber Command: 346, *348*, 372, 374, 375, *401*
   control of operations in Korea: 396–399
   incorporation into SAC: 399
   interdiction missions: 397–398
   losses: 398
   night bombing: 398
FAT MAN: 6, *9*, 118
Fear of flying: 408–410
Fechteler, William M.: 389
Federal Bureau of Investigation (FBI)
   and secret atomic information: 125

Strategic Air Force

Ferebee, Thomas: *11*
Fifteenth Air Force: 25, 53, 63, 80–81, 85, 225
    bombing competition: 224
    headquarters: 280
    training and morale problems: 82–83
Fifth Air Force: 346
Fighter Escort Wings
    27th: 398, 417
Fighter Groups
    82d: 222
    86th: 206
Finletter, Thomas K.: 151, *167*, 341, *343*, 368, 394, 452
    appointed Secretary of Air Force: 330
    base approvals: 432
    expansion and Soviet threat: 381, 384–390
    and fear of flying: 409–410
    overseas basing: 442–444
    reaction to tornado damage: 414
    "task concept:" 395–396
Finletter Commission: 158, 161–162, 164–166, *167*, 465
509th Composite Group: 3–4, *11*, 29
    aircraft of: 65, 168–169
    air refueling training: 225
    in atomic war plan: 148, 215
    and Bikini bombing tests: 67, 81, 118, 121
    organized into SAC: 78
    postwar: 55–56, 59–60
    rating: 403
    as resource and training priority: 233
    security clearances: 220
    tanker units: 268
FLEETWOOD: 287, 307
Flight Refueling, Ltd.: 176–177
Foch, Ferdinand: 16
Forbes Air Force Base, Kansas: 430
Foreign Affairs: 74
Foreign aid
    effect on military spending: 74
Forrestal, James V.: 30–31, 33, *36*, 85, 138, *158*
    and budgets: 159, 162
    and control of military atomic program: 174
    and feasibility of atomic offensive: 294, 465
    gives reasons for B–29 deployment in England: 210–211
    and interservice coordination: 33
    and interservice rivalries: 187–188, 192–194, 203–205
    on military strength: 74–75
    and 1948 budget: 240–241, 249–250
    requests AEC transfer: 204
    resignation and death of: 284, *292*, 301
    as Secretary of Defense: 156
    show of strength: 90
Fort Bliss, Texas: 261
Fox Able III: 417, *423*
Fox Peter I: 419
Fox Peter II: 419
France: 14
    U.S. basing rights in: 53
Franco, Francisco: 443
Fuchs, Klaus: 325

Ganey, Wiley D.: *200*, 201
Gardner, Grandison: 271
GEM/Saddletree: 244
General Electric: 415, 416
Generalized Bomber Study (GEBO): 269–270
George, Harold L: 20, *25*
Germany: 9, 14
    bombing of: 21–22
    four-power government of: 205–206
    occupation of: 49
Gilpatric, Roswell L.: 414, 452
Glenn Martin Company: 98, 99
Glober, George E.: 440
Goose Bay, Labrador: 271, 272
Gorrell, Edgar S.: 14–16
Grand Island, Nebraska: 80
Greece
    civil war in: 190–191
Grenier Field, New Hampshire: 222
Groves, Leslie R.: 7, *51*, 58, 116, 174
    atomic policy: 41–43, 45–46, 48, 124

Index

conflict with AEC: 128
and training: 122, 129
Gruenther, Alfred M.: 172–173,
  190–191, *301*
Guided missiles: 290, 423
Gunn, Paul I.: 64n92

HALFMOON (FLEETWOOD): 199–201,
  205, 211, 287
Hamilton, Pierpont M.: 436
Hansell, Haywood S.: 20, 24, *25*
Harmon, Hubert H.: 295, 305, *307*
Harmon report: 295, 306, 381, 466
Hegenberger, Albert F.: 168, 314, 316
Hickenlooper, Bourke B.: 149, 171, 173
Hipps, William G.: 83
Hiroshima, Japan: 3n1, 4–5, *8*, *18*
Hitler, Adolf: 10, 23
Hobson, Kenneth B.
  reorganization plans: 92–93
Holzapple, Joseph R.: 375, *378*
Hoover, Herbert C.: 455
Hoover, J. Edgar: 445
Hopkins, J. C.: 469n5
Housing
  LeMay's programs to upgrade:
    260–261, 263–265, *268*, *274*, 280,
    406–407, 427
  postwar problems: 71, 82
Hoyt, Palmer: *167*
Hughes Aircraft Company: 403
Hutchinson, David W.: 223
Hydrogen bomb: 322–324, 326, 467

India
  basing problems in: 141
Intelligence
  on Soviet atomic program: 167–168
  on Soviet strategic targets: 140–141
Italy
  communism in: 190

Japan
  atomic bombing of: 5, 7, 9, *18*

deployments to: 91–92
occupation of: 49
surrender of: 24, 54
Jenkins, Reuben E.: 138
Jeppson, Morris R.: 4, *11*
Johnson, Leon W.: 50, 88, *213*, 215,
  229, 273, 342–343, 433
  appointed Secretary of Defense: 284
  and atomic production increase: 322,
    357
  FY 1951 budget: 285, 298–299
  NSC–68: 328–329
  and mandate to cut defense spending:
    316, 317
  and preventive war concept: 347
  resignation of: 348
Johnson-Acheson-Lilienthal reports:
  321–322
Johnson, Lyndon B.: 438
Joint Chiefs of Staff (JCS)
  and Air Force expansion: 388–391
  approval of strategic air offensive
    and direction of SAC: 305
  atomic strategy: 40–44
  on atomic stockpile control: 425
  and balanced forces concept: 388,
    395, 408, 454, 460, 466
  in Berlin Crisis: 211
  BROILER emergency war plan: 168
  Budget Advisory Committee: 203,
    248, 249
  COLOR plans: 135
  and control of atomic forces: 360–368
  control of strategic air warfare:
    289–291, 293
  discussions to resolve interservice
    rivalries: 192–195
  emergency war plans: 198–199,
    286–288
  first statutory chairman: 317
  and interservice rivalries: 187–188,
    192–194, 203–205
  and 1948 budget allocation: 248–250
  and NSC–20/4: 217
  and NSC–30: 218
  and OFFTACKLE: 308–310
  PINCHER planning study: 138–142

505

postwar: 31, 33, 35, 38–39
recommendation to use emergency war plan in Korean War: 345–346
review and approval of SAC emergency war plan: 310–311, 380
SLANT NINE: 360–363
on strategic air offensive: 310
and tactical atomic weapons: 368
Unified Command Plan: 133–134, 272
United Nations peacekeeping role: 13
Joint Research and Development Board: 126
Joint Strategic Plans Committee: 289, 308, 309, 311, 359
identifies atomic targets: 357–360
and 163-wing plan: 387
Joint Strategic Studies Committee: 323
Joint Strategic Survey Committee: 41–42, 51, 127
Report 1745/5: 171–173
Jones, Junius W.: 82
Juin, Alphonse: 436
Jumper, George Y.: *200*, 201

Kadena Air Base, Okinawa: 346, 347, *401*
Kármán, Theodore von: 27
von Kármán Committee: 98, 175
KB-29: 437
first combat refueling: 397
KC-97: *178*
Keflavik, Iceland: 442
Kennan, George F.: 33
containment strategy: 74–75, 190, *192*, 216–217
and invasion of Czechoslovakia: 191
Kenney, George C.: 22n43, *75*, 188, 419–420
and aerial refueling: 180
on aircraft design: 108
on atomic offensive: 170
basing: 222
commands Air University: 229
commands SAC: 63, 68, 84–85, 157
on experimental bombers 100–101

increases strength: 93
management problems of: 219, 221, 227–228
and medium bomber force: 266
objections to B-36: 184–185
public speaking by: 85
and strategic air power: x, 34, 64
success in deployment: 224
at United Nations: 63, 65, 78
and use of B-29: 26
Kepner, William E.
appointed Chief of Atomic Energy Division: 128
on atomic capability: 145–146
and atomic tests: 118, *119*, 120–121
and Special Weapons Group study on atomic offensive: 160, 174
Key West JCS Conference: 192, 290
Kimball, Dan A.: 302
Kim Il-Sung: 339, 340
King, Ernest J.: xiii
Kirkpatrick, Elmer E., Jr.: 142
Kirtland Field, New Mexico: 125, 424
Tactical and Technical Liaison Committee (T&TLC): 128–129
Kissner, August W.: 229, *232*, 443
Knapp, James B.: 171, 172, *200*, 201
Korean War: viii, 339–346, 394–396
crisis period: 347–352
effect on military expansion: 394
end of: 456, 459
negotiated settlement: 352
strategic phase: 346–347
Kuter, Laurence S.: 20, *25*, 393, 452–453
and fear of flying: 409–410
Kwajalein Island: 119

Lackland Air Force Base, Texas: 373
Lajes, Azores: 442
Lake Charles, Louisiana: 375, 430
Landon, Truman H.: 313, 364, 379
Landry, Robert B.: 299, 300
Leach, W. Barton: 302, 321, 344, 448, 454
and defense of Europe: 324
and U.S. military tasks in event of

Index

war: 384–386
Lead crews: 256, 258, *262*, 405
League of Nations: 10
Leahy, William D.: 31, 47, 139, 168, 198
Lee, Robert M., Jr.: 371, 453, 454
LeMay, Curtis Emerson: *64*, 211, *232*
   and AAF atomic responsibilities: 115, 117, 124, 127–128
   on aircraft contract competition: 181
   appointed Deputy Chief of Air Staff for R&D: 58
   appointed SAC Commander: 229
   and Arctic operations: 441
   on atomic strategy: 160
   and atomic tests: 120
   on bomber requirements: 102, 105, 108, 110
   and Compton report: 145
   confers with RAF on war plans: 201
   creates bombing competition: 224, 332, 403–405
   creates new air divisions, 1951: 432
   and deployment of B-29s in England: 344
   at "Dualism" conference: 230–231
   on fear of flying: 409–410
   JCS 2056 and bombing plan 359: 363–364
   leadership approach of: 255–256
   leads XXI Bomber Command: 24
   mission statement: 117
   and new officers to build bombardment unit: 375
   on Pearl Harbor attack: 12
   promoted to full general: 393
   revised organization, 1950: 376–377
   on SAC headquarters: 431
   and SAC ZEBRA: 368
   skepticism about tactical atomic warfare: 369
   and strategic campaign against Japan: 23–24
   success recognized: 332
   on sufficient number of bomb groups: 307
   testimony in B-36 investigation: 303
   training reforms and requirements: 129–130, 233
   and Unified Command Plan: 291
   views on aircraft development, 1952: 421, 422
   views on targets: 361–362
Leo, Stephen F.: 227
Lewis, Robert: *11*
Light Bombardment Wings
   106th: 373
   111th: 373
Lilienthal, David E.: 46, 128–129, 146, 149, 156, 317
   opposes AEC transfer: 204
   opposes use of hydrogen bomb: 323–324
Limestone Air Force Base, Maine: 271–272, 412, 417, 429–430
Lincoln, George A.: 123, 126, 140, 148
Lindbergh, Charles A.: 226–227, *228*, 229, 233, 261, 332
Lindsay, Richard C.: 341
LITTLE BOY: 3–4, 6, *8*
Lockbourne Air Force Base, Ohio: 417, 430
Lodge, Henry Cabot, Jr.: 386, 388
Long, Russell B.: 443
Lovett, Robert A.: 21, 30–31, *37*, 348, 375, 388, 390, 396, 425, 440, 446, 468

MacArthur, Douglas: 64, 132–133
   and atomic bomb: 26
   and Korean War: 346–347, 349
   relieved: 352
   Senate investigation: 386
   wants to attack China: 350–352
Mackay Trophy: 417
MacDill Air Force Base, Florida: 208, 259, *401*, 405, 415–416, 420
   Combat Crew Training School: 420
MacMahon Act: 113–114, 142
McCarthy, Joseph R.: 325
McCone, John A.: 161, 167
McConnell, John P.: 432
   and basing in England: 433, 434
McCoy, N. W.: 415, 417

507

McGrigor, Rhoderick: 449
McGuire Air Force Base, New Jersey: 280
McKee, William F.: 78, 79, 264, 414
McMahon, Brien: 48, 322–323
McMullen, Clements: *86*
   and low ceilings of strength: 87–88, 93
   made Deputy Commander, SAC : 85–87
   management problems of: 219–221, 224, 226
   on medium bombers: 110
McNarney, Joseph T.: 22n43, 79, 188, *324*, 393
   and aerial refueling: 180
   and atomic modification program: 237
   and B–52: 182
   chairs Budget Advisory Committee: 203
   criticizes Special Weapons Group: 174
McNarney-Fairchild Boards: 250–253, 297, 300, *324*
McNeil, Wilfred J.: 240
MAKEFAST: 142–143, 470
MANHATTAN PROJECT: 3n1, 4, 7, 24, 26–27, 41, 42, 48, 51, 60, 464
   dissolution of: 124
   responsibilities of: 116
   secrecy: 115, 125, 126, 145–146
   and testing: 121
   training: 123
March Air Force Base, California: 60, 277, 280, *401*, 426
Mariana Islands: 24, 26
Marshall, George C.: 24, *37*, 305
   and atomic policy study: 41
   and foreign aid: 74
   recalled by Truman: 348
   retirement of: 390
   and UMT: 27, 33–34, 189, 196
Marshall Plan: 74, 91, 113, 189–190, 193, 196
Martin, Glenn L.: 302
Martin, Glen W.: 375, *377*

Martin Company: 431
Masaryk, Jan: 191
Massachusetts Institute of Technology: 64, 121
Mather Air Force Base, California: 258
Matthews, Francis P.: 304, 347
Maxwell, Alfred R.: 44–45, 98
Maxwell Air Force Base, Alabama: 15, 229, 230
MiG–15: 249, *315*, 381, 398–399, 412
Military Air Transport Service (MATS): 370–371, 429, 431
Missiles: 108, 269–270, *428*
Mitchell, William ("Billy"): 15
Mizutani Air Base, Japan: 95
Molotov, Vyacheslav M.: 12
Montgomery, John B.: 229–231, *232*
Morale: 82–83, 233, 405–408
Morocco
   basing in: 432, *433*, 434–439, 467–468
Morse, Wayne L.: 443
Munich crisis: 10, 17
Muroc Field, California: 121

Nagasaki, Japan: 5, 7, *9*, *18*
National Defense Act of 1920: 15
National Security Act of 1947: 110, 135, 149–150, 156, *158*, 194, 317, 330, 463
National Security Council: 191, 210, 457
   in Berlin Crisis: 248
   Joint Nuclear Energy Committee: 316
   NSC–7 on Soviet threat: 216
   NSC–20: 216
   NSC–68: 285, 327–328, 342, 353–354, 385
   NSC–147: 458
   Symington and: 330, 350
Nazzaro, Joseph J.: 375, *377*
Nehru, Jawaharlal: 459
Nelson, Richard: *11*
Newfoundland: 133
New Look: *450*, 455–456, 458–459, 461, 463
Newport JCS Conference: 290, 293, 294

Index

301
Nichols, Kenneth D.: 323
Nimitz, Chester W.: 26, 31, 47
  on atomic strategy: 162
  retirement of: 194
  and Unified Command Plan:
    132–134, 139
Nitze, Paul H.: 326–328
Norstad, Lauris: 26, *45*, 79, *163*, *301*,
    323, 364, 368, 369
  and atomic strike force: 59–60, 146,
    174
  and B–52: 181–183
  as Deputy Chief for Operations: 157
  and interservice rivalry: 203
  as NATO Air Commander: 366, 367,
    369
  and overseas air bases: 437
  on postwar defense needs: 38, 55
  proposed cancellation of Convair
    contract: 237
  strengthening of theater forces: 467
  and targeting: 362
  and training of atomic crew: 123
  and Unified Command Plan: 291
North American Aviation, Inc.: 98
North Atlantic Treaty Organization
    (NATO): 219, 292–293, 384–386,
    395, 447, 451, 454
  responsibility of in Korean War:
    349–350
  SAC and: 312
  Standing Group: 453
  Strategic Guidance: 453
  support for: 386–387
Northeast Air Command: 272, 442
North Field, Tinian Island: 3
Northrop Aircraft, Inc.: 98, 103
Norway
  U.S. basing rights in: 53

Odlum, Floyd B.: 302
O'Donnell, Emmett, Jr.: 346–*348*, 352,
    374
OFFTACKLE: 290, 308–310, 312, 359
Offutt Air Force Base, Nebraska: 228,
    265, *274*, 407, 427, 431
  SAC headquarters: 431–432
Ofstie, Ralph A.: 304
Okinawa
  as base: 201, 202, 222, 273, 288, 442
Old, Archie J., Jr.: 432, *433*, 437
One-way mission concept: 109, 176
Operational Readiness Test: 258
OPERATION CROSSROADS: 118–121
OPERATION STRANGLE: 398–399
Oppenheimer, J. Robert: 323, 358
  and tactical atomic weapons: 367–368
Oppenheimer Committee: 373
Outline Alternate Emergency War Plan,
    SAC: 379–380

P–51: 22, 222
P–80: 111, 184
P–82: 222
P–84: 111, 222
P–85: 112
P–86: 111
P–87: 185
P–88: 112
P–90: 112
Pace, Frank, Jr.: 299
Palestine: 190, 191, 192
Parrish, Noel F.: 458
Parsons, William S.: 4, *11*, 127
Partridge, Earle E.: 69, 91, 102, 109,
    239, 423
  and aerial refueling: 180, *185*
Patterson, Robert P.: 30, *36*, 56, 100,
    156, *158*
  budget requests: 76, 78
Pearl Harbor: 12–13, *18*
People's Republic of China: 325
Pepperel Air Base, Newfoundland: 272
Pershing, John J.: 16
Personal Affairs Officer: 406
Personnel
  spot promotions: 236, 259–260
  standard operating procedures
    (SOPs): 258
Peterson, Howard C.: 43
Philippines

basing rights in: 39
Pick, Lewis A.: 438
Pirie, Sir George: 345
Ploesti, Romania: 50
Porter, John: *11*
Porter-Urquhart: 437
Power, Thomas S.: 109, 133, 120, 144, *184*, *232*, 276, 311
   and aerial refueling: 177
   as Deputy Commander, SAC: 229
Powers, Edward M.: 251
Presidential Air Policy Commission: 151
Preston, Maurice A.: 375, *377*
Princeton University: 40
PROJECT BLUEJAY: 440
PROJECT SILVERPLATE: 4, 7, 65, 67, 123, 125–126, 128
PROJECT SOLARIUM: 459–460
PROJECT VISTA: 376–368, 390
PROJECT WONDERFUL: 49, 52–54, 61, 67, 79–81, 83, 141
Publicity flights: 58, 89–90

Question Mark: 176, *178*

Racial integration and housing: 261
Radar: *404*
   bombing by: 22, 89, 256
   for night operations in atomic war planning: 143
Radar bomb scoring (RBS): 89
Radford, Arthur W.: *301*, 304, 455, 457, 460
Ramey, Roger M.: 60, 86, 115–116, *119*
Ramey Air Force Base, Puerto Rico: 427
Randolph Air Force Base, Texas
   B-29 Combat Crew Training School: 374, 409
Rapid City Air Force Base, Iowa: 208, 271, 277, 373, 412, 429
Rasmussen, Knut: 440
Rated officers
   cross-training of: 86–88
Rating system: 402–403
Rawlings, Edwin W.: 157, *163*, 431

RB–17: 269
RB–29: 269
RB–36: 354, 411, *413*, 428–429
RB–47B: 417
RB–50: 376
Real McCoy: 415
Reconnaissance: 403
   aircraft: x, 239–240, *242*, 252–253, 269
   postwar R&D needs: 105–106
   weakness of units: 333
Reconnaissance Wings
   28th: 404–405, 429
Red Army: 13, 22
Refueling, aerial: 176–186, 201, 245, 247, 267–268, 419–420, 422, 465
Reno Army Air Base (Stead Air Force Base), Nevada
   command survival school: 406
Reserves
   fear of flying: 408–409
"Retardation:" 309–313, 357, 360–364, 366–367
Rhein-Main Air Base, Germany: 90, *213*
Ridgway, Matthew B.: 370, 447
Roark, Robert L.: 125, 129
Robertson, Brian: 208
Robey, Pearl H.: 184
Roosevelt, Franklin D.: *28*
   postwar plans: 12–13
   war strategy: 23
Rosenberg, Anna: 390, 439
Roswell Field (Walker Air Force Base, New Mexico): 56, 118, 224
Round-the-world flights: 222
Royal Air Force (RAF): 15, 183
   B-29 basing at stations: 209–211
   Bomber Command: 91
   in bombing competition: 403–404
   night bombing: 20, 23
Ryan, John D.: 220–221

Sacramento Air Materiel Area: 125
Samuel, J. S.: 366
Sandia, New Mexico: 122
Saturday Evening Post: 316

Index

Saville, Gordon: 319, 321
Schilling, David C.: 419
Schuyler, C.V.R.: 311
Schriever, Bernard A.: 422
Second Air Force
   reconnaissance: 280
Sedalia, Missouri: 432
Semple, David: 118
Searls, Fred, Jr.: 47
Selective Service: 69
Shemya Air Force Base, Aleutian
   Islands: 316
Sherman, Forrest P.: 134, 160, 304–305,
   344, 389, 443
Shumard, Robert: *11*
Simulations
   BECALM atomic bombing exercise:
   334–335
Skidmore, Owings, Merrill: 437
Slessor, Sir John: 342, 449, 451
Slim, Sir William: 449, 451
Smith, Dale O.: 109
Smith, Frederic H., Jr.: xiii, 177, *185*,
   223, 227, 247, 303, 329
Smoky Hill Air Force Base, Kansas: 91,
   206, 222, 223, 280, 432
Smyth, Henry D.: 40
Smyth Report: 40
Spaatz, Carl A.: 37, *45*, *163*
   and aerial refueling: 176
   forms Aircraft and Weapons Board:
   110
   as Air Force Chief of Staff: 156
   and atomic responsibilities: 124, 128
   begins atomic operations: 26
   commands of: 25, 31
   convenes Aircraft and Weapons
   Board: 150
   creates Air Defense Command
   (ADC): 61, 63
   defines SAC's mission: 65–66
   on demobilization: 52
   on development of B–36: 100–102
   and interservice rivalries: 204–205
   on JCS 1745/5: 172–173
   on location of headquarters: 82
   and offensive against Germany:
   21–22
   promotes air power: 386
   promotes Arctic theater: 108
   reorganization plan, 1946: 71
   and SAC combat readiness: 221
   sets rated officer level: 87
   visits England to plan basing:
   141–142
Spaatz Board
   recommends atomic weapons
   strategy: 56–58
Spaight, J. M.: x
Spain
   basing in: 442–443, 467
Spanish Civil War: 32
Spokane Air Force Base, Washington:
   277, 335
Stalin, Josef: xii, 13, *28*, 458
"Standardization:" 236, 255–256, 405,
   469
State Department
   and NSC–68: 327–328
   Policy Planning Staff: 216–217
States' Rights Democratic Party: 215
Stevenson, Adlai E.: 455
Stevenson, John D.: 358
Stiborik, Joseph: *11*
Stimson, Henry L.: 21, *36*
Stone, Charles B., III: 456
Storz, Arthur C.: 228, 431
Strategic Air Command (SAC)
   acknowledged as major arm of
   national strategy: 134
   basing of bomber groups in England
   and Germany: 208
   BECALM: 334–335
   and Berlin crisis: 188
   command elements plan: 365
   debate over role: 1951, 355
   deterrent role of: 385
   Developmental Program: 233
   division in U.K.: 433
   emblem, and other aspects of elite
   character: 406
   emergency war plan: 379–381
   emphasizes professionalism: 408
   established: vii, 63

European flights: 90–91
and exempt units: 370–371
expansion, 1951, 372–381
housing association: 261–262
initial strength: 65
lack of combat readiness: 80–81, 219–233
liaison with Far East Command: 365–366
mission: 65–66, 83
mission in Air Force emergency war plan, 1950: 312
Operational Training Unit (OTU): 374–375
organization plan for atomic strike force: 116–117
overseas duty, 1946: 79
performance and equipment deficiencies, 1948: 225–230
planning group for: 58–60
rating system: 402–403
reorganization, 1949: 280–281
size, 1948: 248
strength, 1947: 93
strength, 1953: 461
wing organization: 377
worldwide role: 364
Strategic Evaluation Squadron 3908th: 405
Stratemeyer, George E.: 398, *441*
and aircraft industry: 150–151
Strauss, Lewis L.: 170, 316, 322
Streett, St. Clair: *86*
and atomic strike force: 59
on lack of urgency: 78
role in SAC: 65
and training and morale problems: 82–83
Sullivan, John L.: 156, *159*, 299
Summerfelt, Milton F.: *200*, 201
Supreme Allied Commander, Europe (SACEUR): 350
Survival in the Air Age: 164, *167*
Swancutt, Woodrow P.: 118–119
Sweeney, Charles W.: 6
Sweeney, Walter C., Jr.: 230, 232
Symington, W. Stuart: 30, *37*, 90, *159*,
 182, *213*, 222, 240, *255*, 458
on autonomous air arm: 150
base closings: 277, 280
becomes Secretary of Air Force: 156
and hydrogen bomb: 324
and interservice rivalries: 203
and NSC–68: 329
and 1951 budget: 318–319, 325
recommends aggressive policy in Korea: 350
supports Vandenberg: 305

Taber, John: 75
Tactical Air Command (TAC): 63–64, 364
Taft, Robert A.: 386, 446, 454–455
Talbott, Harold E.: 456, 457
Tedder, Sir Arthur: 141–142
Tempelhof Air Base, Germany: 215
There Will Be No Time: 322
Thule Air Base, Greenland: *413*, 433, 440–442
 PROJECT BLUEJAY: 440
Thurmond, J. Strom: 215
Tibbetts, Kingston B.: 413
Tibbets, Paul W., Jr.: 4, *11*, *200*, 201
Toward New Horizons: 27
Towers, John H.
and interservice rivalries: 204–205
Trenchard, Sir Hugh: 15, 16
Training
of atomic officers: 122–123
of B–29 groups: 88–89, 92
cross-: 219–221, 233, 266
for handling atomic bomb: 129–130
lead crew concept: 221, 223
in northern latitudes: 133
Training Standard: 84
Travis, Robert F.: 375
Travis Air Force Base (formerly Fairfield-Suisun Air Force Base), California: 429, 431
TROJAN: 28–89, 307
Truman, Harry S.: *167*
announces Soviet bomb detonation: 316

Index

approves NSC-20/4: 217
and atomic production: 355, 359
and atomic stockpile custody: 425
and atomic weapons: 45, 467
bomb production: 322
crisis with Britain over use of atomic weapons: 349
defense budget austerity: 69, 70, 72, 74, 187–193, 197, 285, 314, 317–319, 236, 325, 446–447, 454
defense policy, 1951: 353
election year: 215–216
foreign policy: 46
and Korean War: 341, 344, 347–353
and limited war concept: 347–349
military experience: 30
names Eisenhower SACEUR: 350
1948 budget: 240–241, 248–249
recalls Marshall: 348
relieves MacArthur: 352
and Soviet threat: 326–329
willingness to use atomic weapons: 299
Truman Doctrine: 74, 113, 190
Tu-4: 46, 136, 377
Tunner, William H.: 209
Twentieth Air Force: 26, 114
command structure: 132
delivery of atomic bomb: 3
XX Bomber Command: 26
XXI Bomber Command: 24, 26
Twining, Nathan F.: 101, 362, 364, 365, 393–394, 452
bomber development priorities: 103–105
commands of: 157
and 1954 budget: 457–458
and SAC alternate emergency war plan: 380

Unified Command Plan: 290–293, 465
Union of Soviet Socialist Republics (USSR)
assessed military power of: 135–136
and atomic bomb: 39–42, 45–47, 313–335, 466
atomic tests by: 270, 285
atomic espionage: 325
atomic stockpile: 327, 381
attacks Manchuria: 5
blockades Berlin: 187–188
containment policy: 74–75
estimated strength, 1950: 377–378
involvement in Korean War: 339–347
joint war plan if attacked by: 199–200
night defenses: 381
plans for atomic war against: 216–219
postwar relations with U.S.: 31–33, 32n8, 49, 68, 464
postwar tensions effect on R&D: 105–106
relations with U.S.: viii
strategic air force of: 23n45
strategy against: 447
strategic targets in: 140–141
U.S. planning for atomic war with: 135–149
United Nations Atomic Energy Commission: 46
United Kingdom
as basing site: 114, 141, 146, 148, 168, 175, 208, 261, 276, 288
consultation on use of atomic weapons: 349
deployment of B-29s in Korean War: 342–345
four-power government of Berlin: 205
and global strategy: 449–450
postwar economic problems: 9–10
SAC air division in: 433–434
war plans focused on: 198–201, 273
United Nations
and atomic energy: 46–48
and Korean War: 339, 341, 394–395
Military Staff Committee: 47, 63
need for atomic control under: 144
and nuclear disarmament: 139
peacekeeping role: 12–13, 32, 84
U.S. Air Forces, Europe (USAFE): 91, 276
U. S. Army
on Air Force expansion: 389
and balanced forces budgets: 318

513

Strategic Air Force

  budgets: 392, 395
  command structure disputes with
    Navy: 132–133
  conflicts over role of bombers in
    support of ground forces: 308–309
  dissatisfaction with JCS 2056: 359,
    360
  and exempt units: 370–371
  Ground Forces: 61, 63
  limits on expansion: 468
  1948 budget: 73, 75–76
  objections to Unified Command Plan:
    291
  plans for atomic bomb: 109–110
  postwar recruiting: 69
  postwar role reassessment: 33–34
  Signal Corps: x
  skepticism of Air Force commitment
    to "retardation:" 310–312
  Strategic Striking Force: 49–50
  tactical operations: 366–368
U.S. Congress
  acceptance of 143-wing program: 394
  hearings on B–36 program: 300–306
  Joint Committee on Atomic Energy:
    113, 149, 168
  1949 budget hearings: 158–166
  1950 budget: 297
  Preparedness Subcommittee of the
    Senate Armed Service Committee:
    438
U.S. Navy
  activity in Northeast, 1950: 272
  and atomic tests: 118, 120
  atomic program development,
    rivalry: 48, 169–173, 297–298
  and balanced force budgets: 318
  budgets: 392, 395
  and carrier-based nuclear potential:
    358, 451
  challenges air strategy and B–36
    program: 283–295, 300–306
  challenges strategic bombing
    emphasis: 249
  criticism of SAC: 84
  and emergency war plan: 308
  disputes command structure with

  Army: 132–133
  and exempt units: 370–371
  limits on expansion: 468
  objections to Unified Command Plan:
    291–292
  opposition to Air Force atomic
    strategy: 160–162
  opposition to Air Force expansion:
    389
  plans for atomic war: 137–139
  portion of fleet command: 290–291
  postwar role reassessment: 33–34
  preparedness for war: viii, 12–13
  relationship with Air Force in
    strategic air operations: 192–195,
    199, 203–205
  role in strategic air offensive: 360
  and supercarrier cancellation:
    298–299
  tactical operations: 366–367
United States Strategic Bombing Survey:
    23
Universal military training (UMT): 27,
    33, 54, 189–190, 193, 196–197
University of Chicago: 41
USS *Helena*: 455
USS *Nevada*: 119–120
USS *United States*: 206

Vandenberg, Arthur: 156, 196
Vandenberg, Hoyt S.: *45*, 228, *228*, 229,
    240, 255, 364, 388, 452, 453
  as Air Force Deputy Chief of Staff:
    156–157
  and Air Force view of national
    defense: 305
  and alternative emergency war plan:
    380
  on atomic warfare: 39
  and B–52 contract: 182
  budget requests of: 76
  congressional testimony: 446
  and engine development: 106
  and expansion of SAC: 372
  and fear of flying: 409–410
  and feasibility of atomic offensive:

Index

294–295
on limited strength to extend fighting: 352
on medium bombers: 110
and national defense strategy and Air Force expansion: 386–390
opposes 1954 reduced budget: 457–458, *459*
postwar issues: 55, 59
procurement for 70-group level: 203
removes Anderson: 348
and SLANT NINE: 360–362
and strategic offensive plan: 309–110
succeeds Spaatz as Air Force Chief of Staff: 188
tactical atomic weapons: 367–368
Unified Command Plan: 291–292
Van Kirk, Theodore: *11*
Van Zandt, James E.: 302–303
Vigon, Juan: 443
Viner, Jacob: 41
Vinson, Carl: 302, 388, 440

Walker, Kenneth N.: 20, *25*
Walker Air Force Base (formerly Roswell Field), New Mexico: 215, 224, 268, 430
Wallace, Henry A.: 215
War Department: 146, 149
  postwar role: 33–34
  study of atomic warfare issues: 146
  Victory Program: 20–21
Washington Post: 331
Weapons Systems Evaluation Group (WSEG): 294–295, 306, *307*, 405, 466
Weaver Air Force Base, South Dakota: 227
Webb, James E.: 76
Wedemeyer, Albert C.: 170–171, 209, 211, *301*
Western European Union: 193
Weyland, Otto P.: 142

and atomic warfare: 146, 171–173
Wheelus Air Base, Libya: 442
Wherry, Kenneth S.: 228, 264, 385–386, 407, 431
Wherry Act: 264
Wherry Housing Project: *268*
Whisenand, James F.: 446
White, Edward H.: 71–72
White, Thomas D.: 362, 371, 393
Whitehead, Ennis C.: 84, 91–92, 192, 326
Whiteside, Arthur: 167
Whitney, Cornelius V.: 191
WIBAC (Wichita Boeing Airplane Company): 415, 417
Wilson, Charles E.: 425, *450*, 455, 457
Wilson, Roscoe C.: 58, 174
Wohlstetter, Albert: 444
Wolfe, Kenneth B.: 231, 240, 428–429
Wood, Harold E.: 119–120
World War I
  creation of strategic air force and: 14
World War II
  precision bombing doctrine and: 21–22, 24
Worth, Cedric R.: 302–303
Wray, Stanley T.: 210, 435
Wright Air Development Center: 423
Wright-Patterson Air Force Base (formerly Wright Field), Ohio: 125, 238

XAJ–1: 160
XB–35: *286*
XB–36: 99–100
XB–49: 103, 130, 182–185, 239
XB–52: 99
XF–88: 419
XRB–49A: *242*

Yale University: 39, 40, 322, 362
Yokota, Japan: 346, 347, *348*
Youssef, Sultan Mohammed ben: 436

www.ingramcontent.com/pod-product-compliance
Lightning Source LLC
Chambersburg PA
CBHW020630230426
43665CB00008B/116